THE MAJOR PROPHETS

Old Testament Survey Series

THE MAJOR PROPHETS

JAMES E. SMITH

Library of Congress Catalog Card Number: 91-62386
International Standard Book Number: 0-89900-417-2

DEDICATED TO

MY CHILDREN

KEITH CAMPBELL SMITH

AND

YONA BETH SMITH

CONTENTS

Chapter *Page*

Chapter *Page*

The Book of Ezekiel

The Book of Daniel

Charts and Diagrams

Charts and Diagrams *Page*

Maps

PREFACE

Youngsters are typically taught in Bible school that the Old Testament library consists of thirty-nine books organized into five major divisions: five books of Law, twelve books of history, five books of poetry, five books of Major Prophets, and twelve books of Minor Prophets. Though other schemes have been suggested, the five-fold breakdown is likely to remain the most popular.

The origin of the five-fold organization of the Old Testament is difficult to trace. The earliest manuscripts of the Greek translation—the Septuagint—arrange the books in five divisions. In these manuscripts, however, the Minor Prophets precede the Major Prophets. These manuscripts are of Christian origin. Since no pre-Christian complete Greek manuscripts have survived, it is impossible to say whether or not the five-fold arrangement originated with the Alexandrian Jews who produced the Septuagint version in the second century BC. The familiar five-fold break down of Old Testament books *may* be a contribution of early Christian teachers.

In the first century AD the Jews counted twenty-two or twenty-four books in their Bible (the Old Testament). The double books of 1 & 2 Samuel, 1 & 2 Kings and 1 & 2 Chronicles were counted as only three books. Ruth and Lamentations were sometimes counted as appendices of Judges and Jeremiah respectively. Ezra-Nehemiah were counted as one book. The twelve Minor Prophets were also counted as one book. From as early as the second century BC the Old Testament books were regarded as a tripartite library consisting of *Torah* (the books of Moses), *Nebhi'im* (prophets), and *Kethubhim* (writings). The number of books in these divisions varied from time to time.

In the time of Josephus (ca. AD 90) the three divisions consisted of five, thirteen and four books respectively. Since AD 500, however, eight books have been assigned to the division known as *Nebhi'im.* These eight books are divided into two sub-divisions, the Former Prophets (Joshua, Judges, Samuel and Kings), and the Latter Prophets (Isaiah, Jeremiah, Ezekiel and The Twelve). In this arrangement Daniel and Lamentations are considered part of the third division, the *Kethubhim.*

The Book of Daniel was included among the prophetic literature by Josephus. Why the Rabbis decided to remove Daniel from the prophets and place the book among the *Kethubhim* is not clear. What is clear is that the placement of Daniel after Ezekiel in the Septuagint and subsequently in the Latin Vulgate and English versions is most appropriate. Daniel certainly was a prophet. Geographically, both Ezekiel and Daniel served in Babylon. Chronologically, their ministries overlapped.

Lamentations apparently was counted as part of the Book of Jeremiah by Josephus. For liturgical purposes and for convenience the Rabbis placed the five poems which constitute Lamentations on a scroll by themselves. Lamentations became part of a sub-section of the *Kethubhim* known as the *Megilloth*, (the "scrolls"). The *Megilloth* consists of five small books—Song of Solomon, Ruth, Lamentations, Ecclesiastes, and Esther—each of which was read at one of the annual feast days.

A case could be made for placing Lamentations in the division of poetic or devotional books (Job, Psalms, Proverbs, Ecclesiastes, and Song of Solomon). Its current position in the English Bible between

Jeremiah and Ezekiel is not inappropriate, however. First, this position restores the book to its association with the Book of Jeremiah. Second, the content of Lamentations also makes the placement between Jeremiah and Ezekiel appropriate. Lamentations describes the fall of Jerusalem to the Babylonians in 587 BC. Both Isaiah and Jeremiah anticipated that event and the captivity which followed. Ezekiel and Daniel ministered among the captives in Babylon. Thus it is appropriate that Isaiah and Jeremiah precede Lamentations in the canon, and that Ezekiel and Daniel follow.

That Isaiah, Jeremiah, Ezekiel and Daniel are designated Major Prophets does not mean that they are more important than the twelve Minor Prophets. Rather the four prophets are called *Major* because of their size.The five books of the Major Prophets constitute twenty-two per cent of the Old Testament. The twelve Minor Prophets combined are not as large as Isaiah, Jeremiah or Ezekiel individually. Daniel is over seventy-five per cent longer than the two longest of the Minor Prophets (Hosea; Zechariah).

Each of the five books of the Major Prophets is distinct in style, vocabulary, and to a certain extent, theology. Yet an inter-relatedness is also in evidence. Yahweh's sovereignty over all nations of the earth, even superpowers, is clearly stressed in this section. The false theology combated so valiantly by Jeremiah and Ezekiel had its roots in a misunderstanding and misapplication of the principle of trusting God in national crisis which Isaiah stressed. The concept of world powers executing the will of Yahweh so clearly set forth in Isaiah, Jeremiah and Ezekiel is projected into the distant future by Daniel.

For some fifteen years the author has taught a course which surveyed the Major Prophets in the curriculum of Florida Christian College. At various times exegetical courses focusing on the individual books of this section have also been offered. The author has published major commentaries on three of the books of this section—Jeremiah-Lamentations (1972) and Ezekiel (1979). Key prophecies in the Major Prophets were also discussed in the author's *What the Bible Says About the Promised Messiah* (1984). The material in this survey depends heavily on these earlier studies.

The format of this survey follows that which was earlier employed in *The Pentateuch: A Survey* (1989). The survey of the contents of each of the prophetic books is preceded by an introductory chapter designed to give the student an overview of the book itself and some of the problems associated with it.

Mrs. Linda Stark, librarian of Florida Christian College, has encouraged this project from its inception. She has rendered valuable assistance in proof reading the manuscript. The author's son, Keith C. Smith, has assisted in various ways with solving the problems which arose in translating the text and graphics from one computer program to another. Without the assistance of these two encouragers this work would never have been completed. Appreciation is also extended to Brother Steve Jennings of College Press who granted permission for the use of the maps which appear in this volume. Fred W. Smith, Jr. and Thelma Smith, the elder brother and mother of the author, provided verbal encouragement and financial resources which enabled this work to be published.

THE BOOK OF
ISAIAH

CHAPTER ONE

Getting Acquainted With Isaiah

He has been called "the Prince of the Old Testament Prophets" (Copass), "the Saint Paul of the Old Testament" (Robinson) and "the greatest prophet" (Eusebius). Isaiah son of Amoz was a theologian, reformer, statesman, historian, poet, orator, prince, and patriot. He was "prophet of the gospel before the Gospel" (Robinson), the fifth evangelist. Naegelsbach refers to him as "the great central-prophet." His ministry was central in time. He walked across the stage of history roughly half way between Moses and Christ. Isaiah was central in the events of history. He lived during the days of the mighty Assyrian Empire. He anticipated the downfall of that empire and the rise of its two successors, viz., the Chaldean and the Persian empires. This prophet was central in theological emphasis. He drove home the great principles of salvation through faith, substitutionary atonement, the kingdom and resurrection.

Isaiah was also central among the prophetic books. According to Payne, he ranks third to Ezekiel and Jeremiah in the most predictions

(734 verses), first in the greatest number of separate predictions (111) and second in the amount of material directly anticipatory of Jesus Christ (59 verses).[1] While other prophets were called to illuminate single parts of the near or distant future, Isaiah let the light of his prophetic word fall on the great wide circumference of the entire future of salvation.[2]

THE MINISTRY OF ISAIAH

The message of Isaiah was heralded by his name which means "Yahweh is salvation." The name Joshua has the same two components in reverse order. Isaiah is the only person in Scripture to wear this name. Some English versions in New Testament references to him Anglicize the Greek and Latin spelling of his name as Esaias or Isaias.

Personal information about this prophet is scanty. His father was Amoz, not to be confused with the prophet Amos.[3] According to tradition, Isaiah was from the tribe of Judah. He was a citizen, if not a native, of Jerusalem. Isaiah was married, but the name of his wife is not known. She is simply called "the prophetess" (8:3). His sons were given symbolic names which encapsulated prophecies. The first, Shear-jashub (7:3), means "a remnant shall return." The second son has the longest name to appear in the English Bible—Maher-shalal-hash-baz (8:1). Roughly translated this name means "swift is the booty, speedy is the prey."

Prior to his call to the prophetic ministry, Isaiah served in the royal court as historiographer. He recorded the acts of King Uzziah "from beginning to end" (2 Chr 26:22). Concerning King Hezekiah the record states: "The other events of Hezekiah's reign and his acts of devotion are written in the vision of the prophet Isaiah son of Amoz in the book of the kings of Israel and Judah" (2 Chr 32:32).

Isaiah was called to the prophetic ministry in "the year that king Uzziah died" (6:1). Scholars compute that year to have been 739 BC. His ministry extended for some sixty years through the reigns of Jotham, Ahaz and Hezekiah. According to tradition Isaiah died a martyr's death about 680 BC, early in the reign of the wicked King Manasseh.[4] Legend has it that he was sawed asunder by this king (cf. Heb

11:37).

Among the Major Prophets, Isaiah was the preacher *par excellence.* He exhibits a vocabulary considerably larger than either Jeremiah or Ezekiel. He was a masterful writer as well as an orator. Isaianic expressions have found their way into the speech of many who have never read his book. Sarcasm and irony were tools he used with skill. His words reveal great earnestness, boldness and spirituality. He was a man of deep reverence.

Chart No. 1

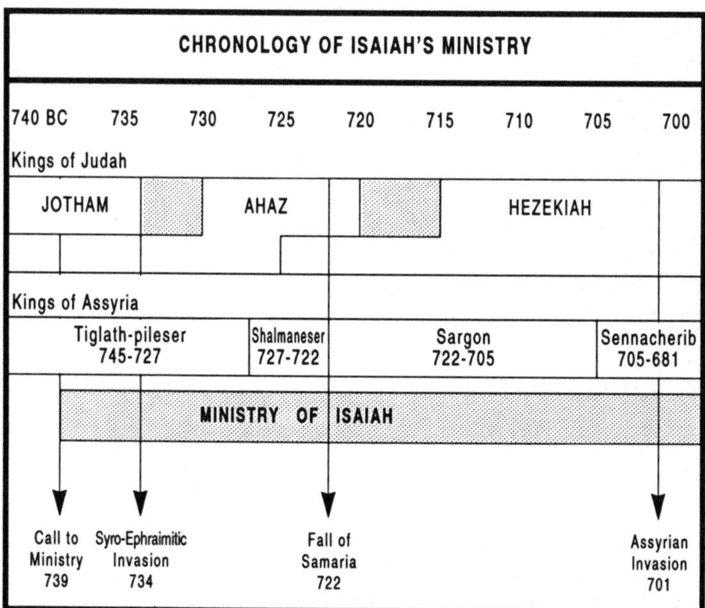

Though Isaiah was known more for what he said than for what he did, action parables are not lacking in his ministry. Once he removed his outer garment and shoes and walked about the streets of Jerusalem in the long linen tunic worn next to the skin (chap. 20). He thus played the role of one who had been taken captive to warn the citizens of Jerusalem against an alliance with Egypt. When Hezekiah was sick unto death Isaiah ordered a clump of figs to be placed on his "boil" to symbolize the beginning of healing (chap. 38). On another occasion he wrote the name of his second son on a large scroll which was serving as a kind of billboard (chap. 8).

Valeton evaluated the ministry of Isaiah in these poignant words: "Never perhaps has there been another prophet like Isaiah, who stood with his head in the clouds and his feet on the solid earth, with his heart in things of eternity and with mouth and hand in the things of time, with his spirit in the eternal counsel of God and his body in a very definite moment of history."[5]

THE BOOK OF ISAIAH

The Book of Isaiah has been called "the Mount Everest of Prophetic Literature." The intrinsic grandeur of this book attracts those who are connoisseurs of great literature. Students of theology find here sublime revelations of God's character. The evangelical emphasis of the book has made it a favorite of Christian preachers through the ages. Those who defend Biblical revelation find in these prophecies abundant evidence of supernatural revelation. Simple believers rejoice in a treasure trove of passages which encourage them in their Christian pilgrimage.

A. Size and Position.

Although the Book of Isaiah has more chapters than either Jeremiah or Ezekiel, by word count it ranks third in size.[6] The Book of Isaiah contains sixty-six chapters which are a microcosm of the Bible. The first thirty-nine chapters, like the thirty-nine books of the Old Testament, speak mainly of condemnation. The last twenty-seven chapters, like the twenty-seven books of the New Testament, speak mainly of redemption.

Because of the respective sizes of the books, ancient Jewish tradition listed Jeremiah and Ezekiel before Isaiah. The placement of the Book of Isaiah as first among the Major Prophets can be justified, however, on chronological grounds. Isaiah's ministry ended about seventy-five years before the call of Jeremiah. The pre-Christian Greek Septuagint was guided by the chronological principle in the arrangement of the Major Prophets. The English translators have followed the lead of the Latin Vulgate, which in turn was based on the Septuagint. The Septuagint, however, had the twelve Minor Prophets before the Major Prophets.

B. The Unity of Isaiah.

The majority of Old Testament scholars are convinced that the Book of Isaiah is not the product of a single author. According to these critics, chapters 40-66 (and several chapters in the first half of the book as well) were written by some anonymous prophet living a century and a half after Isaiah. This anonymous prophet is called "Deutero-Isaiah." Some critics have gone so far as to designate Isaiah as a library of prophetic books compiled by any number of authors over several centuries. One writer refers to the Book of Isaiah as "the garbage can of prophecy."[7]

On what grounds do the critics deny that Isaiah was the author of the entire book which bears his name? An anti-supernatural bias permeates the writers who advocate the multiple authorship theory. They simply do not believe in pin-point predictive prophecy. Their bias is camouflaged in the following dictum: circumstances reflected in a book are evidence of the time of composition. The Biblical view, however, is that God on occasion revealed to a prophet the circumstances of a future period. The multiple authorship theory undercuts the powerful evidence of prediction found in this book.

Critics point to linguistic and stylistic differences between the two halves of Isaiah which they believe support their theory of multiple authorship. Yet a writer's vocabulary and style may vary depending on his age at the time of writing, the subject matter involved, and the audience for whom he is writing. Without question the last chapters of Isaiah were written late in the prophet's life. In these chapters he is addressing new subjects.

Again critics point out that certain theological concepts appear in the latter half of the book which are not attested in the days of Isaiah. Yet this argument begs the question. If Isaiah 40-66 is the product of Isaiah, then the theology found in those chapters would in fact be attested in the days of Isaiah.

Sometimes critics argue that Isaiah's name is not found in the last twenty-seven chapters of the book. While this is true, it is not decisive in determining the authorship of these chapters. A book is presumed to be the product of the person whose name it bears unless overwhelming evidence to the contrary can be produced. Futhermore, most critics who deny that Isaiah wrote chapters 40-66 also deny that he wrote chapter 13, and that chapter *does* contain his name.

The following factors support the traditional view that Isaiah the son of Amoz authored this book.

1. The heading of the book and at least thirteen other places within the book claim Isaiah as the speaker/writer.

2. Jewish and Christian tradition is uniform in attributing this book to Isaiah.

3. The Septuagint, translated about 250 BC, shows no distinction between the two halves of the book.

4. Ben Sirach, writing at about 280 BC, knew of one Isaiah.

5. The two complete Isaiah manuscripts among the Dead Sea Scrolls indicate no break at the end of chapter 39. These manuscripts date to about a century and a half before Christ.

6. Josephus attributes the Cyrus prophecy of 44:28 and 45:1—the most controversial prophecy in the book—to Isaiah the son of Amoz.[8]

7. Jesus in the synagogue at Nazareth read from Isaiah 61 and attributed it to Isaiah (Luke 4:16ff.).

8. In the New Testament several passages from "Deutero-Isaiah" are quoted and attributed simply to Isaiah.

9. The literary style of the second half of Isaiah is so similar to the first that even critics admit that "Deutero-Isaiah" must have been a disciple of Isaiah who tried to imitate his master.

10. A certain circle of ideas appears throughout the book binding it together as the work of one author. The concepts of a highway, Zion, the Holy One of Israel, and pangs of a woman in travail are but a few of the many which might be listed.

11. Many of the passages found in "Deutero-Isaiah" are totally unsuitable to the period of the exile of Judah where they are placed by the critics, but totally appropriate to the days of Isaiah son of Amoz.

C. The Message of the Book.

The theme of Isaiah is the same as the meaning of this prophet's name: "Yahweh is salvation." The immediate purpose of the book was to teach the truth that salvation is by grace.[9] The long range purpose was to demonstrate the role of Judah in the plan of God as the vehicle through which Messiah would come into the world.

The book consists of two major divisions. Chapters 1-35 are concerned primarily with two invasions of Judah. The first invasion was by the combined armies of Syria and Ephraim in 734 BC. This invasion had as its purpose the removal of the reigning representative of the royal house of David. During this crisis Isaiah urged King Ahaz to trust in the Lord. This invasion would come to nothing (Isa 7). A second invasion, however, would be far more devastating. The Assyrians were coming like a flood which would reach all the way to the neck of Judah. The tiny nation would all but be swallowed up by that imperialistic giant. After God had used these foreigners to punish his wayward people he would punish the Assyrians for their brutality, idolatry and pride.

Chapters 36-39 form an historical connecting link between the two major divisions of Isaiah. Chapters 36-37 document the invasion by King Sennacherib in 701 BC and the dramatic, last-minute rescue of Jerusalem by divine intervention. The judgment predictions of chapters 1-35 find fulfillment in these two chapters. Chapters 38-39, however, lay the foundation for the predictions of the last twenty-seven chapters. Here Isaiah announces to King Hezekiah that in years to come his descendants would be carried away to Babylon. Thus the first two chapters of this narrative section look backward to the threats pertaining to Assyria. The last two chapters of the connecting link look forward to the captivity of Judah in the land of Babylon. Furthermore, a careful study of chapters 36-39 indicates that the material is presented in reverse chronological order. The episode recorded in chapters 38-39 occurred before the Assyrian invasion of chapters 36-37. The author apparently sacrificed chronological considerations in the interest of literary structure. By this arrangement of material Isaiah intended to demonstrate how his entire book fits together logically and theologically.

Chapters 40-66 assume that the threat of Babylonian captivity made in chapters 38-39 had come to pass. These chapters were designed to give comfort to the Jews once they had been deported from their homeland. This comfort took the form of (1) explanations of why that terrible judgment was necessary; and (2) anticipations of a complete restoration of God's people which would set the stage for the golden age of Messiah.

Ten major units have been identified in the book.[10] These units or "books" are the basis for the survey of Isaiah found in the following nine chapters.

1. The Book of Mingled Rebukes and Promises (chaps. 1-6).
2. The Book of Immanuel (chaps. 7-12).
3. The Book of Burdens (chaps. 13-23).
4. First Book of General Judgment (chaps. 24-27).
5. The Book of Woes (chaps. 28-33).
6. Second Book of General Judgment (chaps. 34-35).

Chart No. 2

THE STRUCTURE OF ISAIAH			
Threats of Judgment	Historical Connecting Link		Promises of Deliverance
Chaps. 1-35	Chaps. 36-37	Chaps. 38-39	Chaps. 40-66
Coming of Assyrians Anticipated	Assyrian Attack	Coming of Babylonians Anticipated	Babylonian Conquest Assumed

7. The Book of Hezekiah (chaps. 36-39).
8. The Book of Cyrus (chaps. 40-48).
9. The Book of the Suffering Servant (chaps. 49-57).
10. The Book of Future Glory (chaps. 58-66).

D. The Importance of the Book.

For the Christian the Book of Isaiah is extremely important. Forty-seven chapters of this book were directly quoted or alluded to by Christ or the Apostles. With more than four hundred allusions, Isaiah stands second only to Psalms as the most cited book in the New Testament.

According to Payne the book of Isaiah contains 111 separate predictions. Of the 1,292 verses in the book, 754 (59%) deal with future events. Among the more important Messianic prophecies in this book are the following:

1. The future temple which attracts Gentiles (2:2-4).
2. The glorious Branch (4:2-6).
3. The virgin birth of Immanuel (7:13-14).
4. The dawning of a new day in the birth of a child (9:1-7).
5. The Shoot of the stem of Jesse (11:1-10).
6. The conversion of Gentiles (19:18-25).
7. The new Jerusalem (54:9-13; 60:19-22).
8. The marriage supper of the Lamb (25:6-8; 26:19).
9. The ministry of the Messiah (42:1-4).
10. The Servant as a light to the Gentiles (49:1-13).
11. The willing obedience of the Servant (50:4-11).
12. The redemption achieved by the Servant (52:13-53:12).
13. The promises made to David to be fulfilled (55:1-5).
14. Converted heathen to become leaders in worship (66:19-23).

Endnotes

1. J. Barton Payne, *The Encyclopedia of Biblical Prophecy* (New York: Harper & Row, 1973) 674.

2. On the centrality of Isaiah see Carl W.E. Naegelsbach, "The Prophet Isaiah," in vol. 6 of *Commentary on the Holy Scriptures* ed. by John Peter Lange (Grand Rapids: Zondervan, 1960 reprint) 1-2.

3. A seal of "Amoz the Scribe" dating to the eighth century BC has been found. This seal may have belonged to the father of Isaiah.

4. The last dated event in the book of Isaiah was the fourteenth year of Hezekiah (701 BC). The Assyrian King Esarhaddon (681-699 BC) is, however, mentioned in 37:38.

5. Yaleton cited by G.L. Robinson, *The Book of Isaiah* (Grand Rapids: Baker, 1954) 22.

6. Jeremiah contains fifty-two chapters, 42,659 words; Ezekiel has forty-eight chapters, 39,407 words; Isaiah is organized into sixty-six chapters, but contains only 37,044 words.

7. Edwin M. Good, *Irony in the Old Testament* (Sheffield: Almond, 1981) 115.

8. Josephus, *Antiquities* 11.1.2.

9. E.J. Young, *An Introduction to the Old Testament* (Grand Rapids: Eerdmans, 1960) 225.

10. Adapted from B.A. Copass, *Isaiah: Prince of Old Testament Prophets* (Nashville: Broadman, 1944).

11. Payne, *op.cit.* 285-320.

ISAIAH: BIBLIOGRAPHY

Alexander, J. A. *Commentary on the Prophecies of Isaiah.* 2 vols. Grand Rapids: Zondervan, 1953 reprint.

Allis, O. T. *The Unity of Isaiah: A Study in Prophecy.* Philadelphia: Presbyterian and Reformed, 1950.

Archer, G. L. "Isaiah" in *The Wycliffe Bible Commentary.* Ed. Charles Pfeiffer and Everett Harrison. Chicago: Moody, 1962.

Delitzsch, Franz. *Biblical Commentary on the Prophecies of Isaiah.* Biblical Commentaries on the Old Testament. Grand Rapids: Eerdmans, 1949 reprint.

Hailey, Homer. *A Commentary on Isaiah.* Grand Rapids: Baker, 1985.

Jones, Kenneth E. "Isaiah." *The Wesleyan Bible Commentary.* 6 vols. Grand Rapids: Eerdmans, 1969.

Leupold, H. C. *Exposition of Isaiah.* 2 vols. Grand Rapids: Baker, 1968-71.

Lindsey, F. Duane. *The Servant Songs: A Study in Isaiah.* Chicago: Moody, 1985.

MacRae, Allan. *The Gospel of Isaiah.* Chicago: Moody, 1977.

Naegelsbach, Carl W. E. *The Prophet Isaiah.* Commentary on the Holy Scriptures by John Lange. Ed. Philip Schaff. 6 vols. Grand Rapids: Zondervan, 1960 reprint.

Oswalt, John N. *The Book of Isaiah: Chapters 1-39.* The New International Commentary on the Old Testament. Ed. R. K. Harrison. Grand Rapids: Eerdmans, 1986.

Plumptre, E. H. "The Book of the Prophet Isaiah." *An Old Testament Commentary for English Readers.* Ed. C. J. Ellicott. New York: Cassell, 1901.

Rawlinson, George. "Isaiah" (Exposition and Homiletics). 2 vols. *The Pulpit Commentary.* Ed. H. D. M. Spence and Joseph S. Exell. Grand Rapids: Eerdmans, 1950 reprint.

Ridderbos, J. *Isaiah.* Bible Student's Commentary. Grand Rapids: Zondervan, 1985.

Robinson, G. L. *The Book of Isaiah.* Revised ed. Grand Rapids: Baker, 1954.

Watts, John D. W. "Isaiah." *Word Biblical Commentary.* 2 vols. Ed. David A. Hubbard and Glenn W. Barker. Waco: Word, 1985,1987.

Young, E. J. *The Book of Isaiah.* 3 vols. Grand Rapids: Eerdmans, 1965-72.

CHAPTER TWO

Mingled Rebukes and Promises
Isaiah 1-6

Background of the Unit.

The key to the chronological placement of Isaiah 1-6 is found in 6:1. The call of the prophet is dated to the year that King Uzziah died. That Isaiah prophesied prior to his call to be a prophet is unlikely. Therefore, chapters 1-6 contain materials which can be dated immediately after the death of Uzziah in 739 BC. The ruler during this period was Jotham, the son of Uzziah. Jotham had actually been serving as co-regent from as early as 750 BC when Uzziah was forced to live in isolation because of an outbreak of leprosy.

Altogether Jotham reigned sixteen years (2 Kgs 15:33). The sacred historian declares that "he did what was right in the sight of the Lord" (2 Kgs 15:34). The Chronicler adds that he "grew powerful because he walked steadfastly before the Lord" (2 Chr 27:2). Several military campaigns were waged, including a notable one against the Ammonites (2 Chr 27:3-5). These were the times in which Isaiah began his ministry. The economic boom of the preceding reign continued. Major building projects were completed. The rich were getting richer. The poor, however, were being oppressed. The Temple was overflowing with worshipers, but the worship was a sham. Pagan customs were influencing their religious rituals.

In the year that King Uzziah died God called a member of the royal court into the prophetic ministry (Isa 6:1). The report of his call is delayed until chapter 6. Apparently Isaiah desired to first offer examples of his preaching, and then to present his credentials for delivering such stinging condemnation and such glorious predictions.

Outline of the Unit.

A. A Prologue: A Nation Indicted (chap. 1).
B. A Sermon: A People Humbled (chaps. 2-4).
C. A Song: A Vineyard Destroyed (chaps. 5).
D. A Vision: A Prophet Called (chap. 6).

A NATION INDICTED
Isaiah 1

The first chapter of Isaiah serves as a prologue to the entire book. It stresses four concepts which permeate the message of Isaiah: (1) accusation of sin; (2) invitation to repentance; (3) lamentation over disaster; and (4) purgation through judgment.

A. Accusation of Sin (1:2-15).

Isaiah's "vision" begins with an accusation. The prophet took his auditors to court, as it were, and entered against them a three-count indictment.

In count one the charge was ingratitude. God likened his people to rebellious children. They had experienced the loving care of the heavenly Father, yet they had rebelled. Dumb animals have greater loyalty to their masters than did Israel to her God. These people may know *about* God, but they no longer *know* him, i.e., they do not possess experiential knowledge of him (1:2f.).

Corruption was charged in count two. Judah was a sinful nation, loaded down with guilt. They wanted no part of the "Holy One of

Israel" who demanded that his people reflect his holiness. They had snubbed their God, had given him the cold shoulder (1:4).

Count three indicted Judah for incorrigibleness. The children of God had been severely disciplined by their Father. They were covered from head to toe with bruises, wounds and welts. This brilliant but grotesque figure depicts the terrible desolation which God had allowed foreigners to inflict upon the land. Only the grace of God prevented Israel from becoming totally desolate like the once-proud cities of Sodom and Gomorrah (1:5-9).

The mention of Sodom and Gomorrah led to the fourth indictment which focused on hypocrisy. The rulers and people of Israel were so wicked that their counterparts could only be found in those notoriously wicked cities. In spite of their elaborate temple ceremonies they had no standing with God. Every aspect of their hypocritical worship—their sacrifices, offerings, assemblies, and even their prayers—were absolutely detestable to the Lord (1:10-16). Leupold calls this paragraph "the most scathing indictment of formalistic worship to be found anywhere in Sacred Writ."[1]

B. Invitation to Repentance (1:16-20).

The situation was not hopeless, but they must respond quickly. Since their hands where stained with the blood of abused people, God commanded them to "wash" themselves. The figure is immediately explained, first negatively, and then positively. They must stop doing wrong. They must replace that previous wrong with positive action. They must seek justice for the most helpless segments of society—the fatherless and the widow (1:16-17).

As an incentive to repentance the loving Father held out to his beloved children the prospect of forgiveness and reinstatement. God wanted ancient Israel—and indeed modern man as well—to consider two scenarios. In the first, scarlet sin, i.e., the sin of murder itself, becomes as white as snow. Willing obedience could make possible such forgiveness. The forgiven sinner would be able to enjoy life and the blessing of God. He would "eat the best from the land." The second scenario, however, pictures the fate of one who refused God's mercy and rebelled against him. That individual would be devoured by the sword (1:18-20).

C. Lamentation over Disaster (1:21-23).

Isaiah utilized the technique of lamentation to underscore the terrible condition of the nation and its need for repentance. He likened once-faithful Jerusalem to a fallen woman, to silver which had become worthless, and to wine diluted by water. That place which was once the very embodiment of righteousness now harbored murderers. The rulers, who should have been forceful advocates for the less fortunate, accepted bribes from the rich and powerful.

D. Purgation through Judgment (1:24-31).

Only judgment could purge the corrupt city. God would vent his wrath against the rebellious rulers. Like worthless dross they would be swept away. The corrupt leadership would be replaced with dedicated judges like those who served in the early days of Israel's history. Under the leadership of these righteous rulers Jerusalem would come to have a more positive reputation as the city of righteousness and a faithful city (1:24-26).

The penitent people of Zion (Jerusalem) would be redeemed from God's judgment. The rebellious sinners, however, would be crushed by his wrath. They would come to regard their pagan places of worship—the sacred oaks and gardens—with disgust. Their gods would give no sustenance in the day of trial. They would wither under the pressure like vegetation without adequate moisture. Even the mighty man would be consumed in the unquenchable fires of God's judgment (1:29-31).

A PEOPLE HUMBLED
Isaiah 2-4

The opening words of chapter 2 signal the beginning of a new unit of the book: "The word which Isaiah the son of Amoz saw concerning Judah and Jerusalem." Here is recorded a sermon which begins and ends with promise. Sandwiched between are a series of indictments against the values, leadership, men and women of the nation.

A. Promise: A Glorious City (2:2-5).

Isaiah looked beyond the temporal judgment on Jerusalem to the "last days," i.e., the Messianic Age.[2] "The mountain of the Lord's house," the mountain occupied by God's temple, would be established "in the top of the mountains." Mountains often symbolize kingdoms in prophecy. The temple mount here indicates that God's kingdom is spiritual. That kingdom would one day be exalted over all kingdoms of this world (2:2).

Gentiles would stream to that holy mount. They would hunger to know the ways of Israel's God. They would desire to live their lives by his precepts. Zion would be the center of religious instruction for the whole world. The Gentiles would make the Word of God the standard for settling disputes among themselves. The hostility between nations would cease. Instruments of war would be transformed into instruments of commerce. Isaiah used this exciting picture of Zion's future attractiveness to encourage his contemporaries to "walk in the light of the Lord" (2:3-5).

Isaiah's prediction regarding Zion's future has received two very different interpretations. Some see this as a description of the millennial reign of Christ—a thousand years of peace with Christ ruling from the throne of David in Jerusalem. Others see in these predictions a picture of the New Testament Zion, the church of Christ (Heb. 12:22). In any case, where Christ's government prevails, peace follows.[3]

B. Indictment: An Abandoned People (2:6-9).

Since the house of Jacob was not walking in the light of the Lord, he had abandoned them to their fate. This drastic action became necessary because God's people had embraced the superstitions of the heathen. The people trusted in their abundant silver and gold and in their horses, i.e., military might. The land was full of idols and the people unashamedly bowed before these man-made objects. The abandonment of Israel would ultimately result in the humbling of the proud sinners in judgment.

C. Warning: God's Day (2:10-22).

Isaiah predicted the coming of a day when all the sinful pretensions of man would be humbled. The Lord alone would be exalted in that day. Every symbol and object of man's pride would be laid low.

The idols would totally disappear (2:10-18). Whether Isaiah was describing the forthcoming judgment upon Judah, or the final judgment is a matter of debate. The prophets apparently regarded every temporal judgment as a day of the Lord which betokened that final day when God's judgment will be poured out on the entire world.

In that day the Lord would arise to shake the earth. From his dreadful majesty men would flee to the caverns in the rocks. So as not to be impeded in their flight, they would cast away their worthless idols. From God's awesome judgment, however, no escape would be possible. The caves of the mountains and holes in the ground would afford no protection. Since those idols could not avert God's judgment, trusting in them was senseless. Likewise, putting trust in mortal man makes no sense (2:19-22).

D. Warning: Judgment on Judah (3:1-12).

God's judgment would remove every supply and support—every crutch—of Judah. This included material necessities like food and water. Included also were military, political, and religious leaders upon whom the people depended. Naive, inexperienced and immature men—mere children in disposition and ability—would assume the leadership roles. Without strong central government, anarchy would prevail. So desperate would that hour be that men would seize anyone who had the trappings of leadership and draft him for office. No would-be leader, however, would have any solutions for the woes of the nation (3:1-7).

In Isaiah's view Jerusalem was staggering to its destruction. In word and deed these people had fought against God; they had offended his glorious eye. Their sin was blatant, open and defiant. Guilt was written all over their faces. Like the citizens of ancient Sodom, they paraded their sins before God and man. They, therefore, had brought themselves under a prophetic "woe." Disaster was awaiting them. They would reap what they had sowed (3:8-9).

God's judgment would make a distinction between the wicked and the righteous. Those who lived by the standards of God's word would be blessed by God. They would "enjoy the fruit of their deeds." The wicked, however, were under God's "woe," i.e., his threat of destructive judgment. They too would reap what they had sowed.

God's people had been led from the path of obedience by their rulers who were as inexperienced in government as women, and as oppressively selfish as spoiled youths. God accused these leaders of causing "my people" to err, of leading them down paths of destruction (3:10-12).

The Lord stood up to press a lawsuit against the elders and princes of the land. Instead of protecting God's vineyard (the nation) they had consumed it. They had furnished their homes with spoils taken illegally from the poor of the land. In a question addressed to the defendants, the Lord pointedly asked, How could you beat down and crush my people so? (3:13-15).

E. Warning: Judgment on the Women (3:16-4:1).

The women of Judah fell under divine condemnation no less than the men. With cutting sarcasm Isaiah described the haughty walk and look of the leading ladies of the land. In God's judgment they would be stripped of all their finery and forced to don sackcloth. Their beautiful hairdos would give way to baldness and scabs. A stench would replace the sweet odor of their expensive perfumes. Zion, as a destitute widow, would lament the slaughter of all men of war. The women, desperate to avoid the reproach of childlessness, shamelessly would compete for marriage proposals from the few surviving men. They would be willing to eat their own bread, i.e., pay their own way, if only they might have a husband.

F. Promise: A Better Day (4:2-6).

The judgment of which Isaiah had been speaking would not be the final curtain of the divine drama. Three great blessings await those who "in that day," that future time, escape the wrath of God. First, a glorious leader would appear. That he would be divine is hinted at in the title "Branch of the Lord." That he would be also human is suggested by the phrase "the fruit of the earth," i.e., of lowly birth. Those who had been saved from God's wrath—the remnant—would readily embrace him (4:2). The leader in view here is no doubt the Messiah.

Second, those who survived the devastating judgment on Jerusalem would be those who had been "written for life," i.e., chosen by God. They would be called "holy" because by faith they had embraced that divinely appointed leader, the Branch of the Lord (4:3f.).

Third, those who dwell in purified Zion would experience the protection of the Lord. In language borrowed from the Exodus narrative, God promised a cloud by day and a shining fire by night. He would provide his people, as it were, a shelter from storm and heat, i.e., protection through the trials of life (4:5f.).

A VINEYARD DESTROYED
Isaiah 5:1-30

In chapter 5 Isaiah sang parabolically of Israel under the figure of a vineyard. He then delineated some of the sour grapes produced by that vineyard.

A. The Choice Vineyard (5:1-7).

Isaiah referred to God in the most affectionate way: "my loved one" (NIV) or "my well-beloved" (NASB). The gist of his song is that the Lord had a vineyard upon which he devoted constant care. The fertile hillside was properly prepared and planted with the choicest vines. In anticipation of an abundant harvest a wine press was constructed near the vineyard. The vineyard, however, produced nothing but bad fruit. God appealed to the inhabitants of Jerusalem to judge the situation for themselves. What more could have been done for the vineyard? Why did that well-tended vineyard yield only bad grapes? (5:1-4).

Next the vineyard owner announced his intentions regarding his fruitless possession. The hedge and wall which protected the vineyard would be removed. The plot would be trampled by man and beast. Rain would be withheld. No more effort would be expended cultivating the vines. Thorn bushes would soon choke out the vines (5:5f.).

Isaiah made clear the meaning of his parable. The vineyard of Yahweh of hosts represented the house of Israel, and the inhabitants of Judah in particular. The fruit which the Lord anticipated was justice and righteousness. All he saw, however, was violent bloodshed; all he heard was the cry of people in great distress (5:7).

B. The Rotten Fruit (5:8-23).

The parable of the vineyard is followed by six woes which the prophet probably intended to be examples of the wild grapes produced by God's vineyard. The first woe pointed to the insatiable greed of the powerful land barons. They could never acquire enough land. God threatened to vacate their mansions and reduce their crops to only a tenth of the seed sown (5:8-10).

The second woe focused on dissipation and drunkenness. All concern for God's word and work had been quenched by their revelry. Exile to foreign lands awaited these men who lack all spiritual understanding. Sheol (the abode of the dead), like a voracious monster, would swallow the elite and the noisy throngs as well. All the inhabitants of Judah would be humbled in that dreadful day. The Lord, however, would be exalted in his holy act of judgment. Flocks would graze in once populated areas. Strangers would overrun the land (5:11-17).

In the third woe Isaiah condemned Judah's daring defiance of the Lord. They showed willful contempt for all the prophetic denunciations. They brazenly challenged God to do his work of judgment. Only when they saw it would they believe it. These men willingly had hitched themselves to a load of sin and by that load they would be crushed ultimately (5:18f.).

Three brief hammer-like blows completed the series of six woes. The first was a condemnation of Judah's moral perversity. These people had launched a semantical attack on all righteous deeds and had bestowed upon the most despicable acts terms of approbation (5:20). Next Isaiah denounced Judah's arrogant self-conceit. They were wise in their own eyes (5:21). Finally, the prophet mockingly berated Judah's corrupted courage. They were heroes at consuming wine but they had no moral courage to champion the cause of the innocent (5:22).

C. The Bitter Consequences (5:24-30).

Bitter fruit requires a bitter harvest. Isaiah depicted the consequences of spurning the word of the Holy One of Israel in four word pictures. In the first he pictured Judah as a withered vineyard. Against that tinder-dry vineyard the burning wrath of Yahweh would be unleashed (5:24). In the picture of the upraised hand Isaiah depicted God striking down his people with his mighty hand. Mountains shook from the blows.[4] Corpses piled up like refuse in the streets. Stubborn refusal to repent caused God's hand to remain poised for further blows (5:25).

The third word picture was that of the roaring lion. God would summon agents of destruction by means of a signal flag and a whistle. The unidentified enemy soldiers would be alert, well-equipped, swift. This invading army would be as irresistible as a roaring lion (5:26-29). In the fourth picture Judah was compared to a storm-tossed ship. No matter in which direction the leaders looked, no hopeful prospect could be seen (5:30).

A PROPHET CALLED
Isaiah 6

At the conclusion of the Book of Mingled Rebukes and Promises Isaiah presented his credentials for preaching. He indicated the importance of what is recorded here by his precise dating: "the year that King Uzziah died" (c. 739 BC). The vision which is described here has three components.

A. A Vision of God (6:1-3).

Isaiah saw the Lord (*'adonay*, the sovereign one) as an exalted king on the throne of his heavenly temple. His train (robes) filled the whole place (6:1). According to the Apostle John, Isaiah saw Jesus' glory (John 12:39-41).

Seraphim (flame-like angelic beings) stood about the heavenly throne waiting to do the bidding of the King. Each had six pairs of wings. One pair shielded the face from God's glory; one pair covered the lower body parts in modesty; and one pair was used to hover. In their antiphonal singing the seraphim praised God for his holiness and his omnipotence. They extolled him for manifesting his glory throughout all the earth. The heavenly temple shook with the mighty strains of the hymn of these angels. Smoky clouds of incense filled the entire temple and shielded the eyes of the prophet from looking directly upon the glory of deity (6:2-4).

B. A Vision of Self (6:5-7).

Isaiah let his audience know that before he pronounced his woes on others, he had first pronounced a woe upon himself. Having become aware of the holiness of God, he knew that his own sinfulness meant doom ("I am ruined"). He had just heard holy lips praise God; he now became aware of the uncleanness of his own lips. He was unfit to preach, or even to praise God in his wretched condition (6:5).

One of the seraphim touched Isaiah's lips with a hot coal from the altar of incense. In this visional and symbolic gesture the young man received assurance that his sins had been purged (6:6-7). Martin has observed that God does not want and will not use unclean instruments in his service.[5]

C. A Vision of Service (6:8-13).

Isaiah heard the voice of the Lord saying, "Who will go for us?" The plural pronoun seems to point to the pluralistic unity of the Godhead. One God speaks, but three distinct persons in the Godhead are involved. Reverence compels Isaiah to say as little as possible. Two words in the Hebrew give his positive answer (6:8). Martin observes that the *woe* of confession (v. 5) is followed by the *lo* of cleaning (v. 7), and that in turn by the *go* of commission (v. 9).[6]

Men who refuse God's Word become ever more hardened to its influence. Isaiah was warned at the outset that his preaching would "make the heart of this people fat," i.e., their understanding would become dull and sluggish. His auditors would become spiritually blind and deaf (6:9f.).

The pessimistic forecast provoked a despairing question from the fledgling prophet. How long must he continue to preach a message which would cause his people to entrench themselves ever deeper in sin? God's answer: he must continue to preach until his predictions of devastation and deportation had been completely fulfilled. Then only would he be relieved of the responsibility to preach (6:11f.).

One slight glimmer of hope penetrated the dark outlook for Judah. A tithe of the population would survive the judgment. Even that remnant, however, would experience severe persecution. Those who listened to the prophet and embraced God's holiness would be

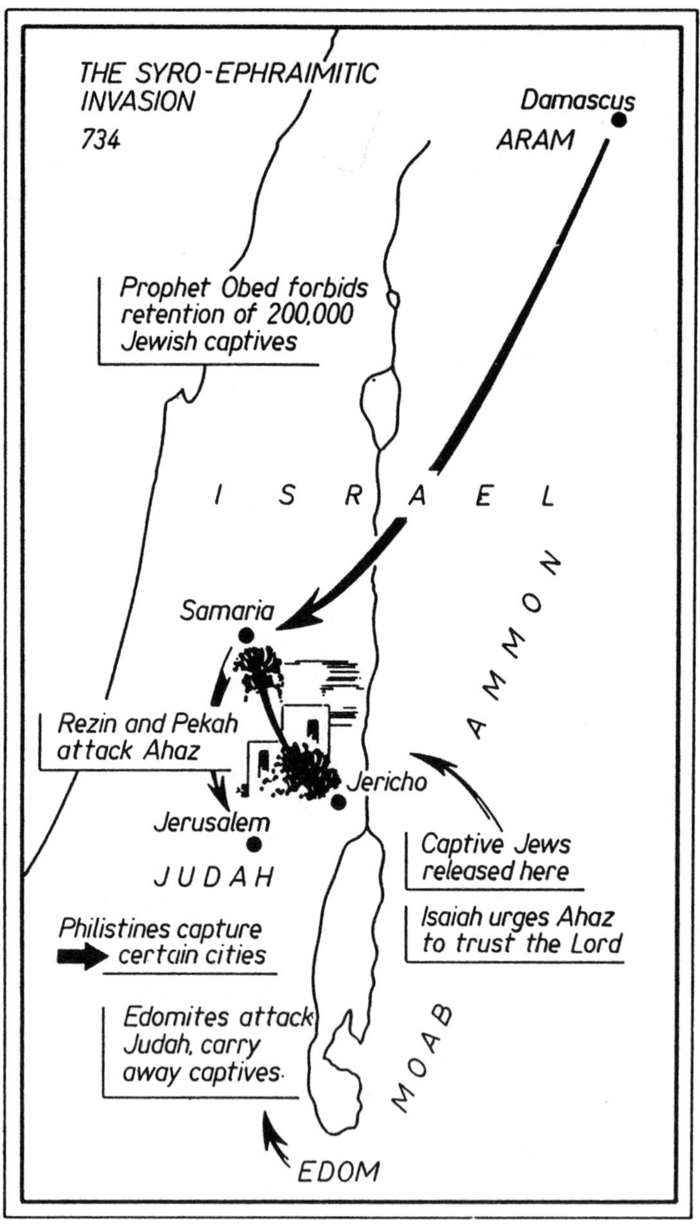
THE SYRO-EPHRAIMITIC
INVASION
734
Damascus
ARAM
Prophet Obed forbids
retention of 200,000
Jewish captives
I S R A E L
AMMON
Samaria
Rezin and Pekah
attack Ahaz
Jericho
Jerusalem
JUDAH
Captive Jews
released here
Isaiah urges Ahaz
to trust the Lord
Philistines capture
certain cities
Edomites attack
Judah, carry
away captives.
MOAB
EDOM

like a stump in the land. From that stump a new Israel would emerge (6:13).

Endnotes

1. H.C. Leupold, *Exposition of Isaiah* (Grand Rapids: Baker, 1968) 1:60.

2. See Acts 2:17; Heb 1:2; Jas 5:3: 1 Pet 1:5,20; 2 Pet 3:3; I John 2:18.

3. Where Christ's government prevails, peace follows. See Acts 10:36; Rom 5:1; Eph 2:14, 15, 17.

4. The reference is probably to the recent earthquake in the days of King Uzziah (Amos 1:1; Zech 14:5).

5. Alfred Martin, *Isaiah: 'The Salvation of Jehovah'* (Chicago: Moody, 1956) 35.

6. *Ibid.*

CHAPTER THREE

The Book of Immanuel
Isaiah 7-12

Background of the Unit.

When the ominous intentions of the Assyrians under Tiglath-pileser III became evident, the states of Syria and Palestine began to band together in a defense league. Leaders of this anti-Assyrian coalition were King Pekah of Israel (740-732 BC) and King Rezin of Damascus (750-732 BC). King Ahaz of Judah (735-720 BC) chose the path of neutrality.

Enormous pressure was brought to bear on Ahaz to join the coalition because Jerusalem was geographically strategic to the defense league. Syria and Ephraim (Israel) attacked Judah with a view to replacing Ahaz with a king who would join the coalition. While thousands of captives were taken in this Syro-Ephraimitic invasion, the attack fell short of its intended purpose. King Ahaz appealed to Tiglath-pileser for assistance, and the Assyrian was not long in coming to his aid (2 Kgs 16:5-8).

On a campaign in 732 BC Tiglath-pileser captured Damascus

and many towns in Israel. Thousands were deported. A vassal king (Hoshea) was put on the throne of Israel (2 Kgs 15:29). The entire unit known as "the book of Immanuel" dates to the years 734-732 BC during the reign of King Ahaz.

Outline of the Unit.

A. The Promise of Immanuel (chap. 7).
B. Attack on Immanuel's Land (chap. 8).
C. Appearance of Immanuel (9:1-7).
D. Deliverance for Immanuel's People (9:8-10:34).
E. The Program of Immanuel (chap. 11).
F. Praise for Immanuel (chap. 12).

THE PROMISE OF IMMANUEL
Isaiah 7

The Book of Immanuel contains what Delitzsch calls "the great trilogy of Messianic prophecies."[1] In chapter 7 Messiah is about to be born; in chapter 9 he is depicted as already having been born; and in chapter 11 he is pictured reigning over his kingdom. Since the days of Delitzsch the ranks of those who believe that Isaiah 7 contains personal Messianic prophecy have dwindled. To see the virgin birth of Christ in Isaiah 7:14 is no longer popular. Modern scholarship notwithstanding, the interpretation which identifies Immanuel as Messiah is superior to those which regard him as a child born in the days of Isaiah.[2]

A. Background of the Promise (7:1-9).

Fear gripped the royal family of Judah when news arrived of the impending invasion by the forces of Rezin and Pekah. In anticipation of a siege, the king began to inspect his defenses and especially his water supply system. Though Ahaz was no paragon of virtue, he was after all the legitimate representative of the house of David. For this reason the Lord dispatched Isaiah to approach the king with a word of encouragement in this moment of national crisis. The prophet conveyed this encouragement by seven means.

First, Isaiah offered encouragement through a symbolic name. The name of Isaiah's son, Shear-jashub ("a remnant shall return") was intended to be a sign of hope (7:3). Second, the encouragement came through four commands. These commands—two positive ("take care, and be calm") and two negative ("have no fear and do not be faint-hearted")—suggest that the king had nothing to worry about. Third, Isaiah brought encouragement through a metaphor. He compared the fierce anger of Pekah and Rezin to smoldering firebrands, i.e., they were of no danger (7:4).

The fourth means through which Isaiah conveyed encouragement was a promise. The plot to overthrow the Davidic dynasty would not succeed (7:7). Fifth, a longer range prediction also brought encouragement. Within sixty-five years Ephraim would cease to be a people (7:8).[3] Sixth, Isaiah offered an encouraging analysis of the situation. Both adversaries ultimately have only human heads over them (7:5). Finally, the prophet offered a simple plan by which Ahaz might escape the dangers posed by the Syro-Ephraimitic invasion. All the king had to do was to believe the promise and he would be established on the throne (7:9).

B. The Sign and the Promise (7:10-16).

Seeing skepticism reflected in the face of the king, Isaiah commanded Ahaz to ask for a sign. The king, however, had the freedom to name whatever spectacular event in the height (heavens) or in the depth (Sheol) which might convince him of the truth of God's Word.

Ahaz was not interested in signs and such. He had already resolved to pursue a political solution to his problem. He would send to Tiglath-pileser, the Assyrian tyrant, for aid against Rezin and Pekah. Ahaz therefore rebelled against the prophet's command, though he couched his rebellion in pious jargon: "I will not ask, nor will I test the Lord." If these words were the resolve of a godly man they would be admirable. In the present circumstances, however, they mask stubborn unbelief and hypocrisy. The royal family of late had tried the patience of God's men (the prophets) again and again. Ahaz's defiant rejection of the gracious offer of a sign was now trying the patience of God himself (7:10-12).

A sign was given to the house of David.[4] A virgin (*almah*) would conceive and bear a son. The word *almah* is never used of a married woman. Strictly speaking the word means a young woman of marriageable age. Logic demands one of two options. The *almah* must be either (1) an unmarried immoral woman; or (2) a virgin. The birth of a child by an unmarried woman is so common it could not be a "sign." For this reason the Greek translators, long before the time of Christ, correctly determined that only the word *parthenos* (virgin) was a suitable translation for *almah* in this context.

Who is the *almah* in Isaiah 7:14? Among the more common modern views are these: (1) Isaiah's wife or wife-to-be; or (2) Ahaz's wife, the mother of Hezekiah. The traditional view of the church is that the *almah* here is the virgin Mary. The Apostle Matthew saw in this verse a direct prediction of the birth of Jesus (Matt 1:22f.).

Concerning the baby of the virgin the prophecy states the following: (1) the child would be male; (2) he would be given the unique name Immanuel, "God with us;" (3) he would grow up in humble circumstances, for his diet would consist of "curds and honey;" (4) he would experience the normal course of growth like any other little boy (7:14f.).

Before the birth of the virgin's child the land of Israel, concerning which Ahaz was upset,[5] would be abandoned by both of her kings (7:16). Isaiah may be prophesying the end of the divided monarchy period.[6]

C. The Punishment of the Unbelievers (7:17-25).

Ahaz willingly submitted to the king of Assyria. That alliance would eventually backfire and bring Judah into a state of humiliation unequaled since the revolt of the northern tribes in 931 BC. In four figures Isaiah described what Judah would face. First, he likened the enemy to killer bees. This plague would be summoned by the divine bee-keeper. The Assyrian killer bees would overrun all the land (7:18f.). Second, Isaiah compared the enemy to a hired razor. The king of Assyria, hired by Ahaz, would shave all the hair off personified Judah. Removal of hair and beard was a sign of deep humiliation (7:20).

The third figure was that of the scanty diet. Only a few milk-giving animals would survive the devastation. The population would be forced to eat only curds (from the milk) and honey found here and there in the land (7:21f.). Finally, Isaiah painted a word picture of an overgrown land. Once valuable vineyards would be covered with brush. They would become hunting preserves. Areas once cultivated would be overrun with cattle and sheep (7:23-25).

ATTACK ON IMMANUEL'S LAND
Isaiah 8

Chapter 8 further develops the theme of chapter 7. The Syro-Ephraimitic invasion would fail. Because Judah, however, had not put her trust in the Lord, she would be faced with even a greater threat, viz., the Assyrian superpower. In the light of these developments, Isaiah urged his people to focus on God alone as the only source of deliverance. The key doctrine taught here is encapsuled in the name Immanuel—God is with us!

A. Revelation for the Present Crisis (8:1-4).

During the Syro-Ephraimitic crisis of 734 BC Isaiah received a four-word revelation which spelled relief for Judah, but doom for the invaders. He made known that revelation in two ways. First, on a large "billboard"[7] Isaiah wrote the four-word revelation: *maher-shalal-hash-baz* ("plunder speeds, spoil hastens"). Two faithful witnesses could attest to the date this symbolic action was performed and the content of the prophecy which accompanied it (8:1f.).

Second, the prophet turned his four-word revelation into a personal name. Nine months later a son was born to Isaiah and his wife ("the prophetess"). Isaiah named his son Maher-shalal-hash-baz. This unusual name conveyed a prophecy concerning the fate of Syria and Ephraim. Before Isaiah's son could utter his first words, the king of Assyria would have carried away the spoil of Samaria and Damascus (8:3f.). Tiglath-pileser fulfilled this prediction in 732 BC.

B. Revelation for the Coming Crisis (8:5-10).

The plot of Pekah of Israel and Rezin of Syria to remove Ahaz from the throne had popular support in Judah. The people had rejected, so to speak, the gently flowing "waters of Shiloah," symbolic of trust in God. Therefore, God would bring against them the mighty waters of the Euphrates River, symbolic of the Assyrian king. Those raging waters would reach to the very neck of Judah. The country would just barely survive. Like a giant bird of prey the Assyrian king would spread his wings over Judah (8:5-8).

The designs of the king of Assyria, however, would not succeed for Judah was really Immanuel's land. In prophetic sarcasm Isaiah addressed all potential enemies of God's people. Whether the invader be from Syria (734 BC) or Assyria (701 BC), he was doomed to defeat. For the sake of Immanuel God would stand by his people (8:9f.).

C. Revelation for Any Crisis (8:11-22).

In the power of God Isaiah received special revelation warning him not to walk in the way of the people. He was not to waver in his position just because the people regarded it as treason. He and his followers were to fear God to such a degree that they would not fear Rezin and Pekah or even Assyria for that matter. Those who trusted in God would find there a mighty sanctuary. To those who refused to believe, however, God would be like a stone of stumbling and a trap. Many would stumble over that stone or be ensnared in that trap (8:12-17).

Isaiah had a ministry to the faithful remnant—here called "my" disciples—as well as to the nation as a whole. He was "to bind up" and "seal" the word of God within them. As one preserves something precious in a purse, so Isaiah deposited his treasure of warnings and teachings with the Lord's disciples[8] (8:16). That the Messiah is the speaker in these verses is indicated in Hebrews 2:13.

Messiah announced that he would wait expectantly while God was hiding his face, i.e., withdrawing his protective intervention on behalf of his people. In the fullness of time, however, Messiah would come. He and his "children" (disciples) would be signs and wonders, i.e., pledges and tokens of future events (8:17f.).

The speaker (Messiah) pointed out the stupidity of seeking occult revelation. Until that day when Messiah would appear God's people should stand steadfastly by the law and the testimony, i.e., the Old Testament revelation. Those who did not allow that ancient Sinai revelation to enlighten their speech were living in absolute darkness. Having rejected God's revelation, they would have a most distressing future of gloom, anguish and fruitless searching for guidance (8:19-22).

APPEARANCE OF IMMANUEL
Isaiah 9:1-7

Chapter 8 concluded with Messiah patiently waiting until the indignation against Judah was past. Now the second member of the great Messianic trilogy sets forth the dawn of a new day, the birth of a wonderful child, and the rule of a glorious king.

A. The Dawn of a New Day (9:1-5).

The gloom of God's judgment upon his people would not be permanent. Those regions around the Sea of Galilee which were the first to be overrun by northern enemies, would be the first to see the dawn of a new day of great light, i.e., a new revelation from God (9:1f.). The passage forecasts the great work of Christ and all the blessings which he would bring (cf. Matt 4:13ff.). In four beautiful word pictures that glorious day is described.

First, the day of Messiah would be a day of expansion. God would enlarge the nation (9:3a). The reference probably is to the incorporation of Gentiles into the new Israel of God, the church of Christ. Second, that would be a day of joy like unto that which follows a successful harvest or battle (9:3b). Third, Messiah's coming would usher in a day of deliverance. The rod and yoke of the Great Oppressor would be shattered as in the day when Gideon crushed the hordes of Midian (9:4). Finally, that would be a day of peace. The picture is that of the clean-up after war. Warrior's boots and blood-stained garments would be consigned to fire (9:5).

B. The Birth of a Miracle Child (9:6).

The glorious day described in the opening verses of the chapter would be ushered in by the birth of a male child. Isaiah identified this child as God's Son who had been given to all people as a deliverer. The weight of government would rest on his shoulders. Four titles would be bestowed on that great ruler: (1) Wonderful Counselor; (2) Mighty God; (3) Everlasting Father; and (4) Prince of Peace. That this son is the virgin's Immanuel of Isaiah 7:14 there can be little doubt.[9]

C. The Reign of a Glorious King (9:7).

The government of this ruler would be ever expanding. Unlike the kingdoms of this world, however, his kingdom would expand by peaceful means. Justice and righteousness would be established and maintained throughout his realm. His kingdom would endure forever. As a descendant of David, he would sit on David's throne and rule David's kingdom. Since David sat on God's throne (1 Chr 29:23) and ruled God's kingdom, these terms are not to be interpreted in a narrow, physical and earthly sense. The New Testament testifies that Christ, the son of David, is now seated on the throne of God in heaven.[10] Only through the zeal of God for his people could these glorious promises be implemented.

DELIVERANCE FOR IMMANUEL'S PEOPLE
Isaiah 9:8-10:34

The name Immanuel ("God with us") captures the theme of this unit. Though Judah would suffer terribly at the hands of her enemies, ultimately neither Ephraim nor Assyria would be able to crush God's people. Both adversaries provoked Yahweh's "woe" because of their pride (10:1,5). After describing God's judgment on Ephraim, the immediate threat, Isaiah described in more detail God's dealings with Assyria.

A. Confrontation with Ephraim (9:8-10:4).

In the midst of the Syro-Ephraimitic invasion Isaiah offered his people a message of hope. Ephraim's fate as a nation was sealed. The point of the unit is that Judah has nothing to fear from Ephraim since Ephraim had troubles of its own. In four artistic strophes Isaiah described Ephraim's impending confrontation with the God of judgment. Each strophe concludes with the thunderous warning, "In spite of all this His anger does not turn away, and His hand is still stretched out" (9:12,17,21; 10:4).

In the first encounter with God the land of Ephraim would be devoured. Prior invasions had made no impact on the arrogant citizens of the Northern Kingdom. They were confident that they could rebuild after any judgment which God might permit to come upon them. Nonetheless, Ephraim must face "the adversaries of Rezin," i.e., the Assyrians. Thereafter the land of Israel would be subject to incursions by Arameans and Philistines alike (9:8-12).

The second encounter with God would leave Ephraim leaderless. The Northern Kingdom faced devastating military defeats in which "head and tail" (elder and prophet) would be cut off. These corrupt leaders had caused the entire nation to err. All classes of society were profane and irreligious and would therefore experience the wrath of God (9:13-17).

A third encounter with God would result in chaotic violence. Anarchy would sweep like a raging forest fire through the land. The major northern tribes (Ephraim and Manasseh) would tear at each other with cannibal-like fury. This internecine strife would only be suppressed as the northern tribes vented their mutual animosity on Judah to the south (9:18-21).[11]

A fourth encounter with the God of judgment would lead to the oppressors being oppressed. Captivity or death awaited those who had misused their office by abusing the disadvantaged. From that day of reckoning there would be no relief from any quarter (10:1-4).

B. Commission of Assyria (10:5-11).

To this point Isaiah had depicted Assyria as a mighty power, dependence upon which would lead to disaster. Now he began to represent Assyria as an instrument of God's wrath, a rod through which God would administer judgment against a godless nation. The Assyrian would trample Ephraim into the mud and enrich himself at the expense of his fallen victim. The Assyrian, however, had more grandiose intentions. His barbarous lust for plunder would drive him to destroy *many* nations, including Judah (10:5-7).

God had given to Assyria a limited commission within his eternal plan. The proud Assyrian, however, had much more grandiose ambitions. Isaiah depicted the arrogant Assyrian boasting of past conquests in Aram and Israel. Great gods (idols) had failed to protect their people from him. Yahweh is but another idol—and not a very grand one at that—who would fail to protect his people. Such arrogance cried out for heaven's judgment (10:8-11).

C. Condemnation of the Assyrian (10:12-19).

Yahweh announced his decision to punish the proud Assyrian once he had used him to bring judgment against Jerusalem. To make clear to the world the need for this punishment, Isaiah did two things. First, he simply let the arrogant king speak. The conqueror claimed that his wisdom was irresistible, his might invincible. He gathered the spoils of nations as easily as men gather abandoned eggs. No one dared to oppose him. Second, Isaiah submitted this argument: The Assyrian was but a tool in the hand of God. Boastfulness on his part was inappropriate and audacious. Therefore, Yahweh would bring judgment upon him (10:12-15).

After justifying the judgment, Isaiah described in dramatic figures what awaited Assyria. A debilitating disease would cause the stalwart warriors to waste away. Like trees consumed by a raging forest fire they would fall in a "single day." So few trees would remain that a child would be able to count them![13] Thus it would become clear that Yahweh was not just another idol, but the Living God, the Light of Israel, the Holy One (10:16-19).

D. The Consequences for Judah (10:20-27).

God's use of the Assyrian at Jerusalem would have both negative and positive results. On the negative side, Judah faced great devastation. Before meeting his own doom, the Assyrian would wreak havoc throughout Judah. Only a small portion of the population would survive. This remnant would consist of those who returned to Yahweh and who trusted only in him, not in political expediencies (10:20-23).

If Judah would experience devastation from Assyria, she would also experience a wonderful deliverance. During the painful chastening the remnant did not need to fear the Assyrians. They could be confident that the punishment of the nation would be over very soon. Then God's wrath would be directed toward the destruction of the adversary. Deliverance would be sure and thorough. History proved that their God was a mighty deliverer. Through Gideon Yahweh had beaten the Midianites into submission in the days of the Judges. Through Moses at the Red Sea he had parted the waters to allow Israel to escape from Egyptian bondage. So the Assyrians also would find God's people to be like a stout ox which could not be subjected permanently to an oppressive yoke (10:24-27).

E. The Coming of the Assyrian (10:28-34).

Isaiah saw in vision the advance of the Assyrian against Jerusalem. He approached from the north. He intended for the village of Nob, within sight of Jerusalem, to be the staging area for the assault against the capital. He shook his fist menacingly toward the city. That, however, would be all the Assyrian would be permitted to do. God, like a mighty Paul Bunyan, would take his axe to that forest of men. The tall trees would be brought low. Assyria would fall.

THE PROGRAM OF IMMANUEL
Isaiah 11

Assyria was doomed, but Judah had a future. Out of the devastation inflicted by powers like Assyria, a great Ruler would arise from the house of David. In this third member of the great Messianic trilogy Isaiah spoke of the appearance of the Ruler. He then described the subjects of his kingdom and the nature of his rule.

A. The Appearance of the Ruler (11:1-9).

From the earliest times God's people anticipated the coming of One who would be Savior, Prophet, Priest and King. Isaiah stressed four points concerning this Coming One. First, Messiah would be of humble origins. At the time of his appearing the royal family of Judah—the house of David son of Jesse—would be reduced to stump-like stature in the world. Out of that stump, however, would come forth a fragile shoot which ultimately would bear much fruit (11:1). Second, Messiah would have supernatural endowments. The fullness of the Holy Spirit would rest upon him. Three pairs of often antagonistic attributes would be marvelously combined in him: wisdom and understanding; counsel and power; knowledge and the fear of the Lord (11:2).

Third, Isaiah stressed the fair judgments which this Ruler would make. In his role as Judge he would be girded about with righteousness and faithfulness. He would long to see in his subjects humble reverence. Knowing the hearts of men, he would be impartial in all decisions. In his omnipotent power he could instantly dispatch the wicked with but a word (11:3-5). Nonetheless, Isaiah indicated that the government of this Ruler would be peaceful. Former enemies would coexist harmoniously. Vicious beasts would be docile. Paradise-like conditions would exist in all God's "holy mountain" (Zion, God's kingdom). This tranquil state would be the result of the dissemination of the knowledge of Yahweh throughout the earth (11:6-9).

B. The Subjects of the Ruler (11:10-14)

The Coming Ruler would have a kingdom and subjects. Isaiah described the citizens of his kingdom in three ways. First, messianic kingdom citizens would be marked by great diversity. The Root of Jesse (cf. 11:1) would become a banner under which Gentiles could rally. His "resting place"—the New Testament temple—would be a glorious attraction to them. In that messianic age the Lord would reclaim the remnant of his Old Testament people from the lands of their captivity just as he had once before gathered them out of bondage to Pharaoh (11:10f.).

Second, Isaiah stressed the unity of Messiah's subjects. The outcasts of the old Northern Kingdom would join the dispersed of Judah. The old rivalries which existed between the northern and southern tribes would cease (11:12f.). Finally, the prophet foresaw ultimate victory. The reunited people of God would conquer their ancient enemies to the east and west. In Old Testament battle language the expansion of Messiah's kingdom is depicted (11:14).

C. The Work of the Ruler (11:15-16).

The barriers standing between people and the promised land of redemption would be removed. Isaiah used the Red Sea and the Euphrates river as symbols of that which impedes the movement of enslaved people to the Land of Promise. At the Exodus under Moses God had made a way through the Red Sea. Under Messiah God would remove "the tongue of the Red Sea," effecting a greater deliverance than that of Moses. The Euphrates river which seemed unfordable would be broken up into rivulets through which pilgrims would be able to walk dry shod (11:15). The point is that nothing can prevent those whom God gathers through the Gospel from enjoying the glories of the promised kingdom.

Those in Assyria, the land of captivity, would have a highway to travel upon to the Land of Promise (11:16). The highway concept, which is common in Isaiah,[16] also appears in the New Testament.[17] A highway is that way which is clearly marked, a way in which God is leading. Though many mysterious passages may perplex believers, the way out of the bondage of sin, through the wilderness of hardship and temptation, across Jordan and home to heavenly Canaan has been clearly revealed in the Word!

PRAISE FOR IMMANUEL
Isaiah 12

The short chapter 12 contains the praise of the redeemed in that day," i.e., the Messianic age, together with one additional precious promise from the Lord. First, the redeemed would break forth into praise because they had experienced the change from divine condemnation to divine comfort (12:1). Second, they would boldly and personally declare their trust in God. They would embrace Yahweh as their strength, song and salvation (12:2). In response to this praise the Lord added another wonderful messianic promise. His people would continue to drink the water of life from "wells of salvation" (12:3).

The added promise stimulated even more vigorous praise on the part of God's people. First, those who had experienced salvation would want all the earth to hear of the mighty deeds of Yahweh (12:4f.). Second, the redeemed would rejoice in the knowledge that the Holy One of Israel dwelled in their midst (12:6).

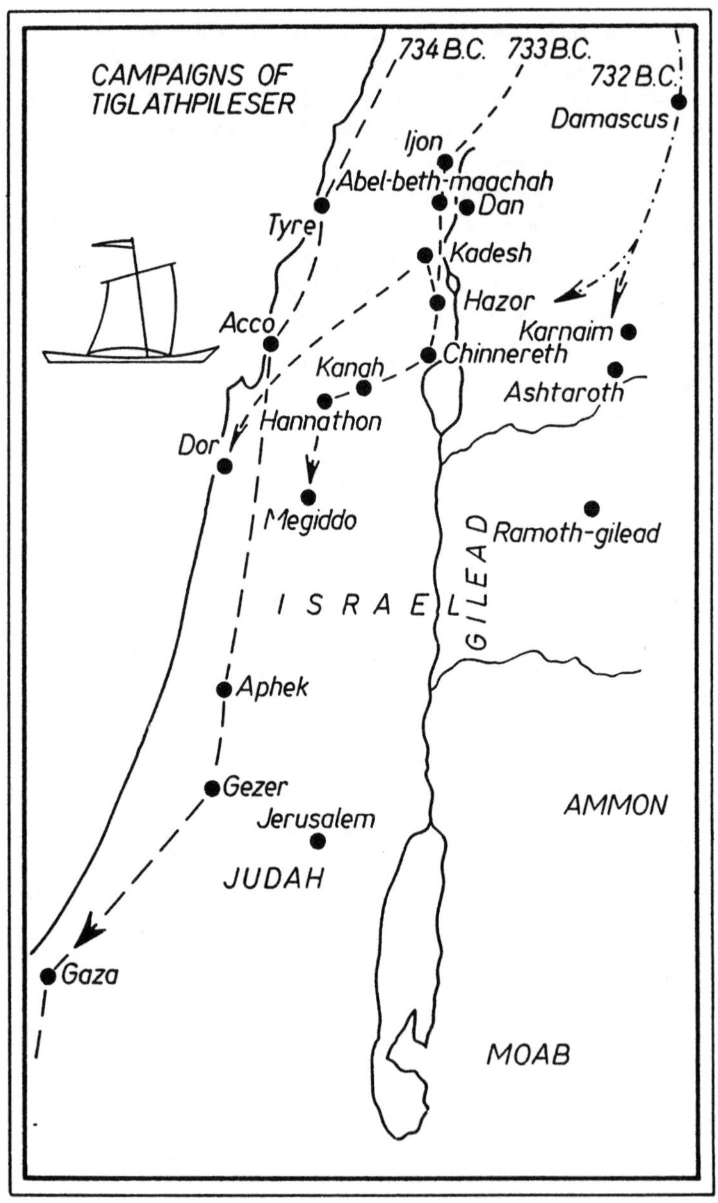
CAMPAIGNS OF
TIGLATHPILESER
734 B.C.
733 B.C.
732 B.C.
Damascus
Ijon
Abel-beth-maachah
Dan
Tyre
Kadesh
Hazor
Acco
Karnaim
Chinnereth
Kanah
Ashtaroth
Hannathon
Dor
Megiddo
Ramoth-gilead
ISRAEL
GILEAD
Aphek
Gezer
Jerusalem
AMMON
JUDAH
Gaza
MOAB

Endnotes

1. Franz Delitzsch, *Messianic Prophecies in Historical Succession* (New york: Scribners, 1891) 143.

2. For a defense of the Messianic interpretation of Isaiah 7:14 see James E. Smith, *What the Bible Says about the Promised Messiah* (Joplin: College Press, 1984) 249-55.

3. Political existence of the Northern Kingdom ceased in 722 BC with the fall of Samaria. When Esarhaddon sent foreign colonists to occupy Samaria about 669 BC he entirely destroyed the nationality of Israel.

4. *You* in 7:14 is plural.

5. Hebrew *qats*.

6. According to J. Barton Payne, the two kings are the king of Israel and the king of Judah. Immanuel would not come on the scene until the monarchy was over. Others take the two kings to be Rezin, who was slain in 732 BC by the Assyrians, and Pekah of Israel, who was assassinated the same year.

7. The Hebrew *gillayon* refers to a flat piece of wood (Ezek 37:16) or metal (Isa 3:23), and thus would be appropriate for posting as a sort of placard.

8. Oswalt takes the children to be Isaiah's sons Shearjashub and Maher-shalal-hash-baz, both of whom wore symbolic names. Ridderbos thinks Isaiah's own name was a sign as well.

9. John D.W. Watts, "Isaiah 1-33," Vol 24 of *Word Biblical Commentary* ed. David Hubbard and Glenn Barker (Waco: Word Books, 1985) 123.

10. On the heavenly rule of Christ see Luke 1:32; Matt 19:28; Acts 2:30; Heb 8:1; 12:2; Rev 3:21.

11. Commentaries struggle with the reference to Aram as an enemy of Ephraim since it is known that the two countries were allies as early as 734 BC. Ridderbos would date this oracle prior to the Syro-Ephraimitic alliance. Oswalt takes Aram as symbolic of enemies to the east counterbalancing the mention of Philistines. Walts surmises that the action taken was against Rezin who controlled Samaria. The view taken here is that Ephraim would be weakened by Assyria to such a degree that incursion on their territory by the Arameans and Philistines would be encouraged.

12. The Assyrians were victorious over Carchemish in 717 BC; Hamath in 720 BC; Damascus in 732 BC; Calno in 738 BC; Arpad in 740 BC; and Samaria in 722 BC. Whether all these conquests were in the past at the time this was written is not clear.

13. The Assyrian empire was dealt a decisive blow by the Chaldeans and Medes in 612 BC when Nineveh was captured. The remnants of the Assyrian army were destroyed by Nebuchadnezzar at the battle of Carchemish in 605 BC.

14. *Erets* could also be translated *land* Cf. John 3:14; 12:32.

15. Several lands are mentioned to which God's people had already been scattered in Isaiah's day. See Hos 9:3, 6; Isa 7:18; 18:1ff.; Joel 3:6ff.

16. See Isa 40:3, 4; 42:16; 49:11; 35:8.

17. See Matt. 7:14; 22:16; John 14:6; Acts 9:2; 16:17; 18:25, 26; 19:9, 23; 22:4; 24:14, 22; Heb 10:20.

CHAPTER FOUR

The Book of Burdens
Isaiah 13-23

Background of the Unit.

The third major division of the Book of Isaiah consists of a series of prophetic oracles most of which concern Gentile peoples. Similar oracles (against Damascus and Assyria) have already appeared; other such oracles are found in subsequent chapters. Collections of this type of material are also found at the conclusion of Jeremiah[1] and the middle of Ezekiel. Isaiah placed this largely negative section immediately following the song of thanksgiving for a glorious future. The prophet clearly saw that the new day celebrated in chapter 12 could come only after every adversary of God's people had been brought low.[2]

The Book of Burdens derives its name from the recurrence of the Hebrew word *massa*, translated "burden" (KJV) or "oracle" (NIV). The word suggests the notion that the consequences of sin are a burden which must be borne by guilty nations. The eleven chapters of this unit contain thirteen "burdens."[3]

The chronological placement of the foreign nation oracles is difficult. The only clue is in 14:28 which refers to "the year King Ahaz died." The oracles would then all date after Ahaz died about 715 BC and therefore would be comparatively late in the prophet's ministry.

The section bristles with difficulties. In some cases the nation being addressed is uncertain. Documenting the fulfillment of some of these prophecies is not possible. While the majority of the material concerns the fate of foreign nations, some passages are addressed to Judah.[4] Why are two "woe" oracles included (17:12-14; 18:1-7)? What principle accounts for the order in which the nations are mentioned? These are but some of the problems associated with the Book of Burdens.

The most important consideration is the purpose of this unit within the overall argument of the book. Isaiah had condemned placing trust in anything or anyone other than God. Ultimately the nations could provide no salvation for Judah. They themselves stood condemned before God.[5] Thus this section underscores the complete folly of trusting in doomed nations. In this respect the unit builds on themes already introduced in the Book of Immanuel. Secondarily, the Book of Burdens serves to stress (1) the disastrous results of pride;[6] (2) the absolute sovereignty of God in the affairs of men; and (3) the ability of God to make good on his promise of a trans-national kingdom headed by a descendant of David.

Outline of the Unit.

Judgment is the major theme of the Book of Burdens. Here Isaiah pronounced God's verdict against every worldly attribute which might form a basis of confidence for any people. Isaiah drove toward the conclusion that all which the world has to offer in the way of culture, wealth, wisdom and power adds up to zero in the final analysis. Overlap between the sub-sections of this unit is apparent. Nevertheless, these oracles have been grouped in such a way as to stress God's judgment against:

A. Worldly Glory: Babylon (13:1-14:27).
B. Worldly Alliances: Near Neighbors (14:28-18:7).
C. Worldly Wisdom: Egypt (chaps. 19-20).

D. Worldly Schemes: Conspiring Nations (chaps. 21-22).
E. Worldly Wealth: Tyre (chap. 23).

WORLDLY GLORY: BABYLON
Isaiah 13:1-14:27

The burden of Babylon stands first in the collection of Gentile oracles. Why this position of prominence for a place not yet mentioned in the book? First, this oracle is the most comprehensive and most important. Second, culturally Babylon dominated the world of Isaiah's day. Powerful Assyrian kings recognized the importance of also being crowned king of Babylon. Third, this ancient city epitomized worldly glory. Fourth, because of its prominence, Babylon was well-suited to symbolize the world in general and Mesopotamia in particular.[7] Fifth, Babylon was involved at every opportunity in fomenting rebellion against Assyria. Just as Ahaz had looked to Assyria for help against the Syro-Ephraimitic coalition, his successors might be tempted to turn to Babylon for aid against Assyria. Finally, Isaiah had already spoken at length about the fate awaiting Assyria. He returned to that theme briefly at the conclusion of this oracle. Isaiah knew, however, that Babylon, not Assyria, would be the power which would destroy Jerusalem (Isa 39; 2 Kgs 20:12-19).

A. The Day of the Lord (13:1-16).

That Babylon is not mentioned until verse 19 in this burden is significant. Isaiah meant to signal his readers that the opening verses of this unit establish a general principle. God hates human pride, and he will bring it to the ground. The judgment on Babylon is but one manifestation of the day of the Lord. All proud nations will one day share her fate.

Isaiah first described the preparation for God's day against Babylon. The language of the Holy War is used to describe the armies which Isaiah foresaw attacking Babylon. God himself would lead the troops of this army of warriors. They are consecrated—set apart by God—to carry out his holy judgment against the super city (13:2-5).

The destruction of Babylon is "the day of Yahweh," i.e., the day of Yahweh's vindication.[8] That would be a day of fear and flight, a tumultuous day, a dark day. That day would be accompanied by commotion in the heavens and on earth.[9] From God's judgment there would be no escape. Soldiers discovered hiding out would be thrust through; children would be slain and wives ravished (13:6-16).

B. The Destruction of Babylon (13:17-22).[10]

Isaiah alluded both to the initial onset of the judgment against Babylon, and to its final result. The Medes would start the process. In Isaiah's day the Medes were giving Assyria some trouble, but they were not a real power. The Medo-Persian coalition defeated the armies of Babylon in 539 BC and took possession of the city. The first ruler of the city after its fall was a Mede (Dan 5:31). That was the first of many conquests of Babylon over the centuries. Eventually the site was deserted. It became the haunt of the desert creatures just as Isaiah predicted.[11]

C. The Future of Israel (14:1-4a).

The fall of Babylon was part of God's plan for his people. Assisted by Gentile nations, God's people would once again settle in the land of Canaan. Israel would one day take possession of Gentiles and they would become servants in the Lord's land. This is best taken to be a reference to the new Israel of God—the church of Christ—conquering the nations through the power of the Gospel.

D. The Fall of the Tyrant (14:4b-21).

The taunt song over the king of Babylon is one of the most remarkable poems in the Old Testament. It contains four stanzas each describing a different scene. In the first, Isaiah depicted the relief of the earth at the news of Babylon's fall. Now that the ruthless tyrant was dead, the earth was again tranquil (13:4b-8). Such was not the case, however, in Sheol where all is astir. In the second stanza Isaiah described how the spirits of dead tyrants greeted the now dead king of Babylon with reminders that his pride had brought him low. He was buried with fanfare only to have his royal corpse eaten by worms (14:9-11).

In the third stanza Isaiah depicted the meteoric fall of the tyrant. Lucifer (KJV)—"Light Bearer"—is actually the king of Babylon, not

Satan. This king fell like a star from the heavens, i.e., from great political height. He aspired to the assembly of gods in the heights of the north. His destiny, however, was to lie abandoned in the depths of the pit of Sheol (14:12-15). While the king's spirit had descended to Sheol, his body on earth remained unburied. In the fourth stanza Isaiah described the astonishment on earth over this ultimate disgrace. The onlookers could not believe the terrible fate which the king of Babylon had experienced. Earth's inhabitants expressed the hope that the name of the tyrant would be forgotten and his heirs destroyed (14:16-21).

E. Epilogue: Yahweh's Promise (14:22-27).

The burden of Babylon concludes with an epilogue which states God's intention regarding the two great Mesopotamian powers. First, he promised to completely cut off Babylon. The great world city would be possessed by porcupines rather than by posterity (14:22f.). Second, the Lord's unalterable purpose was to shatter Assyria upon the mountains of Judah (14:24-27). Isaiah lived to see this prediction fulfilled when the armies of Sennacherib were destroyed while attempting to subdue Judah (Isa 37). The destiny of Assyria was offered as a pledge that Babylon certainly would share the fate which has been the burden of chapters 13-14.

WORLDLY ALLIANCES: NEAR NEIGHBORS
Isaiah 14:28-18:7

Isaiah now took up the burdens of three neighboring nations: Philistia, Moab and Damascus. The first of these oracles is dated in "the year that Ahaz died" (715 BC).[12] These were the nations with whom Judah might be tempted to enter into a defensive pact in an effort to extricate herself from the Mesopotamian powers. These oracles underscore the folly of trusting in military alliance with any nation whose own future is precarious.

A. The Burden of Philistia (14:28-31).[13]

Philistia was warned not to rejoice over some recent Assyrian setback. A worse viper—another Assyrian king—was about to arise and there would be no straggler in his ranks. The reference is probably to the invasion of Sennacherib in 701 BC. The only place of refuge during this crisis would be Zion (Jerusalem).

B. The Burden of Moab (15:1-16:14).[14]

Moab would not be able to offer security to God's people in the coming crisis. Isaiah underscored this point in four movements within the Moab oracle. He first focused on lamentation. Moab would experience a double blast: a devastating invasion and a cruel drought. Throughout the land the wail would be heard. Isaiah raised up a prophetic lament over the national fate of Moab (15:1-9).

Isaiah next described the desperate petition of the Moabites. In their distress fugitives from Moab would appeal to Judah to grant refuge unto them (16:1-4a). Building upon the thought of Judah as a place of refuge, Isaiah announced the Messianic day. Long after the Assyrian oppressor ceased to exist, a throne would be established "in love" (NIV). A descendant of David would occupy that throne and he would rule over his kingdom in perfect justice and righteousness (16:4b-5).

The devastation of Moab occupied the prophet's mind in the next movement of the oracle. Because of pride Moab would experience the judgment of God. The choice vineyards of the land would be trampled by the enemy. Moab would pray for deliverance at her pagan high place, but to no avail. Isaiah again raised up an agonizing lament over the impending devastation of this neighboring nation (16:6-12).

The Moab oracle concludes with a note naming the exact time of fulfillment of the threat. Within exactly three years[15] Moab's "glory" would be despised (16:13f.). The prediction finds fulfillment in 715 BC when Sargon directed a campaign against the Arabians. To reach his destination, Sargon swept through the length of Moab from north to south murdering and plundering as he went.

C. The Burden of Damascus (17:1-14).

Having addressed Judah's two southern neighbors, Isaiah now addressed two neighbors to the north. Damascus and Ephraim were allies in 734 BC. Many in Judah—perhaps most—would have joined this coalition had not King Ahaz refused. Again Isaiah made the point that God's people should not put their trust in alliances.

The focus is first on Damascus. That great city would shortly see desolation. So would the fortified city of Ephraim, i.e., Samaria. The royal power of the Aramean kingdom would disappear (17:1-3). The prophecy was fulfilled with the fall of Damascus to the Assyrians in 732 BC, and the destruction of Samaria by the same forces in 722 BC.

Three *in that day* phrases mark what Ephraim was about to face. *In that day* Jacob (i.e., Ephraim) would gradually waste away. Only a pitiful remnant would survive (17:4-6). *In that day* a remnant in desperation would turn to Yahweh, repudiating any attraction to pagan paraphernalia (17:7f).[16] *In that day* strong cities would be abandoned and the land left desolate (17:9). All this would befall Ephraim because they had forgotten their God. In spite of all their efforts to the contrary, they would experience a bitter harvest (17:10f.).

D. Epilogue: Yahweh's Promise (17:12-18:7).

Two "woes" conclude the second major division of the Book of Burdens. Both oracles say essentially the same thing in different words. The first sets forth this principle: God would not permit his promises to his people to fail no matter what difficulties they might encounter. The first "woe" was pronounced against any who might attack God's people. Many nations might come against Judah like a mighty flood. Yahweh, however, would disperse the attackers like chaff before the wind. At sunset the situation might appear hopeless; by sunrise the enemy would be gone. This is the destiny of any who attack God's people (17:12-14).

The second "woe" (NASB "alas") was pronounced against those who might tempt God's people to depart from the path of faith. Envoys from distant Ethiopia arrived in Jerusalem intent on inciting Judah to join some alliance against Assyria. Isaiah rebuked them and sent them home to proclaim what Yahweh would do without any help from the heathen. When the time was ripe, God would prune back the strength of Assyria. The branches of that once proud bush would be strewn about the mountains providing food for bird and beast alike

(18:1-6). These words undoubtedly point to what God did to the Assyrians in 701 BC.

The second "woe" concludes with a picture of the conversion of the Ethiopians. Those people, once feared throughout the Near East, would send gifts to Mount Zion, the city of the Living God (18:7). The Mount Zion of prophecy often refers to that spiritual city, the New Jerusalem, in which every Christian is a citizen (Heb 12:22). This prediction probably finds fulfillment in the conversion of Ethiopia to Christianity in the early centuries of Church history. Thus the section concludes with the thought: Why turn to worldly alliances when Gentile nations one day will turn to you and to your God.

WORLDLY WISDOM: EGYPT [17]
Isaiah 19-20

In the Egyptian oracle Isaiah followed a pattern which was common in foreign nation oracles. He spoke first negatively of Egypt's confrontation with Yahweh, then positively of Egypt's conversion to the worship of the Living God.

A. Confrontation with Yahweh (19:1-15).

As the threat of Assyria loomed larger and larger, the leaders of Judah looked south to Egypt for assistance. Isaiah first indicated how God would expose the total weakness of all which the world held to be great about Egypt. The land of the Pharaohs would be shown to be bankrupt.

First, God would demonstrate that Egypt was religiously bankrupt. On a cloud chariot Yahweh would ride into Egypt to challenge the gods of that nation. Egypt's idols and practitioners of the occult would be helpless before him. The country would be rent by civil war, and then delivered into the hand of a "fierce king"[18] (19:1-4). Second, Egypt would become economically bankrupt. The annual inundation of the Nile would fail, resulting in a collapse of the basic industries: agriculture, fishing and textiles (19:5-10). Finally, judgment would prove Egypt to be intellectually bankrupt. Unable to explain rationally the series of national calamities, the vaunted Egyptian wisdom would collapse. Isaiah mocked the inability of the wise men to offer some solution. They would be as confused as drunks, and their advice would make the nation stagger in bewilderment (19:11-15).

In these verses Isaiah foresaw the political history of Egypt down to the time of Christ. The Assyrian Esarhaddon ravished Egypt in 672 BC as did Ashurbanipal ten years later. Egypt subsequently was invaded by the Chaldean Nebuchadnezzar, by Cambyses and Xerxes the Persians, and by Alexander the Macedonian. The Romans secured a foothold in Egypt when Pompey came to the aid of Ptolemy XI in 58 BC.

B. Conversion to Yahweh (19:16-25).

In one of the most amazing prophecies in the book, Isaiah depicted the ultimate conversion of the land of Egypt in five paragraphs, each of which begins with the words "in that day." First, *in that day* Egypt would come to recognize the hand of Yahweh in their national destiny. Even a mention of Judah, the people of God, would bring to mind Yahweh, and that would rekindle fear in their hearts (19:16f.).

Second, *in that day* many Egyptians ("five cities") would genuinely repent before God. Some, however, would remain hardened in sin ("city of destruction"). Converted Egyptians would come to speak "the language of Canaan," i.e., the language in which the true God is worshiped. They would speak truth, not falsehood. They would swear allegiance to Yahweh. They would become citizens in God's kingdom. (19:18)

Third, *in that day* Egyptians would worship the Lord in sincerity and truth. An altar to the Lord would be constructed in the midst of the land of Egypt. Isaiah used Old Testament language to depict the establishment of the worship of the true God in Egypt which would result from the preaching of the Gospel. A pillar or monument at the border of Egypt, like Jacob's pillar (Gen 28:16-22) would mark that land as one in which the presence of God had been manifested.[19] As true believers, the Egyptians would experience oppression by the enemies of the Lord (cf. John 15:19); but their cries for help would not go unheeded in heaven (19:19f.). God would send a "savior" and "a champion" to deliver them. In this context such titles must point to Messiah.

By personal experience of deliverance the Egyptians would come to know God. Free will vows—commitments—would be made to Yahweh. The terms *sacrifice* and *offerings* refer to the spiritual worship (cf. Heb 13:15-16) in the kingdom of Christ. As members of the family of God the Egyptians would receive divine correction when they tended to stray (Heb 12:3-17). These converted Gentiles would accept the correction, return to the Lord and he would *heal*, i.e., forgive, them (19:21f.).

Fourth, *in that day* Egypt would enjoy Gospel tranquility. In Messiah's kingdom former enemies would join together in peace. Even Egypt and Assyria, which stood at opposite poles geographically and politically, would experience a new relationship. These ancient enemies would be joined by a highway—a connecting link—by which Isaiah refers to their worship of Yahweh (19:23). The Gospel unites men of all nations. Those who project the fulfillment of this prophecy into the future—the millennium—demonstrate their lack of sensitivity to spiritual realities of the present age.[20]

Finally, *in that day* Egypt would be part of a great spiritual kingdom. Israel, Assyria and Egypt would stand on equal footing before the Lord. This triple alliance—the New Testament people of God—would be a blessing to the whole earth (19:24f.). Thus the blessing promised to Abram some two thousand years before Christ (Gen 12:3) would find fulfillment.

C. An Action Parable (20:1-6).

During the reign of the Assyrian King Sargon, Isaiah acted out a parable. This action parable is dated to the year that Tartan (Assyrian commander) captured the Philistine city of Ashdod c. 711 BC. Normally Isaiah wore a sackcloth garment as a sign of mourning over the captivity of the northern tribes. The Lord told his prophet to remove his garment and his shoes. For three years during the entire siege of Ashdod Isaiah went about barefoot and *naked*, i.e., without his outer garment, but not nude. Isaiah's state of undress was to be a sign against Egypt and Ethiopia (20:1-3).

The removal of the outer garb underscored the humiliation inflicted on the armies of Egypt-Ethiopia by the Assyrians. Those who tried to come to the aid of Ashdod would be carried away captive minus their garments. All of those in Philistia who looked to Egypt for assistance against Assyria would be despondent about prospects for deliverance (20:4-6). The reaction of the Ashdodites depicted here would be an oblique warning to the inhabitants of Judah who also looked to Egypt for support.

WORLDLY SCHEMES: CONSPIRING NATIONS
Isaiah 21-22

The four burdens in chapters 21-22 are extremely difficult to interpret. These oracles share a visionary character. The nations addressed manifested a defiant attitude toward impending calamity. They seem to come from the same historical context as well. Until 702 BC Babylon was the main gadfly to the Assyrian imperial machine. Apparently Dumah, Arabia and Judah were involved in one of the numerous Babylonian conspiracies which characterized the period from 732-702 BC. Isaiah, then, would have his people to avoid putting their trust in worldly schemes.

A. The Defeat of Babylon (21:1-10).

The land of Babylonia was called a *sea* by the ancients because of its many irrigation canals. Judgment, like a terrible desert storm, would turn this *sea* into a *wilderness*. Accumulated acts of treachery which caused so much misery in the world would be brought to account by a coalition of Media and Elam (21:1f.). Isaiah did not gloat over the fate of this enemy. The harsh vision caused him pain, anguish and confusion. He longed for a brighter vision; but instead the mental impression he received from the Lord became more traumatic (21:3f.).

The fall of Babylon would be unexpected. While at a banquet the call to arms would come.[21] Daniel 5 and the Greek historian Xenophon relate that Babylon fell to Cyrus the Great in 539 BC while a banquet was being conducted in the royal palace[22] (21:5). Like a watchman stationed on the wall of a city Isaiah was charged to watch for enemy troop movements. The prophet remained at his post, as it were, day and night. At last he spotted in vision the approach of the enemy. Even as he announced what he had seen the message came back that Babylon had fallen. The great city would be swiftly overcome by her enemies. Her multitude of images would not even be able to save themselves from destruction (21:6-9).

Over the years Israel was threshed by the Mesopotamian powers. With the fall of Babylon God's people would gain relief. Therefore, Isaiah passes along to his people this revelation concerning the fate of Babylon (21:10).

B. A Word for Dumah (21:11-12).

Dumah ("silence") may be a name for Edom.[23] Isaiah heard, as it were, someone in Edom asking him as prophetic watchman about the duration of the night of darkness and oppression. Could the prophet yet see any indication of light (deliverance)? Isaiah's response was purposely ambiguous: "morning comes but also the night." Perhaps he meant that things would worsen before they got better. In any case, further inquiry at a later time might elicit a clear answer.

C. The Devastation of Arabia (21:13-17).[24]

Isaiah described the destitute condition of the Arabian caravans which resulted from an invasion. In exactly one year the splendor of Kedar (Arabia) would cease to exist and her famed bowmen would be reduced to but a few. The Assyrian King Sargon invaded Arabia in 715 BC.

D. The Valley of Vision (22:1-14).

Though Jerusalem is situated on mountains, the capital is here designated "the valley of vision" because it was surrounded by mountains. That an oracle against Jerusalem is found here among the oracles concerning foreign nations is very suggestive. Jerusalem was like Babylon, Dumah, and Arabia spiritually. Her citizens acted like the heathen and must share the fate of the heathen.

The setting of this oracle seems to be 701 BC just after the miraculous deliverance from the invasion of the Assyrian King Sennacherib (cf. chap. 37). The inhabitants are jubilant because the army of the invader had been destroyed. Isaiah could not participate in the celebration. He foresaw a siege of Jerusalem in which soldiers would die of starvation in the city. Troops would desert the place only to be captured by the enemy. Knowing through God's revelation that Jerusalem would be destroyed, Isaiah wept while others laughed (22:1-4).

The prophet received a very definite mental picture of what would take place in that terrible day. He saw contingents of a foreign army—units from distant Elam and Kir—besieging Jerusalem. Archers, chariots, infantry and cavalry were arrayed against the city. The enemy "uncovered the shield," i.e., removed the protective covers from their shields, in preparation for battle. All avenues of escape were cut off (22:5-7).

Isaiah foresaw the desperate efforts of Jerusalem's defenders to prepare for siege. He saw them checking their arsenals, walls and water supply. Houses were torn down to secure materials for patching the breaches in the walls. All these efforts at self-preservation, however, were vain because Jerusalem did not look to God who had brought this disaster upon them (22:8-11).

The near disaster of 701 BC called for national lamentation, not jubilation. The carefree attitude of Jerusalem's inhabitants ("let us eat and drink, for tomorrow we die") was a grim prediction of their fate. Because they were unrepentant, they remained unforgiven. They lived under the divine death sentence (22:12-14).

E. The Royal Steward (22:15-25).

The prophecy against Shebna is the only instance of the denunciation of an individual by name in Isaiah. In this oracle Isaiah cited a particular example of the attitude expressed by Jerusalem's citizens in general. Shebna was a foreigner—most likely an Aramean—in the royal service. As steward he was the ranking officer of the king's court. At the time of his confrontation with Isaiah, Shebna was preparing a rock sepulcher for himself. This man had betrayed his trust as a public official. He was more interested in building lasting monuments to himself than in helping his people face the national crisis which awaited them (22:15-16).

Isaiah announced that Shebna would be expelled from Judah and that he would die in his native land. His replacement as steward would be Eliakim who was called "my servant" because he was sympathetic to the message of Isaiah (22:17-20). By 701 BC Eliakim had in fact replaced Shebna in office (cf. 36:3; 37:2).

A number of honors would be heaped on Eliakim. He would wear the outer insignia of the office of steward. He would possess "the key of the house of David," i.e., unlimited influence in the royal court of King Hezekiah. His family would take pride in his eminence and find security in his firmly entrenched position. Nonetheless, Eliakim was only human, and the nation dared not put its trust in him.[25] Like a peg broken from the wall, all which depended on him would be cut off (22:21-25).

WORLDLY WEALTH: TYRE
Isaiah 23

The Book of Burdens opened with a warning against trusting in worldly glory as illustrated by Babylon on the eastern side of Isaiah's world. Now Isaiah looked to the western side of his world to Tyre. He saw that city as the epitome of worldly wealth in which God's people might be tempted to put their trust. This oracle consists of three main divisions which may be designated by the words lamentation, explanation and restoration.

A. Lamentation (23:1-7) .

Phoenicia was commercial capital of the Mediterranean world. Her two leading cities, Tyre and Sidon, were destined for destruction. Isaiah dramatically described the impact which this disaster would have upon colonies and trading partners along the Mediterranean coasts. Phoenician sailors would become so few that the sea would deny that she ever had any such children (23:1-7).

B. Explanation (23:8-14) .

Yahweh planned the downfall of Tyre in order to humble the pride of that place. The repercussions of the divine destruction decree would be felt as far as Tarshish at the western end of the Mediterranean. That distant colony would be able to develop independently, unrestrained by the mother land. Not even flight to the island of Cyprus would alleviate the vexation of the previously unconquered ("virgin daughter") Sidon (23:8-12).

The blow against the commercial centers of Phoenicia would be delivered by the Chaldeans. These inhabitants of southern Mesopotamia had been conquered by the Assyrians. Nonetheless, the Chaldeans would be the agents of God's wrath against Tyre. The far-flung Phoenician merchant fleets would mourn the destruction of their home port and fortress city (23:13f.). History records the fulfillment of these predictions. The Chaldean King Nebuchadnezzar besieged Tyre for thirteen years (598-586 BC). In the process he completely destroyed the mainland city forcing the inhabitants to take refuge on their island fortress.[26]

C. Restoration (23:15-18).

For seventy years—the duration of the Chaldean empire[27] —Tyre would be forgotten. With biting sarcasm Isaiah urged Tyre to take up the song of an old harlot in an attempt to revive interest in herself. At the end of the seventy years Tyre would again be visited by Yahweh. The city would return to her *harlotry*, her commercial intercourse with the kingdoms of the world (23:15-17).

At some point in this restoration, Tyre's income would be dedicated to the Lord. Specifically, it would be used to feed and clothe the official servants of Yahweh (23:18). Some of the building materials for the second temple came from Tyre (Ezra 3:7). Josephus and Jerome relate how many in the area of Phoenicia were converted and supported the work of the Lord. Paul found godly souls there in New Testament times (Acts 21:3f.). By the second century Tyre had become an important Christian center.

Endnotes

1. In the Greek manuscripts of Jeremiah the foreign nation oracles also have been placed in the middle of the book.

2. B.A. Copass, *Isaiah, Prince of Old Testament Prophets* (Nashville: Broadman, 1944) 51.

3. The term *massa* appears in 13:1; 14:28; 15:1; 17:1; 21:1, 11, 13; 22:1 and 23:1.

4. Judah is addressed in 14:1-4a; 17:4-11; and apparently in 22:1-25.

5. Erlandsson cited by John Oswalt, *The Book of Isaiah: Chapters 1-39* in The New International Commentary on the Old Testament (Grand Rapids: Eerdmans, 1986) 298.

6. The Pride of the nations is partiularly attacked in 13:11, 19; 14:11; 16:6 and 23:9; cf. 10:7-15.

7. From Gen 11:9 onward to Rev 14:8 Babylon becomes virtually synonymous with wickedness and hostile pride. Babylon represents civilization as the stronghold of darkness.

8. The day of the Lord can mean judgment for Israel (Amos 5:18-20; Isa 2:12f; Ezek 5; Joel 1:15; 2:1,11; Zeph 1:7, 14) or for other nations (Jer 46:10; Obad 15). All lesser interventions come to a head in the actual coming of the Lord himself at the end of time.

9. The darkness of heavenly bodies (v. 10), and the shaking of heavens and earth (v. 13) are concrete ways of describing the gloom and upheaval which results from the overthrow of a proud and powerful nation.

10. Other Babylon prophecies are found in Isa 21:1-10; 46:1f; 47:1-5; and Jer 51-52.

11. In 14:22-23 Isaiah clearly indicates (1) that the taunt song for the king of Babylon is not to be taken literally; and (2) that it does not apply to any one individual. It is Babylon as a whole which is brought low.

12. Following Edwin Thiele. E.J. Young gives the year as 727 BC and H.C. Leupold as 721 BC.

13. Other prophetic oracles concerning the Philistines are found in Amos 1:6-8; Zeph 2:4-7; Jer 47; Ezek 25:15-17; And Zech 9:5-7.

14. Other prophetic oracles concerning Moab are found in Jer 48; Ezek 25:8-11; Zeph 2:8-11; Amos 2:1-3; and Isa 25;10-12.

15. The NIV rendering is: "Within three years as a servant bound by a contract would count them."

16. Asherim are sacred trees or poles standing near altars. These, along with sun images, would be abandoned by the remnant.

17. Other prophetic passages concerning Egypt are found in Jer 46 and Ezek 29.

18. The cruel king into whose hand they are delivered may be Shabaka (c. 711-699 BC) the founder of the twenty-fifth or Ethiopian dynasty, or a foreign king like the Assyrians' Esarhaddon or Ashurbanipal who conquered Egypt in 672 BC and 662 BC respectively, or perhaps some later Persian or Greek king.

19. In 160 BC the high priest Onias IV was forced to flee from Judea to Egypt. He referred King Ptolemy to this passage for justification for erecting a Jewish temple in Egypt. Some think that these verses find their fulfillment in the thousands of Jews who resided in Egypt during the intertestamental period.

20. For excellent comments on this verse see Paul Butler, *Isaiah,* Bible Study Textbook Series (Joplin, MO: College Press, 1975) 1:276-77.

21. Greasing the shield was a practice designed to make the blow of swords glance off ineffectively.

22. Xenophon (431-350 BC), *Cyropaedia* 7.5.15.

23. John Oswalt thinks Dumah is an oasis in northern Arabia. *The Book of Isaiah: Chapters 1-39* in The New International Commentary on the Old Testament (Grand Rapids: Eerdmans, 1986) 398. On this interpretation, the inhabitants of Mt. Seir (Edomites) would be expressing great interest in the fate of Dumah. Were that region to fall to the Assyrians, their eastern trade connections would be cut off.

24. Another prophetic oracle against Arabia appears in Jer 49:28-33.

25. On 22:25 following Oswalt (*op. cit.* 423f.). Other commentators think that it is Shebna who is the unreliable peg.

26. Alexander the Great actually destroyed Tyre in 332 BC. Tyre came under attack five times between the days of Isaiah and 332 BC.

27. On the duration of the Chaldean (Babylonian) empire see Jer 25:11f; 29:10; 2 Chr 36:21.

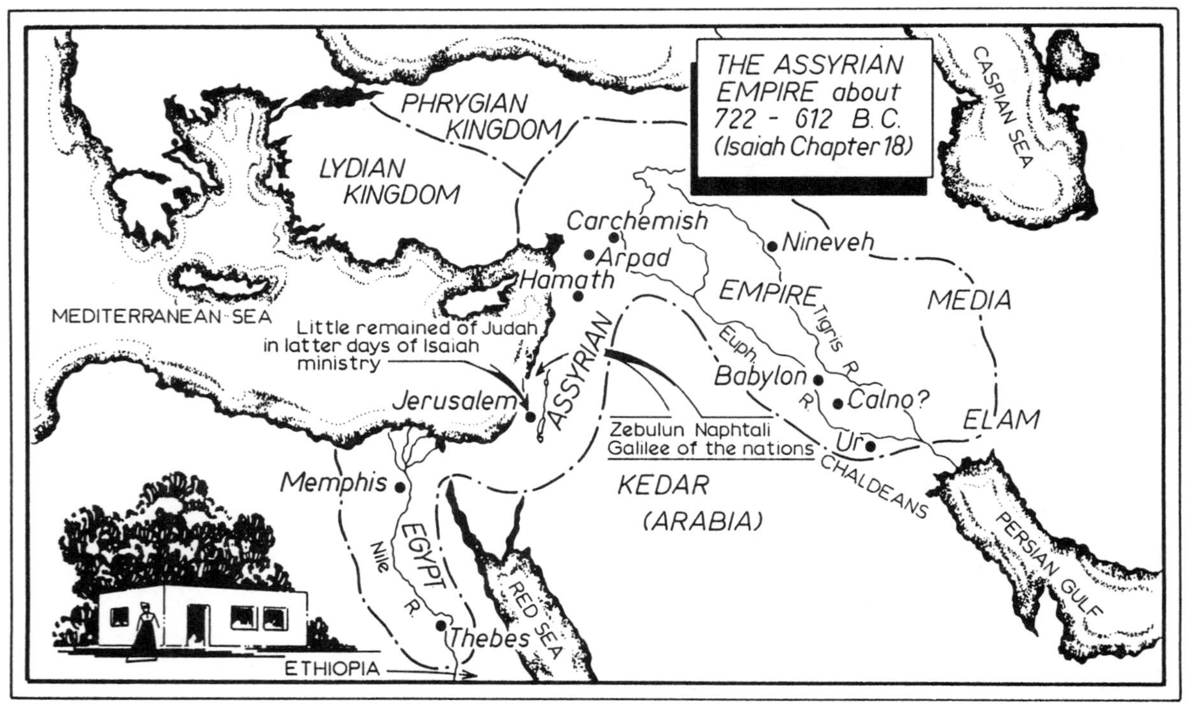
THE ASSYRIAN
EMPIRE about
722 - 612 B.C.
(Isaiah Chapter 18)
CASPIAN SEA
PHRYGIAN
KINGDOM
LYDIAN
KINGDOM
Carchemish
Arpad
Hamath
Nineveh
EMPIRE
Tigris R.
MEDIA
MEDITERRANEAN SEA
Little remained of Judah
in latter days of Isaiah
ministry
Euph. R.
Babylon
Calno?
Jerusalem
ASSYRIAN
ELAM
Zebulun Naphtali
Galilee of the nations
Ur
CHALDEANS
Memphis
KEDAR
(ARABIA)
EGYPT
Nile R.
RED SEA
PERSIAN GULF
Thebes
ETHIOPIA

CHAPTER FIVE

The Books of General Judgment Isaiah 24-27; 34-35

Background of the Units.

Because of the similarity of content, two separate units within the Book of Isaiah are grouped in this chapter. Isaiah loved to portray the final outcome of the flow of history and in these six chapters that is exactly what he does. The dominant theme here is the coming day of the Lord. Both units are marked by "a certain mysterious twilight."[1]

The chronological placement of the books of general judgment within the ministry of Isaiah is uncertain. The literary placement, however, in both cases is appropriate. Locating the First Book of General Judgment immediately following the oracles concerning foreign nations was brilliant. These chapters are like a grand finale such as may close a major musical composition. Here a number of preceding themes are made to re-echo and blend into one harmonious whole.[2] G. A. Smith characterized the language of these chapters as "imaginative, enigmatic and paradoxical."[3] The same can be said for the second unit. It forms an appropriate conclusion to the first half of Isaiah, the dominant theme of which is the futility of trusting in any earthly entity.

Outline of the Units.

A. The First Book of General Judgment (chaps. 24-27).

1. The Judgment of the World (chap. 24).
2. Praise for Yahweh's Triumph (chap. 25).
3. Trust in Yahweh's Protection (chap. 26).
4. The Future of Israel (chap. 27).

B. The Second Book of General Judgment (chaps. 34-35).

1. Judgment on the Unrighteous (chap. 34).
2. Salvation for the Righteous (chap. 35).

THE FIRST BOOK OF GENERAL JUDGMENT
Isaiah 24-27

In the First Book of General Judgment Isaiah oscillates between his own times and the distant future. Judgment on national Israel and the overthrow of world powers would be the prelude to the emergence of the new Israel. Isaiah pictured purified Jews and converted Gentiles joining together in worship on Mt. Zion. What Isaiah saw was, to his mind, certain of fulfillment. Consequently he often described what he saw in vision as accomplished fact.

A. The Judgment of the World (24:1-23).

In chapter 24 the entire "earth" (repeated 17 times) experiences the judgment of God. Four aspects of the world judgment are set forth in Isaiah 24.

1. Universal judgment (24:1-6). Isaiah made a shocking announcement (*behold!*): Yahweh would one day clean (lit., *empty out*) the earth as a man might clean a dirty vessel. All classes and ranks throughout the world would be affected by the judgment. The earth would be completely laid waste. The material world along with its most prominent citizens would wilt before the hot blast of God's wrath (24:1-6). Such judgment was well-deserved in Isaiah's view. Men had polluted the earth by transgressing God's laws and breaking God's *everlasting covenant.* The Noachian covenant (Gen 9) which required execution of murderers seems to be in view here. The inhabitants of earth stood condemned. They lived under the curse of God. Therefore few would survive the fire of God's judgment (24:5f.).

2. Devastating judgment (24:7-16). Throughout the earth the impact would be felt. In the rural areas the vineyards would be ruined. The mirth associated with the grape harvest would cease (24:7-9). In the typical city chaos would reign. Houses would be boarded up. Gloom would hang over the place. The gate would be battered down. Desolation would follow (24:10-12).

Some would survive, but they would be few. They would be comparable in number to olives left on the tree or grapes left on the vine after the professional harvesters had finished their work. Yet throughout the world from west to east the remnant would rejoice over the vindication of the majesty of Yahweh (24:13-15).

Isaiah and his disciples could hear, as it were, the jubilant praise ascending from the ends of the earth. He, however, could not join in that praise. He knew that in his own day the threat of judgment would have no corrective effect on most sinners. They would not survive God's judgment. This preacher had a burden for his lost generation (24:16).

3. Inescapable judgment (24:17-20). Like terrified animals fleeing from a relentless hunter the sinners would attempt to escape. Both pit and snare awaited them. Those who escaped the one would be trapped by the other (24:17-18a). Isaiah depicted this judgment as being like a terrible deluge[4] and a violent earthquake. The earth would shake violently and break open; it would totter like a drunkard and/or like a hut on trembling ground. The earth would reel under the weight of its transgression (deliberate disobedience). This old order of things would pass away, never to rise again (24:18b-20).

4. Orderly judgment (24:21-23). First to taste of divine wrath would be the heavenly host, i.e., those angels who rebelled against God at some point in the distant past.[5] When judgment had been completed "on high," God would turn his attention to the kings of the earth who had been influenced by these demonic creatures to make war against the people of God. All of these enemies would be incarcerated. "After many days" they would be punished (24:21-22). Jude 6 and 2 Peter 2:4 have the same thought.

For Yahweh that will be a glorious day. Once his foes have been subdued, the reign of God will be seen in all of its fullness and wondrous power. He will reign unchallenged "on Mount Zion and in Jerusalem." Since Isaiah has already described the destruction of the physical earth, the reference here must be to the heavenly Mount Zion (Heb 12:22) and the New Jerusalem (Rev 21:1f.). That city will be so bright that it will have no need of the sun or moon (Rev 21:23). In his throne room God will sit in glory "before his elders"—twenty-four of them according to the Book of Revelation (Rev 4). Thus God's people—here represented by the elders—will share in the glory of that day (2 Thess 1:10).

B. Praise for Yahweh's Triumph (25:1-12).

In response to the predictions of the ultimate victory of God over his adversaries, Isaiah (representing the people of God) burst forth into a song of praise. He declared that God is faithful to his purpose. By crushing the forces of evil God had "worked wonders." His ancient plans had reached fruition. He had demonstrated his faithfulness by fulfilling his promises (25:1). This general praise crystallizes around three main ideas.

First, Isaiah described how God would provide protection for his people. He compared the forces of evil to a city which opposes Zion, the city of God. Throughout history again and again God turned such cities (like Nineveh and Babylon) into heaps of ruins. Yahweh's victory over the powerful enemy ultimately would result in the conversion of Gentiles in large numbers (25:2f.). Meanwhile the Lord remained a defense, a refuge, for his people. Isaiah likened the stormy rage of ruthless armies to rain bouncing off a solid wall. Like the shadow of a cloud which brings relief on a hot day, so God would deliver his people from the oppressive heat of persecution. He would silence the boisterous demands, victory songs and arrogant boasts of the enemy (25:4f.).

Second, Isaiah stressed God's provision for his people. A lavish banquet has been prepared for all peoples who accept his invitation.[6] This banquet would be particularly joyous since God would remove the veil which hangs over all nations. Some think the "veil" is ignorance (cf. 2 Cor 3:12-18), others interpret it as mourning. In any case, God would destroy death (1 Cor 15:54; Rev 21:4). The tears and reproach of his people would be removed forever. Seated at that great banquet table the saints of the ages would realize that their patience had been rewarded. They would "rejoice and be glad in his salvation" (25:6-9).

Finally, Isaiah spoke of the punishment which awaited the enemies of Zion. A glorious future awaited Mt. Zion (the redeemed) because God's hand of blessing rested there. While the people of God rejoice on Mt. Zion, however, the enemies of God's people, represented by Moab, would be trampled under foot in "a manure pile." From that terrible pit they would never be able to escape. The fortifications of these arrogant adversaries, along with all else of which they were proud, would be brought low (25:10-12).

C. Trust in Yahweh's Protection (26:1-21).

Chapter 26 is a hymn of trust in God's protection of his people. This hymn moves through three phases.

1. Description of Zion (26:1-6). Isaiah compared Zion to a fortress. She was protected not by walls of stone, but by walls of salvation (cf. Zech 2:5). Her gates were open to a faithful and righteous nation. Her citizens enjoyed a special measure of peace because (1) they were marked by steadfast purpose; and (2) they trusted in God (26:1-3). In view of these facts, Isaiah urged his readers to trust in God forever. He offered two proofs that the Lord was worthy of their trust. First, God is eternal, the "everlasting Rock." Second, God had brought low the lofty and powerful city of evil doers. The poor and lowly (people of God) would walk across the rubble of that once proud place.

2. Reflection by Zion (26:7-15). Isaiah entered into reflective prayer as he contemplated the benefits of God's judgments. First he noted that the way the righteous travel through life becomes level as a result of the just judgments of the Lord. Obstacles and dangers are thus removed from the path. Second, during their earthly pilgrimage the righteous wait for God to perform his judgments. Third, the saints are sustained in their patience by recalling God's memorial name. The name Yahweh—He who Is, The Eternal—was associated with victory over oppressors ever since the days of the Exodus (26:7f.).

Fourth, in the night time of affliction the soul of the righteous man longs for divine intervention. Only through divine judgment are men jarred loose from their hold on unrighteousness. Fifth, if wicked men receive only kind treatment from the Lord, they will not learn righteousness and they will fail to see the majesty of the Lord (26:9f.).

Sixth, even though the hand of God is poised over the head of the wicked, they do not perceive the danger. One day, however, they would see God's zeal for his true saints and his fiery wrath as well. Seventh, judgment upon the wicked means peace for the righteous. Thereby the all-sufficiency of God is impressed anew upon the minds of his people (26:11f.).

Eighth, in periods of foreign oppression ("other lords"), Israel realized the more clearly that she had only one Lord. Through the strength which God supplied, God's people continued to to confess allegiance to Yahweh even in adverse times. Ninth, having experienced the retribution of the Lord, previous oppressors were dead and forgotten. Tenth, Israel had been strengthened numerically and, at times, geographically as a result of the destruction of adversaries (26:13-15).

3. Expectation of Zion (26:16-19). God had been the hope of Israel in past distress. At times the nation had been so beaten down by divine chastisement that all the faithful could do was to whisper a prayer of desperation to the Lord. Though Israel had planned and agonized she could not produce deliverance for herself, much less any other nation. She was like a woman travailing in labor who brought forth only wind. In the context of this prayer, these words underscore the absolute futility of man-made attempts to produce salvation (26:16-18).

Isaiah argued that Yahweh was the hope of Israel's future. He anticipated the dawn of a glorious new day—a day of light and life, a day of shouting and joy. He envisioned a heavenly dew gently but powerfully causing the earth to give forth her dead (26:19). Some think that Isaiah was predicting the final resurrection. Others think that the prophet depicted in poetic language the life-giving power of the Gospel (Eph 5:14; John 5:25). Still others think the reference is to the national restoration of Israel following the captivity (cf. Hos 6:2; Ezek 37:1-14).

4. Exhortation to Zion (26:20-21). In the light of their future hope, Isaiah urged God's people to continue a little longer in the solitude of prayer until "indignation" runs its course (26:20). The period from the time of the Assyrian deportation of the Northern Kingdom (beginning 745 BC) until the destruction of Jerusalem in AD 70 is spoken of in Old Testament prophecy as the period of Jacob's trouble and the period of indignation (Jer 30:7; Dan 8:19). Others think the reference is to what the New Testament calls the great tribulation (Rev 2:22; 7:14). The exhortation of the prophet would be appropriate during any period in which God exercised judgment. The basic idea is that believers must be patient in times of turbulence and prayerfully await God's better day.

Faith demands that the righteous continue to live in the expectation that God is about to come "out from his place" to intervene in human affairs. Divine justice demands that God punish "the inhabitants of the earth," i.e., wicked men, especially powerful empires (26:21). And so he would! Isaiah depicted God using his mighty sword to slay those ugly beasts (governments) which had oppressed his people. The prophet used Leviathan, the mythological sea monster, as a symbol for the world powers of that day. Leviathan the fleeing or gliding serpent probably represented Assyria which was situated on the swift flowing Tigris river. Leviathan the twisted serpent probably symbolized Babylon situated on the winding, relatively slow moving Euphrates river. The "dragon who lives in the sea" most likely should be interpreted as Egypt (27:1).[7]

D. The Future of Israel (27:2-13).

In chapter 27 Isaiah looked beyond judgment to the glorious future which God had in store for his people. What a day that would be!

1. A day of blessing (27:2-6). In the day when the superpowers fell, God would protect his precious vineyard, i.e., the true Israel (cf. Isa 5). He had no wrath against his purified people. The enemies of the vineyard—"the briers and thorns"—had two choices. They could face the Lord in battle and meet with inevitable destruction; or they could embrace his protection by making peace with him. By choosing the path of peace, these enemies became part of Israel, the people of God. The vineyard then would flourish so gloriously that the whole earth would be blessed with its fruit. The fulfillment of these predictions has been realized in the messianic people of God, the church of Christ, whose influence gradually touches the whole earth.

2. A day of pardon (27:7-11). God's chastisements of his people were much less severe than the judgments he brought upon heathen peoples. His purpose in the former was punitive; in the latter, remedial. While heathen nations were annihilated, Israel was sifted by being banished to foreign lands. Forgiveness was possible if "Jacob" would only renounce idolatry. This the nation could do by pulverizing altar stones and dismantling pagan paraphernalia like Asherim and incense altars (27:7-9).

Painful though it might be, the destruction of the land of Judah was a necessary step in God's reclamation program for Israel. The ruins of the once proud fortified city (Samaria? Jerusalem?) would be a place for cattle to graze and women to gather fire wood. This devastation was necessary because Israel was a people without spiritual discernment. Their Creator could show no compassion on them (27:10f.).

3. A day of gathering (27:12-13). Like kernels in a threshing, God's scattered people would be gathered throughout the Promised Land.[8] From distant Assyria and Egypt the scattered people of God would be gathered by means of a trumpet. All of God's people would then unite in worship at Mt. Zion. The trumpet is "the gospel proclamation which gathered (and is still gathering, collecting, picking) the true Israel of God from the far reaches of the world."[9]

THE SECOND BOOK OF GENERAL JUDGMENT
Isaiah 34-35

The Second Book of General Judgment stresses God's sovereignty as manifested in judgment and in salvation.

A. Judgment on God's Enemies (34:1-17).

Chapter 34 presents two pictures of judgment. Isaiah first predicted a world-wide catastrophe; then he focused on one specific victim of that judgment.

1. Judgment generalized (34:1-4). Isaiah called upon all the inhabitants of the earth and nature itself to listen to the divine sentence. God's wrath could no longer be restrained. Like the Canaanites of old, all armies of mankind had been put under the sentence of complete destruction (34:1f.). With gruesome figures Isaiah depicted the results of that world judgment. Rotting corpses would be strewn across the ground. Mountains would be drenched with blood. The "hosts of heaven," i.e., heavenly bodies, would wear away (lit., rot), and wither like a leaf on a tree. Thus the world would be plunged into darkness (34:3f.).

2. Judgment particularized (34:5-15). The sword of divine justice first "is satiated in heaven," i.e., it accomplished its purpose in the heavens. Sun, moon and stars would be destroyed. Then that sword would fall on Edom, representative of all the powers which have been hostile to God's people. The Lord would place these people under the ban (Heb. *cherem*), i.e., would sentence them to utter destruction (34:5).

Isaiah painted three word pictures of the awful fate to befall Edom. First, he unveiled the picture of wholesale death. He compared the inhabitants of Edom to various kinds of animals. The lambs, goats and rams seem to represent the common people; the wild oxen, young bulls and strong ones (mighty bulls) represent the powerful members of society. God's sword of judgment would be directed against them all. Bozrah, capital of Edom, would be the scene of one huge sacrifice, as it were. The soil of the land would be drenched with the blood of the slain (34:6f.). Yahweh's day of vengeance had come! This was a time for the just recompense of countless hostile acts inflicted by the wicked upon the people of God over the years (34:8).

Second, Isaiah painted the picture of complete destruction. Edom would become like Sodom and Gomorrah after the Lord destroyed those cities. Burning pitch and brimstone would cover the land. The fire would be unquenchable. Smoke would ascend forever. Isaiah himself explained the meaning of this picture. The land of Edom would be desolate forever. None would ever again pass through it (34:9f.). That these verses are poetic hyperbole is indicated by the following verses which describe those who inhabit Edom after judgment.

Third, Isaiah presented a picture of permanent desolation. God would hold over that land, as it were, the plummet of desolation, i.e., God would not finish his work there until the land was a complete desolation. He would measure Edom by the standard of absolute desolation. Such human population as might be found there would be lowly and disorganized. The place would be fit habitation only for the wild creatures of the desert (34:11-15).

3. Judgment emphasized (34:16-17). The passage closes by emphasizing the certainty of the judgment against Edom. Isaiah challenged future generations to examine "the book of the Lord," i.e., this very collection of prophecies. They should compare the actual circumstances of Edom with the predictions made in God's book. Every animal named in this prophecy would be found within the precincts of ancient Edom. God himself would bring the animals there; he would, as it were, apportion the land to them.

Edom as a political entity has long ago ceased to exist. The territory once occupied by that proud nation consists of bleak mountain heights and barren table lands. The area swarms with snakes and various desert creatures.[10] Yet these "prefillments" are but a pledge of the doom of all that Edom represented to the prophet's mind. Fulfillment of the prophecy is still future and will be realized when judgment falls upon the abode of all enemies of the Lord (cf. 1 Cor 15:24-28,50).

B. Salvation for God's People (35:1-10).

While the fate of God's adversaries is bleak indeed, that of God's people is glorious to contemplate.

1. The glory of God (35:1-2). In the previous chapter a productive land became a barren waste under God's judgment. In chapter 35 a desert blossoms to symbolize the joy of salvation. The Arabah is the deep cleft on the Jordan valley which runs down through the Dead Sea to the Gulf of Aqabah. This very barren region would "rejoice and blossom." Isaiah used Lebanon (noted for its cedars), Carmel (noted for its oaks), and Sharon (noted for its flowers) as examples of what would happen to the rest of the land.

Why would the wilderness blossom and shout for joy? Because "they[11] will see the glory of the Lord." Israel had seen God's glory during the Exodus (Exod 16:7) and at Mt. Sinai (Exod 24:16f.). God's glory filled the Tabernacle (Exod 40:34f.) and the Temple (1 Kgs 8:11). Thus "the glory of the Lord" refers to a visible appearance by God—a theophany—which usually was accompanied by miraculous signs. That Jesus of Nazareth was the embodiment of God's glory is the teaching of the New Testament (John 1:14; 2:11; 17:5). Thus the prophecy announces the beginning of a new age, the age of Messiah.

2. The work of God (35:3-7). Isaiah urged those who were spiritually perceptive and understood the implications of the preceding prophecy to encourage the people who were discouraged and fearful. In the messianic age God would come to (1) execute vengeance on those who oppose him and his people; and (2) save his people (35:3f.). The latter receives the emphasis here.

The work of salvation would begin with a healing ministry. Blindness, deafness, dumbness and lameness would be corrected (35:5-6a). Jesus cited these verses when he responded to John's question regarding his identity (Matt 11:4f.). By so doing Jesus was claiming to be deity as well as Messiah for it is the coming of God which effects these physical transformations.

The work of salvation involved the provision of abundant water. In that day the dumb would shout for joy, not only because of their own healing, but for another reason as well. Waters would break forth in the wilderness bringing life to barren land (35:6b-7). Isaiah was using concrete imagery to depict the refreshment which Jesus, the Water of Life, would bring to a spiritual waste land (John 4:11-14).

3. The way of God (35:8-10). Isaiah depicted the life of the redeemed in the messianic age as a pilgrimage along a special way. This is a *raised* way—a *maslul*, i.e., something built up above the surface, obvious to all who are looking for it. This is a *holy* way restricted to those who have been cleansed and who desire to live a life of holiness. This is a *plain* way for "the simple will not stray from it" (NIV mar). It is a *safe* way, for no ferocious beast will harm those who stay on it. It is the *freedom* way, for those redeemed from bondage, ransomed by payment of a price, find deliverance from bondage here.

It is a *straight* way, for it has as its sole destination Zion, the city of God. It is a *sure* way, for those who travel it will reach their destination. It is a *joyous* way, for they will enter Zion with singing. It is the *glory* way, for those who arrive in Zion will receive an everlasting crown of joy. Only the redeemed, those ransomed by the Lord, may walk in that way.

Endnotes

1. H.C. Leupold, *Exposition of Isaiah* (Grand Rapids: Baker, 1968) 1:374.

2. Franz Delitzsch, "Isaiah" in *Keil and Delitzsch Old Testament Commentaries; Isaiah XVI to Ezekiel XXIV* (Grand Rapids: Associated Publishers and Authors, n.d.) 79-81.

3. G.A. Smith, *The Book of Isaiah* (Rev. ed. New York: Harper, 1927) 1:438.

4. Paul Butler thinks that the "opening of the windows of heaven" could be a reference to God's sending his Son. *Isaiah* in Bible College Textbook Series (Joplin: College Press, 1976) 2:12.

5. Jude 6; 2 Pet. 2:4.

6. Matt 8:11; 22:2f.; Luke 14:15ff.

7. For E.J. Young, these creatures do not represent specific historic kingdoms, but all the enemies of God, high and low. *The Book of Isaiah* (Grand Rapids: Eerdmans, 1969) 2:235. On the basis of recent research in the Ugaritic text, Oswalt argues only one monster is being symbolically described, "the monster of moral evil." John Oswalt, *The Book of Isaiah: Chapters 1-39* in The New International Commentary on the Old Testament (Grand Rapids: Eerdmans, 1986) 491.

8. From the Euphrates to the River of Egypt were the traditional north-south boundaries of the Promised Land. See Gen 15:18.

9. Butler, *op. cit.* 2:54.

10. Delitzsch, *op. cit.* 167f.

11. The third plural pronoun refers either to the people of God, or to the geographical landmarks enumerated in the previous verse.

CHAPTER SIX

The Book of Woes
Isaiah 28-33

Background of the Unit.

The Book of Woes derives its title from the fact that almost every chapter in this unit begins with the funeral cry "woe."[1] Because the thought here centers about the glorious future of Mt. Zion, von Orelli proposes the more positive title "Book of Zion."[2] The unit appears to have been composed during the reign of good King Hezekiah sometime between the fall of Samaria in 722 BC and the Assyrian invasion of Judah in 701 BC. During this period Judah faced the ever increasing temptation to enter into an alliance with Egypt. The theme of the folly of false trust continues from the preceding two divisions of the book.

Outline of the Unit.

A. The Problem (chaps. 28-29).
   1. Woe to Wanton Rulers (chap. 28).

2. Woe to Worthless Worship (29:1-14).
3. Woe to Wily Schemers (29:15-24).

B. The Proposed Solution (chaps. 30-31).
1. Woe to Willful Children (chap. 30).
2. Woe to Worldly Trust (chap. 31).

C. Interlude: Future Prospects (chap. 32).

D. The True Solution: A Final Woe (chap. 33).

THE PROBLEM
Woe to Wanton Rulers
Isaiah 28:1-29

Chapter 28 points out the problem that existed in the leadership of God's people. Isaiah likened the leaders of Ephraim to drunkards. Then he portrayed the scoffing of the leaders of Judah and the disastrous consequences of the current national policy.

A. The Drunkards of Ephraim (28:1-6).

Situated as it was at the head of a fertile valley, Samaria was the queen city of the northern kingdom, "the proud crown" of the rulers of that realm. To Isaiah, however, Samaria was like a once-beautiful flower in the irreversible process of wilting. The rulers there were so intoxicated with their power they could not perceive the disaster which Isaiah so clearly saw (28:1).

By means of "a strong and mighty agent" (Assyria), God would destroy Samaria. Isaiah likened the force of destruction to a downpour of hail, a blast of wind and a mighty rain. The city would be leveled and trodden under foot. The enemy eagerly would snatch and devour that place like it was a first ripe fig (28:2-4).

Samaria's demise would have one positive result. That national tragedy would cause some men to focus their attention on the true crown of Israel, viz., God himself. Among the surviving remnant God would bring a spirit of justice to those in the judiciary; he would provide strength to those in the military (28:5-6). The point is that a remnant would survive the national catastrophe, and that remnant would experience genuine conversion.

B. The Scoffers of Judah (28:7-29).

The spiritual leaders of Judah share the confusion of the political leaders of the north. The visions announced by the prophets and the judgments rendered by priests were as irrational as the babblings of a drunk. The leaders were sick as well as drunk. Isaiah pictured the tables where these drunken policy makers sat as full of vomit (28:7f.).

1. Countering mockery (28:9-13). The leaders responded to Isaiah's unflattering depiction by attacking the prophet for being simplistic and repetitious. They offered a mocking caricature of the prophet's preaching (28:9f.). "The Hebrew original sounds like the mocking of nursery rhymes or the stammering of drunkards."[3]

Isaiah parried the gibe of his critics with a threat. Indeed God would speak to these people through a foreign tongue which would sound like the gibberish of their mockery. The reference is to the tongue of the Assyrians, the agents of judgment. By rejecting Isaiah, these leaders had rejected God's direction to rest in his word of promise and to trust him for deliverance from national foes. They would therefore have to face the harsh realities of foreign domination. To drive home his point, Isaiah repeated their mocking syllables and imparted to them a sinister significance. These leaders would stumble backward, be broken and taken captive (28:11-13).[4]

2. Countering false security (28:14-19). Faced with an invasion by Assyria ("the overwhelming scourge") Judah felt secure. The leaders had negotiated an agreement which Isaiah sarcastically called "a covenant with death" and a pact with Sheol. Such an arrangement was utterly deceptive (28:14f.). Most likely the prophet was referring to a death-do-us-die treaty with Egypt (cf. chap. 31). By putting these words in the mouths of the leaders, Isaiah suggested that they knew Egypt would provide no help against the mighty Assyrians.

True security could be found only in the stone which God would provide. That stone—tested in every way and costly to set in place—was the cornerstone of the household of faith. That this stone is Messiah is made clear by Romans 9:33 and 1 Peter 2:2f. Anyone who placed his faith in that stone would not "be disturbed," (lit., be in a hurry), whatever judgments might unfold (28:16). The thought is that a believer can face any adversity with calmness since by faith he is anchored to the unmovable Rock.

Judah would shortly need the security of faith in that stone. With the measuring line of justice and the plummet of righteousness God would judge the sinners of that land. The flood tide of judgment would sweep away their man-made refuge. Their secret alliances would not spare them in that day. The Assyrian armies, like a scourge, would again and again come down upon them. Any time, day or night, troops would march through their land. Each visitation would produce terror (28:17-19).

3. Countering presumptuous faith (28:20-22). Some might be inclined to argue that God would come to their rescue against Assyria. The presumption that God owed them deliverance would provide no comfort in that day. That doctrine was like a bed too short for comfortable sleep, like covers too narrow to give warmth to an exposed body (28:20).

Isaiah called the Assyrian judgment a "strange work" (NIV) of God. The Lord would use foreigners to fight against his own people, with the same zeal he had displayed against the Philistines in the battle of Mt. Perazim (2 Sam 5:19-21) and against the Canaanites in the valley of Gibeon (Josh 10:12). Isaiah warned those who took his threats lightly that their indifference would only make the fetters of subordination to Assyria even stronger. Scoff though they may, Isaiah reaffirmed the divine origin of his message and the ominous thrust thereof (28:21f.).

4. Countering theological error (28:23-29). Isaiah used two parables to refute the notion that God's justice would prevent him from bringing judgment upon the entire land. A farmer does not go on plowing forever, but finally sows. So God's judgment would result in the preparation of a seed plot, and in due time plowing would give way to sowing. God would not punish his people forever. The old Israel would be plowed under to make way for the new (28:23-26).

Continuing with his agricultural metaphors, Isaiah made another point. Threshing varies with the material to be threshed. God would not discipline his people beyond what was appropriate. For the sake of the righteous remnant, judgment would be tempered with mercy (28:27-29).

THE PROBLEM
Woe to Worthless Worship
Isaiah 29:1-14

Isaiah's second woe was pronounced against Ariel, the hearth of God. This symbolic name refers to Jerusalem, the sacrificial center of the nation. The city of David was presently gay and festive, but that was about to change.

A. The Distress of Judah (29:2-8).

Perhaps using the great bronze Temple altar as an object lesson, Isaiah announced that Jerusalem would become an Ariel, a sacrificial altar. Joyous songs would turn to lamentation. Why? Because God would direct an enemy (the Assyrians) to launch an attack against Jerusalem. They would come to that place with the intent to kill the inhabitants and burn the city. Proud Jerusalem would be humbled to the dust, unable to speak, except in a ghost-like whisper (29:2-4).

From this distress God miraculously would rescue Jerusalem. Suddenly the Lord would disperse those ruthless enemies as wind scatters the chaff of the threshing floor. He would unleash against the Assyrians the full force of his omnipotent power, symbolized here by the devastating forces of nature. Those who assault Ariel would disappear as suddenly as a nightmare when one awakes. The Assyrians would be disappointed in their aspirations of devouring Jerusalem like a man who dreams of food only to awake and have none (29:5-8).

B. The Disbelief of Judah (29:9-14).

The people of Judah are "stunned and amazed" (NIV) by this message. Their confusion is likened to the staggering about of one who is blind or drunk. God had permitted a deep sleep to fall upon them so that they perceived no danger. Their spiritual leaders (prophets and seers) could offer no guidance for God had shut their eyes (29:8f.).

In their state of confusion and spiritual blindness the nation would not take to heart the message of Isaiah. His vision (i.e., revelation) was like a sealed scroll which the learned would not attempt to open, and the ignorant could not read even if it were to be opened (29:11f.).

Why is Judah so out of tune with God's word? Why have they rejected every effort of this man of God to make them understand? The fault was in their approach to worship. Their devotion was insincere, formal and traditional. They said the right words, but these words did not come from the heart. They recited the proper ritual, but fear of the Lord did not govern their life (29:13).

Since Judah was hopelessly out of touch with the Lord, neither they nor their wise men would be able to fathom the "wondrously marvelous" thing which God was about to do in their midst. Both the distress into which Judah would fall at the hands of the Assyrians, and the miraculous deliverance therefrom, would be inexplicable by political logic or historical precedent (29:14).

THE PROBLEM
Woe to Wily Schemers
Isaiah 29:15-24

The third woe fell on those who challenged the omniscience of God by nefarious schemes. Their secret plans were based on the premise that God could not save. The unit begins with condemnation and concludes with a positive word about future redemption.

A. Condemnation (29:15-17).

The focus here seems to be on the pro-Egyptian party which was attempting to conceal their proposed alliance from Isaiah and from God. Such secretive plans, however, denied the sovereignty of God. The creature must always recognize himself to be inferior to the Creator. Man cannot outsmart God (29:15f.).

The man-made schemes designed to save Judah from the might of Assyria were unnecessary. In a short while the Lebanon forest (representing Assyria) would be cut down to become an ordinary stand of vegetation. On the other hand, the fruitful field (God's people) was destined to become a mighty forest (29:17). The reference must be to the messianic kingdom to which Isaiah has referred repeatedly.

B. Redemption (29:18-24).

Just as the Lord redeemed Abraham from heathen surroundings

(29:22), so Yahweh would rescue Jacob-Israel from their idolatrous surroundings.[5] Concerning that glorious messianic age, Isaiah made five predictions. First, in that day the people of God would be receptive to the divine word. The "deaf" would hear the words of a book, the "blind" would see (29:18). Second, in the messianic age the "afflicted" and "needy"—God-fearing men—would experience fresh joy "in the Lord" (29:19). Third, tyrants and scoffers who had oppressed God's people would be "cut off" (29:20f.).

Isaiah's fourth prediction was that the family of God would be expanded. Jacob is depicted looking over his "house" in the messianic age. He would have no reason to be ashamed. He would observe his children "the work of my hands in his midst." By the divine adoptive process Gentiles would become part of the family of God, the house of Jacob. All the true members of the house of Jacob would stand in awe of "the Holy one of Jacob" as they witnessed this marvelous expansion of the family of redeemed (29:22f.). Finally, in that day errant Jews would be converted. They would come to know the truth (29:24).

THE PROPOSED SOLUTION
Woe to Willful Children
Isaiah 30:1-33

Chapters 28-29 contained three general "woes" which were designed to illustrate the problem faced by Judah. In chapters 30-31 Isaiah became more specific. The fourth woe concerned God's rebellious children who were determined to forge an alliance with Egypt. In these chapters Isaiah continued the denunciation promise pattern which he employed in chapter 29.

A. Denunciation (30:1-17).

Isaiah demonstrated the folly of reliance on Egypt in several ways. Though he makes his point through repetition in verses 1-17, some development in his thought can be detected. The alliance stood condemned because it was man-made, futile, rebellious and ultimately unnecessary.

1. Man-made alliance (30:1-5). The leaders of Judah had not taken counsel of God. Their planned alliance with Egypt was not in harmony with the divine Spirit which through Isaiah had warned of such political entanglements. To the sin of trusting in Pharaoh they were adding the sin of mistrusting Yahweh! (30:1f.).

Since alliance with Egypt was contrary to God's purpose, the plan would fail. Envoys from Judah had already gone to Hanes and Zoan at the extreme limits of Lower Egypt. Their efforts, however, were wasted. Egypt would prove to be a totally unreliable ally. Judah would experience national embarrassment by trusting in the "safety of Pharaoh." The Egyptians would be no help during the coming Assyrian crisis (30:3-5).

2. Futile alliance (30:6-8). In "the oracle concerning the beasts of the Negev" Isaiah elaborated on the trip to Egypt by the envoys of Judah. That trip was difficult, dangerous, expensive, and ultimately futile. Egypt rightly deserved the nickname "Rahab the Do-Nothing" (NIV).[6] Egypt always boasted of more than she could deliver. Her help was vain and empty. In order to verify the fact of the prediction after the fulfillment, Isaiah was told to write down his new name for Egypt (cf. 8:1).

3. Rebellious alliance (30:9-14). The citizens of Judah were rebellious sons who refused to listen to God's word. They wanted the prophets to alter their message, to stop meddling in the affairs of state. They wanted their spiritual leaders to speak more positively about the immediate prospects of the nation. These rebellious sons wanted to hear no more of the theology of God's holiness (30:9-11).

Judgment for those who preferred political alliance to God's word was set forth in two striking figures: (1) a wall with a crack which falls suddenly; and (2) a potter's vessel smashed totally, with no fragment large enough to use for any purpose (30:12-14).

4. Arrogant alliance (30:15-18). As an alternative to reliance upon Egypt, Isaiah advocated calm neutrality in international politics, restful trust in God. He proposed reliance not alliance. He urged repentance with respect to obedience to God's direction (30:15). Trusting God for salvation, however, was far too simple for these arrogant leaders. They spurned God's grace and tried to manufacture their own salvation.

The strategists in Jerusalem thought that the horses which they got from Egypt would be the equalizer in the confrontation with Assyria. On the contrary, declared the prophet, those horses would only aid them in fleeing from their enemy. The Assyrian cavalry would be every bit as swift as any horses they might employ. A handful of enemy soldiers would put to flight thousands. Their disgraceful dispersal would leave Jerusalem alone, undefended, like a flag pole on a barren hill (30:16f.).

The denunciation of the Egyptian alliance closed with an oblique appeal. God longed to be gracious to his people. He was, however, a God of justice. Therefore repentance on their part must precede any change of action on his part. Those who did put their trust in the Lord would be most blessed (30:18).

B. Promise (30:19-33).

Judah's failure to trust God would lead to destruction. Nonetheless, in the midst of judgment God would display his grace. In the long run, and in the short run God had glorious things in store for his people.

1. A glorious Teacher (30:19-26). One day God would hear the cry of the people of Zion—the remnant—and he would respond. In the past the Lord had taught his people by means of hard circumstances. In the future, however, they would actually see their Teacher. This Teacher would provide daily guidance to keep his people on the right path. Under the influence of this Teacher, God's people would develop an absolute abhorrence for all things connected with idolatry (30:19-22). This appears to be a personal messianic prophecy.[7]

Isaiah depicted the blessings of the Teacher's work in terms of agricultural and pastoral prosperity. Abundant water and light symbolize the joy and prosperity of that day (cf. Mal 4:2). At that time God would heal his broken and bruised people through the life-giving Gospel (30:23-26).

2. A marvelous deliverance (30:27-33). In the nearer future, the people of God would experience a wonderful deliverance. Alliance with Egypt was unnecessary because God himself would crush the adversary. To that enemy he would be both a consuming fire and a torrent of water. His actions would shake and sift the political world. Hostile peoples would be led away, as with a bridle, to their ruin. The people of Judah would rejoice with great exuberance over their deliverance from the domination of Assyria (30:27-29).

So that his message could not be misunderstood, Isaiah became more specific. God would unleash a furious storm against the Assyrians. His "voice of authority" (thunder) would be heard, and "the descending of His arm" (lightning) would be seen. Assyria would tremble at this voice of God. Changing figures, Isaiah described how the "the rod of punishment" would fall against Assyria repeatedly. God's people would rejoice in each act of deliverance for they would perceive that Yahweh was fighting against their enemies (30:30-32).

Isaiah repeated his main point as an exclamation mark to the entire chapter. For some time the Lord had been gathering wood at Topheth (the fireplace) for the funeral-pyre of the king of Assyria and his armies. Shortly the breath of God would kindle the fire for the cremation of the corpses (30:33).

THE PROPOSED SOLUTION
Woe to Worldly Trust
Isaiah 31:1-32:20

The fifth woe fell upon those who proposed alliance with Egypt as the solution to Judah's national plight. Isaiah explained here why that policy would not work. The denunciation/promise pattern of the previous two chapters is followed here as well.

A. Denunciation (31:1-3).

The alliance with Egypt was doomed. From the standpoint of political strategy, the move toward Egypt perhaps could be defended. This policy, however, was not of God. Its framers did not recognize that God's wisdom is incomparable, his word is irrevocable, his power is irresistible, and his justice is inexorable. The Egyptians, being mere men, could not resist the power of this One who is Spirit. God must rise against "the house of evildoers" and any who might help them.

B. Promise (31:4-9).

God would wage war upon Mt. Zion. God would be as strong and determined as a lion which had found the prey. He could not be frightened away. At the same time, God was personally attached to his people like a mother bird is attached to her young. Just as a bird circles over her nest to protect the helpless chicks from ravenous birds of prey, so Yahweh would not permit the total destruction of his people (31:4f).[8]

In view of the announcement of God's protection of Zion, Isaiah called for repentance. That implied repudiation of all idolatry. In the crisis of the attack against Jerusalem, all idols would be abandoned anyway. Thus repentance would be the true manifestation of trust in God's promise (31:6f.).

More details were now added about Yahweh's glorious deliverance on Mt. Zion. The Assyrians would fall miraculously, not by the sword of man, but by the sword of divine justice. The reference is to the overnight destruction of Sennacherib's army in 701 BC. The "rock" of the Assyrian army would pass away during the panic of that moment. This could refer to the king, an idol or perhaps to the strength of the army. In any case, panic would seize the leaders of the army. Zion would be the furnace of God's wrath. Those who attacked her would meet their doom (31:8f.).

INTERLUDE: FUTURE PROSPECTS
Isaiah 32

While the prospects for Assyria were bleak, those of the people of God were quite different. In chapter 32 Isaiah spoke in two units of the glories of the messianic age. Sandwiched between these bright foreglimpses is a unit describing the future of the nation before the golden age.

A. Renewal Promised (32:1-8).

The messianic Ruler and his subordinates would rule in justice. In contrast to those leaders condemned in chapter 28, the new leadership would provide refuge and refreshment to people under duress. Those spiritually blind and deaf would come to understand God's truth. They would not hesitate to proclaim that word to others (32:1-4).

True values would be recovered in that future kingdom. Fools no longer would be considered noble. They would be identified clearly by the nonsense they spoke, by their abusive treatment of the less fortunate, and by their devious schemes. The noble man would also be recognized clearly in that day as one who devised noble plans and stood by them. Noble plans would be those which helped, encouraged and built up those who were in need (32:5-8).

B. Renewal Preceded by Disaster (32:9-14).

The complacent women of Judah were urged to listen to the warning of the prophet. In just over a year the supply of grapes (and consequently wine) would be cut off. The women are urged to enter into bitter lamentation over the terrible fate which would befall their land (32:9-12). The scorched earth policy of the Assyrians is reflected here.

Isaiah predicted the complete abandonment of Judah. Thorns and briers would take over the land. Jerusalem would be deserted, the palace abandoned. Animals would find refuge in the ruins of the city (32:13f.). This divine sentence against Jerusalem began to be executed by the Assyrians in 701 BC. For the sake of good King Hezekiah, however, the city was given a reprieve. The destruction here threatened was finally effected by the Babylonians in 587 BC.

C. Renewal Accomplished by the Spirit (32:15-20).

The desolate condition of Jerusalem would in some sense continue until the pouring out of God's Spirit. From 587 to 538 BC the land of Judah was abandoned in the absolute sense. Under the leadership of Ezra, Nehemiah and the postexilic prophets, the Temple was reconstructed and the city was restored. By 445 BC Jerusalem's walls had been rebuilt. The city thrived throughout the intertestamental period. For most of that time, however, Jerusalem was under the domination of some foreign power. First the Persians, then the Greeks and finally the Romans exercised sovereignty over the land. The Shekinah glory no longer resided in the Holy of Holies. The land was without the living voice of prophecy. For these reasons, Jerusalem was still considered to be desolate during the period between the testaments.

With the outpouring of the Spirit on the day of Pentecost a new era was inaugurated.[9] Isaiah portrayed the blessings associated with the coming of the Spirit in terms of fertile fields and lush forests. This metaphorical fruitfulness is explained to represent justice (right relationship between man and his fellows) and righteousness (right relationship between man and God). The creation through God's Spirit of these relationships would result in peace, rest and safety (32:15-18).[10]

Enemies would still be present in the messianic age. Isaiah likened them to a forest (cf. 10:18,33f.) and a city (cf. 24:10; 25:2f.; 26:5). As in the ancient holy war, God would use hail stones to beat down these enemies. On the other hand, those who are citizens in Messiah's kingdom would enjoy blessing in abundance.[11] Again Isaiah used agricultural figures. The crops would be so abundant that a farmer would not have to exercise care in where he allowed his stock to feed (32:19f.).

THE TRUE SOLUTION
Woe to the Wicked Oppressor
Isaiah 33:1-24

Chapter 33 brings the Book of Woes to this grand conclusion: the oppressor would be destroyed and Yahweh would be exalted. The first six verses constitute an introduction to the major themes of the chapter. The remainder of the chapter may be divided into two major units which speak of the exaltation and reign of Yahweh.

A. Introduction (33:1-6).

Unlike the previous five woes, the sixth did not fall upon God's people. The ominous word is used here in regard to the "destroyer," Assyria. For a time by war and stealth this ruthless power had dominated the ancient Near East. That period of oppression, however, would not be interminable. When it ended Assyria would experience what she had inflicted upon others (33:1).

The pronouncement of the woe against the oppressor was followed by a prayer of the faithful. The implication is that the oppressor meets his doom because God's people began to pray. The prayer begins with petition that God would be gracious to his people, that he would be their strength and salvation in the time of distress. The prophet was confident of the outcome of this prayer. He foresaw the army of the tyrant fleeing and the men of Judah, jumping around like grasshoppers, gathering up the spoil (33:2-4).

By his victory over the Assyrians Yahweh would acquire new glory. Once the tyrant was gone, the attributes of the true king would be displayed in Jerusalem, i.e., righteousness and justice. The saved of Zion would come to look upon God as their source of stability and as a veritable treasure trove of salvation, wisdom and knowledge. In response God would bestow upon his people "the fear of the Lord," i.e., complete devotion to him (33:5f.).

B. The Day of Exaltation (33:7-16).

Isaiah now expanded on the theme of God's exaltation. First he sketched the desperate need of the people. Before deliverance, Jerusalem would be reduced to a pitiful state. Even valiant men would weep. Peace envoys would fail in their mission. The Assyrians would renege on solemn covenants. Highways would become unsafe. The land would mourn because of the scorched earth policy of the invaders (33:7-9). Man's extremity, however, is God's opportunity. In the darkest hour, God would arise, i.e., intervene. He addressed, as it were, the Assyrian invaders. Their plans regarding Judah were futile. The struggle to subdue Judah was likened to a painful pregnancy which resulted in no birth. Assyria's angry snorting against Jerusalem came back against them like a consuming fire. The invaders quickly (like thorns) and totally (to lime) would be burned in God's wrath (33:10-12).

Isaiah pictured Yahweh calling upon those far and near to acknowledge his might after the crushing defeat of the Assyrians. Sinners within Jerusalem would be moved to repentance by the divine display of power against Assyria. They would be, and should be, concerned about what kind of person could reside in the presence of this God of consuming fire. Isaiah provided the answer with a six-fold description of the righteous man. On the positive side that man (1) walks righteously and (2) speaks with sincerity. On the negative side, he rejects (1) unjust gain, (2) bribes, (3) even the thought of bloodshed, (4) and evil of any kind. That man would enjoy security in the day of judgment for his refuge was the impregnable rock.

C. The Glorious Reign (33:17-24).

Those who survived the temporal judgment (i.e., righteous men) would look forward with the eye of faith to see "the king in his beauty," i.e., God himself (cf. 33:22). They would behold "a far-distant land" (33:17). That the Messiah and his kingdom are the focus of this anticipation seems clear.

The Zion of Messiah's kingdom would be a safe city. No more would fierce invaders of strange speech threaten the place. Those who counted spoil and plotted demolition would be only a distant memory. The faithful would see the future Zion as a peaceful and permanent habitation. Yahweh himself would dwell there. Unlike historic Jerusalem, this Zion would be situated beside broad rivers, but not rivers which would permit naval attack (33:18-21). The thought is that messianic Jerusalem would have an abundant water supply. The Zion of which Isaiah speaks is that mentioned in Hebrews 12:28.

The presence of the Lord would make that future Zion all that Isaiah said it would be. In that city he would function in three capacities: (1) as judge, like one of those spirit-filled saviors who delivered Israel from foreign oppressors; (2) as lawgiver, i.e., one who regulates life through his instruction; and (3) as king, with absolute sovereignty over all the inhabitants of the place (33:22).

In Isaiah's day Jerusalem looked like a big ship, totally unprepared for the rough waters of Assyrian invasion. Nonetheless, the city would experience a mighty deliverance. Even the physically handicapped would be able to partake of the spoil of the invader. That physical enrichment, however, would not be anything compared to the spiritual blessing which would result from the national repentance induced by the invasion. God would forgive the iniquity of those who dwelled there.

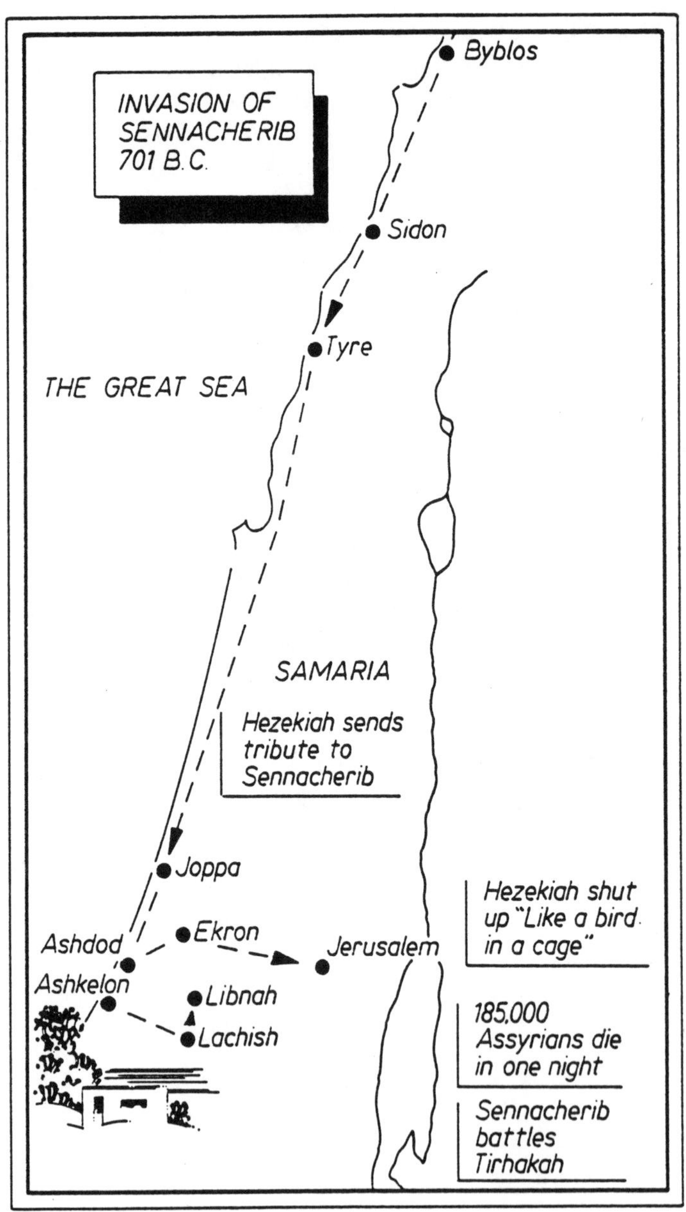
INVASION OF
SENNACHERIB
701 B.C.
Byblos
Sidon
Tyre
THE GREAT SEA
SAMARIA
Hezekiah sends
tribute to
Sennacherib
Joppa
Ashdod
Ekron
Jerusalem
Ashkelon
Libnah
Lachish
Hezekiah shut
up "Like a bird
in a cage"
185,000
Assyrians die
in one night
Sennacherib
battles
Tirhakah

Endnotes

1. Previous woes in Isaiah: 3:9-11; 5:8-11, 20, 22; 10:1; 17:12; 18:1.

2. Cited by H.C. Leupold, *Exposition of Isaiah* (Grand Rapids: Baker, 1968) 1:433.

3. I.W. Slotki, *Isaiah* in Soncino Books of the Bible (London: Soncino, 1949) 128.

4. The threat, however, establishes a principle: when men reject the plan, God employs the unusual to warn them of impending destruction. Thus the Apostle Paul would later say that the speaking in tongues of the first century was a sign, not to believers, but to unbelievers (1 Cor 14:21).

5. George L. Robinson, *The Book of Isaiah* (Grand Rapids: Baker, 1964) 112.

6. Leupold (*op. cit.* 471) renders *rahab hem shaveth* as "Big-mouth that is a Do-Nothing."

7. Most commentators interpret 31:4 as a threat against Jerusalem. God would fight *against* Jerusalem. The Hebrew can be translated *upon,* and the context seems to demand a promise here, not a threat. See John Oswalt, *The Book of Isaiah: Chapters 1-39* in The New International Commentary on the Old Testament (Grand Rapids: Eerdmans, 1986) 574.

8. The word *teacher* is plural in the Hebrew, so most commentators think that the prophets are intended. The verb, however, is singular suggesting that the promise refers to the appearance of the Teacher par excellence, i.e., Messiah. Cf. Joel 2:23.

9. The pouring out of God's Spirit is mentioned in several passages: Isa 44:3; 54:13; 60:21; Ezek 36:26; 39:29; Joel 2:28; Zech 12:10.

10. On peace, rest and safety of Messiah's kingdom see Matt 11:25-30; John 14:27; 15:11; Eph 1:14; 2:11-12.

11. On the abundant blessing of Messiah's kingdom see John 10:10; 1 Cor 3:21-23; Eph 1:3; Rom 8:17-18, 32; 2 Cor 4:16-18.

CHAPTER SEVEN

The Book of Hezekiah
Isaiah 36-39

Background of the Unit.

In 703 BC the Assyrian King Sennacherib marched against and subdued his perpetual antagonist, Merodach-Baladan of Babylon. The following year he conquered Armenia. In 701 BC Sennacherib invaded Palestine.

This unit consists largely of historical narrative. Most of this material appears almost verbatim in 2 Kings 18:13-20:20. The chapters are not in chronological order. Chapters 38-39 speak of events prior to the Assyrian invasion; chapters 36-37 narrate events during and after the Assyrian invasion. Why this arrangement? Isaiah deliberately reversed the order of this material for a literary purpose. Chapters 36-37 form a fitting climax to all the prophet had been saying about the Assyrian ordeal. These chapters document the fulfillment of the several predictions made in chapters 1-35 that God would miraculously deliver Jerusalem from this attack. On the other hand, chapters 38-39 form the background of all that Isaiah would say about deliverance from Babylonian Exile.

At issue in this unit is whether men will continue to trust in God regardless of circumstances. Sennacherib's campaign in Judah forced the issue in the political arena. Would the king, the army and the citizens of Jerusalem continue to believe the predictions of a miraculous deliverance from this menace? A health crisis in the life of King Hezekiah raised the same issue at the individual level.

Outline of the Unit.[1]

A. The Initial Challenge (36:1-37:7).
B. The Intensified Challenge (37:8-38).
C. The Individual Challenge (chaps. 38-39).

THE INITIAL CHALLENGE
Isaiah 36:1-37:7

In the fourteenth year of Hezekiah (701 BC) a massive Assyrian army swept into Palestine. According to 2 Kings 18:14-16 Hezekiah had met the tribute demands of King Sennacherib. Jerusalem should have been given immunity. The Assyrian, however, changed his mind and decided to press for total capitulation. In this crisis King Hezekiah chose the path of reliance upon God. This king demonstrated the attitude and actions for which Isaiah had pressed in chapters 7-35. Thus chapters 36-37 serve as the counterbalance to chapters 7-8 in which prideful and headstrong King Ahaz in a similar crisis chose to place his trust in man.

A. The Rabshakeh's Ultimatum (36:1-20).

Sennacherib had little difficulty conquering all the fortified cities of Judah. By his own count there were forty-six such cities.[2] The Assyrian had his headquarters at Lachish, about twenty-five miles southwest of Jerusalem. While Sennacherib remained at Lachish directing the attack against Philistia, he dispatched three of his top officers, the Rabshakeh, Tartan and Rabsaris (2 Kgs 18:17) with enough troops to intimidate Hezekiah. Isaiah emphasized the irony that the Rabshakeh (NIV "field commander") challenged the trust policy of Hezekiah in the very spot where some thirty-three years earlier Isaiah had challenged King Ahaz to commit himself to such a policy. There the Rabshakeh met with a high-level delegation from Hezekiah's court (36:1-3). He issued two challenges, one to the King Hezekiah and one to the defenders of Jerusalem.

1. The challenge to Hezekiah (36:4-10). The Rabshakeh was the chief propaganda officer of the Assyrian army, and he was a master of his craft. Diplomatic niceties were bypassed as he directed his stinging words to Hezekiah. He did not even refer to the king by proper title (36:4a).

He began his conversation with the Judean nobles by attacking what he perceived to be the motives which prompted the rebellion of Hezekiah. First, he argued that reliance on Egypt would not avail. All who had tried to lean on that "crushed reed" had only pierced their hand (36:4b-6). On this point the Rabshakeh and Isaiah would have been in complete agreement.

Second, the Rabshakeh argued that reliance on Yahweh could not be the basis for rebellion against Assyria. As an idolater and polytheist he could not understand how Yahweh could be pleased with Hezekiah's removal of the rural high places (36:7). Though Hezekiah's efforts at worship centralization were in perfect accord with the Law and the prophets, no doubt many citizens of Judah agreed with Rabshakeh's perspective. The Assyrian intended to exploit the popular discontent created by Hezekiah's religious reforms.

Next the Assyrian pointed out the obvious military weakness of Judah, viz., lack of cavalry. Sarcastically he argued that even if the Assyrians donated two thousand horses to the rebels they would not be able to put riders on them. Hezekiah's strength was not equal to that of one of the lowest officials of the Assyrian Empire, so how could he be brazen enough to defy the Great King? (36:8f.).

In the climax of his argument Rabshakeh claimed to be operating under a commission of Yahweh to destroy the land of Judah (36:10). Did he make this claim on the basis of having heard of some of Isaiah's predictions? Was he arguing from a general theological principle that whatever might happen Yahweh was responsible? In either case, Rabshakeh was employing an argument which was designed to have maximum effect on the rebels.

2. The request by the officials (36:11-12). Hezekiah's representatives interrupted the Assyrian to make a request, viz., that the negotiations be conducted in the international language (Aramaic) not in the language of the Jews (Hebrew). They worried about the effect that these surrender demands might have on the defenders sitting on the walls near-by. With even greater bluster, Rabshakeh rejected this demand. He wanted Judah's soldiers to realize the terrible deprivations which they would experience if their king refused to surrender the city. This Assyrian had not come to negotiate but to undermine Jerusalem's will to resist (vv. 11-12).

3. The challenge to the defenders (36:13-22). The Rabshakeh raised his voice and addressed in the name of his king all the citizens in Jerusalem within earshot. His argument consisted of five points. First, Hezekiah would not be able to save his capital from the Assyrians (36:14). Second, Hezekiah's promises that Yahweh would not allow the city to fall to the enemy were vain (36:15). Third, surrender would mean immediate peace. Jews would be permitted to return to their farms and homes outside the walls (36:16).

The Rabshakeh's fourth argument was that deportation would not be that bad, for they would find themselves in a land of abundance similar to their own (36:17). Finally, the Assyrian argued that no other gods had delivered their cities from the mighty king.[3] Even Samaria, which also worshipped Yahweh albeit in a perverted form, had fallen. Why should the outcome be any different at Jerusalem? (36:18-20).

B. Reaction to the Challenge (36:21-37:7) .

The supreme moment in the drama had now arrived. Would Judah bow to the logic of the Rabshakeh? Or would she renounce all other objects of trust and cast herself on the Lord? Isaiah described the reaction to the challenge of the Rabshakeh on two levels.

1. The reaction of the king (36:21-37:5). Hezekiah's negotiating team was under orders not to engage in debate with Rabshakeh. Upon reentering the palace complex, however, the three officials tore their garments in distress. They then reported to Hezekiah the unconditional surrender demands of the adversary (36:21f.).

Hezekiah was in great distress when he heard the new demands of the Rabshakeh. He tore his clothes, and put on coarse sackcloth to symbolize his agony. He then went to the house of the Lord which was just next to the palace. Several senior officials dressed in signs of mourning were dispatched to Isaiah. This was a dark day for Judah. Hezekiah admitted his utter helplessness before the enemy. The Rabshakeh had reproached the living God by comparing him to the idols worshiped elsewhere. "Perhaps"—they presumed nothing—Yahweh would rebuke those words by taking action against the invading army. Hezekiah's greatest concern was for the honor of God. The emissaries urged the prophet to pray for the terrified remnant which was holed up in Jerusalem (37:1-5).

2. The reaction of the prophet (37:6-7). How would Isaiah react to these leaders who for so many years had mocked his message (cf. 30:8-11)? The prophet did not honor the request for intercession, but only because already he had received divine revelation regarding this crisis. Isaiah directed the dignitaries to take a short reply back to Hezekiah. The king should not be afraid of the words which have been spoken by Rabshakeh. Those words blasphemed God, and God would respond appropriately. He would put a spirit within Sennacherib, a spirit of fear. The Assyrian would hear certain unspecified tidings which would cause him to return to his own country. There he would be assassinated. At this point no explicit mention was made regarding the destruction of the Assyrian army. The focus was on the fate of the king who had dared to blaspheme God. Hezekiah had nothing more to fear from Sennacherib. He should reject the demand for unconditional surrender.

THE INTENSIFIED CHALLENGE
Isaiah 37:8-38

Rabshakeh returned to his master for further instructions. He caught up with Sennacherib at Libnah, about ten miles from Lachish, where the Assyrian army was conducting siege operations. Hearing of the rumored advance of Tirhakah the Ethiopian ruler of Egypt, Sennacherib realized that his time in Palestine might be cut short. He determined to make one last effort to secure the total capitulation of Hezekiah. Messengers were dispatched to Jerusalem carrying a letter from the Great King (37:8f.). This letter represented an intensified challenge to the faith policy of Hezekiah in two respects. First, the written form was taken far more seriously than the oral form in ancient times. Second, whereas Rabshakeh's attack had been upon Hezekiah, the letter was an attack upon the God of Israel.

A. The Contents of the Letter (37:10-13).

As was the custom in the ancient Near East, the envoys first recited the contents of the letter before handing it over to Hezekiah. The letter urged Hezekiah not to be deceived by his God into thinking that Jerusalem would not fall to him. Judah's king was surely not ignorant of the many conquests of Assyrian forces. Sennacherib cited several examples and then asked why the gods of these peoples had not delivered them from the might of Assyria. The Great King obviously regarded Yahweh as an inferior god of an inferior kingdom (37:10-12).

Sennacherib closed his letter with an ominous threat against the person of Hezekiah. He obliquely reminded Hezekiah of what had become of the kings of those nations conquered by Assyria. The king of Judah was all too familiar with the terrible tortures which the Assyrians inflicted on the rebellious kings (37:13). Thus Sennacherib made the issue crystal clear for Hezekiah. Would he continue to trust in Yahweh his God when his life—and the lives of his family members—was on the line?

B. Reaction to the Challenge (37:14-32).

Again the narrative reveals the reaction of both the king and the prophet to the challenge of Sennacherib's letter. Hezekiah's response indicated an even deeper commitment to the policy of trust. He was determined more than ever to place both his own fate and that of his city in the hands of the Lord. Corresponding to this intensity of commitment, the Lord's response through Isaiah was much more detailed and forceful than the initial response.

1. The response of the king (37:14-20). After reading Sennacherib's letter, Hezekiah went up to the Temple and spread it before the Lord. He wished to pray over the letter. The address of this prayer is a marvelous testimony of the faith of the king. He addressed God as Yahweh of hosts, i.e., armies. Though enthroned on Mt. Zion above the cherubim, he was the God of all kingdoms of the earth. His divine sovereignty over all peoples was derived from the fact that he was the Creator of heaven and earth (37:14-16).

Hezekiah made no effort to plead his own righteousness or that of his people. He knew that the real issues here were the honor of God and his sovereignty over all nations. He called upon the Lord to "see" the situation as it was unfolding and to "hear," i.e., take note of the words of reproach contained in the letter of Sennacherib. That the Assyrians had compiled a terrifying record of conquests could not be denied. That they had shown their superiority over the gods of those conquered nations was equally true. The Assyrians contemptuously had thrown the idols of conquered nations into the fire. Those idols, however, were not really gods, but only the work of men's hands. Therefore, Hezekiah called upon Yahweh to demonstrate his commitment to Judah, and his omnipotent power by delivering Jerusalem from the hand of Sennacherib. That would demonstrate to the kingdoms of the earth that Yahweh alone was God (37:17-20).

2. The response of the prophet (37:21-35). Sennacherib had spoken against the Lord; Hezekiah had spoken to the Lord; now at last God spoke. In response to the prayer of the king, the Lord spoke a word of encouragement. Just as Hezekiah's prayer revealed a greater commitment to God than his former words to the prophet, so the prophetic oracle which responded to his prayer was more complete than the initial oracle in 37:5-7.

Sennacherib and his servants had reproached the Holy One of Israel. Shortly the virgin (unsubdued) daughter of Zion would mock the retreating Assyrians (37:21-23). Yahweh was aware of how the Assyrian had boasted of his exploits against the nations of the world. He had taken his chariots into the mountains of Lebanon, as it were. He had chopped down tall and choice trees (nations). Sennacherib's imperial ambition would not be satisfied until he had reached the highest peak of Lebanon, i.e., conquered the most remote nations. Neither lack of water nor water barriers had stopped his advance (37:24f.). Yahweh knew all this, and more.

Isaiah had shocking news for Sennacherib. The very God he had charged with impotence was the one who controlled the entire Assyrian operation. Sennacherib was a mere actor in a drama written and directed by Yahweh. The divine plan was to bring cities to ruins, and to render peoples as helpless to resist Sennacherib as vegetation is powerless before the unrelenting rays of the summer sun. Nonetheless, God kept the Assyrian under constant surveillance. Because of his raging arrogance God would treat him like an animal. A hook in his nose and a bridle in his mouth would force him to turn about at the time appointed by God (37:26-29).

Isaiah addressed a personal word to King Hezekiah. The prophet gave him what his father Ahaz so contemptuously had rejected in chapter 7, viz., a sign.[4] For two harvests the regular operations of agriculture would be suspended. Then normal harvest would be experienced again. Through this word the king learned how long the effects of the Assyrian invasion would last. He was, however, reassured of this: Judah did have a future following the Assyrian devastation. The remnant of Judah, presently holed up in Jerusalem, would go forth from the city. They would take root like a plant and produce fruit. Once again Judah would become a prosperous nation. This dramatic change of fortunes would be due to the "zeal of the Lord of hosts" (37:30-33).

From the long range prospects of Judah, Isaiah returned to the immediate crisis in his concluding words. The Assyrian king would not even come against Jerusalem. Not one arrow would be shot into the city. Sennacherib would return home by the same road which he used to enter Judah. God would defend Jerusalem for his own sake (i.e., for the sake of his reputation). Thus Yahweh would demonstrate his enduring love for David, the founder of the dynasty which ruled Judah (37:33-35).

C. The Prediction Fulfilled (36:36-38).

With marvelous restraint Isaiah described in only three verses what must be regarded as one of the most dramatic moments in the history of Israel. Since chapter 7 Isaiah had been arguing that the only way for Judah to cope with crisis was to trust the Lord. These three verses provide the vindication for that advice. The several predictions of the miraculous defeat of Assyria at Jerusalem[5] find their fulfillment here.

The angel of Yahweh visited the Assyrian camp that night and smote 185,000 of the enemy.[6] With his army decimated, Sennacherib had no alternative but to return home. The Rabshakeh had referred to Sennacherib as "the great king" (36:4); God would reduce him to being merely "the king of Assyria." Some twenty years later, while he was worshiping in the temple of his god Nisroch, Sennacherib was assassinated.[7]

THE INDIVIDUAL CHALLENGE
Isaiah 38:1-39:8

That chapters 38-39 narrate events which were chronologically prior to Assyrian invasion of 701 BC is made clear in 38:6. Deliverance from Assyria which was narrated in the previous chapter as an accomplished fact, is here still future. Furthermore, in 39:2 Hezekiah still had sufficient treasures to impress foreign envoys. That the royal treasury would have that much wealth after the invasion of Sennacherib is difficult to imagine.

In chapter 38 Hezekiah modeled the lifestyle of faith advocated by Isaiah. Yet even here an undertone of warning was evident. As good a man as he was, Hezekiah was a mere man. God's people should not put their trust in men of faith, nor even in faith itself. God alone must be the object of trust. Chapter 38 focuses on Hezekiah's prayer and poem during this crisis in his life.

A. Hezekiah's Prayer (38:1-8).

Hezekiah became mortally ill. Isaiah urged him to set his house in order, because he was about to die. This announcement to the king was designed to humble him. The sick man responded by turning his face toward the wall (for privacy) and by praying as he had never prayed before in his life. Weeping shamelessly, he asked the Lord to consider his walk and his work. His heart had been totally committed to God throughout his life. He had always attempted to do that which was pleasing in the sight of the Lord. Hezekiah prayed, not because he feared death, but because he wanted to see his tiny country through the ordeal of Sennacherib's invasion which he knew was forthcoming (38:1-3).

God heard the prayer of Hezekiah. He was moved by the king's tears. Isaiah was sent back to give the sick man the good news. Fifteen years would be added to his life. Furthermore, God promised to deliver the king and his capital from the hand of the king of Assyria. (38:4-6).

Isaiah offered the king a sign involving the stairway which was used as a sundial to measure time. Hezekiah was given the choice of seeing the shadow go forward or backward on the steps (2 Kgs 20:9f.). At the request of the king, the sun's shadow went back on the stairway ten steps. How much time each step represented is not indicated. Speculation as to how God performed this miracle is useless (38:7f.).

B. Hezekiah's Poem (38:9-20).

After he recovered from his dreadful disease, Hezekiah composed a poem. This composition interrupts the prose story of the healing of the king because in it Hezekiah reflected upon his thoughts during his illness. For this reason the poem is a lament rather than a thanksgiving psalm. It emphasizes the mortality of the flesh rather than the miraculous healing.

1. Hezekiah's condition (38:10-14). The poem begins with the complaint of the dying man. In the prime of life he was about to be (1) consigned to Sheol, the abode of the dead; (2) deprived of public worship ("seeing the Lord in the land of the living"); and (3) cut off from fellowship with his friends (38:10f.). Hezekiah next reflected on the brevity of life. Earthly existence is like (1) a movable Bedouin's tent; (2) a piece of cloth cut from the loom; and (3) the swift passing from day to night (38:12).

The king waited for the inevitable through the night. He likened his impending death to the attack of a lion which breaks all the bones of its prey. Faced with this prospect, Hezekiah gave expression to his anguish through moaning like a dove. Yet he continued to look to God to take action on his behalf and he prayed to that effect (38:13f.).

2. God's response (38:15-20). The tone of the hymn changes in verse 15. God had promised to spare his life, and he had kept his word. Yet Hezekiah acknowledged that his near brush with death had produced five positive results. First, he had been humbled by the experience, and he vowed that he would be humble the rest of his days (38:15b). Second, he came to realize anew that the words of God have the power to create and sustain life (38:16a). Third, He realized his total dependence on God. Thus he continued to pray that his recovery might be complete: "O restore me to health, and let me live!" (38:16b). Fourth, he came to have a greater appreciation for God's grace. God had literally "loved my soul from the pit of destruction" (38:17a). Finally, he perceived in the prolongation of his life that God also had pardoned him of all his sins (38:17b).

Hezekiah's comments on the nature of death have stirred much controversy: "For Sheol cannot thank Thee, Death cannot praise Thee; those who go down to the pit cannot hope for Thy faithfulness" (38:18).[8] Did Hezekiah believe in annihilation of the soul? or soul sleeping? Or was he suggesting that one who enters the afterlife with unremitted sins is eternally separated from God? Then again, perhaps he was saying nothing more than that fleshly praise as he knew it would cease with death. In any case, it is the joyful privilege of the believer to praise God in this life and to teach his children to do the same (38:18f.).

The hymn ends with confident declaration: "The Lord will surely save me." For the rest of their days, he and his associates would continue to sing songs of praise to the Lord in the temple (38:20). In spite of this triumphant conclusion, the major thrust of the poem cannot be escaped. Every human being, no matter how often he may be healed, is still mortal.

C. Explanatory Notes (38:21-22).

Two notes are appended to the account of Hezekiah's illness. These notes may have been copied from the royal annals of Hezekiah's reign. The first indicates that one of the symptoms of Hezekiah's disease was a boil. Isaiah ordered a poultice of figs to be applied to the boil. Some hold that the poultice was medicinal and instrumental to Hezekiah's healing. Others believe that the poultice was symbolic of the fact that the healing process began the moment the poultice was applied. In either case, the note underscores the fact that divine healing is not always instantaneous.

The second note explains why God gave Hezekiah a sign (cf. 38:7). Isaiah had promised the king that he would be in the temple praising God within three days (2 Kgs 20:5). When Hezekiah asked for a sign, the shadow went backward on the stairs. For scoffers to ask for signs is considered sinful in the Old Testament.[9] When one, however, does believe, but needs support for his faith, God takes no offense at the request for a sign.[10]

D. Hezekiah's Failure (39:1-8).

The major theme of chapters 7-38 has been trusting the Lord, not nations nor idols nor anything else. How appropriate, then, that the first half of the Book of Isaiah closes with a warning against misplaced trust. Even such a godly man as Hezekiah can be lured into accepting the world's values. Every human ruler, no matter how many times he may have trusted in God, is still prone to self-reliance. Believers are hereby warned that "trust must be a way of life and not merely a one-time affair."[11] Here Hezekiah seems to be trusting in the accumulation of wealth and perhaps in an alliance with Babylon. Furthermore, the account warns that the believer's trust must be in God himself, not in men of God. Chapter 39 should dispel any idea that Hezekiah was the glorious king promised by Isaiah here and there in the first thirty-eight chapters of the book.

1. The circumstances (39:1-2). Merodach-baladan of Babylon was one of the chief gadflies of Assyrian imperialism. He was constantly rebelling and encouraging others to rebel against the world rulers. He used the occasion of Hezekiah's recovery to initiate contact with one he perceived to be in sympathy with his anti-Assyrian stance. About 703 BC Merodach-baladan dispatched envoys with letters and a gift for the king of Judah (39:1).

The Chronicler relates that in this situation God left Hezekiah alone to test him that he might know all that was in his heart (2 Chr 32:31). The king failed the test. Pride returned to his heart. In a somewhat boastful way Hezekiah put on display before the ambassadors all the wealth and weaponry of his kingdom. Nothing was held back (39:2).

2. The investigation (39:3). As close advisor to the king, Isaiah must have felt apprehensive about not being part of the discussions with the foreign dignitaries. When the envoys had departed he interrogated Hezekiah about them. What did these men say, and where did they come from, he asked. The king answered the second question but not the first. He knew Isaiah's position about alliances with foreign powers, and that subject surely must have been discussed during the visit. The third question of the prophet concerned what these ambassadors might have seen in the capital. Hezekiah, perhaps with some embarrassment, responded, "They have seen all that is in my house" (39:3f.).

3.The announcement (39:4-7). Isaiah then made a dramatic announcement. Assyria would not be the power to conquer Jerusalem and carry off all the treasures of the city. That would be the work of Babylon. Even members of the royal family—Hezekiah's descendants—would be carried off to become officials (lit., eunuchs) in the palace of the king of Babylon (39:5-7). Hezekiah would live out his years realizing that his arrogant display of royal wealth might be one factor which would make some future Babylonian king target Jerusalem for conquest.

4. The reaction (39:8). Hezekiah accepted the prophetic sentence with humility. The judgment he called "good" because it was less severe than he deserved. The exile would not occur in his days (39:8). Some have accused Hezekiah of being selfish for thinking that the judgment would be "good" as long as it did not happen during his reign.

Endnotes

1. This survey of the Book of Hezekiah has been influenced greatly by the very perceptive comments of John Oswalt, *The Book of Isaiah: Chapters 1-39* in The New International Commentary on the Old Teastament (Grand Rapids: Eerdmans, 1986) 627-98.

2. See James Pritchard, ed. *Ancient Near Eastern Texts Relating to the Old Testament* (3rd ed.; Princeton: University Press, 1969) 287f. Sennacherib also claims to have taken 200,105 citizens of Judah captive.

3. The Assyrian conquests mentioned in this chapter were: Hamath, Arpad, Sepharvaim, Samaria, Gozan, Haran, Rezeph, Telassar, Hena and Ivvah.

4. Oswalt (*op. cit.* 664) points out that this sign "is not of the sort which comes before the event in order to create faith for the event, but rather after the fact to demonstrate that God was indeed at work.

5. Predictions of Assyria's defeat at Jerusalem are found in the following passages: 10:5-19, 24-34; 14:24-27; 17:12-14; 18:3-6; 29:7-8; 30:31-33; and 31:4-9.

6. The loss of 185,000 men in this judgment compares with 300,000 men lost during the First Crusade and 238,000 men lost when Napoleon invaded Russia. The army of Assyria is said to have numbered in the hundreds of thousands. See H.W.F. Saggs, *The Greatness that was Babylon* (London: Athlone, 1962) 260.

7. The Biblical account of the assassination of Sennacherib coincides with the Assyrian records. See James Pritchard, *op. cit.* 288-89.

8. Other Old Testament references expressing the idea that the dead do not praise God: Job 10:21f; Pss 6:5; 30:9; 88:10-12; 115:17.

9. On the sin of asking for a sign see Deut 6:16; Mal 3:15; Matt 4:7; 12:39; and John 6:30.

10. Gideon asked for a sign (Judges 6:36-40). In Mal 3:10 God challenges believers to test him by means of tithing.

11. Oswalt, *op. cit.* 673.

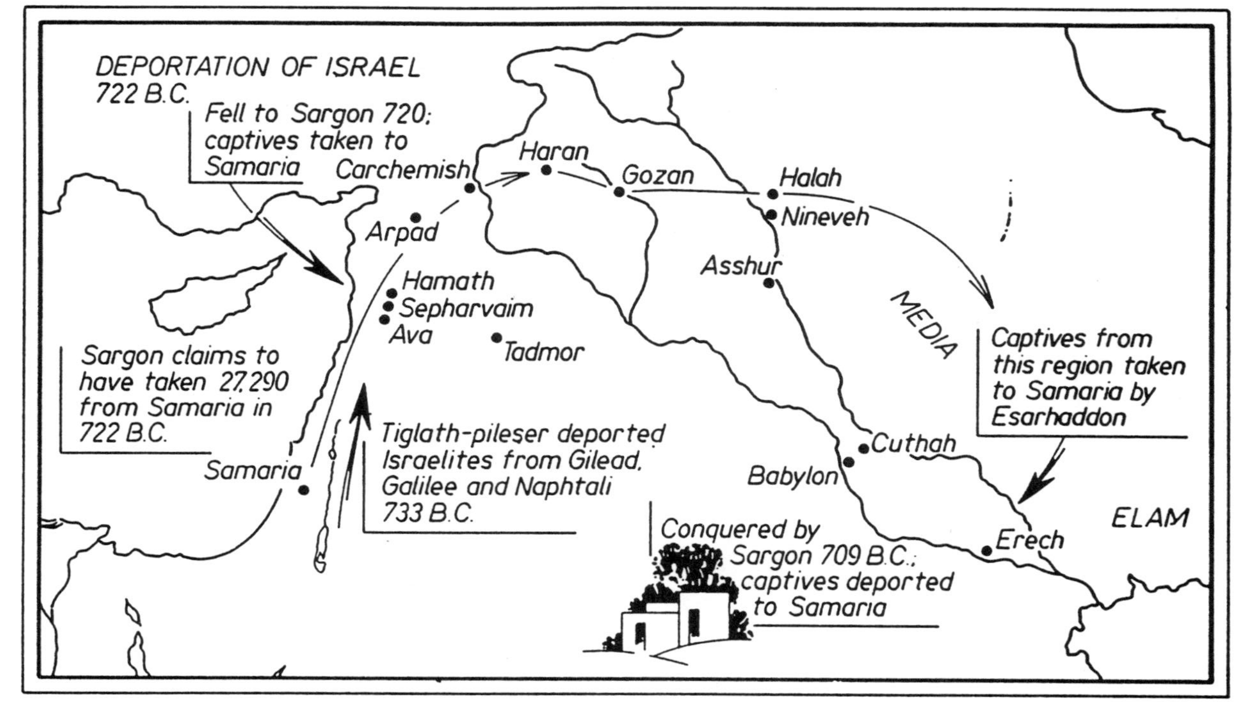
DEPORTATION OF ISRAEL
722 B.C.
Fell to Sargon 720;
captives taken to
Samaria
Carchemish
Haran
Gozan
Halah
Nineveh
Arpad
Asshur
Hamath
Sepharvaim
Ava
Tadmor
MEDIA
Captives from
this region taken
to Samaria by
Esarhaddon
Sargon claims to
have taken 27,290
from Samaria in
722 B.C.
Samaria
Tiglath-pileser deported
Israelites from Gilead,
Galilee and Naphtali
733 B.C.
Cuthah
Babylon
ELAM
Erech
Conquered by
Sargon 709 B.C.;
captives deported
to Samaria

CHAPTER EIGHT

The Book of Cyrus Isaiah 40-48

Background of the Unit.

At the beginning of the seventh century BC a large part of Judah and all of the northern kingdom of Israel were in exile in various parts of the Assyrian empire. In interpreting chapters 40-48 one need not assume that all of Judah was in captivity, nor that the author was among those carried away. The 150 year gap between the writing of chapters 39 and 40, which is postulated by nearly all modern interpreters, is unnecessary.

Sennacherib had stripped Judah bare, had captured all of the fortified cities of the land, and had almost captured Jerusalem in 701 BC. Isaiah, as was his custom, looked to the future for comfort in the present. He could see on the distant horizon a great deliverance from exile, and beyond that, an even greater deliverance from sin.

Deliverance from Babylon is the focus of chapters 40-48. This section has been designated "The Book of Cyrus" because of the several references to that Persian conqueror in this section. The direct mentions of Cyrus (44:28; 45:1) are sandwiched between triads of allusions to him.[1]

Outline of the Unit.

Prologue: God's Incomparable Word (40:1-11).
- A. God's Superiority (40:12-41:29).
- B. God's Servants (42:1-43:13).
- C. God's Grace (43:14-44:23).
- D. God's Agent Cyrus (44:24-45:25).
- E. God's Judgment (chaps. 46-47).

Epilogue: God's Incomparable Word (chap. 48).

PROLOGUE: GOD'S INCOMPARABLE WORD
Isaiah 40:1-11

Isaiah heard, as it were, four voices which set the tone for what he would say in chapters 40-66. Each voice stressed an aspect of God's message to man which makes his communication superior to anything attributed to idols. First, Isaiah heard a voice which directed the prophets to announce a message of comfort to Jerusalem. Her "warfare" (long term of hard service) was over; she had paid "double" for her transgression. According to Exodus 22:9 a man had to pay double for any trespass. Once appropriate punishment had been meted out, God would be ready to pardon (40:1f.).

The second voice announced the coming of one to prepare the way of the Lord. The Evangelists identified this preparatory messenger as John the Baptist.[2] The figure used is that of royal road builders who smooth the way for the king that his journey might be somewhat easier. As a result of the work of this preparatory messenger "the glory of the Lord," a visible manifestation of the presence of God, would be revealed (40:3-5).

The third voice stressed the eternality of God's word. Flesh is temporal, but God's word endures forever (40:6-8). These words were quoted by Peter in the New Testament (1 Pet 1:24f.).

The fourth voice is that of Isaiah himself. He exhorted Zion to announce to the cities of Judah: "Behold the Lord God will come with might." He pictured the Lord coming (1) as a conquering hero; and (2) as a gentle shepherd. The conqueror received as his reward the sheep which he carried in his arm (40:9-11).[3]

THE SUPERIORITY OF GOD
Isaiah 40:12-41:29

The primary aim of chapters 40-41 is to demonstrate that Israel's God is superior to anything else that man might be prone to worship. He is superior in (1) comparison, (2) confrontation, and (3) commitment.

A. Superior in Comparison (40:12-31).

Man is impressed with the magnitude and might of many things in this world. The God of the Bible is superior to them all. First, he is greater than the created world. Isaiah asked a series of questions designed to put man in his proper place. The greatness of God is indicated by the vastness of his creation. God is self-sufficient and independent. He did not solicit advice when he created the world. The Lord does not need man to instruct him about the right course of action (40:12-14).

Second, God is greater than the nations. The great strength of the mightiest nations is like a speck of dust or a drop in the bucket to God. If one were to build an altar fire with all the cedars of Lebanon, and sacrifice every beast in those forests, he still would not have made a sacrifice worthy of such a great God (40:15-17).

Third, Yahweh is greater than the idols. Idols are representations created by man. No matter how beautiful the craftsmanship, no matter how precious the materials, idols cannot capture the essence of God. Idols have difficulty standing erect. How would they then be able to support those who worship them? (40:18-20).

Fourth, God is greater than rulers. From the beginning the knowledge of the sovereign Creator had been handed down. He sits upon his throne "on the circle of the earth" providentially upholding and maintaining all that exists. The heavens themselves are the curtains of his tent! Mighty rulers of this world are under his authority. He can deprive them of power in an instant. He merely breathes on them and they wither like a plant, and are blown off the scene of history like worthless stubble (40:21-24).

Fifth, God is greater than the stars. Heavenly bodies should not be deified as they were in Mesopotamia. Worship belongs only to the Holy One who created the stars. Isaiah likened God to a mighty general who leads his troops across the heavens. Every star is in the exact place God would have it. Implicit in these verses is an attack against the major tenets of astrology (40:25f.).

Finally, God is greater than discouragement. Despondent Israelites must never forget who their God is. He is (1) eternal, (2) omnipotent, (3) omnipresent, (4) omniscient, (5) constantly alert, and (6) compassionate. He can strengthen those who wait for him in faith. This infusion of spiritual power makes believers like (1) an eagle in flight, (2) a runner in competition, and (3) a hiker on a long trek (40:27-31).

B. Superior in Confrontation (41:1-7, 21-29).

Isaiah quoted the words of Yahweh throughout chapter 41. The Lord addressed first the nations, then Israel, and finally the idols. The first and third units are cast in the form of a confrontation.

1. Confrontation with the nations (41:1-7). Yahweh ordered distant nations to listen, then to muster their strength so that they might enter the court of public opinion with him. God announced to the nations his intention to raise up one from the east who would swiftly subdue all his enemies. This is the first allusion to the role of Cyrus the Persian who would not gain world power for yet 150 years. Raising up a conqueror is not difficult for the Lord, for he had brought forth generation after generation from the very beginning. The Eternal was present to welcome the first generation; he will be here when the last one passes from the scene (41:1-4). The approach of the one from the east (Cyrus) would produce panic in the kingdom of Lydia and in the more distant coastal regions. Craftsmen of all types would work in consort to produce new idols which might spare them from the eastern conqueror. No man-made god, however, would be able to detect his advance (41:5-7).

2. Confrontation with the idols (41:21-29). The King of Jacob (God) challenged the idols to present the case for their deity. He urged them to (1) make known former things; (2) make known future things; and (3) do good or evil, i.e., do something. Some understand the "former things" as a reference to events of the past. In that case, God would be asking either for an explanation of past events, or documentation that those past events had been predicted. Others take the "former things" to refer to events of the near future, perhaps within the lifetime of the immediate audience. In either case, the gods failed to meet the challenge. Isaiah therefore pressed the conclusion that idols are non-entities. Those who choose to worship an idol are as loathsome as the idol itself (41:21-24). In contrast to the silence of the idols, Yahweh announced what he was about to do. He would arouse one from the north. That this is the same individual aroused in verse 2 is made clear by the statement "from the rising of the sun he will call on my name." Cyrus' conquests moved from the east to the north, and then south to Babylon. This Persian called on God's name in the decree which he issued allowing the Jews to return to their land (cf. Ezra 1:3). Cyrus would quickly and easily trample under foot all who opposed him (41:25).

Neither idol nor man had been able to foretell the rise of Cyrus. Yet Yahweh had announced these future events to Zion, his people. His announcement had been received as good news. Among the representatives of the idols there is only silence. Since they could not foretell future events Isaiah again pressed the conclusion that idols are empty and vain (41:26-29).

C. Superior in Commitment (41:8-20).

In spite of Israel's disappointing dalliance with idolatry, God remained faithful to his commitment to be their God. He reassured his people of love and support in four areas. First, God assured his people of their position. In spite of all that had happened (judgment on Jerusalem) or would happen (rise of Cyrus), the descendants of Abraham still enjoyed a unique relationship with God. The terms "chosen" and "my servant" apply to Israel because Israel was the descendant of "my friend" (cf. 2 Chr 20:7; Jas 2:23). In the person of Abraham God had called Israel from "the ends of the earth" (i.e., Ur of Chaldees, Acts 7:2f.). God's "servant" need not fear the rise of Cyrus. Yahweh had chosen to identify with Israel as their God. He therefore would strengthen, help, and uphold his servant with his righteous "right hand" (41:8-10).

Second, God assured his people of deliverance. The rise of Cyrus would mean the deliverance of Israel. All nations which were hostile to God's people would be put to shame. They finally would disappear from the scene of history. In whatever difficulties his people might find themselves, God would always be present to sustain and encourage them. Therefore, Israel need not be afraid. The Holy One of Israel was their *go'el,* their redeemer. The word signifies one who has an obligation to another (41:11-14).

Third, God assured his people of victory. After deliverance through the agency of Cyrus, Israel would become a threshing sledge. This instrument was pulled by oxen over the threshing floor in order to break loose the kernels of grain from the husk. Mountains of grain (the nations) would be threshed by Israel. While the wind would blow these worthless husks away, Israel would have occasion to rejoice in Yahweh (41:15f.). Isaiah may be predicting the crushing victories of the Maccabees during the intertestamental period. On the other hand, he may be referring to the conquests in the spiritual realm by the new Israel of God.

Fourth, God assured his people of provision. Whether they be afflicted, needy or thirsty, God would respond to the prayers of his people. He would give them an abundance of waters and turn their deserts into shady woods. God loves to answer the prayers of his people because in so doing men give honor to him. Abundant water in prophetic literature is a figure for spiritual blessing, lush vegetation points to the productiveness of God's people (41:17-20).

THE SERVANTS OF GOD
Isaiah 42:1-43:13

In the last twenty-seven chapters of the book Isaiah introduced two servants of God. One was obedient, the other disobedient. The first was an individual; the second represented the entire nation.

A. The Messianic Servant (42:1-9).

Chapter 42 begins with the first of five poems[4] in which the spotlight is upon one who is called God's Servant. The language is personalized, leading to the conclusion that the prophet was predicting the rise of a unique individual. These five poems are best explained Messianically.

1. The Servant's work (42:1-4). Obedience is the ideal quality of one who is a servant. Isaiah foresaw the coming of one who would be (1) perfectly obedient; (2) upheld by the Lord; (3) specially chosen; (4) in possession of God's Spirit; and (5) devoted to bringing justice to the Gentiles. The ministry of the Servant would be quiet and gentle. He would be tender in dealing with those wounded by the harsh realities of life, yet he would not compromise the absolute standards of justice (42:1-3).[5] These words are applied to Jesus in the New Testament.[6]

Though occasions for discouragement would arise, the Servant would show no signs of weakness till he had fulfilled his objective, viz., the establishment of true justice in the earth. Here Isaiah hinted that the Servant would suffer for his cause, apparently at the hands of his own people. His *instruction* (NASB mar), however, would be eagerly awaited by distant nations (42:4).

2. The Servant's Commitment (42:5-9). Because he would experience difficulties in his ministry, the great Creator addressed words of reassurance to the Servant personally. God called the Servant "in righteousness," i.e., with saving purposes in view. Therefore, he would sustain and protect the Servant in his ministry. The Servant would be the embodiment of a new covenant which he would convey to all people. He would serve as light, the only source of truth, to Gentiles.[7] His ministry would include restoring sight (both physically and spiritually), and releasing those imprisoned in the darkness of sin (42:5-7).

Yahweh alone was worthy of praise for the announcement that the Servant would come. Other prophecies made by the Lord had come to pass.[8] God's people could have every assurance that these "new things" of the distant future would also come to pass (42:8f.).

B. The Messianic Work (42:10-17).

To celebrate God's new work, a new song was in order. Since the work of the Servant would benefit all mankind, all were called upon to join in the song of praise to Yahweh (42:8-12). Isaiah used four word pictures to describe what God's new work would involve. First, he used military language to describe God's furious and successful attack against his enemies (42:13). Second, Isaiah used the figure of a woman in labor. Since Sinai God had been, comparatively speaking, inactive. With the work of the Servant the Lord labors like a woman in travail to give birth to something new (42:14).

In the third picture Isaiah compared God to a trailblazer who would remove all obstacles from the path of his people (42:15). Finally, Isaiah portrayed the Lord as the guide of his people. Though they presently were blind to the ultimate purposes of God, he would lead them "in paths they do not know" (42:16). God's people then could look forward to the active intervention of God on their behalf. Those who clung to idols, however, would be utterly put to shame (42:17).

C. The National Servant (42:18-43:13).

God's national servant Israel was quite a contrast to the messianic Servant. In this unit Isaiah described the present condition of Israel; then he discussed the future prospects of the nation.

1. The present state (42:18-25). Unbelieving Israel was a blind and deaf servant. The nation had a special relationship to God—they were his messenger—but they had failed in their mission (42:18f.).

God had done wonderful things for his people. He had attempted many times to communicate with them but to no avail. With his saving purpose in mind ("for the sake of his righteousness") he had given them his Law. Israel, however, had been disobedient and unresponsive. Therefore Israel had fallen victim to God's judgment. The nation had been robbed and plundered (42:20-22).

Isaiah longed that Israel might take stock of her situation, that she might realize that her devastation was just punishment for a history of rebellion against God. Though the nation had been scorched by the flame of God's judgment, yet she refused to take it to heart (42:23-25).

2. The future prospects (43:1-13). God created Israel, and the nation still figured in his plan. He would redeem them and call them by name,[9] i.e., give them a mission in a very direct way. God had a very special claim on that people (43:1).

No matter what the danger, Israel would survive. Isaiah pictured the nation on a journey. Raging streams and wild prairie fires would not destroy her. Their safety was guaranteed by God's presence. Other nations would be given over to the conqueror as ransom to secure the redemption of Israel (43:2-4). The Persians were reimbursed, as it were, for the release of Israel by being permitted to conquer north Africa.

All who belong to God—who were truly his people—would be gathered from all points of the compass. Isaiah used four verbs to describe the sons and daughters involved in this gathering: *called, created, formed* and *made*. Neither Gentile nor spiritually obtuse Israelite could have forecasted the restoration of Israel. No one could point to past instances of equivalent foretelling (43:5-9).

The reassembled, true Israel of God would testify on behalf of Yahweh before the nations. That was Israel's calling as God's *servant*. They were to testify to (1) his sole divinity; (2) his mighty acts; (3) his revelation; (4) his salvation; (5) his eternality and (6) his power (43:10-13).

THE GRACE OF GOD
Isaiah 43:14-44:23

Isaiah next placed in juxtaposition the unfailing goodness of God and the unworthy recipients of his goodness.

A. Undeserved Promises (43:14-21; 44:1-5).

In the category of undeserved blessing, Isaiah lists three promises which God had made to his people. First, God promised that Babylon would fall. Yahweh controlled the fortunes of other nations, even those of mighty Babylon. Because of his love for Israel, God would make captives of the Chaldeans, and they would be carried away in their own merchant ships (43:14f.).

Second, God promised a new exodus. The God who overthrew Pharaoh and brought Israel through the Red Sea would perform an even greater deliverance. The new Exodus would cause the memory of the Exodus under Moses to fade. God would bring his people through a seemingly impossible desert by supplying water to them en route. Even the desert creatures would glorify God because of the water he supplied for his people. Water here symbolizes all that is essential for their journey home (43:16-21).

Third, God promised the outpouring of the Spirit. Though they had experienced great punishment, Yahweh still would help his servant Israel. He referred to them by a term of endearment—Jeshurun—meaning "righteous."[10] Just as God provided rain when it was needed, so he would pour out his Spirit upon the sons of Jacob. Because of this, Israel would become a flourishing tree. Outsiders would take pride in becoming affiliated with the rejuvenated Israel (44:1-5).

B. An Unworthy People (43:22-28).

Why would God deal so graciously with Israel? Not because of prayer, sacrifice or incense, for worship had degenerated into a tired ritual. Actually the sins of Israel had become a burden to God. For his own sake, he would blot out the transgression of his people (43:22-25)

So that they might appreciate this pure act of grace, Israel was summoned to trial. Isaiah urged the nation to speak up in her own defense if she had anything to say. Jacob, the first father of the nation, was a sinner. Throughout history all the "mediators"—priests, prophets, kings—were sinners. Their sin had forced God to permit the defilement of the sanctuary and the captivity (43:26f.).

C. An Incomparable Patron (44:6-20).

Israel's redemption was guaranteed by Yahweh, the only God who could explain the past and forecast the future. He alone deserved the title *God*. If his claims were true, then there was no ground for fear. Idolatry, on the other hand, was folly. Isaiah foresaw a day when all devotees of idolatry would be ashamed. Meanwhile, no one could put forth a logical defense of idolatry (44:6-11).

The attack against idolatry continued with a satirical description of the manufacture of idols. Idols were constructed by clumsy tools and weak workmen. The same wood used to make an idol is used to make fires for cooking. Those who worshiped idols practiced grand self-deception (44:12-20).

While the heathen fashioned their gods, Yahweh fashioned his people. They must ever remember their calling as God's servant. God had not forgotten his people. In his grace he would blot out their sins. God therefore invites his people to respond to that grace by returning to him with all their heart. The undeserved redemption of Israel called forth universal praise to the Lord (44:21-23).

THE INSTRUMENT OF GOD
Isaiah 44:24-45:25

God had announced three times thus far his intention to raise up a Gentile deliverer for his people (41:2-5; 41:25; 43:14). In one of the most amazing predictions in the Bible, Isaiah now named that emancipator 150 years before he appeared on the scene of history.

A. The Commissioning of Cyrus (44:24-28).

Israel's Redeemer was almighty. He was the one who (1) formed Israel in the womb of Egyptian bondage; and (2) created the heavens and earth. He (3) frustrated the omens of divination; and (4) stood behind his word. This all-powerful God, who could dry up oceans and rivers, announced here his intention to restore the cities of Judah which would be left in ruins by the Chaldeans. The human agent through whom this promise would be fulfilled is specifically named. Cyrus would be the one who would make possible the restoration of Jerusalem and the Temple.

B. The Success of Cyrus (45:1-8).

The sweeping success of Cyrus should be attributed to Yahweh. Through this success Cyrus would come to know God better (45:1-3). Jewish tradition reported by Josephus records that the great Persian king was shown these prophecies after he conquered Babylon in 539 BC. The statements made here by Isaiah do not require that Cyrus embrace the worship of Yahweh. As a matter of fact he did not. In the Cyrus Cylinder he attributed his success to the god Marduk.

All that would be done for and through Cyrus would be done for two reasons. First, God would use this pagan king to bring about deliverance for "Jacob my servant." Second, the work that Cyrus would do was designed to convince all people that Yahweh alone is

God. He alone rules the universe. Either through his direct action or permissive will, all that happens must be attributed to him. This God calls upon the heavens he controls to rain down righteousness (that which is in accord with God's purpose), so that salvation and righteousness might appear on the earth (45:4-8). Particularly in view here is the deliverance of Israel from Babylonian exile.

C. The Perfection of God's Plan (45:9-25).

The remaining verses of chapter 45 defend God's plan to utilize Cyrus. The call of that Persian king would be the first step in a long program to bring all men into submission to his lordship. Five points are made with regard to God's plan. First, God's plan was unchallengeable in its origin. Those who might question God's decision to use Cyrus were rebuked. What audacity to question God about anything! He is, after all, the master designer of all that exists (45:9f.).

Second, God's plan was consistent in its direction. He would raise up Cyrus "in righteousness," i.e., with his saving purpose in view. Without thought of compensation Cyrus would liberate the Jewish captives and permit Jerusalem to be rebuilt (45:11-13).

Third, God's plan was universal in its scope. After the restoration under Cyrus, Zion would enjoy a glorious future. Gifts from distant lands would come to the place. Converts from afar would cheerfully bind themselves as though with chains to Zion because they would come to recognize that Yahweh is the only God (45:14). Depicted here is New Testament conversion through which men come to Mt. Zion (Heb 12:22) and become part of the new Israel of God (Gal 6:16).

Fourth, God's plan was certain in its results. Isaiah burst forth into a prayer of adoration for God's mysterious dealings with his people. God "hides" himself when he allows his people to experience judgment. In the end, however, the idolaters would be put to shame, not those who experienced the everlasting salvation of Yahweh (45:15-17).

Fifth, God's plan was rational in its design. Yahweh appealed to the nations to acknowledge him as the only God. The Lord defended his divinity by pointing to (1) the purposeful creation; and (2) the clear revelation which he has given. On the other hand, Isaiah regards as utter stupidity putting trust in an idol which must be transported. Let idolaters state their case in the court of public opinion. As for the prophet, his main argument is that God had predicted the rise of Cyrus long before it ever took place (45:18-21).

Finally, God's plan was evangelistic in its aim. God yearned for the salvation of all mankind. He promised to save all who would turn to him. Isaiah anticipated a day when all men would submit to his authority. Even those who were his most bitter enemies would turn to him for righteousness and spiritual strength. Only in Yahweh would all the offspring of Israel find salvation (45:22-25).

THE JUDGMENT OF GOD
Isaiah 46:1-47:15

Chapters 46-47 of the Book of Cyrus focus on the judgment of Babylon. Here Isaiah placed in contrast the vindication of Yahweh and the humiliation of Babylon.

A. Yahweh's Vindication (46:1-13).

The overthrow of Babylon would have tremendous theological as well as political consequences. First, the fall of Babylon would reveal the impotence of Babylon's gods (46:1-4). They would not be able to save themselves, not to mention the people who worshiped them. Isaiah depicted Bel and Nebo, two chief gods of Babylon, being carried away into captivity as trophies of war. By way of contrast, Yahweh had carried his people from the day they were born as a nation in Egypt. He would continue to carry them throughout their national existence (46:1-4). Again Isaiah stressed what he had emphasized so often in the Book of Cyrus. Yahweh was in a class by himself. Idols were merely the products of human ingenuity. They were immobile and mute. They could provide no deliverance in time of distress (46:5-7).

Second, the superiority of Yahweh's actions would be revealed in the fall of Babylon. God's people should remember "the former things," predictions which God had made concerning deliverance from Babylon. Long before his birth Yahweh had revealed the rise of "a bird of prey from the east," i.e., Cyrus. The Lord, and no other, can clearly outline the course of events from beginning to end. Omniscience requires sovereignty. Therefore God's people must remember that when God sets his purpose, nothing can thwart it (46:8-11). Isaiah used three words to summarize what God would accomplish through the work of Cyrus: *righteousness, salvation,* and *glory.* The reputation of Yahweh and the fate Israel were intertwined. Liberation for the worshipers would result in vindication for their God (46:12f.).

B. Babylon's Humiliation (47:1-15).

The focus in chapter 47 is on the humiliation which Babylon would experience as a result of the judgment initiated by Cyrus. The chapter consists of four sub-sections each beginning with a sarcastic imperative addressed to Babylon. In each Babylon is depicted as a once proud, but now humiliated, female.

First, Babylon is personified as a tender and delicate virgin daughter who suddenly was forced to become a lowly slave. She would then be compelled to engage in the most menial tasks. As a captive she must lay bare her legs and thighs to cross rivers. This shameful exposure and role reversal is all the more humiliating because it has been brought about by the God of Jewish captives, Yahweh of hosts, the Holy One of Israel (47:1-4).

The second picture is that of a dethroned queen. She who once ruled kingdoms of men now must sit in darkness, i.e., obscurity. Babylon would no longer be called the queen of kingdoms. She must lose her crown because she abused her role as God's agent in the punishment of Judah. Babylon did not exercise mercy in dealing with God's heritage. For example, old men were cruelly treated. Never once did the proud queen give any thought to her accountability before God (47:5-7).

In the third picture of Babylon's humiliation the city is portrayed as a childless widow. Once she had been a sensual and carefree woman. Her numerous children (satellite states) gave her a sense of security. In one day, however, she would lose everything. Without husband or children she would be utterly destitute. Could such an extreme judgment be justified? Isaiah points to the arrogant pride of this woman, a pride which bordered on self-deification. Using language which elsewhere in the book only God uses of himself, Babylon thinks, "I am, and there is no other."[11] The powerful and wealthy Babylon faced a bleak future. She would be unable to prevent this devastating calamity (47:8-11).

The final picture is that of Babylon as the powerless sorceress. Throughout her history Babylon had trafficked in fortunetelling. Highly developed occult "sciences," however, would not save Babylon. The whole company of fortune-tellers amounts to nothing. In the time of judgment they would stray about as if in a daze, unable to save even themselves (47:12-15).

EPILOGUE: GOD'S INCOMPARABLE WORD
Isaiah 48

Chapter 48 closes the Book of Cyrus as it began, with a reminder of the incomparable character of the word of God. Here Isaiah repeats a number of themes from the previous chapters of this unit. The emphasis, however, is on what God had said. The chapter begins with a call for the house of Jacob to hear God's word. The same appeal in slightly different words appears three other times in the chapter (vv. 12,14,16). The contrast throughout is that of a God who speaks clearly and repeatedly on the one hand, and a people who refused to listen on the other.

The Lord had spoken clearly regarding the "former things," but Israel had refused to listen. The Jews had abused their privileges as the people to whom God's oracles had been delivered. They invoked God's name, but not sincerely. They merely leaned on God like a crutch. They were like iron or bronze, i.e., obstinate. Therefore, God took special care to predict certain events long before they happened lest those events be attributed to the work of the idols. Yahweh was about to announce "new things, hidden things," things which were "created now," i.e., revealed for the first time (48:1-7). The reference is to the work of the messianic Servant which is explained in detail in chapters 49-53.

The reason Israel had not heard these things before was because they had been rebels since they came into existence as a nation. Even so, for the sake of his reputation God did not pour out on the Jews the punishment which they deserved. Otherwise they would have been totally cut off. His purpose was to refine his people through affliction. Through their redemption from captivity God's glory would be perceived (48:8-11).

A double imperative called upon Israel to listen when God speaks. He deserved that because of who he is: (1) the Eternal, (2) the Creator, (3) the Judge, and (4) the Revelator of Israel. God deserved to be heard because of the unprecedented character of what he had to say. No pagan god ever had attempted to foretell the future in such detail. He deserved a hearing because his predictions were absolutely assured (48:12-15).

God's instructive word had the potential of averting national judgment. If they had only listened to Spirit-filled men like Isaiah they would have enjoyed peace, prosperity and population growth. Their name among the nations of the world would have never been cut off (48:17-19). Listen, however, they would not. Hence the ultimate national judgment fell upon them: dispersion to Babylon.

The concluding word in this Book of Cyrus comes in the form of an exhortation and a warning. Isaiah urged those who might find themselves in Babylon to take advantage of God's redemption, to leave that place at the earliest opportunity. They should then tell the entire world about what God did for them, how he brought them through deserts and provided their every need (48:20f.). The warning is this: the wonderful peace which those have who listen to God stands in sharp contrast to the restlessness of those who rebel against God (48:22).

Endnotes

1. Allusions to Cyrus are found in 41:2-5; 41:25; 43:14; 45:13; 46:11; and 48:14f.

2. See Matt 3:3; Mark 1:3; Luke 3:4; John 1:23.

3. This according to E.J. Young, *The Book of Isaiah* (Grand Rapids: Eerdmans, 1972) 36-41. Another view is that the conquering hero dispenses rewards to his people.

4. Cf. John 8:8-11.

5. This passage is applied to Jesus in Matt 12:17-21. See also John 5:26; 1 Pet 2:6; Luke 2:40; 3:22; 4:8-21.

6. These words are cited in reference to Jesus (Luke 2:32). In view of this prophecy, Jesus' claim to be the light of the world (John 8:12) had messianic implications.

7. Some interpret "the former things" to refer to the rise of Cyrus and the fall of Babylon. In his mind's eye Isaiah had seen these predictions fulfilled.

8. The Hebrew uses here, as frequently in this section, the prophetic perfect. His predictions were so certain of fulfillment that they could be described as already completed.

9. Jeshurun is used as a term of endearment in Deut 32:15; 33:5, 26.

10. Cf. Isa 45:5, 21; 46:9. The language used here is reminiscent of that used by the boastful king of Babylon in Isa 14:13f.

11. Cf. Isa 45:6.

CHAPTER NINE

The Book of the Servant Isaiah 49-57

Background of the Unit.

The major themes of chapters 40-48 are now laid aside, but one of the secondary themes introduced there is developed in chapters 49-57. In the previous unit two servants of Yahweh were introduced. The first servant was the nation Israel which was deaf, dumb and disobedient to its heavenly calling. The second was an individual who walked in perfect harmony with Yahweh, and who would bring God's justice to the Gentiles (42:1-9). This same individual appears in four other poems in the book, three of which are located in chapters 49-57. The classic explanation of the servant concept in Isaiah was formulated by Delitzsch. He suggested that the concept of the servant could be symbolized by a pyramid. "The base was Israel as a whole; the central section was that Israel, which was not merely Israel according to the flesh, but according to the spirit also; the apex is the person of the Mediator of salvation springing out of Israel."[1]

Outline of the Unit.

A. Declarations by the Servant (49:1-50:9).
B. Encouragements for Zion (50:10-52:12).
C. Sufferings of the Servant (52:13-53:12).
D. Imperatives for Believers (54:1-56:8).
E. Warnings for the Wicked (56:9-57:21).

DECLARATIONS BY THE SERVANT
Isaiah 49:1-50:9

Two speeches are attributed to the Servant in chapters 49-50. The first is addressed to the nations; the second is a soliloquy. Sandwiched between these two speeches is a unit describing the despondency of Zion during the time of her captivity. The doctrine of the coming Servant was God's answer to Zion's discouragement.

A. The Work of the Servant (49:1-13).

The second Servant poem focuses on the work and success of God's Servant. That the Servant would be an individual with a world wide mission of redemption is made quite clear.

1. The task of the Servant (49:1-6). With missionary-like zeal, the Servant would call upon the whole world to hear what he had to say about his work. This one had a sense of vocation. He sensed he had been called before he was born,[2] and named by God (i.e., claimed by him) immediately after his birth (49:1).

The primary instrument for accomplishing the work of the Servant is the spoken word. His mouth would be like a sharp sword (cf. Matt 10:34). His ministry would be a polished arrow when it needed to be "to wound men for their own good."[3] The Servant would be protected throughout his ministry by the shadow of the Almighty's hand. Until the day of his revelation he would remain hidden away in God's quiver (cf. Gal 4:4). He would be totally committed to the will of God. He would be a new *Israel,*[4] the head of a nation. All that he did would reflect glory on God (49:2f.).

The Servant anticipated rejection, yet he left the entire matter in

God's hands. He knew his faithful work would be rewarded. In spite of his rejection, the Lord did not release him from his task, but rather broadened it. Not only was the Servant to bring Israel back to God, he also was to be "a light to the nations" (49:4-6). This text is cited in the New Testament as justification for preaching the Gospel in all the world.[5]

2. The triumph of the Servant (49:7-13). The Servant would be despised of men, abhorred by the nation. Rulers would look upon him with disdain as one far inferior to themselves. Yet the time would come when kings and princes would render homage to him. This radical change of fortune would be brought about because the Holy One would be faithful to his Servant (49:7).

"In a favorable time" God would answer the Servant's cry for deliverance. That would usher in "a day of salvation." In the light of Paul's use of this passage (2 Cor 6:2), the time of God's favor is the Gospel age. In this period the Servant would become "a covenant of the people," i.e., the mediator of a covenant. The servant would (1) "establish" (NASB mar) the land, the messianic kingdom; (2) release captives; (3) provide light; and (4) sustain those who follow him (49:8-10).

People would flow into the Servant's kingdom from all regions, even distant Sinim (Syene), modern Aswan in southern Egypt. The work of the Servant would bring comfort to the afflicted. For this reason the people of God can shout for joy (49:11-13).

B. The Despondency of Zion (49:14-50:3).

The Servant's initial work would be "to raise up the tribes of Jacob, and restore the preserved ones of Israel" (49:6). The spiritual and psychological state of God's people following the exile to Babylon are depicted in the last half of chapter 49. While the return from Babylon mitigated to some extent their sense of abandonment by God, the despondency described here was that which could only be relieved by the coming of Messiah.

1. Zion's complaint and Yahweh's response (49:14-20). Zion complains that God has forsaken her. He, however, can no more forget his people than a mother could forget a nursing child. It is as though God had graven Zion and her walls upon his hand. When in the course of God's providence construction on the walls of spiritual Zion began, the children of Zion would hasten to that place. Those responsible for the destruction of physical Zion—the unbelievers and disobedient—would leave the place as the children of God by faith draw near. The great number of children who approach Zion would serve as ornaments enhancing her beauty. Zion would resemble a bride adorned for her husband (49:14-18). In Christ believers have come to the Zion of this prophecy.[6] The old physical land of Canaan which had been destroyed by enemies would not be large enough to hold the burgeoning population in that new day. The enemies who had carried them off into captivity would be far away geographically and psychologically (49:19f.).

2. Zion's bewilderment and Yahweh's commitment (49:21-23). Zion would be bewildered by her greatly increased population. Mother Israel produced no children during the Exile. So how can her population grow? The answer to this is simple, but glorious. God himself would beckon with his hand to Gentiles. He would establish an ensign for them as a rallying point. Gentiles would come tenderly carrying Zion's sons to her. Kings and princesses would do homage to Zion and serve as guardians and nurses of her sons. Those who continue to wait on the Lord would not ultimately be put to shame.

3. Zion's incredulity and Yahweh's assurance (49:24-26). Zion simply cannot believe that her captives can be liberated from a mighty tyrant like Babylon. Yahweh assures her that he himself would effect the rescue. Anyone who interfered with the extrication would find himself at war with God. The divine strategy would be to set the oppressors against one another. The release of Israel from Babylon would call "all flesh," i.e., both Jew and Gentile, to know that Yahweh is a savior.

4. Zion's depression and Yahweh's power (50:1-3). Zion's children felt that their mother had been divorced from Yahweh. For this, however, no proof could be produced. A separation had taken place, but no divorce. Nor had the Lord been forced by some creditor to sell Zion's children into slavery.[7] The separation of God and his people took place because Israel had transgressed against the Lord. Yahweh cannot be blamed for Israel's captivity. No one had listened when he spoke by the mouth of his prophets (50:1-2a).

Zion's depression grew out of a sense of helplessness. She did not have confidence that Yahweh could deliver her. Thus the Lord raised the crucial question: "Have I no power to deliver?" God had demonstrated his power in nature by drying up water-courses and shrouding the heavens with blackness by causing the eclipse of heavenly bodies (50:2b-3).

C. The Confidence of the Servant (50:4-9).

If Zion lacked confidence in God's program, the Servant did not. The third of the Servant poems is a soliloquy in which the Servant proclaims his confidence in three areas. First, the Servant was confident of his preparation. He was certain that he had received constant revelation from God. He was equally certain that he possessed the God-given ability to communicate what he had received in such a way as to sustain weary souls (50:4). Second, the Servant was confident in God's plan. Thus he willingly would submit his heart and mind to obedience, and his body to abuse (50:5f.).[8] Finally the Servant was confident of vindication. He would set his face like a flint with determination to see through whatever persecution might await him. He knew that he could meet any challenge. His enemies and accusers would not succeed (50:7-9).

ENCOURAGEMENT FOR ZION
Isaiah 50:10-52:12

The thirty-seven verses beginning with 50:10 are some of the most optimistic in the entire book. Through exhortations, spiritual wake-up calls and forthright proclamation of good news God offered encouragement to his people.

A. Exhortations to the Remnant (50:10-51:8).

Four exhortations to Zion follow the third Servant poem. Each is accompanied by promises designed to lift the spirits of God's people during the period of their captivity. First, he exhorted believers to trust in God during periods of darkness. As for those who "kindle a fire" by which to light their own way, they shall be set on fire by their own sparks. They shall lie down in their grave in torment (50:10f).[9]

Second, Isaiah encouraged the remnant to look to the rock from which they had been hewn, i.e., Abraham. He was a solitary man, yet God blessed him beyond measure. History would repeat itself. Though few in number, God would also bless the remnant. Their devastated land would become a veritable Eden (51:1-3). The reference again is to that spiritual, antitypical Land of Promise built up through the efforts of the Servant (51:1-3; cf. 49:8).

Third, Isaiah exhorted the discouraged remnant to be attentive to God's teaching. That instruction would be a light for all people.[10] God's great purposes of salvation speedily were coming to a head.[11] Distant peoples are pictured as longing for that day. The heavens and earth and its inhabitants will pass away, but God's salvation is eternal (51:4-6).

Finally, Isaiah exhorted the remnant to be bold. They should not fear the present reproach of men. Those who revile God's people slowly would be destroyed; but God's salvation endures forever (51:7f.).

B. God's Reveille for Zion (51:9-52:6).

A reveille prayer directed toward heaven is answered by two blasts designed to wake up an indifferent and slumbering people on earth.

1. The wake-up prayer to God (51:9-16). Isaiah called on God to act on behalf of his people. By means of two questions the prophet expressed his faith in what God had done in the past. He had cut to pieces "Rahab the Dragon," i.e., Egypt (cf. 30:7). He had made a path for his people through the sea. What God had done in the past was taken by Isaiah as a pledge of what he would do in the future. Hence the prayer anticipated a positive response. God would redeem his people and they would return to Zion with great rejoicing (51:9-11).

Zion's children feared their oppressors, and that fear grew out of forgetting who God really was. The Creator who stretched out the heavens and laid the foundations of the earth was the one who now comforted his people with promises of deliverance. Their oppressors were weak and short-lived. For the captives the time of release was near. This was no idle wish, but a declaration of the God who controls nature (51:12-15).

God instructed Isaiah "to establish the heavens" and "to found the earth." Just as the removal of heavens and earth speaks of the passing of the old order of things, so these words allude to the ushering in of the new. God would put a protective covering over the prophet[12] and the word he spoke so as to guarantee that his positive predictions would be fulfilled. The reference must be to the new heavens and earth (Isa 65:16-17), the messianic age when spiritual Zion would become the center of the divine program (51:16).

2. The wake-up call to a drunken woman (51:17-23). The Lord did not need to be awakened, but Zion did. The people of God were in a pitiful state, like a woman in a drunken stupor whose children are unable to stir her. Zion had drained the cup of God's wrath. She had no native son to give guidance. Deportation and destruction fell upon her cities, famine and sword upon her citizens. In the siege of Jerusalem strong young men fainted in the streets. The whole nation was under the wrath of God. Yet Zion must arouse herself! (51:17-20).

What news could possibly arouse Zion from her state of self-pity and depression? The remnant could take heart because the cup of God's wrath was about to be transferred to their tormentors. Zion would never again have to drink of *that* cup (51:21-23).

3. The wake-up call to a captive woman (52:1-6). The Lord invited Zion to come up from slave status to become a queen (cf. 47:1ff.). She is to put on "beautiful garments," i.e., garments of holiness (cf. Ps 110:3; Isa 61:10). Messianic Jerusalem would be a holy city. No uncircumcised or unclean person would be permitted to enter that place (52:1f.).[13]

Babylon had not paid anything to acquire Judah. Therefore the people of God could be freed without the payment of a special price, simply on the strength of a divine order. Just as the Egyptians and the Assyrians had no rightful claim upon Israel, neither did the Babylonians. Furthermore, these latest oppressors continually blasphemed the name of Yahweh. He therefore had a right to demand the release of his people. In this deliverance Israel would have a truer and deeper knowledge of God (52:3-6).

C. Good News (52:7-12).

God had two dispatches of the best sort of news for the people who live in Jerusalem and for those who would be carried away to Babylon.

1. Good news for Jerusalem's citizens (52:7-8). Isaiah depicted a messenger racing over the hills of Judah toward the capital (cf. Nah 1:15). Yahweh has won a great victory. Zion's God reigned, and this meant peace, happiness, and salvation to her citizens.[14] Those who had been watching for the messenger broke forth into loud cries of joy. One thing is clear to them. Yahweh had now returned to his people (52:7f.).

Isaiah supplied a victory hymn worthy of the occasion. He called upon all the waste places of Jerusalem to break forth in joyous song. They now could celebrate that God had (1) comforted his people; (2) redeemed Jerusalem; and (3) bared his holy arm, i.e., power, in the sight of all the nations (cf. 51:9). The "ends of the earth" would come to see the salvation of Judah's God (52:9f.).

2. Good news for Babylon's captives (52:11-12). Babylon and all she stood for had to be renounced. The captives must "touch nothing unclean," i.e., they were not to plunder Babylon as they did Egypt at the Exodus (Exod 12:35f.).[15] The holy vessels of the Temple would be returned to Jerusalem. Those vessels must be carried by holy hands. Israel had left Egypt in haste (Deut 16:3). The remnant, on the other hand, would leave Babylon in a leisurely and dignified manner. As in the Exodus from Egypt, Yahweh would lead the way. At the same time he would be their rear guard. Believers can be assured of safe arrival when God is both their vanguard and their rear guard!

AN EXPLANATION OF SALVATION
Isaiah 52:13-53:12

The fourth and greatest of the Servant poems focuses on the suffering and triumph of the Servant by means of which Zion's salvation would become possible. This poem consists of five three-verse paragraphs. The first and fifth paragraphs are in the future (imperfect) tense. Paragraphs two through four are in the prophetic perfect of assured prediction. For a Christian, reading through these verses is a pilgrimage down the Via Dolorosa. That this Servant is Jesus of Nazareth is settled for the believer by New Testament authority.[16]

A. The Success of the Servant (52:13-15).

The Servant would be successful in his mission. First, however, he would be disfigured to the astonishment of onlookers. In his suffering, however, he would "sprinkle," i.e., cleanse, many nations. Because he succeeds in this priestly ministry in spite of suffering, the kings of the earth would be in awe of him and his accomplishments.

B. The Slighting of the Servant (53:1-3).

Isaiah was amazed that so few would (1) believe the prophets regarding the Servant; and (2) take note of the power of God displayed in his life. The Servant would be despised and rejected because of his humble origins and his appearance. This rejection would cause him deep sorrow.

C. The Suffering of the Servant (53:4-6).

The reason for his suffering would be misunderstood. Most would think he suffered for some terrible crime or sin in his own life. Nothing could be further from the truth. His suffering was vicarious and redemptive. Only through that suffering could all the straying sheep be recovered. The *our* and *his* contrast in these verses is striking and moving.

OUR EXPERIENCE	HIS EXPERIENCE
Griefs	Bore
Sorrows	Carried
Transgression	Pierced Through
Iniquities	Crushed
Peace	Chastening
Healed	Scourging

D. The Submission of the Servant (53:7-9).

Isaiah described the Servant as silent during the abuse of his trial. From that oppressive trial he would be taken away to die. No one really would give a great deal of thought to the significance of his death. Though innocent of any crime, he would be sentenced to be buried with evil men. His grave, however, eventually was with a rich man.

E. The Satisfaction of the Servant (53:10-12).

That the Servant should suffer was part of the plan of God. He was to be a sin offering. Yet the Servant would live after death, "he shall see his seed," i.e., his disciples. God's purposes would then prosper in his hand. Many would be justified before God when they learn of what he had done. For this reason the Servant could look with satisfaction upon his work (53:10f.).

The Servant would be regarded as a great conqueror, one who shares the spoils of victory with his followers. Victory, however, would come only through the fact that the Servant was willing to suffer as a sin-bearer and pour out himself in death. Through his death and resurrection he made intercession (53:12).

IMPERATIVES FOR BELIEVERS
Isaiah 54:1-56:8

The agony and grief of chapter 53 give way in chapter 54 to singing and assurance. The sacrificial work of the Servant would redeem and transform. Though not mentioned by name in this unit, there can be no doubt that the joyous imperatives are addressed to Zion-Jerusalem.

A. The Imperative of Enlargement (54:1-3).

Like a barren woman Zion had borne no children during the Exile (cf. 49:14-23). That, however, would change. The family of believers would become so numerous that the tent of dwelling would have to be enlarged (cf. Zech 9:10). Zion would spread abroad in every direction due to the fact that she would "possess," i.e., conquer, the nations with the sword of God's Spirit.[17] Zion's desolate cities would thus be populated.

B. The Imperative of Confidence (54:4-17).

The shame of Zion's youth (idolatry) and her widowhood (exile) would be remembered no more. For a brief time she was separated from her divine Husband. Now, however, because of his great compassion, he would call her to renew the relationship. That reunion would have eternal implications. God's new commitment to Zion would be as irrevocable as the covenant he made with Noah after the Flood. Never again would the Lord be angry with Zion (54:4-10).

In Isaiah's day Zion was afflicted, tossed with tempest, and not comforted. The New Jerusalem—the community of the redeemed—would be constructed of glorious materials (cf. Rev 21:19f.). The citizens of that place would have superior knowledge of God's will (cf. John 6:45). Consequently they would enjoy prosperity and peace. God's people would build upon a foundation of righteousness, and thus they would be secure. Those who might attack Zion would fall. No weapon made by man would be powerful enough to destroy the faithful. Every word spoken against spiritual Zion would be condemned by the truth which abides in God's people (54:11-17).

C. The Imperative of Sustenance (55:1-5).

The Lord offers water, wine and milk—symbols of spiritual blessings—free to all who might desire them (cf. John 7:7). God promised that those who come unto him would "live," i.e., have life more abundant. This new gift of life would be part of a new and enduring covenant which included all the blessings which had been promised to David. Among those blessings the eternal rule of the Messiah, descendant of David, was paramount (55:1-3).

The "sure mercies of David" (KJV) or promises made to David would culminate in one who would be (1) witness, (2) leader, and (3) commander of the peoples. Once this one had been glorified, he would attract other peoples to his cause (55:4f.).

D. The Imperative of Pardon (55:6-13).

Only those who are pardoned would be able to take part in the glorious age anticipated by Isaiah. Thus the prophet called upon both Jews and Gentiles to "seek the Lord," i.e., inquire after his will with the intent of submitting to it. This must be done "while he may be found," i.e., before the expiration of the grace period. Abundant pardon is available to the "wicked" and "the unrighteous" who sincerely repent and ask for it (55:6f.).

Four reasons are given for seeking the Lord. (1) Man's thoughts and ways are not those of God. Man therefore cannot evaluate his own spiritual condition nor can he dictate the terms of his acceptance before the Lord (55:8f.). (2) As moisture accomplishes its purpose in the physical realm, so the word of God will fulfill God's purpose in the hearts of those who humble themselves before him (55:10f.). (3) Those who answer God's invitation "will go out with joy," they will be "led forth with peace." Freedom awaits those who reject sin and embrace the Lord. Even nature is depicted celebrating the redemption of man. Happiness and contentment ("cypress" and "myrtle") replace bitterness and sorrow ("thorn bush" and "nettle") in the lives of obedient believers. These transformed lives would be an everlasting testimony to the power and compassion of the Lord (55:12f.).

E. The Imperative of Service (56:1-8).

Isaiah informed the captives that deliverance was drawing near. Meanwhile, they must be faithful in observing the Law, especially the law of the Sabbath. The rest of the Law is summed up in the general description of refraining from evil (56:1f.).

Those excluded from worship assembly under the old Law (Deut 23:1-6) would be free to participate in the public services of the messianic era. Faithful eunuchs, for example, would have honorable reputation in the future house of God. Also in the New Testament age all strangers who sincerely wish to serve God would be welcome in his house for it would be a "house of prayer for all people." Thus Gentiles would be gathered as well as Israel and both would become one body before the Lord (56:3-8).

WARNINGS TO THE WICKED
Isaiah 56:9-57:21

From surveying the distant peaks of messianic prophecy, Isaiah returned to his own day momentarily. He described in turn (1) the leaders, (2) transgression, and (3) judgment of Judah. Only one brief positive note appears in the unit (57:14-19).

A. Description Judah's Leaders (56:9-57:2).

Judah was about to be attacked by beasts of the forest, i.e., enemy nations. The leaders, however, did not sense the danger. They were like (1) blind watchmen who could not see; (2) dumb watchdogs who could not sound an alarm; and (3) unintelligent shepherds who had no idea what was best for the flock. They were totally given over to greed and self-indulgence. They lived only from day to day with no thought to the future (56:9-12).

God was slowly removing the righteous prematurely by death from the midst of Jerusalem. The leaders did not take note of this warning. Those who had lived upright lives passed by means of death into peace. They rested upon the bed of their graves. Thus God was delivering the faithful from the moral evil of their surroundings, and from the calamity which was about to befall Judah (57:1-2).

B. Description of Judah's Sin (57:3-10).

To underscore their strong attachment to the occult and idolatry, God referred to the inhabitants of Jerusalem as "sons of a sorceress." These hardened sinners mocked those who tried faithfully to adhere to the Law of God (57:3f.).

The majority in Judah was guilty of a wide range of disgusting practices, six of which are cited by way of example. They (1) indulged in the drunken revelry of the tree cult; (2) sacrificed innocent children; (3) participated in some stone cult; (4) engaged in sexual immorality in the high places; (5) set up private deities within their homes; and (6) traveled to distant shrines to honor the King, i.e., the god Molech (57:5-10).

C. Description of Judah's Judgment (57:11-13).

The Jews were driven to idolatry through fear of men. They continued in idolatry because God did not immediately punish them. Speaking ironically, God threatened to bring to light Judah's "righteousness." Unfortunately for them, their deeds were such that no further delay in the judgment could be permitted. In that day all the idols collected together would not avail. Those who trusted in Yahweh, however, would "possess the land."

D. Description of Judah's Hope (57:14-19).

An order is given to prepare for the faithful a road which would lead to the achievement of divine purposes. This order was issued by the eternal, exalted and holy God. This mighty God had chosen to make his abode with those of contrite and lowly spirit. This assertion was a comfort to the humble, but a warning to the spiritually proud (57:14f.).

God's anger against Judah was appropriate because of "iniquity" and "unjust gain." Judah had turned away from God's call to repentance again and again. So finally God "hid" from him and "struck" him. The Lord, however, would not contend with them forever for to do so would mean that man's spirit would be crushed by hopeless despair (57:16f.).

Though God knows the ways of his people, yet he would heal, i.e., forgive and restore them. He would comfort them and lead them as well. On their part, the redeemed of the Lord would respond to God's grace by praising him. They would come to recognize that the peace of God is available to all near and far, i.e., to Jew and Gentile alike.

E. A Final Warning (57:20-21).

The wonderful peace which passes all understanding is not the lot of the wicked. They are like the troubled sea which churns up mire and dirt, i.e., evil thoughts and deeds. They have no peace here, or hereafter.

Endnotes

1. Franz Delitzsch, "Isaiah" in *Keil and Delitzsch Old Testament Commentaries: Isaiah XV to Ezekiel XXIV* (reprint Grand Rapids: Associated Publishers, n.d.) 242f.

2. Homer Hailey thinks the "mother" and "womb" represent the spiritual remnant which returned from Babylon. Cf. Isa 66:7-8; Mic 4:10; 5:2f.; Rev 12:1-6. *A Commentary on Isaiah* (Grand Rapids: Baker, 1971) 2:177f.

3. H.C. Leupold, *Exposition of Isaiah* (Grand Rapids: Baker, 1971) 2:177f.

4. The name "Israel" symbolizes conquest by faith. It was first given to Jacob, then to his descendants. Messiah is also called "David" (Hos 3:5).

5. Simeon cited these words in reference to Jesus (Luke 2:32). Paul and Barnabas used them to prove that they were to go to Gentiles as well as Jews (Acts 13:47).

6. On believers having coming to Zion see Heb 12:22ff.; 1 Pet 2:5-6; and Rev 14:1-5.

7. According to Kenneth Jones, the distinction here is between a divorce that was final and one that was only a separation, and between a sale that was final and one that was revocable. "Isaiah" in *The Wesleyan Bible Commentary,* ed. Charles Carter (Grand Rapids: Eerdmans, 1969) 3:132.

8. On Jesus' willing submission to abuse see Matt 26:67; 27:30.

9. On the torment of the wicked after death compare Matt 25:41.

10. The law of justice which will go forth from Zion (2:3) under the Servant (42:1-4) is the "law of faith" (Rom 3:27), "the law of the Spirit of life" (Rom 8:1-2). See Hailey, *op. cit.* 422.

11. The context is messianic, hence the fulfillment is found, not in the release from Babylonian captivity, but in forgiveness of sin. See Acts 3:24-26.

12. Others think the Servant is being addressed in 51:16.

13. Hailey, op. cit. 430. See Ezek 44:9; Joel 3:17; Zech 9:8-10. All who enter spiritual Zion have received a circumcision not made with hands. See Col 2:11; Rom 2:28-29; and Gal 6:5.

14. The "good news" may include the report that the exiles are returning, but it cannot be limited to that event. Paul rightly applies the verse to the apostolic preaching of the Gospel (Rom 10:15). See Hailey, op.cit. 432.

15. Paul uses the language of the passage to enjoin the sanctification of Christians (2 Cor 6:17-7:1).

16. Acts 8:26-35. Jesus is called "Servant" (Gk. *pais*) in Matt 12:18; Acts 3:13, 26; 4:27, 30.

17. Paul quotes Isa 54:1 in his allegory concerning Sarah and Hagar. See Gal 4:21-31.

CHAPTER TEN

The Book of Future Glory
Isaiah 58-66

Background of the Unit.

Three enneads (nine chapter units) comprise the last twenty-seven chapters of Isaiah. The first and second enneads concluded with the divine declaration that "there is no peace for the wicked" (48:22; 57:21). The major themes of these eighteen chapters have been (1) the captivity to come, (2) the return of a remnant, (3) the work of the Servant, and (4) the glory of Zion. Though a new unit clearly begins in chapter 58, a close relationship exists between chapters 58-59 and the previous chapter. The sins which are condemned here are those which were prevalent in Isaiah's day, the eighth century BC. These chapters serve to remind his listeners of the reasons for the recent humiliating invasion by Sennacherib (chap. 37) and the prophetic threat of Babylonian exile (chap. 39). After describing the present gloom, Isaiah soars again into the heights of prophetic expectation regarding the glorious plans which God had for his people on the other side of captivity.

Outline of the Unit.

A. Hindrances to Salvation (chaps. 58-59).
B. Glories of Salvation (60:1-61:11).
C. Nearness of Salvation (61:12-63:6).
D. Prayer for Salvation (63:7-65:25).
E. Final Words (chap. 66).

HINDRANCES TO SALVATION
Isaiah 58:1-59:21

God wanted to do wonderful things for his people. Difficulties, however, stood in the way. The prophet first identified these obstacles and then predicted their removal.

A. Hindrances Identified (58:1-59:8).

God commanded Isaiah to announce boldly and clearly to the house of Jacob their transgressions (58:1). In response the prophet cried out against three specific sins which were impediments to heavenly blessing.

1. Hypocritical fasting (58:2-12). Judah was guilty of gross hypocrisy. While deliberately disobeying God's commands, they pretended to "seek the Lord" daily. They feigned delight in knowing his will and drawing near to him in worship. In the face of oppression by foreigners, they presented themselves as a righteous nation deserving of God's justice (58:2). Having exposed the general hypocrisy of the nation, Isaiah focused on one example, viz., fasting.

Only one fast day was mandatory under the Law and that was the Day of Atonement (Lev 16:29). Faced with the crisis of the Assyrian invasion, other fast days were appointed. Weeping, confession of sins, and prayer were appropriate accompaniments of effective fasting. The people could not understand why God did not seem to take note of their self-denial. The explanation was simple. On fast days these citizens were (1) doing what they pleased; (2) oppressing their employees; (3) fighting among themselves; and (4) making a big show of the entire enterprise (58:3-5).

Proper fasting must be accompanied by an obedient life. What God wanted was not so much the denial of food for the body, but (1) freeing those illegally enslaved; (2) feeding the hungry; and (3) clothing the naked (58:6f.). These positive acts of compassion were much more important in God's eyes than denying oneself physical sustenance (58:9b-10).

This kind of fasting would be blessed by God to an extraordinary measure. At least nine blessings are enumerated: (1) "Light," i.e., blessing, would break forth. (2) Recovery from all national ailments would speedily spring forth. (3) Righteousness would be their vanguard, and God himself their rear guard. This means that they would have protection in their walk. (4) God would listen to any cry from them (58:8-9a). God would (5) guide them, (6) provide for them, and (7) give them strength. (8) They would be able to rebuild on the ancient foundations the building which had fallen to ruins. (9) Because their efforts would bring such blessing, those who led in this spiritual renewal would gain fame among their brethren. They would be known as the "repairer of the breach" (58:10b-12).

2. Sabbath abuse (58:13-14). Isaiah's contemporaries had failed to sanctify the Sabbath as a special holy day. This calloused disregard for the fourth commandment was a hindrance to divine blessing. Repentance in respect to Sabbath abuse would lead to (1) new fellowship with God; (2) overcoming difficulties and obstacles; and (3) peaceful possession of the Promised Land.

3. Social injustice (59:1-8). Some questioned God's ability to make good on his promises. They wondered whether he really did listen to their prayers. The lack of divine intervention, however, had nothing to do with God's abilities. His "arm," i.e., power, was not too short to reach down and help. He was not hard of hearing. Judah's iniquity and sin caused God to turn away from them. The sin barrier prevented him from hearing their prayers (59:1f.).

All manner of unrighteousness was practiced in Judah. Isaiah presented a head-to-toe evaluation of the sickness of this nation. With their "hands" and "fingers" they practiced iniquity, i.e., crookedness, resulting in bloodshed on occasion. Wickedness and falsehood spewed forth from their "lips" and "tongues." Honesty was lacking even when under oath in a court of law. With their minds they constantly conceived deadly schemes. Their tangled webs of deceit did not hide their true intentions from the Lord. Their thoughts were "thoughts of iniquity." Their feet ran to do evil, even bloodshed, along highways of "devastation and destruction," and "crooked paths." "Peace" and "justice" were totally lacking in their lives (59:3-8).

B. Hindrances Removed (59:9-21).

Eliminating the sin barrier must begin with sincere acknowledgment of sin. Only then can God intervene to rescue his people from humiliating circumstances.

1. Confession of sin (59:9-15a). Straightening matters out with God always begins with admission of wrongdoing. For those who once walked with the Lord, spiritual estrangement is a miserable experience. The remnant recognized that "justice" (the right relationship between men) and "righteousness" (right relationship to God) were nowhere in evidence. Things were dark and gloomy. Without the light of divine revelation they groped like blind men. Depression immobilized them. Men grumbled like bears, they moaned like doves. That which they longed for most—"justice" and "salvation"—seem more remote than ever (59:9-11).

The remnant recognized that their problems stemmed from their numerous sins, transgressions and iniquities. They admitted to (1) sins of the heart—treason and unfaithfulness; (2) sins of the lips—speaking oppression, revolt, and falsehood; and (3) perversion of justice (59:12-15a).

2. Intervention by God (59:15b-21). God was aware of the condition of Israel. The Lord expressed amazement that no one arose to defend the helpless. He, therefore, determined that he must intervene. Isaiah depicted God preparing for the battle against injustice and transgression. He put on righteousness, salvation, vengeance and zeal. He would bring recompense to his enemies both inside and outside Judah. When they saw the irresistible power of his judgment, men in both the west and the east would come to have reverence for Yahweh (59:17-19).

A Redeemer[1] would come to Zion. Those who turn from transgression would recognize him. Associated with this Redeemer is a new covenant.[2] God would anoint this Redeemer with his Spirit (cf. 42:1) and put his words in the Redeemer's mouth (cf. 50:4). The Redeemer would faithfully convey these words to his offspring, i.e., his disciples, and they in turn would pass the words forward through the generations forever (59:20f.). That this Redeemer is Christ Jesus is made clear in Romans 11:26f.

THE GLORIES OF SALVATION
Isaiah 60:1-61:11

Chapters 60-62 are the most optimistic in the book. The Redeemer (59:20) would lead Zion to the heights of glory. What a contrast between the lowly conditions of the inhabitants of physical Zion (chaps. 58-59) and lofty blessings enjoyed by those who would live in the Redeemer's Zion!

A. Zion's Future Glory (60:1-22).

In six masterful paragraphs Isaiah depicted the transformation in Zion after the appearance of the Redeemer. First, Isaiah represented Zion arising to her greet the light of a new day. The glory of Yahweh would shatter the moral and spiritual darkness which enveloped the entire world. In that day the faithful would mirror God's glory (60:1f.). Second, Isaiah predicted that nations and kings would be attracted to the brightness of the New Zion. At the sight of her returning children, Zion would beam with joy. Some would be tenderly carried by Gentiles (60:3-4a).

Third, Isaiah described Zion's wealth. The influx of Gentiles would bring great wealth to Zion. From the east (Midian, Ephah), from the south (Sheba) and from the desert (Kedar, Nebaioth) would come the resources to maintain the Temple and provide adequate sacrifices.[3] On the Mediterranean Sea the prophet could see the sails of "ships of Tarshish" far to the west. Those ships held more converts and additional wealth. All these people have come to know the Lord and therefore would come to Zion singing his praises (60:5b-9).

Fourth, Zion's construction came before the prophet's eye. Foreigners dismantled the walls of physical Jerusalem; foreigners would join in building the walls of the spiritual Zion.[4] The gates of Zion, however, would never close so that there could be a continual flow of people into the place. Kings would willingly join that procession, for they will understand that nations that reject the King of Kings perish. Beautiful construction materials would be brought for the purpose of glorifying God's sanctuary. Descendants of those who had treated God's people so cruelly would humbly bow and submit themselves to Zion and her King. They would recognize this to be uniquely the city of the Holy One of Israel (60:10-14).

Fifth, Isaiah focused on Zion's prosperity. Formerly Zion had been forsaken, but that would change. For many generations to come Zion would be a source of joy and pride. Like a nursing child Zion would gain sustenance from nations and their kings. Far better building materials would be used in the construction of the place thus making it both precious and indestructible. Everything about spiritual Zion would be better than her physical namesake. The city would be without the criminal element. Peace, righteousness, salvation, and praise would be the identifying marks of that holy place (60:15-18).

Finally, Isaiah predicted Zion's crowning glories. In that new day sun and moon would no longer function as they once did, for God would dwell in the midst of his people. He would be their light (cf. Rev 21:23; 22:5). Light symbolizes the presence of God, salvation, and joy. Zion would experience continuous light. Those who inhabit that city would be righteous. They would inherit the eternal Promised Land of which ancient Canaan was but a type. The people would be like a tender shoot planted by God himself. Wholesome growth in numbers is promised. Unimportant individuals would grow into clans and mighty nations (60:19-22).

B. Zion's Wonderful Savior (61:1-3).

The speaker in the opening verses of chapter 61 is not identified, but one can hardly doubt that it is the Servant-Redeemer. These verses should therefore be considered the fifth and last of the Servant poems. In any case, the speaker claims to have been anointed with the Spirit[5] for the purpose of being God's Herald.

In his proclamation the Herald would accomplish seven things. He would (1) preach glad tidings to the afflicted; (2) bind up the brokenhearted; (3) proclaim liberty to the captives (4) and freedom to prisoners; (5) proclaim the year of acceptance, i.e., the period of God's grace; (6) announce the day of judgment; and (7) comfort mourners. In the synagogue at Nazareth Jesus read this passage and announced that it was fulfilled in his ministry (Luke 4:17-21). In place of ashes, mourning and a faint spirit, God's people would receive a garland, oil, a mantle and a new title ("oaks of righteousness"). These are symbols of the joy and strength of the redeemed.

C. Further Blessings of Zion (61:4-11).

Those who have been blessed by the work of the Servant would "rebuild the ancient ruins." The reference is to the building up of the church from the ravages of sin through the ages.[6] Those who were once "strangers" would work for Zion and perform all the work necessary to maintain the Kingdom on earth (61:4f.).

All citizens of Zion would constitute a priesthood to the world. In exchange for this spiritual leadership, Gentiles would supply the physical needs of Zion. In the true Promised Land Zion's citizens would enjoy a double portion of divine blessing. They would experience everlasting joy (61:6f.).

God's absolute justice requires that he destroy his enemies and deliver his people. He would recompense his people for the mistreatment accorded them. To this end he would make with them an "everlasting covenant." This new covenant group would be recognized by all the nations as a people blessed of God (61:8f.).

Isaiah pictured Zion rejoicing over her divinely provided garb. God would wrap his people in "garments of salvation" and in "a robe of righteousness." Isaiah likened these beautiful garments to the attire of a bride and groom. He compared the coming righteousness to a plant which God caused to spring up before the nations (61:10f.).

THE NEARNESS OF SALVATION
Isaiah 62:1-63:6

God promised that he would not keep silent, i.e., be inactive, until he had accomplished his purposes for Zion. Those purposes are summed up in the words "righteousness," i.e., vindication, and "salvation." Isaiah likened this work of God on behalf of Zion to the steady beam of a lamp (62:1).

The Gentiles and their leaders would take note of Zion's change of fortune. The Lord would commemorate the new circumstances by bestowing a special name on his people.[7] The renovated people of God would be utterly glorious, like a crown held and admired by the King. The epitaphs of physical Zion were *`azubhah* ("Forsaken") and *shemamah* ("Desolate"). The names of spiritual Zion would be *"Hephzibah"* ("my delight is in her") and *"Beulah"* ("married").[8] This last title is appropriate from two respects: (1) Zion's sons (individual believers) would be married to Zion (God's kingdom). (2) God would deal with Zion out of an affection like that of a bridegroom for his bride (62:2-5).

God would appoint watchmen, i.e., faithful ministers, on the walls of spiritual Jerusalem. They would warn the citizens of error. They constantly would pray on behalf of the city, and their prayers would not be in vain. Never again would Zion's food and drink fall into the hands of enemies (62:6-9). The reference is to that "food which abides unto eternal life" (John 6:27) which can never be taken away from messianic Zion.

Isaiah urged the citizens of Zion to go out through the gates and prepare the way for the nations to enter.[9] Then they should raise an ensign as a rallying point for the peoples. That ensign has previously been identified as the Root of Jesse, the Messiah (11:10) which God himself would provide (49:22). Throughout the world the Lord would proclaim through his messengers a glorious truth: Salvation has come to the "daughter of Zion" (her citizens). Zion's Savior would bring with him a great multitude, the reward of his own labor. Isaiah identified those who travel the salvation road as the holy people, the redeemed of the Lord. They have been "sought out" because they have been called out of the world. With this vast throng of the saved as her inhabitants, Zion never again would be forsaken (62:10-12).

Zion's enemies (typified by Edom) must be destroyed before the glorious promises made in the preceding chapters can be fulfilled. In a vision Isaiah saw Yahweh striding triumphantly toward Zion. His garments are stained red by the blood of his enemies. This task of judgment he had to undertake alone (63:1-6).

THE PRAYER FOR SALVATION
Isaiah 63:7-65:25

Encouraged by the promises of salvation and future glory, the captives would pray for deliverance. Isaiah first set forth his reflections about God. Then he verbalized to God the feelings which he anticipated would fill the hearts of the captives. Finally, Isaiah recorded God's answer to the captives' prayer.

A. Prelude to Prayer (63:7-14a).

An historical retrospect establishes the setting for the prayer to follow. These verses contain thankful reflection regarding the grace of God, and painful reflection regarding the response of Israel.

1. Thankful reflection (63:7-9). Gratitude and praise should always precede petition. Isaiah recalled the "loving-kindnesses of the Lord," i.e., his great goodness toward the house of Israel. Yahweh had adopted Israel as his people, his very sons. He expressed confidence in their fidelity. He became their Savior. He shared in their adversity. He dispatched "the angel of his presence"[10] to save them (cf. Exod 33:14). He redeemed them from Egyptian bondage and "lifted them and carried them" through the wilderness wandering (63:7-10). What marvelous love!

2. Painful recollection (63:10-14). Unfortunately Israel rebelled against God. They "grieved his Holy Spirit" (NIV) by their iniquity (cf. Acts 7:51; Eph 4:30). He, therefore, became their adversary and fought against them through the agency of foreign powers. Israel's adversity triggered their memory of what God had done for them in the days of Moses. In exile the people were filled with doubts about their God. Why did God help his people during the Egyptian enslavement, but not now? God's Spirit was in their midst then (cf. Num 11:24-30), and he gave them "rest" (Deut 12:9f.; Ps 95:11) in the Promised Land. So why not now? (68:11-14).

B. The Captives' Prayer (63:14b-64:5a).

Isaiah envisioned the prayer which would be on the lips of the penitent captives. The prayer consists of five movements. Four of these are petition, one is a frank confession of sin. First, Isaiah depicted the captives petitioning God for acknowledgement. Only God could be their deliverer. He had led his people in the past and had earned a wonderful reputation. In the present circumstances, however, they had not witnessed God's zeal and mighty works, nor had they sensed his compassion for them. The captives would plead that God might "look down", i.e., intervene, because he was the Father of the nation. Their fathers in the flesh (Abraham, Israel) could not come to their aid; nor were they entitled to deliverance because of physical ancestry. Only Yahweh, who of old had been their Redeemer, could rescue them (63:14b-16).

Second, the captives would petition God for rapprochement. In his patience Yahweh had not punished the wicked. He even had permitted his sanctuary to be trodden down.[11] The apparent injustice of it all had driven many to despair, hardness and unbelief. That they had ever been ruled and upheld by the Lord was hard for them to believe. Therefore, they urged Yahweh to return for the sake of his servants (63:17-19).

Third, the captives would petition God for intervention. They wanted to see the mountains quake like boiling water, their adversaries tremble in Yahweh's presence. The nations had never seen a God who descends in awesome power to aid his people. He meets and aids those who rejoice in him and work righteousness (64:1-5a).

Fourth, the captives would make confession of transgression. They had continued in sin for a long time. Was there any hope of salvation? They felt untouchable (like a leper). Every good deed which any one could name was nothing but a filthy garment.[12] The penitents compared the blighting effects of sin to the wind carrying away a leaf. So unworthy did they feel, the sinners did not believe they could take hold of God in prayer (64:5b-7).

Fifth, the captives would petition God for sympathy. In spite of the fact that prayer seemed useless, yet they prayed. They put forth various reasons why God's anger should be restrained, why he should not continue to remember their iniquity. (1) He was their Father and they were his people. (2) They were but clay in the hands of the divine Potter who had fashioned their nation. (3) The cities of Judah had become a wilderness. (4) The Temple had been burned. Surely God must respond to such misery (64:8-12).

C. God's Answer (65:1-25).

God answered the prayer of his people by offering a perspective on his past relationship to them. He then gave them a promise of better things to come.

1. A perspective on the past (65:1-7). Discovering God's grace through prayer is not difficult. The day would come when Gentiles who have not even sought his grace would discover it (Rom 10:20f.). To his rebellious people, however, God had stretched out his hands in appeal all day long. They preferred to walk a way that was not good, to follow their own thoughts (65:1f.). The irony here is obvious. Gentiles had not sought God, but would find him easily; God sought Israel, but had been constantly rejected.

Far from accepting God's appeal, the sinners provoked him openly. They were guilty of (1) sacrificing in gardens; (2) burning incense on bricks, i.e., the tiled roofs of their houses; (3) sitting in the tombs practicing necromancy; (4) spending the night in secret places in order to gain wisdom from past worthies; (5) eating pork and other unclean meat; (6) thinking that they were holier than others. The exact significance of some of these practices is not known. Like smoke in the nostrils, the sinners were a constant irritation to God (65:3-5).

Judah's misdeeds called forth divine action. Their iniquities piled up from generation to generation. First on God's agenda was the recompense for these blatant transgressions (65:6f.).

2. A promise for the future (65:8-16). So much for the past. What did the future hold for the faithful few who cried out to Yahweh? God would spare a remnant, those stalks in his vineyard which gave some small promise of bearing fruit. Out of Jacob and Judah—the entire covenant people—God would bring forth a "seed, an inheritor of my mountains" (KJV), i.e., my land. God's true servants would inherit the Promised Land of peace and abundance. "Sharon" and "Achor" represent the western and eastern extremes of Canaan and hence here symbolize spiritual Canaan, Messiah's kingdom. Only the people of God who seek him will experience the blessing here envisioned (65:8-10).

For the unfaithful, however, the future was bleak. Those who worshiped Canaanite deities like "Gad" (good luck) and "Mani" (fate) were especially in view. Yahweh alone determines destines. Those who did not respond to his call through the prophets were doomed to the sword of slaughter (65:11f.). Repetition of the interjection "behold" introduces the shocking contrast in the destinies of "my servants" and "you," the wicked.

Chart No. 3

CONTRASTING DESTINIES Isaiah 65:13-15	
God's Servants	**The Wicked**
1. Shall eat. 2. Shall drink. 3. Shall rejoice. 4. Sing for joy of heart. 5. Called by a new name.	1. Shall be hungry. 2. Shall be thirsty. 3. Put to shame. 4. Cry for sorrow of heart. 5. Leave their name as a curse.

What a glorious future the faithful could anticipate! Former troubles would be forgotten. They would recognize Yahweh in that day as the God of Truth (lit., the God of Amen!). They would wish blessings upon themselves in his name (65:16).

3. The new creation (65:17-25). Isaiah called that future age of messianic blessings "the new heavens and the new earth."[13] This spiritual era would be as much "created" by God as was the material universe. According to the New Testament, the new creation began with the work of Christ (2 Cor 5:17; Gal 6:15). The completion of that new creation will follow the final judgment (2 Pet 3:3-13; Rev 20:11-15).

Six wonderful blessings await the redeemed in that new age. First, that would be a time of radical newness. The "former things" would not be remembered with fondness. This would include all the elements of the Mosaic worship system (65:17). Second, the new Jerusalem would be a place of unspeakable joy. Weeping and crying over the wretched condition of the city would not be heard. Even God himself would rejoice in that glorious destiny for his people (65:18f.).

Third, longevity would be another blessing of that day. No premature deaths would occur. Old men would live out their days. The youngest would die a hundred years old (65:20). Longevity for the ancients meant divine approval. The fulfillment as explained by Jesus is even more wonderful than the promise, for he promised to his followers *eternal* life (John 3:15; 6:54).

Fourth, life in the new day would be abundant and totally satisfying. Because of their longevity and the absence of war and calamity, God's people would not be subject to the frustration of not living to enjoy the fruit of their labor. Their long lives would be meaningful and productive. They would use to the full the work of their hands (65:21-23). Fifth, in that day God would answer their prayers before they are even uttered (65:24).[14]

Sixth, messianic Zion would be a safe place. Former enemies would peacefully coexist. Isaiah emphasized this in the picture of meat-eating predators grazing peacefully with domesticated animals. The tranquility, however, would be restricted to "my holy mountain," i.e., Mt. Zion, the kingdom of God (Heb 12:25). The thought here is the same as that in 11:6-9. The phrase "dust shall be the serpent's food" may be an allusion to Genesis 3:15 and the announcement of the complete defeat of the evil spirit called Serpent who tempted the first parents of the human race (65:25).[15]

FINAL MESSAGES
Isaiah 66:1-24

In the final chapter of the book Isaiah addressed the formalists, the remnant and the wicked.

A. The Formalists (66:1-4).

The heavens are God's throne and the earth his footstool. He cannot be confined to a house of worship. He created all the materials from which a temple could be built, and men cannot build from such materials a building worthy of his greatness. Yet this great God condescends to look with favor upon those who are humble and who respect his word. Formal acts of worship apart from wholehearted obedience are as much an abomination to God as murder or swine's blood. Hypocritical worshipers might as well break a dog's neck as offer a sacrificial lamb for all the good it would do them. Those who choose the path of disobedience leave God no choice. He, therefore, would bring their punishment upon them.

B. The Remnant (66:5-14).

The remnant could take some consolation in the fate of their tormentors. Those who persecuted the faithful and mocked their trust in God would come to grief. The prophet could hear, as it were, the outcry of the attackers. The doom of God's enemies had arrived (66:5f.).

A male child would be born. Isaiah had spoken before of the miraculous birth of a scion of the house of David (7:14; 9:6) and of the birth of the Servant (49:1). Almost immediately after Messiah's birth a new "nation," "land," and "her children" appear. Out of the Old Testament Zion would come forth a new people in a single day. God would not permit his eternal plan to be aborted. Zion's travail would end as soon as it began in joyous birth (66:7-9). One is forced to think of the sudden birth of the infant church, the new Israel of God, on the day of Pentecost AD 30.

Such wonderful things were in store for Zion that all who loved her could rejoice. There the faithful would find true satisfaction just as an infant at a mother's breast. By this figure Isaiah described the tranquility ("peace like a river") and nourishment ("the glory of the nations") which the new Zion would enjoy in its infancy. God would comfort his people as only a mother can comfort her child. These were not idle dreams but rich experiences awaiting God's people. The joy would be deep-rooted, going down to the very bones, causing God's people to prosper (66:12-14).

C. The Wicked (66:15-24).

Yahweh was coming against the wicked "with fire," i.e., with judgment.[16] Like a warrior he would go to battle against his foes. The particular sins which aroused God's fury are listed: The cult of gardens and the eating of abominable things (66:15-17).

The time would come for God to cast off apostate Israel and to gather Gentiles. These would witness God's glory as it is revealed in his judgment upon wicked men. A "sign"[17] will be established in their midst. That the "sign" would have "survivors" suggests that the final judgment upon the apostate Jewish nation is intended, viz., the Roman destruction of Jerusalem in AD 70.[18] In any case, "survivors," i.e., the saved, would be sent as missionaries to the far parts of the world. They would declare God's glory among the nations (66:18f.).

The missionary activity of the remnant would bring Gentiles, now considered brethren (cf. Eph 2:14), to the holy mountain (God's kingdom) by every conveyance (cf. 2:2-4). These human souls would be presented as living sacrifices to God. Gentiles would become part of the royal priesthood (66:20f.).[19]

The spiritual Israel would be as enduring as the new heavens and the new earth. "Old Israel will pass away; but from it there will spring the remnant that has survived judgment, and together with it will be a great influx of Gentiles, all of which will form the true Israel of God under the new dispensation."[20] Isaiah represented the faithful worship of the new dispensation under the worship categories of the Old. All mankind, i.e., both Jews and Gentiles, would come at the appointed times ("new moon, sabbath") to express adoration to Yahweh (66:22f.).

Each of the last three enneads of the book conclude with a dark picture of the fate of the wicked (cf. 48:22; 57:20). While gold and silver depict the glories of Zion, so fire and worms depict the fate of the wicked. Those who refuse to render homage to God in his house are dead while they live (cf. 1 Tim 5:6). They are consumed by their own corruption ("worms," i.e., maggots). They are perpetually under the wrath of God's judgment fire (John 3:18). "All mankind," i.e., the Jews and Gentiles who render homage to God, would regard with abhorrence the rottenness of the lifestyle of the unbelievers (66:24). Jesus used the language of this verse to describe the eternal fate of those who reject salvation (Mark 9:48).

Endnotes

1. The term "redeemer" *(go 'el)* is used thirteen times by Isaiah, all in the last twenty-seven chapters of the book. This technical term refers to the person who had the right and obligation to purchase the freedom of a relative who had fallen into slavery. Yahweh is the *go 'el* who would ransom his people from bondage.

2. The "covenant" in view here is the "sure mercies of David" (55:3). This covenant was established in the Servant (42:6; 49:8) and will never be revoked (54:10).

3. Isaiah did not mean to suggest that animal sacrifice would be practiced in the messianic age. He uses the familiar forms of Old Testament worship to describe the spiritual sacrifice of New Testament worship.

4. "Salvation will be appointed for walls and bulwarks" (26:1). See also 60:18.

5. On the role of the Spirit in the life of the Servant, see 11:2; 42:1; 49:8; and 50:4.

6. E.J. Young, *The Book of Isaiah* (Grand Rapids: Eerdmans, 1972) 3:461f.

7. On the "new name" concept see Isa 1:26; Jer 3:17; 33:16; Ezek 48:35; Rev 2:17; 3:12.

8. Both Azubah and Hephzibah were names of women who were mothers of kings of Judah (1 Kgs 22:42; 2 Kgs 21:1).

9. Homer Hailey, *A Commentary on Isaiah* (Grand Rapids: Baker, 1985) 499. Others think the idea is that the captives must leave the world city to claim for themselves the salvation which God supplies.

10. The "angel of his presence" is most likely the person who appears throughout the Old Testament (e.g., Gen 16:7; Num 22:23) as "the angel of Yahweh." This was no ordinary angel, but a visible manifestation of God. Some regard this "angel" as a Christophany. See James Borland, *Christ in the Old Testament* (Chicago: Moody, 1978) 5-33. Ross Price observes: "He who is called God's face (*panim*) can be no less than He by whom God both sees and is seen." *Isaiah* in Beacon Bible Commentary (Kansas City: Beacon Hill, 1966) 4:273.

11. The treading down of the sanctuary could be anticipatory of the Babylonian destruction of Jerusalem in 587 BC. Ross Price (op.cit. 4:278) has proposed that the phrase "the holy people possessed my sanctuary for a little while" refers to the godly reign of Hezekiah. All that suddenly changed when Manasseh ascended the throne.

12. Lit., "a garment of time," a reference to the menstrual periods of a woman (cf. Lev 15:19-24).

13. Hailey (*op. cit.*518f) limits the reference to "the dispensation of the fulness of time" (Eph 1:10) when "the old things are passed away; behold, they are become new" (2 Cor 5:17). Young (*op. cit.* 513f.), however, comments: "The reference is not . . . to be restricted to the first advent but includes the entire reign of Christ, including the second advent and the eternal state."

14. On the answering of prayer before it is even uttered, see Matt 6:8.

15. Hailey (*op. cit.* 521) comments: "The defeat of Satan by Christ (Heb 2:14; 1 John 3:8) guarantees the victory of the saints (Rom 16:20)."

16. According to Exod 19:18 Yahweh descended on Mt. Sinai in fire. Ever after his coming in fire has signified judgment.

17. Various interpretations of the "sign" have been offered: (1) A miraculous sign as in Isa 7:14; (2) the resurrection of Messiah; and (3) the establishment of the Church.

18. Hailey, *op. cit.* 527.

19. Cf. 1 Pet 2:9; Rev 5:9f.

20. Cf. Hailey (*op. cit.* 528): "The prophet now clothes a spiritual truth in the idiom of his day."

THE BOOK OF
JEREMIAH

CHAPTER ELEVEN

Getting Acquainted With Jeremiah

The second of the Major Prophets has been called the Weeping Prophet, the Martyr Prophet, and God's Iron Pillar. He is one of the more interesting prophets simply because so much is known about his life. His biography is a living sermon, and his book is a mini-bible. Saints throughout the ages have been challenged and inspired by his deeds and words.

THE PROPHET JEREMIAH

In order to appreciate the prophet Jeremiah three types of information are vital. One must know something of his personal circumstances, his public ministry and the political context in which he lived and served.

A. Personal Circumstances.

Besides the author of this prophetic book, seven other men in the Bible wear the name Jeremiah.[1] The name means *Yahweh appoints* or *establishes.* Verse 1 of the book gives the basic personal information about this prophet.

Jeremiah was a priest before he was a prophet. His father, Hilkiah, may have been the famous high priest who played such a significant role in the reformation of 621 BC (cf. 2 Chr 34:9).

As a boy, no doubt Jeremiah would have accompanied his father to the Temple from time to time. He would have learned by observation the vocation which he anticipated entering when he reached the age of thirty.

Jeremiah grew up in the priestly village of Anathoth, about three miles north of Jerusalem. This village was part of the tribal area of Benjamin. Perhaps a childhood in this rural area accounts for the numerous agricultural metaphors which Jeremiah used during his ministry.

Chart No. 4

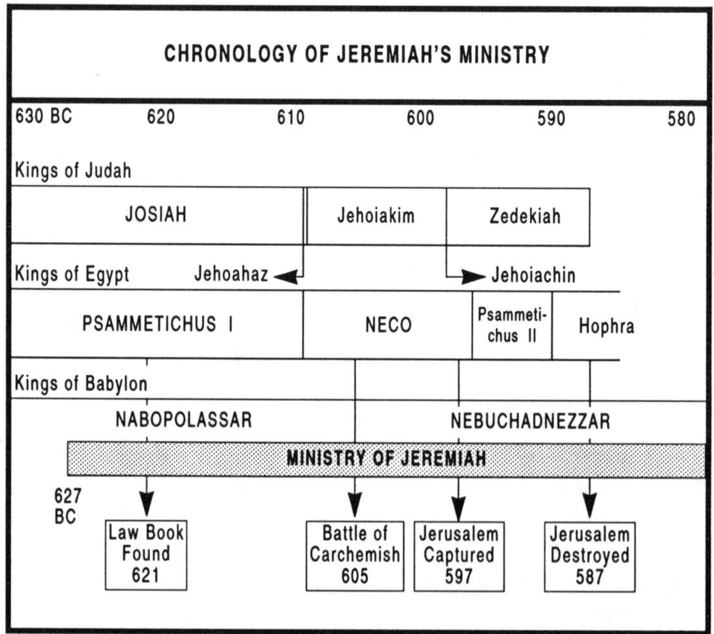

B. Political Backdrop.

Three kings are named in the first verse of the book during whose reigns Jeremiah ministered. Two other kings, who reigned but a year between them, are omitted.

1. Reign of Josiah (640-609 BC). Jeremiah was called to the prophetic ministry in the thirteenth year of King Josiah, i.e., 627 BC. Josiah was a godly man from his youth. Some conjecture that he was tutored by the prophet Zephaniah during his boyhood. He certainly did not learn godliness from his father Amon who did evil in the eyes of the Lord (2 Chr 33:22). When Josiah began to rule, Judah was a vassal state within the great Assyrian Empire. This vassalage required the Jews to venerate Assyrian deities. So idolatry was prevalent in Judah during this period.

In his eighth year of reign, when he was but sixteen years old, Josiah began to seek the God of his father David (2 Chr 34:3). In his twelfth year at the age of twenty the king began to purge Jerusalem of all the paraphernalia of idolatry. His campaign extended to the territory once occupied by the ten northern tribes, territory which had been incorporated into the Assyrian Empire. This was a direct challenge to Assyrian hegemony in the region. Since the Assyrian Empire was at this time weak, Josiah was never compelled to defend his actions on the battlefield.

In the thirteenth year of Josiah, Jeremiah was called by God to be a prophet to the nations. The autobiographical account of that call is recorded in the first chapter of the book. Jeremiah was reluctant to accept the challenge extended to him because he was but a youth. He surely could not have been more than a teenager at the time.

The first milestone in the ministry of the prophet was the major reformation in the eighteenth year of Josiah. A scroll of the Law of God was found by the high priest Hilkiah buried beneath debris in the Temple. After confirming that the threats and curses contained in this scroll were still valid, Josiah intensified his campaign to cleanse his land of idolatry. Jeremiah must have been an active participant in this effort. Much of the sermonic material in chapters 2-7 of the book grew out of the context of this great reformation.

For eighteen years of his ministry, until the end of Josiah's life, Jeremiah had the support of the crown in his preaching efforts. Josiah died when he engaged Pharaoh Neco in battle at the pass of Megiddo in 609 BC. Neco was moving north to reinforce the remnants of the Assyrian army on the Euphrates river. He had no quarrel with Josiah. Yet Josiah felt compelled to confront him. The Judean king was mortally wounded in that battle. Jeremiah was deeply affected by the senseless death of this godly king. He wrote several lamentations which Judean singers employed for years to commemorate Josiah's death (2 Chr 35:25).

2. Reign of Jehoahaz (609 BC). The people of the land anointed Shallum as king in place of his father. Shallum took the throne name Jehoahaz. This king ruled but three months. He was then summoned to Riblah by Pharaoh Neco. There he was put in chains and deported to Egypt. Apparently many people regarded Jehoahaz as rightful king even after his deportation. They expected him to return to claim his throne. Jeremiah, however, announced that Shallum would die in the place where they had carried him captive (Jer 22:11f.).

3. Reign of Jehoiakim (609-598 BC). Pharaoh Neco selected a brother of Shallum, Eliakim, to be the new king. Neco gave the name Jehoiakim to Eliakim. The new king was placed under an enormous annual tribute obligation to Egypt. In 605 BC when Neco was defeated by Nebuchadnezzar in the battle of Carchemish, Jehoiakim switched allegiance to Babylon. This crafty king was able to maintain himself on the throne of Judah for eleven years. Those were miserable years for Jeremiah. The prophet's life was in constant jeopardy. Jehoiakim was the target of some of Jeremiah's most harsh criticism and prediction.

4. Reign of Jehoiachin (597 BC). Jehoiakim died a natural death, apparently, in December 598 BC. He was succeeded by his son Coniah who took the throne name Jehoiachin. After a reign of just over three months, this young king was forced to surrender to Nebuchadnezzar in March of 597 BC. At that time he was deported to Babylon with ten thousand of his subjects. Jeremiah predicted that no descendant of Jehoiachin would successfully sit upon the throne of David in Judah (Jer 22:30).

5. Reign of Zedekiah (597-587 BC). Nebuchadnezzar installed

Mattaniah, another son of King Josiah, as his vassal king in Jerusalem. Mattaniah took the throne name Zedekiah. This last Old Testament king ruled eleven years. He was under constant pressure from his advisors to rebel against Nebuchadnezzar. On the other hand, Jeremiah consistently urged Zedekiah to surrender to Babylon. The king could not resist the pressure to seek an alliance with Egypt against Nebuchadnezzar. This political maneuvering led to the Babylonian destruction of Jerusalem in 587 BC.

C. Public Ministry: Dimensions.

Jeremiah's ministry extended from his call in 627 BC to well beyond the fall of Jerusalem in 587 BC, a period of over four decades. Jeremiah's ministry was multi-dimensional.

1. *Preaching.* He was first and foremost a preacher. Though not as eloquent as Isaiah nor as colorful as Ezekiel, Jeremiah nonetheless was a powerful messenger. His sermons throb with emotion. His metaphors paint vivid pictures of sin and apostasy.

2. *Drama.* Jeremiah was an actor as well as a preacher. He dramatized his message from time to time in order to attract an audience and to underscore the truths he was preaching. Jeremiah's action parables were not so bizarre as those of Ezekiel, but they were nonetheless strange. Among his "props" were a dirty girdle, a pottery jar, a cup of wine, and an ox yoke. To drive home his point he offered wine to a group of teetotalers, buried a stone beneath the pavement before a government building, and purchased a plot of ground in the midst of the siege of Jerusalem.

3. *Writing.* Jeremiah was a writer. He wrote, as noted above, a lament over the death of Josiah. He wrote a letter to Babylon (Jer 29). He wrote the book that bears his name and probably the Biblical books of Lamentations and Kings. Through his writings this prophet has inspired believers for twenty-five hundred years.

4. *Prayer.* Prayer was yet another dimension of Jeremiah's ministry. He was persistent in intercession in spite of repeated indications of the hopelessness of his efforts (chap. 14; 18:20). This prophet has recorded for posterity his prayers of complaint (4:10), perception (5:3), praise (10:6f.), and clarification (32:16-23). Perhaps more teaching on prayer is found in the Book of Jeremiah than in any

other book of the Bible.

5. Statesmanship. Jeremiah was a statesman. He supported the national reformation efforts of King Josiah. After the battle of Carchemish, he urged his nation to recognize Babylon as world ruler. He battled the majority in the royal court who thought that Egypt would provide relief from Babylonian oppression. Jeremiah saw clearly that Babylon would rule the world for seventy years. Although he consistently urged submission to Babylon, Jeremiah was no traitor. After Jerusalem's fall he was given the option of spending the rest of his days under royal patronage in Babylon. He chose to remain with the tattered remnant of his people in the devastated land of Judah.

6. Counseling. Jeremiah ministered privately to individuals as well as to the masses. He was a counselor. He was equipped for this ministry by his personal victory over depression in a mid-ministry crisis. Five times Jeremiah cried out to God from the black depths of doubt and discouragement. God answered the prophet's "confessions" in such a way that Jeremiah was was able to "get back on track" in his ministry. Using the insights which grew out of these dialogues with God, Jeremiah advised Baruch, his secretary, during one of his periods of discouragement. King Zedekiah sought Jeremiah out on numerous occasions to ask for his advice in dealing with national crises.

D. Public Ministry: Agony.

Not without reason has Jeremiah been called the weeping prophet. This man suffered as no other Biblical character save the Son of God himself. Three distinct aspects of his personal suffering can be identified in the book.

1. Ministerial aspect. Jeremiah experienced the agony of his message of judgment. He saw clearly in vision the total destruction of the land he loved. He saw the suffering of men, women and children. Emotionally he was drained each time he shared those dire visions with his audience (9:1; 13:17).

If his message was painful to deliver, the reception which that message received was even more painful. The people he loved—the people he knew were standing on the brink of national destruction—

refused to listen. The men of his own hometown plotted his demise (11:19,21). He could not even trust members of his own family (12:6). For his assertion that Jerusalem and its temple would be destroyed Jeremiah was branded a heretic and threatened with death (26:7-9). When his predictions failed to materialize immediately, they branded him a false prophet and scoffed at his doomsday threats (17:15). To his contemporaries Jeremiah was a joke—a sad, pathetic, anachronistic joke (20:7b). The crowds cheered when a representative of the more "enlightened" clergy publicly humiliated Jeremiah in the temple courts (chap. 28).

2. Psychological aspect. Jeremiah's personal loneliness intensified his agony. If ever a man needed a sympathetic spouse, this prophet surely did. Yet God ordered him not to marry (16:2). The preacher's lifestyle must match his proclamation. For this preacher to marry and father children would be inconsistent with his announcement that shortly Jerusalem would be destroyed by Nebuchadnezzar. For the same reason God prohibited Jeremiah from attending social gatherings, whether feasts or funerals (16:5-9). This prophet was to be a "loner" and through his loneliness he would preach a sermon. This was no time for parties, for there was nothing to celebrate. On the other hand, funerals would soon be impossible. So many people would die in the imminent judgment that conducting individual memorial services would be impractical. Thus Jeremiah preached as much by what he refused to do as by what he did or said. He was a sermon in shoes!

3. Physical aspect. Jeremiah's agony had physical as well as psychological dimensions. The chief officer of the Temple had him seized, flogged and put in the public stocks overnight (20:1ff.). During the last days of Jerusalem, Jeremiah was arrested on the charge of treason. Again he was beaten, then was thrown into a subterranean dungeon. He nearly died in that foul place (37:11ff.). Shortly after that ordeal he again was charged with treason for urging Jerusalem's defenders to desert to the Babylonian armies. The king permitted ruthless princes to have their way with this man of God. They cast him into an empty cistern and left him there to starve to death (38:6). A humble black servant of the king risked his life to rescue the prophet from certain death (38:11ff.).

THE BOOK OF JEREMIAH

By word count the Book of Jeremiah is the largest of the prophetic books of the Old Testament. Because of its size, this book was placed at the head of the Major Prophets in some ancient lists and manuscripts.[2] In some ways Jeremiah is an easy book to read. The exciting accounts of the prophet's vicissitudes during his forty plus years of ministry are compelling. The sermons of the prophet, filled as they are with brilliant metaphor, are pregnant with devotional application. Yet even a surface reading of the book reveals several problems which are not easily solved.

A. Composition of the Book.

Jeremiah had been preaching for twenty-three years before he was instructed to record his sermons on a scroll. The prophet dictated his messages to the scribe Baruch. This first edition of the Book of Jeremiah was destroyed in 604 BC by the tyrant King Jehoiakim. God, however, commissioned Jeremiah to produce another scroll. This second edition of the book contained all the words of the first scroll and "many similar words" as well (36:32).

A third edition of the book must have been produced by Baruch in Egypt after the death of Jeremiah. This Egyptian edition must have been considerably larger than the second edition. It would have contained the record of the last twenty years of the prophet's ministry. The third edition of Jeremiah was produced about 560 BC.[3] A hasty copy of this edition of the book was made before Baruch emigrated to Babylon. There he produced the fourth edition of the book. Certain additional oracles of the prophet were added and all the material was reorganized. This Babylonian edition became the prototype for the standard Hebrew form of the book which has been translated into English.

Who, then, is actually responsible for the writing of this book? Baruch certainly performed the mechanical work of a stenographer. Did he do more? The last verse of chapter 51 clearly indicates that Jeremiah was not responsible for the authorship of chapter 52. Baruch most likely added that chapter in order to document the fulfillment of Jeremiah's most dramatic and controversial prediction, viz., the destruction of Jerusalem and the deportation of the people of God. At some point Baruch may have functioned more like a modern editor. To what degree was he responsible for arranging the material in the book? The data available does not permit a definitive answer to this question.

The above reconstruction of the composition of the Book of Jeremiah may help to explain why the Greek translation—the so-called Septuagint—is so different from the standard Hebrew edition of the book. This version was translated about 250 BC in Alexandria Egypt. It is about one eighth shorter than the Hebrew form of the book. The major sections of the book are arranged in a different manner,[4] and even within the various sections the material is in a different order.[5] Some blocks of material found in the Hebrew are absent in the Greek version.[6] Much of the repetition found in the Hebrew version is absent in the Septuagint. These facts lead to the conclusion that the Alexandrian translators had before them a very different Hebrew manuscript. Perhaps they based their translation on the Egyptian edition of the book which was hastily copied by the Jews in Egypt before Baruch emigrated to Babylon. This hypothesis would account for the rather substantial differences in the the two forms of the text.

B. The Plan of the Book.

The arrangement of materials in the Book of Jeremiah has been called the most confused in the Old Testament.[7] Large blocks of the material are in chronological order. Here and there, however, chapters are inserted which jump forward or backward in time. Jeremiah or his editor Baruch must have grouped material at times according to a topical rather than a chronological principle. This survey does not permit an extensive discussion of all the particulars regarding the organization of the book. That chapter 1 is intended to be an introduction to the entire book is clear enough. This chapter narrates the prophetic call of Jeremiah in 627 BC. The remaining chapters are arranged in two main divisions.

Chapters 2-25 form the first major division of the book. These chapters are *mainly* pre-605 BC.[8] This was the year of the battle of Carchemish, the fourth year of King Jehoiakim of Judah and the first year of Nebuchadnezzar of Babylon. For the most part these chapters contain excerpts from sermons and oracles delivered by Jeremiah. The title which appears in 1:1 ("the words of Jeremiah") is appropriate to this first division. These twenty-four chapters may be subdivided according to contents as follows: (1) public pronouncements (chaps. 2-10); (2) personal discouragement (chaps. 11-20); (3) corrupt government (chaps. 21-24); and (4) coming judgment (chap. 25).

Chapters 26-51 form the second major division of the book. These chapters are more biographical in form. For the most part they are dated after 605 BC.[9] Although some sermon excerpts are found here, this division might be entitled "The Deeds of Jeremiah." The subdivisions of the second division are as follows: (1) Jeremiah's suffering (chaps. 26-29); (2) special prophecies regarding Judah (chaps. 30-35); (3) Jeremiah's suffering (chaps. 36-45); and (4) special prophecies regarding foreign nations (chaps. 46-51).

Chapter 52 is an appendix describing the fall of Jerusalem in 587 BC and the deportation of many Jews to Babylon. The purpose here is to vindicate Jeremiah by showing that all the calamity which he had predicted concerning Jerusalem and Judah had come to pass.

Chart No. 5

THE STRUCTURE OF THE BOOK OF JEREMIAH			
Introduction	THE WORDS OF JEREMIAH	THE LIFE OF JEREMIAH	Appendix
THE CALL	*Mostly before 605 BC*	*Mostly after 605 BC*	THE FALL
627 BC	Public Pronouncement 2-10 Private Discouragement 11-20	Jeremiah's Suffering 26-29 Judah Prophecies 30-35	587 BC
Chap. 1	Corrupt Government 21-24 Imminent Judgment 25	Jeremiah's Suffering 36-45 Nations Prophecies 46-51	Chap. 52

C. Predictions in the Book

According to Barton Payne,[10] the Book of Jeremiah contains ninety different specific predictions. This total ranks second only to Isaiah. Some 812 verses, sixty per cent of the total, are predictive. The majority of these predictive verses (222) focus on the fall of Jerusalem to the Babylonians. Among the more outstanding political prophecies of the book are the following: (1) the seventy years of service to Babylon (25:11f.); (2) Nebuchadnezzar's invasion of Egypt (43:8-13); (3) the capture of Babylon by Cyrus (25:12-14); and (4) the defeat of Pharaoh Neco at Carchemish (46:5f.).

The Book of Jeremiah does not contain nearly as much Messianic prophecy as does Isaiah. Yet prophecies pointing to Christ and his kingdom are not lacking. Perhaps the most important of those is the famous new covenant prophecy of 31:31.[11] Two prophecies are noteworthy in the personal Messianic category. A future leader, the Righteous Shoot, will rule over the united tribes (23:5). This ruler will enjoy priestly as well as royal privileges (30:21).

Endnotes

1. The seven other Jeremiahs are mentioned in the following references: (1) 2 Kgs 23:31; 24:18; Jer 52:1; (2) 1 Chr 5:24; (3) 1 Chr 12:4; (4) 1 Chr 12:10; (5) 1 Chr 12:13; (6) Neh 10:2; 12:1, 12, 34; (7) Jer 35:3.

2. In the Talmud, the Jewish repository of oral tradition, Jeremiah is listed first among the prophets. On the numerous Hebrew manuscripts reflecting this same tradition, see H.E. Ryle, *The Canon of the Old Testament* (second edition; London: Macmillan, 1895) 237.

3. The suggested date for the Egyptian edition of Jeremiah is based on the assumption that it contained chapter 52. The last event mentioned in this chapter is the release of the Judean king Jehoiachin which can be dated to 560 BC.

4. In the Septuagint the section containing oracles against foreign nations is found in the middle of the book following 25:13 rather than at the conclusion of the book.

5. The foreign nation oracles, for example, appear in a different order in the Septuagint.

6. Jeremiah 33:14-16 is absent in the Septuagint.

7. Clyde T. Franscisco, *Introducing the Old Testament* (Nashville: Broadman, 1950) 145.

8. 21:1-10 comes from the reign of Zedekiah. Possibly 13:18-27 is also post-605 BC.

9. Chapter 26 comes from "early in the reign of Jehoiakim," which probably means prior to 605 BC.

10. J. Barton Payne, *Encyclopedia of Biblical Prophecy* (New York: Harper & Row, 1973) 674.

11. Other passages which speak of the new covenant are 3:16; 30:22; 31:1, 33-34; 32:40.

JEREMIAH-LAMENTATIONS: A BIBLIOGRAPHY

Blackwood, Jr. Andrew W. *Commentary on Jeremiah.* Waco: Word, 1977.

Bright, John. *Jeremiah.* The Anchor Bible. Ed. W. F. Albright and D. N. Freedman. Garden City, NJ: Doubleday, 1965.

Brueggemann, Walter. *To Pluck up, To Tear Down.* International Theological Commentary. Ed. F. C. Holmgren and G. A. F. Knight. Grand Rapids: Eerdmans, 1988.

Carroll, Robert P. *The Book of Jeremiah; a Commentary.* The Old Testament Library. Philadelphia: Westminster, 1986.

Cawley, F. "Jeremiah," *The New Bible Commentary.* Grand Rapids: Eerdmans, 1953.

Feinberg, Charles. *Jeremiah: a Commentary.* Grand Rapids: Zondervan, 1982.

Gray, C. Paul. "The Book of the Prophet Jeremiah," vol. 4, *Beacon Bible Commentary.* Kansas City: Beacon Hill, 1966.

Hall, Bert H. "The Book of Jeremiah," vol. 3, *The Wesleyan Bible Commentary.* Ed. Charles Carter. Grand Rapids: Eerdmans, 1969.

Harrison, R. K. *Jeremiah and Lamentations.* Tyndale Old Testament Commentaries. Ed. D. J. Wiseman. Downers Grove: Inter-Varsity, 1973.

Holladay, William L. *Jeremiah 1: A Commentary on the Book of the Prophet Jeremiah Chapters 1-25.* Hermeneia. Ed. Paul Hanson. Philadelphia: Fortress, 1986.

Kaiser, Jr. Walter C. *A Biblical Approach to Personal Suffering.* Chicago: Moody, 1982.

Keil, Carl F. "Jeremiah," *Keil and Delitzsch Old Testament Commentaries: Isaiah XV to Ezekiel XXIV.* Grand Rapids: Associated Publishers, n.d.

Kidner, Derek. *The Message of Jeremiah.* The Bible Speaks Today. Ed. J. A. Motyer and J. R. W. Stott. Downers Grove, IL: Inter-Varsity, 1987.

Kuist, H. T. "The Book of Jeremiah," vol. 12, *The Layman's Bible Commentary.* Ed. Balmer Kelly. Richmond: John Knox, 1960.

Laetsch, Theo. *Bible Commentary: Jeremiah.* St. Louis: Concordia, 1965.

Martens, Elmer A. *Jeremiah*. Believers Church Bible Commentary. Scottdale, PA: Herald, 1986.

Naegelsbach, C. W. Edward. "Jeremiah," *Commentary on the Holy Scriptures, Critical, Doctrinal and Homiletical*. Edited by John Peter Lange. Grand Rapids: Zondervan, n.d.

Smith, James E. *Jeremiah and Lamentations* in Bible Study Textbook Series. Joplin: College Press, 1972.

Thompson, J. A. *The Book of Jeremiah*. The New International Commentary on the Old Testament. Ed. R. K. Harrison. Grand Rapids: Eerdmans, 1980.

CHAPTER TWELVE

The Call and Early Ministry Jeremiah 1:1-4:4

Background of the Unit.

Jeremiah was called to prophetic ministry in the thirteenth year of King Josiah, 627 BC (Jer 1:2). As early as his eighth year, when he was but sixteen years of age, Josiah began "to seek the God of his father David." In his twelfth year Josiah launched a religious reformation. He removed the Baal altars and chopped down the sacred poles (Asherim) beside them. He began to purge Judah and Jerusalem. He even carried his crusade into the territories formerly occupied by the tribes of the Northern Kingdom (2 Chr 34:1-7). The reform efforts—and especially the campaign outside his borders—were a direct challenge to the authority of the Assyrians who had dominated Judah for over half a century.

Jeremiah was called to ministry to aid this last heroic effort to change the direction of Judah. While the king was attacking the external and public aspects of idolatry, the preacher would attempt to root out idolatry from the hearts of the people. Five years after the call of

Jeremiah, in 621 BC, the reformation efforts were intensified after the discovery in the Temple archives of a copy of the ancient scriptures penned by Moses (2 Chr 34:8-33).

The material in the first unit of the Book of Jeremiah comes from the earliest period of the prophet's ministry. Josiah must have applauded, if not actively encouraged, the work of the young preacher. The sermon excerpts recorded in chapters 2-10 should be assigned to the years 627-609 BC. Precise dating for smaller units in this section is not possible.

Outline of the Unit.

A. Appointment of the Prophet (chap. 1).
B. Accusations against Judah (chap. 2).
C. Appeals by the Lord (3:1-4:4).

APPOINTMENT OF THE PROPHET
Jeremiah 1:4-19

The call of Jeremiah was not as elaborate as those of Isaiah and Ezekiel. He simply affirms that "the word of the Lord came unto me" without bothering to explain the mechanics of that process. This autobiographical narrative describes how God (1) summoned him to service, (2) assured him of support, (3) confirmed him in ministry, and (4) exhorted him to action.

A. Summons to Service (1:4-6).

The first revelation which came to Jeremiah concerned him personally. God had "formed" him in his mother's womb, i.e., he was a unique person, endowed with attributes to accomplish what no other man could accomplish. God "knew" him, i.e., recognized his strengths and weaknesses, yet chose him anyway. God "consecrated" him, i.e., set him apart from all others to fulfill a specific mission. This series of divine affirmations impressed upon Jeremiah's mind the fact that he and he alone could do the job which God had in mind for him (1:5a).

Jeremiah had been appointed "a prophet," i.e., an official ambassador of God who spoke in his name and by his authority. Though other prophets spoke to and about foreign nations, Jeremiah is the only one to receive the title "a prophet to the nations." The fate of tiny Judah was so inextricably intertwined with the super powers that anything he would say to or about his country would of necessity involve the nations of the world (1:5b).

Jeremiah understood immediately the basic involvements of this appointment and he was intimidated by them. In an emotional outburst ("Alas Lord God!") he expressed his keen sense of unworthiness. His age was against him ("I am a youth").[1] Culture dictated that young people listen but not speak in public affairs. He also did not "know how to speak," i.e., he lacked natural abilities (1:6).

B. The Assurance of Support (1:7-10).

To ease the apprehension of this reluctant servant, God reassured him in four areas. First, the Lord gave to his prophet assurance of direction. Jeremiah was instructed not to focus his attention on his own weaknesses, but on God's strength. God would direct both the where of his ministry and the what. He would go where God directed him. He would speak what God revealed to him (1:7).

Second, Jeremiah received assurance of deliverance. God looked beneath the surface excuses of Jeremiah and saw the fear in his heart. That fear was not unfounded. At times Jeremiah would need to be rescued from the machinations of those who hated the truth. God, however, promised to be with him, to deliver him, not *from* any difficult circumstances, but *through* those circumstances (1:8).

Third, God gave to the young man assurance of power. Whether in the visional or physical realm, the young man felt his lips touched by God's hand. The touch of Isaiah's lips was for cleansing; that of Jeremiah's was for empowerment. From this day forward he could preach boldly because God declares: "I have put my words in your mouth" (1:9).

Finally, God gave assurance of authority to prophesy. Jeremiah's appointment involved the authority to verbally "pluck up, break down, destroy and overthrow" the nations of his day. This he would do by preaching God's word of judgment against them. Once the old order had been removed, Jeremiah's preaching would become more optimistic. He would "build and plant" the basic principles of a new era, the age of Messiah (1:10).

C. Confirmation in Ministry (1:11-16).

On two occasions subsequent to the initial summons Jeremiah's call was confirmed by visions. In the first vision his attention was directed to an object which he correctly identified as an almond *(shaqed)* rod. Since the almond was the first tree to "wake up" in the spring, it was sometimes known as the "wakeful tree." Employing a play on words, God declared that he was watching *(shoqed)* over his word to perform it. The prophet could speak the divine word with the assurance that God was alert and awake, that his word would not fail (1:11f.).

In the second vision Jeremiah's attention was directed to a boiling pot in the process of tipping over. It was "facing away from the north," i.e., its contents were about to be spilled southward. This symbol meant that "out of the north the evil," i.e., calamity, "would break forth" on all the inhabitants of Judah. The boiling pot symbolized the political turmoil which would arise north of Judah when the Assyrian empire fell and the Babylonian empire arose on the scene of history. God would employ "the kingdoms of the north" to conquer the cities of Judah. Through those foreign agents God would pronounce his judgments on the Jews because of their unfaithfulness (1:13-16).

D. Challenge to Action (1:17-19).

The call narrative concludes with a series of exhortations designed to challenge Jeremiah to begin his ministry. "Gird up your loins," i.e., tuck your long robe into your belt so as to be prepared for strenuous activity. "Arise," so as to be heard, and "speak to them all which I command you." He must not only gird up, stand up, and speak up, he must also bear up. "Do not be terrified by them" (NIV). His audience would try to intimidate him, and if they sensed that they were succeeding, God would permit them to crush his ministry through fear (1:17).

God would prepare the prophet for his confrontation with an

hostile audience. They would find this man to have a God-given fortitude and determined purpose. Before his adversaries he would appear to be as invincible as a fortified city, as indestructible as an iron pillar, and as impregnable as a bronze wall. Kings, princes, priests and prominent people of the land would fight against him by every means. They would not be able to overcome Jeremiah. The Lord would be with him every step of the way to deliver him out of any danger. Thus the last implied exhortation of the call narrative was to look up to God as the source of strength (1:18f.).

ACCUSATIONS AGAINST JUDAH
Jeremiah 2:1-37

Chapter 2 contains excerpts from several early sermons of the prophet. The material is largely accusatory. Jeremiah here skillfully painted word pictures of the waywardness of God's people. He spoke of the fact, the fruit, the form and the fault in Judah's apostasy.

A. The Bitter Fact (2:1-13).

Jeremiah presented three pictures which underscored the fact that Judah had departed from the Lord. First, he depicted Judah as an unfaithful wife. God reminded his bride (God's people collectively) of the youthful love which she had for him in the earliest period of their involvement with one another. That betrothal love caused Israel trustingly to follow God's leading out of Egypt and into a barren wilderness. If Israel loved God in those days, God loved Israel even more. He regarded them as holy to himself, i.e., set apart for him exclusively. He took pride in them as much as a farmer would in the first of his harvest. Any nation which attempted to devour that harvest incurred guilt and calamity (2:1-3).

Second, Jeremiah pictured Judah as an ungrateful heir. Apostasy was nothing new in Israel. The fathers of the nation had departed from the Lord, and that for no good reason. They walked after "worthless idols" (NIV) and became like that which they worshiped. The Lord had brought them through a barren desert into the fruitful land (Canaan); but they "defiled" God's land. They made his inheritance "an abomination." Even the priests did not seek God's will; they had no experiential knowledge of him. The rulers transgressed against the Lord. The prophets spoke in the name of the god Baal. All of them followed the unprofitable paths of idolatry (2:4-8).

Third, Jeremiah represented Judah as a speechless defendant. The Lord entered into a legal dispute with the sons of Israel. He charged them with having committed an unprecedented crime. Neither in the far west (Kittim) nor in the eastern desert (Kedar) could be found an example of a nation turning its back upon its gods. Yet Israel had exchanged its true glory (God) for unprofitable idols (2:9-11).

Jeremiah described the heavens as appalled at what they had witnessed in Israel. God's people had committed *two evils*. They had "forsaken the fountain of living waters" (i.e., Yahweh), and they had hewn out for themselves "cisterns" which were broken and could hold no water (2:12f.). Spring water here represents God-given religion; cistern water is man-made religion. The latter can never meet the needs of man in times of emergency.

B. The Bitter Fruit (2:14-19).

Having established the fact of apostasy, the prophet then mentioned what had already happened to Israel, the Northern Kingdom, and what was about to happen to Judah. Israel was supposed to be a son not a slave. Yet they had become a "prey" to foreign powers. Powerful nations ("young lions") had plundered the land leaving cities desolate (2:14f.). From 745-722 BC the Assyrians had systematically destroyed the Northern Kingdom and deported most of her citizens.

Jeremiah next spoke of Judah's future. Humiliation would be inflicted on the *head* of Judah by the men of "Memphis and Tahpanhes," i.e., the Egyptians. The reference may be to the humiliating defeat of Josiah by Pharaoh Neco at the battle of Megiddo in 609 BC and the subsequent deportation of King Jehoahaz to Egypt (2 Kgs 23:29-34). Because of the certainty of prophetic vision, Jeremiah could describe the fate of Judah as a *fait accompli* (2:16).

Any blows to be struck against Judah were self-inflicted. God had done his part. He had led them in their national journey. They, however, had chosen to go the way of political entanglements. They would drink "the waters of the Nile" (Egypt), then that of the

Euphrates (Assyria). In their awe of the great powers, they had lost their fear of God. They had forsaken Yahweh. Such treachery God regarded as "evil and bitter." This "wickedness" and "apostasy" was the real cause of any discipline which the nation might experience (2:17-19).

C. Bitter Forms (2:20-28).

Apostasy takes many forms. Jeremiah flashed a series of word pictures before his readers which were designed to reveal the true nature of turning away from God. First, he likened Judah to a rebellious ox. Israel broke away from the yoke of God's law and refused to serve the Master (2:20a). Second, he pictured Judah as an unrelenting harlot. Under leafy trees on hill-top high places Israel, like a common harlot, indulged in sexual acts. Ritual prostitution was practiced in the Baal cult (2:20b). Third, Judah was also like a degenerate vine. God expended much effort in cultivating Israel. He expected that vine to produce a high-quality red grape. Instead, the vine became degenerate, producing strange fruit (2:21).

Fourth, Jeremiah pictured Judah's apostasy as an indelible stain. Lye and much soap could not remove the stain of their iniquity (2:22). Fifth, Jeremiah painted the picture of the roving camel. Secret devotees of Baal thought that they were undefiled as long as they attended to Temple ritual. The proof of their involvement in the Canaanite cult could be found in the valley of Hinnom in Jerusalem. They were like a young camel. That unreliable and unpredictable animal, for no apparent reason, will run hither and yon (2:23). In the sixth picture Judah's apostasy was compared to a donkey. The wild donkey when in heat searches desperately for a mate, sniffing the wind to catch the scent of the male. The male of the species does not have to exert much effort to find the female under those circumstances. So Judah seemed determined to stay involved in the fertility cult (2:24).

In the seventh picture Jeremiah likened Judah to a persistent paramour. They *loved* strange gods and pursued them until their shoes were worn out and they were faint with thirst. Like a drug addict, they were "hooked" on Baal worship. Pleading with them to change directions was useless (2:25). Finally, Judah was compared to an embarrassed thief. A thief is ashamed when he is caught in his theft. So Judah would one day be put to shame because of attachment to idolatry. How ridiculous to regard a *tree* or a *stone* as the creators of life! The "tree" was the Asherah or wooden pole which represented the female Canaanite deity; the "stone" was the standing pillar representing the male Canaanite deity. Veneration of these pagan symbols was tantamount to turning the back on Yahweh. In times of real national emergency they would discover these gods to be totally impotent (2:26-28).

D. The Bitter Fault (2:29-32).

Who was to blame for the deplorable spiritual condition of Judah? The people "contend" with Yahweh, i.e., they seek to make a legal defense of their conduct. Yet the evidence was clear. All of them had transgressed against the Lord (2:29). With a new series of word pictures Jeremiah assessed the blame for Judah's estrangement from God. First, he compared Judah to a son who refused discipline. God had administered discipline to Judah as needed. Physical calamities called the nation to repentance, but these calls were ignored. Verbal chastisement from the prophets was silenced by violence (2:30).

Second, Jeremiah compared Judah to a pilgrim who rejects guidance. God had not left his people to grope about in a wilderness or in darkness without guidance. Yet they wanted freedom. They defiantly declared their intention never to return to their heavenly Guide (2:31). Third, he compared Judah to a bride who forgets her status. Eastern women wore certain tokens which marked them as married. These tokens were cherished by the young women as reminders of love bestowed and love pledged. Judah, however, had forgotten the love of her divine husband and the sacred vows that bound her to him. Her willful amnesia was not of recent origin, nor was it temporary. This bride had forgotten her husband "days without number" (2:32).

Finally, Jeremiah likened Judah to a harlot who denies her sin. She had no love for her husband, but she was anxious to seek liaisons with every other deity. Even the street walkers could learn a trick or two from Judah! Her love for Baal induced the harlot even to kill innocent people. Taking a life was considered justifiable manslaughter if the victim was caught trying to break into a house. The victims of the Baal-cult zeal, however, were innocent children! (2:33f.). Because

God had not thus far brought down his holy wrath upon them, Judah considered herself innocent of serious wrong doing. This arrogant attitude of innocence in spite of clear evidence to the contrary would force God to come against them in judgment (2:35).

APPEALS BY THE LORD
Jeremiah 3:1-4:4

No matter how absolute the threats of judgment may be, no matter how inextricable the entanglements of sin, repentance opens the door of possibility that judgment can be averted.

A. The Possibility of Repentance (3:1-5).

Under the Law of Moses a woman who had been divorced and married to a second husband could not be reclaimed by the first husband under any circumstances (Deut 24:1-4). Such an action would pollute the land. Judah, however, acted worse than the situation envisioned in the Law. She had not been divorced (Isa 50:1), but she had played the harlot with many lovers. Yet God was willing to take her back! What amazing grace! (3:1).

Everywhere, even out in the open ("bare heights"), evidence of Judah's idolatrous harlotry abounded. As desert Arabs rush forward to greet strangers, so Judah threw herself into the arms of other deities. God had disciplined Judah by withholding the showers which supposedly the storm god Baal controlled. Yet Judah was unashamed of her conduct. She had the brazen face of a prostitute who could engage in the most disgusting perversion and yet show no shame (3:2f.).

God called upon Judah to acknowledge him as Father and Husband right now. They had, as a matter of fact, used these titles for God, but at the same time they had done evil things. They had gotten by with this hypocrisy so far, but God would not restrain his anger for ever (3:4f.).

B. The Need for Repentance (3:6-10).

"Faithless Israel" (the Northern Kingdom) had given herself totally over to the fertility cult. She had practiced her harlotry throughout the land. God had waited in vain for her to return to him. Eventually God had divorced faithless Israel, i.e., sent her off into captivity. Judah observed all this, but failed to learn from it. She took the matter of fidelity to Yahweh lightly and committed adultery with gods of wood and stone. Attempts at reform in Judah were at best half-hearted, at worst hypocritical.

C. The Call for Repentance (3:11-14).

Under the principle that the greater the light, the greater the guilt, "faithless Israel" was considered more righteous in God's eyes than "treacherous Judah." To dramatize this fact, Jeremiah was commanded to "proclaim these words toward the north." He was to invite the scattered tribes of the north to return to the Lord. He promised that he would not look upon them any longer in anger (3:11f.).

To avail themselves of God's grace, they needed to acknowledge and to renounce their previous apostasy. They were still his sons, though woefully disobedient. He would gather the few who recognized him as *Master* and he would bring them to Zion (3:13f.). Some individuals from the scattered northern tribes returned to Jerusalem during the Persian period. The reference, however, appears to be to the messianic Zion (Heb 12:22ff.). The purpose of this call to the northern tribes is to underscore this truth: for individuals there is hope on the other side of national judgment. God would still have a people even after the destruction of physical Jerusalem.

D. The Blessings of Repentance (3:15-18).

The individuals who responded to God's call for repentance would experience wonderful blessings. The down payment on these promises was made in the postexilic period of Old Testament history (c. 538-445 BC). Only in the age of Messiah, however, would the full scope of these blessings be realized. First, God would provide a new leadership ("shepherds") for his people. These leaders would be thoroughly committed to God ("men after my own heart"). Under their leadership the people would be able to grow in knowledge and understanding (3:15). The godly leadership of men like Ezra and Nehemiah was the down payment on this promise. Full realization was found in Messiah, the chief shepherd, and the apostles he appointed to be the teachers of the Church.

Second, once having returned to Canaan, God's people would experience wonderful growth in population "in the land." This was true during the postexilic period. Canaan, however, was but a symbol of the realm over which Messiah would rule (3:16a). Third, a far better worship system would be introduced. The ark, the centerpiece of Mosaic worship, would be absent, but it would not be missed. The Second Temple, which was built during the postexilic period, did not contain the ark. That which the ark symbolized, viz., God's presence among his people, would be realized in the person of Jesus Christ (3:16b).

Fourth, the new age would be characterized by a new revelation (3:17a). The New Jerusalem would be known as "the throne of Yahweh" for there would be his "name," i.e., his revelation of himself. "All nations," i.e., Gentiles, would be attracted to that place. Fifth, a new humility would mark those who inhabited the new Jerusalem. They would no longer walk "after the stubbornness of their evil heart" (3:17b). Sixth, a new unity would be in evidence among Zion's citizens. Representatives of the house of Israel and the house of Judah would jointly return from the land of the north to their ancestral land (3:18). Again, Canaan here is a symbol of that spiritual realm ruled by Messiah. Citizens in his kingdom are all one in the Lord (Gal 3:28).

E. The Plan of Repentance (3:19-25).

The question now raised and answered by God himself is this: How can an apostate people be restored to sonship and inheritance? A good start would be to recognize Yahweh as "Father." Then they must continue from that day forward to walk with the Lord daily. The entire house of Israel had "dealt treacherously" with her husband, and only a radical change on her part could restore the relationship (3:19f.).

Some would respond to God's call for repentance. Jeremiah could hear, as it were, those penitent ones making earnest supplication on the mountain heights. He mentioned that here in order to suggest that "weeping and supplications" are part of genuine repentance. He encouraged those "faithless sons" who were distraught over their spiritual condition to "return." God promised to heal the disease of apostasy if they would heed his call (3:21-22a).

Jeremiah provided for the penitent a model prayer by which they might present appropriately their petition before the Lord. First, they needed to accept Yahweh as their God. This involved a repudiation of the loud Baal-cult festivals as "a deception," i.e., a "rip off." They needed to acknowledge that Yahweh is the only "salvation of Israel." They must confess frankly the depths to which they had been involved in the Baal cult. From the very beginning of their nation they had lavished gifts upon Baal. They had even offered to him as sacrifices their own sons and daughters. They frankly must state how ashamed they were of their long-standing disobedience (3:22b-25).

F. The Rewards of Repentance (4:1-4).

Repentance for Judah involved four specific acts: (1) returning to God; (2) removing abominations; (3) being faithful; and (3) making true oaths. If Judah complied with these requirements, then the nation would be blessed. As a result Gentiles would turn to the God of Judah as a source of blessing (4:1f.).

This long section closes with three dramatic figures for repentance: (1) breaking up the hardened soil of the heart; (2) weeding the heart so that the seed of the word might fall on good ground; and (3) circumcising the heart. The external mark upon their physical body had no significance unless accompanied by internal change (4:3-4a). Jeremiah concluded with a warning: The alternative to repentance was the unquenchable fire of God's wrath (4:4b).

Endnote

1. The Hebrew term *na 'ar* can refer to a person from infancy (Exod 2:6) to about forty-five (Exod 33:11). Estimates of Jeremiah's age at the time of his call range from eight to eighteen.

CHAPTER THIRTEEN

The Power of Preaching
Jeremiah 4:5-8:17

Background of the Unit.

Excerpts from the preaching of Jeremiah continue in the second unit of the book. No compelling reason has been given for dating any of this material to the period after the death of Josiah. Most likely then these materials represent the substance of Jeremiah's preaching during the years 627-609 BC. During this period the power of the crown was on the side of religious reform. No hint of any overt opposition to Jeremiah is found here.

Outline of the Unit.

A. Preaching Regarding Judgment (4:5-6:26).
B. Preaching Regarding Worship (7:1-8:3).
C. Preaching Regarding Knowledge (8:4-17).

PREACHING REGARDING JUDGMENT
Jeremiah 4:5-6:26

Jeremiah grouped his sermon excerpts in a logical progression. In the previous unit he (1) described the desperate sin problem in Judah; and urged the people to repent in order that God might be able to bless them nationally and individually. In this unit he described in detail the alternative to repentance, viz., judgment.

A. Announcement of Coming Judgment (4:5-18).

Jeremiah used three dramatic figures to announce that the judgment of God was coming against Judah.

1. *The lion (4:5-10).* Jeremiah began by describing in second person action verbs the frenzied flight to fortified cities. An unidentified enemy was approaching. As the fortresses of Judah were threatened, people would take final refuge in Jerusalem. This was "the evil from the north" about which Jeremiah was instructed at his call (1:14). The enemy would approach Jerusalem like a lion which leaves its jungle abode to harass men. This "destroyer of nations" would wreak havoc on the cities and countryside as well (4:5-7).

Lamentation would be appropriate in that day as the people come to realize that they are experiencing the unrelenting "fierce anger of the Lord." Kings and princes would be immobilized with fear; prophets and priests dumbfounded, unable to explain the national calamity (4:8f.).

In response to this first distinct revelation of judgment, Jeremiah utters a prayer of complaint. He felt that God had "greatly deceived" the nation. God had given his people reason to believe that the nation would have "peace," i.e., prosperity, security. Jeremiah must be referring either (1) to his own optimistic forecast in 3:14-18; or (2) to the false prophets which God permitted to preach a message of peace (cf. 4:10; 6:14; 8:11). In either case, the charge was ridiculous, and God did not even bother to answer it (4:10).

2. *The tempest (4:11-13).* The hosts of enemy soldiers are envisioned approaching Jerusalem like a blasting whirlwind from the desert. This strong wind would be sent by God, and through it he would pronounce judgments against his people. Jeremiah imagined

what the desperate cry of the people would be in that terrible day: "Woe to us, for we are ruined!"

3. The keepers (4:14-18). Inserted into the midst of this dark judgment passage is another appeal for repentance: "Wash your heart from evil, O Jerusalem." The city personified continued to harbor wicked thoughts in her mind. If she was to be spared, she would need to rid herself of these thoughts (4:14).

Without repentance Jerusalem faced a terrible fate. Jeremiah painted a word picture of that day when the news would be relayed toward Jerusalem from the north (Dan; Mount Ephraim) that the enemy was rapidly approaching. The attackers would besiege Jerusalem, sitting like prison keepers around the perimeter of the capital. No one would be allowed to leave Jerusalem. When this bitter day arrived, Jerusalem would have no one to blame but herself. Her heart, which could not be moved to repentance, in that day would be touched with sorrow (4:15-18).

B. Description of the Coming Judgment (4:19-31).

In describing the judgment which Jerusalem must face, Jeremiah emphasized three points.

1. Terrifying judgment (4:19-22). Through his prophetic gifts Jeremiah could mentally experience the terrors of that judgment day. His heart pounded within him as he heard the sounds of war. One piece of bad news would follow another. The land would suddenly fall to the enemy, as suddenly and completely as a collapsing tent (4:19f.).

Jeremiah protested these terrifying visions of judgment. "How long" must I see them, he asked. Though the complaint is not addressed to God, it is the Lord who answered the question. Visions of judgment must continue because God's people were "foolish." They were "stupid children" who had no walk with God ("know me not") nor spiritual "understanding." They were utterly brilliant when it came to plotting wrong doing; but they did not know the first thing about doing what was right (4:21f.).

2. Devastating judgment (4:23-26). Jeremiah saw in vision the desolate condition of Judah during the exile to Babylon (587-538 BC). He described what he saw with two words taken from the creation vocabulary of Genesis 1, "formless and void." The idea is that the land of Judah would be unorganized and uninhabited as a result of the execution of the fierce anger of Yahweh.

3. *Inevitable judgment (4:27-31).* The poetic description of the devastation of the judgment was not to be taken literally. God would not execute "a complete destruction," but it would be bad enough. Heavens and earth would mourn over the sight. Of this God plainly had spoken, and he would not relent (4:27f.). Judah as a political entity would cease to exist.

Again Jeremiah alluded to the panic of that day. People would hear the approach of cavalry and flee to safety wherever they might find it. In these dark days Judah, like a harlot attempting to woo lovers, would try to seduce foreign nations to come to her aid. Her "lovers" (allies), however, would turn against her and seek her death. Instead of an attractive harlot, Judah would be more like a woman travailing in delivering her first child. Her desperate cries for relief would go unanswered. She would in the end realize that she was at the mercy of ruthless murderers (4:29-31).

C. Causes of the Coming Judgment (5:1-31).

In chapter five the focus is on six reasons why the terrible judgment was necessary.

1. *Moral corruption (5:1-6).* God wanted Jeremiah to see the necessity for the judgment. He instructed him to make a personal investigation. If he could find one righteous man God would spare the city. The prophet's search turned up men who used the name of God in oaths, but only to swear to that which was not true. He knew that God was looking for *justice* in men's dealings with their fellows, and *truth* or faithfulness in their dealings with God. For the lack of these two essential qualities Judah required and received divine discipline. They, however, had refused correction. No matter how severe the disaster, they had hardened their face like a rock (5:1-3).

Jeremiah was still not ready to concede that no righteous man could be found in the nation. He thought that among the wealthy he would find those who had the leisure time to study and know the way of God. He found, however, that they too had "broken the yoke," i.e., they were lawless. Only one fate awaited an ox that broke loose from its yoke and headed for the forest. The wild beasts would rip it to pieces. Because of their many "transgressions" and "apostasies," such would be the fate of Judah at the hands of the ferocious Babylonians (5:4-6).

2. Sexual impurity (5:7-9). Even though Yahweh provided all the material needs for his people, yet they flocked to the house of the temple harlot to participate in the fertility rites of Baal. Their "worship" practices had spilled over into everyday life. Sexual desire had become an uncontrollable animal appetite. Like mindless horses they neighed after the wives of their neighbors. Such a breakdown of sexual mores is an affront to God. He must punish any nation which permits this corruption to take place.

3. Treacherous unbelief (5:10-18). God himself would direct the enemy into his vineyard (Judah) to begin a ruthless pruning process. Those who had been unfaithful to the Lord would be removed by death or exile. A restriction, however, was imposed upon the pruners. They were not to make "a complete destruction" (cf. 4:27) of Judah (5:10).

The entire covenant people (Israel and Judah) had "dealt very treacherously" with the Lord. The most sacred relationship—Israel's marriage to Yahweh—had been violated, and that due to no fault of the Lord. These people did not believe that God could or would bring any calamity upon them. They regarded his spokesmen who prophesied such things as nothing but windbags. They threatened the messengers with the same judgment which had been pronounced on them (5:11-13).

The threats of Jeremiah's preaching were not idle. God assured him that his words would be a judgment fire to consume his skeptical audience. God would bring a mighty nation from afar against the house of Israel. They would overrun the land devouring everything in their path including the fortified cities in which the Jews had put their trust. Yet a remnant would survive; God would not make of them "a complete destruction"[1] (5:14-18).

4. Religious apostasy (5:19-24). Once the divine calamity began to fall, people would seek out the prophet to inquire as to the reason for it. His answer was to be along the following lines. The punishment would be appropriate to the crime. They had served foreign gods in

Canaan; God would make them serve strangers in a foreign land (5:19).

Jeremiah was preaching to a "foolish and senseless people." They were totally insensitive to the creative handiwork of God. They had no reverence for the God who controls the movements of the sea and "gives the rain in its season." While the mighty ocean obeys the will of God, Israel did not. This people had "a stubborn and rebellious heart;" they had departed from the boundaries established by the Law of Moses. They were totally dependent on God for the harvests, but they had no intention of reverencing him[2] (5:20-24).

5. Social injustice (5:25-29). Judah's sins had caused the rains to be withheld. By devious means the wealthy were taking advantage of the innocent. Their houses were full of their ill-gotten gain. They were totally inconsiderate of the rights of the helpless minorities. Acts of injustice are offenses against God and he must avenge them.[3]

6. Corrupt leaders (5:30,31). Jeremiah concludes his list of reasons for judgment with "an appalling and horrible thing." Prophets prophesied falsely and the priests were at their beck and call. The people, however, were as guilty as their leaders for they encouraged the deliberate perversion of divine truth. In the end they all must face God.

D. Approach of Judgment (6:1-30).

Chapter 6 focuses on the enemy which would invade Judah and carry out the judgment decreed by God. Jeremiah developed this theme in six paragraphs.

1. The advance of the foe (6:1-5). Like some merciless brute, evil looked down from the north on "the daughter of Zion," i.e., the inhabitants of Jerusalem. This comely daughter was "dainty," i.e., not accustomed to the deprivations to which she now would be exposed. Even Jerusalem no longer provided safety. In dramatic second person verbs Jeremiah called upon the the "sons of Benjamin" to leave the capital. Warning trumpets should be sounded in the villages south of Jerusalem (6:1f.). The point is that the northern enemy would not stop until he had reached the southern border of Judah.

The invaders would be like "shepherds" who graze their flocks undisturbed in the portion of the city assigned to them. Jeremiah imagined the the attackers urging each other to undertake a surprise attack at noontime and at night when normally both sides would desist from battle. The point is that the attack would be relentless (6:3-5).

2. The siege of Jerusalem (6:6-8). God ordered the attacking force to build the high mounds from which they could shoot into the city. This order was justified on the grounds that oppression continuously bubbled forth like a fountain in Jerusalem. Throughout the city victims of mistreatment lay sick and wounded. Such a situation called for the righteous judgment of God. Jerusalem should be forewarned. The city was nearing the point of totally alienating God. If that were to happen, Jerusalem would become a desolation without inhabitant.

3. The success of the foe (6:9-15). Only a remnant of the once proud nation survived in Judah. Now that remnant was about to be gleaned like grapes from a vine. God urged the grape gatherer to continue his work. The figure pressed home the idea that Judah would experience repeated calamities (6:9).

Jeremiah knew that the people of Judah were paying no heed to his warnings. Their ears were "uncircumcised," i.e., closed. They regarded the word of the Lord as a "reproach;" they had no delight in it. Jeremiah tried to hold back the message of doom, but he could not. He was filled with the message of divine wrath. In self-exhortation the prophet urged himself to "pour it out"[4] on the entire population from the children in the street to the aged (6:10f.).

The hand of God was stretched out against Jerusalem and justifiably so. Everyone, even the spiritual leaders, was guilty of greed. The religious leaders tried to heal the serious wounds of the nation with assurances of peace. The leaders felt no shame over their conduct. They "did not even know how to blush." When God punished them, however, they would share the humiliating fate of those they misguided (6:12-15).

4. Prescription for deliverance (6:16-21). Could Jerusalem be delivered from the ravishing invasion? Yes indeed! The nation at this moment was at a crossroads. Only the old paths of fidelity to God would give them rest for their souls. The problem was that Judah adamantly refused to walk in those paths. God had set "watchmen," i.e., prophets, over the people to warn them of impending invasion.

They stubbornly refused to listen to the warning (6:16f.).

In view of the intransigence of his people, God really had no alternative but to unleash judgment. The nations of the world were called upon to hear God's pronouncement against Judah: "I am bringing disaster upon this people." This judgment would demonstrate the folly of refusing to hear God's spoken word through the prophets, and his written word in the Law (6:18f.).

Disobedient people can render no meaningful worship to the Lord. Judah orchestrated elaborate worship rituals. They sent to distant lands to secure Temple incense. Yet their burnt offerings and other sacrifices were not acceptable to the Lord. Because that was true, God was about to lay before them a stumbling block which they could not avoid (6:20f.). The stumbling block is the invasion in which many would perish.

5. *Description of the foe (6:22-26).* Jeremiah described the unnamed enemy from the north in terrifying detail. He pictured them coming "from the remote parts of the earth." The ruthless hordes would be armed to the teeth. Their approaching cavalry would sound like the roar of the ocean. This mighty invader would swoop down upon the defenseless "daughter of Zion," i.e., the population of Jerusalem (6:22f.).

At the approach of the invader the population of Jerusalem would be thrown into panic. In the dramatic first and second person, Jeremiah describes that panic. He likened it to the experience of a woman beginning the travail of childbirth. No one would be able leave the city for the enemy would control the countryside. In view of the sad fate awaiting Judah, Jeremiah called on his countrymen to lament (6:24-26).

6. *The hopeless task of the prophet (6:27-30).* In an aside to the prophet, God warned Jeremiah that his task would not be easy. He fearlessly could continue to test the way of the people by his preaching, for God had made him a "tower" and a "fortress"[5] in their midst. He would find this people, however, were "stubbornly rebellious" and "corrupt." They were as hard as iron in their sin, especially talebearing. Even a smelting fire heated to its hottest could not separate the dross ("wicked") from the precious. Since the impurities could not be removed, this "silver" must be cast aside as worthless.

PREACHING REGARDING WORSHIP
Jeremiah 7:1-8:3

One's attitude toward worship is reflected in his attitude toward life in general. At the root of the sin problem in Judah was worship which presumed that God had an obligation to continue being gracious to Judah.

A. Presumptuous Worship (7:1-15).

Jeremiah was directed by God to stand at the main entrance to the Temple and to proclaim God's word to the throngs. These smug worshipers believed that since the Temple was in Jerusalem, they were safe from destruction. Jeremiah shocked them by insisting that only if they "amend" their ways and deeds would they be allowed to remain in their land. Chanting "This is the temple of the Lord" in response to every call for repentance was deceptive. The mere presence of that sacred building could not spare Judah from judgment (7:1-4). Why was this so?

First, the presence of the Temple could not spare Judah because the land promise was conditional. Judah needed to start practicing "justice between a man and his neighbor." Specifically, they were not to oppress the helpless (alien, orphan, widow). They were to cease shedding the blood of innocent children in sacrifice to Baal. They were not to walk after other gods. The land promise made to the Patriarchs was conditional. Only if Israel lived righteously would they be allowed to dwell in the land (7:5-7).

Second, any theology which said Jerusalem was safe because of the Temple failed to take note of the hypocrisy practiced there. Those who came to the Temple had been guilty of stealing, murder, adultery, and false swearing. They had sacrificed to Baal and walked after other gods as well. Yet because they went through the motions of rendering homage to Yahweh, they thought they were safe. What was worse, they thought this hypocritical lifestyle could continue unabated. They had turned the Temple into a refuge for those who had committed criminal acts. That sacred place was nothing but "a den of robbers!" Their spiritual duplicity had not gone unnoticed by Yahweh (7:8-11).

Third, history refuted their theology. Jeremiah cited two examples which should have refuted the notion that the presence of the Temple guaranteed national survival. First, he urged his auditors to consider the fate of the sacred town of Shiloh. For over three hundred years after Joshua had conquered the land, Shiloh had been the worship center of Israel. In the days of Eli and Samuel that sacred place had been destroyed by the Philistines "because of the wickedness of my people Israel." Judah had done similar wickedness, and had spurned every effort of God to call them to repentance. God therefore would do to the Temple and to Jerusalem what he had done to Shiloh (7:12-14).

The second example from history concerned the fate of the Northern Kingdom (Ephraim). They too could trace their descent to Abraham. They too worshiped Yahweh, albeit in a corrupted form under the image of a calf (1 Kgs 12:28). Yet God "cast them out" of their land. The same would happen to Judah (7:15).

B. Pagan Worship (7:16-20).

Prayers of intercession on behalf of corrupt Judah were of no avail. No longer would judgment be postponed unless, of course, there was massive repentance. Why? Because the influence of paganism was obvious throughout the land. The entire population had engaged in the worship of false gods. Children gathered wood for sacrificial fires. Women made little sacramental cakes to honor the Queen of Heaven (the goddess Ashtoreth). Men poured out libations to other gods. Since idolatry was inherently ridiculous, they must have engaged in these activities for one purpose: "to provoke," i.e., hurt, Yahweh (7:16-18).

In reality the sinners were hurting only themselves by participating in pagan worship. God would "pour out" his wrath on Judah, its inhabitants, its flora, and its fauna. The burning anger of God would not be quenched until the place had been destroyed (7:19f.).

C. Priorities in Worship (7:21-28).

Thus far Jeremiah has attacked the spiritual overconfidence of Judah by arguing two points: neither the presence of the Temple nor the prayers of those who worshiped there could deliver Judah from judgment. But what about other acts of worship? Jeremiah argued that worship ritual in general was not as important as willing obedience to the word of God. Let them increase the number of sacrifices! That would accomplish nothing. Their sacrifices had lost all religious significance. At Sinai God had not spoken to their fathers "concerning," i.e., out of concern for, sacrifices.[6] Obedience in daily walk was the fundamental obligation of the Mosaic covenant. According to that covenant national well-being depended on their willingness to heed the voice of God. The fathers, however, paid no heed. They "went backward and not forward" (7:21-24).

Nothing had changed since the day God had brought the fathers out of Egypt. He had urgently[7] dispatched "my servants the prophets" to proclaim the divine word. His people, however, did not listen. In fact, they were more evil than their fathers. The current generation would not listen to Jeremiah any more than their fathers had listened to earlier prophets. All Jeremiah could do was publicly to accuse them of obstinacy. Faith or truth had vanished from their prayers and praise (7:25-28).

D. Polluted Worship (7:29-8:3).

The prospects of Judah called forth lamentation. Jeremiah urged his auditors to "cut off your hair and cast it away" as a sign of agony. Because their worship had been tainted by paganism, Yahweh had rejected "the generation of his wrath." "Detestable things," i.e., idols, had been set up in the Temple (cf. 2 Kgs 21:5-7). Special high places of *Topheth* ("fireplace") had been built in the valley of Hinnom on the west side of Jerusalem. Here God's people offered up their sons and daughters to the god Molech. Such a practice was totally contrary to everything for which Yahweh stood (7:29-31).

God's wrath would be poured out on the perverted worship at Topheth. So many would die there that the valley of Hinnom would come to be called the valley of Slaughter. Burial places for all the corpses would be impossible to find. The unburied bodies would be ravished by beasts and birds. The entire land of Judah would become a ruin, a place of gloom and sadness (7:32-34).

The enemy in search for treasure would violate the tombs of nobility. The bones of these people would be scattered across the face of the ground. The sun and moon, objects of their worship, would look down helplessly upon the gruesome scene (8:1f.).

Would any escape this judgment? Yes, but their lives would be hard. Those who fled to neighboring lands would be so persecuted that they would prefer death to life (8:3).

PREACHING REGARDING KNOWLEDGE
Jeremiah 8:4-17

Men may learn hard spiritual lessons by heeding the word of God. That is the easy way. Judah chose to reject God's word and learn these truths the hard way, viz., through their national suffering. In 8:4-17 Jeremiah pointed out Judah's willful ignorance of God's word. He described the self-deception and public deception of the spiritual leaders. Finally, he depicted the harsh circumstances under which Judah would finally comprehend the enormity of her sin.

A. A Willful Ignorance (8:4-7).

Men who fall down normally attempt to get up. Men who get off the right path normally try to get back on track. Yet Judah persisted in apostasy. Jeremiah listened in vain for some sign of repentance. What he observed instead was each individual recklessly pursuing his own interests like a horse charging into battle. In their migratory instincts the birds routinely follow God's will. Judah, however, did not know "the ordinance of the Lord." To use a proverbial expression, they did not have the sense that God gave geese! (8:4-7).

B. An Arrogant Boast (8:8-10).

The leaders of Judah boasted of their wisdom. They had the Law of God; they did not need a prophet like Jeremiah. Such a boast was inappropriate for two reasons. First, "the lying pen of the scribes" had attempted to alter, nullify or circumvent the written Law. Second, these men rejected the prophetic word of God. When "wise" men do that, "what kind of wisdom do they have?" Third, when these worldly-wise leaders fell into the hands of their adversaries they would be put to shame. In that day all would be lost, loved ones as well as possessions. Fourth, all the spiritual leaders were "greedy for gain." They were not objective in the advice which they dispensed (8:8-10).

C. A Deceptive Forecast (8:11-12).

Jeremiah cited an example of the deceitful messages of the priests and prophets. The kingdom of Judah faced invasion, siege, exile, and political extinction. Jeremiah likened this fate to a disease which he called "the brokenness of the daughter of my people." The spiritual leaders were attempting to "heal" this disease superficially. They promised *shalom* (peace, well-being) when in fact the future held in store the very opposite. For them to create in the minds of trusting souls a false sense of security was abomination. Yet these men had no shame for what they had done. They did not "know how to blush!" In the day of judgment they would fall along with those they had misled. They would be brought down. That was God's revelation.

D. A Painful Discovery (8:13-17).

Having described the fate of the religious leaders, Jeremiah turned to the nation they had deceived. Judah was unproductive. God, therefore, would give them into the hands of an overpowering army. In that day the residents of the countryside would be forced to flee to the cities for safety. In gloomy fatalism, there they would expect to die by pestilence, i.e., plague. They would understand full well that this "poisoned water" was theirs to drink because they had sinned against Yahweh (8:13f.).

Judah listened to her false prophets and expected "peace" and national "healing." Instead she faced "terror." Jeremiah could hear, as it were, the thundering hooves of the enemy cavalry at Dan, the northern most city of Canaan. This horde was coming to devour both the rural regions and the cities. Just as God had sent fiery serpents among his people in the days of Moses (Num 21:6), so these enemies would be like poisonous snakes throughout the land. None of the political leaders of Judah would be able to charm them into harmlessness (8:15-17).

Endnotes

1. That God would not make a complete destruction of Judah is stated in 4:27 and 5:10, and with slight variation, in 30:11 and 46:28.

2. "They did not say" in 5:24 is an example of what Sheldon Blank called "unprayer," i.e., things God would like to have heard his people say in prayer, but which they never said.

3. The expression "on a nation such as this shall I not avenge myself" occurs three times: 5:9, 29; 9:9.

4. Some think that 6:11 is a prayer calling on God to pour out his wrath. The distinguishing mark of prayer, however, is address to God. That is missing from this verse. This suggests the interpretation that Jeremiah is employing the technique of self-exhortation.

5. The KJV rendering *tower* and *fortress* is defended by Theo. Laetsch, *Bible Commentary Jeremiah* (St. Louis: Concordia, 1965) 89f. NASB renders the words *assayer* and *tester.*

6. Critics have forced on 7:22 an interpretation which makes Jeremiah deny the Mosaic origin of the Old Testament sacrificial system. For a refutation of this view see James E. Smith, *Jeremiah and Lamentations* in Bible Study Textbook Series (Joplin, MO: College Press, 1972) 232-235.

7. The literal expression is *rising early and sending* which appears, with slight variation, eleven times in the book.

CHAPTER FOURTEEN

Prophetic Agony and Prayer
Jeremiah 8:18-13:27

Background of the Unit.

Dating the contents of Jeremiah 8-13 is extremely difficult. Most of the material seems to come from the early reign of Jehoiakim, prior to the battle of Carchemish.[1] Chronologically that would place this unit between 609 and 605 BC.

Good King Josiah died as a result of wounds received in the battle of Megiddo in 609 BC. The "people of the land," i.e., the landed aristocracy, then took Josiah's son Jehoahaz and placed him on the throne. Pharaoh Neco, who was still campaigning in northern Syria, did not like this choice. He summoned the young king to Riblah, and then deported him to Egypt. Neco selected Eliakim, another son of Josiah, to install as his vassal on the throne. The Pharaoh gave Eliakim the throne name Jehoiakim. Judah was placed under heavy tribute obligations to Egypt (2 Kgs 23:28-35).

Jehoiakim was as evil as his father was righteous. Because he no longer had the backing of the throne, Jeremiah's ministry became intolerably painful. The audience which had rebuffed him for eighteen years, now began to plot his demise.

Outline of the Unit.

A. The Prophet's Pain (8:18-9:22; 10:17-25).
B. The Prophet's Preaching (9:23-10:16; 11:1-17).
C. The Prophet's Problem (11:18-12:17).
D. The Prophet's Parables (chap. 13).

THE PROPHET'S PAIN
Jeremiah 8:18-9:22; 10:17-25

The unbearable pain of Jeremiah rises to the surface in this section. His spiritual agony was triggered by the revelation of Judah's impending destruction, national corruption, complete desolation, and ruthless deportation.

A. Impending Destruction (8:18-9:1).

Jeremiah experienced a sorrow beyond healing because of the revelations of future judgment. He seemed to hear a dialogue between the future captives and God. The former questioned why God, if he really lived in Zion, would permit the city to fall. The Lord responded by pointing to the chief cause, viz., the idols by which they had "provoked" him to wrath. The future exiles responded with a complaint of unfairness. They felt that they were continuing to suffer even after the harvest of judgment was past (8:18-20).

The despair of the people caused Jeremiah to despair. The wound of Zion was deep. No medicine (balm) or physician could heal her. Jeremiah wished that he could produce an inexhaustible supply of tears so that he might lament the inevitable doom of his people (8:21-9:1).

B. National Corruption (9:2-8).

Jeremiah longed for a hermit's life away from the corruption of society. In his opinion the men of Judah were all "adulterers," i.e., they are idolaters. Even when gathered in their religious assemblies these men were "treacherous," i.e., hypocritical and untrustworthy. The tongue of each man was a deadly bow hurling deceit and falsehood. They proceeded from one evil enterprise to the next without interruption. They did not "know" the Lord, i.e., have a daily walk with him (9:2f.).

Jeremiah thought that no one in Judah could be trusted. Brothers (kinsmen) and neighbors were involved in fraudulent schemes and slanderous attacks. No one spoke the truth; they had "taught their tongue to speak lies." They worked so hard at committing iniquity that they had wearied themselves (8:4f.).

The Lord concurred with Jeremiah's negative assessment of his society. The prophet lived "in the midst of deceit." This deceit had prevented this people from "knowing" God, i.e., having an experiential walk with the Lord (9:6).

A radical refining process was the only alternative for those who refused to know the Lord. Those who used their tongues as a deadly weapon were dross which must be purged away. God must bring punishment on a nation which had obliterated the distinction between truth and untruth [2](9:7-9).

C. Complete Desolation (9:9-22).

Because of the impending disaster, a lamentation for the "mountains" and "pastures" of Judah was in order. These areas would be left so desolate by the vengeance of God that the sounds of birds and cattle would no longer be heard there. Jerusalem and the other cities of the land would be left in ruins inhabited only by wild animals (9:10f.). Shortly after 587 BC this prophecy was fulfilled.

Conventional wisdom could not explain the disaster which would befall Judah. Those who pretended to receive divine revelations had no word of explanation. Yahweh alone could answer the question "Why is the land ruined?" The people of Judah had forsaken God's Law and had refused to obey his voice as he spoke through prophets. They chose rather to walk "after the stubbornness of their own heart," i.e., after the god Baal. This behavior they had learned from their fathers (9:12-14).

Because of their apostasy the Lord would feed this people with "wormwood" and give them "gall" to drink. These two poisonous substances were symbols in the Old Testament for bitter affliction. Judah would be carried away captive. Even in captivity, however, the sword of divine retribution would pursue them until every unrepentant sinner among them had been annihilated (9:15f.).

Since judgment was inevitable, lamentation was appropriate. The professional mourning women should be summoned so that they might stimulate sorrow in this people who were impervious to prophetic announcements of doom. Though no one would weep now, Zion in that day would wail in her agony over her ruin, shame, and expulsion from the land (9:17-19).

Jeremiah exhorted the women of Judah to teach their daughters how to weep. They would need that skill in the day of judgment. What a day that would be! Pestilence would appear to come through the windows. Children and youth would be cut down by the plague in the streets. Outside the city the fields would be littered with the unburied corpses of soldiers fallen in battle (9:20-21).

D. Ruthless Deportation (10:17-22).

Those who would experience the future siege of Jerusalem should not hold out for deliverance. They should pack their meager belongings in a bundle, hobo style, and prepare to be deported from the land. The inhabitants of Judah were about to be violently expelled from their land. This deportation would cause God's people much distress, but it would also have a positive result. Those who were truly the Lord's would be *found*. Their experience would drive them back to the Lord (10:17-18).

Jeremiah's knowledge of what would befall his people was like a "wound" or "sickness" which he must bear. He pronounced a "woe" upon himself, i.e., he laments his own misery. He compared Judah to a tent which had collapsed because the cords had been cut. No one remained to help erect the national tent again (10:19f.).

The "shepherds" (political leaders) were responsible for the threatened judgment. They had become "stupid." They had not "sought the Lord," i.e., sought his counsel. Acting on human wisdom alone, the shepherds had not been successful in steering an independent course. Therefore, the flock would be scattered far and wide. In his mind Jeremiah could hear the report from the north. The enemy which would make Judah a desolation was on its way (10:21f.).

E. The Fairness Issue (10:23-25).

Jeremiah was a great intercessor. In the prayer which concludes chapter 10 Jeremiah empathized with his people. He acknowledged man's weakness and waywardness and urged this as a ground for God's mercy. Man cannot guide himself in moral and religious matters; he needs divine direction which sometimes may come in the form of discipline. Jeremiah pled for a measured punishment of Judah, one which would not totally destroy the small nation. Judah may deserve discipline; but the Gentiles deserved God's full wrath. Justice demanded destruction of those nations which had "devoured Jacob and laid waste his habitation."

THE PROPHET'S PREACHING
Jeremiah 9:23-10:16; 11:1-17

Jeremiah has collected several sermon notes on various themes in this section of the book. These samples demonstrate the power of this man as a proclaimer of God's Word.

A. Sermonettes on Priorities (9:22-25).

Two sermonettes set forth what for Jeremiah were the great priorities of life. The first emphasizes the importance of knowing God. The most important thing in life is not wisdom, strength or wealth. If one must boast about anything it should be that he understands and knows (by experience) the Lord. The God of the Bible exercises loving kindness, justice, and righteousness on earth. To know him means to put into practice these fundamental principles in which he delights (9:22-23). This passage is cited by Paul in 2 Corinthians 10:17.

The second sermonette stresses the importance of hearing God. Even though they were circumcised physically, the men of Judah were uncircumcised spiritually, i.e., their hearts were closed to the word of God. Their circumcision meant no more to God than the circumcision of some of the Gentile nations of the day. God planned to punish all who were uncircumcised of heart whether or not they were circumcised of flesh (9:24-25).

B. Sermon on Idolatry (10:1-16).

God's people are not to imitate pagan practices. They are not to be terrified by the "signs of the heavens" as are heathen people. Pagan customs are but superstition. Idols originate in the craftsman's shop. They are ornate but impotent. They must still be fastened down so they will not totter. They are as mute and immobile as a "scarecrow in a cucumber field." God's people are not to fear them, for they cannot help or hurt anyone (10:1-5).

As Jeremiah reflected upon the greatness of Israel's God, he broke forth into a spontaneous prayer of praise.[3] Yahweh has no equal among the gods of the nations. He is great. His name, i.e., the sum of his revealed attributes, is great in might. He is rightfully addressed as "King of the nations." Fear or reverence is the appropriate response to such a God. No wise man or prince among all the nations can be compared to the Lord (10:6-7).[4]

As the sermon resumed, Jeremiah amplified his previous remarks about the origin of idols. Wisemen and princes who worship lifeless lumber are stupid and foolish in the delusion of idolatry. True, the idols may be objects of beauty, decorated with the most expensive silver, gold[5] and even clothing. They evidence the most exquisite craftsmanship. Idols are, however, only the creation of men. On the other hand, Yahweh is "the true God, the living God, the everlasting King." His wrath sometimes is displayed in mighty earthquakes which the nations of the world cannot endure (10:8-10).

Created gods will perish from the earth. Only Yahweh, who created the heavens and earth by his wisdom and power, is eternal. This Creator, not Baal, is responsible for the rain storms upon which Canaan was so dependent (10:11-13).

Every man who engages in idolatry is stupid. In the day of judgment even those who manufactured the idols would be ashamed. In that day the idols would prove themselves to be "worthless, a work of mockery" unable even to save themselves. That would not be the case with Yahweh. What is more, this one who created everything is "the Portion of Jacob." He belonged to Israel in a special way (10:14-16).

C. Sermon on the Covenant (11:1-17).

Jeremiah was to hear and then proclaim throughout Judah the

"words of this covenant." The reference most likely is to the law-book discovered in the Temple during the reformation of Josiah in 621 BC. The one who did not "hear," i.e., obey, this covenant was under the curse of God (11:1-3).

The covenant which Jeremiah was to preach was ancient. It had been given by Yahweh to their forefathers in that day when he had brought them out of "the furnace of fire," i.e., Egypt. Agreement to abide by this covenant was what made the Israelites God's people. The land promises made to the Patriarchs were conditional. Only if Judah remained faithful to the covenant could the nation continue to dwell in the land flowing with milk and honey (cf. Deut 7:8ff; 8:18ff.). In the shortest prayer in the book, Jeremiah indicated his agreement with the terms of the covenant and his readiness to preach it: "Amen, O Lord!" (11:4f.).

Jeremiah was to deliver his message on the covenant throughout the land of Judah. He was to call upon his audience to "hear the words of this covenant and do them." From the day God had brought their fathers out of Egypt until that day God had persistently and urgently admonished the Israelites to "listen to my voice." They, however, did not obey and chose to walk in the "stubbornness of their evil heart." Through the years God had brought upon his people all of the disasters which were stipulated in the covenant as the punishment for unfaithfulness (11:6-8).

Jeremiah's generation had joined as it were the original generation and former northern kingdom in conspiracy (treason) against their King. Therefore, God would bring upon them an inescapable calamity. They may cry to him in that day, but he would not listen. Their new gods to whom they burned incense would not be able to save them in that day. Every city in Judah had its patron god. Every street in Jerusalem had an incense altar to Baal, "the shameful thing." Neither individually nor collectively would these deities provide any aid in the day of Yahweh's wrath (11:9-13).

Jeremiah might as well cease making intercession for the impenitent people of Judah. Prayer could not hold back any longer the grinding wheels of justice. God's beloved wife, i.e., Judah, no longer had any right to reside in God's house, i.e., the Temple. All the sacrifices in the world were useless when the worshipers actually rejoiced over their evil ways (11:14-15).

At one time God had regarded Judah as "a green olive tree." The form and fruit of this tree were a delight to easterners. The tree, however, was now worthless. The branches would to be broken off and burned. None other than the Lord, who planted that tree in the beginning, pronounced "evil," i.e., calamity, against those who had committed *evil* against him. What evil had they done? They had offered sacrifices to Baal in order to "provoke" the Lord (11:16f.).

THE PROPHET'S PROBLEM
Jeremiah 11:18-12:17

During the reign of Jehoiakim the underlying animosity against Jeremiah bubbled forth in overt attacks. The first situation arose in the prophet's hometown of Anathoth. Faced with this new development, Jeremiah (1) presented his case to God; (2) made a complaint to the Lord; and (3) finally received divine correction.

A. The Case Presented (11:18-23).

Yahweh made known to Jeremiah that a plot had been devised against him. The prophet was totally naive and unsuspecting, like a lamb being led to slaughter. The plot was to "destroy the tree" (Jeremiah) "and its fruit" (any who might be listening to the prophet). Their intention was to "cut him off from the land of the living," i.e., kill him, "that his name be remembered no more." Faced with this serious threat, Jeremiah turned to the Lord. He knew that God judges righteously because he alone can see the internal motive as well as the external act. In faith he asked for God's "vengeance on them," i.e., his righteous sentence. He was content to leave the entire matter in God's hands, for he said, "to Thee have I committed my cause" (11:18-20).

Those who were plotting against Jeremiah were from his hometown at Anathoth. Once their intentions were revealed, they made their threats public. "Do not prophesy in the name of the Lord, that you might not die at our hand!" Since the attack here was against his chosen messenger, Yahweh himself pronounced sentence against the conspirators. They would be punished. Their young men would die by the sword in battle. Other family members would die by famine holed up in fortified cities. Not even a remnant would be left to those evil men in that day when God brought upon Anathoth the time of its punishment (11:21-23).

B. The Complaint Registered (12:1-4).

Some time must have elapsed, and the men of Anathoth continued to thrive, and presumably harass Jeremiah. Again the prophet brought his complaint to the Lord. He started by acknowledging that God is righteous in all that he does. Nonetheless, from Jeremiah's perspective a grave injustice had been done. Jeremiah asked the age-old question, "Why has the way of the wicked prospered?" He charged that the Lord actually had "planted" these wicked men. That they had taken root, grown and produced fruit was therefore God's fault (12:1-2a).

Jeremiah was further perplexed by God's leniency with his enemies when he compared himself to them. They were hypocrites who talked much about God, but did not have him in their hearts. On the other hand, God knew Jeremiah; his heart was an open book before the Lord. Therefore, God should punish the adversaries, should "drag them off like sheep to the slaughter." Jeremiah was asking for the execution of the sentence which God already had pronounced in the concluding verse of chapter 11 (12:2b-3).

Still another consideration argued for God's immediate action against the plotters. The Anathoth enemies intended to kill Jeremiah so that "he will not see our latter ending," i.e., they would kill him before any of prophetic threats against the land came to pass. Because of their attitude, God had sent a famine upon the land. The vegetation was withering; the animals were suffering. The innocent suffered because of the wickedness of these incorrigible cutthroats (12:4).

C. The Correction Received (12:5-13).

By means of two questions the Lord pointed out to Jeremiah that his present difficulties with the men of Anathoth ("run with footmen; land of peace") were relatively minor compared to what he would experience in the future ("compete with horses; thicket of Jordan").

Even members of his own family would conspire against him. They may say nice things to him, but they would treacherously betray their own flesh and blood (12:5f.).

Jeremiah was full of self-pity because of the persecution which had been unleashed against him. God helped him put his own hurt in proper perspective by revealing to him the greater hurt which the Lord had experienced. He had forsaken his house, the Temple. He had abandoned his inheritance, the land of promise. He had given his beloved people into the hand of their enemies. Nothing which Jeremiah had experienced could approach this pain (12:7).

Three figures were used to depict the current status of God's inheritance (his people). (1) They had become like a hostile lion encountered in the forest. They had defied God, and he had come to "hate" his people, i.e., treat them as an object of his hatred. (2) Judah was like an odd-colored bird which other birds of prey (nations) plucked to pieces and which scavenger beasts then devoured. (3) Judah was a vineyard or pleasant field which had been trampled down into a desolate wilderness (12:8-10).

God was grieved over the condition of the land. None of the leaders of the nation, however, were concerned about the impending disaster. Even in the most remote areas of the land the sword of divine judgment wielded by the enemy would do its deadly work. No one was safe from the spoiler. But why such tragedy? With their political scheming the leaders thought they had sown "wheat," i.e., something beneficial. Because of the fierce anger of the Lord they would in fact reap "thorns," i.e., humiliation, ruin, destruction and death (12:11-13).

God continued to correct the thinking of Jeremiah by revealing to him the ultimate objective of the forthcoming judgment. God would punish the wicked who laid hands on his inheritance by uprooting those nations from their lands. Of course Judah would be uprooted along with those Gentile nations. Judgment, however, would be followed by compassion. Each nation would be allowed to return to its own inheritance (12:14f.).

Nations which were converted to the worship of Yahweh would "be built up in the midst of my people." As evidence of their conversion they would swear by the name Yahweh. To swear by the name of a deity implied recognition of the supremacy of that deity. Nations which refused to obey the Lord would face continual uprooting by God (12:16f.).

THE PROPHET'S PARABLES
Jeremiah 13:1-17

Five parables of Jeremiah are recorded in chapter 13. The first is an action parable; the others are verbal. The date of this material is hard to determine, but most likely it comes from the reign of King Jehoiakim (609-598 BC).

A. Parable of the Linen Girdle (13:1-11).

Jeremiah was told to purchase for himself a linen girdle, but not to put it in water. This colorful waistband was used to hold the loose upper garment in place. Why he was not to put the garment in water is unclear. Jeremiah carried out the instructions. For some time the prophet wore the girdle about his waist (13:1f.).

A second word from the Lord directed Jeremiah to make a three hundred mile journey to the Euphrates river.[6] There he was to bury his girdle "in a crevice of the rock." Jeremiah carried out these instructions. "After many days" the Lord directed the prophet to retrieve his girdle from its hiding place at the Euphrates. He found the garment to be "ruined." It was "totally worthless" (13:3-7).

God had intended that the whole house of Israel "cling" to him, as a girdle clings to a man. They were to be God's people, a source of "renown, praise and glory" to the Lord. Israel, however, would not listen. They stubbornly walked after other gods. Therefore, God would destroy the pride of Judah which made them as worthless as the rotten girdle of the prophet (13:8-11).

B. Parable of the Wineskins (13:12-14).

A commonplace observation by Jeremiah provoked ridicule. He pointed out the obvious truth that empty wineskins were refilled with wine. The inhabitants of Judah were spiritually empty. They would be filled with the wine of God's wrath. They would stagger over one another to their own destruction. This catastrophe faced Judah in spite of God's compassion.

C. Parable of the Path (13:15-17).

One who is walking a narrow mountain path hopes for more light as the sun begins to set. Pitch darkness in such a situation would mean sure disaster. Such was the precarious condition of the proud citizens of Judah. Jeremiah urged them to "give glory" to the Lord before the complete darkness of judgment fell upon them. The prophet knew that if his plea for repentance was not heeded the destruction of the nation was inevitable. All he could do was weep over their stubborn pride and the fate to which it would lead.

D. Parable of the Royal Family (13:18-19).

Jeremiah was commanded to address a message to "the king and the queen mother."[7] The anonymity of this address and the lack of specificity as to chronological setting give to these words a parabolic quality. With prophetic sarcasm Jeremiah urged the king and queen mother to get down from their throne. The point is that the royalty of Judah was about to be humbled. The land would be overrun. In the face of this invasion even the gates of cities in the Negev to the south would be locked. All Judah would be carried into exile. These predictions began to be fulfilled in March of 597 BC when King Jehoiachin surrendered Jerusalem to the Babylonians and marched into captivity with ten thousand of his countrymen.

E. Parable of the Delinquent Daughter (13:20-27).

The daughter of Zion was commanded to lift up her eyes and see that vast horde approaching from the north. Jeremiah asked five questions which were designed to point out the plight of Jerusalem in this desperate time. First, Jerusalem would be like a shepherd who cannot account for his lost sheep. The cities for which Jerusalem was responsible would fall to the enemy. Second, Jerusalem would be embarrassed when her "companions" (allies) become her oppressors. Third, when faced with the predicted crisis, Jerusalem would be like a woman facing the travail of childbirth (13:20f.).

Fourth, Jerusalem would be perplexed by all which befalls her. She would ask, "Why have these things happened to me?" The answer can be given in advance: "Because of the ingratitude of your iniquity." The daughter of Zion would be treated as an adulteress. She would be stripped, even of her shoes, and forced to go into captivity naked. The fifth question pointed to the tenacious hold that sin had on the nation. Doing evil had become second nature. For them to do anything good seemed as impossible as for a leopard to change his spots or an Ethiopian the color of his skin (13:22f.).

Jerusalem's fate was to be scattered like chaff before the wind. This was "the portion" which God had measured to them because they preferred the falsehood of idolatry to the Lord. As an adulteress was shamed by having her garments removed prior to stoning, so God would expose the shame of Judah. Of Judah's guilt there could be no doubt. God himself had seen her "adulteries" and "neighings," i.e., passionate cravings for illegitimate objects of worship. God had seen her "abominations" on the hills throughout the land. As long as she remained unclean, Jerusalem was living under a divine "woe," i.e., threat of judgment (13:24-27).

Endnotes

1. A placement prior to the battle of Carchemish in 605 BC is proposed because the Chaldeans are not mentioned by name in this section.

2. The language of 9:9 is found also in 5:9, 29.

3. The prayer in 10:6, 7 is a rhetorical prayer, i.e., a prayer used for audience impact within the context of a sermon.

4. It is not clear at what point the prayer in chapter 10 ends and the sermon resumes. Verses 8-9 might be part of the prayer, possibly also verse 10.

5. "Tarshish" generally is thought to be located on the southwest coast of Spain. "Uphaz" is an unknown location, likely in the opposite direction from Tarshish, i.e., east of Judah.

6. For a defense of the literal interpretation of this command see James E. Smith, *Jeremiah and Lamentations* in Bible Study Textbook Series (Joplin, MO: College Press, 1972) 294-96.

7. The king here is usually identified as Jehoiachin who reigned three months in 587 BC. The queen mother would then be Nehushta (2 Kgs 24:8).

CHAPTER FIFTEEN

Problems and Prayer Jeremiah 14-20

Background of the Unit.

Jeremiah 14-20 most likely should be dated to the reign of Jehoiakim between 605 and 597 BC. Jehoiakim had been placed on the throne by Pharaoh Neco. When Neco was defeated by the Chaldeans (Babylonians) at the battle of Carchemish in 605 BC, Jehoiakim shifted his allegiance to Nebuchadnezzar. This move was the better part of wisdom since Nebuchadnezzar controlled all of Syria-Palestine subsequent to Carchemish.

After serving Nebuchadnezzar for three years, Jehoiakim rebelled by withholding the annual tribute. He died or was assassinated late in the year 598 BC just before Nebuchadnezzar arrived to punish him for his rebellion. The accounts of the reign of Jehoiakim are found in 2 Kings 24:1-7 and 2 Chronicles 36:5-8.

Outline of the Unit.

In this unit the discouragement of Jeremiah which began to

appear in chapter 12 intensifies. The prophet was ready to quit on more than one occasion. He said things to and about God which no believer ought ever to utter. Yet God was patient with his man. Mingled here among the agonizing cries of discouragement are some very practical suggestions for dealing with ministerial depression.

A. The Rejected Intercessor (14:1-15:9).
B. The Lonely Herald (15:10-16:21).
C. The Scorned Preacher (17:1-18).
D. The Urgent Exhorter (17:19-18:17).
E. The Slandered Servant (18:18-23).
F. The Dramatic Prophet (chap. 19).
G. The Afflicted Martyr (chap. 20).

THE REJECTED INTERCESSOR
Jeremiah 14:1-15:9

Judah experienced a drought during the reign of Jehoiakim. The nation went into mourning over the increasingly severe conditions. Servants of the powerful nobles scoured the land in vain search of cisterns which still contained water. The farmers were confused because they could not produce a crop. Men covered their heads with dust as a sign of mourning. Lack of vegetation caused the wild animals to suffer. The tender doe forgot her young in search of food and water. The rough wild ass sniffed the air for the scent of water, then languished and died (14:1-6). Faced with this desperate situation Jeremiah petitioned God on behalf of his people.

A. The First Petition (14:7-12).

Jeremiah frankly confessed the sins of the nation; then he asked God to aid Judah "for Thy name's sake," i.e., for the sake of his reputation. The prophet firmly believed that God was the only hope of the nation; but he could not understand why God showed no more interest in the plight of his people than a stranger might show in a land he merely visits. He did not doubt that God was in the midst of Israel. Why then was God acting like a warrior who has become so terrified that he cannot function? Why was God doing nothing when the people who belonged to him ("called by Thy name") were totally dependent on him? (14:7-9).

God explained that he had abandoned his people because they had first abandoned him. They had not "kept their feet in check." They loved to wander. Judgment had been decreed already. God would "call their sins to account." For Jeremiah to continue to pray for Judah's deliverance was futile. Fasting, prayer and sacrifice could not avail at this point. God had determined to "make an end of them" by means of "sword, famine and pestilence" (14:10-12).

B. The Second Petition (14:13-18).

In his second drought prayer Jeremiah blamed the apathy of the people on the prophets who promised a rosy future. God totally disassociated himself from these prophets. He denied that he sent these men, commanded them or spoke to them in any way. Their message was totally wrong headed. They were prophesying "a false vision, divination, futility, and the deception of their own minds" (14:13f.).

The prophets kept saying that neither famine nor sword would come upon Judah. As a matter of fact, the prophets and those who listened to them would experience both. So many would die that there would not be enough people left to bury them. To drive home this point, God instructed Jeremiah to enter into a rhetorical lament. In this lament Jeremiah called upon himself to cry night and day for "the virgin daughter of my people." They would receive a crushing blow which would result in "a sorely infected wound." Outside the city the "sword," i.e., war, would take its deadly toll. Inside the city people would starve to death. Both prophet and priest would have to "rove about" (lit., peddle their wares) in a foreign land (14:15-18).

C. The Third Petition (14:19-15:9)

In his third petition Jeremiah asked God three questions designed to move him to intervene during the drought. In the first he asked if God utterly had rejected Judah. In the second he asked if God loathed Zion. The third question inquired as to why God had stricken the nation beyond healing. Misled by the false prophets, the people were expecting national "healing." The drought, however, continued unabated (14:19).

Again Jeremiah frankly acknowledged the sin of his people. They were indeed worthy of punishment. Then, however, he presented a four-fold appeal for leniency. (1) He prayed that God would not continue to despise his people "for Thine own name's sake" (cf. 14:7). (2) He asked that God not disgrace "the throne of Thy glory," i.e., Jerusalem. (3) He pled for God to "remember Thy covenant with us." (4) He argued that God alone could send the rains. He, therefore, was the only hope of the nation (14:20-22).

For the third time God categorically rejected any further intercession for mercy on Judah. The problem was not in Jeremiah's prayer technique. Even the greatest intercessors of Israel's history ("Moses and Samuel") would not be able to move God to continue showing pity to that sinful generation. God's decree was that these sinners should be sent away to their appointed destinies: death, sword, famine, and captivity. Those slain by the sword would be torn and eaten by bird and beast (15:1-3).

As they witnessed what befell Judah, other nations would be horrified and fearful for their own safety. The sins introduced by Manasseh and perpetuated by all his successors (save Josiah), demanded such harsh treatment. No other nation in the world really would care when Judah fell (15:4f.).

These people who had forsaken their God continued to go backwards. God would therefore stretch out his hand against them. He was weary with the business of making threats and then withholding the stroke at the last possible moment. A winnowing process would begin "at the gates of the land" where young men would be slain making a stand against the enemy. Parents would thus be separated from their children. God would destroy his people because they had not repented of their ways (15:6f.).

What a slaughter that would be! Widows would be more numerous than the sand of the sea. Jerusalem would be like a mother who suddenly experienced anguish and despair. At the most unexpected time ("high noon") a destroyer would come against this mother. The woman who had given birth to "seven sons," i.e., numerous sons, would develop labored breathing and slowly die. For her the sun would set while it was yet day, i.e., she died prematurely. Those who survive the demise of the mother city would be given over to the sword of their enemies (15:8f.).

THE LONELY HERALD
Jeremiah 15:10-16:21

No work is so lonely as the ministry. No prophet was so lonely in his work as Jeremiah. Throughout his ministry this servant experienced psychological stress. Of that fact the text now gives a prime example.

A. Lamentation and Consolation (15:10-14).

Jeremiah wished he had never been born. The gentle prophet had become a controversial figure, a man of "strife" and "contention." His message of doom had accomplished no more than arousing animosity against him. He was cursed as much as a ruthless lender or an irresponsible borrower (15:10).

God promised to release Jeremiah from the hostility which he had been experiencing in this phase of his ministry. His enemies would actually seek him out for aid in a time of distress. Furthermore, he need have no fear about the accuracy of the threats he had pronounced. The invincible foe from the north would be like iron or bronze which men could not smash. That enemy would roam throughout the land looting. Because of God's burning anger the inhabitants of Judah would be carried away to a foreign land (15:11-14).

B. The Second Confession (15:15-21).

Jeremiah began his second confession by acknowledging that God is omniscient. Yet he called upon the Lord to take note of his difficult situation. He asked for vengeance, i.e., execution of divine justice, upon his persecutors. If God continued to exercise patience with these evil men, Jeremiah would be killed. He pointed out that all of his suffering was because of his commitment to God (15:15).

In a narrative prayer Jeremiah described his situation to the Lord. Many years earlier he had eaten God's word, i.e., he took it in and made it part of himself. At first he experienced real joy in knowing that word and sharing it with others. He found satisfaction in knowing that he belonged to God in a special way. God's hand had touched him and set him apart. The message which God gave him to preach, however, was one of indignation against sin. This caused people to shun him. He was not welcome at their social gatherings. Now he felt totally alone. His mental suffering was perpetual. He felt that God had become to him "like a deceptive stream, i.e., had failed him, had not lived up to his promises (15:16-18).

In comparing God to a deceptive stream, Jeremiah had gone too far. He needed to repent if he wanted to continue to "stand" as a servant in God's court, i.e., maintain his unique relationship to the Lord. He must separate the vile (doubt, mistrust) from the precious (faith, love, and trust). He must not allow the skeptical citizens to drag him down to their level. If Jeremiah made these adjustments, then the Lord would honor the promise he had made to him at his call. Jeremiah would be "a fortified wall of bronze." No matter how much men might attack him, they would not prevail. God would always deliver him from the hand of the wicked (15:19-21).

C. Directions for the Prophet (16:1-13).

Although Jeremiah had complained of his loneliness, God immediately gave him instructions which must have increased his sense of isolation. First, he was forbidden to marry. In the short run this command seems harsh. If any man ever needed a compassionate helpmate, this prophet did! In the long run, however, the prohibition was in the best interest of Jeremiah. In the coming judgment wives and children would suffer tremendously. Worries about the safety of family would only increase the burdens of the prophet (16:1-4).

Second, Jeremiah was forbidden to attend social gatherings. He was not to attend funerals. His non-attendance was to underscore one of the major thrusts of his warnings. In the coming judgment so many would die that normal funeral rites would not be possible. This included the funeral feast which was conducted in the home of the bereaved after the funeral (16:5-7). Jeremiah was also not to participate in festive occasions. Again his non-participation was to underscore the threats which he made in his predictions. In the day of judgment all sounds of celebration would be absent from the land (16:8f.).

Third, Jeremiah was commanded to preach an unpopular message. If he were to be challenged about the justice of the coming calamity, the prophet was to have a ready answer. The fathers had been unfaithful, and the present generation stubbornly had persisted in apostasy. God would therefore hurl them out of their land. In exile in a strange land they could serve their idols to their hearts' content (16:10-13).

D. Explanation for the Prophet (16:14-18).

Seeing light at the end of a dark tunnel can lift the spirits of those in the throes of discouragement. God now revealed to Jeremiah some of what was on the other side of the national judgment on Judah. After the exile would come restoration to Canaan. The return of God's people would eclipse in significance the Exodus under Moses. This regathering would involve, not just one land as in the case of Moses, but multiple lands, "the land of the north" and "all the countries where he had banished them" (16:14f.). The restoration of God's people after the exile culminated in the work of the great liberator Jesus Christ.

Jeremiah compared the conquerors of Judah to fishers and hunters who seek out every sinner. The people could not hide their sin from God. To the penalties which Judah had already experienced, God would add the penalty of mass deportation. This double penalty was necessary because their lifeless idols, like dead carcasses, polluted the land (16:16-18).

E. Affirmation by the Prophet (16:19-21).

Jeremiah conquered depression temporarily and burst forth into a triumphant prayer of faith. He confessed that Yahweh was his "strength, stronghold, and refuge in the day of distress." He looked forward to the day when Gentiles would turn to God and totally renounce their idolatry as "falsehood" and "futility." They would recognize that idols are utterly worthless, "things of no profit." To think that a man could create gods for himself was ridiculous to Jeremiah (16:19f.).

God responded to Jeremiah's prayer of faith by assuring him that the Jews would also come to know his "power" and "might." When he brought judgment on Jerusalem and subsequently restored the faithful to the land, they would come to know the real significance of God's name Yahweh (16:20).

THE SCORNED PREACHER
Jeremiah 17:1-18

Chapter 17 contains excerpts from Jeremiah's preaching during the middle period of his ministry. Three of these sermonettes are brief and unrelated. The chapter concludes with a longer sermon summary.

A. Sermonettes (17:1-11).

The sermonettes in chapter 17 deal with (1) the guilt of the nation, (2) the contrast between believers and unbelievers, and (3) the deceitful human heart.

1. National guilt (17:1-4). The record of Judah's sin was written indelibly ("iron stylus with a diamond point") on their stony hearts and on the most sacred parts ("horns") of their altars. All the children could remember were the pagan altars with the sacred Asherahs[1] beside them (17:1f.).

Because of her record of sin and rebellion, all the wealth of Jerusalem ("my mountain") and all her high places (pagan worship centers) would be given as spoil to an enemy. The citizens of the place would be carried off to become servants of a foreign power. By their perpetual rebellion they had kindled the fire of God's anger, and by it they would be scorched (17:3f.).

2. Believers vs. unbelievers (17:5-8). In what amounts to a psalm, Jeremiah set forth the contrast between believers and unbelievers. The man who trusts in flesh and departs from the Lord is cursed. Like a twisted desert shrub he does not live, he merely survives. On the other hand, the man who trusts in the Lord is blessed. He is like a flourishing tree with roots by a stream. That man continues to bear fruit even during the "heat," i.e., the difficult times of life.

3. The human heart (17:9-11). The heart of man is deceitful and desperately sick. God alone understands the human heart. This is why he can be absolutely just in his judgment. Evil men will be deprived of ill-gotten gain as surely as the hapless partridge is deprived of her eggs by her natural enemies.

B. The Third Confession (17:12-18).

At this time Jeremiah fought another bout with depression. His third confession began on a positive note. He praised God as "the glorious throne on high," i.e., the ruler of the earth, "from the beginning." The Lord is "the place of our sanctuary" because true worship is grounded in him. He is the "hope of Israel." Those who forsake the Lord are ultimately put to shame. Those who turn away from the Lord would be "written in the dust" (NIV), i.e., quickly obliterated. The prophet who called God "a deceptive stream" in his previous confession (15:18) now called the Lord "the fountain of living water" (17:12f.).

Since God was the object of his praise, again the discouraged prophet cried out for God to "heal" him of his mental torment, to save him from his adversaries. In narrative prayer he related the situation to his God. His adversaries keep mocking his predictions: "Where is the word of the Lord? Let it come now!" In spite of this mockery Jeremiah had not forsaken his post as undershepherd to God. On the other hand, he took no malicious delight in announcing the doom which would befall Judah. He was utterly sincere in his ministry. God knew his every word (17:14-16).

Jeremiah desired and prayed for the salvation of Judah as a nation. At the same time, he prayed for the immediate demise of that group of hard core antagonists who were the enemies of both God and his prophet. He longed to see them "put to shame" and "dismayed." He asked God to bring on them "a day of disaster, twofold destruction," i.e., total or complete destruction. Jeremiah knew that he personally had nothing to fear in that day of judgment for God would be a "refuge" to him (17:17f.).

THE URGENT EXHORTER
Jeremiah 17:19-18:17

In the next two messages of the book exhortation is prominent. Jeremiah urgently was attempting to get his generation to manifest some sign of repentance so that God might then spare the city from the calamity which had been forecast.

A. Sermon on Survival (17:19-27).

In the gates of Jerusalem Jeremiah was to preach a sermon on national survival. He was to address his message to the kings of Judah, to all Judah and especially to the inhabitants of Jerusalem. The message emphasized three points. First, Jeremiah exhorted the people to start sanctifying the sabbath. This they could do by ceasing to carry loads in or out of the city or their homes. God had commanded their forefathers to "keep the sabbath day holy," but they did not listen. They "stiffened their necks"; they would not "take correction" (17:21-23).

Second, Jeremiah promised his audience they could chart a new course if they only would. A manifestation of repentance regarding sabbath observance would cause God to spare Jerusalem. Business would continue as usual in terms of the activity of kings and princes, and the worship activities of the Temple. The city would be "inhabited forever" (17:24-26).

The sermon on survival concluded with a threat. If Judah showed no sign of repentance regarding sabbath observance, then the city would experience the fires of judgment. That fire would not be quenched until it devoured "the palaces of Jerusalem" (17:27).

B. A Parable (18:1-17).

Jeremiah was commanded to go to the potter's house where he would learn a very important principle relating to his own promises and threats. When the prophet arrived at the potter's house he observed that the craftsman was making something on his wheel.[2] He was impressed by the ease with which the potter would begin a new project if something went wrong with the clay he was working (18:1-4).

The house of Israel was clay in the hands of the divine Potter. He could do as he pleased with this clay. His decisions, however, were based on the conduct of the nation. If he threatened destruction of a nation, and they repented, then God would relent concerning the calamity which he had announced. On the other hand, if God announced a blessing upon a nation, and it turned from him, then the blessing would be canceled (18:5-9). The point is that all the threats and promises of God are conditional.

With this in mind, Jeremiah was told to announce that the divine Potter was "fashioning calamity" against Judah and Jerusalem. He earnestly pled with his people to "turn back" and "reform your ways and your deeds." They, however, were defiant in their response: "It is hopeless!" Jeremiah should not waste his time trying to coax them into changing their lifestyle. They intended to follow their own plans and stubbornly to do whatever their heart might desire (18:11f.).

Judah's horrible sin, unheard of among the nations, was that she had rejected her God. The Lebanon mountains are snow-capped the year around and swift-flowing streams constantly flow down those slopes. Nature is constant; but God's people were not. They had departed from the old paths of faithfulness to blaze new trails into idolatry where they stumbled in their ways (18:13-15).

Judah would suffer the consequences of the decision to abandon the Lord. Their land would become a desolation, and as such it would become an object of derision. They would scatter before their enemies as leaves before wind. In the day of their calamity God would show them his back and not his face, i.e., he would turn his back upon them in that crisis (18:16f.).

THE SLANDERED SERVANT
Jeremiah 18:18-23

Active opposition to Jeremiah arose in Anathoth (cf. 11:21), but it spread throughout the nation. These enemies now conspired to make lying accusations against this man of God which might trigger governmental action against him. After all, they had their counselors and spiritual leaders: priests, prophets and wise men. They had no need for a troublemaker like Jeremiah (18:18).

This new threat caused Jeremiah to plunge for the fourth time into the depths of depression. He urged the Lord to hear him, and to listen to his opponents as well. He could not understand why some were so antagonistic toward him. He had done only good for them; but they had repaid him with evil. Indeed, they had dug a pit, i.e., set a trap, for him to ensnare him with the intent that he might be executed. Yet in his role as God's servant,[3] Jeremiah had only spoken good on behalf of the nation. He had interceded with God to "turn away His wrath" from Judah (18:19f.).

Speaking from the bitterness of his soul, Jeremiah asked God to unleash his wrath against the enemies who plotted his death. He called for the invasion which he had threatened so many times. In gruesome detail he described how that invasion would affect civilians ("children, wives") as well as the men of war. They deserved whatever the raiders might do to them because they had tried to entrap a man of God (18:21f.).

Jeremiah was confident that God knew about all the deadly schemes which had been devised against him. He asked God not to forgive their iniquity, i.e., fail to punish it. These mockers must be "overthrown" because they had rebelled against the word of God, the messenger of God, and thus God himself. Jeremiah wanted God to deal with them "in the time of Thine anger" (18:23).

THE DRAMATIC PROPHET
Jeremiah 19:1-13

Jeremiah was told by the Lord to purchase "a potter's earthenware jar." He was to take some of the elders of the people and some of the senior priests with him to the Potsherd Gate which overlooked the valley of Ben-Hinnom. In this valley children were regularly sacrificed to Baal (19:1f.).

A great calamity was about to befall Judah, one so terrible that the ears of those who heard about it would tingle. This judgment was appropriate because they had (1) forsaken God; (2) made Jerusalem alien; (3) burned sacrifices to other gods; and (4) filled this place with the blood of the innocent. They were actually burning their sons in the fire as "burnt offerings to Baal." The very thought of child sacrifice was totally foreign to Yahweh (19:3-5).

The day was coming when Topheth ("fireplace") and the valley of Hinnom would become known as the valley of Slaughter. God would "make void" (lit., empty out) the political counsel of Judah. Those who advised resistance to Babylon would be proved wrong. They would fall by the sword before their enemies. Corpses of slain soldiers would lie about everywhere. Birds and beasts would feed upon them. Jerusalem would be such a desolation that it would cause astonishment among passersby. At that time some would be reduced to cannibalism (19:6-9).

Jeremiah was told by the Lord to smash the vessel which he had purchased in the sight of the men who had accompanied him to the gate. This symbolic act dramatized the prediction that the people of Judah and Jerusalem would be smashed like an irreparable vessel. "Topheth" in the valley of Hinnom would become a graveyard and the whole city would be a "Topheth." Dead bodies would desecrate the place where once on the flat-roof houses they burned incense to the astral deities and poured out libations to other gods (19:10-13).

THE AFFLICTED MARTYR
Jeremiah 19:14-20:18

After the death of good King Josiah in 609 BC Jeremiah's life was a living martyrdom. He had experienced threats against his life (11:21) and reputation (18:18). He had plumbed the depths of depression on four previous occasions (12:1-4; 15:15-18; 17:12-18; and 18:19-23). He knew the strain of mental anguish. Now for the first time he experienced a physical attack and bodily pain. Publicly he remained an iron pillar through this ordeal. Privately he was a broken man.

A. Public Attack (19:14-20:6).

Jeremiah returned from Topheth perhaps encouraged by the response of the elders and senior priests to his dramatic message. He attempted to continue preaching this message of doom in the precincts of the Temple. In the name of the Lord he announced the calamity which God was about to bring upon Jerusalem because "they had stiffened their necks," i.e., they had been stubborn, in refusing to heed his word (19:14f.).

When Pashur, the chief officer of the Temple, heard this threatening message, he ordered Jeremiah arrested and beaten, i.e., scourged. Then the prophet was put in the "stocks" in a public place near the northern gate of the Temple precincts. Although the exact nature of these stocks is not known,[4] they obviously were some sort of restraining device which at the same time twisted and thus tortured the body (20:1-2).

Though beaten physically, Jeremiah was not subdued by his priestly adversary. When Pashur released the prophet from the stocks the next morning, the prophet pronounced a symbolic name change over the priest. He would no longer be called Pashur, but "Magomassabib," i.e., "terror on every side." Pashur would live to see the invasion of Jerusalem and the Temple area which Jeremiah had been predicting. He would look on in terror as his close friends were cut down by the sword (20:3-4a).

For the first time Jerusalem's conqueror was named. God would give all Judah into the hands of "the king of Babylon" who would slay some and deport others. All the wealth of Jerusalem would be plundered. Both Pashur and his family would be among those taken into Babylon. There this priest and all his friends to whom he had "falsely prophesied" would die and be buried (20:4b-6).

B. Private Discouragement (20:7-18).

The fifth and final "confession" of Jeremiah moves through three phases: (1) complaint, (2) conviction, and (3) curse.

1. His complaint (20:7-10). Privately Jeremiah reached a low point in his ministry. He felt that God had deceived him about his ministry, had overpowered and forced him into his service. Everyone was mocking him because his predictions of violence and destruction had not materialized. Fidelity to the word of God had earned him "reproach and derision all day long" (20:7f.).

Jeremiah wanted to quit, to forget his heavenly call. The message, however, kept burning like fire in his heart and bones. He could not stand to hold it within himself. He had to preach it! He knew full well that people were plotting against him. From every direction he was under attack. He was routinely denounced as enemy and traitor. Even his closest "friends" were watching for one wrong step which would enable them to take revenge on him. He could trust no one (20:9f.).

2. His conviction (20:11-13). Suddenly the darkness of Jeremiah's despair was broken by a light. God was after all on his side! As a "dread champion" the Lord would defend his servant. The plots of his enemies would fail. Ultimately they would be put to shame. Their disgrace in having opposed the messenger of God would endure forever (20:11).

Jeremiah regarded the Lord as the faithful Judge who looked on the heart. He was confident that he would live to see God's "vengeance" on these tormentors.[5] To this Judge Jeremiah had presented his case and he knew the Lord would do what was just. Therefore, he could sing praises to him for deliverance "from the hand of evildoers" (20:12f.).

3. His curse (20:14-18). In but a moment Jeremiah plummeted from the lofty heights of praise to the lowest depths of depression. Why? Because he took his eye off of God. He focused anew on his own miserable situation. Therefore, he cursed the day of his birth, and the man who announced his birth. He wished he had died in the womb. For this martyr, life was nothing but trouble, sorrow and shame.

Endnotes

1. Asherah was a female deity symbolized by a wooden pole implanted beside Baal altars.

2. The potter's wheel consisted of two circular wheels connected by a vertical axis. The lower disk was worked by foot.

3. "I stood before Thee" refers to the custom of servants to always stand in the presence of their king.

4. That detainment in the stocks became a common punishment is indicated by 2 Chr 16:10 which speaks of a "house of stocks" in the reign of King Asa.

5. NASB and NIV make these words a petition: "Let me see Thy (Your) vengeance on them."

CHAPTER SIXTEEN

Corrupt Leadership
Jeremiah 21-25

Background of the Unit.

Up to this point the material in the Book of Jeremiah has been arranged more or less in chronological order. Beginning with chapter 21 the prophet appears to have arranged his material topically. The oracles in chapters 21-25 are concerned mainly with political matters. They come from the reigns of three kings, Jehoiakim, Jehoiachin and Zedekiah.

Chapter 25 is dated to the fourth year of Jehoiakim (605 BC), the year in which the Babylonians defeated the Egyptians at the Battle of Carchemish. Shortly thereafter Jehoiakim switched allegiance from the now defeated Pharaoh Neco to Nebuchadnezzar, the new master of the world. After the battle of Carchemish Jeremiah identified Babylon as the "enemy from the north" and forthcoming destroyer of Jerusalem.

One brief oracle (22:24-30) can be assigned to the reign of King Jehoiachin. In December of 598 BC just before Nebuchadnezzar came to punish him for rebellion, Jehoiakim either died a natural death or was assassinated. His eighteen-year-old son Coniah succeeded him under the throne name of Jehoiachin. Shortly after he assumed the throne the Babylonians arrived and began siege operations against Jerusalem. Jehoiachin held out until March 597 BC when he surrendered the city to the enemy. He, his family and ten thousand of his countrymen were deported to Babylon. There Jehoiachin lived the rest of his life as ward of the government.

Nebuchadnezzar placed as his vassal on the throne of Judah an uncle of Jehoiakim who took the throne name Zedekiah. This last king of Judah was under constant pressure to throw off the yoke of Nebuchadnezzar and to align himself with Egypt. After almost a decade of reluctant vassalage Zedekiah withheld tribute. Nebuchadnezzar besieged Jerusalem for eighteen months after which he razed the city and deported the remaining leaders of the nation. The opening verses of chapter 21 belong to the reign of Zedekiah.

Outline of the Unit.

A. God and the Rulers of Judah (chaps. 21:1-23:8).
B. God and the Prophets of Judah (23:9-40).
C. God and the Exiles of Judah (chap. 24).
D. God and the World Ruler (chap. 25).

GOD AND THE RULERS OF JUDAH
Jeremiah 21:1-23:8

The first subsection begins with an oracle addressed to Zedekiah, the last king of Judah. Chapter 22 is chronologically prior to chapter 21. In this chapter 22 Jeremiah first spoke concerning the royal house in general, then concerning Jehoahaz, Jehoiakim and Jehoiachin. Finally he contrasted these worthless rulers with the coming of one who would faithfully fulfill the expectations of the royal office.

A. A Reply to King Zedekiah (21:1-10).

During the final siege of Jerusalem King Zedekiah dispatched two messengers to Jeremiah. Nothing further is known of the first messenger, Pashur the son of Malchijah.[1] The second was a priest named Zephaniah.[2] The messengers requested that Jeremiah "inquire of the Lord," i.e., make entreaty and ascertain God's will. The situation in Jerusalem was desperate. Perhaps God would intervene with a miraculous overthrow of the Chaldeans as he had done in 701 BC when he destroyed the Assyrian invaders (21:1-2).

Chronologically chapter 21 is displaced and commentators have puzzled over its location here. The editor seems to have regarded this episode as an appendix to the previous unit. In the preceding chapter Jeremiah named Babylon as God's agent to punish Judah. Chapter 21 documents the fulfillment of that prediction. In the "confessions" Jeremiah complained that people were laughing at his predictions regarding the enemy from the north. Chapter 21 documents that his predictions were now taken seriously. God had promised that if Jeremiah remained stalwart, someday his adversaries would turn to him (15:19). Chapter 21 illustrates how this came to be. At the end of chapter 20 Jeremiah cursed the day he was born. He was so discouraged he was ready to quit. Chapter 21 testifies that he stayed with his ministry and ultimately was vindicated.

1. A word for Zedekiah (21:3-7). Jeremiah sent the messengers back to Zedekiah with a response the King would not want to hear. God would thwart all efforts to defend Jerusalem. He actually would aid the Chaldeans to breach the walls and enter the very heart of the city. God declared that he himself would war against Jerusalem "with an outstretched hand and a mighty arm." Through the Chaldean conquest he would display his "anger, wrath and indignation" against Jerusalem (21:3-5).

God threatened to "strike down" the inhabitants of the city. Many would die of pestilence. Zedekiah and others who survived the sword, famine and pestilence would fall into the hand of Nebuchadnezzar who would execute still more by the sword. He would show no compassion upon them (21:6f.).

2. A word for the people (21:8-10). The people of Jerusalem had only two options which Jeremiah characterized as "the way of life and the way of death." Those who elected to remain in the city chose the way of death. The only hope of personal survival was surrender to the enemy. He who chose this option would lose all earthly possession; but "he would have his own life as booty." To attempt to weather the storm behind the massive walls of Jerusalem was to commit suicide. God's face had been set against the city and he would give the place into the hand of the king of Babylon.

B. Remarks Concerning the Royal House (21:11-22:9).

Two chronologically separate oracles give a sampling of the preaching which Jeremiah directed toward the royal family in general throughout his ministry.

1. A word to the royal family (21:11-14). Jeremiah offered a program which would mitigate the effects of the burning wrath of the Lord. The royal house must see to it that two things were done immediately. First, they must practice justice. For example, they must deliver those who had been robbed from the "the power of the oppressor" (21:11f.). Second, they must cease trusting in the inviolability of Jerusalem. The Almighty had declared his hostility against "the valley dweller,"[3] the rock fortress, i.e., Jerusalem. Though they boast of safety within her walls, they should know that God would punish them according to their deeds. The houses in Jerusalem, like trees in a forest, would burn down to the ground (21:13f.).

2. A word for the government (22:1-9). Jeremiah was commanded to go down to the house of the king of Judah. There he was to deliver a message to the king, his servants, and his family. God required the government to do "justice and righteousness." Specifically, God expected the king to deliver those who had been robbed from the power of the oppressor. Stranger, orphan, and widow were not to be mistreated in any way. The shedding of innocent blood in child sacrifice or by unjust execution must cease (22:1-3).

If the house of David would implement these social reforms, God would permit the royal family to continue ruling in Jerusalem. If, on the other hand, they ignored these directions, God swore that he would make the palace "a desolation." Because of its height and cedar-wood construction, that palace was figuratively called "Gilead, top of Lebanon." Yet God would make that lofty forest a wilderness. Destroyers would cut down those cedar beams and pillars and cast them into the fire (22:4-7).

Visitors to the area would inquire as to why Yahweh had allowed such a total destruction of this city. The answer would come back, Because they "forsook the covenant of the Lord their God and bowed down to other gods" (22:8f.).

C. Remarks Concerning Specific Kings (22:10-30).

At various times during his ministry Jeremiah received divine revelation concerning Jehoahaz, Jehoiakim and Jehoiachin. These oracles were here collected in a sub-section of the book.

1. Concerning Jehoahaz (22:10-12). Jehoahaz (Shallum) reigned but three months after the death of Josiah in 609 BC. He was then summoned to Riblah, put in chains, and deported to Egypt by Pharaoh Neco (2 Kgs 23:30ff.). Apparently some believed that Jehoahaz shortly would return from Egypt to resume his reign. Not so. Jehoahaz would never see his native land again. He would die in Egypt.

2. Concerning Jehoiakim (22:13-19). Jeremiah pronounced a "woe" on Jehoiakim because he launched a renovation of the palace using unpaid labor. This king wanted a more spacious dwelling, one which was paneled, and painted red. Building luxurious palaces would not preserve the reign of this king. His father Josiah had enjoyed the trappings of kingship, but at the same time he had been concerned about establishing justice and righteousness. He "pled the cause of the afflicted and needy; then it was well." That is the essence of "knowing" God (22:13-16). When this good king died the entire nation lamented his death (2 Chr 35:25).

By way of contrast, Jehoiakim was concerned only about oppression and violence. He had his heart set on dishonest gain, shedding innocent blood and on practicing oppression and extortion. Therefore, when Jehoiakim died no one would be moved to sorrow. He would receive "a donkey's burial," i.e., he would not be buried at all. Rather he would be dragged off and thrown out beyond the gates of Jerusalem (22:17-19).

3. Concerning the nation (22:20-23). Jeremiah compared Judah to a woman who is called upon to ascend the heights and bewail the fate of the nation. The Chaldean army would shortly pass through Lebanon, Bashan and Abarim (southeast of the Dead Sea).

Allied nations (lovers) would desert Judah in this situation (22:20).

In times of national prosperity God had spoken to Judah, but they had refused to hearken. The shepherds (leaders) would be swept by the wind (Chaldeans) into exile. Then the people would be ashamed of their previous conduct. Jeremiah compared the residents of Jerusalem to the birds which make their nests in the tops of the cedars of Lebanon. This proud city was about to suffer a terrible ordeal (22:21-23).

4. Concerning Jehoiachin (22:24-30). Coniah (Jehoiachin) briefly followed his father Jehoiakim on the throne early in 597 BC. Even if Jehoiachin were a signet on his right hand,[4] i.e., extremely precious, he would be handed over to the Chaldeans. God would "hurl" this young king and the queen mother into a foreign land where they would die (22:24-27).

Jeremiah expressed his astonishment over this tragedy with a series of questions. "Is Coniah a despised, shattered jar" that one might throw on a trash heap? "Why have he and his descendants been hurled out," i.e., deported? Jeremiah solemnly called upon the *land* to hear the word of the Lord on this matter. As far as the throne is concerned, Coniah would be written down in the public records as "childless," i.e., he would have no heir to inherit the throne from him. This man would not "prosper in his days," for he would not be able to hand his throne over to a son. No man of his descendants would "prosper" sitting on the throne of David or ruling again in Judah (22:28-30).

D. The Ideal Ruler (23:1-8).

The current leaders of Judah were under the divine "woe" because they were "destroying and scattering" God's sheep. Though the shepherds had not attended to the needs of the sheep, God would shortly attend to the shepherds because of the evil of their deeds (23:1f.).

God himself would gather the flock from all the countries where he had scattered them. They would return to their "pasture," i.e., Canaan, where they would "be fruitful and multiply." God would raise up new shepherds who would devote themselves to the welfare of the flock. The sheep would no longer have cause to be afraid, nor would any of the sheep be found missing (23:3f.). The reference is to the great leaders of the postexilic period, men like Zerubbabel, Ezra, and Nehemiah.

An ideal king of the house of David would rule over the remnant after the return from exile. He is called "righteous" because of his character and purpose. He is called "branch" (lit., sprout) because, like a tender plant, his origins would be humble and fragile. As a king he would always "act wisely," i.e., act in such a way as to guarantee the success of his mission. His reign would be characterized by "justice and righteousness." He would be Judah's savior, Israel's protector. Under his leadership the fractured people of God would be reunited. His subjects would recognize that in this king God had provided for sinful man a righteousness which no man can earn or deserve. Therefore, this ideal ruler would be called "the Lord Our Righteousness" (23:4-6).

For two reasons the return from Babylon would come to exceed in significance the Mosaic Exodus. First, the Exodus involved one country, Egypt, while the gathering predicted here involved "all the countries where I had driven them." Second, the return from exile in Babylon would be a necessary stage anticipating the appearance of Messiah (23:7f.).

GOD AND THE PROPHETS OF JUDAH
Jeremiah 23:9-40

In general the prophets supported the political decision to resist the Babylonian hegemony. They countered Jeremiah's threats of invasion and destruction with theological reasons why God could never permit Jerusalem to be overthrown. Jeremiah now turned his attention to these charlatans who professed to have received revelation.

A. The Menace of the Prophets (23:9-15).

Jeremiah expressed great distress over what he observed around him as well as what had been revealed to him by God. He felt a mixture of sympathy ("my heart is broken within me") and trepidation ("all my bones tremble"). He lost self-control, and in that respect was like an intoxicated man. He was disheartened by the sinfulness of the masses for "the land was full of adulterers." Because of the presence of these sinners, the land itself was suffering from drought. The nation was headed in the wrong direction. They used their might for that which is not right (23:9f.).

Even their priests and prophets were "polluted." They practiced their wickedness in the Temple precincts. God would make the way of the spiritual leaders slippery and dangerous as they plunged forward into the darkness of sin. God would bring "calamity" upon them in the "year of their punishment" (23:11f.).

In the eyes of God the prophets of Judah were more wicked than the prophets of Samaria. Those Northern Kingdom prophets had prophesied by the god Baal and thus had led "my people Israel astray." On the other hand, the Judean prophets professed to be spokesmen for God. Their lifestyle, however, betrayed their profession. They were immoral ("the committing of adultery") and unscrupulous ("walking in falsehood"). By their false prophecies they "strengthened the hands" of those who engaged in evil practices. Without the moral restraint imposed by faithful preaching of God's word, Jerusalem had become a virtual Sodom. "Pollution" had spread from the prophets into all the land of Judah. Therefore, because they had failed as spiritual leaders, God would make these prophets eat "wormwood" and drink "poisonous water," i.e., they would be forced to partake of the divine judgment (23:13-15).

B. The Message of the Prophets (23:16-22).

Jeremiah urged his audience not to listen to the popular prophets. These men were leading the nation into "futility." They spoke a "vision of their own imagination," not a revelation from the "mouth of the Lord." They kept assuring those in rebellion against God that "the Lord has said, You will have peace." The person whose life followed a path of stubborn self-will was assured by spiritual leaders that "calamity will not come upon you" (23:16f.).

Jeremiah raised a question which must have been on the minds of those who were hearing conflicting prophetic messages. "Who has stood in the council of the Lord," i.e., who has been made privy to inside information direct from the throne room of heaven? Who actually has been granted visions of future events and has heard the divine word? "Behold," he cried. This word introduces the shocking revelation which Jeremiah had been granted. He saw a terrible storm brewing which would eventually "swirl down on the head of the wicked." God's anger would not "turn back" until his purpose of judgment had been accomplished. To his contemporaries this seemed inconceivable. Popular theology argued that God would not and could not abandon his people to their enemies. In the latter days (the messianic age), however, men would have a better comprehension of the plan of God (23:18-20).

So what about the many prophets who promised peace? God declared, "I did not send them, I did not speak to them." Yet they were zealous ("they ran") in their mission and bold ("they prophesied") in their proclamation. If they had truly received revelation from God as they claimed they would be preaching the same message as Jeremiah. The supreme proof that God had not sent these "prophets" was that they made no effort to get people to repent (23:21-22).

C. The Methods of the Prophets (23:23-32).

God is fully aware of what the prophets have done in his name. After all, he is transcendent, omniscient and omnipresent. He had heard the lying claims of the prophets to have had a dream revelation (23:23-25).[5]

With disgust Jeremiah asked rhetorically how much longer these "prophets" would continue their deception and falsehood. Was it their purpose to make God's people turn their backs on the Lord? Whether or not that was their intention, their "dreams" were as dangerous as Baalism had been in an earlier generation (23:26f.).

Spokesmen for God need to make a clear-cut distinction between their own opinions and the word of the Lord. So Jeremiah taught. Prophets may share their own dreams so long as they label them as personal wishful thinking. The wheat of God's word must be separated from the chaff of human speculation. Faithfully proclaimed, the word of the Lord is as powerful as "fire" and as a "hammer" (23:28f.). It burns away falsehood; it smashes delusion.

Three times God declared his hostility toward the false prophets.

These men caused the simple people to err because (1) they stole parts of their message from prophets like Jeremiah; and (2) they formulated their messages in the technical language of prophecy. They used the phrase "the Lord declares" (lit., oracle of Yahweh), which was the most solemn assertion that the message came directly from God. They spoke, not oracles from Yahweh, but "false dreams." Their "reckless boasting" and falsehoods led God's people astray. They certainly had not been sent by God. Their presence was of no value to the people (23:30-32).

D. The Mockery of the Prophets (23:33-40).

Prophet, priest and people mocked Jeremiah's message. They constantly asked him what new "oracle" (lit. *burden*, i.e., weighty saying) he might have for them. He was instructed to reply, "You are the burden!"[6] This was one burden the Lord would be glad to shed (23:33).

Those who continued mockingly to use the word "burden" would be punished along with their households. On the other hand, those who sincerely sought God's revelation from the prophet should employ new terminology. They should ask, "What has the Lord answered?" or "What has the Lord spoken? Those who persisted in using the term "burden" would find their own words to be a burden which would crush them to the ground. Such punishment was deserved. These men had not only mocked the messenger of God, they had "perverted the words of the Living God" (23:34-36).

Jeremiah was to challenge the false prophets to see if they would dare to use the word "burden." He was to inquire as to what the Lord had said to them. If in their answer they employed the word "burden," he was to announce to them that both they and their city would be cast away from God's presence. When that judgment was poured out, these "prophets" would be shown to be deceivers. Thus they would become an object of "reproach" and "humiliation" forever (23:37-40).

GOD AND THE EXILES OF JUDAH
Jeremiah 24:1-10

In March 597 BC Nebuchadnezzar deported ten thousand Jewish

captives to Babylon. Among these captives was "Jeconiah" (Jehoiachin), his officials and most of the skilled working class. Jeremiah learned a lesson about those captives when he observed near the entrance to the Temple two baskets of figs. One basket contained choice figs; the other rotten figs. God directed Jeremiah to note the difference between the contents of the two baskets. This alerted Jeremiah that a revelation of importance based on those baskets would be forthcoming immediately (24:1-3).

The conventional wisdom of the self-righteous citizens of Jerusalem was that those who had been carried off by Nebuchadnezzar in 597 BC were terrible sinners. They got just what they deserved. God, however, declared just the opposite. The good figs represented the captives who had been carried away to the land of the Chaldeans. God regarded those people as "good." He would set his eye on them for good, i.e., he had positive plans for them. Eventually those exiles would return to their land. God would "build them up, and not overthrow them;" he would "plant them and not pluck them up." God would "give them a heart" so that they might "know" him. He would use them to begin the process of rebuilding the nation because they would "know" God, i.e., they would repent and have their relationship to God restored (24:4-7).

The bad figs represented Zedekiah, those who remained in Jerusalem, and those who had fled to Egypt. God would abandon the bad figs. They were due to be destroyed by famine, sword and plague. So pitiful would be their lot that Gentiles would use them as a proverb or curse (24:8-10).

GOD AND THE WORLD RULER
Jeremiah 25:1-38

Chapter 25 is dated to the fourth year of Jehoiakim, the year 605 BC. This was the year of the battle of Carchemish when Nebuchadnezzar defeated the Egyptians and became ruler of the world. Shortly after the battle he succeeded his father as king of Babylon (25:1f.). The chapter speaks of God's judgment against Judah, Babylon, surrounding nations and the entire world.

A. Judgment against Judah (25:3-11).

Jeremiah now had been preaching for twenty-three years. He had again and again spoken (lit., rising early and speaking) to his countrymen "the word of the Lord" which had come to him. Other prophets had been sent as well. The people of Judah, however, refused to listen to any of God's servants (25:3-4).

The message of the true prophets consisted of appeals to "turn from your evil way and the evil of your deeds." Only then could these people continue to dwell in the land which God had sworn to give to their forefathers forever. Specifically, they were to quit following after other gods. The making of idols did nothing but provoke the Lord to anger against them. God would do them no harm if they turned away from idolatry. The people, however, refused to listen. They continued to do that which provoked God to anger (25:5-7).

Serious consequences awaited Judah for failing to obey the words of God. God was about to bring against Judah and surrounding nations a multi-national force led by "Nebuchadnezzar the king of Babylon my servant." The Babylonian would crush all in his path. The lands which he invaded would be left as "everlasting desolation,"[7] as a object of horror and astonishment. Silence would reign supreme in these lands. The nations of Syria-Palestine would serve the king of Babylon seventy years (25:8-11). This period probably is to be measured from 605 to 538 BC.

B. Judgment against Babylon (25:12-14).

After seventy years the Chaldeans would pay for their iniquity. The land of the Chaldeans also would become "an everlasting desolation." All that God had spoken about Babylon's judgment would be fulfilled. Babylon would be enslaved by "many nations." Among those who conquered Babylon were Medes and Persians, then the Greeks, and still later the Parthians.

C. Judgment on Surrounding Nations (25:15-29).

Jeremiah was commanded to take from God's hand "the cup of the wine of wrath." He was to pass this cup among the nations designated by God. The nations which drank from that cup would "stagger and go mad." Such would be the utter chaos which would result from "the sword," i.e., invading army, which God would send into their midst. Jeremiah records that he took the cup from the Lord's hand and made all the nations to which God sent him to drink of it. Did he visit capitals? Probably not. Did he carry out these instructions in a vision? Possibly. He may also have taken a wine cup to the foreign ambassadors of the various nations who resided in Jerusalem (25:15-17).

The list of nations which must drink the cup extends as far south as Egypt and as far east as Elam and Media. Seventeen are mentioned specifically. The thought was thus conveyed that all nations in the known world must drink the cup. The last to drink it would be the king of "Sheshach," a cryptic name for Babylon (25:18-26).

The nations had no option but to drink the cup, for God's sword was coming into their midst. If God was about to destroy the city which belonged to him in a special way (i.e., Jerusalem), he could not allow heathen kingdoms to go unpunished (25:27-29).

D. Judgment on the World (25:30-38).

Jeremiah painted four pictures of the Lord executing judgment on the wicked. He compared God to (1) a roaring lion about to pounce upon a sheepfold; (2) a victorious conqueror who has crushed his enemies like grapes beneath his feet; (3) a prosecutor reading his indictment against the guilty; and (4) a righteous judge pronouncing sentence against the guilty (25:30f.).

An "evil" or calamity was going forth from nation to nation. Like a whirlwind the divine wrath would sweep across the world until it finally reached "the uttermost part of the earth."[8] Everywhere unburied and unlamented corpses would lie about on the ground (25:32f.).

Shepherds (leaders) as well as sheep suffer in the judgment. They would fall and be shattered like a choice vessel. No escape would be possible for these shepherds. They would wail in grief as they saw their "pasture," i.e., the land they governed, invaded and destroyed. All would be silent in the "folds" where once the sheep thrived. The Lord, like a lion, would give vent to his fierce anger. The resulting devastation would be a cause of astonishment (25:34-38).

Endnotes

1. Pashur son of Malchijah was not the same Pashur who had Jeremiah beaten and thrown into the stocks back in the days of Jehoiakim (cf. 20:1).

2. Zephaniah son of Maaseiah was the second ranking member of the priesthood (52:24). He is mentioned again in 29:25 and 37:3.

3. Jerusalem is called the "valley dweller" in 21:13 because the city was built on hills rising abruptly out of the surrounding valley.

4. Because of its importance the signet ring in antiquity was highly valued and guarded against any possible loss. That ring impressed into a bit of warm wax on a document made the document legally binding. The signet was the equivalent of the modern day signature.

5. Jeremiah seems to suggest that the "prophets" were discredited because they claim to receive their revelation through dreams. Cf. Deut 13:1; Num 12:6.

6. The Hebrew supports the reading, "What burden?" The Greek and Vulgate read, "You are the burden."

7. The Hebrew language does not contain a word which is the exact equivalent to the English word *everlasting*. The word used in 25:9 *('olam)* has the meaning "long-lasting."

8. In 6:22 Babylon comes from the "uttermost part of the earth." This may indicate the horizon of the world which Jeremiah envisions as being under God's wrath. On the other hand, the expression may have its broadest possible meaning.

CHAPTER SEVENTEEN

Mounting Opposition
Jeremiah 26-29

Background of the Unit.

Having digressed in chapters 21-25 to treat topically Jeremiah's political pronouncements, the editor in this unit reverts to chronological arrangement. Thus chapter 26 would appear to come from the same period as did chapter 20, i.e., "the beginning of the reign of Jehoiakim" (26:1). The date could be any year between 609 and 605 BC.[1] Prior to the battle of Carchemish (605 BC), King Jehoiakim was a vassal of Pharaoh Neco. The "confessions" of chapters 12-20 point to the fact that Jeremiah was facing increasing opposition during this period of his ministry.

A gap of about fifteen years exists between chapters 26 and 27. In the "fourth year of Zedekiah" (28:1) Jeremiah publicly challenged the policy of the government. Ambassadors from neighboring states had come to Jerusalem to plan a revolt against Nebuchadnezzar. How Zedekiah responded to these overtures from the foreign ambassadors is not known. Zedekiah did make a trip to Babylon in that same year to present personally the tribute money and renew his oath of allegiance to Nebuchadnezzar (51:59). Did he do so because he had been moved by Jeremiah's preaching to distance himself from the rebels? Was he summoned by Nebuchadnezzar because the Great King had heard rumors of revolt? These questions cannot be answered. In any case, strong sentiment existed in the royal court of Judah throughout the reign of Zedekiah to revolt against Nebuchadnezzar as soon as was practicable. Jeremiah adamantly was opposed to this sentiment.

Outline of the Unit.

A. Addressing a Theological Issue (chap. 26).
B. Addressing a Political Issue (chaps. 27-28).
C. Addressing a Practical Issue (chap. 29).

ADDRESSING A THEOLOGICAL ISSUE
Jeremiah 26

In the beginning of the reign of Jehoiakim, Jeremiah was dispatched by the Lord to the Temple precincts. This must have been the time of some festival for "all the cities of Judah" had come to the Temple to worship. Jeremiah was warned that he was not to "omit a word" (26:1f.). This warning was appropriate in view of the change in government religious policy. Josiah had been a fervent supporter of revival; Jehoiakim viewed religion as a tool for supporting state policy. He intended to silence any voice which created religious controversy or challenged state policy.

The desired outcome of this public proclamation was worth the personal risk to the prophet. "Perhaps they will listen." At least they would not be able to plead ignorance. God desired that everyone "turn from his evil way." Should that happen, God could then relent concerning "the calamity which I am planning to do to them" (26:3). The God of the Bible does not delight in judgment. He looks for reasons not to pour out his wrath.

The message which Jeremiah delivered in the Temple courts was essentially the same sermon he had preached there a decade or so earlier (cf. 7:1-8:3). The Temple would be completely destroyed.

Jerusalem would become ruins like Shiloh, the original Israelite center of worship in the land of Canaan. To avoid that calamity they must walk after the written law and hearken to the voice of God's contemporary spokesmen. The threatened destruction would be so great that the name Jerusalem would be used in curse formulas (26:4-6).

In his audience on this occasion Jeremiah had priests and prophets as well as the people who had come as worshipers. When he had finished speaking, this crowd seized him saying, "you must die!" They could not fathom the audacity of anyone standing in the Temple precincts to announce the destruction of the sacred house and city. "All the people gathered about Jeremiah in the house of the Lord" (26:7-9). Their intent was to stone him on the spot, or perhaps to force him to leave the Temple area where they could execute him with better conscience.

The "701 theology" held that God would never permit the Temple to be destroyed. At the last minute he would always intervene to rescue the place just as he had done in the days of good King Hezekiah in 701 BC. The "701 theology" had a tenacious grip on the minds of Jeremiah's generation. To contradict this basic belief was to be labeled "traitor" and "blasphemer." This explains why the mob was about ready to kill Jeremiah in the Temple courts. When he last attempted to preach in the Temple area, he was arrested, beaten and placed in the public stocks (19:14-20:2). He no doubt had been threatened at that time with death should he ever again attempt to preach in God's house. This may have been his first appearance there since that episode.

Some fair-minded officials heard the commotion in the Temple and rushed in to rescue Jeremiah from certain death. They organized a formal trial for the prophet in which accusations were presented, and the prophet was given an opportunity to defend himself. As far as the prophets and priests were concerned the only appropriate sentence for Jeremiah was "death." He had dared to prophesy against Jerusalem! (26:10-11). According to popular theology anyone who spoke against the holy city was guilty, not only of treason, but of blasphemy.

Speaking in his own defense Jeremiah made five points. First, he affirmed that he had spoken against the Temple and city because God had sent him to do so. Second, he pointed out that the fate of their city was in their own hands. If they would "amend" their ways and deeds, and obey the voice of the Lord, God would relent concerning the misfortune which he had announced. Third, Jeremiah was willing to die for what he had to say. He would not physically nor legally attempt to resist what they desired to do. Fourth, he assured them that if they carried out their intentions to kill him, they would be bringing the guilt of innocent blood upon the whole city. Fifth, he concluded his defense by reiterating his claim that his message came from God (26:12-15).

Jeremiah's defense swayed the princes and the people. They were not willing to execute a man for speaking in the name of the Lord. The elders cited a legal precedent for this stance. In the days of King Hezekiah, Micah of Moresheth too had threatened Jerusalem in the name of the Lord. The elders actually were able to quote the words of Micah: "Zion shall be plowed as a field, and Jerusalem will become ruins" (Mic 1:14). Hezekiah was moved to "fear the Lord and entreat" his favor. The Lord then relented concerning the misfortune which he had pronounced against them. Thus they underscored one of the points which Jeremiah had made in his own defense (26:16-18).

The prosecutors were not yet ready to give up on their intent to execute Jeremiah. They cited more recent legal precedent. Under King Jehoiakim prophets like Jeremiah had not fared very well. Uriah was forced to flee to Egypt for refuge from the king. Jehoiakim had him extradited and executed. His body was cast into the burial place of the common people (26:19-23). That Jeremiah had escaped a similar fate might be due to his family connections[2] or to the fact that he had spent considerable time out of the country carrying out instructions of the Lord (cf. 13:1-7).

The counterprecedent swayed the crowd again, this time in the direction of execution. Jeremiah's life, however, was a series of rescues from unexpected sources. In the Temple court crisis the deliverer was Ahikam the son of Shaphan. His "hand," i.e., power, "was with Jeremiah, so that he was not given into the hands of the people to put him to death" (26:24). Ahikam was a faithful official who had been carried over from the administration of King Josiah (cf. 2 Kgs

22:14). His prestige and authority were such that the enemies could not execute Jeremiah.

ADDRESSING A POLITICAL ISSUE
Jeremiah 27-28

After 605 BC the burning political issue in Syria-Palestine was this: What will be the relationship with the new world power Babylon? For some reason the royal counselors in the various kingdoms of the area thought that Babylonian hegemony was soft and temporary. The rulers were being advised to resist Babylon. Religious functionaries assured their kings of success if the path of resistance was chosen. Jeremiah had a different view regarding Babylon. In this unit he attempts to impress that view on the neighboring nations and on the people of Judah.

A. Instructions to the Kingdoms (27:1-11).

In the beginning of the reign of Zedekiah[3] Jeremiah was directed by the Lord to make for himself and then wear an ox yoke. He was to send "them," i.e., replicas of the yoke which he wore, to the kings of five neighboring kingdoms by means of their ambassadors. These foreign dignitaries had come to Jerusalem to encourage Zedekiah to participate in an anti-Babylon coalition (27:1-3).

The ambassadors were told to declare to their masters that Yahweh, the God of Israel, was sovereign over the whole world. He had created all which is upon the face of the earth "by my great power and by my outstretched hand." He therefore had the right to "give" the earth to whomever he chose. God had determined to give all lands, along with the wild animals which dwell there, into the hands of Nebuchadnezzar "my servant." All nations were required to serve him and his sons until such time comes as Babylon became servant to another nation. Nations which refused to put their necks in the yoke of Babylon would be destroyed by sword, famine and pestilence (27:4-8).

B. Warnings against False Optimism (27:9-22).

At the same time Jeremiah performed his action parable with the yoke, he issued warnings concerning those who were pushing their agenda of rebellion against Babylon. First, he warned Judah's neighbors. Each kingdom represented in Jerusalem had its own brand of prognosticators and political advisors. Apparently throughout Syria-Palestine the unanimous advice to the kings was that "you shall not serve the king of Babylon." This advice, Jeremiah insisted, was wrong. It was a lie which would result in the deportation of any people which resisted Nebuchadnezzar. Only the nations which submitted to the yoke of Nebuchadnezzar would survive. (27:9-11).

Second, Jeremiah issued a warning to Zedekiah. The Judean king, like his counterparts in surrounding kingdoms, must also bring his neck under the yoke of the king of Babylon. For Zedekiah to allow his people to perish by sword, famine and plague was absolutely senseless. Yet that was exactly what would happen to every nation which refused to serve the king of Babylon. Zedekiah was listening to the wrong advice. The prophets who were advocating rebellion against Babylon were lying. God had not sent them. They were prophesying falsely in the name of God. The result would be that the royal family along with the prophets who prophesied falsely would be driven from the land (27:12-15).

Finally, Jeremiah warned the priests and people. Again Jeremiah pled with his audience not to listen to the lying prophets. These prophets confidently were asserting that the Temple vessels which had been carried away to Babylon in 597 BC shortly would be returned to Jerusalem. Jeremiah urged these citizens to serve the king of Babylon so that they might live. Why would they be so stupid as to rebel and bring ruin to Jerusalem? True prophets would be praying that no further looting of the Temple and city would take place (27:16-18).

Jeremiah now made a shocking announcement. Nebuchadnezzar would return to finish the job of dismantling the Temple which he had started in 597 BC when King "Jeconiah" (Jehoiachin) surrendered the city to him. This included (1) the huge bronze Temple pillars;[4] the molten "sea," a huge stationary laver in the courtyard;[5] and the bronze "bases" which supported the ten portable lavers. God declared that all of the valuable objects from palace and Temple would remain in Babylon "until the day I visit them," i.e., until God brought judgment on Babylon. Then the vessels would be returned to Jerusalem (27:19-22).

C. Confrontation with a False Prophet (28:1-17).

In the fourth year of Zedekiah a dramatic confrontation took place in the Temple area between Jeremiah and one of the prophets he had been denouncing. Hananiah addressed Jeremiah in front of a large audience of priests and people. With a "Thus says the Lord of hosts," this brazen liar contradicted everything which Jeremiah had been preaching. According to Hananiah, (1) God had "broken the yoke of the king of Babylon;" (2) the Temple vessels would be returned within two years; and (3) King Jeconiah (Jehoiachin) and the ten thousand captives soon would be returning. Hananiah repeated for emphasis his prediction that God would shatter the yoke of the king of Babylon (28:1-4).

Jeremiah responded to Hananiah by uttering a hearty "Amen!" He sincerely wished that the prophecy of Hananiah would come to pass. Such optimistic forecasts of the immediate future, however, did not comport to the general trend in the prophetic movement. Prophets from ancient times had "prophesied against many lands and great kingdoms of war and of calamity and of pestilence." A prophet like Jeremiah stood in the mainstream of the prophetic movement. A prophet like Hananiah who "prophesied of peace" could only be confirmed as a true man of God by the fulfillment of his forecasts. Thus Jeremiah was giving the audience a simple test to apply when trying to determine who really did speak the word of the Lord (28:5-9).

Hananiah dramatically reinforced his prediction of the imminent return from Babylon. He seized the symbolic yoke from the neck of Jeremiah and broke it over his knee. Again Hananiah played to his audience. "Thus says the Lord," he declared. "Even so will I break within two full years, the yoke of Nebuchadnezzar king of Babylon from the neck of all the nations." Since Hananiah had swayed the audience with his antics, Jeremiah simply walked away. This was not the time nor the place for a response (28:10-11).

After the incident in the Temple, Jeremiah received directions from the Lord to carry a divine word to Hananiah. The gist of the message was that Hananiah had "broken yokes of wood," but he had made instead of them "yokes of iron." Optimistic forecasts of Babylon's imminent demise only encouraged rebellion which in turn provoked the Babylonians into more harsh hegemony. The yoke which was on the neck of the nations was put there by Yahweh. Like it or not, these nations will serve the king of Babylon (28:12-14).

Jeremiah made two charges against Hananiah: (1) Yahweh had not sent him; and (2) he had made the people "trust in a lie." Without the crowds to support him, the bombastic Hananiah was docile as Jeremiah delivered his stinging personal rebuke. The announcement of his personal fate was both ominous and specific. Because he had counseled rebellion against the will of Yahweh, the Lord declared, "I am about to remove you from the face of the earth." Hananiah would die within the year. A note appended to chapter 28 documents that Hananiah did in fact die two months later (28:15-17).

ADDRESSING A PRACTICAL ISSUE
Jeremiah 29

Communication between the ten thousand captives in Babylon and the residents of Judah was fairly routine. Chapter 29 contains a summary of a letter sent by Jeremiah to the captives. It alludes to two other letters which were provoked by the initial correspondence.

A. A Letter to Babylon (29:1-23).

Nebuchadnezzar had deported ten thousand Jews to Babylon in 597 BC. When a official delegation was sent to Babylon by King Zedekiah, Jeremiah used the occasion to address a communication to "the rest of the elders of the exile, the priests, the prophets and all the people" who had been carried to Babylon. The letter was secretly carried to Babylon by Elasah and Gemariah, two of Jeremiah's few supporters[6] (29:1-3).

The message to the exiles was very practical. First they should realize that God had sent them into captivity. That being the case, they should make the best of their situation. The normal activities of life should be resumed. Specifically he mentioned building houses, planting gardens, and marrying their children. Jeremiah directed them to pray for the welfare of Babylon, because as Babylon prospered, so also would the captives who were there (29:4-7).

Among the captives, as in Judah, nationalistic prophets kept stirring up hope of a quick overthrow of Babylon. They urged the captives to maintain a posture of non-cooperation with the Babylonians. Jeremiah warned that the prophets and diviners[7] were prophesying falsely. Only when seventy years had been completed for Babylon would God fulfill his promise to bring them back to the homeland (29:8-10).

God's plans for the captives were positive but not immediate. He was planning for their "welfare, future and hope." The experience in Babylon would lead these Jews to genuine conversion. They would "call upon" the Lord and he would listen to them. When they sought God with all their heart, he would be found. God does not play hide-and-seek with penitent people! Once they were spiritually attuned to their God, he would restore their fortunes. That would begin when God gathered them up wherever they have been scattered and brought them back to their land (29:11-14).

Jeremiah anticipated that some would reject his advice and argue that God had raised up prophets for the captives in Babylon. Thoroughly grounded in the "701 theology," these prophets kept assuring the captives that God would never allow Jerusalem to fall to Nebuchadnezzar. Jeremiah assured the readers of his letter that those who remained in Jerusalem were not favored by God. They would experience untold suffering because they were like rotten figs, good for nothing but destruction (29:15-17).

The inhabitants of Jerusalem were destined for a terrible fate. God would "pursue them" into foreign lands with "the sword, with famine and with pestilence." Their national condition would strike fear into surrounding nations. When people wished to curse or humiliate someone, they would compare them to the inhabitants of Jerusalem. Such punishment would be theirs because they consistently had refused to listen to the voice of prophecy with which God repeatedly and urgently tried to communicate with them. Jeremiah pled for the captives in Babylon to chart a new course, to begin to listen to what God said through his true prophets (29:18-20).

One specific and short-range prediction should verify for the captives that Jeremiah was a true prophet. Ahab and Zedekiah, two of the lying Babylonian prophets, would be delivered into the hand of Nebuchadnezzar. They would be executed by being thrown into a fiery furnace and "roasted in the fire" in full view of the captives (cf. Dan 3). Their gruesome death would come to be used in curses by the captives when they desired to wish upon someone a terrible fate (29:21f.).

Ahab and Zedekiah would be remembered as those who "acted foolishly in Israel." Even though they had "committed adultery with their neighbors' wives," with some they still had credibility as God's spokesmen. God, however, knew the facts in the case. He bears witness against the two. They were speaking falsely in God's name things which he had not commanded them to speak (29:23).

B. A Letter from Babylon (29:24-32).

Jeremiah's letter to Babylon must have created quite a stir. Shemaiah fired letters back to Jerusalem addressed to influential people, and especially Zephaniah the overseer of the Temple. In his letter to the Temple official Shemaiah argued that Zephaniah had the responsibility to punish any mad man who attempted to prophesy in the Temple precincts. Such a one should be placed "in the stocks and in the iron collar." Yet Zephaniah had not even so much as rebuked Jeremiah of Anathoth. Perhaps the subtle jab here is that Zephaniah the priest had been derelict in his duty when it came to punishing the prophet who came from the priestly town of Anathoth (29:24-28).

The priest Zephaniah must have respected Jeremiah, for he merely read the letter to him without implementing its suggestions. Jeremiah fired back another letter to the captives. Shemaiah had prophesied falsely in the name of the Lord. He had "preached rebellion against the Lord." He therefore would be punished in two ways. (1) He would have no male offspring; and (2) he would not live to see the restoration of the people (29:29-32).

Endnotes

1. That the phrase "beginning of the reign" does not necessarily mean either the accession year or the first full year of reign is indicated by the dating of chapter 28. There "the beginning of the reign of Zedekiah" is specified as the fourth year.

2. The high priest during the days of Josiah was Hilkiah (2 Kgs 23:4). Jeremiah was a priest and the son of Hilkiah. The possibility then exists that Jeremiah came from one of the most prominent families in the land.

3. Most Hebrew manuscripts read "Jehoiakim" instead of "Zedekiah" in 27:1. The rest of the chapter (vv. 3, 12, 20) make it clear that Zedekiah was the king. The name "Jehoiakim" was inadvertently carried over from the previous chapter by a careless scribe early in the transmission of the book.

4. The bronze pillars were twenty-seven feet high and eighteen feet in circumference.

5. The molten sea was forty-five feet in circumference.

6. Elasah was the son of Shaphan and the brother of Ahikam who rescued Jeremiah in chapter 26. Gemariah *may* have been the brother of Jeremiah.

7. A "diviner" is one who attempts to predict the future by means of external, physical objects. Examining the entrails of animals was a common form of divination in the ancient world.

CHAPTER EIGHTEEN

Visions of a New Age
Jeremiah 30-33

Background of the Unit.

The material in chapters 30-33 is largely optimistic regarding the future of God's people after the destruction of Jerusalem. The unit can to be dated to the tenth year of Zedekiah. Nebuchadnezzar's siege of Jerusalem was under way. Jeremiah has been imprisoned in the court of the guard along with others whose loyalty to the crown was suspect (32:1-2).

Jeremiah was commanded to "write all the words which I have spoken unto you in a book" (30:2). This suggests that the material in chapters 30-33 was never part of public discourse. In written form these chapters must have been an encouragement to the captives during the long years of exile in Babylon. Originally this material may have circulated as an independent document. Its placement at this point in the Book of Jeremiah, however, is altogether appropriate. Even while Jerusalem was suffering through her death throes, Jeremiah was revealing the next thrilling chapters in God's dealings with his people.

Chapters 30-33 have been entitled The Book of Consolation. In this section Jeremiah began to build and to plant (cf. 1:10). The grand themes which are developed in this section are set forth concisely at the very outset. "Behold, days are coming" in which God would (1) reverse the fortunes of his people; (2) reunite Judah and Israel; and (3) bring them back to the land which he had given to their fathers (30:1-3).

Outline of the Unit.

A. The Need for Divine Intervention (30:4-31:1).
B. The Blessings of Restoration (31:2-40).
C. The Certainty of Restoration (chap. 32).
D. Promises Reiterated (chap. 33).

THE NEED FOR DIVINE INTERVENTION
Jeremiah 30:4-31:1

The first chapter of the Book of Consolation underscores the need for God's intervention on behalf of his people. They are enslaved and in desperate straits. Yet God has a glorious future in store for them.

A. The Promise to Enslaved Israel (30:4-11).

Mentally Jeremiah could hear the approach of an enemy host. He visualized the mighty men of Judah as terrified as a woman in travail. Jeremiah uttered a mournful "Alas!" over that terrible "day," i.e., period of Israel's history. "This is the time of Jacob's distress." That gloomy period, however, would not last forever. "Jacob [i.e., the nation] shall be saved from it" (30:4-7). The text does not indicate the beginning nor end of this period and commentators are not agreed about it. Probably Jeremiah referred to that long period when God's people began to be dominated by ruthless powers. The first Israelites were deported in 733 BC. That is most likely the *terminus a quo* of the "time of Jacob's distress." The *terminus ad quem* is perhaps the final emancipation of God's people from the fear of death by the Lord

Jesus Christ.

The period of Jacob's trouble would end when the yoke of the oppressor was smashed. No more would God's people be enslaved by foreigners. They would serve "the Lord their God, and David their king" whom God would raise up for them (30:8f.). The thrust here is that a delivered people will demonstrate genuine conversion by serving God and a scion of the house of David. That New Testament salvation is in view here can hardly be questioned. Saved from the power of sin, Satan and death, God's people focus their service on none save their God and his Son—David's son—Jesus of Nazareth.

In view of the ultimate deliverance here announced, "Jacob, my servant," i.e., God's people, need not be terrified at the horrors of their present circumstances. Though they be scattered to distant lands, yet God promised, "I will save you from afar." Jacob would return to his own land there to dwell in safety. This deliverance would be possible because (1) God is with them to deliver them; and (2) God would destroy completely the nations which had taken Israel captive. God's purpose was to chasten his people with measured punishment. They would survive the exile. On the other hand, those nations to which God had scattered them he would destroy completely (30:10f.).

B. The Plight of Apostate Israel (30:12-17).

That God could not leave Judah unpunished should have been evident to the impartial observer. Israel had received an "incurable wound." No one could plead her cause, i.e., speak up on her behalf. Her "lovers," i.e., allies, had abandoned her because her situation was hopeless. God had inflicted upon Israel a wound such as an enemy might inflict. His punishment was like that which a cruel person might administer. This treatment, however, had been necessary because of the enormity of their sin problem. Further cries for help and healing were useless. Their pain would not quickly go away (30:12-15).

Israel could not heal herself, nor could her allies cure her deadly wound. Therefore, God himself, the great physician, would intervene on their behalf. The adversaries who with such cruelty had "devoured" and "plundered" Israel would themselves be devoured. They would experience the captivity which they inflicted on Israel. Because the enemies had ridiculed Zion's abandonment and helplessness, God would restore Zion to health and wholeness (30:16f.).

C. The Picture of Regenerate Israel (30:18-22).

God would "restore the fortunes of the tents of Jacob," i.e., the dwelling places of his people. Cities would be rebuilt on their original sites. Those cities would be inhabited by a joyful and grateful people. Their numbers would continue to increase. God would honor them in the sight of surrounding peoples. As a people they would have the stature and security which they had enjoyed in "days of old" (NIV), i.e., the glorious days of David and Solomon. All of their oppressors would be punished by the Lord (30:18-20).

The restoration would reach its climax with the rise of a wonderful ruler, a native son who would be able to "approach" God. This is the language of priesthood. The future ruler would be priest as well as king. Under the Old Testament Law a prince who tried to serve as a priest would have been risking his life (cf. 2 Chr 26:18ff.; Zech 5:13). Not so this future prince. Under his priestly leadership God's people would enter into a new relationship with God (30:21-22). That this is a personal messianic prophecy can scarcely be challenged.

D. The Plan for Israel (30:23-31:1).

The judgment against Judah would continue like a whirlwind until God had accomplished his purposes. Only in the "latter days," i.e., the New Testament age, would men really be able to comprehend the significance of the Babylonian exile. All that befell Israel and Judah was designed to make possible a unification of God's people and a restoration to the proper relationship to God.

THE BLESSINGS OF RESTORATION
Jeremiah 31:2-40

In chapter 31 Jeremiah continues to expand upon the theme of restoration. He depicts seven blessings which would follow the return of the people of God to their homeland.

A. New Concord (31:2-6).

In the "wilderness" of exile the remnant would experience heaven's grace. God would give rest in Canaan to those who repent while in captivity. In distant Babylon the captives would discover anew the love of God. They would feel God wooing them with his words: "I have loved you with an everlasting love!" He would draw them to himself by his loving kindness. He would build up his people. He would address his adulterous wife as though she were a chaste virgin. This language suggests a new relationship between God and his people. The virgin of Israel would respond to these undeserved favors with music and dance (31:2-4).

The new concord between God and his people would be matched by harmony within the covenant people themselves. The region of Samaria would be reinhabited. The hills of the area would be covered with vineyards as in the days prior to the captivity. The men of Ephraim, i.e., the old Northern Kingdom, would anxiously await the opportunities to go up to Zion to worship Yahweh (31:4-6). During the intertestamental period the region of Ephraim was full of Jews who took every opportunity to travel to Jerusalem to worship at the Temple. In Old Testament prophecy, however, to "go up to Zion" embraces the New Testament church which is called by the Apostle "Zion" in Hebrews 12:22. Jew, Gentile and Samaritan found their ultimate spiritual kinship in the body of Christ.

B. New Consolation (31:7-20).

The prophet foresaw a day when salvation would be accomplished and a new joy would fill the hearts of God's people. Jacob, i.e., Israel, is "the greatest of the nations" (NIV) because God had chosen them from among all nations for special privileges and obligations. Thus Jeremiah called for shouts of joy and praise among all those who loved the Lord. Part of that praise was the petition that God would save his people, the remnant of Israel (31:7). The verses that follow offer consolation to four groups of people.

First, Jeremiah offered consolation for the distressed. From remote parts of the earth the Lord would bring his people to Zion. In that great gathering the distressed of the earth would not be overlooked. The "blind, the lame, the woman with child" would be included. With tears of repentance and supplication those who had been called together by the Lord would follow his leading. He would "make them walk by streams of water," i.e., provide for their needs in the way. He would provide for them a "straight path," one in which "they shall not stumble." The reason for God's concern for the distressed was that a Father-son relationship existed between the Lord and his people (31:8f.).

Second, the passage gives consolation to the disheartened. The prophet alerted the nations of the world that he who scattered Israel would also gather them. He would keep his people as a shepherd keeps his flock. The gathering would be possible because Yahweh had "ransomed Jacob," had "redeemed" him from the grip of those who were stronger than he. To state the matter another way, first would come the defeat of the captors, then liberation, then the gathering of God's people. The goodness of God would then attract a steady stream of former captives. They would not lack for any good thing. Mourning would be turned to joy. Abundant sacrifices at the Temple would mean adequate provision for the priests. God's people would be satisfied with his goodness in that day (31:10-14).

Third, Jeremiah had consolation for the disconsolate. Rachel, the tribal mother of Benjamin, lived on in her descendants. She would weep bitterly over her dead children. The weeping would be heard all the way to Ramah, north of Jerusalem (31:15). Matthew (2:17f.) furnishes the key to the interpretation of this obscure prophecy. He saw here a reference to the lamentation of the mothers of Bethlehem over the slaughter of their infants by Herod.[1] The Bethlehem mothers were the first to suffer great loss for the sake of Christ. Their labor in bearing children, however, would not be in vain. They could have hope for the future. In the resurrection those children would return from the land of the enemy (death) to inherit their own territory (31:15-17). The inheritance here is no doubt the New Heavens and New Earth of which Old Testament Canaan was a pledge and guarantee (Heb 11:14-16).

Finally, Jeremiah offered consolation for the despondent. God had heard Ephraim's inhabitants lamenting their waywardness. They knew they had been chastened like a rebellious animal for their stubbornness. Ephraim prayed for divine aid in the process of repentance. That prayer was answered. Through the discipline of exile Ephraim came to recognize his miserable condition. He smote his thighs in consternation and contrition. He became desperately ashamed of his spiritual condition (31:18-19).

God responded to Ephraim's desperate spiritual agony. First, he acknowledged that Ephraim had not been the kind of child in whom a Father could delight. Yet as often as God spoke of Ephraim he remembered the close relationship which in the past had existed between them. He yearned for association with Ephraim. Repentance would open the door for God's compassion on his wayward people (31:20).

C. A New Creation (31:21-22).

The virgin of Israel (the population) was urged to mark clearly the road they would walk into captivity. Someday they would want to retrace their steps. The Lord urged them to return to their cities. Only a faithless daughter would dillydally when the opportunity for return presented itself. As an incentive to encourage them to return the Lord declared his intention to "create" something new in the earth: "a woman shall encompass a man." The people would miss out on the opportunity to participate in the wondrous event if they remained in Babylon. This may be an allusion to the virgin birth of Messiah which Isaiah had predicted over a century earlier.

D. New Conditions (31:23-30).

Judah would be restored as well as Ephraim. Once again inhabitants would pronounce blessings upon Zion, the holy hill. Peace and harmony would exist between farmers and nomads who frequently were at odds in the ancient world. The weary would find rest and the sorrowful, comfort. Jeremiah foresaw this glorious future in revelatory dreams. At this point the prophet awoke, and found his sleep to be pleasant (31:23-26).

As the dream continued, Jeremiah foresaw a time of great fruitfulness. People and cattle would multiply rapidly. It would seem as though they sprang up from seed. The reunification of Israel and Judah would make this growth possible. God had "watched over" his people to bring judgment ("pluck up, break down, overthrow, destroy"); so he would "watch over them" to "build and to plant" (cf. 1:10). The fact that he fulfilled his word of judgment guaranteed that he would also fulfill his word of promise (31:27f.).

Many in Judah thought that they were being punished for the sins of their fathers. They capsulized this misunderstanding in a proverb: "The fathers have eaten sour grapes, and the children's teeth are set on edge."[2] In the messianic age no one would have occasion to think such a thing. Each individual would be responsible before God for his own sin (31:29-30). The teaching of the New Testament would make this principle abundantly clear.

E. A New Covenant (31:31-34).

Even though the Lord had been a faithful husband to Israel, yet she had broken the Sinai marriage covenant. Therefore the united people of God would live under a new covenant in the days to come. The Law would be written upon their hearts, not on tables of stone like the Ten Commandments. Men would respond to the divine will from inward rather than outward compulsion. Those with God's Law upon their hearts would enter into a new relationship with him. Everyone under the new covenant would know the Lord personally as savior for they would have their sins forgiven by him. This basic knowledge of God would not need to be taught to those under the covenant, because such knowledge would be essential to gaining admission to the New Covenant Israel.

F. A New Commitment (31:35-37).

The God who makes promises about the future is the God who established the laws of nature. The pattern of night following day, the changing ocean tides are part of a fixed order. Jeremiah declared that the seed of Israel was eternal, as eternal as the laws of nature. God could no more cast off the "offspring of Israel" than a man could measure the heavens or search out the earth's foundations. The outward form of Israel may change, but the nation continues. Because they rejected their Messiah, God took the kingdom from the Jews (Matt 21:43) and bestowed it on a new nation (1 Pet 2:9), the church of Jesus which is the new Israel of God (Gal 6:16).

G. A New City (31:38-40).

Jeremiah sketched the borders of the Jerusalem of that future age. He spoke in concrete terms of the borders of the city in order to make the following points: The new Jerusalem would (1) be larger than the old city; (2) include certain areas around old Jerusalem which were considered unclean; and (3) be holy to the Lord. That the prophet is speaking symbolically of the New Testament Jerusalem (Heb 12:22), is indicated by the prediction that "it shall not be plucked up, or overthrown any more forever" (cf. Zech 2:1-5; 8:3-6).

THE CERTAINTY OF RESTORATION
Jeremiah 32

The circumstances out of which the Book of Consolation (chaps. 30-33) arose are set forth in detail at the beginning of chapter 32. The tenth year of King Zedekiah (the eighteenth year of Nebuchadnezzar) equates to 588 BC. The Babylonian armies were besieging Jerusalem. Jeremiah was under detention in the "court of the guard" which was located near the "house of the king of Judah." The prophet had been "shut up" because he had continued to preach that God would give both the city and its king "into the hand of the king of Babylon." King Zedekiah would be forced to confront "face to face" the one against whom he had rebelled. He would be taken to Babylon. There he would remain until God visited him, i.e., set him free (32:1-5).

A. The Purchase of a Field (32:6-15).

By revelation Jeremiah learned that his cousin Hanamel would offer for sale to him a piece of property in Anathoth. Jeremiah had "the right of redemption," i.e., purchase option, over this property. That Hanamel would want to convert inaccessible real estate to cash is not hard to understand. The family hometown of Anathoth was at this time behind enemy lines! The prophet was instructed to purchase the field. The arrival and offer of Hanamel confirmed in Jeremiah's mind that he had indeed received the word of the Lord in this matter (32:6-8).

All the legal requirements for transfer of property were followed. Payment of seventeen shekels of silver was publicly weighed out. Jeremiah signed and sealed the deed. He called in witnesses before whom he again weighed the shekels. Duplicate copies of the deed were made and given to Baruch who was instructed to place the documents in "an earthenware jar, that they may last a long time."[3] The significance of this legal transaction is made clear to the prophet: "houses and fields and vineyards shall again be bought in this land" (32:9-15).

B. The Prayer of Jeremiah (32:16-25).

Jeremiah was a man of prayer. He was not reluctant to confess his perplexities to the Lord. After purchasing the field and announcing the significance of his action, Jeremiah prayed for further light (v. 16). His prayer began with an exclamation of utter confusion ("Ah Lord God!"). It then moved through praise to confession and narration.

1. Praise (32:17-22). First, Jeremiah praised God for his "power" as revealed in the creation of "the heavens and the earth." He rightly concluded that "nothing is too difficult" for the God of creation. Second, the Lord is the God of justice. He dispenses grace to the thousands who turn to him, and punishment to those who follow the path of iniquity, both fathers and their children. He gives to every one "according to his ways and according to the fruit of his deeds." Third, he is the God of wisdom, "great in counsel and mighty in deed," i.e., he has the power to execute his counsel. Fourth, he is omniscient for "his eyes are open to all the ways of the sons of men." Fifth, he is the God of all the earth whose wonders had been performed in Egypt as well as Israel and whose fame is universal and lasting. Sixth, he is the God of history who brought forth his people from bondage in Egypt "with signs and with wonders and with a strong hand and with an outstretched arm, and with great terror." Seventh, he is the God who honors his word for he kept the oath he had made to the forefathers by bringing Israel into a land flowing with milk and honey.

2. Confession (32:23). After entering and possessing the land of Canaan, the Israelites had not obeyed God. They ignored his law. They virtually did nothing which he commanded them to do. Therefore, the calamity at hand rightly would befall them.

3. Narration (32:24-25). In the prayer context Jeremiah described the desperate situation of Jerusalem. His purpose was not to tell God something he did not already know. Rather, the narration constitutes an implied petition that God would explain the action parable which had just been carried out in the court of the guard. How could houses and land be bought and sold again in Judah when the capital itself was about to fall? The siege mounds of the Babylonians had already reached the city. Earlier predictions of the desperate conditions produced by siege were being fulfilled. The city had been weakened by sword, famine and plague; it would fall to the Chaldeans shortly. Yet God had commanded the prophet to purchase a field! Why?

C. The Plan of God (32:26-44).

Jeremiah had commenced his prayer with the affirmation that nothing is too hard for God (32:17). The Lord began his reply by asking the prophet if he really believed that proposition. Mouthing the right words is easy; developing the depth of conviction which those words suggest is not (32:26-27).

The Lord next made clear that Jeremiah's action parable did not imply that God would rescue Jerusalem from impending destruction. God was about to give the city into the hands of Nebuchadnezzar. The Chaldeans would enter Jerusalem, and then destroy the place. All of the places where pagan rites had been conducted would be burned to the ground (32:28-29).

The justice of the catastrophe was next addressed. From "their youth," i.e., the earliest days of the nation, the sons of Israel and Judah had "provoked" God to anger by "the work of their hands," i.e., their idols. Because of "all the evil" of its citizens, Jerusalem had been a perpetual provocation which challenged divine holiness from the time it was founded as a city. These people had turned their back on God; they had refused to accept correction. They had defiled the Temple with "detestable things," i.e., idols, and built "high places," i.e., pagan shrines, about the city. In the valley of Ben-Hinnom they "caused their sons and daughters to pass through the fires" to the god Molech. The practice of child sacrifice was an "abomination" to the Lord (32:30-35).

While the present prospects were bleak, the distant future would be bright for God's people. God would gather his people from the lands to which they had been scattered. He would restore them to their land. In that day they would experience a new relationship with the Lord. The allegiance of the people would no longer be divided for they would have "one heart" (inward disposition) and "one way" (outward manifestation). God would enter into a new and "everlasting covenant" with his people, one in which he committed himself never to turn away from them. This act of God's grace would produce in the hearts of his people reverence and fidelity. The new Israel would be a joy to the heart of God. He would manifest that joy by gladly doing good for them. He would "plant them in this land" (32:36-41).

The same degree of certainty which attends the threats of divine judgment also attends the promises of divine favor (cf. 31:28). Though the city was now about to become "a desolation," though the Chaldeans were about to capture the place, yet God would reverse the fortunes of his people. The buying and selling of properties and other business transactions would once again be common in Judah (32:42-44).

PROMISES REITERATED
Jeremiah 33:1-26

Jeremiah received a second revelation while he was detained in the court of the guard (33:1). In this revelation the themes of the previous three chapters are reiterated.

A. General Promises (33:2-13).

Yahweh created the future.[4] He certainly would be able to fulfill his promises. His very name means "he who is." It is a pledge that he would keep his word. This God encouraged perplexed souls to inquire of him. He alone could declare the great and unsearchable things to come (33:2-3).

At the moment Jerusalem's situation was grim. Buildings were being dismantled to secure materials to strengthen the walls. An heroic effort was being made to defend those walls, but the net result was only an increase in corpses. These painful events gave evidence of God's "anger and wrath." The Lord had hidden his face from them because of their wickedness. God promised, however, to heal the grievous wound inflicted by the Chaldeans. He would "restore the fortunes" of both Israel and Judah. He would rebuild them as they were at the first, i.e., when they first came out of Egypt. He would cleanse, pardon, and bless his people. The restored Jerusalem would have a reputation for joy, praise, and glory. Nations which heard of what God had done at Jerusalem would come to fear, i.e., reverence, him (33:4-9).

The entire land of Judah would be blessed in that day. The curse pronounced against Jerusalem (7:34; 16:9; 25:10f.) would be removed. The streets of the cities would once again echo with the sounds of mirth, marriage and worship. Rural areas would likewise prosper. Sheep would again find pasture there; shepherds would again count their flock. God promised to restore the "fortunes of the land as they were at the first" (33:10-13).

B. Special Promises (33:14-26).

A happy future awaited Israel and Judah. The words "Behold, days are coming" are something of a messianic pointer in this book. God had spoken a "good word" concerning his people, and he would fulfill that word (33:14). Three paragraphs amplify this good word which God had for his people. Redundancy is found here for the sake of emphasis, but new aspects of the promise emerge in each paragraph. Clearly the focus is on the promises made to David.

1. Two offices (33:15-18). The glorious future which God promised to his people was wrapped up in the appearance of a scion from the house of David. God repeated the promise of 23:5 that he would "cause a righteous branch of David to spring up." The term "righteous" points to the character of the coming Ruler; the term "branch" (lit., sprout) to his humble origins. This one would "execute justice and righteousness on the earth," i.e., he would be the ideal Ruler. He would be a savior to his people. The city, saved by his power and grace, would wear a name which would bear testimony to her trust in God: "Yahweh is Our Righteousness."[5] That which would make possible the salvation and protection of the people was not their own righteousness but that of God himself (33:15f.).

Because of the appearance of the Righteous Branch, "David shall never lack a man to sit on the throne of the house of Israel." Several truths are suggested by this brief assertion. First, the Davidic line would continue beyond the exile as an identifiable family at least until the appearance of the Righteous Branch. Second, the royal office would be part of the new order. Third, he who would occupy the throne in the new order would be from David's family (33:17). The fulfillment of this promise is not difficult to find. Jesus of Nazareth was of the house of David. At his ascension he occupied God's throne ruling the New Testament Israel of God.

The new order would have a priesthood as well as a royal family. The Levitical priests as a distinct body survived the exile. Once the Temple had been rebuilt they officiated in the sacrificial ritual. This of itself, however, does not fulfill the prediction that "the Levitical priests shall never lack a man to stand before me" in sacrificial service. The old Levitical priesthood was removed from the scene when Jerusalem finally fell to the Romans in AD 70. The ministerial function of that priesthood, however, had already been assumed by "a man" who lives forever, even Jesus Christ (Heb 7:11; 10:19-22). He epitomizes what the Old Testament priesthood only approximated. He offers better sacrifices, in a better sanctuary and with better results.

Since the Righteous Branch is priest as well as king, those who belong to him belong to a royal priesthood (1 Pet 2:5). This priesthood would offer "burnt offerings" and "grain offerings" to the Lord (33:18). In the Old Testament system these offerings symbolized commitment and thanksgiving. The Christian priesthood continues the work of the Levitical priesthood by offering more excellent sacrifices (Rom 12:1; Phil 4:18) in a more excellent Temple (Eph 2:21). A Christian is a true son of Levi in the same spiritual sense in which he is a true son of Abraham (Gal 3:7).

2. Two covenants (33:19-22). As Jeremiah wrote, the representative of the Davidic dynasty, Zedekiah, was facing defeat and exile. Had God revoked his ancient covenant with David (2 Sam 7:12-16)? Not at all. The covenant with David was as irrevocable as the God-ordained succession of day and night. David was God's servant. He would always have a son to sit on his throne. David's throne was God's throne (1 Chr 28:5; 29:23), the seat of authority over the people of God. Thus when Christ ascended to sit on God's throne, he was in effect sitting on David's throne, i.e., the throne once occupied by David.

The same permanence attached to the covenant made with the Levitical priests.[6] That these words must be understood spiritually is indicated by the categorical affirmation in the New Testament that the Levitical priesthood has passed away (Heb 7:11). Jeremiah went on to say that both the Davidic and Levitical families would be as numerous as the host of the heavens and the sand of the sea. Christians are members of a royal priesthood (1 Pet 2:9) and as such are the spiritual descendants of both David and Levi.

3. Two families (33:23-26). The Lord directed Jeremiah to take note of what the people were saying. They were discouraged, thinking that "the two families which the Lord chose," i.e., Israel and Judah, had been completely rejected by God. For this reason Gentiles despised God's people. They no longer regard Israel as a nation. In response to this despondency the prophet renewed his assurance of the permanence of God's relationship with his people. The Lord would no more reject the descendants of Jacob and David than he would revoke the day-night sequence or annul the "fixed patterns of heaven and earth." In the future the "seed of Abraham, Isaac and Jacob" would be ruled by "the seed of David." This restoration of Davidic rule was regarded as part of God's plan to "restore their fortunes." At the same time, it was a manifestation of God's mercy upon them.

Endnotes

1. Most commentators see in 31:15 only an analogy. What happened to the mothers at the fall of Jerusalem would be repeated by the mothers at Bethlehem. See for example C.F. Keil, "Jeremiah" in *Keil and Delitzsch Old Testament Commentaries* (Grand Rapids: Associated Publishers, n.d.) 941ff.; J. W. McGarvey and P.Y. Pendleton, *The Fourfold Gospel* (Cincinnati: Standard, n.d.) 52. Theo. Laetsch defends the view that Jeremiah was predicting the massacre of the Bethlehem infants. See *Bible Commentary: Jeremiah* (St. Louis: Concordia, 1965) 248ff.

2. Ezekiel 18 attacks the validity of the popular proverb cited in 31:29.

3. To prevent tampering with legal documents two copies were made. The *seal copy* was encased in the *open copy*. The procedure would be like recording the contents of a letter on the envelope. If anyone suspected that the document on the outside *envelope* had been altered, the seal could be broken and the sealed copy checked against the open copy.

4. The object of the verb in 33:2 is the third feminine singular pronoun. NIV and NASB interpret the pronoun to be a reference to the earth.

5. In 23:6 it is the Davidic Ruler (Messiah) who wears the name "Yahweh is Our Righteousness."

6. The covenant with Levi probably refers to the promises made to Phinehas, grandson of Aaron, in Num 25:13. This covenant is again mentioned in Mal 2:4, 5, 8.

CHAPTER NINETEEN

The Destruction of Jerusalem Jeremiah 34-39

Background of the Unit.

Chronologically the material in chapters 34-39 is disjointed; logically it fits together brilliantly. Chapter 34 begins with a brief announcement to King Zedekiah in the earliest days of the siege of Jerusalem in 588 BC. The final blow had begun to fall. Then in reverse chronological order Jeremiah cited examples of the stubbornness and disobedience of the people and kings of Judah which have as their purpose the justification of the final blow.

The first example (34:8-22) comes from the period of the siege of Jerusalem, in the summer of 588 BC. The second piece of evidence (chap. 35) comes from the reign of King Jehoiakim about a decade earlier, 598 BC. The last illustration (chap. 36) is precisely dated to the fourth year of Jehoiakim, 605 BC, the same year in which Nebuchadnezzar defeated the Egyptians at Carchemish.

After he cited his evidence justifying the destruction of Jerusalem, Jeremiah described his ministry during the terrible siege (chaps. 37-38). To this he appended a concise narrative describing the actual capture of the city (chap. 39).

Outline of the Unit.

A. Announcement of the Disaster (34:1-7).
B. Justification of the Disaster (34:8-36:32).
C. Pronouncements During the Disaster (chaps. 37-38).
D. Description of the Disaster (chap. 39).

ANNOUNCEMENT OF THE DISASTER
Jeremiah 34:1-7

The long-standing predictions that an enemy from the north would invade Judah came to pass when Nebuchadnezzar and his multi-national army began "fighting against Jerusalem and against all its cities." Early in 588 BC, before his confinement in the court of the guard (32:1-3), Jeremiah took the initiative and went to King Zedekiah with a message.[1] God declared that Jerusalem would fall to the invaders and be burned. After a face to face confrontation with Nebuchadnezzar, King Zedekiah would be carried away to Babylon. There he would die a natural death. Fellow captives would burn incense for him and bewail his death with traditional laments (34:1-5).

The message to Zedekiah is dated to the early part of the Babylonian invasion. Already the Babylonians controlled the countryside. Only two Judean fortified outposts beyond Jerusalem remained unconquered (34:6-7).

JUSTIFICATION FOR THE DISASTER
Jeremiah 34:8-36:32

Before he described the terrible ordeal of Jerusalem's fall, Jeremiah cited three incidents from recent history which demonstrated why Jerusalem had to be destroyed.

A. The Hypocritical Princes (34:8-22).

During the first weeks of the siege of Jerusalem the king and princes "got religion." Zedekiah entered into a solemn and sacred covenant with the inhabitants of Jerusalem "to proclaim release." Each man was to set free his Hebrew servants who were being held illegally. All who entered into this covenant obeyed and released the servants.

When the siege was lifted temporarily in the summer of 588 BC these princes went back on their solemn commitment and forced these men and women back into slavery (34:8-11).

God's covenant with Israel stipulated that Hebrew servants were to be released after six years of service, or "every seventh year" (NIV). This law had been ignored by their forefathers. That the princes had recently, albeit belatedly, released their slaves, pleased the Lord. They had entered into a sacred covenant before the Lord in the Temple. When those same princes reneged on their sacred oath they *profaned* God's name by which they had taken their oath (34:12-16).

Since the princes had failed to proclaim release to their servants, God would proclaim a release to these covenant breakers. They would be released from divine protection and handed over to the sword, plague and famine. Judah would experience all the horrors of war and become a terrifying object lesson to surrounding nations. The princes who participated in the covenant ceremony of marching through the severed carcasses of animals would be slain[2] and their bodies left exposed to the bird and beast (34:17-20).

The Babylonian invaders who had departed from their siege would return. They would capture Jerusalem and destroy it. The other cities of Judah would become "a desolation without inhabitant." Zedekiah and his officials would fall into the hands of their enemies (34:21-22).

B. The Disobedient Sons (35:1-19).

Chapter 35 antedates the previous chapter by some ten years. The episode can probably be assigned to 599 or 598 BC. Jeremiah was told to go the "house of the Rechabites." This was an ascetic group which normally refused to live in houses, plant vineyards or drink wine. Jeremiah was to take this group to one of the large chambers of the Temple and publicly offer them a large bowl of wine to drink (35:1-2). The prophet was not placing a temptation before this stalwart band. He knew what their reaction would be. Jeremiah wanted to use these devout souls as an illustration.

The prophet carried out his instructions. He took the Rechabites to "the chamber of the sons of Hanan" in the Temple. There he set before them "pitchers full of wine and cups" and invited them to drink. The Rechabites refused to touch the wine. They explained that their ancestor Jonadab[3] had commanded them not to drink wine forever. Through all the years the Rechabites faithfully had followed the instructions of their ancestor. Only when roving bands of Chaldeans and mercenaries made the countryside unsafe did these noble nomads leave their tents to take refuge in the capital (35:3-11).

Jeremiah was told to take a message to the "men of Judah and the inhabitants of Jerusalem." The Lord asked this question: "Will you not receive instruction by listening to my words? Jonadab had spoken once and his descendants obeyed him for two hundred years. By contrast the Lord had spoken repeatedly and earnestly, but the men of Judah paid him no heed. God's servants the prophets consistently had urged each citizen to "turn from his evil way, amend your deeds, do not go after other gods." Only national repentance would guarantee their right to continue to dwell in Canaan. Because Judah had refused to listen to God's call to repentance, the land would experience all the calamities which his messengers and his Law had threatened (35:12-17).

The Rechabites were models of parental respect and obedience. Because these people had obeyed the command of their distant ancestor Jonadab, God had a word of promise for them: "Jonadab the son of Rechab shall not lack a man to stand before me always." To *stand before* God means to be active in his service (35:18-19). Through the centuries those who respect the instructions of their godly parents are spiritual descendants of Jonadab.

C. The Defiant King (36:1-32).

The head of the nation was wicked to the core. In chapter 36 Jeremiah went back in time to 605 BC to relate an incident in the reign of King Jehoiakim. The attitude of the king toward the written word of God was cited as another reason which justified the destruction of Jerusalem.

1. The scroll written (36:1-4). Shortly after the battle of Carchemish in 605 BC Jeremiah was told to write all the words which God had given him "concerning Israel, concerning Judah and concerning all the nations." His scroll would have contained a summary of his twenty-three years of preaching. Since the written word was given far more credence than the spoken word in antiquity, the hope was that the house of Judah would at last give heed to God's call to repentance. To facilitate this project Jeremiah employed a scribe named Baruch to whom he dictated the words he had been preaching.

2. The scroll read (36:5-15). For some unexplained reason Jeremiah could not go to the Temple. He instructed Baruch to read the scroll there on a fast day when there would be large throngs present. The prophet yet hoped for a dramatic national repentance which would turn away God's wrath (36:5-7).

The scroll was read in the fifth year of Jehoiakim, the ninth month.[4] Thus a gap of at least nine months intervened between the writing of the scroll and the reading of it. Baruch read the document from the chamber of Gemariah who came from a family which earlier had demonstrated support for the prophet (cf. 26:24). The son of this Gemariah was present and was moved by the words of the scroll. He reported what he had heard to a group of princes who were holdovers from the administration of good King Josiah. Wishing to hear for themselves the words of the scroll, these friendly princes sent for Baruch and asked him to read it to them (36:6-15).

3. The scroll discussed (36:16-19). The princes were moved to fear by the words of the scroll. They felt compelled to inform the king of the warnings contained therein, for only the king had the authority to alter the direction of the nation. They inquired precisely as to the origin of the document. Baruch informed them that the words were dictated by the prophet Jeremiah. Anticipating the reaction of the king, the princes urged Baruch and Jeremiah to go into hiding.

4. The scroll attacked (36:20-26). The princes deposited the scroll in the chamber of Elishama the scribe, and then went to convey its words to the king. When Jehoiakim heard of the scroll he demanded to see it. Before three or four columns of that scroll had been read in his presence, Jehoiakim slashed it with a scribe's knife and threw it into the brazier fire. None of the servants about the king felt any fear about destroying the word of God, although the princes who had reported the scroll to the king pled with him not to burn it. After he had burned the document, Jehoiakim issued orders that Jeremiah and Baruch be seized.

5. The scroll restored (36:27-32). God directed Jeremiah to prepare a second scroll which was to contain all that the first had contained. He was, however, to add a special message to the king. Jehoiakim had burned the scroll because he did not like Jeremiah's predictions that the king of Babylon would come to destroy the land. God had a special word of judgment for this brash king. First, he would have no descendant to follow him successfully on the throne.[5] Second, the corpse of Jehoiakim would not be buried. Jehoiakim, his seed, i.e., descendants, and his servants would be punished for their iniquity. The entire calamity which had been declared by the Lord would most certainly befall the inhabitants of Jerusalem and the men of Judah (36:27-31).

Jeremiah did as God directed him. He took another scroll and dictated "all the words of the book which Jehoiakim king of Judah had burned in the fire." He added in this second scroll "many similar words" (36:32).

PRONOUNCEMENTS DURING THE DISASTER Jeremiah 37-38

Coniah (Jehoiachin) the son of Jehoiakim reigned briefly after his father died or was assassinated late in the year 598 BC. When Jehoiachin was deported to Babylon in March of 597 BC, Nebuchadnezzar placed Zedekiah, another son of Josiah, on the throne as his vassal. In terms of his willingness to listen to the word of God as spoken by Jeremiah, Zedekiah was no better than his immediate predecessors (37:1-2). Chapters 37-38 document how the prophet of God suffered for his testimony during the last half of the Babylonian siege.

A. Jeremiah Consulted (37:3-10).

In the summer of 588 BC the Chaldeans lifted the siege of Jerusalem in order to deal with an Egyptian relief column which was marching northward to aid Zedekiah. Jeremiah had not yet been imprisoned for the final time. A two-man delegation was sent to Jeremiah to request prayer.[6] Perhaps they were hoping for an Egyptian victory over the Chaldeans. They certainly expected reassurance that the Babylonian menace was over (37:3-5).

Jeremiah sent the two messengers back to their master with a message of doom. Pharaoh's army would return to the land of Egypt. No help could therefore be expected from that quarter. The Chaldeans shortly would return to capture and destroy Jerusalem. Belief that the Chaldeans would now leave Jerusalem alone was nothing but a vain delusion. Even if every Chaldean soldier were wounded, the Chaldeans would still have enough strength to capture and burn the city (37:6-10).

B. Jeremiah Confined (37:11-38:28).

The prophet had his freedom only a short time during the lull in the siege of Jerusalem. He was destined for re-arrest and harsh treatment during the last nine months of the siege.

1. Arrested by the guard (37:11-16). Jeremiah had business to conduct in Anathoth, his hometown. Probably he was going there during the lull in the siege to take possession of the property which he had purchased from his cousin in chapter 32. While attempting to leave the city by the Benjamin gate, Jeremiah was arrested by the captain of the guard. The charge was treason: "You are going over to the Chaldeans." Jeremiah vigorously denied the charge both to the captain and to the princes before whom he stood trial. These officials now had an excuse to vent their anger against the prophet. Jeremiah was beaten, i.e., scourged, and thrown into a subterranean dungeon beneath the house of one of the scribes. The prophet was there "for many days."

2. Summoned by the king (37:17-21). The Chaldeans came back as Jeremiah had predicted. In desperation King Zedekiah ordered that Jeremiah be brought to the palace. The king secretly asked Jeremiah this crucial question: "Is there a word from the Lord?" The "701 theology" of last minute divine intervention was thoroughly ingrained in the king. He expected finally to hear from Jeremiah a positive word regarding the fate of Jerusalem. The prophet affirmed without a moment's hesitation that indeed there was a word from the Lord, but it was not the word which the king expected nor wanted. In fact, the word had not changed since Jeremiah had confronted Zedekiah earlier in the siege (cf. 34:1-7): "You will be given into the hands of the king of Babylon" (37:17).

Having delivered his official word to Zedekiah, Jeremiah made a personal request. He had committed no wrong against the government or the people. The "prophets" who had wrongly predicted that Nebuchadnezzar would not come against the land were the ones who should be punished. Jeremiah politely requested that he not be returned to the dungeon of Jonathan the scribe. If the king forced the prophet to return to that dungeon, he would surely die (37:18-20).

Zedekiah listened to the plea of Jeremiah. He commanded that Jeremiah be detained in the court of the guard, presumably a much more hospitable detention area. He was given a ration of bread as long as there was any bread left in the city (37:21).

3. Imprisoned by the princes (38:1-6). Detention did not silence Jeremiah. At every opportunity he urged the soldiers defending the walls to surrender to the Chaldeans. Only by so doing could these soldiers save their lives. He who remained in the city would die by sword, famine and pestilence. Jerusalem would certainly be given into the hand of the army of the king of Babylon. Jeremiah's actions enraged the princes (38:1-3).

The princes[7] went to the king and demanded the death penalty for the traitor. In their view he was hurting the war effort. The king handed Jeremiah over to the powerful princes; he was too weak to resist them. The princes then threw Jeremiah into an empty cistern in which he sunk into the mud (38:4-6).

4. Rescued by Ebed-melech (38:7-13). An Ethiopian servant named Ebed-melech ("servant of the king") rushed from the palace to the Benjamin gate where Zedekiah was sitting. The king may have been engaged in some form of judgment or perhaps military planning. Ebed-melech informed Zedekiah about the treatment Jeremiah had received from the princes. The servant insisted that Jeremiah would die of the famine if left in the cistern since no more bread was left in the city. If this is a logical argument and not merely an emotional outburst the thought might be this: prisoners would be the first to be cut off from any rationing of what little bread could be found in Jerusalem. Mustering some degree of moral outrage, the king authorized his servant to rescue the prophet. He warned Ebed-melech, however, to protect himself from the princes with thirty bodyguards (38:7-10).

Ebed-melech and his assistants stopped at a palace storeroom en route to the cistern. There the servant thoughtfully secured some tattered garments which could be used to protect the prophet from rope burn when he was pulled up from the cistern. After his rescue Jeremiah remained in the detention area known as the court of the guard until Jerusalem fell to the Chaldeans (38:11-13).

5. Interviewed by the king (38:14-26). As the siege conditions worsened King Zedekiah sought one last time to find some ray of hope in the message of Jeremiah. The prisoner was brought to the third entrance of the Temple for a secret meeting with the king. Zedekiah urged Jeremiah not to hide anything from him. For his part, the prophet was pessimistic about the results of telling the king the word of God. Zedekiah had shown no inclination on previous occasions to give heed to divine directives. The king, however, gave solemn assurances that he would not execute Jeremiah, nor turn him over to those who were his enemies (38:14-16).

In the name of God Jeremiah gave the king two alternatives. If he surrendered to the Chaldeans, the city would be spared from destruction and Zedekiah would live. On the other hand, if he continued to resist, the Chaldeans shortly would capture Jerusalem and burn it. Zedekiah would not escape from their hands (38:17-18).

Fear prevented King Zedekiah from following the advice of the prophet. Many Jews already had defected to the Chaldeans. They would be angry with the king for having caused the city to endure such agony. Zedekiah was afraid that the Chaldeans might hand him over to his own former subjects for torture and humiliation. Jeremiah assured the king that his fears were unfounded. He begged the king to surrender. If he did not, even the palace women would mock him when they were taken captive. They would liken him to one who was led forth by friends he trusted into the mire, and then abandoned there. Worse still, these palace attendants would turn on the royal family and deliver them over to the Chaldeans as well (38:19-23).

Zedekiah ordered Jeremiah to keep silent about this meeting. If questioned by the princes he was to say only that he had petitioned the king not to return him to the dungeon in the house of Jonathan where he had been a few weeks earlier (38:24-26).

6. Questioned by the princes (38:27-28). Through their spy network, the princes did learn of the meeting between Zedekiah and Jeremiah. They came to the prophet and questioned him about the meeting. Jeremiah gave to them the response which the king had commanded. In so doing Jeremiah was not guilty of lying. He told the truth, but not all of the truth. The princes did not have the right to know the full contents of the privileged conversation between the king and his spiritual counselor. The princes had no basis upon which to dispute the report since the conversation had not been overheard. So Jeremiah was left in the court of the guard until Jerusalem was captured.

DESCRIPTION OF THE DISASTER
Jeremiah 39:1-18

Chapter 39 contains a concise account of the Chaldean siege and capture of Jerusalem. The purpose of this chapter is to underscore the fact that Jeremiah was indeed a true prophet of God. All that he had predicted about the city came to pass. To the account of the destruction of Jerusalem a message of hope for Ebed-melech has been attached.

A. The Fall of Jerusalem (39:1-14).

The siege of Jerusalem began in January of 588 BC. In July of 587 BC the walls were breached. A military government was established by the conquerors. All that remained was the storming of the higher parts of the city where Zedekiah and the remnant of the army were still holding out (39:1-3).

After the walls were breached Zedekiah knew that it would be futile to attempt to defend the rest of the city. The king fled by night toward the Arabah or plains. He was captured near Jericho and taken to Riblah in the land of Hamath. There Nebuchadnezzar passed sentence against him. He witnessed the execution of his sons and nobles before having his own eyesight taken from him. He was then bound with fetters of bronze and led away captive to Babylon (39:4-7).

Jerusalem was destroyed totally by the armies of Nebuchadnezzar. The king's palace and the houses of the people as well were burned. The walls were dismantled. Many were taken captive. Only the poor were left in the land by the Babylonian commander Nebuzaradan (39:8-10).

Finally, the chapter mentions the command of Nebuchadnezzar regarding Jeremiah. The conqueror viewed the prophet as a Babylonian partisan. He gave orders that Jeremiah receive favorable treatment. Consequently he was given over to the care of Gedaliah[8] to be escorted home. Jeremiah was free at last! (39:11-14).

B. A Message for Ebed-melech (39:15-18).

Just after his rescue from the cistern, while Jeremiah was confined to the court of the guard, he received a special word from the Lord regarding Ebed-melech. Jeremiah was to go to this servant who apparently worked in the vicinity of the detention area. He announced to this royal servant that Jerusalem was indeed about to fall to the Chaldeans. The royal servant, however, need not worry. Because he had rescued Jeremiah from certain death in the cistern, Ebed-melech was promised that God would rescue him when Jerusalem fell. The implication of including this prediction after the account of Jerusalem's fall is that Ebed-melech was indeed spared by the Chaldeans just as Jeremiah had predicted. God rewards those who demonstrate daring faith for him.

Endnotes

1. The chronological arrangement of the interviews between Zedekiah and Jeremiah during the last days of Jerusalem is difficult. The following arrangement is probable: (1) early summer of 589 when Nebuchadnezzar was advancing against Jerusalem (21:1-10); (2) early in 588 when most of the military outposts of Judah had been captured (34:2-7); (3) summer 588 when the siege of Jerusalem was temporarily lifted (37:3-10); (4) fall of 588 after Jeremiah's release from the dungeon (38:14-28).

2. The covenant ceremony of marching through the bodies of severed animals is first attested in Gen 15. The action was a self-malediction in which the participant called upon God to make him like those severed animals if he should violate the oath or covenant.

3. Jonadab lived nearly two hundred years earlier. He was associated with the exploits of King Jehu of Israel (2 Kgs 9:15-31).

4. The ninth month corresponds roughly to December on the present calendar.

5. As a matter of record, Jehoiakim did have a son who occupied the throne for about three months.

6. Zephaniah the deputy high priest is mentioned in 21:1; 29:25; 52:24, 26; and 2 Kgs 25:18, 20, 21. Jehucal shortly would join other princes in demanding the death sentence for Jeremiah (38:4).

7. This much is known about the princes who complained to the king about Jeremiah's preaching: Gedaliah was the son of the Pashur who had Jeremiah beaten in 20:1-2; Jehucal and Pashur had asked Jeremiah to pray for the city a few weeks earlier (21:1). Shephatiah is mentioned only here.

8. This Gedaliah is the son of the Ahikam who had rescued Jeremiah from certain death in the Temple (26:24).

CHAPTER TWENTY

Tragedy Beyond Tragedy
Jeremiah 40-45

Background of the Unit.

This unit is introduced with the words, "The word which came unto Jeremiah from the Lord." What follows, however, is essentially historical narrative. From this one can conclude that history as well as prophecy is the word of the Lord.

The unit begins with an incident related to Jeremiah personally. The prophet was permitted to join the pitiful remnant which remained in the land after the destruction of Jerusalem. He went to Mizpah to support the efforts of Gedaliah who had been appointed governor by the Babylonians. How long Jeremiah remained at Mizpah with Gedaliah before the latter's assassination is difficult to determine from the available data. Some think Gedaliah governed until 582 BC; others envision a governorship of only a few months.

After the assassination of Gedaliah, Jeremiah was forced to accompany the remnant to Egypt. His last recorded sermons were on foreign soil. There he confronted the same old hypocrisy and bent toward idolatry which he had battled before the destruction of Jerusalem. Jeremiah concluded his ministry laboring among the same kind of audience which he had faced for forty years prior to the destruction of 587 BC. Though well into his sixties, Jeremiah had lost none of his fire and fervor. A date of about 560 BC for Jeremiah's death seems to fit all the available data. Chapter 45 is a special appendix addressed to Baruch. It dates back to the crucial fourth year of Jehoiakim when Jeremiah first put his sermons into writing (chap. 36) and Nebuchadnezzar defeated Egypt in the battle of Carchemish. The placement here is a testimony to the faithfulness of God in keeping his word to Baruch throughout the ordeal of Jerusalem's fall and even beyond.

Outline of the Unit.

A. Post-fall Events in Judah (40:1-43:7).
B. Post-fall Events in Egypt (43:8-44:30).
C. A Personal Note to Baruch (chap. 45).

POST-FALL EVENTS IN JUDAH
Jeremiah 40:1-43:7

The destruction of Jerusalem did not end the suffering for the remnant in Judah. The text now relates how Jeremiah came to be part of that remnant after almost being deported to Babylon. The unit then describes the assassination of the governor Gedaliah and the plight of the remnant following that most unfortunate event.

A. Jeremiah's Choice (40:1-6).

Some subordinate Chaldean officer did not recognize Jeremiah among the Judean captives. Perhaps he had not heard the order which had been given regarding the treatment of Jeremiah by the military government. In any case, the prophet was taken in chains to Ramah where the captives were being processed prior to deportation to Babylon. One of the Chaldean generals recognized him there and ordered his release (40:1).

Nebuzaradan seems to have heard of the predictions of Jeremiah for he said, "the Lord your God promised this calamity against this place." He was familiar with the reasons which the prophet had cited for the fall of Jerusalem: "You people sinned against the Lord and did not listen to his voice." The captain set Jeremiah free from his chains and gave him three options. First, he could go to Babylon where the captain promised to look after him the rest of his days. Second, he could go back to join Gedaliah in the devastated land. Third, he could go anywhere he wished. The captain gave "a ration and a gift" to Jeremiah and then dismissed him. Jeremiah chose to go to Mizpah to join Gedaliah the provincial governor (40:2-6).

B. Gedaliah's Program (40:7-12).

Small guerrilla bands of Jewish soldiers were hiding out in remote regions of the land. When the commanders of these units heard that Gedaliah had been appointed governor by Nebuchadnezzar, they began to bring their men out of hiding. Obviously they had confidence in the ability of Gedaliah to rebuild the country. Among those who came to Mizpah to join Gedaliah, two were to play a prominent role in subsequent events, viz., Ishmael and Johanan (40:7).

Gedaliah was a wise and able leader. His first priority was to unite the various factions into which the remnant had fractured. Gedaliah gave his solemn word that if these people would remain in the land and serve the king of Babylon all would be well. He pledged that he would serve as a representative for them before the Chaldean officers who might come through the land from time to time to conduct the business of their king. He urged the remnant to gather the summer harvest and occupy the cities of the land. In response to this positive program, refugees from surrounding lands began to return to Judah. They "gathered in wine and summer fruit in great abundance" (40:8-12).

C. Ishmael's Plot (40:13-41:16).

The king of Ammon, Baalis, employed a radical member of Judah's royal family to assassinate Gedaliah. The plot was revealed to the governor by the guerrilla commanders with Johanan as their spokesman. Gedaliah, however, refused to believe the report. Johanan privately proposed to the governor that he be authorized to assassinate Ishmael. He understood that should Ishmael succeed with his plot, the tattered remnant would be scattered to the point of perishing altogether. Gedaliah refused to authorize the counterplot. He branded the reports about Ishmael as a lie. Gedaliah could not believe that anyone could possibly contemplate an attempt to reestablish the monarchy (40:13-16).

In the seventh month (presumably of the year Jerusalem fell), Ishmael and ten other princes rose up at a banquet to slay Gedaliah. All the other Chaldean and Jewish officials who were there at Mizpah also died by the hand of the cutthroats (41:1-3).

Eighty mournful pilgrims who were making their way to the ruins of the Temple became the next victims. Ishmael went out to meet them feigning mourning. He invited them to come to Gedaliah within Mizpah. The eighty were thus diverted into the city, slain and thrown into a cistern. Ten of the pilgrims bargained for their lives with provisions they had stored during the tumultuous years of the Babylonian invasion (41:4-9).

Ishmael and his men took captive the people who resided in Mizpah. Among the hostages were some daughters of the former king. Presumably Jeremiah was also among them. The plan was to herd the captives down to the Jordan, then across the river to Ammon. Somehow Johanan and other soldiers heard what had happened. They pursued Ishmael. Near the pool of Gibeon the rescue units caught up to the kidnappers. The hostages were rescued, but Ishmael and eight of his men escaped (41:10-16).

D. The Remnant's Plight (41:17-43:7).

The Babylonian governor was now dead. Fearing Chaldean retaliation, the remnant started south toward Egypt. Near Bethlehem somebody got the idea that before proceeding any further, they should stop to seek God's will about their actions. They presented their petition to Jeremiah and requested that he pray for the remnant. They wanted the Lord to "tell us the way in which we should walk and the thing that we should do" (41:17-42:3).

Jeremiah agreed to the request. He assured the remnant that he would tell them "the whole message that the Lord will answer you." He promised that he would not "keep back a word from you." To this the remnant responded with strong assurances that they "would act in accordance with the whole message with which the Lord your God will send you to us." The remnant leaders piously committed themselves to listen to the voice of the Lord whether his word was pleasant or unpleasant. They professed to realize that only through obedience to the divine word would they be able to secure their well-being (42:4-6).

After ten days the answer came. Jeremiah summoned Johanan, the other commanders, and the people to hear God's word. If they continued to dwell in the land God would build them up and plant them. He would relent concerning the calamity which he had inflicted upon them. They would have no reason to fear the king of Babylon. God would be with them, and deliver them from the hand of Nebuchadnezzar. God would show them compassion, and so would the king of Babylon (42:7-12).

The other alternative was to continue their flight to Egypt. There they hoped to escape war and famine. Their abandonment of the land, however, would be a manifestation of disobedience to God and lack of faith in his word. Their plan would not succeed. Sword and famine would follow them to Egypt. All who set their minds on this course of action would die in Egypt "by the sword, by famine and by pestilence." No one of them would survive this calamity (42:13-17).

Jeremiah could tell by the reaction of those before him that the remnant had no intention of remaining in Judah. Therefore, he amplified his warning. Just as God had poured out his wrath on Jerusalem, so he would pour out his wrath on the remnant which entered Egypt. Their fate would be so wretched that people would use them in curses and imprecations (42:18f.).

God had spoken clearly his will and Jeremiah had "testified" faithfully against the remnant. They should not migrate to Egypt. Jeremiah reminded them of their request ten days earlier. He quoted to them their commitment to do whatever the Lord told them they should do. By making that request and that commitment these men were only deceiving themselves. Their minds were made up before they ever requested prayer. The proof of that accusation was obvious. They were in the process of disobeying again a direct, simple, unambiguous directive given to them by their God through his messenger.

In the last recorded words spoken in his native land, Jeremiah wanted the remnant clearly to understand the consequences of their action. Egypt for them would mean more sword, famine and pestilence (42:20-22).

The commanders trusted human logic more than divine revelation. For this reason they are called "arrogant men." They had the temerity to accuse Jeremiah of lying to them in the name of the Lord. They simply could not believe that God would be opposed to their plan to migrate to Egypt. For some unexplained reason, they accused Baruch of having incited the prophet against them. In their twisted logic, they accused Baruch of opposing migration to Egypt so that the remnant could be punished by the Chaldeans for the murder of Gedaliah. As far as they were concerned, death or exile to Babylon were the only alternatives if they remained in the land (43:1-3).

Led by Johanan, the remnant disobeyed the voice of the Lord and departed for Egypt. The commanders "took the entire remnant" with them, all who had formerly been under the authority of Gedaliah. Apparently individuals did not have the option of heeding the words of the prophet. Among those forced to make the trip were Jeremiah and his faithful secretary Baruch. The group moved into Egypt as far as Tahpanhes. This detail is mentioned perhaps to underscore that these men did not just flirt with disobedience, they plunged headlong into it (43:4-7).

POST-FALL EVENTS IN EGYPT
Jeremiah 43:8-44:30

Jeremiah continued his prophetic ministry among the remnant in Egypt. The narrative centers around an announcement, an admonition and an affirmation which he made in that land.

A. A Prophetic Announcement (43:8-13).

At the entrance of a government building in Tahpanhes, Jeremiah performed his last action parable. He buried some stones beneath the pavement. His actions were probably ignored by the Egyptians as the work of a madman. The prophet, however, intended to convey to the refugees in Egypt a serious message. At that very spot Nebuchadnezzar, who functioned as God's servant, would set up his throne in Egypt (43:8-10).

Jeremiah predicted a devastating Babylonian invasion of Egypt. Some would die of the sword in battle, others by exigencies of war; still others would be deported to Babylon. Through his agent, the king of Babylon, God would burn the temples of the gods of Egypt. The great stone pillars at the religious center of Beth-shemesh (Heliopolis) would be shattered. Nebuchadnezzar would "wrap himself with the land of Egypt as a shepherd wraps himself with his garment," i.e. he would completely dominate Egypt. Then he would depart in safety to his own land. Ancient sources testify that Nebuchadnezzar invaded Egypt twice, once in 582 BC and again in 568 BC (43:11-13).[1]

B. A Prophetic Admonition (44:1-19)

From their initial settlement in Tahpanhes the Jews scattered throughout the land of Egypt.[2] On some holy day when they gathered at one location for worship, Jeremiah addressed his countrymen (44:1).

1. Explanation of past calamity (44:2-6). Jeremiah began by reminding the Jews in Egypt what had happened to their homeland. The cities of Judah were uninhabited ruins. This calamity had befallen them because they had provoked God to anger by offering sacrifices to the gods of Canaan. The apostasy continued in spite of the urgent and persistent effort of God's prophets to persuade them to cease this "abominable thing." They did not listen, nor did they turn from their wickedness. Therefore, the wrath of God had been poured out on the cities of Judah.

2. Expostulation regarding the present (44:7-10). The conduct of the refugees in Egypt was absolutely incredible to Jeremiah. Why would they want to bring more calamity upon themselves? That remnant in Egypt was in danger of being totally exterminated. Once again they were provoking the Lord to anger with their idolatrous worship. Had they forgotten the wickedness which had permeated Judah through the years? Never had these people shown any contrition. They had not feared the Lord nor walked in his Law.

3. Declaration regarding the future (44:11-14). Since the remnant was continuing in the wickedness of their fathers, God declared himself to be against them. "Behold, I am going to set my face against you for woe, even to cut off all Judah." These refugees would meet their end in the land of Egypt. Both small and great would fall by the sword or perish in famine. That group would suffer so much that they would be mentioned in curses and imprecations. They would suffer a fate similar to that which Jerusalem experienced. Although these Jews longed to return to their native land, only a very few would ever be able to return to Judah.

4. *Rejection of the warning (44:15-19).* The remnant made no pretense of accepting the warning from Jeremiah. They declared: "We are not going to listen to you." They had every intention of continuing to worship the queen of heaven, i.e., Ishtar. In defense of their practice they argued that (1) this had been the practice of their forefathers and leaders; and (2) when they had worshiped the queen of heaven, they had prospered. They interpreted the recent calamities in Judah as due to the cessation of pagan worship forced on the populace by the reforms of King Josiah. The women argued that all which they did—sacrifices, libations, and sacramental cakes—they did with the knowledge and approval of their husbands.

C. A Prophetic Affirmation (44:20-30).

Jeremiah repeated his contention that the destruction of Jerusalem resulted from God's anger against their idolatry. God remembered the crimes they had committed in the reign of Manasseh. He delayed executing the sentence because of his longsuffering. Finally, however, the Lord "was no longer able to endure it." They flaunted their disobedience. They refused to walk in his Law or listen to his voice. Therefore the calamity fell on Judah and this remnant was still suffering the repercussions of that calamity (44:20-23).

In bitter sarcasm Jeremiah urged the refugees to fulfill their vows to the queen of heaven. The Jews in Egypt were no longer God's people; they had lost their right to call upon the Lord. God would watch over those Jews for evil not for good. Most of them would perish. Only a very few would escape the sword to return to their homeland. Those few would recognize then that God's word endures eternally; man's word is overturned by circumstances (44:24-28).

A sign was given that the complete prophecy concerning the

Egyptian Jews would be fulfilled. Pharaoh Hophra would fall into the hands of his enemies just as God earlier had given Zedekiah into the hands of Nebuchadnezzar (44:29f.). Hophra was taken hostage by Amasis the succeeding Pharaoh about 570 BC. About a decade later he was strangled to death.

A PERSONAL NOTE TO BARUCH
Jeremiah 45

So far as the record goes, Baruch first became associated with Jeremiah in the fourth year of King Jehoiakim. That was the year that Nebuchadnezzar defeated Pharaoh Neco at Carchemish (cf. 25:1; 36:1). That was also the year when Jeremiah first dictated his messages to the scribe Baruch (45:1). That Baruch believed the words of the prophet is clear enough. That he entertained notions of sharing honors which he thought would be bestowed on the prophet also seems clear. The purpose of this brief note is to correct that mistaken notion. In all of his concern for the great international events of his day, Jeremiah was not too preoccupied to be concerned about the spiritual crisis of a single disciple.

Baruch was experiencing a period of discouragement perhaps triggered by the arrest order of King Jehoiakim (36:26). The ministry was not what he thought it would be. The message of the impending destruction of Jerusalem was depressing to him. Privately he was complaining that the Lord had added sorrow to his mental pain. He had become weary with groaning. He could find no rest. Baruch's self-pity here is reminiscent of that depression which Jeremiah experienced shortly before in his ministry. Here is one believer who had traversed the dark valley of spiritual depression helping another weary pilgrim find his way through that same terrain (45:2f.).

God responded to Baruch's depression much as he earlier had dealt with that of Jeremiah. To help this faithful secretary put his personal agony in proper perspective, God revealed to him the divine hurt. God must destroy the land which he had built up. What agony that must have been to him (45:4). Whatever the pain of ministerial rejection, the messenger of God must always realize that the agony of God is infinitely worse. God is not willing that any should perish.

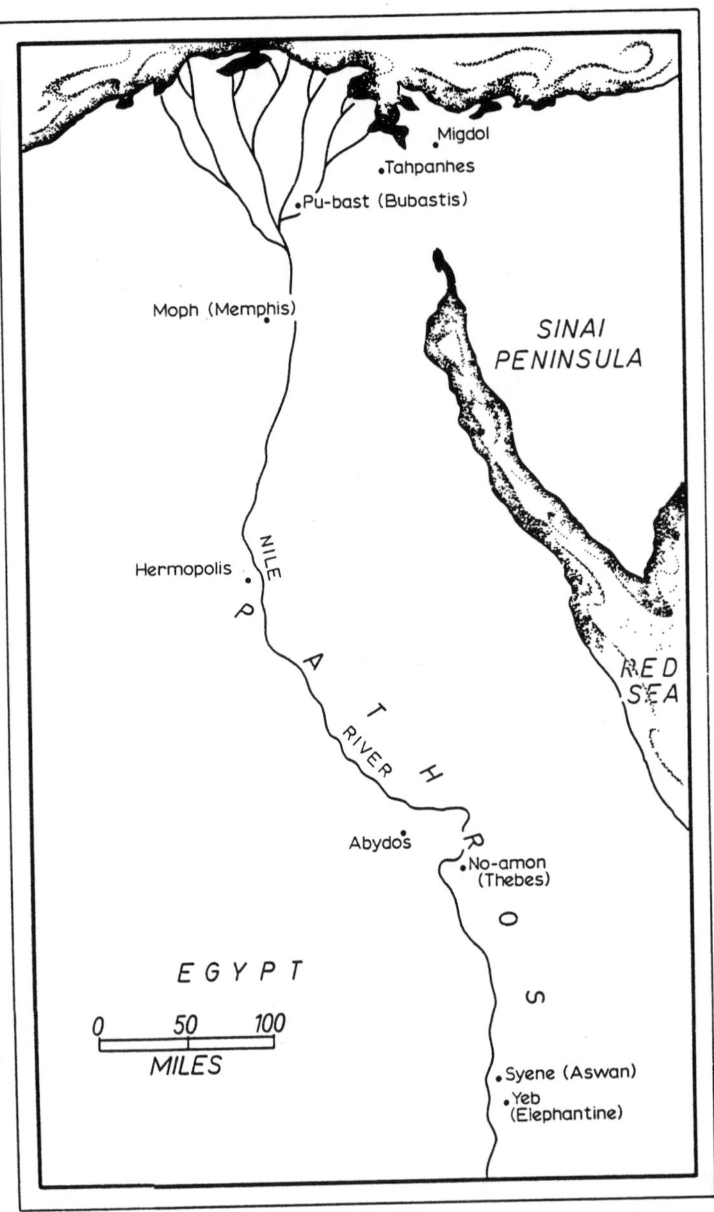
Migdol
Tahpanhes
Pu-bast (Bubastis)
Moph (Memphis)
SINAI PENINSULA
NILE
Hermopolis
PATHROS
RIVER
RED SEA
Abydos
No-amon (Thebes)
EGYPT
0 50 100
MILES
Syene (Aswan)
Yeb (Elephantine)

Most, however, do not love him and will not serve him.

Baruch, like many young servants of the Lord, had grandiose personal ambitions. Those ambitions would never be realized. He must put them aside. He must be realistic about the future. The entire land of Judah would experience a disaster, i.e., the judgment of God. The Lord, however, does make a promise to Baruch. He would survive the destruction of his city and land (45:5). God kept his word. Baruch was part of the small group which the Chaldeans left in the land after Jerusalem fell. Along with Jeremiah, he was forced to emigrate to Egypt. Jeremiah has inserted this personal note here in the text to demonstrate that God keeps his promises to individuals as well as to nations.

Endnotes

1. Josephus tells of an invasion of Egypt by Nebuchadnezzar in 582 BC (*Antiquities* 10.9.7.) A fragmentary inscription from the archives of Nebuchadnezzar tells of another invasion in 568 BC (*Ancient Near Eastern Texts,* 308).

2. Migdol is located near the northeastern boundary of Egypt. Noph or Memphis was located about 125 miles south of the Mediterranean Sea. Pathros means "land of the south" and refers to the region still further south of Memphis called Upper Egypt. The gathering probably took place in Tahpanhes.

CHAPTER TWENTY-ONE

God and the Nations
Jeremiah 46-52

Background of the Unit.

The Book of Jeremiah concludes with a collection of oracles concerning foreign nations from various periods of the prophet's ministry. In the Greek version this section appears in the midst of chapter 25. Similar collections of foreign nation oracles appear in Isaiah (chaps. 13-23) and Ezekiel (chaps. 25-32). That Jeremiah's ministry would have an international dimension was indicated clearly at the time of his call (1:5).

This section is closely related to chapter 25. There Jeremiah was told to take the cup of God's wrath and pass it among the nations of his day. The nations would drink that cup, stagger and fall to their destruction. Last of all the king of Babylon would drink and perish. The foreign nations in chapters 46-51 are treated in roughly the same order in which they are listed in chapter 25.

The foreign nation oracles in this unit seem to be organized in a definite pattern. Jeremiah placed first a small collection of oracles against Egypt, Israel's archenemy to the south. Then he collected the oracles against smaller nations which were more or less pawns in the struggle between the great powers of the day. The climax of the unit is the lengthy oracle against Babylon in chapters 50-51. Here Jeremiah announced God's judgment against the greatest power of his day.

The following chart indicates the approximate chronological placement of the various oracles of this unit.

Chart No. 6

CHRONOLOGICAL SEQUENCE OF JEREMIAH'S FOREIGN NATION ORACLES		
Time Frame	**Oracles**	**Location**
Sometime Before the Battle of Carchemish	Philistine Oracle	47:1-7
Just Prior to the Battle of Carchemish	First Egypt Oracle Moab Oracle Ammon Oracle Edom Oracle Damascus Oracle	46:1-12 48:1-47 49:1-6 49:7-22 49:23-27
Just After the Battle of Carchemish	Kedar-Hazor Oracle	49:28-33
Early Reign of Zedekiah	Elam Oracle	49:34-39
After the Emigration to Egypt	Second Egypt Oracle	46:13-28

Outline of the Unit.

A. Oracles against Egypt (chap. 46).
B. Oracles against Smaller Countries (chaps. 47-49).
C. Oracles against Babylon (chaps. 50-51).
D. Appendix: The Prophet Vindicated (chap. 52).

ORACLES AGAINST EGYPT
Jeremiah 46:2-28

Jeremiah recorded two oracles against Egypt. The first was composed just prior to the battle of Carchemish in 605 BC. The second, the latest oracle in the book, was composed after Jeremiah was forced to emigrate to Egypt with the refugees from Judah.

A. The First Egypt Oracle (46:2-12).

In his first oracle concerning Egypt Jeremiah twice depicted the defeat of Pharaoh's forces at Carchemish. First he described the elaborate preparation of the Egyptians before the battle. Jeremiah expressed his amazement at what he saw. The mighty Egyptian army would be destroyed at the river Euphrates (46:2-6).

The second picture was that of the Egyptian army rolling northward toward Carchemish like the mighty Nile in flood time. Jeremiah urged Pharaoh's troops and mercenaries to march forward. At Carchemish they would experience the day of the Lord's vengeance against his adversaries. In describing their defeat as a "slaughter for the Lord God of hosts" Jeremiah was indicating the religious significance of the battle. At Carchemish God inflicted on Egypt an incurable wound. What shame! The soldiers of Egypt would stumble over one another in their haste to retreat (46:7-12).

B. The Second Egypt Oracle (46:13-26).

The second Egypt oracle is chronologically the last oracle in this unit. It comes from the period after Jeremiah had been abducted to Egypt. The oracle announces that Nebuchadnezzar would invade Egypt (46:13). It develops three themes.

First, the oracle speaks of the certainty of the invasion. Jeremiah called on the major cities of Egypt to prepare for invasion. The "mighty ones" of Egypt would be thrown down. Mercenary soldiers would stumble over one another in flight to their homelands for they have come to see Pharaoh as nothing but a windbag. Egypt's appointed time for glory on earth had passed. The true King, Yahweh of hosts, had sworn that Nebuchadnezzar would tower over Egypt as surely as Mt. Tabor and Mt. Carmel tower over the landscape of Canaan. The capital of Egypt (Memphis) would be laid waste, and the citizens would be taken captive (46:14-19).

The oracle next moves to a description of the consequences of the invasion. In this unit Jeremiah presented four pictures of Egypt's plight. First, he compared Egypt to a beautiful heifer fleeing from the sting of the tiny gadfly, i.e., from Nebuchadnezzar. Second, he pictured the fat calves (mercenary soldiers) of Egypt fleeing to their homelands. Third, Jeremiah depicted woodsmen (Babylonians) coming to demolish the territory of the serpent (Egypt) which can only hiss in defiance. Fourth, he likened the Babylonians to a great swarm of invading locusts (46:20-23).

Egypt's plight would expose the futility of her idolatry. She would be put to shame when Yahweh declared war on her gods. Amon the sun god would be humbled; No (Thebes), the religious capital, would be brought to ruins. Pharaoh, who was regarded as a god by his countrymen, would be brought low. He and those who trusted in him would be given into the power of Nebuchadnezzar. After this judgment, however, Egypt would be inhabited as in older days, i.e., the land would enjoy peace (46:24-26).

The oracle concludes with a promise to the captives of Judah. Quoting the words of 30:10-11, the Lord urged "Jacob my servant" not to fear nor be dismayed. Egypt's troubles would be temporary; so also Israel's captivity. After corrective discipline against Israel, God would make a "full end" of the nations where Israel had been taken captive (46:27f.).

ORACLES AGAINST SMALLER NATIONS
Jeremiah 47-49

Seven oracles against smaller nations are contained in this unit.

Most of them were vassal states of Nebuchadnezzar which were plotting rebellion. The longest is that against Moab. Six of the seven nations were neighbors of Judah.

A. Oracle Against the Philistines (47:1-7).

The exact date is uncertain, but the Philistine oracle seems to come very early in Jeremiah's ministry. It is the earliest of the foreign nation oracles. Here the massive armies of a northern enemy (Babylon) are likened to an overflowing stream which destroys Philistia. The sound of rumbling chariots and galloping hoofs would strike paralyzing fear in the hearts of the Philistines. They would not be able to fulfill treaty obligations to neighboring states. They would not even be able to rescue their own children (47:1-4).

Jeremiah was sympathetic with the fate of the Philistines. Twice he expressed his concern with the query, "How long?" Upon further reflection he realized that the sword of justice cannot be ensheathed until it has done its work in the land of the Philistines (47:5-7).

B. Oracle Against Moab (48:1-47).

The Moabites lived east of the Jordan River and south of the Arnon River. They were descended from Lot, the nephew of Abraham. The Moabites seem to have been allies of Judah during the period of Jeremiah. The lengthy oracle against Moab can be analyzed in seven paragraphs. The first paragraph depicts the advancing devastation. Jeremiah envisioned the invaders pushing southward into Moab. He heard the enemy soldiers exhorting themselves: "Let us cut her off from being a nation." He heard the weeping of the refugees fleeing before the invaders (48:1-6).

In the second paragraph an urgent exhortation is addressed to Moab. The Moabites were urged to flee because neither their works (strongholds), nor their treasures, nor their national god (Chemosh) would be able to save them. The "destroyer" would come to every city of the land. Moab would need wings to help her escape. The destruction of Moab would be a work of Yahweh. Thus the destroyer must perform his job thoroughly (48:7-10).

The third and fifth paragraphs explain the calamity which was about to befall Moab. Heretofore Moab had remained comparatively undisturbed. Like wine allowed to stand on its lees (sediment), they had become a strong and proud culture. Now, however, "tilters" (RSV) would come to pour out Moab to the ground. In that day two aspects of Moab's pride were doomed to disappointment: (1) her confidence in her god Chemosh; and (2) her pride in military might. The judgment of Moab prophesied by Balaam (Num 24:17), Amos (2:1-3), Isaiah (chaps. 15-16) and now Jeremiah was close at hand. All who were friends of Moab were urged to bemoan the fate of the land (48:11-17). Moab's arrogance was an affront to God and he declared in the fifth paragraph that he must deal with it (48:29f.).

The fourth paragraph underscores the complete degradation which Moab would experience. Jeremiah likened Dibon, the royal city of Moab, to a delicate damsel. She was told to sit in the dust. The news would sweep southward from city to city. The horn of Moab (symbol of power) and arm (symbol of authority) had been broken. Just as Moab mocked Israel in her hour of humiliation, so at that time Moab would be mocked like a drunken man wallowing in his own vomit. Jeremiah urged the Moabites to seek refuge in the high mountains where the birds nest (48:18-28).

In the sixth paragraph Jeremiah took up a lament over Moab. He was distressed to think that the beautiful vineyards of that land would be ruined. Wine vats would be empty; worship activity would cease; everywhere gloom and despair would prevail. Jeremiah shared the agony (48:31-38).

The oracle concludes by emphasizing that Moab's destruction was inescapable. Surrounding nations would mock the fate of Moab. The conqueror would swoop down like an eagle and spread his wings over the whole land. This fate would befall Moab because he had "exalted himself against the Lord." Fugitives would fly from one danger to another. An ancient proverb (cf. Num 21:28) would again be applied to Moab. Centuries earlier the Amorite king Sihon launched his attack against Moab from the city of Heshbon. So now the Chaldean flame would spread forth from Heshbon (48:39-45). The prediction points to Nebuchadnezzar's conquest of Moab in 582-81 BC.

The prophecy ends as it began with a woe against Moab. Those who worship Chemosh would go into captivity. In the latter days (messianic age) Moab would find its situation reversed. The reference is to the hearing of the Gospel and conversion of former Moabites (48:46-47).

C. Oracle Against Ammon (49:1-6).

Malcam, the god of Ammon, had tried to take possession of the tribal territory of Gad on the eastern side of the Jordan. Now Rabbah, capital of Ammon, and satellite cities would be destroyed. Malcam and his worshipers would go into exile. Then Israel would be able to recover her lost territory. For this reason Jeremiah called upon the land of Ammon to lament (49:1-3).

Ammon prided herself in natural resources and treasures. Her false confidence would be shattered when Yahweh brought the fearful enemy against them. After the judgment, however, a reversal of circumstances would transpire. These words probably have messianic implications (49:4-6).

D. Oracle Against Edom (49:7-22).

The calamity would come on Edom with such suddenness that the counselors would have no helpful advice to offer. Jeremiah urged Dedan, a merchant people south of Edom, to withdraw deep into the desert to escape the calamity (49:7-8).

The enemy would do a more thorough job in devastating Edom than grape-gatherers do to a vine, or thieves do when they clear out a house. The warriors of Edom would be cut off; but the gracious God of Israel would care for their orphans and widows if they looked to him (49:9-11).

The chosen people had to drink the cup of God's wrath. Edom surely could not escape. Furthermore, the doom of Bozrah (chief city in northern Edom) was sealed by a divine oath. Jeremiah had been informed that God was arousing the nations to come against Edom. God had decreed that Edom would be small among nations (49:12-15).

The pride of the Edomites would be humbled. The high mountains of their land would not protect them from God's wrath. Their destruction would be as permanent as that of Sodom and Gomorrah. Jeremiah likened Nebuchadnezzar to a lion who attacks Edom. No leader (shepherd) would be able to stand before him (49:16-19).

Edomites would be taken captive, their land made desolate. At the Red Sea, where Edom conducted foreign trade, the cry of her destruction would be heard. The enemy would be swift as an eagle. The warriors of Edom would be as terrified as a travailing woman (49:20-22).

E. Oracle Against Damascus (49:23-27).

Consternation would fill the cities of Syria all the way to sea shore. The enemy was approaching. Because the inhabitants of Damascus did not flee, there would be a great slaughter.

F. Oracle Against Kedar and Hazor (49:28-33).

Jeremiah urged Nebuchadnezzar's troops to plunder Kedar and the other Arab tribes of the desert. All the booty would fall into his hand. The prophet urged the Arabs to flee deep into the desert. Again he urged the attackers to go up to take the spoil from the Arab tribes. Hazor would become a permanent desolation.

G. Oracle Against Elam (49:34-39).

Elam was located two hundred miles due east of Babylon. The Elamites were attempting to rebel against Nebuchadnezzar. The Jewish captives in Babylon saw this as an indication that the collapse of the Babylonian empire was near at hand. Jeremiah, however, corrected that notion. The strength of Elam would be demolished. The inhabitants of the place would be dispersed. The Elamites would be dismayed; the rulers, destroyed. The real Ruler of the world would set up over Elam one of his own choosing. The prophecy was fulfilled when Cyrus (Isa 44:28; 45:1) incorporated Elam into his empire. "In the latter days," however, the situation in Elam would change. The reference is probably to the messianic age.

ORACLE AGAINST BABYLON
Jeremiah 50-51

Although Jeremiah advocated submission to Babylon as the world power appointed by God, he was no Babylonian partisan. He regarded Nebuchadnezzar as only a tool which God was using to accomplish his purpose. Justice demanded that the Babylonians taste the wrath of God.

A. The Defeat of Babylon (50:1-34).

The Babylon oracle begins with a series of four contrasts between the fate of Babylon and the future of Israel.

1. Destruction vs. deliverance (50:1-10). The god of Babylon—Bel Marduk—would be put to shame by the fall of his sacred city. A nation coming from the north would wreak havoc upon the land. The entire place would become desolate (50:1-3).

"In those days," i.e., the time of Babylon's destruction, God's people would be delivered from captivity. Both Israel and Judah would join together in genuine repentance to return to Zion and to enter an eternal covenant with God. Abandoned by their shepherds, God's people had wandered from the fold. On the mountains they had worshiped their false gods. The enemies used this apostasy as an excuse to abuse God's people. The future of the two nations, however, would be totally different. Israel would flee Babylon in the hour of deliverance. At the same time, Babylon would be plundered by a company of great nations (50:4-10).

2. Desolation vs. restoration (50:11-20). The Chaldeans chastised Israel with malicious glee. Therefore, their "mother" (the city of Babylon) would become a desolation. Jeremiah addressed the attackers, urging them to unleash their deadly arrows against this nation which had sinned against Yahweh. The defenses of the city would be broken down, the agricultural regions destroyed. What Babylon had done to others would be done to her. Then the exiles of all nations would be able to flee to their respective lands (50:11-16).

Assyria and Babylon, like two mighty lions, had devoured Israel. Assyria had already fallen; Babylon would soon fall in like manner. Then the scattered sheep of Israel would return to graze in the pasture land of Canaan. "In that day" God would grant to the remnant pardon for the sins committed against him (50:17-20).

3. Visitation vs. vindication (50:21-28). Rhetorically Jeremiah urged powerful armies to go up against Merathaim *(double ruin)* and Pekod *(punishment),* i.e., Babylon. Following his summons Jeremiah heard the terrible noise of war and destruction. He sarcastically raised a lament over the fate of the city. "How sad it is" that this hammer which once smashed the nations of the world into submission, would be "cut off and broken" (50:21-23).

Babylon would be suddenly caught like a wild animal in a hunt. All the weapons of God's armory would be unleashed against her. God would do a work in the land of the Chaldeans. Babylon had exceeded the bounds of the divine commission and in so doing had "striven against Yahweh." Again Jeremiah urged the enemy of Babylon to do the job thoroughly. The doomed warriors of Babylon would become like sacrificial animals destined for slaughter (50:24-27).

Jewish captives would return to Zion to declare that the destruction of God's Temple had been avenged (50:28).

4. Recompense vs. redemption (50:29-34). Jeremiah urged the enemies of Babylon to blockade the city and let no one escape. Babylon thus would be recompensed for her ungodly pride in respect to Yahweh. That metropolis was pride personified. "The arrogant one will stumble and fall with no one to raise him up." The fire of war would devour the whole land of Babylonia (50:29-32).

The covenant people (Israel and Judah) were held fast in the grip of the Mesopotamian power. Their strong Redeemer, however, would "plead their case." By disquieting the Babylonians, the Lord would bring rest to the earth (50:33f.).

B. The Destruction of Babylon (50:35-51:26).

The destruction of Babylon is described in detail in this unit in three paragraphs. The description at one point is interrupted with an exhortation to Israel.

1. Thorough destruction (50:35-40). Yahweh would use the agents of sword and drought through the centuries to destroy all which supported Babylon's power and glory. The site of the great city would be permanently destroyed like Sodom and Gomorrah (cf. Isa 13:19-22). The place would be fit only for desert creatures.

2. Ruthless destruction (50:41-51:5). Jeremiah pictured those who would attack Babylon through the centuries coming against that city from the north. They would surge forward like the sea. They would have no mercy on the daughter of Babylon (the inhabitants of the city). The king of Babylon would be petrified at the news. The

God-appointed conqueror, like a lion, would come against his capital. No shepherd (political leader) would be able to resist him. All the earth would tremble when the dying gasp of Babylon was heard (50:41-46).

Jeremiah predicted the demise of Leb-kamai, a cryptogram for *Chaldeans*. He compared Babylon's enemies to a "destroying wind" by which the land would be winnowed. Jeremiah exhorted the invader to do his deadly work at Babylon. The result would be corpses all over the place. The reason for this slaughter is twofold. First, by means of the destruction of Babylon the Lord would prove that Israel and Judah had not been "forsaken" (lit., widowed). Second, he would demonstrate that Babylon was guilty before the Holy One (51:1-5).

3. An exhortation to Israel (51:6-10). When Babylon's enemy approached, God's people were to flee lest they suffer the vengeance of God on that place. That city had once been a beautiful cup from which all the nations drank the wine of God's wrath. Now God would smash that vessel. Sympathetic bystanders would not be able to heal the wound of the king of Babylon. They must flee the city as well. With their faith in Yahweh completely vindicated, God's people would urge one another to return to Zion to declare what God had done at Babylon.

4. Divine destruction (51:11-26). The first wave of Babylon's adversaries were the Medes. About 548 BC Cyrus united the Medes and Persians and the combined force toppled Babylon in 539 BC. Yahweh himself gave the command to launch the siege of Babylon. His divine purpose was to destroy Babylon (51:11f.).

Neither the waters surrounding Babylon nor the treasures gathered by Nebuchadnezzar would avert the disaster. The enemy would overwhelm the city like locusts. Men would be helpless to resist the forces of the Almighty who created the world and who controls all the forces of nature. Man-made gods are stupid, lifeless and worthless. "The Portion of Jacob," however, "is not like these." He created everything including "the tribe of his inheritance," i.e., Israel (51:13-19).

Jeremiah rhetorically addressed the Medo-Persian king. He would be God's battle axe; no one could stand before him. Through him Babylon would be repaid for the evil done against Zion. That great city was once an active volcano in world politics; but it would become a burned out crater. So desolate would the place become that its stone would not be used for building purposes (51:20-26).

C. The Doom of Babylon (51:27-58).

After a description of the attack against Babylon, Jeremiah again developed the thematic contrasts between the fate of that city and the future of Israel.

1. The attack of the enemy (51:27-33). Wars in antiquity commenced with sacred rites. So God ordered these rites to take place. The Medes would approach Babylon with their allies from Ararat, Minni and Ashkenaz. Jeremiah pictured the land heaving as though it were experiencing an earthquake. This invasion would demonstrate that "the purposes of the Lord against Babylon stand, to make the land of Babylon a desolation without inhabitants" (51:27-29).

The mighty men of Babylon would be petrified as news came that the gate bars had been shattered and the passages across the Euphrates seized. The reedy swamps around Babylon would be burned to prevent escape. Babylon would be a threshing floor. The time of the harvest and subsequent threshing was near (51:30-33).

2. Complaint and response (51:34-40). The captive Jews complained that Nebuchadnezzar had swallowed them like some great sea monster. Israel stood before the Judge to demand that justice be done. Jerusalem pled that "my blood be upon the inhabitants of Chaldea." God responded favorably to this petition. He declared his intention "to plead your case and exact full vengeance for you." Babylon's "seas" and "fountains," i.e., the Euphrates and irrigation canals, would be dried up. Babylon would become a total devastation (51:34-37).

Presently the Babylonians were like lion whelps celebrating the acquisition of spoil. God would give them a different kind of banquet. They would drink the wine of wrath and fall into perpetual sleep. The devouring lion would become like a lamb led to slaughter (51:38-40).

3. Demolition vs. liberation (51:41-46). A sea of invaders would sweep through Sheshach, i.e., Babylon (cf. 25:26), leaving behind total devastation. Bel, the chief god of that place, would be forced to vomit up all the nations he had consumed (51:41-44).

God's people were instructed to flee when they saw God's judgment approaching Babylon. Until then, they should not be disturbed by rumors of collapse (51:45f.). Numerous upheavals and throne changes plagued Babylon after the death of Nebuchadnezzar in 562 BC.

4. Retribution vs. return (51:47-53). All the idols of Babylon fall under the judgment of God. Idolaters would be put to shame. The universe would rejoice over Babylon's fall. Many from all over the land would be slain in that day (51:47-49).

Those who had escaped the sword of divine justice in Jerusalem should remember the Lord from afar in Babylon. Those who tried to remain faithful, however, were ridiculed by their neighbors because the sanctuaries of Yahweh had been overrun. The day was coming when God would vindicate himself by punishing Babylon's graven images. No matter what defensive precautions were taken, Babylon could not escape the divinely appointed destroyers (51:50-53).

5. The final pronouncement (51:54-58). Jeremiah envisioned the cry at Babylon as the destruction commenced. The foe would sweep into Babylon like a great sea. They would shatter the military might of Babylon. The leaders would drink the cup of divine wrath and fall into a helpless stupor. The enormous walls of Babylon would be razed. All the weary labor of Babylon would prove in the end to be vain.[1]

D. The History of the Babylon Oracle (51:59-65).

King Zedekiah went to Babylon to pay tribute in 593 BC. Seriah, the king's chamberlain, was a brother of Baruch (cf. 32:12) and a friend of Jeremiah. He carried the Babylon oracle with him to Babylon. Apparently this material was originally written on a separate scroll. Seriah was to read the scroll in Babylon, probably to carefully selected witnesses. Then he was to summarize the contents of the scroll, bind a stone about it, and stink it into the Euphrates river. This act symbolized the demise of Babylon.

APPENDIX: THE PROPHET VINDICATED
Jeremiah 52

Chapter 51 closes with the words, "Thus far are the words of

Jeremiah." The final chapter was probably added by Baruch[2] to show (1) how Jeremiah's prophecies against Jerusalem were fulfilled; and (2) how the prophet's hope for the future was justified. The material here is similar to that recorded in the Book of 2 Kings (24:18-25:30).

A. The Fall of Jerusalem (52:1-23).

The single most important event which vindicated Jeremiah as a prophet was the fall of Jerusalem. Though much of this material is found elsewhere in the book, Baruch thought it wise to rehearse one last time the details of this momentous event.

1. The reign of Zedekiah (52:1-11). At twenty-one years of age Zedekiah was placed on the throne of Judah by Nebuchadnezzar in 597 BC. He was no better than his wicked brother Jehoiakim who preceded him.[3] In his ninth year he rebelled against Nebuchadnezzar. The latter brought Jerusalem under siege for eighteen months. When the city's food supply was exhausted and the outer walls had been breached, Zedekiah and the few loyal troops fled the city. The king was caught in the plains of Jordan. Zedekiah was taken to Riblah in the land of Hamath. There Nebuchadnezzar pronounced sentence against him. Zedekiah witnessed his sons and loyal princes slain. Then Nebuchadnezzar put out the eyes of Zedekiah. He was bound in chains and taken to Babylon where he died in prison.

2. The destruction of Jerusalem (52:12-16). A month after the capture of the city, a staff officer arrived from Riblah with orders concerning the fate of Jerusalem. He was to destroy Jerusalem and to prepare its inhabitants for deportation to Babylon. The entire city, including the Temple area, was put to the torch. The walls were razed. Jews who had surrendered or who had been captured were prepared for the long trip to Babylon. Only the very poorest people were left in the land to serve as "vinedressers and plowmen."

3. The plunder of the Temple (52:17-23). Jeremiah's predictions regarding the fate of the Temple had been a controversial issue throughout his ministry. Thus here Baruch expanded upon the treatment of the Book of Kings regarding the fate of that place. The larger items[4] of Temple furnishings were broken up by the conquerors to facilitate transportation. The smaller Temple vessels of bronze, gold and silver[5] became trophies of victory in the temples of the gods of

Babylon. The amount of bronze hauled off was so amazing that the writer gave special attention to it.

B. Events Subsequent to Jerusalem's Fall (52:24-34).

Following the fall of Jerusalem several events took place which more or less directly related to predictions made by Jeremiah during his ministry. First, the leaders of Judah were executed. Baruch named several of those who were slain at Riblah. They included Seriah, the chief priest, and Zephaniah the second priest and a number of prominent officials of state. Apparently the Chaldeans also selected sixty representatives from the ranks of conscripted soldiers to be executed as a warning to the rest of the troops (52:24-27).

Second, Baruch documented the deportations to Babylon. Three deportations are mentioned. They are dated according to the years of

Chart No. 7

DEPORTATIONS TO BABYLON Jeremiah 52:28-30			
Year of Nebuchadnezzar	**Date**	**Family Heads Deported**	**Notes**
Seventh	597 BC	3,023	Included Ezekiel; total involved: 10,000. (2 Kgs 24:11-16)
Eighteenth	587 BC	832	These were *from Jerusalem*. No doubt thousands of others were taken too.
Twenty-third	582 BC	745	May have been taken from refugees who fled to Egypt.

Nebuchadnezzar's reign. He omitted the earlier taking of hostages in 604 BC. Scholars are divided over the issue of whether the first and second deportations mentioned here are the same as the two deportations mentioned in 2 Kings 24-25, or whether these were in addition to those mentioned in Kings (52:28-30).[6]

The book closes on an optimistic note with the citation of 2 Kings 25:27-30. King Jehoiachin had been taken captive in 597 BC. He was kept in prison in Babylon until the end of the reign of Nebuchadnezzar. When Evil-Merodach ("stupid one of Marduk")[7] became king, he released Jehoiachin and granted to him special favors in the royal court. As long as he lived Jehoiachin received a royal allowance of all that he needed for himself and his family besides the food which he enjoyed at the king's table. Perhaps this account has been incorporated here as evidence that the reversal of fortunes for the captives which Jeremiah had predicted was beginning to take place.

Endnotes

1. The words "so the peoples will toil for nothing, and the nations become exhausted only for fire" are taken from Hab 2:13.

2. For a discussion of the problem of the authorship of Jeremiah 52, see James E. Smith, *Jeremiah and Lamentations* in The Bible Study Textbook Series (Joplin, MO: College Press, 1972) 89-90.

3. Three sons of Josiah followed their father on the throne of Judah: Jehoahaz, Jehoiakim and Zedekiah. Zedekiah's immediate predecessor was his nephew Jehoiachin who reigned but three months before being carried off to Babylon in 597 BC.

4. The "pillars" refer to the two eighteen-cubit bronze pillars which stood immediately in front of the Temple. The "bases" were the supports of the ten portable lavers at which animals were washed before sacrifice. The "bronze sea" was a huge laver at which the priests washed their hands and feet before offering sacrifice (cf. 1 Kgs 7:23-26).

5. The bronze vessels which were taken were these: The "pots" and the "shovels" were used in the Temple for carrying away the ashes after sacrifice. The "basins" were probably used in the sprinkling of the sacrificial blood. The "spoons" were incense-cups. The word translated "snuffers" (NASB) is of uncertain meaning (52:18). The gold and silver vessels were these: "pots," "basins" and "spoons" (mentioned a second time because they were made of silver and gold as well as bronze); ten "lampstands" (which illuminated the interior of the Temple); and "libation bowls" (which were connected with the table of showbread, 52:19).

6. For a discussion of the various chronological and numerical issues connected with Jeremiah's list of deportations, see James E. Smith, *op.cit.* 829-834.

7. Nebuchadnezzar's son was actually named Amel-marduk ("man of Marduk"). To the Jews he was known as Evil-Merodach ("stupid one of Marduk").

8. Contemporary economic documents discovered in Nebuchadnezzar's palace contain lists of the daily rations of food given to the royal prisoners and hostages from various lands. Jehoiachin and his five sons are mentioned in these texts. See *Documents from Old Testament Times,* ed. D. Winton Thomas (New York: Harper & Row, 1961) 84-86.

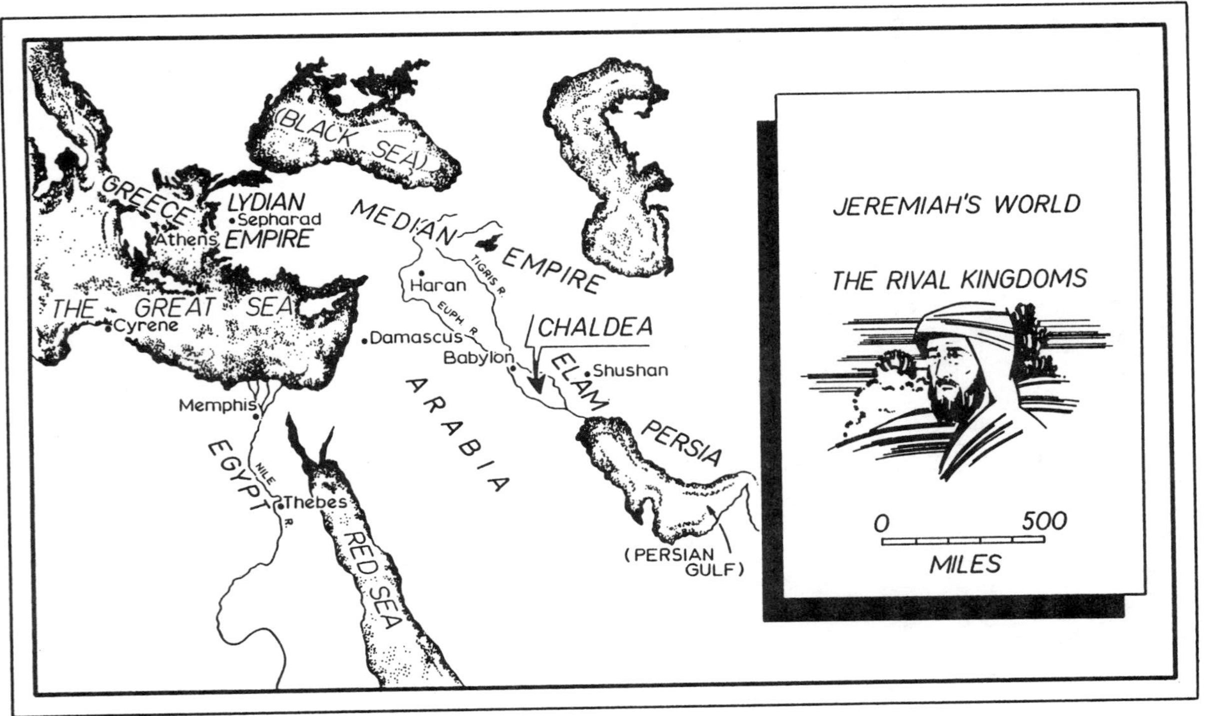
JEREMIAH'S WORLD
THE RIVAL KINGDOMS
0
500
MILES
GREECE
Athens
LYDIAN
Sepharad
EMPIRE
(BLACK SEA)
THE GREAT SEA
Cyrene
Memphis
EGYPT
NILE
R.
Thebes
RED SEA
MEDIAN
EMPIRE
Haran
TIGRIS R.
EUPH R.
Damascus
Babylon
ARABIA
CHALDEA
ELAM
Shushan
PERSIA
(PERSIAN GULF)

THE BOOK OF
LAMENTATIONS

CHAPTER TWENTY-TWO

The Lamentations of Jeremiah

The collection of poems known as the Book of Lamentations has received scant attention in Christian teaching. Children memorize the title as part of the books of the Bible. Few homilies or lessons, however, are based on this book. In general the body of Christ is not familiar with its contents. Lamentations is truly the "orphan book" of the Bible.[1] Why is this so? Perhaps because this book is perceived to be extremely somber and gloomy. The Lamentations are the painful outburst of a suffering people, so it is said.

Actually Lamentations is much more than the cheerless protest of the inequities of life. These poems are really an affirmation of faith in the justice and goodness of God. The author has experienced the worst that life can offer in the way of pain, sorrow, senseless violence and loneliness. Yet his eye of faith penetrates the despair and focuses on the Living God. No book in the Bible is better designed to help believers cope with calamities of all kinds.

GETTING ACQUAINTED WITH LAMENTATIONS

The Book of Lamentations is "one of the most comprehensive surveys of the problem of suffering found anywhere."[2] A general familiarity with Lamentations is essential to an understanding of the message of the book.

A. History of the Book.

Lamentations, like several other Old Testament books, originally took its title from its first Hebrew word: *ekhah* ("alas"). This same word is found at the beginning of the second and fourth chapters as well. Later Jewish teachers gave the book the title *qinoth* ("Laments"). From this the Greek translators in the second century before Christ gave the book the title *Threnoi* ("Lamentations").

Very early the book came to have the expanded title, The Lamentations of Jeremiah. Early Jewish teachers apparently considered these five poems as an appendix to the Book of Jeremiah.[3] By the time of the writing of 2 Esdras (c. AD 100)[4] Lamentations had been removed from its position as an appendix to Jeremiah and placed in the third division of the Hebrew Bible—the *kethubhim* or Writings. There it found its place alongside of Ruth, Esther, Ecclesiastes and Song of Solomon as part of the *megilloth* or "Scrolls."[5] In the Greek and Latin versions of the Old Testament Lamentations reassumed its position immediately after the Book of Jeremiah.

B. Background of the Book.

Only one proper name appears in Lamentations, that of Edom in 4:22. Yet it is clear that the fall of Jerusalem to the Chaldeans in 587 BC forms the background of Lamentations. The connections with 2 Kings 25 and Jeremiah are too obvious to permit any other conclusion.[6] The physical suffering associated with the eighteen months of siege was bad enough. The spiritual implications of the loss of Zion and the Temple, however, made this event psychologically devastating.

Jews were stunned to stupefaction when they saw their beloved city and sacred Temple go up in flames. The unthinkable—the impossible—had happened! In spite of the preaching of prophets like

Jeremiah the Jews were unprepared to cope with this tragedy. Events had demonstrated that the basic tenet of their theology—the inviolability of Jerusalem—was erroneous. A feeling of abandonment by God made the natural shock and grief over their national and personal loss that much harder to bear. Lamentations underscores the comfort which the Bible has for those who suffer, viz., that where pain and hurt are, there God is also.

C. Theme of the Book.

Lamentations consists of four dirges (chaps. 1-4) and one prayer (chap. 5) designed to capture the sense of outrage and despondency which the people felt after Jerusalem had fallen. To accomplish his purpose the writer did not have to exercise much imagination for he seems to have shared the experience of his people. For the most part, the book contains description of national suffering. Here and there are confessions of sin, declarations of penitence and appeals for divine aid.

D. Form of the Book.

Lamentations is entirely poetry. This is not a poetry of rhyme but of thought. The second or third lines of a verse either (1) repeat the thought of the first line, (2) build on that thought, or (3) state a contrast to that thought. Some writers believe that these poems reveal the *qinah* or lament rhythm.[7] These five poems have been declared to be "without peer" among the collective laments of the ancient Near East.[8]

The first four chapters in the book are in the form of alphabetic acrostics in which the author begins each verse with successive letters of the Hebrew alphabet. Chapters 1, 2 and 4 have twenty-two verses, one for each letter of the Hebrew alphabet. Chapter 3 contains sixty-six verses since three consecutive verses begin with each successive letter of the Hebrew alphabet.[9] Though it contains twenty-two verses, chapter 5 is not an acrostic.

The author of these poems was not a slave to form. He varied the number of lines per verse as well as the number of verses to be assigned to each Hebrew letter. In three of the poems he reversed the order of two Hebrew letters apparently in order to maintain his sequence of thought.[10]

Why did the author utilize the acrostic pattern in his first four poems? His reasons were practical, psychological and literary. First, the acrostic served as a mnemonic device to aid the memory as these laments were publicly recited. Second, it aided in grief management by enabling the sufferer to specify the particulars of his inner hurt in a systematic manner. Third, the acrostic pointed to the final resolution of the grief. Just as the verbalization of the hurt concludes with the final letter of the alphabet, so the actual hurt would finally run its course. Thus this technique was adopted in order to create a sense of continuity and completeness to the expression of grief.[11] Finally, the author is indicating by the choice of this unusual form that the event which he was commemorating was itself unusual, in fact unprecedented.

E. Authorship of the Book.

The Book of Lamentations does not expressly identify its author. Substantial external and internal evidence, however, points to Jeremiah as the writer of this material. That this prophet was acquainted with the techniques of lamentation is attested by the Book of Jeremiah itself and by 2 Chronicles 35:25. The Greek version of the book, translated about 200 BC, contains a heading which attributes the book to Jeremiah. Jewish and Christian tradition is all but unanimous in assigning Lamentations to the famous prophet. That Jeremiah was capable of great outpourings of grief has caused him through the centuries to be dubbed "the weeping prophet" (cf. Jer 9:1).

The internal evidence of Jeremiah's authorship is as strong as the external. The character and spirit of the two books is the same.[12] Both books are full of sympathy for the people of God in their hour of judgment. Both books attribute the destruction of Jerusalem to the sin of the people. In addition to these general similarities, several parallels within the two books have been identified.[13]

F. Purpose of the Book.

In one respect, Lamentations was not unique among the literature of the ancient world. Several laments over the fall of great cities have been uncovered in Mesopotamia.[14] On two levels Lamentations shared the purpose of these kindred documents. Psychologically, Lamentations served the purpose of giving expression to the agony of a distraught people. Liturgically, these poems served as the means by which the congregation of Israel could express sorrow over their national loss.

With the Biblical book, however, another dimension of purpose is evident. Theologically, the book served to help the people maintain their faith in God in the midst of overwhelming disaster. The author desires that his people recognize the righteousness of God's dealings with them. He teaches them how to submit to the judgment that has befallen them. He aims to lead those to God who would not let themselves be brought to him through his previous testimony regarding that judgment while it was yet impending. He yearned for them to cast themselves upon the mercy of the Lord.[15]

G. Structure of the Book.

Each of the chapters in Lamentations is an independent composition. Yet a certain pattern in the arrangement of these chapters is evident. In chapters 1-2 each three-line stanza begins with the succeeding letter of the Hebrew alphabet. In chapter three, all twenty-two letters of the Hebrew alphabet appear at the beginning of verses three times in succession. This intensification of the acrostic functions to bring to a climax the agony of the sufferer. Chapter four contains only two lines to a stanza. Here the intensity begins to subside. The final chapter simulates the form of an acrostic in that it contains twenty-two verses. The acrostic pattern, however, is abandoned in chapter 5. In this final chapter the nation casts its grief burden upon the Lord in communal prayer.[16] Kaiser sees in the chapter arrangement a chiastic or crisscross pattern. Chapters 1 and 5 are overall summaries of the disaster, chapters 2 and 4 are more explicit, and chapter 3 occupies the central position.[17]

Outlining the book is difficult because the theme does not show significant variation from one poem to another. The outline adopted here is based on that proposed by C. Paul Gray.

A. A Widowed City (chap. 1).
B. A Broken People (chap. 2).

C. A Suffering Prophet (chap. 3).
D. A Ruined Kingdom (chap. 4).
E. A Penitent Nation (chap. 5).

A WIDOWED CITY
1:1-22

As to form, the first poem is an acrostic. Every fourth line begins with a new letter of the Hebrew alphabet. As to theme, one monotonous phrase "there is no comforter" (vv. 2,9,16,17,21) "rings like the heavy gong of a funeral bell."[19] The poem has two units. In the first the prophet laments the destruction of Jerusalem. In the second unit the city laments its fate. Both units end in prayers which call upon God to execute vengeance upon the enemies of Zion.

A. A Lament Over the City (1:1-11).

The prophet's lament over the condition of Jerusalem moves through three stages. First, he described the present condition of the city. Then he explained that condition. Finally he prayed for God to take note of the plight of his people.

1. Description of the present condition (1:1-7). Jeremiah depicted Jerusalem as a widowed princess who sat alone in the night weeping over the loss of her husband and children. Once she was a "princess among the provinces"; now she had become "a forced laborer." Her "lovers" (political allies) had deserted her, her "friends" (neighboring nations) had become her enemies. Judah had been carried away to "harsh servitude" among the nations. The disasters which she had experienced in her homeland—famine, plague, war—would pursue her even in the distress of exile (1:1-3).

Zion was widowed spiritually as well as politically. The roads to Zion wept because no pilgrims traversed them. Since Jerusalem had been destroyed, the appointed feasts of the Law of Moses could no longer be observed. The city gates which once bustled with business during the festival season were now desolate. The priests mourned because they could no longer officiate in Temple ritual. The maidens who danced in celebration of the annual festivals were now sorrowful. Only Zion's enemies took delight in what had transpired. They were happy that Yahweh had made Jerusalem suffer because of her many transgressions. They rejoiced to see Zion's children carried off into captivity (1:4f.).

Zion was also widowed psychologically. Her beauty, which made her the envy of the ancient world, had disappeared. Zion's miserable present was made all the worse when she remembered all the wonderful privileges which once were hers as God's chosen city. She ceaselessly replayed in her mind that fateful day when her citizens fell into the hands of the enemy. She could not forget how helpless she felt when her leaders ran like terrified deer before the enemy. She could still hear the vicious gloating of the enemy which watched her suffer (1:6f.).

2. An explanation of the present condition (1:8-9a). The poet now developed that to which he alluded in verse 5. Zion's present woes could be traced to her grievous transgressions. As her outer garments of respectability were removed, the filth of blatant sin and vice became apparent. Those who once respected Zion now despised her for truly "sin is a reproach to any nation" (Prov 13:34). Even Zion herself cannot stand the sight of her own corruption.

For a time she had hidden her filthiness beneath her skirts. During that period of prosperity she had given no thought to the ultimate consequences of her evil ways. She resolutely refused to believe God's warnings through his servants the prophets. In haughty pride she regarded herself as God's favorite, a city exempt from the accountability required of others. Thus Zion's end came as a total shock. This was what made the fall of Jerusalem so terrible. What made matters worse, in that sorrow which approached stupefaction Zion had no one to comfort her! Grief is compounded when there is no one who cares.

3. A prayer concerning the present condition (1:9b-11). In narrative prayer the poet summarized the plight of the widow Zion. The enemy had become haughty and overbearing. All the gracious gifts which God had bestowed upon Zion had fallen into the hands of the enemy. Gentiles had desecrated the sacred precincts of the Temple. Citizens used their most precious possessions to barter for enough bread to keep alive. As spokesman for his people, Jeremiah called upon God to take note of the misery of his people and the distress of his prophet.

B. A Lament by the City (1:12-22).

Jeremiah now portrayed the lonely, tearful widow Zion taking up her lament. First, she appealed for sympathy to passers-by. Zion's agony was all the worse because none of the travelers who passed by Jerusalem seem to realize the depths of her agony. She complained bitterly that no other city had suffered what she had suffered. Yahweh had brought this calamity upon Zion "in the day of his fierce anger." Zion then used a series of figures to describe what God had done to her: lightning bolts, an ensnaring net, a heavy yoke, a solemn assembly of adversaries, a wine press. This may appear to be an appeal to passers-by, but in reality it was a complaint against God. The paragraph ends as it began, with a note that there is no comforter (1:12-16).

Second, Zion appealed to neighboring nations. She spread forth her hands in a pitiful gesture of solicitation, but there was no comforter. Neighboring nations had become her enemies. The city was now regarded as something filthy. Even those nations which were "lovers," i.e., allies, had failed Zion. Consequently, the younger citizens had been carried off into exile; the older had been left behind and now must struggle for survival in the destitute city. Yet as harsh as this suffering was, it was justly deserved because the city had rebelled against God. Yahweh was righteous in executing this judgment (1:17-19).

Finally the weeping widow turned her eyes heavenward and presented a petition before God. Her heart was now contrite. She accepted her punishment. She pointed out the malicious glee which the enemies showed as they executed the judgment. Yet she was confident that one day these enemies would receive their just deserts. She called upon the Lord to execute similar judgment upon them. Only then would the sorrow of Zion be alleviated (1:20-22). This appeal to God should not be interpreted as vindictive imprecation, but as a plea for mercy.[20]

A BROKEN PEOPLE
2:1-22

The second lament focuses on the anger of God as it relates to the tragic events of 587 BC.[21] The chapter contains (1) description of the judgment upon God's people; (2) sympathy for their condition; (3) exhortation and rebuke to the people; and (4) petition for the broken people.

A. Description of the Judgment (2:1-10).

The opening verse sets the tone of the second poem in three mighty metaphors. In the first Jeremiah compared what had happened to Judah to a solar eclipse. Yahweh had "covered the daughter of Zion with a cloud." In the second metaphor he compared the collapse of Judah to a falling star. Thus God had "cast down from heaven to earth the glory of Israel." In the third metaphor Jeremiah depicted Jerusalem as God's "footstool" which had been forgotten in the day of divine wrath. Thus Judah had experienced befuddlement, debasement and abandonment. Jeremiah made this generalization emphatic by enumeration in verses 2-10.

The intensive verb "swallow" (*billa*) heads a list of powerful verbs describing what God had done to Judah in his wrath. The same verb is repeated at the conclusion of the list where it is linked with the concept that Yahweh had become the enemy of his people. In his wrath God had cut down "the horn of Israel," i.e., their national strength. Habitations, strongholds, palaces, and rulers had fallen. Those who were "pleasing to the eye," i.e., the youth of the nation, had been slain. God had withdrawn his right hand of help in the face of the enemy. Even worse, he had used that right hand in a gesture of hostility toward his people (2:2-5).

The Temple had been dismantled as easily as a garden hut. With the destruction of the Temple came the cessation of festival, sabbath, king[22] and priest. The sacred altar and sanctuary had been treated with disdain. The noise which emanated from the Temple precincts was not that of worshipers, but that of Gentile destroyers (2:6f.).

The divine demolition of Jerusalem was carried out by Yahweh. He used the precision normally employed in building a city, for "he stretched out the measuring line." The massive gates now lie beneath rubble. The bars which sealed those gates closed are broken and useless (2:8-9a).

The kings and princes of Judah had been carried into foreign lands "where there is no law," i.e., no divine revelation. The false prophets who had been so positive about Jerusalem's deliverance from Babylon no longer pretended to be receiving revelation from the Lord. No sage counsel was available from the elders who had been overwhelmed by the calamity. The joyful songs of the maidens had been silenced (2:9b f.).

B. Sympathy for the People (2:11-16).

The prophet Jeremiah, who had labored so hard to avert the disaster of 587 BC, now expressed his unrelenting sorrow over what had happened. He was moved particularly by the plight of the innocent babies. Unable to supply food for their babies, mothers had abandoned their offspring to die on the streets of the city. The prophet knew of no similar calamity from which he might derive a comforting word for Jerusalem. Zion's destruction was as unfathomable as the ocean itself (2:11-13).

Who would heal the wound of Zion? Certainly not the false prophets. They had preached falsehood and foolishness through the years. They had made no effort to turn Jerusalem away from her path of ruin. Even less were local travelers or neighboring nations able to extend any aid to her. The former added to the misery by mocking the destitute condition of the city. The latter actually had been coveting the territory of Judah which now lies undefended before them (vv. 14-16).

C. Exhortation to the People (2:17-19).

Verse 17 is the heart of chapter 2. All that had befallen Judah was God's doing. "Yahweh has done what he planned." He had fulfilled the word he had spoken long before. On the surface these words seem to add to the tragedy. Beneath the surface, however, there is consolation here. If God had made good on his threatening words, he would also make good on his words of promise. Here, then, was a glimmer of hope in the blackness of Zion's agony.

The people now turn to God in prayer. Jeremiah encouraged them to join him (cf. v. 11) in shedding tears night and day. They should lift up their hands in earnest entreaty before the Lord on behalf of the little ones who were suffering so severely (2:18f.).

D. Prayer for the People (2:20-22).

Jeremiah concluded his second poem with a model prayer. This was how he hoped the nation would pray to the Lord. First, he asked God to consider that it is his own people who were suffering. Then he specified the suffering experienced by the different segments of the population. The women had been reduced to cannibalism. Holy men had been slain in the sanctuary. Young and old lay in the streets dying of starvation. Vigorous men and maidens had been cut down by the sword. The slaughter had no regard to age nor sex. No one had escaped, not even the babies in the arms of mothers. This rehearsal of Judah's suffering was an implied petition for mercy and deliverance.

A SUFFERING PROPHET
3:1-66

Chapter 3 stands out both as to form and content. Here the acrostic form appears in intensified form. The sixty-six verses are arranged in twenty-two triplets each verse of which begins with the same letter of the alphabet. In content this chapter contains a personal lament presumably by Jeremiah himself.[23] In this lament the prophet presented his (1) cry of desperation; (2) confession of faith; (3) call for repentance; (4) condition of suffering; and (5) prayer for deliverance.

A. Cry of Desperation (3:1-18).

The opening verses establish the theme of the third lament. The poet had suffered along with his people. He affirmed, "I am the man who has seen affliction by the rod of his wrath." Then in a series of ten brilliant metaphors and similes this sufferer painted a vivid picture of his mental and physical agony. He compared his experience to (1) darkness, (2) being smitten repeatedly, and (3) the frailties of old age. He likened himself to (4) a city under siege, (5) a dead man in eternal darkness, (6) a prisoner, and (7) a traveler forced to walk uncharted detours. He felt (8) he was the victim of a ferocious beast, and (9) a target for the arrows of the divine Archer. He compared his anguish (10) to unpalatable food and drink with which he had been filled to the point of nausea (3:2-16).

The prophet was overwhelmed by the disaster. He had lost all inner peace. He had forgotten what prosperity meant. His confidence in Yahweh had been shaken (3:17f.). Yet the very mention of the precious name of God helped the poet regain a solid footing for his faith.

B. Confession of Faith (3:19-39).

Since the prophet's outlook was so bleak, he tried the uplook. In this unit he reflected upon God and the nature of suffering.

Though he could not forget the sufferings which he had experienced, yet the poet dared to hope in God. That any had survived the tragedy of 587 BC was due to the loving kindness of God. The daily provision of the necessities of life was evidence of his unceasing mercies. In the final analysis the faithfulness of God to his people was great beyond human understanding. Though this believer had nothing in the way of this world's goods, yet he could rejoice because the Lord was his portion. The knowledge that he possessed God, and God possessed him was the foundation of this man's hope. He was confident that the Lord is always good to those who wait for him, i.e., place their trust in him (3:19-25).

Growing out of his reflections about God, the prophet made five great observations about suffering. First, patience and hope open channels of deliverance (3:26). Second, youthful self-discipline has positive benefits if one will accept it without complaint (3:27-30). Third, affliction sent by God is measured and purposeful. He takes no delight in afflicting men. Compassion follows affliction (3:31-33). Fourth, God does not approve of punishment which is not just or purposeful. He will punish those who are guilty of political atrocities, legal injustice or social inequities (3:34-36). Fifth, nothing is done in this world without God's permission. He does not force men to choose the path of disobedience with its resultant punishment. No one can then complain when he is punished for his sin (3:37-39).

C. Call for Repentance (3:40-47).

Personal suffering is the appropriate time for self-examination and earnest prayer. The prophet provided for his readers a model prayer to use in their desperate circumstances. First, they should frankly acknowledge their sin. Second, they should acknowledge the terrible consequences of sin. Sin cuts off the mercies of God, stirs up divine wrath, severs the communication lines to heaven, and ultimately brings humiliation, panic and ruin.

D. Personal Suffering (3:48-54).

Again the prophet burst forth into tears over the destruction of "the daughter of my people." He determined to continue this flow of tears until God looked down and took note of his distraught prophet. Three things particularly disturbed Jeremiah: (1) the shameful defilement of the young maidens of Jerusalem; (2) the vicious and undeserved persecution of the prophet; (3) the personal jeopardy of the prophet in the pit. The reference may be to the time when Jeremiah nearly died in an empty cistern (Jer 38:6-13).

E. Prayer for Deliverance (3:55-66).

God had heard the prophet's desperate plea from the midst of that pit of death. He had reassured Jeremiah with the words, "Do not be afraid." He had redeemed the life of his prophet. Therefore, Jeremiah had confidence that God would listen to his present appeal for help (3:55-58).

Though Jeremiah prayed in the first person singular, he had assumed the role of an intercessor. The *me* was really *us*. He began by acknowledging the omniscience of God. The Lord had seen all the wrong done to his people—the vengeful acts and taunting words of Judah's enemies. Jeremiah called upon God to judge those who had committed wrongs against the Jews, to repay these enemies for the deeds they had done. He asked that these adversaries experience "blindness of heart," i.e., intellectual confusion. He wanted the curse of God to rest upon them. He asked God to destroy them from off the face of the earth (3:59-66). This was not a desire for personal vengeance, but a plea for justice.

A RUINED KINGDOM
4:1-22

The fourth lament is an acrostic like that found in the first two chapters with the exception that the stanzas here have two lines instead of three. Here the tragedy of 587 BC is described in a more matter-of-fact manner. The level of emotional intensity is somewhat diminished.[24] The poem has three natural divisions: description, explanation and expectation.

A. Description of the Calamity (4:1-10).

Chapter four laments the afflictions that fell on the whole populace of Judah. (1) The youth, the most valuable asset of the nation, lay dead and scattered about like broken bits of pottery. (2) The little children starved from lack of bread and milk. (3) The wealthy, accustomed to the finest food and clothing, were forced to scavenge in the city garbage dumps. (4) The princes of Judah once had been the picture of health. Now they were nothing but skin and bones. No one could even recognize them in the streets. Better for them had they been thrust through by the enemy sword rather than waste away in the famine. (5) The once tender-hearted mothers of Judah had resorted to cannibalizing their own offspring. Jerusalem's chastisement was worse than that of Sodom. Whereas Sodom's fall had been sudden, Jerusalem's agony was prolonged over several months.

B. Explanation of the Calamity (4:11-20).

The ultimate cause of Zion's downfall was the burning wrath of Yahweh. Virtually no one considered it possible that God would permit the holy city to be destroyed (4:11f.). This notion probably grew up after the miraculous deliverance of Jerusalem from the Assyrian King Sennacherib in 701 BC (2 Kgs 19:35ff.). Both Jeremiah and Ezekiel battled mightily against the "701 theology."

The poet points out two major reasons God's anger was stirred up against the inhabitants of Jerusalem. First, he mentions the sins of the spiritual leaders. Because of the evil counsel of the priests and prophets, many innocent persons had been executed by the government. Now those religious leaders were totally confused. They were so defiled by blood that they were now treated as though they were lepers. They were discredited in Jerusalem, spurned in neighboring nations, and rejected by God (4:13-16).

The stubborn resistance of the city was the second reason cited for the severity of the calamity. The inhabitants rejected the light of divine revelation and stumbled on in four delusions: (1) that some foreign nation would rescue them; (2) that they could successfully resist the might of Babylon; (3) that they would be able to flee the falling city; and (4) that King Zedekiah[25] would be able to provide protection for them (4:17-20).

C. Expectation Regarding the Calamity (4:21-22).

Edom, Judah's traditional enemy, sarcastically was urged to enjoy the hour of Jerusalem's humiliation. The poet hastened to predict, however, that Edom shortly would be forced to drink the cup of divine wrath (cf. Jer 25:18-28). Because of that cup the Edomites would experience confusion and shame. For Judah the darkness was over. A new day would dawn. For Edom, however, the future held nothing but the prospect of punishment.

A PENITENT NATION
5:1-22

The fifth poem of Lamentations differs from the previous four in three major respects. First, this chapter is not an acrostic. Second, whereas the stanzas in chapters 1-3 had three lines each, and those in chapter 4 had two lines each, the stanzas here consist of only one line. Finally, the fifth poem is a prayer, not a dirge. Kaiser sees this chapter as a "decrescendo," a winding down of the intense sorrow expressed in the previous poems. He notes that whereas chapters 1-3 end with a prayer, chapter 4 does not. The prayer which is missing from Lamentations 4 is now supplied by the entire fifth chapter.[26]

The first verse of the poem sets the tone for the chapter. The poet calls upon the Lord to "remember," i.e., intervene, on behalf of his people. The prayer then moves through two major phases as (1) the reproach of Zion is described; and then (2) the restoration of Zion is requested.

A. Reproach of Zion Described (5:2-18).

The inhabitants of Zion described their plight in narrative prayer.[27] Their inheritance (land, houses) had fallen into the hands of foreigners. The wholesale decimation had left Judah largely a nation of orphans and widows. Basic necessities of life were worth their weight in silver. The constant harassment by the conquerors left the inhabitants weary. They had to submit themselves in servitude to Egyptian and Assyrian caravanners in order to secure food. Babylonian mercenaries, some of whom had been former slaves of the Jews, now ruled the land. Because of marauding bands from the desert, the harvest could be brought in only at great risk. Scarcity of food made for famine-like conditions. The entire population was showing the effects of prolonged hunger (5:2-10).

The generalities of the preceding verses are now individualized. All segments of the population had suffered in the calamity. Women had been raped. Princes had been impaled and left to die a slow and shameful death. Elderly people had received no compassionate consideration. Youth had been forced to do the work of animals (5:11-13).

Elders could no longer exercise their leadership in the city gate. Young men could no longer sing. Dance had turned to mourning. Like a crown toppling from the head of a deposed monarch, the glory of Zion had been completely removed. The population sensed they were under a divine "woe" because of their sin. Their hearts were sick with sorrow, their eyes darkened by tears because of what had happened. The hill where once stood proudly the Temple of God was now the habitation of wild animals (5:14-18).

B. Restoration of Zion Requested (5:19-22).

The poet first anchored his appeal in the truth that Yahweh is enthroned forever. Earthly things may pass away, but God remains and rules. The poet then presented his appeal in the form of a question: "Why have you forgotten us forever? What for God might be a passing moment, for his suffering people can seem like an eternity. The poet then strengthened his appeal with an attitude of submission. He called upon God to aid his people to turn back to him. With his faith soaring, the poet next elevated his appeal to request complete restoration of Zion: "Renew our days as of old." Finally the poet supported his appeal with an oblique reminder of God's past commitment to his people. Only if God had abandoned his people totally—a thought foreign to all previous revelation—could he fail to intervene on their behalf.

Endnotes

1. Walter C. Kaiser, Jr., *A Biblical Approach to Personal Suffering* (Chicago: Moody, 1982) 10.

2. *Ibid.*

3. Josephus (*Against Apion* 1.8) states that there were twenty-two books in the Old Testament canon of his day (end of first Christian century) — five books of law, thirteen books by prophets, and four books of "songs and hymns." In the Jewish count the double books (1—2 Sam; 1—2 Kgs; 1—2 Chr) and the Ezra-Nehemiah combination are counted as one book each. The twelve Minor Prophets were also counted as one book. Taking all this into account would yield a total of twenty-four books. The only method of arriving at the figure twenty-two is to count Jeremiah-Lamentations as one book and Judges-Ruth as one book.

4. Esdra gives twenty-four as the number of canonical books. This means that Ruth had been separated from Judges and Lamentations from Jeremiah.

5. In Hebrew manuscripts the arrangement of the five *megilloth* differs. Some reflect a chronological order: Ruth, Cant, Eccl, Lam, Esth. Others reflect a liturgical order, i.e., the books are arranged according to festival at which each was publicly read; Cant (Passover); Ruth (Pentecost); Lam (Ninth of Ab commemorating the destruction of Jerusalem); Eccl (Tabernacles); and Esth (Purim).

6. For a tabulation of the connections between Lamentations, 2 Kgs 25 and Jeremiah, see Kaiser, *op. cit.* 18. A description of the actual conquest of Jerusalem is found in three passages in addition to 2 Kgs 25: Jer 39:1-11; Jer 52; and 2 Chr 36:11-21.

7. In *qinah* rhythm the second line of each verse is one stress shorter than the first line. As a rule in Lamentations the pattern is three stresses in the first line, two in the second, and three in the third line. This meter is obscured by English translations.

8. Norman Gottwald, *Studies in the Book of Lamentations* (Chicago: Allenson, 1954) 111.

9. Thirteen acrostics appear in the Old Testament. Besides the four in Lamentations, the acrostics are Pss 9-10; 25; 34; 35; 111; 112; 119; 145; Prov 32:10-31.

10. In Ugaritic abecedarian documents from as early as the twelfth century BC *pe* comes before *'ayin* just as it does in Lam 2, 3 and 4. See Kaiser, *op. cit.* 37.

11. Howard Kuist, *The Lamentations of Jeremiah* in vol. 12 "The Layman's Bible Commentary" ed. Balmer Kelly (Richmond: John Knox, 1960) 141. In Kaiser's words, the acrostic technique "itemizes, organizes and finalizes" grief (*op. cit.* 17).

12. The most radical critic cannot deny that the character and spirit of Jeremiah are the same as that of the author of Lamentations.

13. See James E. Smith, *Jeremiah and Lamentations* in Bible Study Textbook Series (Joplin, MO: College Press, 1972) 853.

14. For example, the laments over Ur, Sumer, and Nippur. See James Pritchard, ed., *Ancient Near Eastern Texts Relating to the Old Testament* (3rd. ed. Princeton; University Press, 1969) 455-63.

15. C.F. Keil, "The Lamentations of Jeremiah" in *Keil and Delitzsch Old Testament Commentaries: Isaiah XV to Ezekiel XXIV* (Grand Rapids: Associated Publishers, n.d.) 1084.

16. Kaiser, *op. cit.* 16f.

17. *Ibid* 21.

18. C. Paul Gray, "The Lamentations of Jeremiah," in vol. IV of *Beacon Bible Commentary* (Kansas City: Beacon Hill Press, 1966) 506.

19. Kaiser, *op. cit.* 43.

20. Smith, *op. cit.* 867.

21. The first ten verses of chapter 2 alone contain forty descriptions of God's judgment and anger. The theme of the anger of God is elsewhere treated by this poet in 1:12; 3:1, 43, 66; 4:11; and 5:22.

22. Since the construction of the Temple by Solomon a close relationship existed between the Davidic kings and that structure. Promises made to David regarding his descendants were celebrated in the songs sung in the Temple ritual.

23. Commentaries have interpreted the individual as (1) a typical sufferer; (2) a collective personage, i.e., Zion represented as an individual; and (3) an individual, perhaps the author of the book.

24. Delbert Hillers, *Lamentations* in The Anchor Bible (Garden City, NY: Doubleday, 1972) 86.

25. Because the life of the kingdom depends upon having a king, Zedekiah is called by the poet "the breath of our nostrils" (v. 20). The people were supremely confident that God would not allow the house of David to be completely overthrown.

26. Kaiser, *op. cit.* 109.

27. First person plural pronouns appear twenty times in verses 2-10.

THE BOOK OF
EZEKIEL

CHAPTER TWENTY-THREE

Getting Acquainted With Ezekiel

The Book of Ezekiel stands in the English Bible fourth among the Major Prophets. It ranks second in actual word count among the prophetic books (39,407 words as compared to Jeremiah's 42,659), and ranks third in size in the entire Bible. In spite of its size, this book is one of the most neglected in the sacred library.

THE STUDY OF EZEKIEL

A casual perusal of this material has convinced many readers that Ezekiel has little spiritual value and even less contemporary relevance. Those who attempt to make a more serious study of the book often fail to make it past the intricate visionary details of the first chapter. This is most unfortunate. Ezekiel has a vital message for God's people, a message not duplicated anywhere else in God's Word.

While Ezekiel has been neglected by the church at large, it has come to be the happy hunting ground of cultists, critics and curiosity mongers. The modern negative critics regard Ezekiel as pivotal in their topsy-turvy reconstruction of Old Testament history which views the tripartite priesthood as a scribal concoction from Babylon rather than a divine revelation from Sinai. Ezekiel is cited by self-styled "students of prophecy" as proof that God's plan for the future includes the modern Zionist movement (Jews returning to Palestine in unbelief), an imminent Russian invasion of Israel, and the reinstitution of the Old Testament animal sacrificial system in a Temple shortly to be constructed in Jerusalem. Science fiction buffs have scoured this book in search of spaceships and extra-terrestrial beings who pawned themselves off as God. Mormons regard Ezekiel 37:15-23 as the prophetic allusion to the Book of Mormon (stick of Ephraim) being joined to the Bible (stick of Judah). If for no other reason the Book of Ezekiel merits careful study so that the man of God may be able to silence these modern day "empty talkers and deceivers" who are upsetting so many families today (Titus 1:10f.). The best defense against a thousand and one errors is the truth.[1]

There is something more positive to be said in favor of diligent study of Ezekiel. The book is full of profound theology, not the least of which is the doctrine of individual responsibility. God's sovereign grace, his absolute holiness and justice, and his universality are presented here as clearly as in any other portion of Scripture. In spite of difficult details, the theme of ultimate victory for God's people is forcefully developed in this prophecy. These mother lode truths, plus priceless nuggets of revelation too numerous to mention will make the serious student of this book spiritually wealthy. Those who would prospect for this treasure should not be discouraged by the exegetical bogs which here and there challenge the resolve as well as the intellect.

Ezekiel invites investigation not only because of what he said, but also because of how he said it. The book is fascinating, replete with visions, allegories, and action parables. Not without reason has Ezekiel been dubbed the "audio-visual aids prophet." If a picture is worth a thousand words, then Ezekiel must be regarded as artfully verbose. His prophecy is a gallery of word pictures interspersed with mini-stages upon which the prophet performed divinely inspired monodramas. His delightful antics should draw students to his book in these days even as they attracted observers to his door his his day.

BACKGROUND OF EZEKIEL

Ezekiel was born in the eighteenth year of King Josiah, 621 BC. That was the year that the young king launched a vigorous religious reformation in Judah. Visible signs of idolatry were purged from the land, but not, as it turned out, from the hearts of the people. Josiah was mortally wounded by Pharaoh Neco at the pass of Megiddo in 609 BC. Reformation momentum abruptly halted. The nation shifted into spiritual reverse. Evidence of idolatry began to reappear throughout the land.

Josiah's second son Shallum was elevated to the throne by the people of the land. He assumed the throne name of Jehoahaz. At the end of three months Jehoahaz was deported by Pharaoh Neco to Egypt. He lived in exile there until the day of his death. Neco placed Eliakim, another son of Josiah, on the throne as his vassal. Eliakim took the throne name Jehoiakim.

Neco was defeated by Nebuchadnezzar at the battle of Carchemish in 605 BC (Jer 46:1). Jehoiakim shortly thereafter shifted his allegiance to the Babylonian conqueror. Daniel and several other prominent hostages were sent to Babylon at this time (Dan 1:1). For three years Jehoiakim served Nebuchadnezzar (2 Kgs 24:1). When the Babylonian king experienced a setback on the borders of Egypt, Jehoiakim withheld the annual tribute and declared himself to be independent.

Nebuchadnezzar marched against Jerusalem to punish his rebellious vassal. Jehoiakim, however, either died or was assassinated just prior to the arrival of the Babylonian. Jehoiakim's eighteen-year-old son Jehoiachin held out for three months. Finally Jerusalem was surrendered to Nebuchadnezzar. The king and ten thousand of the leading citizens were carried away to Babylon. Among the captives was Ezekiel the son of Buzi. Nebuchadnezzar then installed Mattaniah, a third son of Josiah, as his vassal in Jerusalem. Mattaniah took the throne name of Zedekiah (2 Kgs 24:10-17).

THE LIFE OF EZEKIEL

The name Ezekiel means *God strengthens* or *God is strong*. In the Bible Ezekiel is mentioned only in the book which bears his name, and there only twice (1:3; 24:24).[2] Whatever may be known about the prophet's life must be gleaned from the book.

A. His Family and Station.

Like Jeremiah, Ezekiel was of a priestly family. His father's name was Buzi, but nothing further is known about him. Unlike Jeremiah, Ezekiel was married. The Lord refers to his wife as "the desire of your eyes." This suggests that Ezekiel had a warm and tender relationship with his wife. The text mentions no children who might have been born to this union. In the ninth year of his captivity, four years after he had begun his prophetic ministry, Ezekiel's wife died (chap. 24).

B. His Ministry.

Ezekiel was thirty when he received his call to the prophetic ministry in 593 BC (1:1). He continued to carry out his assigned mission until at least his fifty-second year. How long he lived after that cannot be determined. Ezekiel was a contemporary of Jeremiah, though he never mentions the name of his co-laborer. He does mention Daniel three times (14:14,20; 28:3).

Ezekiel ministered to the Jewish captives in Babylon. The fall of Jerusalem in 587 BC was the pivotal event in the prophet's career. That disaster divided Ezekiel's ministry into two distinct phases. In the first phase (593-587 BC) Ezekiel was a prophet of doom. He fought valiantly against the devastating delusion that God would never destroy Jerusalem. He dashed to pieces the hope of the exiles that they would swiftly be returned to their homeland. Following the destruction of Jerusalem, the tone of Ezekiel's ministry changed radically. Now that the unthinkable had happened, the prophet attempted to reassemble the shattered pieces of Israel's faith. He marked out clearly the path that would take the truly penitent back to the Lord.

As with most of the prophets, preaching played the primary role in the ministry of Ezekiel. Dozens of times the prophet was told to verbalize the message which God laid on his heart. When he was told to write (24:2; 37:15f.) or draw something (21:18-23) it was only to underscore or illustrate the spoken word. The book is rich in the variety of the prophetic oracles which it contains.[3]

Chart No. 8

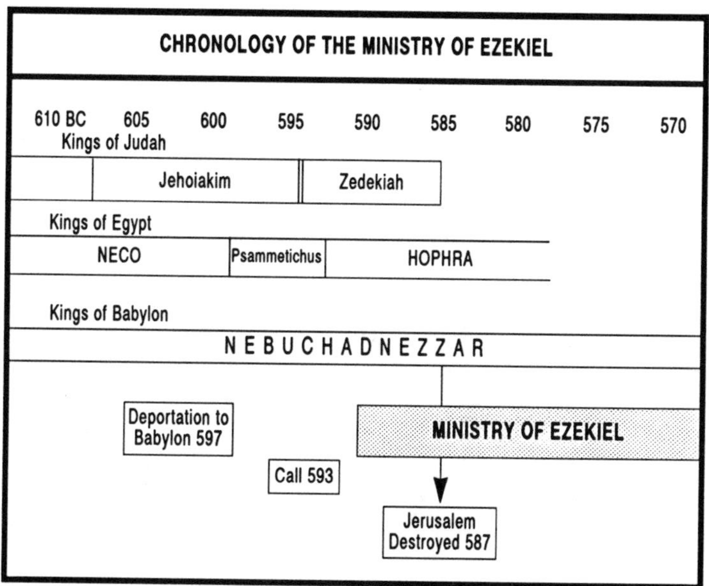

More than any other prophet Ezekiel communicated his message through symbolic actions. His strange behavior served the twofold purpose of (1) arousing interest in his message; and (2) illustrating the main points in the oral word. As a rule Ezekiel appended to his symbolic action an interpretative oracle which expanded upon the meaning of what he had done. These mini-dramas should not be attributed to the creative genius of Ezekiel. They were ordered by God himself.

Visions also play a prominent role in the ministry of Ezekiel. In a vision categories of time and space become meaningless. The prophet could be physically in Babylon, for example, but then suddenly in Jerusalem. Scenes change rapidly. Time is compressed. The book begins (chaps. 1-3) and ends (chaps. 40-48) with such visions.

Chapters 8-11 contain an extended vision of the terrible corruption in the Temple back in Jerusalem. Perhaps the most famous vision in the book is that of the valley of dry bones in chapter 37. This vision sets forth in the most bold symbolism the resurrection of the nation Israel following the Babylonian exile.

THE MESSAGE OF EZEKIEL[4]

The basic message of Ezekiel is that God is faithful to his eternal purpose. The sinful nation must be destroyed, yet God will not forsake his own. At first Ezekiel's messages were not well received. In time, however, his prophecies brought about a fundamental change in the idolatrous tendencies of the nation.

A. Doctrine of God.

Feinberg points out that whereas Isaiah emphasized God's *salvation,* Jeremiah his *judgment,* and Daniel his *kingdom,* Ezekiel stressed the *glory* of the Lord.[5] To Ezekiel Yahweh was no mere local or national divinity. Israel's God was the supreme, self-existent, almighty (1:24) and omniscient (1:18) One. He was infinitely exalted above the earth, clothed with honor and majesty. Three points are especially stressed by this prophet.

First, Ezekiel proclaimed that God is sovereign. He rules the celestial hierarchies and all the dwellers on earth. Men and nations yield to his sovereign decisions. Egypt, Babylon and all heathen peoples were bound to obey him. Nebuchadnezzar was but a tool in his hand.

Second, Ezekiel stressed that God is holy (39:7). His name is holy (36:21f.; 39:25). Ezekiel's God could not overlook sin. Because of the corruption of Jerusalem, he had withdrawn his glory from the Temple (10:18; 11:23). This holy God placed blistering denunciations against the sin of Judah on the lips of Ezekiel. If anything, this prophet's condemnation of spiritual waywardness was even more severe than that of Jeremiah.

Third, Ezekiel understood that God is gracious beyond comprehension. Yahweh has no delight in the death of the wicked (18:23,32; 33:11). In the midst of thundering threats, he woos his wayward people to repentance (14:22; 16:63; 20:11). Though his people were undeserving of his mercy (36:32), yet he promised to them a glorious future.

B. Doctrine of Messiah.

The Messiah is not so prominent in Ezekiel as in Isaiah. Nonetheless, striking teaching concerning the Coming One is found in this book. The Messiah is represented as a "tender twig" taken from the highest branch of the cedar of Judah's royalty, then planted upon a high mountain (17:22-24). He is the one to whom the diadem of Israel's sovereignty rightfully belonged and to whom it would be given after it had been removed from the head of the wicked Zedekiah (21:27). The Messianic "David" would be a faithful prince among God's restored people. He would perform all the functions of a true and faithful Shepherd (34:23f.), ruling over them as king (37:24). This Prince would eat and drink before the Lord in his capacity of special representative of God's people (44:3).

C. Doctrine of Man.

Ezekiel viewed man as God's creature and property (18:4). He shows awareness of the Biblical teaching of the original innocence of man (28:15,17). Man, however, had fallen. Hence, man is sinful (18:21-30). His heart needs to be softened and renewed (18:31). For his wickedness he is held individually accountable (18:4,13,18). He is a free moral agent and is therefore responsible for his own reformation of life and purification of heart (33:11: 43:9). To those willing to receive it God would give a new heart (11:19; 36:26; 37:23). Rightly has Ezekiel been called "the champion of individualism."

D. Doctrine of the Kingdom.

The terminology "kingdom of God" never appears in the book. Ezekiel, however, clearly points to the concept of God's reign over the hearts of redeemed men. Much to the dismay of his countrymen, Ezekiel stressed that the kingdom of God was not inseparably connected with the political existence of Judah. He saw an inner spiritual kernel of the nation existing in the lands of the dispersion (12:17). This nucleus was growing constantly as penitent men were added to it

(34:11-19). Eventually Ezekiel saw a new Israel with Messiah as its prince (34:23f.; 37:24). That new Israel would walk in the law of the Lord (11:20; 16:61; 20:43; 36:27) and dwell in the land of Canaan (36:33; 37:25). God would enter into a new covenant with that people (37:26-28), and he would walk in close fellowship with them (39:29; 46:9). Upon them the Lord would pour out his Holy Spirit (36:27; 39:27).

THE BOOK OF EZEKIEL

Several introductory issues need to be addressed before a survey of Ezekiel can be undertaken.

A. Authorship of the Book.

The Book of Ezekiel claims several times to be the product of a sixth century prophet who was the son of Buzi (1:1; 8:1; 33:1; 40:1-4). A unity of theme is observable throughout the forty-eight chapters, viz., God's vengeance in Israel's destruction and God's vindication in Israel's restoration. Thirteen prophecies are dated and localized in such a way as to point to the life and times of Ezekiel. Similarity of thought, style, phrasing and arrangement make it clear that the entire book is the work of one mind. The evidence for the authenticity of Ezekiel is so convincing that some scholars who otherwise take a critical view toward the Old Testament have written in support of the book's claims for itself.

The traditional view regarding the authorship of this book is clouded by two curious statements which are found in ancient Jewish literature. The Talmud (fifth century AD) states that "the men of the Great Synagogue wrote Ezekiel and the Twelve."[6] This probably means nothing more than that the men of the Great Synagogue in the days of Ezra edited and copied the original scroll of Ezekiel. The second curious statement is found in Josephus (first century AD). He states: "But not only did he [Jeremiah] predict to the people [the destruction of Jerusalem], but also the prophet Ezekiel who first wrote two books about these things and left them [for posterity]."[7] The *two books* are probably the two major divisions of the present Book of Ezekiel, viz., chapters 1-32 and chapters 33-48.[8]

B. Canonicity of the Book.

The Book of Ezekiel was one of five antilegomena—books spoken against—in the Hebrew canon. Certain rabbis were convinced that the teaching of the book was not in harmony with Mosaic law. Rabbi Hananiah, however, vigorously defended the book before those who argued that it should be removed from the canon. Legend has it that he burned the midnight oil—three hundred jars of it—in harmonizing Ezekiel with the books of Moses in regard to the sacrificial ritual. Hananiah's effort at harmonization must not have satisfied all Jewish scholars. The Talmud states that when Elijah comes (cf. Malachi 4:5) the discrepancies between Ezekiel and the Pentateuch would be explained.[9]

The Book of Ezekiel certainly belongs in the Bible. The book was included in the Greek translation of the Old Testament which was initiated about 280 BC. Josephus numbered Ezekiel among the books held sacred by the Jews in his day.[10] The majority of rabbis defended the book against those who were concerned about the discrepancies with the Pentateuch. Ezekiel was listed among the canonical books in the Talmud. In Christian circles the canonicity of Ezekiel has never been seriously questioned.

C. Literary Characteristics.[11]

Critics give Ezekiel low marks on literary style. That this prophet was not a poet of the same ability as Isaiah, or even Jeremiah for that matter, is clear. His sentences are often long and involved. Ezekiel sometimes smothers his readers with tedious details and redundancy. Yet here and there are passages sublime in both content and expression. Specifically, the Book of Ezekiel is marked by seven stylistic characteristics.

First, the book emphasizes the supernatural. Ezekiel claimed repeatedly that he was the recipient of divine communication. Second, Ezekiel is marked by highly idealistic coloring. The book is full of visions, allegories and parables. His form of discourse was ideal for capturing the attention of reluctant listeners and impressing vividly upon their minds the truths of God. Third, the book makes extensive use of earlier Scripture. Ezekiel certainly was acquainted with the Pentateuch. He knew the eighth century prophets—Hosea, Amos and Isaiah—as well as those of his own century—Jeremiah and Zephaniah.

The fourth stylistic characteristic is a cosmopolitan outlook. This prophet exhibits a remarkable acquaintance with several foreign nations. Fifth, the book reflects a sophisticated diction. Ezekiel was an aristocrat, and there is something aristocratic about his writing style. Sixth, originality of expression characterizes the book. A long list of Hebrew verbs, nouns and expressions peculiar to Ezekiel could be produced. Seventh, in this book there is a deliberate redundancy. Ezekiel employed the technique of emphasis by repetition.

D. Structure of the Book.

The fall of Jerusalem in 587 BC is clearly the pivotal point in the Book of Ezekiel. R. K. Harrison[12] has proposed a two-fold arrangement for the Book of Ezekiel. He leans heavily on the testimony of Josephus cited above that Ezekiel left *two books*. These originally independent productions have been combined, Harrison thinks, in the present Book of Ezekiel. Chapters 1-23 constitute Book One, and chapters 24-48 constitute Book Two. Harrison regards the mention of the prophet by name in chapter 24 as a clue that the second volume began with this chapter.[13] The prophet is re-commissioned (33:1-9) in the second book, and this is followed by release from the dumbness imposed at his initial commissioning (3:25f; 33:21f.). Whereas the first book speaks of the vengeance of God against his people, the second underscores his vindication through those same people.

Chart No. 9

THE STRUCTURE OF EZEKIEL		
Oracles Concerning Israel	Oracles Concerning Foreign Nations	Oracles Concerning Israel
Chapters 1-24	Chapters 25-32	Chapters 33-49
Prior to the Fall of Jerusalem	During the Siege of Jerusalem	After the Fall of Jerusalem
Condemnation and Catastrophe		Consolation and Comfort

More traditional is the tripartite structure which has been attributed to the Book of Ezekiel. That would make this book similar to Isaiah in the Hebrew Bible and Jeremiah in the Greek translation. The oracles against foreign nations are grouped in the middle of the book. The above chart illustrates the structure of the book.

Chronology of the Book.

The Book of Ezekiel contains a chronological system unparalleled in any prophetic book. Fifteen dates are given in thirteen passages.[14] The dating is based on the month, years and days of the deportation of King Jehoiachin who was carried away to Babylon in 597 BC. Apparently Jehoiachin was regarded by many as the legitimate king even after Nebuchadnezzar put Zedekiah as his vassal on the throne of Judah. In Chart No. 10 the chronological references are tabulated and converted into the modern calendrical system.

Chart No. 10

CHRONOLOGICAL REFERENCES IN EZEKIEL			
REF.	YR/MO/DA	EVENT	DATE BC
1:2	5/4/5	Prophet's Call	Jul. 31, 593
8:1	6/6/5	Jerusalem Vision	Sep. 17, 592
20:1	7/5/10	Elders' Inquiry	Aug. 9, 591
24:1	9/10/10	Slege Begins	Jan. 15, 588
29:1	10/10/12	Egypt Oracle	Jan. 7, 587
30:20	11/1/7	Pharaoh Oracle	Apr. 29, 587
31:1	11/3/1	Pharaoh Oracle	Jun. 21, 587
26:1	11/?/1	Tyre Oracle	Feb. 12, 586
32:1	12/12/1	Pharaoh Lament	Mar. 3, 585
32:17	12/?/15	Pharaoh Lament	Mar. 17, 585
33:21	12/10/5*	News of Fall	Jan. 8, 585*
40:1	25/1/10	Last Vision	Apr. 28, 573
29:17	27/1/1	Egypt Oracle	Apr. 26, 571

* Some MSS and the Syriac read "eleventh year" rather than "twelfth year" which would yield a conversion date of Jan. 19, 586 BC. Conversion table based on John Taylor, *Ezekiel* in Tyndale Old Testament Commentaries (London:1969) 36.

EZEKIEL: BIBLIOGRAPHY

Blackwood, Jr. Andrew W. *Ezekiel, Prophecy of Hope*. Grand Rapids: Baker, 1965.

Currey, G. "Ezekiel" in vol. 6 *The Holy Bible Commentary*. Ed. F. C. Cook. New York: Scribners, 1892.

Eichrodt, Walther. *Ezekiel, a Commentary* in The Old Testament Library. Philadelphia: Westminster, 1970.

Ellison, H. L. *Ezekiel: The Man and His Message*. Grand Rapids: Eerdmans, 1956.

Fairbairn, Patrick. *An Exposition of Ezekiel*. Grand Rapids: Sovereign Grace, 1971.

Feinberg, Charles Lee. *The Prophecy of Ezekiel*. Chicago: Moody, 1969.

Frisch, S. *Ezekiel* in Soncino Books of the Bible. Ed. A. Cohen. London: Soncino, 1950.

Grider, J. Kenneth. "The Book of the Prophet Ezekiel" in vol. 4 of *Beacon Bible Commentary*. Kansas City: Beacon Hill, 1966.

Hall, Bert. "The Book of Ezekiel" in vol. 3 *The Wesleyan Bible Commentary*. Ed. Charles Carter. Grand Rapids: Eerdmans, 1969.

Smith, James E. *Ezekiel* in Bible Study Textbook Series. Joplin, MO: College Press, 1979.

Stuart, Douglas. "Ezekiel" in vol. 18 *The Communicator's Commentary*. Ed. Lloyd Ogilvie. Dallas: Word, 1989.

Taylor, John B. *Ezekiel* in Tyndale Old Testament Commentaries. Ed. D. J. Wiseman. London: Tyndale, 1969.

Zimmerli, Walther. *Ezekiel* in Hermeneia. Ed. Frank Moore Cross. Philadelphia: Fortress, 1979.

Endnotes

1. Adapted from James E. Smith, *Ezekiel* in Bible Study Textbook Series (Joplin, MO: College Press, 1979) ix.

2. Another Ezekiel—a priestly dignitary of David's day—is mentioned in 1 Chr 24:16.

3. An oracle is a type of prophetic speech in which the prophet became the mouthpiece for God. In an oracle Yahweh speaks in the first person. For a list of the various types of oracles found in Ezekiel see James E.. Smith, *op. cit.* 14f.

4. The theological summary in this section is adapted from Thomas Whitelaw, *Ezekiel* in The Pulpit Commentary (New York: Funk and Wagnals, 1909) 1:xxix.

5. Charles L. Feinberg, *The Prophecy of Ezekiel* (Chicago: Moody, 1969) 12.

6. *Baba Bathra* 15a.

7. Josephus, *Antiquities* 10.5.1.

8. Edward J. Young, *An Introduction to the Old Testament* (Grand Rapids: Eerdmans, 1960) 256.

9. *Menachot* 45a.

10. Josephus, *Against Apion* 1.8.

11. Material in this section has been adapted from the discussion of Whitelaw, *op. cit.* 1:xxv-xxvi.

12. R.K. Harrison, *Introduction to the Old Testament* (Grand Rapids: Eerdmans, 1969) 848f.

13. Such a renewed claim to authorship was made by Thucydides in his *History* (5.26), the probable beginning of the second roll of his work.

14. A double dating is found in 1:1-2 and 40:1 in which two different counting systems are employed.

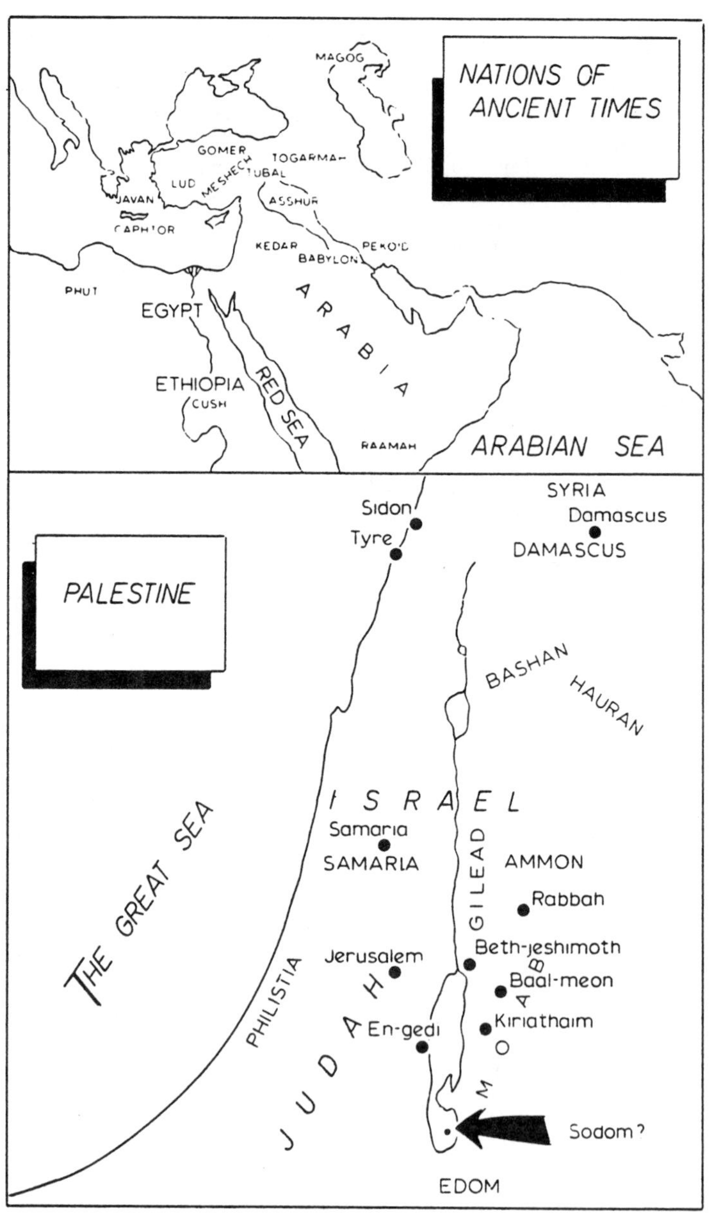
NATIONS OF ANCIENT TIMES
MAGOG
GOMER
TOGARMAH
MESHECH
TUBAL
LUD
JAVAN
ASSHUR
CAPHTOR
KEDAR
PEKOD
BABYLON
PHUT
EGYPT
ARABIA
ETHIOPIA
CUSH
RED SEA
RAAMAH
ARABIAN SEA
PALESTINE
SYRIA
Sidon
Tyre
Damascus
DAMASCUS
BASHAN
HAURAN
ISRAEL
Samaria
SAMARIA
GILEAD
AMMON
Rabbah
THE GREAT SEA
Jerusalem
Beth-jeshimoth
Baal-meon
PHILISTIA
JUDAH
En-gedi
Kiriathaim
MOAB
Sodom?
EDOM

CHAPTER TWENTY-FOUR

The Call of Ezekiel
Ezekiel 1-3

Background of the Unit.

Ezekiel precisely dated his call to prophetic service to the fifth year of the captivity of Jehoiachin, the fourth month and the fifth day. On the modern calendar that is equivalent to July 31, 593 BC. For him the captivity of King Jehoiachin in 597 BC was a crucial event. Ezekiel had been among the ten thousand Jews taken away to Babylon at that time. He was thirty years of age at the time of his call. At that age he would have begun service in the Temple as a priest had he still been living in Jerusalem.

Ezekiel was geographically as well as chronologically precise about his call. He was by the river Chebar, an irrigation canal which cut across Babylonia joining together the Euphrates and Tigris rivers. While he was there among the exiles, the "the heavens were opened" and he saw "visions of God." Two things happened during the course of these visions. First, "the word of the Lord came expressly" to him. Second, "the hand of the Lord came upon him" (1:1-3).

Outline of the Unit.

A. The Chariot of God (chap. 1).
B. The Call of God (2:1-3:3).
C. The Commission of God (3:4-27).

THE CHARIOT OF GOD
Ezekiel 1

Ancient Jewish writers found in this passage what they called the *merkabhah*, the divine throne chariot. The chapter is rich in symbolism which underscores various attributes of God. Modern science fiction writers who attempt to find here a vehicle from outer space have missed the whole point of the account. The one who appears riding atop the *merkabhah* is not some alien astronaut, but rather the Living God. The focus of attention here should not be the mechanics of the divine chariot, but the message it conveys. Ezekiel describes in detail five things which he saw on that fateful day.

A. The Cloud (1:4).

Ezekiel first noticed a "storm wind" coming from the north. Then his eye caught a great cloud with "fire," i.e., lightning, "flashing forth continually." In subsequent revelation Ezekiel learned that this ominous black cloud symbolized God's judgment against Jerusalem which Jeremiah had represented as coming from the north. The cloud was surrounded by a "bright light." In the middle of the cloud Ezekiel saw "something like glowing metal in the midst of the fire." Through the blackness of judgment Ezekiel could see the splendor of God. Storm, cloud and fire are all used in the Old Testament as symbols of God's coming judgment.

B. The Cherubim (1:5-14).

Ezekiel's attention next focused on four figures which resembled "four living beings." Later (10:20) the living beings are identified as cherubim, angelic beings which are always depicted guarding something sacred. These living beings were stationed in a square pattern. Their very persons formed the supports for the mysterious *merkab-*

hah. Not all the details in the text are clear, nor are they meant to be. The very purpose of the *merkabhah* is to inspire wonder and contemplation. Such details as are given stretch the human imagination to its limits.

1. In general the bodies of these cherubim had a human-like appearance.

2. Each had four faces facing in different directions. These were the faces of (1) man, (2) lion, (3) eagle, and (4) ox. The four represent all sentient creation. Man is the highest creature God made. Lion, eagle and ox dominate the wild animal kingdom, the skies, and the domesticated animals respectively. Since God sits on a throne above the cherubim, the thought is that all sentient creation is subordinate to him.[1]

3. Each had four wings. Two were used to cover the naked bodies of these creatures. In flight the second pair of wings stretched to the right and left and touched the wing tips of the other creatures, implying unity of purpose.

4. Their legs were "straight," i.e., unjointed. The soles of their feet were like the hoof of a calf, i.e., rounded. These feet glistened like polished bronze.

5. Under their wings on four sides were human hands. Whether each creature had two hands or four hands is not clear.

6. The creatures seemed to glow. Inside the hollow square formed by them was a bright fire which seemed to move back and forth among the living beings.

7. The creatures darted about with the speed of lightning. Since the creatures had four faces, they did not need to turn their heads no matter what direction the *merkabhah* might be going.

C. The Wheels (1:15-21).

Beside each creature was a "wheel on the earth." The four wheels were beautiful in workmanship. They were the color of "beryl," i.e., topaz. They appeared to Ezekiel as though one wheel were within another bisecting it at right angles. This seems to be the prophet's way of explaining that the four wheels were omnidirectional. Like a ball-bearing they could move in any direction without any steering mechanism (1:15-17).

The wheels were huge in comparison to the total vehicle. They were terrifying because of their size. Their rims were "full of eyes round about." The wheels moved in conjunction with the living creatures because "the spirit of the living beings was in the wheels." The *merkabhah* could move on the ground or through the air (1:18-21). The wheels symbolize God's omnipresence; the eyes, his omniscience.

D. The Expanse (1:22-25).

Over the heads of the creatures was an "expanse," lit., something stretched out. This expanse was the platform upon which the throne of God rested. It glittered "like ice." The platform symbolizes the glories of heaven. The entire persons of the creatures including their outstretched wings were under the platform. When the *merkabhah* was in motion the whirring wings sounded like roaring waters or like "the voice of the Almighty," i.e., loud thunder. The movement of the *merkabhah* was directed by the voice of God from above the platform (1:22-25). The symbolism points to God as high and lifted up above the heavens, far removed from this world. Yet he still gives direction and order to his creation from his heavenly throne.

E. The Throne (1:26-28).

The most important aspect of the vision has been put last for emphasis. Above the platform was a sapphire-like throne (cf. Exod 24:10), the majestic throne of God himself. Ezekiel reverently backs away from describing in detail the one who sat on the throne. He says only that he had "the appearance of a man." From his waist and upward the figure resembled "glowing metal" that looked like it was full of fire. From the waist and downward Ezekiel saw only fire. Around the entire figure was a radiance. This brilliant light was multicolored like the colors of a rainbow. The rainbow in this vision suggests that mercy as well as judgment was in the offing (1:26f.).

Ezekiel identified what he saw there beside the river Chebar as "the glory of the Lord." This is a technical term for the presence of God among his people. The basic idea conveyed through this entire vision is that God is present with the captives in Babylon. Ezekiel fell on his face in the presence of this awesome sight (1:28).

THE CALL OF GOD
Ezekiel 2:1-3:3

Chapters 2-3 make clear the purpose of the vision in chapter 1. Once Ezekiel had been humbled by his vision of the grandeur of God, he was prepared to hear the voice of his Maker. The voice called him to preach God's word, and then directed him to perform an action which symbolized the divine origin of his message.

A. The Mission (2:1-7).

To prepare him for his mission to the sons of Israel, God first strengthened Ezekiel. The Lord addressed Ezekiel as "son of man." This title which occurs over eighty-five times in the book underscores the human frailty of the prophet. Most of the time this title precedes a direct command of God. The first command which God gave to Ezekiel was this: "Stand on your feet that I may speak with you!" Service, not servility, was what God desired from this man. In those days servants always stood in the presence of their Master. Even as he issued the command, God supplied the inner strength which enabled the terrified captive to comply. Empowered by the Holy Spirit, Ezekiel rose to his feet to listen to the voice of God (2:1f.).

Second, God warned Ezekiel about what he would face in his role as prophet. God was sending him to "the sons of Israel."[2] His audience was a "rebellious people." They had even rebelled against God himself. They had transgressed against the Lord "to this very day." They were still God's children, but they were "stubborn" (lit., hard of face) and "obstinate" children. Their hard faces revealed their hard hearts! To this antagonistic audience Ezekiel was to say "Thus says the Lord God." Whether or not they listened, he was to preach with authority so that they would know "that a prophet has been among them" (2:3-5).

Third, God charged Ezekiel. Four times the Lord told his messenger that he must not fear his audience. He might have cause to fear them, however. God compared his audience to thorns, thistles and scorpions. Ezekiel must expect to be pierced through on many occasions and stung by their criticism and personal attacks. Such conduct was consistent with the fact that this was a rebellious people. As

God's representative, however, Ezekiel must not be intimidated, neither by their fierce looks nor by any threatening words which they might hurl at him. He must continue faithfully to proclaim God's words "whether they listen or not." God's justice demanded that the people be confronted with an indictment of their sins. Even if his audience rejected his message and lashed out against him, Ezekiel would be fulfilling God's purpose by the proclamation of the divine word (2:6f.).

B. The Message (2:8-3:3).

The first requirement of a man of God is absolute obedience to God. Ezekiel was told to open his mouth and eat what God was about to give him. In his vision Ezekiel saw a hand extended to him from the *merkabhah*. Whether this was the hand of God or of one of the cherubim is not indicated. The hand contained a scroll. God spread the scroll out before the prophet and he noted that it was "written on the front and back." He further noted that the scroll contained messages of "lamentations, mourning and woe." The scroll came from God, and it was not very pleasant. It symbolized the message which Ezekiel was to deliver in the early part of his ministry. Ezekiel's early sermons were largely negative and condemnatory. That the scroll was written on the backside as well as the front indicated that God had much to say to his people (2:8-10).

God directed Ezekiel to eat what he saw before him. He must make God's word part of himself before he tried to share it with the house of Israel. Ezekiel obediently opened his mouth. Then God enabled him to eat the scroll. In preparation for ministry, man must do his part and then God will do his. The message was not forced on Ezekiel; he willingly received it. That God fed him the scroll suggests divine aid in comprehending and preserving the message. Ezekiel was told to feed his stomach, to let the word of God fill his body. The preacher must digest and assimilate the message he proclaims. Since it was God's word, Ezekiel found the scroll sweet to his taste. He did not delight in the morbid thrust of his message. He did rejoice, however, in the fact that God had chosen him as a recipient of divine revelation (3:1-3).

THE COMMISSION OF GOD
Ezekiel 3:4-27

A fourfold commission followed the divine call. The emphasis in each was on Ezekiel's obligation to speak the word of the Lord. Each command, however, revealed a slightly different aspect of his work. Ezekiel was commissioned as a preacher, an observer, a watchman, and a prisoner.

A. As a Preacher (3:4-9).

Ezekiel was now equipped to go to the house of Israel and speak the word of God. That was exactly what he was to do. God warned him, however, about the nature of his mission. He was not being sent to a divergent group of peoples scattered over great distances. Unlike Jonah, he was not dispatched to a people of "unintelligible speech or difficult language." He would not have to spend years in language study nor learn the customs of a strange land. The mechanics of language would be no problem. He was being sent to a people who should listen to him. Yet God warned Ezekiel again about the reaction of his audience. They would not listen to Ezekiel because they would not listen to God. The preacher should never take rejection personally. These people were "stubborn" (lit., of a hard forehead) and "obstinate" (lit., of a hard heart) (3:4-7).

God promised to equip Ezekiel emotionally and intellectually to deal with the anticipated rejection. God had made the prophet's face and forehead just as hard as theirs. He would be able to "butt heads" with his antagonists. If they were as hard as flint, Ezekiel would be as hard as a diamond. He was to be as stubborn for truth as they were stubborn in evil deeds. Therefore, for the second time (cf. 2:6) God directed his prophet not to fear his audience (3:8f.).

B. As an Observer (3:10-15).

An effective servant of God must know two things. He must know (1) the word of the Lord; and (2) the needs of God's people. The first priority of any preacher is to be attuned to God's word. The word of God is that which fortifies the messenger against the hostilities of the enemy. So Ezekiel was told to take into his heart "all my words which I shall speak to you." He must "listen closely" whenever God spoke to him (3:10f.). A good preacher must first be a good listener. This will enable him to speak with authority and credibility to his contemporaries. The words "thus says the Lord God" will not ring hollow from the lips of one who is the epitome of an obedient servant.

The servant of God must also be attuned to the needs of his audience. For this reason God commissioned Ezekiel "to go to the captives." The prophet was reluctant to leave the scene of his dramatic encounter with God. He was not anxious to undertake the hard service to which he had been assigned. So God took matters into his own hands. Ezekiel felt himself being "lifted up" and taken away by the Spirit of God. At the same time the *merkabhah* departed amidst a cry of praise apparently from the cherubim: "Blessed be the glory of the Lord in his place." Ezekiel heard the noise of great shaking as the wings of the cherubim were raised and began vibrating. The wheels of the *merkabhah* rumbled as the visionary chariot began its take off (3:12f.).

Ezekiel described how he felt as he departed from his mountain top experience. He went "embittered in the rage of my spirit." Perhaps he was angry because the blessed experience had so quickly come to an end. Like Isaiah and Jeremiah before him, he was initially reluctant to undertake the task to which he had been called. Another interpretation is that he was filled with righteous anger over the sin of Israel. In any case, he was very conscious that "the hand of the Lord was strong" on him. He felt God's power filling him (3:14).

Guided by the Spirit Ezekiel returned to his countrymen at Tel-abib near the Chebar canal. For seven days he sat among them, perhaps motionless and dumb, as he awaited further instructions. During this period he was "overwhelmed" (NIV), i.e., astonished, amazed and silent.[3] What was the purpose of this seven-day period which God forced on the reluctant prophet? Ezekiel needed to develop sympathy and empathy before he began to preach. He needed to see these people as God saw them. This was a time of reflection and observation such as many great men of God experienced prior to launching their ministries. Those days of silence changed his attitude about his mission. He learned patience; he came to accept responsibility (3:14f.).

C. As a Watchman (3:16-21).

At the end of the seven days of silence, God commissioned Ezekiel to be "a watchman to the house of Israel."[4] Every fortified city had a sentinel whose task it was to warn the citizens of approaching enemies. What an appropriate figure to describe the work of Ezekiel. Whenever God spoke a threatening word against Israel, Ezekiel was to warn his countrymen of the impending danger. He had an obligation to warn the wicked even if they did not give heed. If he failed to sound the alarm he would stand guilty before God for that lost soul. Nonetheless, the wicked man would still pay for his sin. "He will die in his iniquity." Death here is more than premature death. A sinner who dies in his iniquity, impenitent and unforgiven, is lost for eternity (3:16-19).

Ezekiel also had the responsibility to warn righteous men who might wander into sin. God would place "an obstacle" in the path of that man, i.e., some trial, difficulty or test. That man must be warned that he would "die in his sin" if he did not remain faithful. God would not remember to his credit "his righteous deeds." Ezekiel knew nothing of the doctrine of eternal security as taught by John Calvin. If Ezekiel failed in his duty to warn such a man, God said he would hold the prophet "accountable." On the other hand, if the righteous man accepted the warning and repudiated the sin, he would live. In that case Ezekiel would have delivered himself from any guilt in the matter (3:20f.).

D. As a Prisoner (3:22-27).

The "hand," i.e., power, of God came upon Ezekiel. He was directed to go out to the plain. There God would communicate to him his message. When Ezekiel went out to the plain he saw that "the glory of the Lord was standing there." This second appearance of the *merkabhah* engendered in the prophet the same response as the first. He fell on his face in reverence. Again the Spirit entered him and made him stand up to hear what God would say. The command of the Lord was strange indeed: "Go shut yourself up in your house." This man was to make himself a prisoner! (3:22-24).

Ezekiel was told that his fellow captives would put ropes on him and bind him with them, "so that he could not go out among them"

(3:25). Is this warning to be understood literally? Perhaps the captives thought that he was insane and so they restrained him for a time in his house. Perhaps this refers to a persecution of the prophet (cf. Jer 20; 29:26). Others understand the warning metaphorically. By their unbelief and hostility the captives restricted the freedom with which Ezekiel could conduct his ministry. Or again, they tried to imprison him to their way of thinking. Ezekiel, however, was to be a prisoner of the word of God, not to the whims of men.

God then declared that he would make Ezekiel's tongue "stick to the roof" of his mouth. The prophet would be "dumb," unable to rebuke the exiles because they were a rebellious house. From time to time God would speak to Ezekiel. In such an event Ezekiel was to present that word to his audience as a "thus says the Lord God." His audience would then have the freedom to hear, i.e., obey the prophetic word, or to refuse it. Most would choose the latter alternative because they were "a rebellious house" (3:26f.).

Some understand these words to mean that Ezekiel experienced a literal period of silence in his ministry. The passage seems to say that Ezekiel would communicate with his fellow exiles only at such times as he received a divine communication. The fetters symbolically represented this restraint which God placed on Ezekiel. This restraint is removed in 33:22.

Bert Hall[5] offers an effective summary of the commissioning of Ezekiel by paraphrasing the commands given to him in this unit:

1. "Go, and speak" (3:4).
2. "Go, and sit" (3:11).
3. "Go, and watch" (3:17).
4. "Go, and wait" (3:24).

Endnotes

1. Others think the cherubim represent the irresistible forces of Nebuchadnezzar which would be God's agents in the destruction of Jerusalem. See J. Kenneth Grider, "The Book of the Prophet Ezekiel" in *Beacon Bible Commentary* (Kansas City: Beacon Hill, 1966) 4:538f.

2. After the deportation of the northern tribes, the citizens of Judah, even those in captivity, are called *Israel*.

3. NASB understands the passage to be saying that Ezekiel was "causing a great consternation among them," i.e., the captives.

4. Other prophets were called watchmen: Habakkuk (Hab 2:1); Isaiah (Isa 56:10); and Jeremiah (Jer 6:17).

5. Bert Hall, "Commentary on Ezekiel" in *The Wesleyan Bible Commentary* (Grand Rapids: Eerdmans, 1969) 3:380.

CHAPTER TWENTY FIVE

Ezekiel's Early Ministry
Ezekiel 4-7

Background of the Unit.

The material in chapters 4-7 represents the earliest ministry of Ezekiel among the captives. These parables and discourses probably should be dated to the same year as the call—593 BC. This was the fifth year of King Jehoiachin's captivity. False prophets among the captives continued to peddle the "701 theology" which affirmed the inviolability of Jerusalem. Jeremiah had already sent his controversial letter to the captives to counter the influence of these prophetic deceivers. Most of the captives, however, continued to cling tenaciously to the illusion that the captivity would be of short duration.

In Jerusalem King Zedekiah was ruling as the vassal of Nebuchadnezzar. The preceding year Zedekiah had entertained ambassadors from neighboring countries (Jer 29:1-3). A move was afoot to coordinate a rebellion against Babylon. Zedekiah was required personally to bring the tribute money to Babylon (Jer 51:59). Apparently Judah's policy was to look for the earliest opportunity to cast off the cast off the yoke of Babylon.

Outline of the Unit.

A. Silent Demonstrations (4:1-5:4).
B. Discourse One: Siege and Suffering (5:5-17).
C. Discourse Two: Disobedience and Desolation (chap. 6).
D. Discourse Three: Chaos and Calamity (chap. 7).

SILENT DEMONSTRATIONS
Ezekiel 4:1-5:4

The prophets of Israel employed the technique of action parables in order to attract attention to their message and underscore the main points which they wished to impress on the minds of their audience. Ezekiel used this technique more than any other Old Testament prophet. As he inaugurated his ministry Ezekiel used a series of dramatic actions to dramatize various predictions regarding the siege of Jerusalem.

A. Siege Operations (4:1-3).

In his first action parable Ezekiel used as a prop a clay brick on which he had sketched a diagram of Jerusalem. He then was told to lay siege to the city which he had sketched in the drawing. He used camps of attacking soldiers, assault forts, mounds and battering rams to carry out these instructions. These were common sights when a city was under siege in that day. He either made models of various siege instruments or else depicted them on the brick (4:1f.).

The prophet was then told to secure a flat iron plate. He was to set it up as a barrier between himself and the city depicted on the brick. This plate has been interpreted to represent (1) Jerusalem's wall; (2) the barrier between God and Jerusalem; or (3) the shield used by attacking soldiers as they approached the walls of a city. Ezekiel was then told to "besiege" (lit., press the siege) his model city. This may have entailed the gradual movement of the clay models of siege instruments toward the city.[1] Ezekiel's actions were to be "a sign," i.e., have symbolic import, to the house of Israel (4:3).

B. Siege Duration (4:4-8).

The second action parable was performed simultaneously with the first. Ezekiel was to lie on his "left side" for 390 days. If his head was toward the east, the orienting direction of the ancients, then his back would be toward the north. During those days on his left side Ezekiel was illustrating the years of the iniquity of the "house of Israel." Here the expression "house of Israel" is used in its narrow sense of the Northern Kingdom. After the death of Solomon in 931 BC the northern tribes had broken away from Judah to form their own kingdom. The Assyrian King Sargon finally destroyed that kingdom in 722 BC and incorporated the territory into the Assyrian empire. Each day the prophet remained positioned on his left side represented a year which Israel had been estranged from God. From its inception in 931 BC the Northern Kingdom stood under the condemnation of God because they abandoned the worship of God in his Temple in Jerusalem. This estrangement would last in round figures for 390 years. Subtracting 390 from 931 BC yields a date of 541 BC. Israel's estrangement from God would end with the rise of Cyrus, the fall of Babylon in 539 BC, the liberation of the captives, and the return of the remnant to Jerusalem (4:4f.).

When he had completed his 390 days on his left side, Ezekiel was to reverse positions and lie on his right side for forty days. This would mean that his back was now to the south. Ezekiel was now illustrating the estrangement of Judah, the Southern Kingdom, from the Lord. Again each day represented one year of actual time. According to Jeremiah 52:30 the last contingent of Jews was deported to Babylon in 582 BC five years after the destruction of Jerusalem. For roughly the next forty years Jews, like their ancestors before them, were in a wilderness—the wilderness of exile in a foreign land. During those years they were denied access to the Promised Land (4:6).

Jeremiah had predicted that Nebuchadnezzar would rule the world for seventy years (Jer 25:11). Ezekiel was focusing on the last forty years of that period. The entire nation would be outside the Promised Land for that period. By 542 BC Cyrus, the anointed of God (Isa 45:1) was on the scene. Through his conquests he prepared the way for God's people to return to their homeland. The following chart illustrates how this first time prophecy in Ezekiel was fulfilled.

Chart No. 11

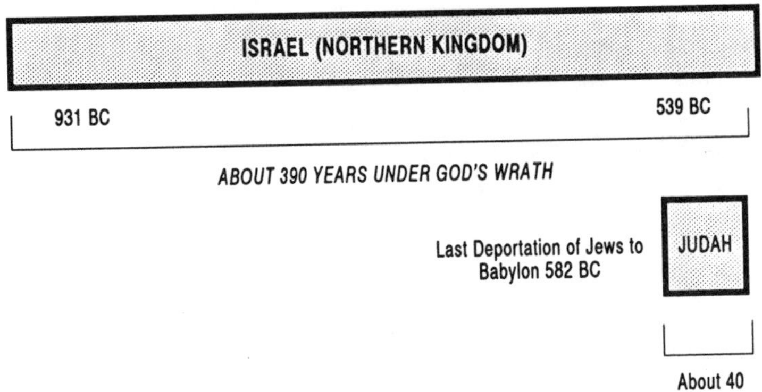

During the 430 days of his action parable God told Ezekiel to set his face toward the siege of Jerusalem. Apparently he was to be facing the brick which was inscribed with the diagram of Jerusalem. He was to bare his arm, a gesture of hostility. By his actions he was prophesying against the city. During this time God rendered him immobile. Ezekiel appeared as if God had placed ropes on him to restrain him. He was not able to turn from one side to the other until the 430 days of his siege were completed (4:7f.).[2]

C. Siege Conditions (4:9-17).

During the days of his siege[3] Ezekiel was to observe a restricted diet. He first received instructions from the Lord regarding his diet; then the Lord explained to Ezekiel the two-fold meaning of this action parable.

1. Dietary instructions (4:9-12). Contrary to the dietary laws, Ezekiel was to gather various kinds of grains into one vessel and then make from that mixture his bread. The quantity as well as the quality of his food was restricted. He was to weigh out for himself only twenty shekels of food per day, about ten ounces. He was to drink only the sixth part of a hin of water per day, i.e., a little more than a pint.[4] He was to sip this water "from time to time" (4:9-11).

Ezekiel was instructed to bake his bread over stones heated by human excrement "in their sight." This is evidence that the prophet remained in the prone position only a portion of each day. Under God's Law, contact with human dung rendered a person unclean (cf. Deut 23:12ff.). Yet in spite of the quality of the product and the wretched circumstances of its preparation, Ezekiel was to eat it "as barley cake," i.e., just as he might eat a regular meal (4:12).

2. Divine explanations (4:13-17). God first explained why he had directed the prophet to eat food which, according the the Law of Moses, was unclean. The prophet's actions were designed to underscore the fact that the sons of Israel would "eat their bread unclean among the nations" where God would banish them (4:13).[5]

In the first words attributed to Ezekiel in the book, the prophet protested the use of human dung as cooking fuel. Throughout his thirty years he had always observed the dietary provisions of the Law of Moses. No unclean meat had ever entered his mouth. God heard this complaint of his prophet. He canceled the most abhorrent aspect of the initial directive. The Lord gave Ezekiel permission to substitute cow's dung, which was used for cooking fuel in some quarters, for human dung (4:14f.).

The second aspect of the lesson from the parable of food has to do with conditions in Jerusalem just prior to the fall of that city. God declared his intention "to break the staff of bread in Jerusalem." Because outside food supplies would be cut off during the siege, the city would be forced to ration food and water. People would eat and drink their meager provisions "with anxiety" and "in horror" because of grave concern over the food supply. Gradually the lack of basic necessities would take its toll. People would be "appalled" as they observed the effects of the famine on their neighbors. Gradually they would "waste away" from lack of proper nutrition (4:16f.).

D. Siege Results (5:1-4).

Chapter 5 begins with directions for an action parable which was to be performed "when the days of the siege are completed," i.e., after the 430 days. Ezekiel was told to take a razor-sharp sword and use it as a barber's razor to shave his head and beard. He was then to take scales and divide the shaven hair into three equal piles. After the 430 days of his symbolic siege of Jerusalem, he was to take the first pile of hair and burn it "at the center of the city," i.e., in the middle of the brick which had on it the diagram of Jerusalem. The second pile he was to spread around the diagram of the city, and then chop with a sword. The last pile of hair he was to scatter to the wind. God declared that he would "unsheathe a sword" after these, i.e., they will not escape suffering by fleeing from the land (5:1f.).

Ezekiel was to take a few of those hairs which had been scattered to the wind and bind them in the edge of his garment. Here is hope! A remnant would survive. Some of those hairs, however, were again to be burned. The remnant would suffer persecution. The remnant in Babylon would constitute the "whole house of Israel" after the destruction of Jerusalem (5:3f.).

DISCOURSE ON SIEGE AND SUFFERING
Ezekiel 5:5-17

Partial explanations accompanied the divine directive to perform the silent symbolic acts. Now the Lord began to respond to the many questions which must have been filling the mind of Ezekiel. For the sake of emphasis this unit contains much repetition. Two more or less distinct units can be identified. The first focuses on the reasons for the siege, the second on the results of it.

A. Reasons for the Siege (5:5-12).

The prophet uses a "because . . . therefore" pattern to underscore three reasons for the terrible siege. Included here is verbal explanation and amplification of the symbolic acts just performed.

1. Rejection of divine guidance (5:5-8). So there could be no misunderstanding, the city to which Ezekiel had been symbolically laying siege for 430 days was again identified as Jerusalem (cf. 4:1). Geographically she was "in the midst of nations." Throughout history Palestine had been a crossroads between Africa and Asia. God intended for this people to be a shining example to the "lands around her." To them God had imparted his "ordinances" and his "statutes." Yet in spite of her position and privilege Jerusalem had "rebelled." In God's sight she was more evil than her heathen neighbors. She had rejected God's ordinances and had refused to abide by his statutes (5:5f.).

Refusing divine standards resulted in moral and spiritual "turmoil." In some respects Jerusalem fell below the standards of her neighbors. Heathen peoples were far more loyal to their gods than Israel was to the Living God. For this reason God made a declaration of hostility against Jerusalem: "Behold, I, even I am against you." The Lord was about to enter into mortal combat with this city. Since God had been publicly profaned by the citizens of Jerusalem, there he would be publicly vindicated in the "judgments" which he brought upon the place (5:7-8).

2. Abominations (5:9-10). A second reason for the threat against Jerusalem is captured in the word "abominations." Idols and idolatrous paraphernalia and worship were considered abomination by the Lord. Jerusalem's involvement with the gods of the nations justified the unprecedented judgment which God was about to unleash against the place. Though Jerusalem would fall many times after 587 BC, never again would God bring upon that place a judgment which would, in all of its components, be the equivalent (5:9).

Two particularly gruesome aspects of the siege of 588-87 BC are predicted. The first is cannibalism: "fathers will eat their sons among you, and sons will eat their fathers."[6] The second is total depopulation. God said that he would scatter all their remnant to every wind (5:10).

3. Defilement of the sanctuary (5:11-12). The people of God had "defiled" the sanctuary, i.e., the Temple, with "detestable idols" and "abominations." By so doing they were in effect repudiating any special relationship to Yahweh. The Lord, therefore, would "withdraw" from them. The presence of his Temple in Jerusalem would not guarantee their safety. He would no longer show them any pity nor spare them from the atrocities of war. A third of the population would die by plague or famine during the siege. Another third would fall by the sword in the battle to defend the city. Another third would be scattered to every wind. Some of these would flee of their own volition; others would be led away in chain gangs. Yet even on foreign soil they would not escape the relentless sword of divine justice.

B. Results of the Siege (5:13-17).

The siege and consequent fall of Jerusalem would have impact in three areas. These areas are marked off in the text by the expression "I the Lord have spoken" (vv. 13,15,17). Vindication of the prophetic word spoken in God's name is a major theme in this book.

First, the judgment against Jerusalem would have an impact on God himself. God gave triple emphasis to the fact that the judgment against Jerusalem would bring an end to his wrath against them.[7] "My anger will be spent, and I will satisfy my wrath on them, and I shall be appeased." These words contain an oblique note of hope. God's people would realize that God had spoken in his "zeal" prior to the event. Through men like Jeremiah and Ezekiel God had warned his people repeatedly that he would destroy their Temple and capital. The Lord is zealous *for* truth, and *against* evil. The judgment against Jerusalem, then, would result in an enhanced appreciation for the true nature of God (5:13).

Second, the judgment against Jerusalem would have an impact on the nations. Jerusalem would become a "desolation" and consequently "a reproach among the nations" which surrounded her. All who passed by the ruins would show nothing but contempt for Jerusalem. How could a people be so wicked as to provoke their God to execute judgments against them "in anger, wrath and raging rebukes!" At the same time, the Gentiles would look upon the ruins of Jerusalem as "a warning and an object of horror." What happened at Jerusalem could happen to them. There the nations would learn that Yahweh is in control of history (5:14f.).

The overthrow of Jerusalem would have an impact on the populace. The "deadly arrows of famine," i.e., all calamities which lead to food shortages, would be hurled against Jerusalem with the intent of destroying the place.[8] The famine would gradually intensify until finally "the staff of bread" was broken. Because of depopulation resulting from the war for survival, "wild beasts" would become a menace to their children. Plague and violent death would pass through the midst of the city doing their deadly work. Finally they would face the "sword," i.e., the Chaldeans, God's agent who would execute the final blow against the city (5:16f.).

DISCOURSE ON DISOBEDIENCE AND DESOLATION
Ezekiel 6:1-14

The second discourse may have been delivered during the course of the 430 days of siege. More likely, however, it followed shortly after the execution of those symbolic acts. The discourse begins with a dire prediction and concludes with a prophetic lamentation. Sandwiched between is a note of hope regarding the remnant. Each of the three units concludes with the so-called recognition formula: "you/they will know that I am Yahweh."

A. A Dire Prediction (6:1-7).

The divine word directed Ezekiel to set his face "toward the mountains of Israel and prophesy against them." Apparently he was to look in a westwardly direction as he spoke these words. He actually called upon the mountains to hear the word of the Lord! Those mountains, hills, ravines and valleys were the places where Israel had practiced idolatry in "high places." Josiah had made a valiant effort to rid the land of these pagan shrines. When he died, however, the high places rapidly reappeared. The "sword" of divine punishment would fall upon these rural areas as well as the city of Jerusalem (6:1-3).

God spoke very specifically about what he was about to do to the mountains of Judah. The sacrificial altars would be left desolate, the incense altars smashed. The slain would lie unburied before the blockheads[9] they worshiped as gods. Sacred worship areas would be defiled by the bones of those who once worshiped there. Cities once teeming with people would be waste places. Popular high places would be desolate. Their idols would be broken and cease to exist. All of this would transpire so that their evil "works may be blotted out" (6:4-6).

For emphasis Ezekiel again alluded to the slaughter about to take place in the mountains of Israel: "The slain shall fall among you!" Then he introduced a new thought: "and you will know that I am the

Lord." This so-called recognition formula, which occurs some sixty times in the book, captures the theme of this prophet. God's motive in all that he does is that he might be recognized as the only God. He desires more than anything that his people have a true understanding of his nature (6:7).

B. A Confident Expectation (6:8-10).

Though the nation as a whole had been rejected, faithful individuals would be spared. Some would escape the tribulation which Ezekiel had been describing. God would leave a "remnant," though they would be scattered "among the nations." These captives would "remember" the Lord, i.e., they would seek to restore their relationship with God. They would realize how deeply their dalliance with pagan idols had hurt the Lord. Their "adulterous hearts" and wandering eyes had brought pain to the heart of God. They would come to regard idolatry as nothing less than spiritual harlotry. Because of this change of attitude, they "will loathe themselves in their own sight for the evils which they have committed, for all of their abominations." This is Ezekiel's way of describing genuine repentance. Most important, however, they would come to recognize the true nature of Yahweh as the God of truth and justice.

C. A Distressing Lamentation (6:11-14).

God directed Ezekiel to dramatize an agonizing lament. He was to clap his hands, stamp his feet, and cry "Alas!" He was to publicly lament "all the evil abominations of the house of Israel" which would precipitate the fall of the nation "by sword, famine, and plague." He who was near the battlefield would die by the sword. He who was far away from the battle would die by plague. Those who experienced the siege would die by famine. Only then would God's wrath come to an end (6:11f.).

When they had experienced the full impact of God's judgment, Israel would come to recognize that Yahweh is faithful to his word. Ezekiel cited two aspects of the calamity which would produce this recognition by way of example. First, they would see corpses scattered about among their idols in the hilltop shrines and shady sanctuaries where they had offered incense to their gods. Second, they would see their land become a desolation (6:13f.).

DISCOURSE ON CHAOS AND CALAMITY
Ezekiel 7:1-27

The third discourse is organized in two unequal divisions. First Ezekiel briefly announced the coming calamity at Jerusalem; then he described at length the various components of that calamity. Again the overriding theme is that men would come to have a correct assessment of Yahweh. The recognition formula ("you/they shall know that I am the Lord") occurs in this discourse three times (vv. 4, 9, 27).

A. The Calamity Announced (7:1-9).

The messenger formula "thus says the Lord God" marks two announcements of the coming calamity. For the land of Israel "the end" has come! The destruction would extend to "the four corners of the land," i.e., it would be complete. The word "now" indicates that the destruction was close at hand. "The end" to which Ezekiel refers is the judgment of God, a righteous retribution for all their abominations, i.e., idols. Even when the judgment unfolded they would still cling to their "abominations," i.e., idols. Therefore, God would show no mercy on the sinners in that day. This judgment would correct their faulty notions about the nature of God (7:1-4).

The second announcement emphasized the uniqueness of the coming disaster. This disaster was described as "an end, the end, doom, the time" and "the day." The prophet used the expressions "is coming,""has come" and "has awakened" to announce the nearness of the time of reckoning. The clamor and confusion of military invasion would replace the "joyful shouting" associated with the religious shrines in the mountains (7:5-7).

The disaster faced by Israel would be no accident of history. God announced his intention to pour out his "wrath" on Judah. They would experience the full extent of God's "anger." This, however, would be no capricious unleashing of divine hostility. God declared that he would judge according to their ways. He would bring on them all their abominations. In this day of retribution God threatened to show no pity nor mercy. He could not, for even as the judgment unfolded, the "abominations," i.e., idols, still would be in their midst. When these predictions come to pass, God's people would realize that Yahweh actually executed this "smiting" (7:8f.).

B. The Calamity Described (7:10-27).

Ezekiel next described the social, military, economic and political impact of the calamity which was about to befall Jerusalem.

1. Social disruption (7:10-13). The day of Jerusalem's judgment would begin with the blossoming of the arrogant superpower Babylon, God's judgment "rod." The wickedness and violent deeds of the citizens of Judah created the need for this rod of correction. Babylon's rise would bring disaster to Judah. None would remain in the land. National wealth would be confiscated. Those who survived would experience a grief beyond tears (7:10f.).

That day of accountability was at hand. Every economic institution would be shaken. Real estate transactions, normally sad for the seller and joyous for the buyer, would cease altogether. Sellers would never return to properties they once owned.[10] They would die in captivity. This threatening "vision" regarding the multitudes of sinners would not be averted! (7:12f.).

2. Military dismay (7:14-18). In that day of calamity organized resistance to the invaders would fail. Outside Jerusalem the "sword" of the enemy would cut down all who stood in the way. Inside the city plague and famine would take their toll. The few who escaped would bemoan their iniquity in lofty heights and deep ravines. With sackcloth on their bodies and heads shaven in humiliation they would sit in fear and trembling as they contemplated what worse fate might still be awaiting them.

3. Economic distress (7:19-22). Silver and gold would become worthless in the day of judgment, an actual liability to the one who was attempting to flee. Fugitives would cast it away like some unclean thing. No amount of wealth would deliver them in the day of the Lord's wrath. Food would be unavailable at any price (7:19).

They had abused the wealth which God had given them. From their gold and silver they fashioned jewelry which became objects of pride. They made from their precious metals "images of their abominations and their detestable things," i.e., idols. This abused wealth would become to them worthless, foul, and unclean. God would take their silver and gold from them and give it to the foreign invaders, i.e., the Babylonians. Sacred objects would be put to profane use by the conquerors. Since God would turn his face from his people, even the secret treasuries of the Temple would be ransacked by the invaders (7:20-22). What a terrible judgment! Yet, as Blackwood has observed, "the death of material property turned out to be the resurrection of faith."[11]

4. Political disorder (7:23-27). In view of the bloodshed and violence which he had been describing, Ezekiel called sarcastically upon the leaders in Jerusalem to "make the chain." The chain was used to deflect battering rams as a last ditch defensive maneuver of besieged cities.[12] In the case of Jerusalem, this effort would not succeed. God had brought against them "the worst of the nations." The thought is that Judah must be wretched if God selected as the agent of punishment the worst of the nations. Those ruthless invaders would overrun Jerusalem. They would take possession of private houses. They would humble proud rulers, and profane sacred sanctuaries (7:23f.).

In the coming "anguish" the Jerusalemites would sue for peace, but there would be none. Disaster would follow upon disaster. Rumors would abound. Neither priest nor elder would be able to give any authoritative advice. In desperation men would look for prophets who might have "a vision" from the Lord. The civil authorities and "people of the land," i.e., land owners, would tremble before the bombardment of the enemy. Yet the terrible judgment was not inappropriate. God would deal with these sinners "according to their conduct." They would learn through this horrible experience that Yahweh is sovereign, awesome in power and justice (7:25-27).

Endnotes

1. H.L. Ellison, *Ezekiel: The Man and His Message* (Grand Rapids: Eerdmans, 1956) 33.

2. Most likely this was his condition only during the hours when leaders came to his home for instruction. Cf. 8:1.

3. He was to observe his dietary restrictions for 390 days. Probably the diet continued during the 40 days as well. Some writers think that the 430 days of symbolic siege represent a prediction of the actual duration of the siege of Jerusalem in 587 BC. The siege lasted eighteen months (cf. 2 Kgs 25:1-30, but was interrupted by a withdrawal of unreported duration (Jer 37:7-9).

4. A *hin* was equal to about six and a half pints.

5. Foreign lands were regarded as unclean since the first fruits of crops could not be dedicated to the Lord at the Temple. Cf. Hos 9:3; Amos 7:17.

6. Predictions of cannibalism are found in Lev 26:29 and Deut 28:53. Lam 4:16 documents the fulfillment.

7. The idea that God's wrath would be assuaged through judgment is found also in 16:42; 21:22; 24:13.

8. The NASB marginal reading of 5:16 is preferred. NIV reads: "I will shoot to destroy you."

9. The Hebrew *gillulim* lit., block gods, is a term of derision for idols used thirty-nine times in the book.

10. According to Jer 32:15 and 37:43 properties would again be bought and sold in Judah. Ezekiel's point is that the sinful land owners of his day would never live to reinhabit their property.

11. Andrew W. Blackwood, Jr., *Ezekiel, Prophecy of Hope* (Grand Rapids: Baker, 1965) 70.

12. Yigael Yadin, "The Mystery of the Unexplained Chain," *Biblical Archaeology Review* 10 (July/August, 1984): 65-67.

CHAPTER TWENTY-SIX

Visions of Jerusalem's Judgment Ezekiel 8-11

Background of the Unit.

Chapters 8-11 contain a series of visions designed to demonstrate the justice of God's destruction of Jerusalem. This unit is precisely dated (8:1) to the fifth day of the sixth month of the sixth year of King Jehoiachin's captivity, i.e. September 17, 592 BC. Fourteen months have elapsed since the call of the prophet. He would have been in the 413th day of the symbolic siege of Jerusalem (cf. 4:5,6). The situation in Jerusalem had not changed. Zedekiah was still ruling. The national policy was to cast off the obligations to Nebuchadnezzar at the earliest opportunity.

Ezekiel recited in detail the circumstances of his visionary experience. He was sitting in his house. Elders from among the captives were sitting before him as his students. On one particular day the "hand of the Lord God," i.e., power of God, fell on Ezekiel. He immediately saw in his prophetic trance a fiery, glowing, man-like figure. No doubt this was the same one he had seen on the throne in his call vision, i.e., God himself (cf. 1:26). This theophanic figure stretched forth "the form of a hand" and took hold of the prophet by a lock of hair. Ezekiel felt himself being lifted up into the air. When he came back to earth he found himself (in vision) in Jerusalem at the entrance of the northern gate of the inner court of the Temple. Before the reforms of good king Josiah an "idol of jealousy," i.e., an idol which provoked God's jealousy, had once stood there. "The glory of God," i.e., his presence, was now there. The Lord had already abandoned the Holy of Holies of the Temple, but he was still at this point near the Temple. This is the same vision of God which Ezekiel had earlier seen in the plain (3:23) and beside the river Chebar (1:1ff.) in Babylon (8:1-4).

Outline of the Unit.

A. Introduction to the Vision (8:1-4).
B. The Defilement of the Temple (8:5-18).
C. The Doom of the City (9:1-10:8).
D. The Departure the Glory (10:9-22).
E. The Denouncement of the Leaders (11:1-21).
F. Conclusion to the Vision (11:22-25).

THE DEFILEMENT OF THE TEMPLE
Ezekiel 8:5-18

In his vision Ezekiel was conducted to various locations where he witnessed the abominations of Jerusalem. Based upon this visionary investigation, Ezekiel announced again the destruction of the city.

A. The Abominations of Jerusalem (8:5-16).

At four different locations in and around the Temple Ezekiel witnessed the abominable practices of the leading citizens of Jerusalem. First, God directed his attention to the area north of the altar gate. There he saw a new "image of jealousy" in the entrance. Though the image is not further identified, most likely it was the representation of the fertility goddess Asherah. Those approaching the altar of God passed beside this image. An abomination like this was sufficient to justify Yahweh's departure from his sanctuary. The Lord assured Ezekiel, however, that he would see yet greater abominations (8:5f.).

Next the Lord brought Ezekiel to the entrance of the inner Temple court. There he saw a hole in the wall of the Temple. He was told in his vision to dig through that hole. When he did so he found inside an entrance to a secret chamber. Entering that door, Ezekiel saw idolatrous carvings on the wall "of creeping things and beasts and detestable things, with all the idols of the house of Israel" (8:7-10). The fact that these carvings consisted of animals suggests some Egyptian animal cult. Perhaps this religion was adopted by the national leaders during the reign of Jehoiakim who was a vassal of Pharaoh Neco (2 Kgs 23:34ff.).

Chart No. 12

THE ABOMINATIONS OF THE TEMPLE

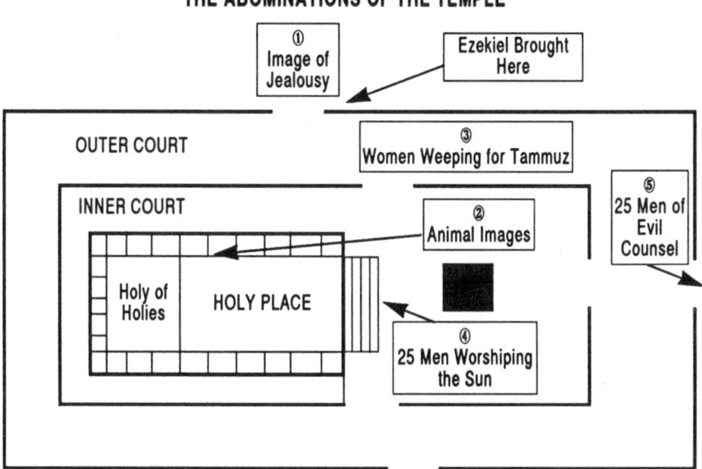

Ezekiel saw standing before those carvings seventy elders of the house of Israel offering the incense of worship before the representations on the Temple walls. Among the seventy was Jaazaniah, a black sheep from the godly family of Shaphan.[1] The elders not only practiced their religion collectively "in darkness," i.e., in secret, each also worshiped in his own individual chamber. They justified their actions, to themselves if not to others, by two arguments: (1) "the Lord does not see us," and (2) "the Lord has forsaken the land." Their first argument was blasphemous because it questioned the omniscience of God. The second was hypocritical because these same leaders were publicly arguing that God could never abandon Jerusalem and the Temple. Yet in spite of the audacity of Egyptian animal cult worship in the sacred precincts of the Temple, Ezekiel was assured that he would see yet greater abominations (8:11-13).

The Lord then brought Ezekiel to the door of the north gate of the Temple. There the prophet saw the women sitting and weeping over the god Tammuz. The annual death and resurrection of this vegetation god was mourned by his consort Ishtar. The worst kinds of immoralities were employed by this cult in a effort to magically control nature. Yet Ezekiel was assured that he would see yet greater abominations (8:14f.).

Finally the Lord brought Ezekiel to the inner court of the Temple. Between the porch of the Temple and the brazen altar of sacrifice Ezekiel noticed twenty-five men. Because of their location in the inner court these men were most likely priests. The number twenty-five perhaps represents the twenty-four courses of priests plus the high priest. In any case, these men had their backs to the Temple and their faces to the east. They were worshiping the sun god Shamash (8:16).

B. The Announcement of Judgment (8:17-18).

The inhabitants of Judah were not content to provoke the Lord with their abominations. They had also filled the land with "violence," i.e., social chaos and injustice. They were "putting the twig to their nose." This is obviously an offensive practice, but the precise meaning of it is not known. These people would experience the full wrath of God. No compassion would be shown. God would not hear their loud prayers of desperation.

THE DOOM OF THE CITY
Ezekiel 9:1-10:8

Ezekiel saw two aspects of Jerusalem's destruction in his visionary experience. He learned that the overthrow of Jerusalem would be bloody and fiery.

A. Bloody Destruction (9:1-11).

In a loud voice the Lord ordered the executioners to approach Jerusalem, each with his battle axe in his hand. Ezekiel then saw six ruthless executioners enter through the northern gate of the city. These men symbolized the Babylonian armies which would attack Jerusalem from the north. Among the six executioners was a scribe dressed in linen, symbolic of purity. He had a writing case at his side. The entire group went into the Temple and stood beside the bronze altar. The idea conveyed here is that both salvation and judgment come from the altar of God (9:1f.).

Ezekiel saw "the glory of God" leave the "cherub" in the Holy of Holies. The Lord positioned himself at "the threshold of the Temple." He would personally direct all operations against Jerusalem. The Lord first commissioned the scribe to go through the midst of Jerusalem. He was to "put a mark on the foreheads" of all those who were truly concerned about the abominations of the city. These were destined to survive the destruction of Jerusalem (9:3f.).

The six executioners were commissioned to follow the scribe through the city. They were to spare no one. Pity was to be extended neither to old nor young, neither to women nor children. The slaughter was to start right in the Temple with the religious leaders who had fallen away from the Lord. Only those whose foreheads bore the identifying mark were to be spared (9:5f.).

Ezekiel witnessed the beginning of the slaughter. The elders of the people fell first. At the direction of God the Temple courts were defiled by the corpses of the slain. Then the Lord ordered his agents to go out from the Temple precincts to do their deadly work throughout the city. Observing the expanding slaughter, Ezekiel was moved to intercessory prayer. The words "Alas, Lord God!" indicate the emotion which he felt as he saw this vision. An oblique petition is couched in the form of a question: "Art Thou destroying the whole remnant of Israel by pouring out Thy wrath on Jerusalem?" Ezekiel was asking that Jerusalem might be spared (8:7f.).

The Lord explained to his prophet why the agents of slaughter must be unleashed. For one thing, the iniquity of Israel was "very, very great." The land was "full of blood," i.e., violent bloodshed of the innocent. The city was full of "perversion," i.e. miscarriage of justice. People were denying the omniscience of God. They were wrongly blaming him for abandoning the land (cf. 8:12). God had determined that he would "bring their conduct upon their heads." He would show no mercy to the wicked citizens (9:9f.).

Ezekiel observed the scribal agent returning from his mission. He had completed his assignment. The next event on God's calendar would be the actual destruction of the city (9:11).

B. Fiery Destruction (10:1-8).

Ezekiel then saw the *merkabhah*, the throne chariot of God. For the first time he identifies the "living beings" (1:5) as "cherubim." Cherubim were angels who are always depicted in the Scriptures as guarding something sacred. In the *merkabhah* the cherubim supported and guarded the throne of God. That sapphire-like throne was at the moment empty (10:1).

"The man clothed in linen" who had just completed his mission of marking those who were to be spared had another mission to perform. The Lord directed this agent to "enter between the whirling wheels under the cherubim." There he was to fill his hands with "coals of fire." Then he was to scatter those hot coals over the city of Jerusalem. Ezekiel observed the scribe obediently enter the *merkabhah* (10:1f.).

Parenthetically, Ezekiel described in more detail the scene. The cherubim which formed part of the *merkabhah* were standing "on the right side of the Temple" when the man entered. The "glory of the Lord," i.e., the manifestation of God himself, went up from the cherub in the Holy of Holies to "the threshold of the Temple." The cloud which signaled divine presence filled the Temple and inner courts. The "brightness" of the glory of the Lord filled the outer court. This awesome sight was accompanied by an awesome sound. The sound of the wings of the cherubim which formed the *merkabhah* was heard as far as the outer court. The sound was like "the voice of God almighty when he speaks," i.e., like thunder (10:3-5).

The man clothed in linen entered among the whirling wheels and cherubim of the *merkabhah*. He stood beside one of the wheels. One of the cherubim stretched forth his hand from beneath his wing to the fire which burned in the midst of the *merkabhah* (cf. 1:13). He took some of the fire, i.e., coals of fire, and put it in the hand of the man dressed in linen (10:6-8). The stage was now set for the fiery destruction of Jerusalem which here is symbolically represented as coming from the Lord himself.

THE DEPARTURE OF THE GLORY
Ezekiel 10:9-22

In this unit Ezekiel again describes in detail the *merkabhah*, the throne chariot of God. The description is almost identical with that in chapter 1. The repetition underscored the impression which this symbolic chariot made on the prophet. It also served to make the point that the same glory of God which once had occupied the Temple, now abode with the captives in Babylon.

The description of the *merkabhah* here differs from that in chapter 1 in a few details. In reference to the wheels, Ezekiel added one point. They had the gleam of a Tarshish stone. The identity of the Tarshish stone is not known. The bodies, backs, wings and hands of the cherubim were full of eyes as well as the wheels (cf. 1:18). Whereas the cherubim in chapter 1 each had the faces of an ox, a man, a lion, and an eagle, here the face of the ox has become "the face of the cherub." This suggests that the primary or normal face of a cherub resembled that of an ox (10:9-17).

Ezekiel then observed as the "glory of the Lord" left the threshold of the Temple and "stood over the cherubim" who were stationed in the courtyard. The divine rider had rejoined his chariot! The *merkabhah* then rose from the earth as the cherubim "lifted up their wings." The *merkabhah* with the "glory of the Lord" above it paused momentarily at the eastern gate of the Temple (10:18f.).

Ezekiel concluded this unit by making explicit what had been implicit throughout. He had seen these cherubim before in Babylon by the river Chebar. They were the living beings which he had seen "beneath the God of Israel." The faces, wings, hands and movements were exactly the same (10:20-22). Thus Ezekiel made the point that

God had deserted the Jerusalem Temple. He had now taken up residence among the captives in Babylon.

THE DENOUNCEMENT OF THE LEADERS
Ezekiel 11:1-25

Jerusalem's leaders were diametrically opposed to the revelation which God had given to men like Jeremiah and Ezekiel. In his visionary state, Ezekiel blasted the false counsel that Jerusalem was inviolable. Then he responded to the false confidence of those who wrongly considered themselves the chosen of God.

A. False Counsel Condemned (11:1-6).

Ezekiel felt himself being lifted up and transported from the inner court of the Temple to its eastern gate. There he saw twenty-five leaders of the realm. Among them were the princes Jaazaniah[2] and Pelatiah. These most likely are not the same twenty-five men whom Ezekiel saw with their backs to the Temple worshiping the rising sun (cf. 8:16). The first twenty-five were most likely priests while these twenty-five appear to be lay leaders. They were "men who devise iniquity and give evil advice in this city." They were arguing that life in Judah would shortly get back to normal. Economic prosperity would enable people to build their houses. Jerusalem, they continued, was like a giant pot. The people within the city were like meat within the pot. They were adequately protected by the city's massive walls from any threat which the Babylonians might pose. This group of lobbyists was no doubt urging rebellion against Nebuchadnezzar, and alliance with Egypt.

The Spirit of the Lord came upon Ezekiel in his vision. He was told to declare to those conspirators that God knew the things which they had been saying. He also knew their thoughts. In a predictive accusation, Ezekiel announced that the counsel of these men would result in multitudes of slain filling the streets of Jerusalem (11:4-6).

B. A False Concept Exposed (11:7-12).

In view of the fact that the policy advocated by the twenty-five men would bring disaster on the city, they should take a second look at the pot/meat metaphor which they had been using (cf. 11:3). Jerusalem's walls would afford no safety. Many would die in the city during the siege. They were the meat in the pot. Others would be brought forth from the walled city by the enemy (11:7).

The "sword" which they feared—the Babylonians—God would bring against them in all of its might. Furthermore, God would deliver them into the hand of these "strangers." The Lord himself would execute judgments against them. Many would fall "at the border of Israel." The terrible fulfillment of this prediction would cause God's people to have the correct perspective on the nature of God (11:8-10). The reference is to the executions ordered by Nebuchadnezzar at Riblah on the northern border of the promised land (cf. 2 Kgs 25:18ff.).

These predictions make it clear that Jerusalem would not be "the pot" in the sense that these advisors used the word. The walls would afford no protection from deportation. Again the prediction is repeated: God would judge the citizens of Jerusalem at the border of Israel. This jarring judgment would force a reassessment of the true nature of God. To know God meant to know his law and to practice his ordinances. This was exactly what Israel had *not* been doing. They had been acting according to the ordinances of the surrounding nations (11:11f.).

C. A Death and a Prayer (11:13).

As Ezekiel delivered his sermon in his vision, Pelatiah, one of the twenty-five counselors, dropped dead.[3] Ezekiel was shocked. He immediately assumed the posture of an intercessor. He fell on his face and cried out with a loud voice, "Alas, Lord God!" He asked the Lord a question which really constituted an oblique petition: "Wilt Thou bring the remnant of Israel to a complete end?" Ezekiel interpreted the death of Pelatiah as a signal that the judgment was beginning to unfold. He was praying for a postponement or at least a softening of that fateful blow.

D. A False Claim Refuted (11:14-21).

The Jerusalem Jews felt superior to the ten thousand who had been taken captive in 597 BC. They regarded themselves as the chosen of God because they had been spared such humiliation. In regard to the captives the Jerusalemites were saying in effect, "Good riddance! Their departure just gives us more land to divide among ourselves" (11:14f.). Partly to refute these claims upon the land of Israel, and partly to respond to Ezekiel's prayer-question about the remnant (11:13), the Lord revealed to the prophet an optimistic forecast regarding his people who were in captivity.

God had a very positive attitude toward the captives of Judah in Babylon. He acknowledged that the deportation of these people was a divine work. That, however, did not mean that the Lord had rejected the captives. Though these thousands had been denied access to the physical Temple in Jerusalem, God promised that he himself would be their sanctuary "for a little while," i.e., during the duration of their captivity (11:15f.). The point is that one did not have to live in Palestine in order to have a vital relationship with the Lord.

God had a plan for his people after the exile. He would gather and assemble them. He would give to the exiles the land of Israel. The converted captives would return to cleanse the land of all her "detestable things" and "abominations." Those returnees would be united in heart. This unity would be achieved through a "new spirit" of fidelity to God. "A heart of flesh," i.e., a submissive heart, would replace the old "heart of stone," i.e., stubborn heart. God's people would live a new life. They would walk in the "statutes" of the Lord and observe his ordinances. Because of all this, a new relationship would exist between God and Israel. They would claim Yahweh as their God, and he would acknowledge them as his people. On the other hand, God assured those who clung to idols that he would "bring their conduct down on their heads" (11:19-21).

CONCLUSION OF THE VISION
Ezekiel 11:22-25

Once again the *merkabhah* began to move. The cherubim "lifted up their wings." The "wheels" moved beside them. The "glory of God" atop the *merkabhah* moved from Jerusalem to "stand over the mountain which is east of the city," i.e., the Mt. of Olives. In his actual experience in the land of captivity Ezekiel already had learned that the ultimate destiny of the *merkabhah* was Babylon (11:22f.).

In his vision Ezekiel then felt himself being transported "in the Spirit of God" back to the captives in Babylon. So the lengthy vision which commenced in chapter 8 came to an end. Ezekiel then reported to his fellow captives all the things which God had showed him in the vision (11:24f.).

Endnotes

1. Four men are said to be sons of Shaphan: (1) Gemariah, one of the princes sympathetic to the reading of scroll written by Jeremiah (Jer 36:10-12); (2) Ahikam, who rescued Jeremiah from certain execution in the Temple (Jer 26:24); (3) Elasah, who carried a letter from Jeremiah to the exiles in Babylon (Jer 29:3); and (4) Jaazaniah, who was among those elders worshiping animals in the secret chambers of the Temple. Presumably the Shaphan in all these cases was the famous scribe who supported the reform efforts of King Josiah (2 Kgs 22).

2. The Jaazaniah in 11:1 is not to be confused with the Jaazaniah of 8:11. The former was the son of Shaphan; the latter, the son of Azzur.

3. Scholars debate whether this is strictly a visionary death or whether Pelatiah actually died at the very time Ezekiel was delivering his visionary sermon.

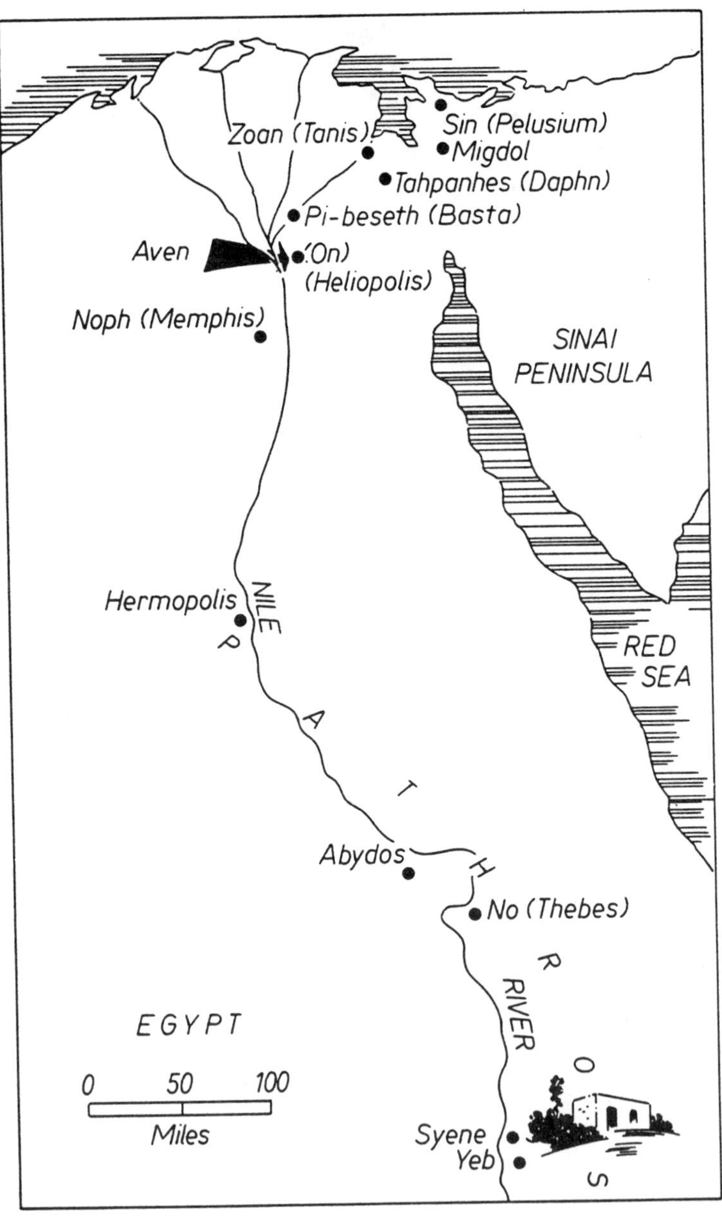
Zoan (Tanis)
Sin (Pelusium)
Migdol
Tahpanhes (Daphn)
Pi-beseth (Basta)
Aven
(On)
(Heliopolis)
Noph (Memphis)
SINAI
PENINSULA
Hermopolis
NILE
P
A
T
H
R
O
S
RED
SEA
Abydos
No (Thebes)
RIVER
EGYPT
0
50
100
Miles
Syene
Yeb

CHAPTER TWENTY-SEVEN

Parables and Proclamations
Ezekiel 12-15

Background of the Unit.

Ezekiel did not date the material in this unit. Most likely these symbolic acts, sermons and allegories were presented to the captives in the summer or fall of 592 BC just after the completion of the 430 days of symbolic siege (cf. 4:5-6). Conditions in Babylon and back in Jerusalem remained unchanged. King Zedekiah was still being manipulated by his princes. They were determined to throw off the Babylonian yoke with the aid of Egypt. The concept of the inviolability of Jerusalem had a firm grip on the minds of the Jerusalemites and the captives in Babylon. The purpose of this material was to reinforce the announcement of Jerusalem's impending destruction, and further underscore the justification of that judgment.

Outline of the Unit.

A. Two Symbolic Actions Performed (12:1-20).

B. Two Popular Sayings Corrected (12:21-28).
C. Two Scathing Oracles Delivered (chap. 13).
D. Four Objections Answered (chaps. 14-15).

TWO SYMBOLIC ACTIONS PERFORMED
Ezekiel 12:1-20

Two action parables underscored the trauma which Ezekiel predicted would characterize the final days of Jerusalem. The need for dramatic actions and not mere rhetoric was clear. Ezekiel was living in the midst of a "rebellious house." These people had eyes, but they refused to analyze the desperate situation of Jerusalem. They had ears, but they refused to listen to the prophetic warnings. Ezekiel's action parables had shock value which might penetrate the mental barrier which this rebellious house had erected in order to shield themselves from unpleasant realities (12:1f.).

A. Parable of the Fugitive (12:3-17).

For his action parable Ezekiel needed a prop. He was told to prepare for himself "baggage for exile," i.e., such things as one might be permitted to take into exile. In the presence of his daily visitors he was to stage a deportation. He was to take the meager items of exile baggage and move from his own house to another place. Perhaps this action would make this rebellious people realize that those left in Jerusalem would shortly be joining those who had been deported to Babylon (12:3).

Ezekiel was to prepare his baggage by day before the eyes of his audience. That evening he was to assume the role of an exile. He was to dig through his clay courtyard wall and carry his baggage through the hole that evening. Then he was to carry his baggage over his shoulder through the dark. He was to cover his face, probably with some cloth, as he made his mock trip. In doing all of these things Ezekiel would be a *sign* to the house of Israel. As always, the prophet obeyed these directions and performed the symbolic act (12:4-7).

In the morning Ezekiel received a divine revelation which explained his actions of the previous night. His auditors had been asking for the meaning of what they had witnessed. This "burden," i.e., prophetic oracle, had an application both to the "prince in Jerusalem," i.e., Zedekiah, and to his subjects. Ezekiel was a sign to testify that those who dwelled in Jerusalem would do in reality what he had done in symbol. They would go into captivity (12:8-11).

The prince also would become a captive. He would try to escape from the city at night through a hole in the wall. His face would be covered so that he would not be able to see the land. He may have worn a hood over his head to shield his identity from those of his own people who might wish to kill him for prolonging the agonies of Jerusalem. His efforts, however, would not be successful. The Lord would see to it that Zedekiah was ensnared. He would be brought to land of the Chaldeans. Yet he would not *see* Babylon, though he would die there. His aides and personal bodyguards would "scatter to every wind" when the "sword" of the Lord, i.e., the Chaldean soldiers, began to pursue them (12:12-14). The fulfillment of this prediction is recorded in the Book of Kings. Zedekiah fled from Jerusalem at night once the Chaldeans had made a breach in the walls. He was captured in the plains of Jordan. He was taken to Riblah, his eyes were blinded, and he was deported to Babylon in chains (2 Kgs 25:4-6).

The deportation to Babylon would cause the Jews to have a true understanding of the nature of God. The remnant which God spared from sword, famine, and pestilence had a mission to perform in their exile. Among the heathen these would openly confess all of their abominations, the folly of their addiction to idolatry. Through their testimony the heathen also would come to know the true nature of Yahweh (12:15f.).

B. Parable of the Suffering Citizens (12:17-20).

God directed Ezekiel to eat his bread with "trembling" and drink his water with "quivering and anxiety." In so doing he was illustrating what would happen to the citizens of Jerusalem. The "violence," i.e., social chaos, would bring on an invasion which would strip their land of its fullness. The cities would be laid waste and the land would be a desolation. When these unspeakable disasters befell their land, the inhabitants of Jerusalem would eat and drink in anxiety and horror. Yet through this bitter experience they would learn something about the true nature of Yahweh.

TWO POPULAR SAYINGS CORRECTED
Ezekiel 12:21-28

The citizens of Jerusalem had created two proverbs which constituted the standard rebuff to prophetic threats against the nation of Judah.

A. The First Saying (12:21-25).

The first saying was this: "The days are long and every vision fails." The argument was that long years had elapsed and the prophetic threats of Jerusalem's destruction had not materialized. As events unfolded, the mouths of false teachers would be stopped. This skeptical proverb would no longer be heard in the land. To replace it, Ezekiel suggested his own proverb: "The days draw near as well as the fulfillment of every vision" (12:21-23).

"False vision" and "divination" would fail. God, however, would speak a certain revelation. Whatever word which God spoke would be performed. The destruction of Jerusalem would not be delayed. In the days of that very generation God would speak his word of judgment, and he would execute that judgment as well (12:24f.).

B. The Second Saying (12:26-28).

Some were willing to grant that the predictions of destruction of Jerusalem might be a genuine word from the Lord. They, however, argued that such predictions were for the distant future: "He prophesies of times far off." God's response was that the divine word would not be delayed any longer. Any word which God spoke definitely would be performed.

TWO SCATHING ORACLES DELIVERED
Ezekiel 13

The main stumbling block to the acceptance of the prophetic call to sober thinking and repentance was the optimistic forecast of false prophets. In a nutshell the theology of these "prophets" was that God was inseparably bound to the Temple in Jerusalem. He could never abandon that place. In chapter 13 Ezekiel addressed a word to these prophets. Then he blasted their female counterparts.

A. Condemnation of the Prophets (13:1-16).

Ezekiel was directed to prophesy against "the prophets of Israel." In both Jerusalem and in Babylon among the captives (cf. Jer 29) these men "prophesied," i.e., proclaimed messages which they claimed to be oracles from God. This group, however, prophesied from their own heart. They were foolish because they had confused their own desires and hopes with divine communication. These prophets had "seen nothing," i.e., they had not received any special revelation from God. They were following "their own spirit," not the Holy Spirit of God (13:1-3). These prophets deserved a divine "woe" for several reasons.

First, the prophets were undermining the nation. They were like foxes among the ruins of a city. These little creatures had no concern about their habitat. They made no effort to repair the ruins, but in fact did further damage to them. So it was with the false prophets (13:4).

Second, the prophets had shown no courage in battle. In time of war a brave soldier would rush to any break in the defensive perimeter and defend it until the position could be secured. These prophets, however, had not "gone up into the breaches" in the moral and spiritual walls of the nation. They did not cry out against sin, nor call for repentance. They made no effort to extend or strengthen that wall. The physical walls of Jerusalem did not protect God's people from hostile attack. Rather their faith in God and obedience to his word were their protection. Yet that wall had been severely eroded. God needed faithful preachers to stand in the gaps in the wall, to defend those gaps, to rebuild the walls at those points by calling the nation back to obedience (13:5).

Third, these prophets were making false claims. They were using the vocabulary of true prophets when they said, "the Lord declares" (lit., oracle of Yahweh). The Lord, however, had not spoken to them. What they were proclaiming was "a false vision" which had no more authority behind it than "a lying divination."[1] They could only "hope for the fulfillment of their word." In a point-blank question Ezekiel asked these prophets whether or not this accusation was true (13:6f.).

Because they had dared to present lies in the name of God, the prophets stood condemned. Ezekiel had a real oracle of the Lord for them: "Behold I am against you!" God's powerful "hand" would be against those who saw false visions and uttered lying divinations. These men, so popular at present, would one day be excluded from citizenship among the people of God. Their names would not appear in the national registry. They would not return from captivity to the land of Israel. This punishment would bring to these deceivers a true knowledge of the God with whose word they had trifled (13:8f.).

To justify his harsh words against these religious leaders, Ezekiel became more specific in his accusations. The prophets had misled God's people by promising "peace" when there was no peace. He likened them to wall builders. The national wall of false hopes and clever political schemes had been plastered over with "whitewash" by these prophets. A wall held together by whitewash rather than mortar could not possibly stand for long. A terrible storm of divine judgment was brewing, a storm of "violent wind, flooding rain" and "hailstones." The wall would fall! When it did these false prophets would be mocked for using "plaster," i.e., their lying visions, to hold together a wall. Ezekiel was charging the prophets with lending credibility to a national policy which was doomed to failure (13:10-12).

So that wall, crafted by the national counselors and held together by the assurances of the "prophets" would fall. God would tear it down; he would lay bare its foundations, i.e., the false theological notions upon which their national policy was built. The "prophets" would be destroyed along with their wall. Through this terrible experience men would learn the true nature of God. They would see that the Lord had poured out his wrath on both the wall and its plasterers. To jar the memory of his people in that day, and to stimulate sober reflection, God would say to them, "the wall is gone and its plasterers are gone." The false prophets who saw "visions of peace" for Jerusalem would be nowhere to be found when that delusion was shattered by the harsh realities of God's judgment (13:13-16).

B. Condemnation of the Prophetesses (13:17-23).

Prophetesses were also on the scene. Like their male counterparts, they prophesied "from their own heart." Unlike the prophets, they were not so much preachers as practitioners of occult arts. They sewed magic bands full of incantations and charms on the wrists. They made veils of various sizes to put over the heads of their clients. Perhaps this was some sort of mind control measure. They made a living for themselves by hunting down the lives of God's people. This probably means that for a price, they would use their witchcraft to harm the innocent (13:17f.).

Ezekiel offered a specific example of how these women worked. They would examine handfuls of barley and bread crumbs for "signs" that sick people would either live or die. On the basis of these auguries the prophetesses would forecast the death of the righteous and promise life to the wicked. They "profaned" God before his people by their (1) methodology, (2) motives, and (3) message. They lied to God's people, and the people were only too eager to listen to their lies. Thus these women were doing serious damage to the faith of Israel (13:19).

The Lord declared his hostility to these prophetesses. He would rip off their bands and veils. The souls held captive by magic spells would be liberated. These women had "disheartened the righteous with falsehood." At the same time they had "encouraged the wicked not to turn from his wicked way" which was his only hope of salvation. When the judgment began to unfold these women would no longer "see false visions or practice divination." God would deliver the faithful from the clutches of these ruthless women. When they saw their hold on the population shattered, they would come to know the true nature of God (13:20-23).

FOUR OBJECTIONS ANSWERED
Ezekiel 14-15

As in 8:1, the elders again came to Ezekiel's home in Babylon and sat before him as his students. God directed the prophet to answer four anticipated objections to his message of judgment. Two of these objections are found in the first oracle in chapter 14, the third is found in the second oracle. The fourth anticipated objection was answered by means of another parable in chapter 15.

A. First Objection (14:3-8).

By sitting at the feet of the prophet the elders appeared to be seeking the Lord's will. Surely Ezekiel's warnings did not apply to them. The Lord, however, exposed the hypocrisy of these men. They had "set up idols in their hearts." They secretly pined for the old pagan ways. They put right before their faces "the stumbling block of their iniquity," i.e., they were constantly thinking about idols. No positive word of encouragement was possible for such hypocrites. God would deal with such men directly and personally, not through a prophetic intermediary like Ezekiel. God's purpose in these warnings was "lay hold of the hearts of the house of Israel." He desired to recapture the hearts of those who had become estranged from him because of idolatry (14:3-5).

Reconciliation to God can only be effected by repentance. Therefore Ezekiel called upon the elders to "repent and turn away" from their idols and abominations. He repeated the warning that God would personally deal with hypocrites who pretend to seek his will, but who love idolatry. God would set his face against such men, i.e., be their adversary. He would make them "a sign and a proverb" by cutting them off from among their people. The hypocrite would experience such a fate that his name would become a proverbial warning to others. Through that experience of judgment, however, others would come to have the correct understanding of the nature of God (14:6-8).

B. Second Objection (14:9-11).

A second objection to the harsh rhetoric of Ezekiel might be paraphrased like this: "How can you be so hard on us? We have only been listening to men who claim to be prophets!" Ezekiel responded to this objection decisively. These "prophets" had been "enticed" to speak in God's name. Ezekiel even went so far as to say that Yahweh was the one who had enticed them! The Old Testament frequently does not distinguish between primary and secondary causation. What God permits to happen, he sometimes is said to have caused to happen. That the enticement of the false prophets was the permissive and not the active will of God is indicated here in the context. God would stretch out his hand against the prophet who had been enticed to speak falsehood in his name. He would destroy that man from among his people. That God would directly entice a prophet to speak falsely, and then punish him for that act would be inconceivable (14:9).

Consulting one who claimed to be a prophet could not be offered as an excuse for not obeying the Lord. Both the "prophet" and the one who inquired of him would bear the punishment of their iniquity. Again Ezekiel stressed that this judgment had a positive purpose. The judgment would cause the house of Israel no longer to stray from the Lord or defile themselves by their transgressions. Once their dalliance with idolatry was over, their former relationship with the Lord could be restored. He would be their God and they would be his people (14:10f.).

C. Third Objection (14:12-23).

The third anticipated objection to Ezekiel's message of judgment was that some righteous men were still living in the midst of the nation. How could God destroy those righteous ones along with the wicked? Ezekiel answered this objection by affirming that even the presence of Noah, Daniel and Job could not spare an unfaithful land once the wheels of judgment were set in motion. Whether the judgment was famine, wild beasts, the sword, or plague, such righteous men would not be able to deliver their sons and daughters. Righteous men can save only their own lives, not those of their families. The principle here is that righteousness is not inherited (14:12-20).

God was about to send a four-fold calamity against Jerusalem consisting of sword, famine, wild beasts and pestilence. A remnant would survive this judgment, but they would be carried away into captivity to join the Jews already there since 597 BC. Those later captives would bring "comfort" to the earlier captives. This "comfort" was the sense of understanding which results when new light is brought to bear on an otherwise perplexing situation. When they see the spiritual condition of the second wave of captives, they would realize that God's judgment against Jerusalem was just (14:21-23).

D. Fourth Objection (15:1-8).

The fourth objection which Ezekiel anticipated can be paraphrased like this: "How can God forsake his covenant, the vine of his planting?" Ezekiel answered this objection with another parable, the parable of the worthless wood.

Through a series of questions the Lord directed Ezekiel's attention to the value of a vine tree. In comparison to other trees of the forest the vine tree was insignificant. Its wood was useless, incapable of being fashioned by craftsmen. One could not even make a peg from the wood of a vine tree. It was good for nothing except fuel. A charred vine was doubly worthless.

The inhabitants of Jerusalem were like that vine tree. They had been appointed by God as fuel for the fire of judgment. God's face was against them, i.e., he was hostile towards them. Once they had escaped from the fire, so to speak, when Nebuchadnezzar came against the city in 597 BC. Now the fire would consume them. When Jerusalem was in the throes of the ordeal of judgment, the inhabitants would realize the true nature of Yahweh. Lest there be any mistake about the application of his parable, God declared that he would make the land of Judah a "desolation." Such severity was justified because these people had "acted unfaithfully."

Endnote

1. Divination is the use of any external and physical object to predict the future. This pagan form of prognostication was condemned in the Old Testament. Interpreting omens was decidedly inferior to direct revelation from the Deity.

CHAPTER TWENTY-EIGHT

Parables and Pictures
Ezekiel 16-19

Background of the Unit.

In chapters 16-19 the justification for the announced destruction of Jerusalem continues. Ezekiel was still laboring to smash the delusion that Yahweh would not and could not destroy his Temple in Jerusalem. The unit is not dated. The last recorded date was September 17, 592 BC (8:1). The next date in the book equates to August 14, 591 BC (20:1) The material at hand most likely falls somewhere between these two dates. The situation both in Babylon and Jerusalem remained unchanged. Zedekiah was still ruling Jerusalem as a vassal of Nebuchadnezzar. He and his advisors were intent on rebellion. Ezekiel, as well as Jeremiah, saw this as the ultimate folly and the act which would precipitate the destruction of Jerusalem. In this unit Ezekiel used five verbal parables to drive home his point. Four of these parables were negative, i.e., they painted a dismal picture of the spiritual and moral climate in Jerusalem.

Outline of the Unit.

A. Apostasy Parables (chap. 16)
B. Political Parables (chap. 17).
C. Proverb of the Sour Grapes (chap. 18).
D. Dirge Parables (chap. 19).

APOSTASY PARABLES
Ezekiel 16:1-63

In the two apostasy parables Ezekiel made known to Jerusalem her "abominations" (16:1f.). In both parables Jerusalem is compared to a woman. In the first the woman was a wayward wife; in the second, a fallen sister.

A. Parable of the Wayward Wife (16:3-43).

In the first masterful allegory Ezekiel traced the history of God's people from their earliest days as a nation to Ezekiel's day in five paragraphs. The language is blunt at places. Westerners find it offensive. No passage, however, underscores more forcefully the ugliness, filthiness and treachery of spiritual adultery.

1. The unwanted foundling (16:3-6). Ezekiel pictured Jerusalem as a baby born in the land of Canaan. The father of the child was the Amorite; the mother, the Hittite. Though the Israelites had lived there for centuries, Jerusalem had been influenced from the very beginning by Canaanite culture (16:3).

From the moment of birth Jerusalem was an unwanted child. No one showed any compassion to perform customary hygienic and medical procedures for the infant. She was was not washed, salted[1] nor wrapped.[2] She was cast out upon the surface of the ground to become the victim of infanticide. She was abhorred on the day of her birth. Yet the Lord passed by and saw the infant squirming in the blood of birth. Though repulsive to look upon, God decreed that this baby should "live" (16:4-6).

2. The beautiful marriage (16:7-9). The Lord nurtured the child in her growth. She flourished "like plants of the field." She grew tall. Her hair grew long. Her breasts developed. Yet this beautiful young lady was still "naked and bare," i.e., insufficiently clad, just like a poor desert girl. Again the Lord passed by and observed that the young lady had come to "the time for love," i.e., she was of marriageable age. Performing an ancient marriage custom, the Lord spread his skirt over her and covered her nakedness, i.e., he provided all her material needs. Following the pattern of true marriage God "swore," i.e., pledged his fidelity, to her. He entered into a "covenant" with her, i.e., the two exchanged vows of commitment and obligation. Thus did Jerusalem, i.e., the Israelites, become the people of the Lord. He then performed for his bride the ritual purification which accompanied marriage, and anointed her with the oil of gladness.

3. The adornment of the bride (16:10-14). The Lord clothed his wife with the finest garments—with linen, silk, embroidered cloth, and shoes of porpoise skin. He bestowed on her jewelry of all kinds. He set before her the finest foods. Israel, God's bride, became exceedingly beautiful. She even "advanced to royalty," i.e., developed into a monarchy. Her reputation for beauty spread among the nations because she in reality reflected the splendor of God. What made Israel truly attractive was her faith in the true and living God.

4. The infidelity of the bride (16:15-34). In the indictment against God's bride eight charges were made. First, God's bride came to trust in her beauty, i.e., her material prosperity (16:15). Second, in her association with other nations she "played the harlot," i.e., she was unfaithful to God. She had an affair with every willing passer-by. Ezekiel vividly depicted Israel's involvement with every idolatrous cult of the ancient Near East (16:15).

Third, the bride of the Lord misused everything with which he had blessed her. She used her garments to make and decorate high places where she committed harlotry with Canaanite gods. Gold, silver and jewels were fashioned into idols which became objects of harlotry. She gave her clothing and food as gifts to her gods (16:16-19). Fourth, God's bride even took sons and daughters whom she had borne to the Lord and offered them as sacrifices to their idols. Jerusalem's harlotries were no light matter. She actually slaughtered God's children and caused them to "pass through the fire" (16:20f.).

Fifth, in addition to all her abominations, Israel was guilty of the worst sort of ingratitude. She did not remember the days of her youth when God in his grace had taken pity on that naked, bloody and unwanted infant (16:22). Sixth, platforms and high places were built on every street in Jerusalem (16:23-24a).

Seventh, Jerusalem made herself sexually available to every suitor who passed by. First the sensuous Egyptians, then the Assyrians and finally the Chaldeans were Israel's lovers. Even the godless Philistines were shocked at the conduct of Jerusalem. Because of her conduct the unfaithful wife of Yahweh was under a double "woe." God had stretched out his hand against her. He had delivered her into the hand of her enemies (16:25b-29). Finally, Jerusalem was a brazen, wanton harlot. She was willing to sleep with anyone except her husband. She did not commit harlotry for payment like a prostitute. In fact she paid her lovers to come in unto her! (16:30-34).

5. The punishment of the harlot (16:35-43). Jerusalem was deserving of divine punishment. She had "poured out" her lewdness and "uncovered her nakedness." She had been involved in harlotries with her lovers (foreign nations) and idols. She had given the blood of her sons to her idols. For these reasons God would gather all her lovers—those she had loved, i.e., the Egyptians, and those she had hated, i.e., the Chaldeans. These would come against Jerusalem from every direction. God would expose Jerusalem's "nakedness," i.e., her deprivation and need. Jerusalem would be as harshly punished as women who commit adultery or shed blood. She would experience a violent bloodshed such as one might experience who was punished in "wrath and jealousy" (16:35-38).

The executioners of the harlot would be her former lovers. They would destroy Jerusalem's pagan shrines. They would confiscate the clothing and jewels which the harlot had misused in pagan worship. The harlot would be left naked and bare. Then a "crowd," i.e., a great throng, would stone the harlot and thrust her through with swords. The daughters of the harlot, i.e., satellite cities, would be burned. "Many women," i.e., neighboring nations, would observe this execution. No longer could Jerusalem play the harlot. No longer could she "pay her lovers" (16:39-41).

By the execution of this sentence God's "fury" and righteous "jealousy" would depart from his people. Once the problem of unfaithfulness had been corrected, God would be angry with his people no more. Whatever he would do to them, however, they would deserve. Their failure to remember their youthful association with the Lord and consequent infidelity had "enraged" the Lord. They had added "lewdness" to their "abominations." His justice demanded that he repay them in accordance with their sin (16:42f.).

B. Parable of the Three Sisters (16:44-63).

The parable of the three sisters is similar in some details to the preceding one. Parable mongers in the future would say regarding Judah, "like mother, like daughter." As in the preceding parable, Jerusalem's mother is a Hittite, her father is an Amorite (cf. 16:3). Here is added that Samaria was Jerusalem's older sister, Sodom her younger sister. Both the mother and sisters loathed their husbands and children. The prophet accused Jerusalem of being worse than her sisters. Jerusalem had not merely "walked in their ways or done according to their abominations." Jerusalem had actually "acted more corruptly" in all her conduct than they (16:44-47).

1. The record of the sisters (16:48-52). In order to underscore his charge that Jerusalem had acted more corruptly than Sodom or Samaria, Ezekiel examined the record of the three sisters. The sexual misconduct of the Sodomites is well documented in the Book of Genesis (Gen 19). Ezekiel added to that picture. Because of "abundant food" and "careless ease" Sodom was filled with "arrogance." She made no effort to "help the poor and needy." This heartless pride caused Sodom to commit "abominations" before the Lord. Because of this, Sodom was "removed" from the face of the earth. Yet Jerusalem's transgressions exceeded that of Sodom. Samaria, her northern sister, did not commit half of the sins committed in Jerusalem. All the abominations committed in Jerusalem made Sodom and Samaria appear righteous by comparison. Jerusalem would forever bear the disgrace of being considered morally and spiritually worse than her wicked sisters (16:48-52).

2. The future of the sisters (16:53-63). Though Sodom and Samaria had long since disappeared from the stage of history, and though Jerusalem was about to be destroyed, yet the three sisters had a future. God would "restore their captivity," i.e., restore their fortunes. That act of God's grace would cause Jerusalem to be ashamed of the abominations she had committed. All three sisters would return "to their former state" (16:53-55). This symbolic prophecy looked forward to the salvation of Jew, Samaritan and Gentile in the kingdom of Christ.

A new relationship would exist between the three sisters in that messianic age. In former times self-righteous Jerusalem would not even mention the name of Sodom. Jerusalem, however, was humbled when her own wickedness was made public through divine judgment. Singers in surrounding nations made her the object of ridicule.[3] Jerusalem had suffered much already from her lewdness and abominations. She would yet suffer much for having broken the marriage covenant with God (16:56-59).

Though Jerusalem had forgotten her national youth and the marriage covenant with God, the Lord would remember that covenant. He would therefore establish an everlasting covenant with his people (cf. Jer 31:31). This new covenant would be with those who were genuinely ashamed of their old ways. Under this covenant Samaria and Sodom would be regarded as daughters of Jerusalem. This is what is meant by the restoration of Samaria and Sodom (cf. 16:53). The idea here is that citizens of the former Northern Kingdom, and the heathen in general would become part of the new covenant through the instrumentality of the Jews. The establishment of this covenant would be a solemn act of God which would aid God's people in knowing his true nature. Under this covenant the unfathomable grace of God in forgiving past sin would forever silence self-justification (16:60-63).

POLITICAL PARABLES
Ezekiel 17

Ezekiel was told to propound a "riddle" or "parable" to the house of Israel (17:1f.). The prophet compared the royal family of Judah to a cedar tree in "Lebanon," a symbolic name for Jerusalem. The parable has two distinct parts, and is perhaps better regarded as two distinct but closely related parables. The first depicts the immediate past and immediate future of the Davidic line. The second predicts the long range future of the royal family.

A. Parable of the Eagles (17:3-21).

Ezekiel used two eagles to symbolize the two great powers of his day, viz., Babylon and Egypt. The parable described what took place in 597 BC when Nebuchadnezzar deported the king of Judah and ten thousand captives. The parable also predicted what was about to happen in 587 BC when Jerusalem was destroyed and the Davidic ruler was deported to Babylon. After presenting the parable itself, Ezekiel provided the interpretation.

1. The parable presented (17:3-10). Ezekiel began by describing a great eagle. It had multi-colored feathers, great wings, and long pinions. It came to Lebanon and broke off the top most twig of the cedar there. It carried the twig to the land of merchants and commerce. It then implanted the seed of the land of Lebanon as a willow beside many waters. That implanted seed became a spreading vine (17:3-6).

The vine could have prospered had it stayed in its own domain. A second great eagle, however, came along. It also had great wings and many feathers. The vine inclined toward the second eagle. Because of this, the vine could not prosper. The vine would be plucked up by the first eagle. Its fruit would be cut off. It would wither. No great power would come to the aid of the vine (17:7-10).

2. The parable explained (17:11-21). Ezekiel wanted his audience to be crystal clear about the meaning of his parable. The first eagle represented the king of Babylon. He came to Jerusalem and carried off the king (Jehoiachin) and princes to Babylon. He put one of the royal family (Zedekiah) under oath. He allowed Judah to continue as a lowly kingdom. Zedekiah rebelled against Nebuchadnezzar by sending envoys to the second eagle, Egypt (17:11-15).

Because he despised his oath and broke his covenant, Zedekiah would die in Babylon. Pharaoh would not be able to provide any relief from the siege of Jerusalem in which so many would die. Violation of a sacred oath was an offense against Yahweh. God would bring down on Zedekiah's head all the stipulations of self-malediction which he pronounced upon himself in his oath to Nebuchadnezzar. Through his agent, the king of Babylon, God would ensnare Zedekiah and deport him to Babylon. By these actions God would enter into judgment with Zedekiah regarding "the unfaithful act" which he had committed when he violated his oath. The army would fare no better than their king.

They would fall by the sword, and the few survivors would be scattered to every wind. This terrible judgment would throw new light on the true nature of God (17:16-21).

B. Parable of the Stately Cedar (17:22-24).

Ezekiel compared the Davidic family again to a cedar. That royal family would not cease to exist with the deportation of Zedekiah. God himself would take a tender twig from the top of that cedar and set it out "on a high and lofty mountain," i.e., in Israel. The twig would grow to maturity, bring forth boughs, bear fruit, and become a "stately cedar." The tender twig was a symbol for Messiah. Birds of every kind, i.e., all races and nations of people, would nest in the shade of its branches. These events would have an impact on other trees, i.e., royal houses. They would see the lowly and withered tree (David's family) flourish. They would see the green and high trees (proud kingdoms) dry up. When this occurred the other trees would be forced to acknowledge that Yahweh is the God who announces the future and then brings it to pass. He is sovereign over all the trees of the forest.

THE PROVERB OF THE SOUR GRAPES
Ezekiel 18

As indicated earlier (cf. 12:22), the people of Israel responded to the preaching of men like Jeremiah and Ezekiel with cliches and proverbs, not with reasoned argument. In chapter 18 Ezekiel refuted another such proverb: "The fathers eat the sour grapes, but the children's teeth are set on edge." The Lord expressed shock that anyone would think that he would punish one generation for the sins of another. When all the events unfold and the full implications of the judgment were known, they would not use this proverb any longer in Israel (18:1-3). In refuting the implications of this proverb Ezekiel touched on two basic doctrines of Scripture.

A. Doctrine of Personal Responsibility (18:4-20).

The basic principle of divine justice is simply this: "all souls are mine." Each person is a separate entity before God. "The soul who sins will die." Each person is accountable for his own life (18:4). After stating this basic principle, Ezekiel offered three illustrations of what he meant.

1. The fate of a righteous man (18:5-9). A man who was righteous by the standards of the Old Testament law would live. Ezekiel cited sixteen identifying marks of a righteous man. Seven are negative characteristics, or things a righteous man did not do. A righteous man did not (1) eat on the mountains in pagan rituals; (2) lift up his eyes to idols; (3) defile his neighbor's wife; (4) approach a menstruous woman; (5) oppress anyone through fraudulent dealings; (6) commit robbery; nor (7) lend money to a needy person on express condition of receiving interest. On the other hand, the righteous man possessed nine positive attributes. He (1) executes justice; (2) practices righteousness; (3) restores to the debtor his essential collateral; (4) feeds the hungry; (5) clothes the naked; (6) keeps his hand from iniquity; (7) executes true justice between men; (8) walks according to the law of God; and (9) deals faithfully, i.e., he is sincere.

2. The fate of the wicked son (18:10-13). A righteous man might have a wicked son who was so violent that he actually shed blood. He was the exact opposite of his father. Concerning this man the verdict must be death! Although temporal judgment is in the forefront here, in the light of the New Testament the eternal consequences of his actions cannot be overlooked. His blood would be on him, i.e., he must bear full responsibility for his conduct.

3. The fate of the righteous son (18:14-18). Occasionally a wicked man might have a son who repudiated the deeds of his father. He manifested all the characteristics of a righteous man. In no case would he die for the sins of the father. The wicked father, however, would "die for his iniquity" because he practiced extortion and robbery and "did what was not good among his people."

The basic question, then, was this: "Why should the son not bear the punishment for the father's iniquity?" Simply because God is impeccably fair. The son who was just, righteous and obedient to the law of God would live. "The soul that sins," however, would die. "The son shall not bear the iniquity of the father, nor shall the father bear the iniquity of the son." Each person bears the ultimate responsibility for his own conduct. The "righteousness of the righteous shall be upon himself, and the wickedness of the wicked will be upon himself."

B. Doctrine of Free Will (18:21-32).

Men are not locked into a life of sin. They can change. A wicked man can turn from all his sins. He may determine to live his life by the Book, i.e., the law of God, and to deal justly and righteously with his fellow man. The penalty for that man would be canceled. None of his transgressions would be remembered against him. Because of his righteousness he would live. God had no delight in the death of the wicked. On the contrary, the Lord has always delighted to see a wicked man turn from his evil way (18:21-23).

A righteous man may choose to turn from his righteousness to iniquity, to all the abominations of the wicked. Such a man's righteousness would not be remembered because of his "treachery." He would die in his sin (18:24).

This raised the objection that "the way of the Lord is not right." The argument seems to be that if a man once saved is subsequently lost, then God is inconsistent. Ezekiel responded to this argument decisively. God's ways were consistent; Israel's ways were inconsistent. Backsliders would die in their sin. Penitent sinners would live. God would judge each individual separately. A man's fate is determined by his own free choices (18:25-30a).

The doctrine of free will implies that a sinner can repent. Ezekiel concluded this section of his book with a strong appeal for repentance. He urged Israel to "return," to go back to the point where they got off the path. He exhorted those who repented to cause others to turn from their transgressions.[4] He called upon his audience to "cast away" all their transgressions. On the positive side, he encouraged them to make for themselves "a new heart and a new spirit," i.e., develop a firm resolve to be faithful and obedient. The alternative to such repentance was death. Yet God did not delight in the death of the wicked. Therefore, he urged them one last time to repent so that they might live (18:30b-32).

THE DIRGE PARABLES
Ezekiel 19

Chapter 19 contains two parables in poetic verse which are actually lamentations over the vicissitudes of the kings of Judah.

A. Parable of the Lion Cubs (19:1-9).

The first parabolic lament concerns the princes of Israel. Ezekiel likened the royal house of Judah to a lioness which reared her cubs in the midst of the lions (other royal houses). The first cub became a young lion. Nations gathered against him, captured him, and "they brought him with hooks to the land of Egypt." The lioness was disappointed in the loss of her progeny (19:1-4). The reference here is to Jehoahaz, the son of Josiah, who briefly succeeded his father on the throne in 609 BC. Pharaoh Neco and his allies took Jehoahaz captive to Egypt (cf. 2 Kgs 23:33; Jer 22:10-12).

Since her hope for her first cub was disappointed, the lioness reared a second cub to maturity. He became a ruthless young lion. He devoured men and "knew their widows," i.e., caused many women to lose their husbands. He "laid waste their cities" by causing the king of Babylon to come against the land. Because of the "sound of his roaring," i.e., his boasting, he brought desolation upon the land. Nations beset the young lion and captured him. They put him in a cage and took him to the king of Babylon (19:5-9). The reference here is to the father/son kings Jehoiakim and Jehoiachin. The policies of the father brought the armies of Babylon to the gates of Jerusalem in 597 BC. The son was deported to Babylon after a brief reign of three months.

B. Parable of the Vine (19:10-14).

In the second parabolic lament Ezekiel likened the "mother" of the royal house to a vine full of "blood," i.e., sap. This vigorous vine flourished beside the waters. It produced "strong branches" for scepters of rulers. The vine grew to great height. Then, however, it was plucked up and cast to the ground. Its fruit was withered by the east wind (19:10-12a). The reference here is to the heavy taxation which Nebuchadnezzar imposed on Zedekiah.

The "strong branch" was torn off so that it withered. The fire (of war) consumed the branch, i.e., Zedekiah. Now the vine, i.e., the people of Judah, was planted in a wilderness, i.e. the exile in Babylon. Fire had gone out from its branch to consume its fruit and shoots. The foolish rebellion of Zedekiah against Babylon was the cause of the ruin which befell Judah. No strong branch remained on the vine to serve as a scepter to rule. The deportation of Zedekiah brought a temporary halt to the rule of the house of David. This sorrow over the fate of the nation and her royal house became the general theme of lamentation after the destruction of Jerusalem in 587 BC (19:12b-14).

Endnotes

1. Newborn infants had their skins rubbed with salt water, apparently to harden the skin.

2. Every seven days through day forty the body of the infant was wrapped in bandages, perhaps as a protection against disease or injury.

3. The reference may be to the Syro-Ephraimitic invasion of 734 BC. Cf. Isaiah 7; 2 Kgs 16:5f; 2 Chr 28:5f.

4. NASB renders the last half of 18:30: "Repent and turn away from all your transgressions." The second Hebrew verb, however, is causative.

CHAPTER TWENTY-NINE

Israel: Past and Future
Ezekiel 20-23

Background of the Unit.

The material in this unit is precisely dated by Ezekiel to the seventh year of the captivity of Jehoiachin, the fifth month, and the tenth day of the month. This equates to August 14, 591 BC on the modern calendar. Eleven months had elapsed since his previous oracles. Again the elders of the captives had come to the home of Ezekiel "to inquire of the Lord." They were sitting before Ezekiel as students sit before their master (20:1). Politically not much had changed either in Babylon or in Jerusalem. Zedekiah had not yet had the courage to withhold his annual tribute from Nebuchadnezzar. He was, nonetheless, secretly negotiating with Pharaoh.

As in 14:1-4, Ezekiel again was told not to indulge the curiosity of the elders concerning the future. He was first to "make them know the abominations of their fathers." Then he was to pronounce judgment upon them. Defilement and judgment are the overriding themes in this unit.

Outline of the Unit.

A. Israel's Arraignment (20:5-44).
B. Israel's Judgment (20:45-21:32).
C. Israel's Defilement (chap. 22).
D. Israel's Debasement (chap. 23).

ISRAEL'S ARRAIGNMENT
Ezekiel 20:5-4

Chapter 20 places in juxtaposition two contrasting pictures: the corruption of Israel and the grace of God. Ezekiel spoke here of the past, present and future of God's dealings with his people.

A. God's Grace in the Past (20:5-29).

Ezekiel led the elders in a review of Israel's spiritual history from the birth of the nation in Egypt to his own day. Were it not for God's amazing grace the nation would have been abandoned to its fate long ago.

1. Israel in Egypt (20:5-9). In the land of Egypt many centuries earlier God had chosen Israel as his own people. He bound himself to them by an oath. He made himself known to them in mighty ways. He pledged himself to bring them out of Egyptian bondage to a glorious land, one which was "flowing with milk and honey." In view of his commitment to them, he asked them to commit themselves to him. He appealed to each of them to "cast away the detestable things of his eyes," i.e., the idols which he venerated. Since he was their God, he asked them not to defile themselves with the idols of Egypt (20:5-7).

There in Egypt Israel "rebelled" against God. They refused to listen to him, refused to abandon their idols. The Lord resolved to pour out his wrath upon them right there. Grace, however, prevailed. God declared, "I acted for the sake of my name." He did not wish for his holy name to be "profaned in the sight of the nations" among whom his people dwelled. Had Yahweh failed to keep his word and bring his people out of Egypt as he announced that he would do, the heathen would have mocked the God of Israel. Therefore, God kept his word.

He brought his people out of Egypt even though they had done nothing to deserve this favor (20:8f.).

2. Israel in the wilderness (20:10-17). God brought his people out of Egypt and into the wilderness. He led them to Sinai where he gave them a life-giving code of conduct. He established the sabbaths as a sign of the bond between himself and his people. In the law he revealed himself to them as Yahweh, the God who sanctifies. Nonetheless, Israel rebelled against their God in the wilderness. They refused to follow his life-giving code. They profaned the sabbaths (20:10-13a).

Again the Lord resolved to destroy his people. Grace, however, prevailed. He acted for the sake of his name. He did not wish his name to be profaned among the Gentiles. Because of their sin he swore that he would not bring that generation into the Promised Land. Only because of God's grace did Israel escape complete destruction in the wilderness (20:13b-17).

3. The second generation (20:18-26). As they grew up in the wilderness God warned the sons of the condemned generation to be faithful to him. He urged them not to walk in the way of their fathers, nor to defile themselves with idols. He urged them to follow the divinely revealed Law, to sanctify the sabbaths as signs of the covenant relationship between the Lord and themselves. By following these instructions that second generation would come to know by personal experience that Yahweh was their God (20:18-20).

The second generation was no better than their fathers. They too rebelled against God and refused to follow his law. They too profaned the sabbaths. According to the Book of Numbers, the culmination of their sin occurred at Baal-Peor in the plains of Moab (Num 25). Once again God was minded to pour out his wrath upon them. He withdrew, however, his hand and acted again for the sake of his name. He did not wish his name to be profaned among the Gentiles (20:21f.).

To that second generation God revealed his plan for the righteous punishment of Israel's sin. If they continued their rebellious ways, some day he would "scatter them among the nations" (cf. Deut 28:64ff.). He would give them (i.e., allow them to have) "statutes that were not good and ordinances by which they could not live." The pagan law codes which they substituted for the life-giving law of God would become a severe taskmaster. God would pronounce them "unclean" because of the way they used the gifts he bestowed upon them. Their participation in child sacrifice would make necessary the desolation of their land (20:23-26).

4. Israel in Canaan (20:27-29). God kept his word. He brought those unworthy people into Canaan. Even then they refused to serve him. They "blasphemed" the Lord by "acting treacherously" against him, i.e., they departed from the Lord to serve other gods. They saw the pagan shrines in the high hills and among the leafy trees and worshiped there. They provoked the Lord with their sacrifices, their libations and incense offerings which were presented to pagan deities. God called them to account for their conduct by asking, "What is the high place to which you are going?" That was how those pagan shrines came to be called *bamah,* i.e., high place.

B. God's Plan for the Present (20:30-39).

How could God cancel the threats which he had made through the years against the infidelity of his people? Ezekiel's generation had defiled itself in the same way as their fathers before them. They were playing the harlot with their "detestable things," i.e., their idols. They were continuing to present their gifts to these gods and to make their sons "pass through the fire," i.e., burn them alive. God could grant them no favorable insights into the immediate future. Some both in Babylon and in Jerusalem desired the complete paganization of Israel. Their motto was this: "We shall be like the nations serving wood and stone." God would not allow this to come about (20:30-33).

As paradoxical as it might seem, God's program of judgment was designed to guarantee the survival of his people. He would manifest his kingship over Israel in judgment "with a mighty hand, and with an outstretched arm and with wrath poured out." The reference is to the destruction of Jerusalem in 587 BC. Then the Lord would bring his wayward people "into the wilderness of the peoples," i.e., into exile. There he would "enter into judgment" with them (20:34f.).

Centuries before in the wilderness of Egypt the Lord had discriminated between those who were destined to enter the land of promise, and those who were not. So now the Babylonian exile would serve to discriminate between those who were to be permitted to return, and those who would be denied. The divine Shepherd would make his sheep "pass under the rod" so that he might identify those who were truly his. With this remnant he would enter into "the bond of the covenant." Rebels and transgressors would not be permitted to join the remnant on their trip back home. This purging process would reveal the true nature of the Lord (20:36-38).

God's purpose in having a holy people in this world would not be frustrated by the idolatry of that generation. Therefore, the Lord sarcastically challenged them to continue apace with their idolatry if that be their choice. He assured them, however, that the day would come when God's holy name would no longer be profaned by the idolatrous practices of his people (20:39).

C. God's Plan for the Future (20:40-44).

Looking beyond the exile Ezekiel described the relationship between God and Israel. He saw the high and holy "mountain of Israel," i.e., Zion. He saw "the whole house of Israel" serving the Lord faithfully in that mount "in the land." In that place the Lord would accept his people and all the offerings which they presented. They would become to him as a living sacrifice creating a "soothing aroma." Because of this, God promised "I will prove myself holy among you," i.e., demonstrate his presence, "in the sight of the nations" (20:40f.).

The regathering of Israel to their land would cause his people to understand the Lord as never before. They would look back upon their evil conduct prior to the captivity and they would "loathe" themselves. True repentance thus would be indicated. The grace of God finally would impact upon their minds. They would see that God had dealt with them for the sake of his name. They deserved nothing. They would understand that the Lord had not punished them to the extent that their "evil ways" and "corrupt deeds" deserved (20:42-44).

ISRAEL'S JUDGMENT
Ezekiel 20:45-21:32

Four brief parables depict the inevitable judgment which would come against Israel at the hands of Nebuchadnezzar. To these is appended a forthright declaration of judgment against Ammon, Israel's neighbor across the Jordan river.

A. Parable of the Fire (20:45-21:5).

God directed Ezekiel to set his face toward the south and to prophesy against "the forest of the southland" (NIV), i.e., Judah. God was about to kindle a fire against this forest. That fire would consume every green tree as well as every dry one. The thought is that both the righteous and the wicked would suffer from the devastation caused by the Chaldean invaders. That blazing inferno could not be quenched. "Every face" (NIV) throughout the land would be seared by the flames. This judgment on Judah would reveal the true character of Yahweh to all flesh (20:45-48).

At this point Ezekiel offered to the Lord a prayer of complaint (cf. Jer 4:10). People were ignoring what the prophet had to say. They were brushing it aside because he used the parabolic form of teaching. Ezekiel's complaint contained an implied petition that he be allowed to preach plainly (20:49).

Ezekiel's prayer was answered. He was allowed to preach in such a way as to explain the parable of the fire. He was to set his face toward Jerusalem and prophesy against the land of Israel. He was to preach against the pagan sanctuaries in particular. He was to announce God's hostile relationship to his people: "Behold, I am against you." The divine sword was unsheathed, i.e., the agents of Yahweh were about to invade the land. Both righteous and wicked would be cut off in that judgment. "All flesh," i.e., other peoples, would also feel the effects of that sword. The sword would not return to its sheath until the destructive work was finished (21:1-5).

The teaching here regarding the cutting off of both righteous and wicked does not contradict the teaching of chapter 18 that only the soul that sins shall die (cf. 18:20). The former passage spoke of final judgment, while this passage speaks of temporal judgment. As regards final judgment, the righteous will not be destroyed along with the wicked. In temporal judgments, however, both often suffer equally.

B. Parable of the Sigh (21:6-7).

God told Ezekiel to give vent to his emotions, to groan as a mourner might groan "with breaking heart and bitter grief." His actions were designed to provoke an inquiry on the part of the captives. He was to explain that his actions dramatized the behavior of the captives when they would hear the news that their Temple had been destroyed in Jerusalem. The tidings would be such as would cause every heart to melt and hands to droop. Spirits would be faint and knees would be as weak as water. As shocking as this sounds, it would happen. Yahweh himself declared it to be so. Five years after Ezekiel performed this action parable, the news of the destruction of Jerusalem reached the captives in Babylon.

C. Parable of the Sword (21:8-17).

The thought of the unsheathed sword earlier in chapter 21 gave birth to this unit. This parable may have been accompanied by sword brandishing. In any case, Ezekiel pointed to a "sword." It was sharpened and polished. Its dazzling brightness and sharpness added a fresh element of terror. This sword was designed to fit snugly into the hand of the slayer. Perhaps responding to smiles on the faces of his audience, Ezekiel asked rhetorically, "Shall we rejoice?" i.e., Do you think I am joking? The sword which Ezekiel was describing was no laughing matter. It would serve as a rod to correct God's son Israel who had rejected lesser forms of discipline (21:8-11).

God told Ezekiel to manifest the signs of deep mourning. He was to "cry out and wail" and "strike" his thigh. That sword was coming against God's people. The princes would fall in that day with the people. This would be a "testing" or trial for Judah. The "rod which despises," i.e., King Zedekiah who despised God's word, would cease to exist. The people would be without a king! (21:12f.).

Ezekiel was told to clap his hands to summons the sword of judgment. He was to "let the sword be doubled the third time," i.e., brandish his sword three times. This may represent the three times Nebuchadnezzar would invade the land of Judah. In any case, that sword would surround Judah like a besieging army. The point of that sword at every gate would cause consternation. God had provided that glittering sword. It was designed to strike with lightning-like speed. As Ezekiel spoke that sword was ready for its work of slaughter (21:14f.).

The Lord addressed his sword, the king of Babylon. He urged

the sword to demonstrate its sharpness and to move in any direction. Babylon was being urged to get on with the judgment. God clapped his hands to order that the sword begin its work. Only when that work was completed could the wrath of Yahweh be appeased (21:16f.).

D. Parable of the Crossroads (21:18-27).

The Lord directed Ezekiel to sketch a road with a fork in it. That represented the road which the "king of Babylon" would travel. The prophet was to make a sign post which pointed out the destinations of the two roads. One road lead to Rabbah, capital of Ammon; the other led to Jerusalem. At that fork in the road the king of Babylon would resort to his pagan divination to determine which direction he should go with his army. He would shake the arrows,[1] inquire of the "household gods" *(teraphim),* and look at the liver of a sacrificial animal. The king's divination pointed the way to Jerusalem. There he would set up his battering rams, cast up mounds and build a siege wall. There he would "open the mouth for slaughter," i.e., lift up the battle cry (21:18-22).

The citizens of Jerusalem regarded Nebuchadnezzar's divination as vain. In the past they had escaped Babylon's wrath by swearing oaths of allegiance to the Chaldean king. The king of Babylon, however, would now bring "iniquity to remembrance," i.e., he would remember the oaths which the leaders of Judah had broken. The citizens of Jerusalem would be "seized" by Nebuchadnezzar. Their more recent transgressions cause God also to remember their whole record of rebellion. They would be "seized with the hand" of divine justice as well (21:23f.).

The coming of Nebuchadnezzar would also be the climax of the punishment for Zedekiah, Judah's profane and wicked prince. The insignia of his rank—the turban and crown—would be removed. Socially, things would be thrown into confusion. The lowly would be exalted, the high brought low. The monarchy would be a total ruin. The throne of Judah would be empty "until he comes whose right it is." Then the Lord would give the throne to that individual. The reference here is to the Messiah (21:25-27).

E. The Sword and Ammon (21:28-32).

The Ammonites lived on the eastern side of the Jordan river. They were taunting the Jews because of all the misfortune which had befallen their land. The same lightning-swift, polished sword of divine justice which fell on Judah would also fall on Ammon. The soothsayers of Ammon promised peace. That, however, was not what the Lord had in mind for Ammon. He depicted the Ammonites hanging from the neck of the wicked Jews who would be slain in the time of punishment. At this point God told Ezekiel to return the sword to its sheath (21:28-30a).

Ezekiel then expanded upon his predictions of the judgment of Ammon. The Ammonites would be judged on their own soil. There God would pour out his indignation on Ammon. His anger would grow ever more intense as a flame blown by bellows. The destroyers of Ammon would be ruthless men, skillful destroyers. Ammon would be consumed in the fire of God's judgment. The blood of her people would be shed throughout the land. She would be remembered no more. For her there was no hope of restoration such as the prophet envisioned for Israel (21:30b-32).

ISRAEL'S DEFILEMENT
Ezekiel 22:1-31

Chapter 22 serves to underscore the necessity of the judgment against Judah which has just been described. The land was absolutely, irredeemably corrupt.

A. The Bloody City (22:1-16).

Before Ezekiel could pronounce judgment, he must inform his people of the charges against them. Again he was to "cause her to know all her abominations" (cf. 20:4).

The first two charges against Jerusalem were serious indeed. She was "a city shedding blood in her midst." The reference is to any wrongful death, especially one resulting from a corrupt judicial system and from child sacrifice. That the latter was probably in the foreground here is indicated by the second charge. She "makes idols" which cause her to be defiled before the Lord. These two major transgressions had brought near to Jerusalem the day of reckoning. Jerusalem would become a "reproach" to those near and far. She had the reputation of a city "full of turmoil," i.e., lawlessness (22:3-5).

The indictment continued with a catalog of sins committed in the midst of Jerusalem. Political leaders abused their power even to the point of bloodshed. Children treated their parents with contempt. The alien, widow and orphan had been mistreated. The city had shown no respect for sacred things. Sabbaths had been profaned consistently. Slanderers had sent many men to their deaths. Inhabitants had frequented the pagan shrines in the mountains (22:6-9a).

"Acts of lewdness" had been performed in Jerusalem. Men had "uncovered their fathers' nakedness," i.e., they had committed incest with a member of the family. A double sin was committed when men "humbled," i.e., raped, a woman during her menstruous period. Adultery and illicit sex within the family circle were also common (22:9b-11).

Ezekiel charged Jerusalem with bribery which led to executions. Oppression of neighbors through excessive profits or interest was yet another fault. The root sin which produced all the others in this terrible list was that Jerusalem had forgotten the Lord (22:12).

Their illicit gain and bloodshed had caused the Lord to clap his hands to summons the agents of his judgment. To drive home the implications of this statement, the Lord asked a rhetorical question. "Can your heart endure, or can your hands be strong, in the days that I shall deal with you?" By no means would they be able to stand against the enemies which God has summoned. The day of judgment on Jerusalem was certain because the Lord had spoken (22:13f.).

The judgment would serve a cleansing function for Israel. The Lord would scatter them among the nations. By this process he would rid the land of its uncleanness. The sinful people would "profane" themselves, i.e., be humiliated and debased, "in the sight of the nations." Through this experience they would come to learn the true nature of Yahweh (22:15f.).

B. The Blast Furnace (22:17-22).

The people of Israel had once been like precious silver to the Lord. Now they had become worthless dross. So the house of Israel would be gathered into Jerusalem just as contaminated silver is placed in a smelting furnace. There the Lord would pour out on them the fire of his anger and wrath. The nation would melt before that heat. In the fire of God's judgment the dross (impurity) would be removed from the silver. As the events of 587 BC were seen in retrospect, no one would doubt that the Lord himself had poured out his wrath on that city.

C. The Corrupt Land (22:23-31).

Judah was a land not cleansed, i.e., defiled. She had not been "rained on," i.e., spiritually blessed. She was facing the indignation of God. Prophets, priests, princes, and the people of the land were all to blame (22:23f.).

The prophets had entered into a "conspiracy" to preach only promises of peace. Like roaring lions tearing the prey, so they had devoured souls. They had amassed a fortune in treasure. By urging the leaders to revolt against Babylon they had brought the horrors of war upon the nation. Thus they had multiplied widows (22:25).

The priests were just as bad. They had done violence to the law of God by their self-serving interpretations. They had profaned the holy things of God. They failed in their duty to teach the people the difference between the unclean and the clean. They hid their eyes from God's sabbaths, i.e., they ignored the sabbath day. By all of these actions they had profaned God (22:26).

The vicious princes were like wolves tearing the prey. They were guilty of "shedding blood and destroying lives" in order to acquire "dishonest gain." The prophets worked hand in glove with the princes in two ways. They (1) whitewashed their despicable lives; and (2) manufactured a false vision to further government policy whenever called upon to do so (22:27f.).

The "people of the land," i.e., the landed aristocracy, were guilty as well. They too engaged in oppression and theft. They wronged the poor and needy, oppressed the alien unlawfully (22:29).

Throughout the entire nation God was searching for a real man (cf. Jer 5:1), someone who would "build up the wall," i.e., the moral and spiritual wall which was Judah's true protection from external threat. The Lord was looking for a national leader to "stand in the gap before me," someone who would personally intervene where that wall had fallen into decay. Someone who put his life on the line. Someone who would beseech the Lord to spare the city, and who would match that prayer with mighty works of reformation. Such a national leader could avert the destruction which God had been threatening. God, however, could find no one who could or would fill this role (22:30).

The moral collapse of Judah would be followed by physical destruction. The judgment was so certain that God could speak of it as though it had happened already. He declared: "I have poured out my indignation on them; I have consumed them with the fire of my wrath; their way have I brought upon their heads" (22:31).

ISRAEL'S DEBASEMENT
Ezekiel 23

In a lengthy allegory reminiscent of chapter 16 Ezekiel underscored the debasement of Israel. The prophet spoke of two sisters who played the harlot in their youth in the land of Egypt. "Their breasts were pressed," i.e., fondled, which points to sexual license. The sisters lost their virgin chastity even before leaving Egypt. The names of the sisters were Oholah and Oholibah. They both belonged to God, i.e., were married to him, and both bore him children. Lest there be any mistake about the meaning of this allegory, Ezekiel revealed the identity of the two sisters. Oholah was Samaria; Oholibah was Jerusalem (23:1-4).

A. Their Lewdness (23:5-21).

Ezekiel used sexual terms like lewdness, adultery, and harlotry to depict Israel's intimate association with idolatry. He first focused on the harlotry of Oholah, the northern sister, and then on Oholibah, the land of Judah.

1. Samaria's harlotry (23:5-10). Oholah committed harlotry from under the authority of God. She threw herself on her "lovers," i.e., political allies. She was especially attracted to the Assyrians who came to her with handsome and dashing young warriors. Yet Oholah did not forsake her Egyptian lovers with whom she had committed harlotry in her youth. Her political entanglements always involved defilement by the idols of her allies. Therefore, God gave Samaria into the hand of her Assyrian lovers. They "uncovered her nakedness," i.e., ravished the land. They took captive the sons and daughters of Oholah. They slew Oholah with the sword, i.e., destroyed the Northern Kingdom. Thus did Oholah become a "byword among women," i.e., an object of reproach among other nations.

2. Jerusalem's harlotry (23:11-21). Oholibah became even more corrupt than her northern sister. She too became attracted to the handsome and dashing warriors from Assyria. Yet even during her liaison with the Assyrians, her lust was kindled by wall pictures of the Chaldeans in their native dress. She sent messengers to Chaldea (Babylon). The "Babylonians came to her to the bed of love," i.e., they entered into an alliance with Judah. Oholibah was then defiled by the harlotry (idolatry) of the new lover. The affair with the Chaldeans, however, was temporary. Oholibah soon "became disgusted with them" (23:11-17).

Oholibah became yet more degenerate. "She uncovered her harlotries," i.e., she began to openly seek alliances with other nations. In an attempt to attract lovers who could free her from Babylon, she "uncovered her nakedness." In spite of warnings that she was alienating her God, she continued to multiply her harlotries. She recalled her early harlotry in Egypt and so she made overtures in that direction. She lusted after the Egyptians who had a reputation for sexual potency, i.e., military power. She relived the "lewdness" of her youth in Egypt, i.e., she revived Egyptian cults and customs long forgotten (23:18-21).

B. Their Punishment (23:22-35).

The punishment of Samaria's lewdness was past. Her sister Jerusalem was about to experience a similar fate. Ezekiel first described her punishment; then he underscored that description by means of a parable.

1. Jerusalem's punishment described (23:22-31a). God was about to bring against Oholibah her alienated lovers, i.e. the Chaldeans. The attacking army would be multi-national. They would be dashing in appearance as they came to do their deadly work.

These soldiers, however, would be armed for war and they would deploy themselves for siege about Jerusalem. To this army the Lord had committed the judgment of Jerusalem. They would judge the place "according to their customs." This force would execute the jealous wrath of God against Jerusalem. "Nose and ears," i.e., the leading citizens, would be removed from the city. Captivity, sword and fire awaited the inhabitants of Jerusalem. The attackers would strip the harlot of garments and jewels, i.e., take all her wealth, and leave her naked and bare. Under this attack the lewd Egyptian harlotries would be forgotten for it would be clear that no relief would come from Pharaoh (23:22-27).

For emphasis and with even greater clarity Ezekiel repeated the threat he had just made. Jerusalem was to be given into the hand of those whom she hated, i.e., the Chaldeans. They would deal with Jerusalem in hatred. They would confiscate all properties leaving Oholibah nothing. That day would uncover the full extent of Jerusalem's "lewdness and harlotries." This terrible fate awaited Jerusalem because she had "played the harlot with the nations" and because she had "defiled" herself with idols. Oholibah had followed the path of her notorious sister to the north (23:28-31a).

2. Jerusalem's punishment illustrated (23:31b-35). God placed in the hand of Oholibah the same cup of judgment which her sister had consumed. That cup was deep and large and full to the brim. Drinking that cup would result in national "drunkenness," i.e., confusion, which in turn would lead to scorn and derision by other nations. That cup would produce sorrow, astonishment and desolation. Not only must Oholibah drain the cup, she must even gnaw the shards of the container. She would experience every last bit of punishment which God had decreed for her. Then she would tear her breasts, i.e., be plunged into anguish and despair. The cup depicted the terrible consequence of having forgotten God, of having deliberately cast the Lord behind their back. This was the punishment for Oholibah's harlotries and lewdness.

C. Their Lewdness (23:36-44).

The second round of indictment against the two sisters is more specific. The language of allegory gives way to specific examples of what the prophet had in mind. The two sisters had committed adultery with their idols. Their hands were stained with the blood of their own children—Yahweh's children—whom they offered as food to their pagan gods in the sacrificial fires. On the very days when they committed these atrocities they entered into the God's sanctuary hypocritically to render homage to the Lord. They had thus profaned that sacred place and the sacred sabbaths as well (23:36-39).

Judah actively pursued idolatry. She sent messengers to distant places to invite idolaters to come and teach them pagan rites. Like a harlot, Judah attempted to attract new lovers. She prepared herself by bathing, putting on eye makeup, and bedecking herself with beautiful ornaments. She prepared her table with incense and oil. The irony was that she used the gifts which God had bestowed upon her to advance the cause of idolatry. She created a festive atmosphere, the sound of a multitude at ease. The harlot was not particular about who shared her table and her bed. Men of the common sort and even drunkards from the desert were all welcome (23:40-42).

The Lord hoped that the idolatrous pattern of behavior might stop when Judah became "worn out by adulteries." Surely foreign nations would find her attractive no more! Yet foreigners continued to go into Oholah and Oholibah as they would go in to a harlot (23:43f.).

D. Their Punishment (23:45-49).

In comparison to the sisters, those who brought judgment were "righteous men." Both sisters deserved the judgment of adulteresses and the judgment of women who had shed blood. Therefore, the Lord called for a company to come against the sisters. They were to be given over to "terror and plunder." The company would stone them, then cut them down with swords. Their sons and daughters would be slain, their houses burned. By this radical means God would force the lewdness to cease from the land. Through the experiences of Oholah and Oholibah other women, i.e., nations, would learn not to commit lewdness. The Lord would requite the lewdness of the sisters. They would bear the penalty of worshiping idols. In this experience they would come to have a better understanding of the nature of God (23:45-49).

Endnote

1. Shaking the arrows probably involved placing the name "Jerusalem" on one arrow, "Rabbah" on the other. The arrows would then be placed in a quiver, and shaken. The arrow which was drawn from the quiver indicated the direction which the gods would have the king go.

CHAPTER THIRTY

A Turning Point for Ezekiel
Ezekiel 24-28

Background of the Unit.

Another precise date according to the captivity of King Jehoiachin is given in 24:1, viz., the ninth year, tenth month and tenth day of the month. This equates with January 15, 588 BC on the modern calendar. This date was crucial to Ezekiel. On this day many miles removed from Babylon Nebuchadnezzar "laid siege to Jerusalem." God told Ezekiel to record this date so as to verify the fulfillment of his prediction after news from Jerusalem reached the captives in Babylon some weeks later. For years afterward this date would be commemorated by the Jews with fasting (cf. Zech 7:19).

Three important events transpired in Ezekiel's ministry on that date. He related yet another parable. He experienced the death of his wife. He received revelation that shortly his dumbness would be removed. During the interim between the beginning of the siege of Jerusalem and the arrival of the news that the city had fallen, Ezekiel turned his attention to foreign nations and expounded God's revelations concerning them.

Outline of the Unit.

A. Focus on the Prophet (chap. 24).
B. Focus on Neighboring Nations (chap. 25).
C. Focus on Phoenicia (chaps. 26-28).

FOCUS ON THE PROPHET
Ezekiel 24

On the day that Jerusalem came under siege, Ezekiel was busy about his ministry in Babylon. He related to the captives another verbal parable. He also performed another symbolic act on that day (24:1f.).

A. A Parabolic Message (24:3-14).

The parable began with a command to "put on the pot and also pour water into it." Then Ezekiel urged his auditors to put choice pieces of meat into the pot, build a fire under it, and make it "boil vigorously." By way of explanation of his parable, Ezekiel pronounced two "woes" against those who trusted in the strength of Jerusalem (24:3-5).

1. *The first woe (24:6-8).* The rust-covered pot represented Jerusalem the "bloody city." She had been stained with the blood of the innocent, especially children offered to Baal. The filth of the city had not yet been removed by centuries of preaching and chastisement. Now Jerusalem had reached the ultimate extreme. Piece by piece the chunks of meat would be brought out of the pot, i.e., the citizens would be carried away into captivity. This deportation would be indiscriminate (24:6).

Jerusalem's fate was well deserved. She had become so calloused that she made no effort to hide her crimes of bloodshed. As if to flaunt her transgression, she "placed it on the bare rock," i.e., she performed her acts of bloodshed openly. Through the messages of his prophets, God would preserve those bloodstains in plain view until his wrath fell on the place (24:7f.).

2. The second woe (24:9-14). In the second woe God assures his people that he would heap up the fuel for the burning of Jerusalem. He would see to it that both the meat (citizens) and the bones (leaders) within the pot were burned. Then he would set the pot on the coals so the filth could be melted out. The Lord was weary with previous half-hearted efforts at reform. The uncleanness of the place could only be removed by the drastic process of melting down the pot, i.e., totally destroying Jerusalem (24:9-12).

At this point the Lord would make no further effort to purge the nation by prophetic admonition. All that remained was for the wrath of God to be poured out on Jerusalem. This threat was irrevocable because the Lord had spoken, and he would not change his mind. He would have no pity upon them. He would hand Jerusalem over to the Chaldeans for the judgment appropriate to her sins (24:13f.).

B. A Parabolic Action (24:15-24).

On that fateful day when Jerusalem came under siege by Nebuchadnezzar, Ezekiel experienced a personal loss. In the morning the Lord announced to him that his beloved wife—"the desire of your eyes"—would be suddenly taken from him. The prophet was to use this occasion of personal grief to teach the captives yet another truth. When he heard of his wife's death he was not to manifest any of the traditional signs of mourning. He was not to publicly lament, weep or shed tears. He was not to alter his normal dress, nor allow his hair to hang down over the face to cover his mustache. He was not to eat the bread which was traditionally offered by friends to one who mourned. He was to "groan silently" (24:15-17).

Even though he knew that his wife would die at any moment, Ezekiel spoke to the captives in the morning, presumably delivering the parable of the pot mentioned earlier in the chapter. At evening his wife died. In the morning the prophet carried out the difficult commands which the Lord had given him. By this time the captives were familiar enough with Ezekiel's methodology to realize that the absence of emotion at the death of his beloved wife must have some prophetic meaning. They therefore asked the prophet to explain his conduct

(24:18f.).

Ezekiel's conduct following the death of his wife illustrated the reaction of the Jews to the terrible news which they would shortly receive. God was about to profane his sanctuary by giving it into the hands of wicked men. Westerners have a difficult time appreciating the deep attachment which the Jews felt toward that Temple. Ezekiel described the Temple in three ways: (1) "the pride of your power," i.e., that which guaranteed the security of Jerusalem; (2) "the desire of your eyes," i.e., that which was most precious to them; and (3) "the delight of your soul," i.e., that which they most missed by being in Babylon. Another blow would also fall. Their sons and daughters who still lived in Judah would fall by the sword (24:20f.).

The news from Jerusalem would be utterly shocking. When the captives heard that news, they would behave as Ezekiel had behaved at the death of his wife. They would experience a grief which is beyond tears, a despondency which could not be expressed with outward acts. To make matters worse, they would "rot away" in their iniquities, i.e., be totally consumed by a guilty conscience. The only outward expression which would be heard among them would be a quiet moan (24:22f.).

In his actions after the death of his wife Ezekiel was a "sign" to the captives. When the news arrived from Jerusalem they would know that the event had been decreed by the Lord. As terrible as the shock would be, the destruction of Jerusalem would help the captives gain a true perspective on the character of God (24:24).

C. A Personal Promise (24:25-27).

God was about to deliver to the Jews a double blow. He would take from them their Temple. That sacred sanctuary was the very "stronghold" of their faith, the "joy of their pride." He would also take from them their sons and daughters. A fugitive from Jerusalem would come to Babylon bringing the sad news. "On that day" Ezekiel's mouth would be opened (cf. 3:26,27). His ministry would change. He would be able to comfort and encourage them with words of hope rather than oracles of doom and stony silence. This prophet who previously had been so negative would become at that time the great encourager.

FOCUS ON NEIGHBORING NATIONS
Ezekiel 25

During the days when he was awaiting the arrival of the messenger with the news from Jerusalem Ezekiel directed his attention to neighboring nations. A section of foreign nation oracles like that which follows here appears also in Isaiah (chaps. 13-23) and Jeremiah (chaps. 46-51). Ezekiel devoted eight chapters to this material. Seven different nations were addressed, with Phoenicia and Egypt receiving the most attention. Commentators puzzle over the absence of any word concerning the fall of Babylon. Perhaps such an oracle would have stirred foolish resistance among the captives. Ezekiel began with the smaller nations which surrounded Judah.

A. God's Word to Ammon (25:1-7).

Ammon was located just to the east of the Jordan river. This nation was charged with mocking the plight of God's people when they experienced the judgment at the hands of their God. The Ammonites mocked when the Temple was profaned, when the land of Israel was made desolate, and when Judah was taken into captivity. Because of this, the Ammonites would be given to "the sons of the east" for a possession. These desert tribes would set their encampments and make their dwellings in the land of Ammon. They would take what they pleased of the fruit and milk of the land. Even Rabbah, capital of Ammon, would become a pasture for the camels and flocks of the invaders. Those who observed the fulfillment of this prediction would know that Yahweh alone is the only God (25:1-5).

God cannot stand the gloating of one people over the misfortune of another, especially if the misfortune had befallen *his* people. The Ammonites had clapped their hands, stamped their feet and rejoiced with all the scorn of their soul against the land of Israel. Therefore, Yahweh had stretched out his hand against Ammon. That nation would be given as spoil to other nations. The Ammonites would cease to exist as a distinct people. The fulfillment of these threats would cause those who knew of these predictions to recognize Yahweh as sole divinity (25:6f.).

B. God's Word to Moab (25:8-11).

The sin of Moab was the failure to recognize the distinctiveness of Israel. Therefore, God was about to bring judgment on that land. The cities of Moab would be invaded by desert tribes from the east. Moab and her cousin Ammon would disappear from the pages of history. Moab's demise would not be due simply to the passing of time. The judgments of Yahweh would bring that nation to an end. Moab would then be convinced that Yahweh was God.

C. God's Word to Edom (25:12-14).

Edom's sin is that of vengeful conduct toward Judah (cf. Amos 1:11). By "avenging" themselves on the children of Judah the Edomites had incurred enormous guilt. Therefore, God would stretch out his hand against Edom to cut off both man and beast from that land. The land would be laid waste by an invader. From Teman in the north to Dedan in the south Edomites would fall by the sword. The vengeance of Yahweh would be executed on Edom by the hand of the Israelites. The history of Edom subsequent to Ezekiel indicates the accuracy of this prediction. Edom fell to the Arabs in the fifth century BC, to the Nabataeans in the third century BC. In the second century the great Jewish general Judas Maccabaeus conquered the area and forced the inhabitants there to accept circumcision. This brought to an end the existence of Edom as a distinct people.

D. God's Word to Philistia (25:15-17).

The Philistines lived in the coastal plains to the west of Judah. Their sin was acting in revenge. In fact they had "taken vengeance with scorn of soul," i.e., mockery accompanied their vengeful acts. Their intent was to "destroy" the people of God because they had "everlasting enmity" toward them. Therefore, God's hand was against the Philistines. He intended to cut off the Cherethites who were close allies of Philistia. He would destroy "all the remnant of the seacoast," i.e., everyone else living in Philistia. They would experience the "great vengeance" of the Lord "with wrathful rebukes," i.e., repeated acts of furious chastisement. Through these experiences the Philistines would come to know the Lord. History records an attack against Gaza by Pharaoh Hophra in the sixth century BC. In the second century the

Jewish armies overran the area and incorporated it into Judea.

FOCUS ON PHOENICIA
Ezekiel 26-28

Some seventy-six verses in this book speak of Tyre, and four additional verses of Tyre's sister city Sidon. Why Ezekiel devoted so much space to this small northern neighbor of Judah has puzzled commentators. The suggestion has even been made that Ezekiel used Tyre as a symbol for Babylon.[1] Be that as it may, four distinct messages are contained in this unit. Two of these concern the city of Tyre and two concern Tyre's ruler.

A. The Destruction of Tyre (26:1-26).

The Tyre material is dated to the eleventh year of King Jehoiachin's captivity, and the first day (26:1). The month is not indicated. The material probably should be assigned to September 18, 587 BC,[2] three weeks after the fall of the city of Jerusalem. This word to Tyre unfolds in five movements.

First, Ezekiel cited the reason for the destruction. Tyre was a center of commerce in Ezekiel's day. When the Babylonians destroyed Jerusalem, Tyre gloated. "She who was the door of peoples is broken," i.e., the major trading center of Jerusalem had fallen. Tyre rejoiced over Jerusalem's fall because she would be "filled with the one who has been laid waste," i.e., she would reap the profits of Judah's fall (26:2).

Second, Ezekiel indicated the extent of the destruction. The prophet made five specific predictions relating to the destruction of Tyre. (1) Many nations would come against Tyre. History records that the Babylonians, Alexander, Antigonus, the Arabs and the Crusaders all inflicted their blows against this place. (2) Tyre would be made a bare rock. (3) Fishermen would spread their nets at Tyre. (4) Tyre would become spoil for the nations. (5) Tyre's satellite villages would be slain by the sword. The destruction of Tyre was certain because God had spoken. Through this experience the citizens of Tyre would come to know that Yahweh is the only God (26:3-6).

Third, Ezekiel focused on the agents of destruction. God would bring Nebuchadnezzar against Tyre. The resources at his disposal included horses, chariots, horsemen and a mighty company. He would destroy Tyre's satellite cities and then lay siege to Tyre itself. He would break down the towers of the city. His forces would be so vast that the dust stirred by their feet would cover the city. The noise of his cavalry, wagons and chariots would shake the walls. Finally he would smash through the gates. The hoofs of his horses would tread down the streets of Tyre. The inhabitants of Tyre would be slain with the sword. The "strong pillars," i.e., leaders of the city, would be brought down to the ground (26:7-11). Nebuchadnezzar besieged Tyre for some fifteen years (587-574 B.C.). He destroyed the mainland city, but was not able to conquer the island fortress.

The prophecy now shifts to Tyre's attackers subsequent to Nebuchadnezzar.[3] They would ransack Tyre and tear down all the structures of the place. The rubble of those walls and buildings would be dumped into the midst of the waters. History records that Alexander razed mainland Tyre and built from its debris a causeway out to the island fortress where most of the leading citizens were holed up. God would silence the revelry of that city. Tyre would become a bare rock, a place for the spreading of fishing nets. Phoenician Tyre would never be rebuilt.[4] This prediction would certainly come to pass because it had upon it the verbal signature of the Lord (26:12-14).

Fourth, Ezekiel described the reaction to the destruction. Tyre presided over a network of trading colonies throughout the Mediterranean world. These island colonies would shake and tremble when they heard the news of Tyre's fall. Their princes would sit stupefied and astonished. All her former allies would take up a lamentation over the demise of that powerful merchant city (26:15-18).

Finally, Ezekiel spoke of the result of destruction. Tyre was to become an uninhabited desolation. The ruins of the place would be washed by the waves, i.e., her sea wall would be destroyed. Tyre was personified and pictured descending into "the pit," i.e., the nether world, the abode of the dead. Tyre thus would descend to the "lower parts of the earth." There she would join "the people of old," i.e., other civilizations which passed on before. The language here is highly figurative. The point is that Tyre would disappear from the land of the living—from the stage of history—and never be found again. By way of contrast, God declared that he would "set glory in the land of the living." The glory of man-made kingdoms fades but the Lord's kingdom endures forever (26:19-21).

B. Parable of the Sinking Ship (27:1-36).

Ezekiel next employed an allegorical dirge to underscore his predictions regarding the ultimate fall of Tyre. Because of her excellent harbor, Ezekiel addressed Tyre as the one who dwells "at the entrance of the sea." Tyre was the "merchant of the peoples" who lived throughout the Mediterranean region. Since Tyre boasted of her beauty, i.e., attractiveness to commercial partners, Ezekiel likened the city to a beautiful ship (27:1-3).

The builders had constructed the most beautiful ship possible. Materials from distant lands were imported for use in the vessel. Her planks were of fir, her mast of cedar, her oars of oak and her deck of box wood inlaid with ivory. Her sail was of embroidered work, her awning of imported blue and purple. Accompanying the rowers and pilots from Phoenicia was a multi-national crew: repairmen, sailors and marines from distant lands. The ship's glory was enhanced by a display of shields and helmets (27:4-11).

Ezekiel named twenty-four nations, cities and peoples as being the ports of call for this allegorical ship. Among those mentioned are Judah and Israel. An impressive array of products was transported between these ports of call including foodstuffs, metals, livestock, wool, spices, precious stones and manufactured goods. The point is that the Phoenicians had trading relations with peoples all over the ancient Near East. To a large extent the economy of the entire region depended on these commercial experts (27:12-25).

The overloaded ship encountered a storm while in deep waters. The crew and cargo of the vessel were lost at sea. All over the world a lament arose over the loss of the ship. The countryside quaked in fear over the news. International shipping came to a halt. Tough sailors throughout the world were distraught. Tyre's clients were confused. Commerce was disrupted. The inhabitants of the coast lands were appalled. Kings were afraid and troubled, merchants astonished. In these pictures Ezekiel portrayed the reaction to the destruction of Tyre (27:26-36).

C. The Death of the Prince (28:1-10).

In his third Tyre oracle Ezekiel condemned the pride of the prince of Tyre. That ruler, like many of his counterparts in the ancient Near East, considered himself a deity. He regarded himself as completely safe in his island fortress. He thought that he was as wise as God. Ezekiel conceded that the prince was as wise as Daniel who had already achieved a reputation in the royal court at Babylon. No secret seemed too difficult for him. By that wisdom he had been able to amass great wealth, to build a commercial empire. With the increase of his riches, however, came a corresponding inflation of his ego (28:1-5).

The arrogant prince would experience punishment at the hands of God. Ruthless strangers would come against him. The splendor of this ruler would be defiled. The vainglorious prince would be slain in battle. He would go down to the pit, i.e., Sheol, the afterlife. He would die on his island fortress "in the heart of the seas." Ezekiel wondered if this prince would argue the case for his deity in the face of the men who were about to slay him. Only a confrontation with death will deflate the ego of the arrogant. At that time the prince would realize, as all rational men must, that he was mortal, not God. So this glorious prince would "die the death of the uncircumcised," i.e., the most ignominious death. This was certain to happen, because the Lord had spoken (28:6-10).

D. Parable of the Garden Dweller (28:11-19).

The parabolic lament over the king of Tyre is one of the most difficult passages in the book. Ezekiel developed two thoughts: the privileges of the king, and his sin.

1. *Privileges of the king (28:12-14).* The king had "the seal of perfection," i.e., he was perfect in physical form. He lived in a paradise which Ezekiel symbolically called Eden, the garden of God. On the day he was created, i.e., enthroned, he wore dazzling apparel made up of every precious stone. He was "the anointed cherub," i.e., guardian, of his city. In the eyes of his subjects he achieved deity, thus he is said to be "on the mountain of God." There he "walked in the midst of the stones of fire," i.e., precious stones which flashed like lightning.

2. The sin of the king (28:15-19). From the day he was "created," i.e., enthroned as king of Tyre, he was blameless. Then, however, "unrighteousness" was found in him. Ezekiel leveled four charges against the king. First, the king's numerous trading ventures led to violence, i.e., goods being taken by violent means. Because of his sin God would cast him forth like something profane from "the mountain of God," i.e., his island fortress. This guardian cherub of Tyre would be "destroyed" from the midst of the "stones of fire" (28:15f.).

Second, the heart of the king of Tyre was lifted up because of his "beauty," i.e., the splendor of his surroundings. Third, he corrupted his wisdom, i.e., he misused his business acumen for evil purposes. True wisdom cannot be exercised where there is arrogance. The Lord would cast this proud king "to the ground" before kings, i.e., humble him (28:17).

Fourth, the king profaned sanctuaries with the ill-gotten gain of his international merchandising. The evil of the king would be like a fire which would reduce Tyre to ashes. All who knew the king would be appalled at his sudden change of circumstances. This mighty king who thought himself to be a god, would be terrified as he faced the end. He would "be no more," i.e., the monarchy of Tyre would cease forever (28:18f.).

E. Judgment on Sidon (28:20-26).

The Lord now directed Ezekiel to turn his attention to Tyre's sister city Sidon. The God of Israel was hostile towards Sidon too. By executing judgments on that place God would be glorified. A siege of the city would result in pestilence. Blood would be shed in the streets. The sword of judgment would be against Sidon on every side. Thus would God remove this painful thorn in the side of Israel. All sources of danger, opposition, and ridicule for Israel would be removed from Canaan. Then they—both the antagonists and the Israelites—would realize that Yahweh alone is deity (28:20-24).

In contrast to Canaanite culture represented by Sidon, God's people would have a future. The Lord would gather them from where they were scattered. In so doing he would manifest his "holiness" in them in the sight of the nations. God would execute judgments upon all the surrounding nations who had scorned his people. Therefore they would be able to dwell safely upon the land which God gave to their ancestor Jacob. Then they would realize that Yahweh was their God (28:25f.).

Endnotes

1. H.L. Ellison, *Ezekiel: The Man and His Message* (Grand Rapids: Eerdmans, 1956) 106f.

2. James E. Smith, *Ezekiel* in Bible Study Textbook Series (Joplin, MO: College Press, 1979) 307.

3. The change is indicated by the shift from the singular to the plural pronoun.

4. This prediction is not negated by the existence of a modern Arab fishing village named after the famous commercial metropolis of Tyre. The prophecy is that *Phoenician* Tyre would be destroyed.

CHAPTER THIRTY-ONE

The Eclipse of Egypt
Ezekiel 29-32

Background of the Unit.

Ezekiel devoted seven oracles consisting of ninety-seven verses to the announcement of the downfall of Egypt. Each of the seven oracles begins with the phrase, "the word of the Lord came unto me, saying." All but one of these oracles are dated precisely between tenth and twenty-seventh years of the exile, i.e., January 587 BC when Nebuchadnezzar besieged Jerusalem, and April 571 BC when he lifted his siege against Tyre. The latest of the Egypt oracles—in fact the latest oracle in the entire book—is the second in the group.

From the human point of view, Egypt was Judah's last hope of salvation from being crushed by Babylon. Those in Babylon and Jerusalem who advocated rebellion against Nebuchadnezzar were trusting in Pharaoh to provide the military assistance which would make rebellion possible. Ezekiel desired to smash these false hopes in order that Judah might realize that they should be turning upward to God for help, not southward to Egypt.

Outline of the Unit.

A. The Future of Egypt (29:1-16).
B. The Judgment of Egypt (29:17-30:19).
C. The Fall of Egypt (30:20-31:18).
D. The Lament for Egypt (chap. 32).

THE FUTURE OF EGYPT
Ezekiel 29:1-16

The first Egypt oracle is dated to Jehoiachin's tenth year of exile, the tenth month, the twelfth day of the month. This equates to January 7, 587 BC on the present calendar. The Babylonian siege of Jerusalem had been underway for one year. God told Ezekiel to set his face against Egypt. He was to declare God's hostility toward that land and its ruler (29:1-3a).

A. Condemnation (29:3b-9a).

Ezekiel used two brief parables to point out the sins for which Yahweh condemned Egypt. First, Ezekiel compared Pharaoh to a giant crocodile which lay in the midst of the rivers. This monster boasted that the river belonged to him, that he himself had made the river. That was tantamount to a claim to deity. Pharaoh regarded himself as responsible for all the wealth of Egypt. This crocodile, however, was about to be captured. Hooks would be placed in its jaws. The beast would be hauled forth out of its rivers. Its carcass would be cast into the wilderness and left unburied to be consumed by beasts and fowl. The fish clinging to its scales, i.e., Pharaoh's allies and mercenaries, would suffer the same fate (29:3b-6a).

The judgment on Pharaoh would bring the inhabitants of Egypt to the knowledge that Yahweh is God. That judgment would befall them because they had been nothing but a "staff made of reed" to the house of Israel, i.e., they failed Israel in a time of need. When the Jerusalemites took hold of that staff it broke and pierced their hand. The point is that every time God's people attempted to lean on Egypt they got hurt. For this reason the Lord would bring against Egypt "a sword," i.e., a military force, which would cut off both man and beast.

The land of Egypt was destined to become a desolation in order that they might know that Yahweh is God (29:6b-9a).

B. Desolation (29:9b-12).

Pharaoh's pride which boasted of deity necessitated the punishment which God had decreed. God was hostile to Pharaoh and the rivers which he claimed to have created. The land would become a "desolation and waste" from one border to the other. For forty years the cities of Egypt would be abandoned. Egyptians would be scattered among the nations. Thus far the Egyptian records, which are very skimpy in this period, do not provide documentation for such a time in Egyptian history.[1]

C. Restoration (29:13-16).

At the end of forty years the Lord would gather the scattered Egyptians. They would return to Pathros, i.e., southern Egypt, the region of their origin. Restored Egypt, however, would only be a shadow of the once mighty empire of the Pharaohs. Never again would Egypt lift itself over other nations. Never again would the Israelites repeat their past iniquity by putting their confidence in Egypt.

THE JUDGMENT OF EGYPT
Ezekiel 29:17-30:19

The second and third Egypt oracles focus on judgment. The second word concerning Egypt is the latest oracle in the book. It is dated to new year's day of the twenty-seventh year of Jehoiachin's captivity, which equates to April 26, 571 BC on the modern calendar. The third oracle is undated, but likely comes from the same time frame as the second.

A. The Prize of Egypt (29:17-21).

For thirteen years Nebuchadnezzar had besieged the island fortress of Tyre. Every soldier's head was made bald by ill-fitted helmets. Every shoulder was raw from carrying heavy timber and stone. Yet in spite of years of effort, Nebuchadnezzar and his army had not adequately been rewarded with the spoils of war. Because he did the bidding of the Lord at Tyre, Nebuchadnezzar would be rewarded. He would be given all the wealth of Egypt to use as wages for his army (29:17-20). Though Egypt would be humiliated, the Lord would make a "horn sprout for the house of Israel," i.e., he would begin the process of restoring the power of Israel.[2] In the day Nebuchadnezzar invaded Egypt the Lord would open Ezekiel's mouth.[3] This seems to mean that the skepticism of the captives regarding Ezekiel would be removed and they would come to regard him as a true prophet. He would therefore be able to speak freely to them (29:21).

B. The Woes of Egypt (30:1-19).

In the third word concerning Egypt Ezekiel listed the woes which were about to befall Egypt. The oracle begins with an announcement of the approach of the day of Yahweh. Ezekiel pictured that day as gloomy, a day when a sword would come upon Egypt and her allies. An enemy would take away the wealth of the land. The very foundations of the land would be shaken. Egypt's allies would also fall in that day (30:1-5).

For Egypt that would be a time of great slaughter. All of Egypt's helpers, those who were the "pride of her power," would fall by the sword throughout the land. Egypt and her cities would be desolate. This devastating judgment would bring Egypt to experiential knowledge of who the Lord really was. News of the fall of Egypt would be carried by messengers to the neighboring Ethiopians. These complacent people would be terrified and confused by what they heard. The day of Egypt was certainly at hand (30:6-9).

Again Ezekiel identified Nebuchadnezzar as the agent of Yahweh's wrath against Egypt. His army consisted of "the most ruthless of the nations," "evil men," and "strangers." This force was coming to empty their swords against Egypt, to destroy the land and fill it with slain Egyptians. Yahweh promised to "make the Nile canals dry," i.e., remove every obstacle from before Nebuchadnezzar. The Lord would deliver Egypt into the hand of the invaders (30:10-12).

The idols of Egypt would suffer along with the land which venerated them. Never again would that nation have a native prince, i.e., Egypt would be ruled by a succession of foreign rulers.[4] Ezekiel identifies the leading cities of Egypt and succinctly predicted how the judgment would impact on each of them. An interesting contrast is predicted for two major capitals, Noph or Memphis in the north, and Thebes or No in the south. The Lord threatened that he would "make the images cease from Memphis." Thebes would be torn asunder and its population would be cut off. A visit to the ruins of these ancient sites demonstrates that images of various kinds still stand at Thebes, but they are nowhere to be found at Memphis save for one huge statue of Ramses lying prone under a modern shelter (30:13-17).

God would thus break the yoke which Egypt had imposed on other nations. The pride of that superpower would cease forever. A cloud of gloom would cover the land. Egypt's daughters, i.e., her cities, would go into captivity. Through the judgments which Yahweh would execute there, Egypt would learn that Yahweh is God (30:18f.).

THE FALL OF EGYPT
Ezekiel 30:20-31:18

The fourth and fifth words addressed to Egypt came from the eleventh year of Jehoiachin's captivity. On the modern calendar the dates would be April 30, 587 and June 21, 587 BC, respectively. The fall of Jerusalem was only weeks away. The fourth word focuses on Pharaoh, the fifth on his nation.

A. The Defeat of Pharaoh (30:20-26).

The Lord had broken the arm of Pharaoh, i.e., his military might. The reference is probably to the defeat of Pharaoh Hophra when he tried to come to the aid of Jerusalem in 587 BC (cf. Jer 37:6-10). The Pharaoh's wound had not been healed, i.e., he had not yet recovered from his defeat by Nebuchadnezzar in Palestine in 587 BC. He could not hold a sword, i.e., muster any strength, to further resist Nebuchadnezzar (30:20f.).

Since Yahweh was against Egypt, that land would experience yet other setbacks. Pharaoh's other arm would be broken, i.e., he would be rendered totally powerless. The sword would fall from his hand, i.e., his armies would be scattered. While Egypt decreased, however, Babylon would increase. The Lord would uphold the arms of Nebuchadnezzar, and he would wield the sword of God's justice. When that sword was stretched out against Egypt, and the Egyptians were scattered among the nations, they would know by experience that Yahweh is God (30:22-26).

B. The Downfall of the Nation (31:1-18).

The fifth word concerning Egypt is a combination of prose and poetry. It compares Pharaoh to the mighty Assyrian empire which in turn is compared to a great cedar tree. The thought is that even though Pharaoh's army was as formidable as the mighty cedar of Lebanon, yet they would be cut down and cast into Sheol by the Chaldeans (31:1f.).

1. Description of the cedar (31:3-9). The oracle begins with a rhetorical question: "Whom are you like in your greatness?" Only Assyria was comparable to Egypt in pomp and power. Ezekiel compared Assyria to a giant cedar tree with beautiful and shady foliage.[5] This tree was exalted above all the trees of the forest, i.e., every other kingdom. The numerous boughs and long branches provided shelter for bird and beast alike, i.e., "all great nations lived under its shade" (31:3-6).

No other tree in the "garden of God," i.e., the world, could compare to it. In fact all other trees (nations) were jealous of the giant cedar. As part of God's garden, the kingdoms of this world needed to recognize that they had been planted and nurtured by the Lord. The cedar (Assyria) spread its branches and boasted of its beauty. The cedar forgot the source of its life. By extolling the beauty and majesty of the cedar, Ezekiel condemned the proud spirit of Assyria and of Pharaoh who was like Assyria (31:7-9).

2. Downfall of the cedar (31:10-14). The Assyrian king had an ego which matched the might of his empire. The cedar's heart was "haughty in its loftiness." Therefore, the Lord had delivered the Assyrian king into the hand of "a despot of the nations," i.e., Nebuchadnezzar. The giant tree had been cut down. Its remains filled mountains and valleys. People had abandoned the tree. Birds and beasts fed on its remains. This happened to Assyria so that no other tree should exalt itself in its height. Nations must learn that they are mortal. In time they will die and descend into the lower parts of the earth—the pit, i.e., they will depart the scene of history.

3. Descent of the cedar (31:15-18). The fall of the great cedar caused great concern throughout "Lebanon," i.e., the garden of God or the world. The rivers which nourished the great tree were dried up. All the other trees of Lebanon mourned and wilted away. Nations were shaken at the fall. The descent of the cedar brought comfort to the trees of Eden, the choicest and best of Lebanon, which were already in Sheol. The idea here is that previous world powers took consolation in the demise of Assyria. The allies of Assyria (those who were his arm, who dwelt in his shadow) also descended into Sheol (31:15-17).

The oracle ends with a question similar to the one with which it began (cf. v. 2): "To which among the trees of Eden are you thus equal in glory and greatness?" The point of the lengthy parable of the great cedar is simple. Regardless of his grandeur, Pharaoh would fall like others before him. He would surely descend to join the trees of Eden in Sheol, the abode of the dead. Pharaoh would "lie in the midst of the uncircumcised, with those who were slain by the sword." Since the Egyptians practiced circumcision, to spend eternity with those who were uncircumcised would be the ultimate humiliation (31:18).

THE LAMENT FOR EGYPT
Ezekiel 32

The sixth and seventh words concerning Egypt are dated to the twelfth year of the captivity of Jehoiachin. The month is not given for the seventh word, but most likely Ezekiel delivered it the same month he spoke the sixth word. On the modern calendar the dates would be March 4 and March 18, 585 BC. Both of these oracles are parabolic laments.

A. Parable of the Crocodile (32:1-16).

In his own estimation, Pharaoh was "a young lion of the nations." In truth he was nothing but a clumsy crocodile. Usually the crocodile remained submerged in the seas, i.e., the rivers of Egypt. Occasionally, however, he would venture forth, muddying the waters, i.e., confusing the political situation, as he did (32:1f.). Ezekiel had made this same comparison two years before (cf. 29:1-6).The great crocodile of Egypt faced a terrible fate. It would be captured in a net by a company of many peoples. It would be cast forth into a field and left for dead. Bird and beast, i.e. smaller nations, would pick the bones of the helpless creature. Mountains and valleys would be filled with the huge carcass. The blood of the beast would saturate the ground and rivers (32:3-6). The meaning of these frightening images is explained by the prophet himself.

The fall of Egypt would be a dark day. Sun, moon and stars would refuse to shine. Other nations and kings would tremble before God's unsheathed sword. When they saw Egypt fall, they would realize that the situation was hopeless for them. That sword was the king of Babylon who made expeditions against Egypt in 582 and 568 BC. Ezekiel called his armies "the mighty ones, tyrants of the nations." This army would devastate the pride of Egypt, her multitude and her cattle. Egypt would become a desolation with neither man nor beast to trouble her waters any more. This was the lamentation which "the daughters of the nations" would chant over Egypt in that day (32:7-16).

B. Parable of Sheol (32:17-32).

The final word concerning Egypt is dated two weeks after the previous one. The prophet was to feign a lament. Through his prophetic message he was to bring down to the nether world the multitude of Egypt and the "daughters of powerful nations," i.e., he was to announce the ultimate demise of these peoples. The oracle has to do with the place of Egypt among the various uncircumcised nations, i.e., Gentiles, in Sheol. The terms "nether world," "Sheol" and "pit" are all Hebrew ways of referring to the afterlife, the abode of the dead (32:17f.).

1. Egypt's descent inevitable (32:19-21). The prophetic lament began with a rhetorical question: "Whom do you surpass in beauty?" Egypt was no different from any other nation of that period. She must make her bed with the uncircumcised, i.e., Gentile nations. Though the Egyptians embalmed their dead and made other elaborate provisions for the afterlife, they would have no privileged position there (32:17-19).

Egyptian soldiers would fall by the sword. Ezekiel pictured the inhabitants of Sheol pulling Egypt down, as it were, into the pit. There she would be greeted with mocking words by "the strong among the mighty ones," i.e. the chiefs of the nations. The mockery involved four points: (1) "they have gone down," i.e., the Egyptians had entered Sheol; (2) "they lie still," i.e., they are dead; (3) they are among "the uncircumcised," i.e., those who had been treated as though they were uncircumcised;[6] and (4) they are treated like those "slain by the sword" in battle (32:20f.).

2. Other occupants of Sheol (32:22-27). The Egyptians would join the six nations which were already in Sheol. Assyria[7] with its multitude was there in the graveyard of tyrants. These were the graves of those slain by the sword. They lie in the uttermost part of the pit, an area reserved for those who caused terror in the land of the living. The thought is that those who were ruthless in life are repaid with utter contempt in the life to come. Elam[8] was also there in shame, "in the midst of them that are slain." Meshech and Tubal[9] experienced an even more humiliating fate for they had been even more ruthless. They were "the terror of the mighty in the land of the living." Therefore Meshech and Tubal rested with those who had been stripped of their weapons.

3. Pharaoh's burial place (32:28-32). Pharaoh was buried near the Assyrians. He was not among the mighty ones, but among the leaders of Edom, the princes of the north and the Sidonians. Pharaoh, however, could take some measure of comfort in the fact that others had shared his fate. For a time God had instilled a terror of Pharaoh in the land of the living. The fall of Egypt would mean shame and disgrace. The oracle closed as it opened (cf. v. 17) with the declaration that Pharaoh and all his multitude, i.e., subjects, would be made "to lie down among the uncircumcised."

The key phrase in this difficult passage is "by the sword" which occurs twelve times. This parable illustrates the words of Jesus: "all they that take the sword shall perish with the sword" (Matt 26:52). The passage thus underscores the futility of war.

Endnotes

1. Keil suggests that the forty years are a symbolic period of punishment. If actual years are intended the period between the conquest of Egypt by Nebuchadnezzar and its restoration under the Persians seems to fit. *Keil and Delitzsch Old Testament Commentaries; Ezekiel XXV to Malachi* (Grand Rapids: Associated Publishers, n.d.) 64.

2. Egypt's humiliation ended about 530 BC. Israel's restoration took place about five years earlier in 538 BC. Some regard the passage as a messianic promise.

3. This opening of Ezekiel's mouth has nothing to do with the sealing of his lips in 3:26-27. Rather here the opening of the mouth refers to the authentication of his prophetic office through the fulfillment of his prophecy.

4. Egypt was invaded by Cambyses (525 BC) who made it a Persian satrapy. Subsequently Egypt was ruled by the Greeks, the Romans, and the Arabs.

5. To compare kings and nations to trees is common in the Old Testament. See Isa 14:4-8; Dan 4:1f; Ezek 17:3f.

6. The Egyptians practiced circumcision and considered those who did not to be totally uncivilized. The term *uncircumcised* then is a term of derision.

7. The Assyrians fell from world power when their capital Nineveh was captured in 612 BC by a coalition of Medes and Chaldeans. The remnant of the Assyrian army was destroyed by Nebuchadnezzar at Carchemish in 605 BC.

8. Elam is southern Persia. Its capital was at Shushan (Susa). Elamites had joined the Assyrians in the attack against Jerusalem in 701 BC (cf. Isa 22:6). The country eventually gained its independence from Assyria. It became part of a coalition which conquered the mighty Babylon in 539 BC.

9. Meshech and Tubal were the remnants of the old Hittite Empire of Asia Minor. Ezekiel later would utter a long prophecy concerning Gog, the prince of Meshech and Tubal.

CHAPTER THIRTY-TWO

Preparation For Restoration
Ezekiel 33-35

Background of the Unit.

Jerusalem had fallen. A new phase of Ezekiel's ministry now began. From condemnation and threats of judgment the prophet turns to consolation and hints of hope. Chapter 33 is the transition from the one to the other.

Outline of the Unit.

A. Prophetic Commission Renewed (chap. 33).
B. Corrupt Leadership Replaced (chap. 34).
C. National Enemies Removed (chap. 35).

PROPHETIC COMMISSION RENEWED
Ezekiel 33

The second phase of Ezekiel's ministry began like the first, with a description of his role as watchman to the nation (cf. 3:16-21). A preacher needs to be reminded from time to time about the serious role he has in God's program. God reminded Ezekiel of his mission, message, manner and ministry as prophetic watchman for the house of Israel.

A. Mission of the Watchman (33:1-9).

God restated Ezekiel's primary responsibility as a watchman, i.e., to warn of approaching danger. A man who failed to heed the warning of the watchman was responsible for his own death. The watchman would not be held accountable. On the other hand, a watchman who failed to sound the alarm was held accountable for every life lost within the city (33:1-6).

Ezekiel had been appointed by God as a watchman for Israel. When he heard a divine word, he must warn the nation. Failure to warn a wicked man of the consequences of his conduct made the prophetic watchman responsible. The watchman delivered his own soul by sounding forth the divine warning (33:7-9).

B. Message of the Watchman (33:10-20).

The message of the watchman/prophet was to be responsive to the needs of his audience. The captives in Babylon had fallen into the depths of despair because of the news of the siege of Jerusalem. For the first time they acknowledged their transgressions. They attributed their present circumstances to the sins they had committed against their God. They had lost all hope that they would survive as a distinct people (33:10).

Ezekiel's message was to focus on the hopeful possibilities of repentance. He had good news for those depressed captives, news which was reinforced with a divine oath: "as I live, declares the Lord God." God did not delight in the death of wicked men! Rather he delighted in the repentance which leads to life. Repentance for the captives was possible, and God appealed for it (33:11).

The message also spoke of responsibility. The basic principle here articulated is this: A man's past does not of itself determine future relationship with the Lord. The righteousness of the righteous man would not deliver him in the day of his transgression. God's promises to that man were conditional. Therefore, he dared not trust in his own righteousness. A man who had been living a righteous life might suddenly choose to commit iniquity. In that case his righteousness would not be remembered. He would die in the iniquity which he had done. In God's view every man is responsible for his present conduct and standing with God (33:12f.). Ezekiel knew nothing of the doctrine of "once in grace always in grace" or "eternal security."

Ezekiel was to speak of the possibility of remission. Threats of judgment upon a wicked man were not irrevocable. A wicked man could respond to the word of God and repent. True repentance would manifest itself in such actions as restoring items which have been illegally retained, restoring items taken by violence, and walking in the statutes of life, i.e., the Law of God. Because God took note of his changed life, that sinner who truly repented would live! His sins would not be remembered against him (33:14-16).

The message was to stress God's righteousness in his dealings with men. The captives objected that Ezekiel's doctrine made God out to be inconsistent. The prophet declared that it was men who are inconsistent, not God. Wicked men sometimes do repent, and consequently reap the reward. Righteous men do sometimes backslide and then pay the price. Ezekiel argued that God deals with men as they are in the present, not as they once were, whether good or evil. Furthermore, the Lord declared that he judged men individually: "I will judge each of you according to his ways" (33:17-20). "There is no group insurance against God's judgment."[1]

C. Manner of the Watchman (33:21-22).

In the twelfth year of Jehoiachin's exile, the tenth month, the fifth day, a fugitive arrived from Jerusalem with the sad news (33:21). In modern reckoning the date would be January 8, 585 BC. This would be some eighteen months after the actual fall of the city (cf. Jer 39:2). Commentators have difficulty explaining why it would have taken eighteen months for the news to reach Babylon.[2] A general report of the destruction of Jerusalem may have reached Babylon somewhat earlier, but this would be an eyewitness report from one who actually had been through the ordeal. This fugitive may have been detained for some time by the Babylonians.

The previous dated oracle was delivered in the ninth year of the exile, the tenth month and the tenth day, i.e., January 15, 588 BC (24:1). That was the day when Jerusalem came under siege by Nebuchadnezzar. In that oracle Ezekiel explained his silent sorrow over the death of his wife. From that date until the fugitive arrived with details of the fall of the city, the prophet's mouth had been closed from speaking to the Israelites. During those three years of silence Ezekiel composed most of his oracles against foreign nations (chaps. 25-32). The evening before the messenger arrived the silence imposed on the prophet at the outset of Jerusalem's siege was removed (33:22).[3] This fulfilled the prediction made to the prophet in 24:26ff. News of Jerusalem's destruction vindicated the first half of Ezekiel's ministry. He was now authorized to open his mouth in a new series of utterances. He could now move freely among the captives offering consolation in the midst of their depression.

D. Ministry of the Watchman (33:23-28).

During his first commission the Lord described to Ezekiel in detail the nature of the audience to whom he would be ministering (cf. 2:3-7). The watchman's work of restoration would be no easier than his earlier work of condemnation. The Lord now revealed to Ezekiel the character of those who had survived the destruction of Jerusalem, and those who had been carried away to Babylon. The one "possessed hope without holiness," the others were "hearers of the word, but not doers of the work."[4]

1. The survivors in Palestine (33:23-29). Those who had survived the destruction of Jerusalem had unrealistic optimism regarding their future. Originally, they argued, God had given the land of Palestine to a single individual, viz., Abraham. How much more claim did these survivors have upon the land since they were many! (33:24). The survivors did not take into account the fact that God's promises always have the implied condition that men faithfully serve the Lord.

The survivors were not entitled to that land for they continued committing transgression against the Lord. They ate meat from which blood had not been properly drained. They lifted up their eyes to idols. They shed blood, probably in child sacrifice. They lived by violence. They committed various other abominations including the defilement of the wife of their neighbor (33:25f.).

Nothing but further disaster awaited the survivors of Jerusalem's fall. God swore an oath that they would yet face the sword of divine justice, or they would be devoured by wild beasts, or they would die by pestilence. The land of Judah would become desolate. The pride of Judah's power, i.e., her favored position as a nation, would cease. No one would even make a trip through Judah. This would bring the survivors to see the true nature of God. Then they would realize that they had been justly punished for their abominations (33:27-29).

2. The captives in Babylon (33:30-33). Now that Jerusalem had fallen, Ezekiel was very popular among the exiles. They talked about him throughout the community. They were anxious to hear new revelations from God. They sat before Ezekiel as God's people seeking instruction. They regarded the prophet as an accomplished entertainer. Yet there were no signs of repentance. They implemented none of the measures demanded by the prophet. The heart of the exiles was bent toward covetousness. God warned Ezekiel not to be deceived by their words of love. Only when all of Ezekiel's prophecies came to pass would the attitude of the captives change. Then they would know that a true prophet had been in their midst.

CORRUPT LEADERS REPLACED
Ezekiel 34

In the parable of the evil shepherds Ezekiel described the corrupt leadership which was responsible for Judah's national destruction. As in Jeremiah 23 the term "shepherds" includes such persons as kings, princes, judges, priests and false prophets. In contrast to the evil shepherds, the prophet depicts the work of the divine Shepherd in regathering his sheep. Building on that thought, he predicts the coming of the messianic Shepherd.

A. Evil Shepherds (34:1-22).

God directed Ezekiel to prophesy against the shepherds of Israel, i.e., the leaders of the nation. These men were under a divine "woe." They were guilty of four crimes. (1) They used the flock of God for their own purposes. They ate the fat, i.e., the choicest parts of the animals. They clothed themselves with the wool. (2) They showed no concern for the flock of God. They did not strengthen the weak, heal the sick, bind up the broken, nor go after those who strayed. (3) They ruled the flock with force and rigor. (4) They were responsible for the scattering of the flock. The straying sheep became prey to every beast of the land, i.e., to the Assyrian and Babylonian kings who took the nation captive. They were scattered over the face of the land. No one searched them out (34:2-6). In short, the shepherds were both unfaithful and unconcerned.

Because of this dereliction of duty, the Lord pronounced a word of judgment against the evil shepherds. The threat contained therein was certain to come to pass for it was sealed with a divine oath. The Lord found the sins of the shepherds intolerable. He announced his opposition to these shepherds. He held them accountable for the fate of the flock. Therefore, God would remove these evil shepherds from office. They would not feed the sheep any more, nor would the sheep be food for those shepherds again (34:7-10).

B. The Divine Shepherd (34:11-22).

During the period of the exile, God himself would serve as the Shepherd of the flock.[5] In this role he would take eight actions: (1) He would seek out his sheep. (2) He would deliver them from the places where they had been scattered "on a cloudy and gloomy day," i.e., the dark day when they were carried away captive. (3) He would bring them out from among the peoples. (4) He would restore them to their fold, the land of Israel. (5) He would feed them upon the mountains and beside the streams "in good pasture, in rich pasture" (34:11-14).

The divine shepherd would also (6) lead his flock "to rest," i.e., to safety. (7) He would give special attention to the weak among the flock by seeking out the lost sheep, bringing back the stray, binding up the the wounded, and strengthening the sick. (8) The fat and strong sheep, however, he would "feed with judgment" and thereby destroy them. The powerful and wealthy would receive no favoritism (34:15f.). Clearly these words predict the return from captivity triggered by the edict of Cyrus in 536 BC (cf. Ezra 1:1f.).

In the day of restoration the Lord would administer fair judgment in two areas: he would judge "between one sheep and another," especially between the fat, i.e., the powerful, and the lean, i.e., the poor (vv. 17,20,22). He would also judge between "the rams and the male goats," i.e., between true sheep and those who were not really members of the flock. Neither the fat sheep nor the male goats deserved any special favors from the Lord. They had seized the good pasture for themselves. They had ruined the rest of the pasture and water for the flock. They had used force against the weak with shoulder and horns. Therefore, the Lord would destroy these powerful ones and rescue his true sheep from oppression by them (34:17-22). These predictions may refer to the turbulent times of intertestamental history when the people of God suffered immeasurably at the hands of their own leaders as well as from foreign invaders.

C. The Future Shepherd (34:23-31).

At some point after the restoration, God would set up over his flock "one shepherd." This shepherd is identified as "my servant David," i.e., he would be a second David or one from the line of David. He personally would feed the flock. Yahweh would be their God, but this new David would be "prince among them" (34:23f.). Jesus of Nazareth, who was descended from David (Matt 1:1), claimed to be the good shepherd (John 10:11,14).[6] That God would restore the Davidic dynasty in the person of an incomparable king is a prominent teaching of Old Testament prophetic literature.[7]

In conjunction with the rise of the Davidic Prince the Lord promised to make a new covenant with his people (cf. Jer 31:31). The covenant would be one characterized by "peace." The implications of this covenant of peace were presented in word pictures appropriate to the pastoral and agricultural mind-set. (1) Vicious beasts which threatened the flock would be eliminated from the land. Therefore, the flock of God would be able to dwell safely in wilderness and woods alike. (2) The inhabitants of Mt. Zion and the region around that hill would be blessed of God. Ezekiel described this blessing in terms of rains which come at appropriate times. "Showers of blessing" would fall throughout the land. (3) Abundant crops would make food plentiful thus eliminating the insecurity of uncertain harvests (34:25-27a).

In slightly less metaphorical language the Lord repeated the promises of blessing and security. God would set his people free from the yoke of bondage. No longer would Israel be "a prey to the nations, the beasts of the earth." They would live securely and no one would make them afraid. Shame would give way to fame, for God would "establish for them a renowned planting place," i.e., a place famous for its fertility. Famine would be a thing of the past. No more would they have to endure the insults of the Gentiles who were confident that Yahweh had failed his people in times of dire need. They would be secure in the knowledge that the Lord had redeemed them and was with them. They would understand that they were the sheep of God's pasture (34:27b-31). Some believe that these predictions are yet to be fulfilled, that they will not be realized until the Millennium. Others with more probability see in these words poetic descriptions of the new Israel of God, the church of Christ, which enjoys peace, security and blessing under the present-day rule of the scion from David's house.

ENEMIES REMOVED
Ezekiel 35

Yet another step in God's reconstruction program was the removal of national enemies. For the second time (cf. 25:12-14) the Lord rebuked and sentenced the Edomites, the descendants of Esau.[8] Here Edom seems to be singled out as one specific example of all the enemies who might attempt to thwart the restoration of Israel to her homeland. The fate of this people was placed in juxtaposition to the future of Israel. A general announcement of judgment was followed by two specific counts of an indictment with corresponding punishments.

A. Desolation of Edom (35:1-9).

Ezekiel was told to set his face toward Mt. Seir, i.e., Edom, and prophesy. He was to announce that Yahweh was against Mt. Seir. Shortly the Lord would stretch out his hand in judgment against that place. He would "lay waste" the cities of Edom. Thereafter that land would become a desolation. In this bitter experience the Edomites would come to know that Yahweh alone was God (35:1-4).

The Edomites had an "everlasting enmity" toward Israel. This hostility had manifested itself recently in the aid which they had given to the Babylonians during the siege of Jerusalem. They had "delivered the sons of Israel to the power of the sword during the time of their calamity," i.e., they had handed over to the enemy any fugitives who fell into their hands. The calamity was further described as "the time of the punishment of the end," i.e., the time when Judah's iniquity reached full measure and thus brought about her downfall (35:5).

Punishment for this national hatred was certain. It is confirmed by a divine oath ("as I live!").[9] God had prepared for Mt. Seir a bloody death. Since these people did not hate bloodshed, they would be pursued by bloodshed. The slain would fall throughout the mountains and valleys of Edom. Mt. Seir would thereby become "a waste and an everlasting desolation." Her cities would be uninhabited. Even travelers through that land would be cut off. Then they would know by experience that Yahweh is God (35:6-9).

B. Condemnation of Edom (35:10-15).

The Edomites coveted the land once occupied by Israel and Judah.[10] They fully intended to take possession of that abandoned area. God, however, was still in that land watching over it, protecting it, until the day he would bring his people back there. It belonged to him. The Edomites offended him by attempting to annex this territory. They reviled the mountains of Israel when they said: "they are laid desolate; they are given to us for food." By claiming God's land as their own the Edomites were speaking "arrogantly" against Yahweh. The Lord had heard their words. He would therefore deal with the Edomites in measures appropriate to their anger, envy and hatred against Israel. By bringing judgment upon Edom, God would make himself known among his own people. At the same time the Edomites would realize that God had heard all of their blasphemous words (35:10-13).

The Edomites rejoiced over the desolation of the inheritance of Israel. So all nations would rejoice over the desolation of Edom. Mt. Seir and all Edom would be a desolation. Then they would realize that Yahweh is God (35:14f.).

Endnotes

1. Walter R. Roehrs, "Ezekiel" in *The Biblical Expositor* (Philadelphia: Holman, 1960) 2:251.

2. Some prefer the reading of the Septuagint and Syriac manuscripts which read "in the eleventh year." Others believe that Ezekiel was using a system of counting years which had new year's day in the autumn. This would narrow the gap from eighteen to six months. See Herbert G. May, "The Book of Ezekiel" (Exegesis) in *The Interpreter's Bible* (New York: Abingdon, 1951) 6:247f.

3. An alternative interpretation is that the relative silence imposed upon Ezekiel at the time of his initial call (3:26f.) was lifted when the fugitive arrived from Jerusalem.

4. Bert H. Hall, "The Book of Ezekiel" in *The Wesleyan Bible Commentary* (Grand Rapids: Eerdmans, 1969) 3:456.

5. The comparison of Yahweh to a shepherd and his people to a flock is common in the Old Testament. See Pss 23, 100; Jer 23:1-8; Zech 11:4-17.

6. On the concept of Jesus as shepherd, see also Heb 13:20 and 1 Pet 2:25.

7. On the idea of a future ruler from the house of David see Amos 9:11; Hos 3:5; Isa 9:7; 55:3; Jer 23:5, 30:9; 33:15.

8. Edom stood under prophetic condemnation also in Obad, Jer 49:7-22 and Isa 34:1-17.

9. The phrase "as I live" is used frequently in the second phase of Ezekiel's ministry (e.g., 33:11, 27; 34:8; 35:6). This oath formula points to the most fundamental characteristic of Yahweh. In contrast to the lifeless idols worshiped among the heathen, Yahweh is the *living* God.

10. Others think that "these two lands" refers to Mt. Seir and Canaan.

CHAPTER THIRTY-THREE

Transformation and Restoration Ezekiel 36-39

Background of the Unit.

God's plan for the restoration of his people to their own land continues to unfold in this unit. Ezekiel put no date upon this material. These oracles could have come from almost any time after January 8, 585 BC, when the fugitive reached Babylon with an eyewitness account of the destruction of Jerusalem (33:21). Interpreters are sharply divided about the interpretation of these chapters. Have they already been fulfilled? or do future events hold the key to unlocking the mysteries of these chapters?

Outline of the Unit.

A. Restoration to the Land (chap. 36).
B. Rebirth of the Nation (chap. 37).
C. Rescue of the Faithful (chaps. 38).
D. Results of the Victory (chap. 39).

RESTORATION TO THE LAND
Ezekiel 36

Chapter 36 is the brightest chapter in the Book of Ezekiel. Here the prophet spoke of the redemption, repopulation and purification of the land of Israel.

A. Redemption of the Land (36:1-7).

Ezekiel began by describing the plight of the land after the fall of Jerusalem. The enemy coveted and claimed the mountains of Israel as their own. The land was desolate, the cities forsaken. The land had been swallowed up by the nations to which Israel had been prey. Observers now spoke derisively about the land (36:1-4).

How did the Lord react to the plight of the land? He had spoken against the surrounding nations, especially Edom, in the fire of his jealousy or zeal for his people. He regarded with anger the joy of their heart and the disdain of their soul as they contemplated the occupation of Israel. He could not restrain himself when Israel suffered the reproach of the nations. The Lord had taken an oath that the nations would soon bear their own reproach, i.e., they would experience the same fate which Judah had experienced (36:5-7).

B. Repopulation of the Land (36:8-15).

Yahweh is now *for* the land. Therefore the land of Israel would yet be tilled and sown, would yet be fruitful. God's people were about to return to that land. The Lord would multiply "all the house of Israel" upon that land. Cities would be inhabited, waste places built up. Men and cattle would be multiplied so that the land would be inhabited as in former times. In fact, the Lord promised to treat the land better than he had treated it before. Those who repopulate the desolate land would be "my people Israel." God would cause his people to walk on that land, to possess it. The land would again be their inheritance. No more would those hills rob God's people of their children through war, pestilence or famine. This turn of fortune would help the people have a better perspective on the true nature of God (36:8-12).

A popular saying about the land would be silenced in that day.

Because of what had happened to those who dwelled there, people were saying to the land: "You are a devourer of men and have bereaved your nation of children." That may have been true once, but not any more. No longer would the land hear the insults of surrounding nations. The land would not again devour its people because she would never again cause the nation which dwelled upon it to stumble into idolatry. The same judgment which devastated Judah, devastated the Canaanite population which had led God's people so frequently into sin (36:13-15).

C. Purification of the Land (36:16-38).

When the house of Israel was living in their own land they defiled it by their ways and deeds. Their idolatry rendered the land as unclean as a menstruous woman before God. From Canaanite religion the Israelites learned calloused disregard for human life. Because of the blood shed on the land, God poured out his wrath upon his people. He scattered them among the nations. He judged them according to their ways. This judgment, however, resulted in the profanation of God's name among the nations. Gentiles mocked a God who would allow his people to be cast forth from their land. God was concerned about his "holy name," i.e., his reputation (36:16-21).

Israel was totally undeserving of any favorable action on the part of the Lord. Yet he was about to act for the sake of his holy name. What God planned to do would vindicate the holiness of his great name which had been profaned among the nations. Gentiles would come to realize that Yahweh was God when he demonstrated his holiness by acting in grace on behalf of his people (36:22f.).

What dramatic move did God plan to make? He would gather up his people and bring them back to their land. He would then cleanse his people from the filthiness of idolatry. Like a priest performing a purification rite the Lord would sprinkle clean water upon them. From those purified souls the Lord would remove the heart of stone, i.e., obstinate heart, and replace it with a "new heart, a heart of flesh," i.e., one which was tender and responsive. He would fill them with a "new spirit," his Holy Spirit which would enable them to walk in his statutes. This new people would be conscientious about observing all of the divine ordinances (36:24-27).

Ezekiel outlined several consequences of the regeneration of Israel. They would dwell in the land which God had given their fathers. They would enjoy a very special relationship with the Lord. God would save them from uncleanness, i.e., help them to overcome it. God would restore fertility to the land. He would speak to the grain on their behalf. There would be no more famine, and no more reproach caused by famine. On the contrary, God would increase for them the "fruit of the tree and the produce of the field." Overwhelmed by the love of God, the redeemed would loathe their former life of sin; they would be ashamed and confounded because of their ways. They would understand the grace of God (36:28-32).

The land as well as the people would be restored. The regenerate people would repopulate the desolate land of Canaan. Cities would be inhabited and fortified. The land would be tilled. Those who passed by would marvel at the beauty of the place, comparing it hyperbolically to the garden of Eden. The restored land would bear testimony to the power and faithfulness of God (36:33-36).

The restored people of God would pray for an increase in the population. God would answer that prayer. He would increase their numbers like a holy flock such as filled Jerusalem during festivals. The waste cities would be filled with flocks of men. This glorious increase in the numbers of the people of God would give further insight into the true nature of Yahweh (36:37-38).

REBIRTH OF THE NATION
Ezekiel 37

The vision of the valley of dry bones is perhaps the best-known passage in the book. Many are familiar with the Negro spiritual which made this chapter famous. Actually chapter 37 contains two powerful passages, one a vision, the other a parable. Both depict the rebirth of the nation of Israel after the devastation of exile.

A. Vision of Dry Bones (37:1-14).

Ezekiel felt again the "hand of the Lord," i.e., the power of God, upon him.[1] In the spirit, i.e., in a visionary experience, he was taken to the edge of a valley (37:1). There he not only saw a spectacular vision, he heard an authoritative explanation thereof.

1. Presentation of the vision (37:2-10). The valley to which Ezekiel visionally was transported was full of bones. As in his lengthy visionary trip back to Jerusalem (chaps. 8-11), Ezekiel was an active participant in the vision. Here the Lord caused the prophet to pass through the midst of the bones in his vision. He made two observations: (1) there were very many bones on the surface of the valley, i.e., unburied and open to public view; and (2) the bones were very dry, i.e., in an advanced state of decomposition. The Lord piqued Ezekiel's curiosity in the meaning of the bones by asking a question: "Son of man, can these bones live?" A man of lesser faith would have responded negatively. Ezekiel, however, wisely responded: "O Lord God, Thou knowest." For the Lord nothing was impossible. If he so willed, even those decaying bones could be resurrected to life (37:2-3).

The Lord then commanded Ezekiel to prophesy over those bones, to call upon them to hear the word of the Lord. God promised those bones that he would enable them by his Spirit to live again. He would put sinews upon them, and cover them with flesh. Those resurrected bones would know for certain that Yahweh alone is God (37:4-6).

Ezekiel carried out his instructions. With dramatic swiftness things began to happen. He first noticed a noise—a rattling—as bones came together "bone to its bone," i.e., each bone joined the appropriate bone in the skeleton. As he continued to look at this weird scene he noticed sinews coming upon the skeletons followed by flesh rapidly covering the bones. Still there was no evidence of life in these corpses for "there was no breath in them." The double use of the word "behold" suggests Ezekiel's amazement and shock at what he was witnessing (37:7f.).

Ezekiel was now directed to prophesy to the "breath" or spirit of these dead ones. He was to command their breath to come from "the four winds," i.e., from four directions, and "breathe on these slain that they come to life." Ezekiel did as he was told. The breath or spirit came into the corpses and they lived. When they rose to their feet Ezekiel could see that they were an exceeding great army (37:9f.).

2. Explanation of the vision (37:11-14). Fortunately the explanation of the vision of dry bones is given in the text. The bones represent "the whole house of Israel." As a nation the captives regarded themselves as dead and disjointed. In spite of the promises of restoration which Ezekiel had been making since the fall of Jerusalem, they were convinced that their nation could not live again. They felt that forever they were "cut off" from their land, their Temple and even one another (37:11).

God assured these discouraged captives that he would resurrect his people from this death-like captivity. He would open their graves and then cause his people to come out of their graves. Then the Lord would bring them back to their land. This miraculous transformation would be accomplished through the Holy Spirit of God which God would put within his people. When these glorious events transpired they would know that Yahweh was God, and that he was absolutely faithful to his word (37:12-14).

B. Parable of the Sticks (37:15-28).

The Lord directed Ezekiel to perform his last action parable. This one would involve two sticks which had been appropriately labeled. On the first stick he was to write, "for Judah and for the sons of Israel, his companions." On the second stick he was to write, "for Joseph, the stick of Ephraim, and all the house of Israel his companions." He was then to hold the two sticks together so that they appeared to be one stick in his hand (37:15-17).

The strange action of Ezekiel would provoke inquiry on the part of the captives. He was to explain that the sticks were being used as object lessons. The stick of Ephraim represented the former Northern Kingdom. The stick of Judah represented the Davidic kingdom. The joining of the sticks pointed to a time when all God's people would be united in one kingdom (37:18-20). Certainly no basis exists in this text for the strange Mormon teaching that the sticks refer to two scrolls. According to the convoluted interpretation of this cult, Ezekiel was prophesying that one day the Book of Mormon (the stick or scroll of Ephraim) would be joined to the Bible (the stick or scroll of Judah) to form the complete revelation of God.

The parable of the sticks means just this: God will reunite his fractured people. The distinction between Ephraim and Judah, Northern Kingdom and Southern Kingdom, would no longer exist. God would gather the true "sons of Israel" from all the lands where they had been scattered over the years and bring them back to their own land. They would be "one nation" in the land, "on the mountains of Israel," i.e., their unity would transcend any of the old geographical barriers. This reunited people would constitute one kingdom, ruled by one king (37:21-22). This prophecy was fulfilled over a span of years. God began to gather his people in 538 BC. The "one king" who would be king for all of them is an obvious allusion to the Messiah. Jesus announced that the kingdom was at hand. When he died, rose and ascended he began his kingdom rule over the new Israel of God.

Ezekiel cited several factors which either contribute to the national unity, or else grow out of it. (1) God's people would share a common aversion to pagan practices. They would no longer defile themselves with their idols, with their "detestable things," nor with their "transgressions." (2) They would experience a common salvation. God would "deliver them from all their dwelling places in which they have sinned." This may be an Old Testament way of saying that God would translate them out of the kingdom of darkness and into the kingdom of his dear son (Col 1:13). (3) They would share a common cleansing and (4) a special relationship to God (37:23).

That unity of God's people would be possible because (5) they would be united in loyalty to the rightful king. Ezekiel designated that king as "David my servant," i.e., a king like David and from the line of David. This Davidic ruler would be the one shepherd of the flock of God. (6) The kingdom would be governed by the ordinances and statutes of God to which every citizen would be committed.

(7) They would share a common inheritance, viz., "the land which I gave to Jacob my servant, in which your fathers lived." They would live on that land "forever," ruled by the Davidic prince "forever" (37:25). The close tie between the *land* and its ruler suggests that *land* in this and similar prophecies points to the kingdom of the future king. The geographical boundaries of that kingdom then must be defined by later revelation. A "forever" kingdom ruled by a "forever" prince points to a new order of things. Certainly no thousand year millennium can be read into this prediction. The New Testament expands on the land promise by affirming that Christ's authority, i.e.,

his kingdom, is world-wide in scope (Matt 28:18). Actually Abraham and his descendants were heirs "to the world" (Rom 4:13), of which Old Testament Canaan was but the token and type. Those who follow King Jesus shall inherit the earth (Matt 5:5). New Testament Israel anticipates the ushering in of the new heavens and earth wherein dwells righteousness (1 Pet 3:12).[2]

Still other factors would bind together the people of God in the future. (8) They would all live under the "covenant of peace"[3] which is described as "an everlasting covenant."[4] This is that new and better covenant of which Jeremiah prophesied (31:31). Jesus is the mediator[5] and the Apostles are the ministers of this covenant (2 Cor 3:6). God would "place" (NASB) or "establish" (NIV) his people under this covenant. He would "multiply"[6] them. The reference is probably to the influx of Gentiles who become part of the New Testament Israel of God (37:26).

(9) The unified people of God would worship at the "sanctuary" which God would set in their midst "forever." Ezekiel further described this sanctuary as God's "dwelling place."[7] The presence of this sanctuary "sanctifies Israel," i.e., sets God's people apart from the world at large. Nations, i.e., Gentiles, will come to have a better understanding of the nature of Yahweh when they observe the way in which he sanctifies his people (37:26-28).

Ezekiel focused on the messianic sanctuary in the closing chapters of his book. Indeed, the restoration of the sanctuary is the climax of all that this prophet had to say. Ezekiel had already demonstrated that the term *sanctuary* need not be restricted to the physical building constructed by Solomon and reconstructed after the exile by Zerubbabel. In 11:16 God himself is the sanctuary for his people. Here the announcement of the establishment of the sanctuary is followed immediately by the clause, "I will be their God and they will be my people" suggests that the *sanctuary* here is the presence of God among his people. In the person of Jesus, God dwelled in the midst of his people (John 1:14).[8] Given the messianic thrust of the present passage, the *forever* sanctuary which will be in the midst of the new Israel of God is best interpreted as a reference to that spiritual temple described by New Testament writers.[9]

THE RESCUE OF THE FAITHFUL
Ezekiel 38

Chapters 38-39 correct the mistaken notion that God's people would face no further difficulty after the restoration. Indeed, Ezekiel painted a picture here of the intense danger to which the people of God would be subject. At some point the territory of Israel would be invaded by hordes from the north intent on destroying God's people completely. These chapters are apocalyptic, i.e., highly symbolic.

At least four very different attempts have been made to solve the difficult questions posed by these chapters. (1) Some hold the historical or preterist view which identifies the attacking force with some great enemy of Israel during the restoration or intertestamental periods.[10] Though not too popular today, this approach to the chapter is not easily refuted. (2) Others take a literal futuristic view of the passage. Ezekiel is describing an invasion which has not yet occurred. Usually this invasion is placed after the Millennium by these writers. They frequently identify *Rosh* here as Russia, and Gog as some leader of Russia. They contend that this prophecy depicts a Russian invasion of the modern state of Israel. A number of writers, however, have pointed out that hard etymological evidence linking Russia and *rosh* is lacking.[11] (3) According to the prophetic parable view, chapters 38-39 illustrate a great truth. No specific invasion is intended. The chapters should be viewed as a general promise of God's deliverance of his people from any and every attack by external enemies. (4) In the future idealistic view Ezekiel is here describing a final climactic struggle between the forces of good and evil. The notes which follow are based on this fourth approach to these difficult chapters.

A. Introduction to the Foe (38:1-2).

The leader of the invading forces is called Gog. He is from the land of Magog. He is "chief prince of Meshach" (NIV). Meshach has been identified as the country of Lydia (in Asia Minor) whose first king was Gyges (Midas). Gog is also leader of the country of Tubal which likewise is situated in Asia Minor. The exact meaning of the name *Gog* is unknown.[12] Gog is probably best not identified with any specific individual past, present or future. He is simply the leader of the last all-out effort to exterminate God's people.

After introducing the leader of the forces opposed to God's people, the lengthy Gog oracle proceeds through seven thought units each of which begins with the messenger formula "Thus says the Lord God."

B. Preparation of the Foe (38:3-9).

The Lord declared his hostility to Gog. This invader would be forcibly turned back like a wild beast (cf. 29:4). The same was true of Gog's handsome, well-equipped allies. Gog's army was made up of contingents from all over the known world.[13] This was probably intended to symbolize the world as it opposes the people of God. Thus the prophet announced the result of Gog's plan even before he describes the invasion itself (38:3-6).

These forces were commanded to prepare themselves. "After many days" they would be summoned by the Lord. They were merely pawns in his hand. In "the latter years" this force would undertake the invasion.[14] The land which they would attack is described as one that had been "rescued from the sword," a land that had suffered greatly already, a land which enjoyed serenity. The Lord gathered this force to the mountains of Israel. Gog and his troops would cover the entire land like a threatening storm cloud (38:7-9).

C. Motivation of the Foe (38:10-13).

Ezekiel described the planning which went into Gog's attack against the people of God. Gog would devise an "evil plan." The plan was militarily feasible. The tyrant anticipated sweeping down upon a people who are both defenseless and unsuspecting. He believed that such an attack was potentially rewarding. He anticipated confiscating all the wealth which those who had been gathered out of the nations had acquired. Furthermore, to conquer this people would place Gog at "the center of the world," i.e., in a strategic position. In this endeavor Gog was encouraged by other nations of the area which hoped that some of the plundered wealth would rebound to them. To summarize, Gog calculated that the attack against the people of God would be relatively easy and extremely profitable.

D. Invasion by the Foe (38:14-16).

God's people would be enjoying peace and serenity at the time Gog and his forces swooped down upon them "out of the remote parts of the north." Ezekiel represented the final attack against God's people as coming from the north because that was the direction from which the enemies of Israel traditionally came.[15] The invaders would move with lightning speed for all of them would ride upon horses. This vast army would cover the land of Israel like a cloud. The situation would seem desperate. Yet Gog would not realize that Yahweh was maneuvering him into a situation which would rebound to the recognition of God. "In the last days" the Lord would be "sanctified," i.e., recognized as God and treated with reverence, by the Gentiles because of what he would do to the forces of Gog.

E. Confrontation with the Foe (38:17-23).

Ezekiel next explained how Yahweh would be sanctified in the destruction of Gog. A question was directed to Gog, the implication of which is that this invasion had been anticipated by the prophets of God who spoke "in former days." The reference is probably to the predictions of Isaiah (34:2; 66:15-18), Jeremiah (e.g., 4:5ff.) and Zephaniah (chap. 1). The point is that this invasion would not take God by surprise. He was waiting for Gog's advance with "fury," "anger" and "blazing wrath." In his zeal to defend his people the Lord would unleash against Gog a great "earthquake." Mountains would be thrown down, every wall would crumble. All creation, and especially all the men who were on the face of the earth, would tremble in the presence of the Lord (38:17-20).

The Lord would enter into judgment with Gog with other weapons in addition to earthquake. God would call for a "sword" against the invaders. The result would be that "every man's sword will be against his brother," i.e., the enemy would fight against one another. The Lord would bring pestilence and bloodshed against the armies of Gog. He would rain hailstones, fire and brimstone upon them. In these mighty acts the God of Israel would "magnify" and "sanctify" himself, he would make himself known in the sight of "many nations." Gentiles would come to know that Yahweh alone is God (38:21-23).

RESULTS OF THE VICTORY
Ezekiel 39

The address to Gog continues in chapter 39 with some repetition of the themes of chapter 38, but with a different emphasis. The closing verse of chapter 38 sets the theme for this chapter: "And I shall magnify myself, sanctify myself, and make myself known in the sight of many nations; and they will know that I am the Lord." Thus chapter 39 focuses on the results of the victory over Gog.

A. Dramatic Destruction (39:1-8).

Ezekiel used brilliant word pictures to emphasize the ultimate and complete destruction of the enemies of God's people. Like the first word addressed to Gog, this one also begins with a declaration of divine hostility: "Behold, I am against you, O Gog." Again the prophet emphasized that Gog's movements were being orchestrated by God. The Lord would strip the invaders of their weapons. Then Gog and all of his troops would fall upon the "mountains of Israel." Predatory birds would feed upon the corpses of the fallen host of Gog. Furthermore, even while Gog was attempting to conquer the people of God, judgment fire would fall upon the lands from which the invaders came (39:1-6).

The destruction of Gog would once again reveal to Israel the holiness of God's "name," i.e., his person. Never again would that holy name be profaned by those who regarded Yahweh as no different than the gods of this world. Gentiles would know that Yahweh is God, "the Holy One in Israel." That day of vindication for the Lord was sure to come. God declared it through Ezekiel just as he had done through the prophets who had preceded him (39:7f.).[16]

B. Complete Destruction (39:9-10)

The completeness of the destruction of Gog is driven home with four word pictures. First, Ezekiel depicted Israel taking from the fallen foe an immense quantity of spoils. For seven years the people of God would have no need for ordinary fuel for they would be able to burn the weapons lost by the enemy in their defeat. The number *seven* conveys the ideal of completeness (39:9f.).

A second picture focuses on the lengthy efforts to cleanse the land. God would provide a valley[17] for the purpose of a mass burial site. Because of the number of corpses buried there the place would be called Hamon-Gog, "multitude of Gog." Persons wishing to transverse that valley would not be able to do so because of the number of corpses. This mass burial effort would last for "seven months." The symbolic number hints that literal interpretation is not appropriate here. The entire population of Israel would be involved in the effort. Their noble efforts would gain for themselves notoriety. At the same time their efforts would underscore the glorious victory of God (39:11-13).

In a third word picture Ezekiel described a commemorative city which would be built. After the seven months, a permanent committee would handle the burials of corpses scattered throughout the land. Travelers would aid the committee by marking the location of human bones. A city would be built near the burial site to commemorate the victory. The city would be called "Hamonah," i.e., "multitude" (39:11-16). The thought is that not a trace of Gog's army would remain to remind the Lord's people of that fearful invasion (39:14-16).

Ezekiel's fourth picture of the complete destruction of Gog is the most gruesome. That picture might be entitled "The Judgment Banquet." God invited the birds and beasts to come to the mountains of Israel to feast upon the flesh of the mighty and to drink the blood of the princes of the earth. Ezekiel likened the mighty warriors of Gog to rams, lambs, goats and bullocks. The Lord promised his invited guests that they would eat until full and drink to the point of intoxication. They would be filled at God's banquet table with horses and horsemen, with mighty men of war (39:17-20). Chronologically this description should come before the picture of the burial of the fallen armies of Gog. Its placement here signals the astute interpreter that these judgment scenes are not to be pressed literally.

C. Ultimate Vindication (39:21-24).

The destruction of Gog would be the vindication of Yahweh in three specific areas. First, the nations would regard the mighty deliverance as an act revealing God's glory, his judgment and his hand or power. Second, Israel's faith would be confirmed by what happened to Gog. From that day forward they would know beyond the shadow of doubt that Yahweh alone is God. Third, the nations (Gentiles) would come to have a proper perspective on the exile of Israel. No more would they assume that Israel's exile resulted from the impotence of Yahweh. Rather they would realize that Israel had been taken into exile because they had (1) committed iniquity and transgression; and (2) dealt treacherously with their God. According to their uncleanness and transgression Yahweh had dealt with them. He hid his face from them, i.e., no longer aided them against their enemies. What is more, he actually "gave them into the hands of their adversaries." Thus the exile revealed the justice of God. It was part of his long range plan for his people (39:21-24).

D. Final Consolation (39:25-29).

The rehearsal of the reasons for the tragic exile to Babylon triggered a need to conclude the oracle concerning Gog with consolation for the captives. First, the Lord assured these discouraged people that his attitude toward them had changed. He was about to restore the "fortunes of Jacob" by showing his mercy to the "whole house of Israel." He promised to be "zealous" for his holy name which had been profaned by the lowly circumstances of the people who honored that name (39:25).

Second, the Lord assured the discouraged captives that their attitude toward him would change. Once they had been restored to their homeland eventually they would forget those disgraceful deeds and treacherous acts which precipitated the exile. Dwelling securely in their own land, these people would be prime evidence of the power and compassion of God. The restoration of the exiles would cause Gentiles to "sanctify" Yahweh, i.e., revere him as holy and worthy of worship (39:26f.).

Third, God would have a new relationship with his people in that day. They would have a new understanding of God as they saw his providence at work first in the deportation to Babylon, then in the restoration to Canaan. Not one of the true people of God would be left behind in foreign lands. The restoration would mark the time when God ceased to hide his face from them. This new relationship would be possible because the Lord would pour out his Holy Spirit upon the house of Israel (39:28f.).

Endnotes

1. Four other times Ezekiel noted that the hand of the Lord came upon him: 1:3; 3:14, 22; and 8:1. This special overwhelming power of God enabled Ezekiel to be transported in body or spirit to other places and to see spectacular visions.

2. Martin Wyngaarden points out the latent spiritualization of the Holy Land or inheritance concept. He cites the following passages: Num 18:20; Deut 18:2; Pss 73:26; 16:5; 142:5; 119:57; Jer 10:16; and 51:19. He comments: "Hence we see that in the Old Testament the primary inheritance, the real portion of Israel was not Canaan, but Jehovah himself, and only in a secondary way whatever Jehovah might give to his people." The concept of the inheritance for God's people receives "evident spiritualization" in the following New Testament passages: Matt 5:5; Rom 4:13; Col 3:14; Gal 3:29; Heb 9:15; 11:10; 1 Pet 1:3-5. Wyngaarden concludes: "Thus the Messiah's prophesied rule over the land of Israel's inheritance becomes his rule over the new heavens and new earth." See *The Future of the Kingdom in Prophecy and Fulfillment* (Grand Rapids: Baker, 1955) 91-93.

3. The terminology *covenant of peace* was used earlier by Ezekiel in 34:25 and by Isaiah in 54:10. For a similar concept see Hos 2:18.

4. The future covenant is called *an everlasting covenant* by Isa (55:3; 61:8; cf. 59:21) and Jer (32:40) as well as by Ezek (16:60; 37:26). See also Ps 89:3f.

5. On the new and better covenant under which Christians live, see also Heb 7:22; 8:6-10; 9:15-20; and 12:24.

6. Other references to the messianic multiplication of God's people: Isa 9:3; Jer 3:16; 23:3; 30:19; 33:22; Ezek 36:10f.; 36:37.

7. Isaiah also spoke of the house of the Lord in conjunction with the messianic age. See Isa 56:5-7; 60:7; 66:20.

8. Jesus clearly referred to himself as God's temple in John 2:19-21.

9. The New Testament temple stretches from earth to heaven. Christ sits now upon his throne in its holy of holies (Heb 9). On earth this spiritual house is built of precious stones carved from the quarry of life by the Gospel of Christ (1 Pet 2:5). The church of Christ is the temple of the Holy Spirit of God (2 Cor 6:16).

10. Cambyses the Persian, Alexander the Great, Antiochus the Great and Mithridates king of Pontus have all been nominated. The best case can be made for identifying Magog as Syria and Gog as Antiochus Epiphanes, that ruthless invader of Palestine who is mentioned so prominently in the Book of Daniel (Dan 8:9-27; 11:21-35).

11. *Rosh* appears six hundred times in the Old Testament, never as a place name. Not until the Middle Ages did anyone suggest that *rosh* was a name for Russia. In several modern versions *rosh* is not even translated as a noun but as an adjective modifying *prince*. Cf. the NIV, *chief prince of Meshach*. Even if it is a noun, *rosh* is linked here with *Meshech* and *Tubal,* places now generally accepted as being in Anatolia. The phrase *uttermost part of the earth* cannot be forced to support the Russia view. In Jeremiah that phrase meant a country no more distant than Babylon. See Jer 6:22.

12. Some trace Gog to a root meaning "darkness." Others think it is an artificial name derived from the name of his country Magog. Still others point out the similarity between the name Gog and Gyges, the first king of Meshach=Lydia.

13. The allies of Gog were (1) Persia; (2) Cush or Ethiopia; (3) Put or modern Libya; (4) Gomer, i.e., the Cimmerians who had settled in central Anatolia; and (5) the house of Togarmah, a city in eastern Anatolia.

14. Some argue that the reference here is to the *latter years* of the Old Testament age, and thus they find in this passage a prediction of the invasion of Palestine by Antiochus Epiphanes in 168 BC. Others think the reference is to the *latter years* of all the ages.

15. On the enemy from the north see Jer 1:14f.; 4:6; 6:1, 22; 10:22; 13:20; 16:15; 25:9, 26.

16. On "the day of the Lord" see Joel chs. 2 and 3; Zeph 1; Amos 5:18; Isa 24; Jer 25:32-38.

17. A number of suggested identifications for the valley have been proposed ranging from the valley of Abarim near Mt. Nebo to the valley of Megiddo. The valley is said to be *east of the sea,* but whether the Dead Sea or the Sea of Galilee is not clear. The text may be suggesting that the Lord would create a new valley as a burial place, perhaps by means of earthquake (cf. 38:19).

CHAPTER THIRTY-FOUR

Vision of a New Age
Ezekiel 40-48

Background of the Unit.

In chapters 40-48 Ezekiel reached the climax of his hope for the future. The restored people of God would have a Temple and God would be in it. Chronologically these are most likely the last words which Ezekiel addressed to the captives, but not the last words which he spoke (cf. 29:17). This section is dated to the twenty-fifth year of the exile, the first month, the tenth day of the month. On the modern calendar this would equate to April 28, 573 BC. For some twelve years Ezekiel had been engaged a hope-inspiring ministry (cf. 33:21).

On his visionary trip to Jerusalem (chaps. 8-11) Ezekiel saw the Temple profaned by idol worship of the worst sort. He saw the Lord depart from that once sacred place. Since the Lord was no longer in his Temple, any expectation that he would defend that place against Chaldean attack was wishful thinking.

After the destruction of Jerusalem Ezekiel began to encourage the captives to look forward to a new age. He had announced the restoration of the captives and the rebirth of their nation. He had hinted that in their homeland they would have a sanctuary (cf. 37:26,28). Now he expanded upon these themes in glorious detail. The Temple of the future would again be a holy place, and God would take up residence in it (43:5). That Temple would be part of a holy land, a land abundantly and supernaturally blessed by the Lord.

A. Interpretation of the Unit.

The last vision of Ezekiel is particularly difficult to interpret. The tedious details become manageable only with the aid of diagrams. Major translations utilize the measuring units of Ezekiel's day, and the significance of these is often lost on the modern reader. Even more difficult is the application of this entire section. How did the Holy Spirit intend for these chapters to be understood? Three main positions have been taken.

First, some believe that Ezekiel intended these chapters to be the pattern of a new Temple to be built by the exiles who would return to Canaan. Some arguments, however, weigh against this approach. (1) Those who led the Jews back to Canaan built their Temple on the foundations of the old Temple, and fashioned their worship according to the Mosaic not Ezekielian instruction. (2) Some aspects of Ezekiel's depiction could not have been executed even had the leaders so desired. For example, how would they have constructed the stream of living water which Ezekiel described in chapter 47?

A second approach sees the fulfillment of Ezekiel 40-48 as yet future. Prior to the second coming of Christ, Jews will convert to Christ in large numbers. They will return to Canaan and divide it among themselves as here specified. They will then erect a Temple after the specifications here set forth and institute a worship program in accord with the teaching of Ezekiel. In the light of the Book of Hebrews, however, the animal sacrificial system was but a temporary provision to prepare the way for the perfect sacrifice of Christ. That this system would be revived and that Christ would in some way preside over these sacrifices is difficult to imagine.

The best approach is to see these chapters as illustrative of spiritual truths. The main points thus symbolized in these chapters are these: God would provide for his people a Temple, a priesthood and a worship system related to, but different from, that which they had formerly known. A united people, including Gentiles, would occupy the inheritance which God had promised to their forefathers.

Outline of the Unit.

A. Introduction to the Vision (40:1-4).
B. The Future Temple (40:1-43:17).
C. The Future Worship (43:18-44:31).
D. The Future Service (chaps. 45-46).
E. The Future Land (chaps. 47-48).

INTRODUCTION TO THE VISION
Ezekiel 40:1-4

On April 28, 573 BC, the hand of the Lord came upon Ezekiel and he experienced another visionary transmigration. In his vision he was brought to the land of Israel for the second time (cf. 8:1-3). He was taken to "a very high mountain." Since the highest peaks in Canaan are only about 3500 feet, this language is best taken as symbolical. On the southern end of that mountain he saw "a structure like a city." Old Testament prophets frequently represent the Messianic city of God as being on a high mountain.[1] The idea is that God's kingdom would be exalted over all the kingdoms of this world (40:1f.).

In his vision Ezekiel was brought closer to the city. In its gateway he observed "a man whose appearance was like the appearance of bronze," i.e., his entire body glistened in the sunlight. This "man" appears to have been an angelic being. He is clearly distinguished from Yahweh in 43:6. The man was holding in his hand two measuring instruments: a line of flax and a rod. The rod was six cubits long, but each cubit was a hand span (six inches) longer than the usual eighteen inches. The angelic figure admonished Ezekiel to hear, see and pay close attention to everything he was about to show him. The prophet was told that he had been brought to that spot so that he might see these sights and then subsequently declare to the house of Israel all that he had seen (40:3f.).

THE FUTURE TEMPLE
Ezekiel 40:5-43:17

The angelic guide conducted Ezekiel on a tour of the visionary Temple. Each area was carefully measured and described. These details are regarded by westerners as boring; but eastern people loved to describe their sacred buildings in minute detail. Ezekiel's experience might be likened to a young couple who go frequently to the site of their future dream home. They step off the dimensions of the home, perhaps sketch in the dust its configuration. They relish every moment of the anticipation. In their minds they can visualize that home in all its grandeur. Every effort expended, every penny saved, brings the dream closer to realization. So Ezekiel is given the mental picture of that sacred house which was so dear to the hearts of the Jews (cf. 24:25).

The angel guide spoke very little during the measuring of the future Temple.[2] Apparently not much else needed to be said. Having come from a priestly family, Ezekiel was very familiar with the Temple environment. The guide may have called out the measurements of the Temple areas and furniture. On the other hand, Ezekiel simply may have observed the actions of the man and then made his own calculations. After Ezekiel saw the glory of Yahweh return to the Temple (43:4), he received extensive direct communication from the Lord.

That which was not mentioned in the Temple description is significant. No building materials were named. No command was found to follow this pattern. The ark of the covenant is not mentioned, nor are the lamp stand, table of showbread and court lavers.

A. The Temple Courts (40:5-47).

The sacred house or Temple proper was surrounded by two courts, an outer court where even Gentiles might worship, and an inner court where the priests officiated at the sacred altar.

1. The outer court (40:5-27). Ezekiel observed first the wall which enclosed the outer court (40:5). It was one reed (about ten feet) thick and one reed tall. The prophet was taken to the eastern gate of the outer court. He walked up seven steps into and then through a gatehouse. The walkway through the gatehouse was twenty-two feet wide. It was flanked on both sides by three guard chambers (40:5-16). Passing through a porch of pillars Ezekiel was ushered into the outer court (40:17-19) which extended about 850 feet from north to south and about 170 feet from the porch of the outer gatehouse to the gatehouse of the inner court. Ezekiel noted that the wall of the outer court contained northern (40:20-23) and southern gate complexes (40:24-27) which were identical to the one on the eastern side of the court.

2. The inner court (40:28-47). The inner court was a square of about 170 feet. It also had three entrances or gatehouses, one on its southern (40:28-31), eastern (40:32-34) and northern sides (40:35-37). Ezekiel ascended eight steps to enter one of these gatehouses. The tables[3] and instruments for the preparation of sacrifices were kept in these gatehouses (40:38-43). Chambers for Temple singers and priests[4] were adjacent to the inner court (40:44-47).

B. The Temple Proper (40:48-41:26).

The angelic guide next led Ezekiel up the ten steps to the *house*, i.e., the Temple proper. They passed through the large porch (35 x 20 feet) which featured two huge pillars at the entrance (40:48-49). The building itself was divided into two unequal rooms, the holy place (70 x 35 feet) and holy of holies which was a square of thirty-five feet (41:1-4).[5] As in Solomon's Temple, three stories of small chambers were constructed on the exterior wall of the sacred building on three sides. Each story contained thirty chambers which were entered from the court on the north and the south. These chambers probably served as storage rooms (41:5-11). Behind the sacred building was a building or court called the separate area (41:12).[6] The sacred building with free space on three sides formed another square of 170 feet (41:13-15).

The sacred house was decorated with wall and ceiling paneling which had inlays of alternating cherubim and palm trees. Each cherub had two of its four faces exhibited (since four could not be conveniently represented on a plain surface)—a man's face directed toward the palm tree on one side, and a young lion's face turned towards the palm tree on the other side (cf. 1:5-10). This ornamentation was employed from the ground to above the door (41:16-21).

Chart No. 13

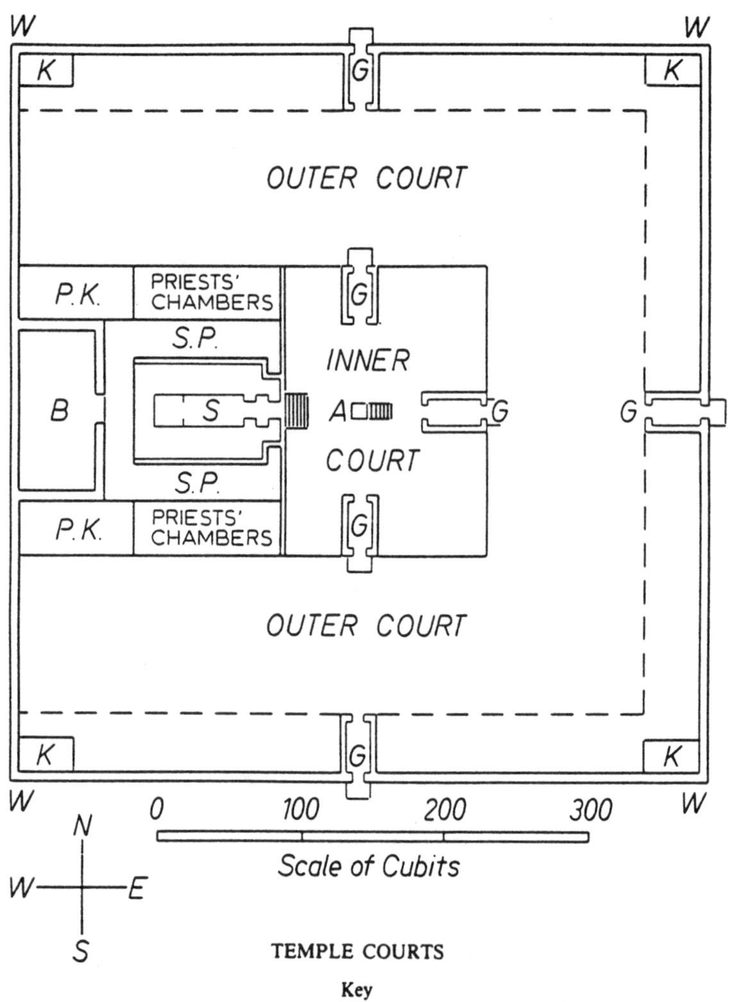

TEMPLE COURTS

Key

A. Altar
B. Building mentioned in 41:12
G. Gatehouse
K. Kitchens
P.K. Priests' Kitchens
S. Sanctuary
S.P. The Separate Place
W. Surrounding Wall

The altar of incense in the Holy Place was made of plain wood (41:22).[7] The swinging doors in front of the Holy Place and the Holy of Holies were decorated with cherubim and palm trees (41:23-25). The porch had recessed windows and palm tree decorations on its walls (41:26).

C. The Temple Buildings (42:1-20).

Ezekiel was taken back to the outer court to witness the measuring of the priests' chambers. Two three-storied buildings flanked the rear of the Temple area on the north and south. A third identical building may have flanked the inner court on the east.[8] These chambers served as dining halls and robing rooms for the priests when they officiated at the Temple (42:1-14).

Having completed his tour of the courts and buildings of the Temple area, the guide took Ezekiel through the eastern gate. His final measurements were those of the outer wall (cf. 40:5) which surrounded the entire Temple area. This wall was found to form a square of five hundred reeds which equals about 3,062,500 square yards (42:15-20).

D. The Temple Glory (43:1-12).

After completing the trip around the outer wall, the angelic guide brought Ezekiel back to the eastern gate of the Temple, the same gate from which he saw the divine glory depart some twenty-five years earlier (cf. 11:1,22f.). He now was privileged to witness the divine glory coming from the east to occupy the Temple which he had just toured. He heard a roaring sound as of many waters. The dazzling glory of God illuminated the entire area. Ezekiel likened what he saw here to his original vision beside the river Chebar (chap. 1), and his subsequent vision when he witnessed the destruction of Jerusalem (cf. chaps. 8-11). Thus for the third time Ezekiel saw the *merkabhah*, the throne chariot of God. The prophet reacted to the approach of God as he had on previous occasions. He fell on his face. He watched as the glory of God entered through the eastern gate. Then the Spirit brought Ezekiel into the inner court. There he noted that the glory of God "filled the house" (43:1-6).

The Lord himself now made three declarations regarding the future Temple: (1) "This is the place of my throne." This expression is peculiar to Ezekiel but it is based on a concept expressed by earlier writers, viz., that Yahweh was dwelling between the cherubim in the Holy of Holies.[9] (2) "This is the place of the soles of my feet." This expression is used in earlier material to denote the ark of the covenant.[10] (3) This is "the place where I will dwell among the sons of Israel forever." The word *forever* made this declaration more far-reaching than anything which was spoken concerning the Tabernacle of Moses or the Temple of Solomon (43:7a).[11]

The Lord announced the result of his perpetual habitation of the future Temple mount. The new Israel would not again "defile" the name of God through their "harlotry," i.e., idolatry. Because the Temple would occupy the entire hill, one major source of pollution from the old order would not exist. The kings of Israel had committed all kinds of abominations in the royal palace which was located immediately adjacent to the old Temple. For example, the graves of kings had been used as shrines in some cult of the dead. Because the Lord's holy name had been defiled in this way, he had "consumed" his people in his anger. If they would have the Lord dwell in their midst forever they must now put away such provocations (43:7b-9).

The purpose for the lengthy description of the future Temple was now set forth. Ezekiel was to describe the Temple to the house of Israel "so that they might be ashamed of their iniquities." The excitement generated by the promise of a new Temple would kindle spiritual fervor in the hearts of those who received this message. Therefore he should encourage them to "measure the plan," i.e., note the spiritual significance of the structure. If he observed signs of repentance, he should unfold to them all the details of the house and the ordinances which governed it. He should write down all the information contained in this vision "so that they may observe its whole design and all its statutes and do them" (43:10f.).

The future Temple had one "law" which governed its construction and usage. The entire Temple mount was to be a virtual holy of holies consecrated as such by the abiding presence of Yahweh himself (43:12).

E. The Temple Altar (43:13-17).

In his vision Ezekiel was still in the inner court (cf. 43:5). At some point his angel guide had measured the altar of sacrifice. He now revealed the measurements. This information was delayed until this point so that a description of the altar could be viewed as a climax to the portrait he had been painting of the future Temple.[12] Since the ark of the covenant was absent, (cf. Jer 3:16), the altar was the most important piece of furniture in this Temple. The description of this four-tier altar corresponds closely with the bronze altar of Solomon's Temple. The text gives no indication, however, as to the material from which this altar was constructed (43:13-17).

THE FUTURE WORSHIP
Ezekiel 43:18-44:31

After Ezekiel received the detailed design of the future Temple, he was instructed regarding the ordinances which would govern the worship in that house. In this section the guide became the prophetic teacher. He used the messenger formula ("Thus says the Lord") to introduce his messages in which he is actually quoting the very words of God. He spoke of the statutes of the altar, the gate, the house, and the ministry of the Temple.

A. Statutes of the Altar (43:18-27).

The angel first set forth the "statutes for the altar." The paragraph ordains the rites which were to be performed before regular worship commenced at that place. The statutes were addressed to Ezekiel as though he personally were to conduct the consecration rites. Why this should be the case is not entirely clear.[13] Perhaps the thought is that as the prophet of God he is to direct that certain actions should be taken with regard to the consecration of the Temple.

In a ceremony reminiscent of Mosaic days (cf. Exod 36; Lev 7), the altar was to be consecrated over a seven-day period. Each day a "sin offering" and a "burnt offering" were to be offered. The former represented the expiation of sin and iniquity; the latter, the removal of uncleanness (43:18-26).

Once the altar was purified and consecrated, the people would bring their burnt offerings and peace offerings. The former symbolized complete consecration to the Lord; the latter, the fellowship of a believer with his God (43:27). Believers today offer to the Lord that which the old sacrifices symbolized. They present their bodies as living sacrifices (Rom 12:1) and continually offer to him the sacrifice of praise (Heb 13:15).

B. Statutes of the Gate (44:1-3).

From the inner court in which he had received the statutes of the altar Ezekiel was conducted back to the eastern gate of the outer court. The last time he had stood by this gate it was open (cf. 43:1). Now Ezekiel noticed that the gate was closed (44:1). This was the principal entrance to the Temple and as such already it had been described to him and measured (cf. 40:6). At this spot Yahweh himself instructed Ezekiel regarding some of the privileges of the future prince.

The eastern gate of the former Temple always had remained opened. In the future Temple that gate would be closed in perpetuity. Yahweh had passed through that gate (cf. 43:4), thus rendering it holy. That closed gate would forever be an object lesson to underscore the sanctity of the future Temple now that the Lord had taken up permanent residence there. "The prince," however, would be permitted to enter the gate complex. He thus possessed a sanctity like no other. Here he would "eat bread before the Lord," i.e., eat those foods reserved under the Law for the priests (cf. Lev 2:3; 24:9). Thus this prince had priestly prerogatives. Ezekiel has already indicated that a glorious Ruler would appear in the future age. That Ruler is David, i.e., a descendant of David, or Messiah.[14]

C. Statutes of the House (44:4-14).

Ezekiel was next conducted back to the front of the house through the northern gate of the inner court. Here he perceived anew (cf. 43:5) the awesome presence of the glory of the Lord. The prophet fell in reverence at the sight. For the second time (cf. 40:4) Ezekiel was summoned to "mark well" (lit., set your heart on) all that God would show him and tell him with regard to the "statutes of the house." He was especially to take note of the "entrance of the house and all the exits of the sanctuary" (44:4-5). What follows is a discussion of the various persons who would have the right to participate in the Temple services.

Ezekiel was to deliver a scathing denunciation to the house of Israel concerning one of the "abominations" which had been committed in the first Temple. They had permitted uncircumcised heathen to be present as witnesses and/or worshipers in the outer court while the sacred sacrificial rituals were being performed.[15] Even worse, those aliens had been allowed "to keep the charge" of Yahweh's sanctuary, i.e., they had been admitted to the inner court as assistants of the priests. To prevent such an abuse in the future Temple, the edict is given that no alien uncircumcised in heart or flesh would be permitted to approach the altar of the Lord. The future Temple would be restricted to those who had complied with the initiatory commands of the Lord and who had surrendered their hearts to him.

When Israel fell into apostasy, a large number of the Levites, including several who were priests, led the way. These Levites would "bear the punishment for their iniquity" in the new order. Though forgiven of their sins, they would be permitted to minister only in menial tasks around the sanctuary, tasks which the lowest order of Levites performed in the first Temple. They would not be permitted to approach the altar to sacrifice or to enter the holy place (44:10-14).

During the period of Israel's apostasy a few of the priests remained steadfastly faithful to the Lord. Those few were the descendants of Zadok, the great priest of David's day. In recognition of their faithfulness, God assigned priestly rights to the Zadokites in the new Temple. These Zadokites would not necessarily be biological sons of the great priest. Rather they would be his moral and spiritual progeny. The thought is that in the messianic age moral and spiritual resemblance to the sons of Zadok would be the prime qualification for service in the priesthood (44:15f.).

D. Statutes of Ministry (44:15-31).

The Lord spoke next of the priesthood in the messianic Temple. Of interest is the fact that Ezekiel made no mention of a high priest. First, he set forth the priestly requirements. Definite regulations were stipulated regarding priests' garments, hair style, sobriety and marital status. When engaged in Temple service the priests were to wear "linen garments," emblematic of purity (cf. Rev 19:8,14). They were to wear nothing which would make them sweat, for that would render them unclean. Before leaving the inner court they were to remove these service garments. Otherwise they would transmit holiness to the common people which would in turn render them temporarily unfit to fulfill the ordinary duties of life. The hair of the priests was neither to be shaven nor allowed to grow long. When on duty the priests were to abstain from wine. A priest could marry only a virgin or the widow of another priest (44:17-22).[16]

Second, he set forth four official duties of the priests. They were to (1) educate the people in the fundamental principles of their faith, viz., the distinction between "the holy and the profane;" (2) serve as judicial officers; (3) regulate all festive assemblies in accordance with divine statutes; and (4) hallow the sabbath by offering appropriate sacrifices and by refraining from unnecessary work (44:23f).

Third, he spoke of priestly purity. Priests were not to touch a corpse. An exception was made in the case of close relatives. A priest defiled by contact with the dead had to undergo a seven-day cleansing ceremony (Num 19). Under the new regulations he was required then to present a sin offering before he could be restored to priestly service (44:25-27).

Finally, Ezekiel mentioned the priestly inheritance. As under the Mosaic law, the priests would have no territorial possession, no tribal tract such as would be assigned to other tribes. Yahweh himself was their inheritance. Portions of certain offerings brought to the Lord were assigned to the priests for their sustenance. The Mosaic prohibition against eating any animal which had died a natural death or which had been mangled is here repeated (44:28-31).

THE FUTURE SERVICE
Ezekiel 45-46

Five matters pertaining to the future service of the Temple were next addressed. These include the matters of worship maintenance, festivals, leadership and regulations. A concluding note speaks of the Temple kitchens.

A. Worship Maintenance (45:1-17).

The new system of worship would be sustained by the provision of a special district in the midst of the land, and by the faithful contribution of the Prince and his people.

1. The central portion (45:1-8). The land of Canaan was divided by lot after the conquest (Josh 13:6). This same method was to be employed after the land was repossessed following the exile.[17] The first portion to be marked off, however, was the Lord's. On this portion the Temple would be built as well as the houses of the priests. This area was to be 25,000 cubits square or roughly 8.3 square miles.[18] This district was to be divided into three parts. The northern part (25,000 x 10,000 cubits) was for the Levites. The middle portion had in its midst the Temple area (500 cubits square) surrounded by an open space. The southern section (25,000 x 5,000 cubits) was reserved for the new city (45:1-6).

The land on either side of the sacred district was delegated to the Prince. This land grant would enable the Prince to support himself and meet his responsibility as head of the community to provide public offerings. He would leave the rest of the territory to the house of Israel according to their tribes. The confiscation of private property so characteristic of the pre-exilic rulers would be unknown in the future age[19] (45:7-8).

2. The offerings of the people (45:9-17). The future princes were reminded that whatever they obtained from the people for the sanctuary was not be be extorted from them by violence. Temple assessments should be levied with "justice and righteousness." The princes were to stop the "expropriations" from the people which were common before the exile. The exhortation to the princes was expanded to include the people as well. They must see that all business transactions throughout the realm were based on honest weights and measures (45:9-12).[20]

In order to maintain the necessary sacrificial worship in the new Temple the worshipers were to bring special oblations. Plumptre has made a detailed analysis of the requirements here as compared with similar demands of the Law of Moses. He concludes that "the demands of Ezekiel's Torah surpass those of the earlier or Mosaic Torah in quantity as well as quality."[21] These offerings were not considered taxes on the people, for no penalty attaches to non-compliance. That they are free-will offerings is plain from the fact that there is no hint that these generous offerings would be withheld. The point seems to be that the generosity of God's people in the future age would far exceed that which Old Testament Israel had demonstrated (45:13-17).

B. Worship Festivals (45:18-25).

In the new era three great gatherings would constitute the annual festival cycle. (1) Each year was to begin with a New Year festival in which, through a sprinkling of blood, cleansing was effected for both the sanctuary and the worshiper. (2) The Passover festival began on the fourteenth day of the first month. The Prince led in this occasion of remembering the past deliverance of God's people from bondage. (3) The Feast of Tabernacles in the seventh month was a harvest feast, a time of thanksgiving, which lasted seven days.

C. Worship Leader (46:1-7).

The gate of the inner court was to be shut on work days but open on the sabbath and new moon. The Prince was worship leader on these occasions. He would eat his sacrificial meal on the porch of the outer gate. Then he would cross the outer court, and stand by the post of the gate of the inner court. There he would look into the inner court to watch the priests offer his sacrifices before the Lord. On sabbath days the Prince offered seven animals as burnt offerings accompanied by appropriate cereal offerings. These offerings expressed thanksgiving for the past week and its blessings. Similarly on the new moon the Prince provided a series of burnt, cereal, and oil offerings.

D. Worship Regulations (46:8-18).

Three blocks of text set forth the regulations which would govern worship in the new Temple. First, the law of entrance and exit is set forth. No worshiper was to depart the court by the same gate through which he entered. This regulation may have been made to preserve order among the large throngs at the annual festivals. On the other hand, the rule may be intended to enforce worship symbolism. Each should leave worship a different person than he came in. At these great festivals the Prince would stand on a level with the people for he would enter and exit by the same gates as they (46:8-10).

The worship regulations regarding sacrifices were next revealed. The Lord stipulated the appropriate offerings to be made at the major festivals. Should the Prince wish to make a private free-will offering, the eastern gate of the inner court would be opened for his view as on sabbath days. The community was to present sacrifices every morning to the Lord (46:11-15).[22]

Three regulations would govern the property of the Prince. (1) The Prince could make a gift of part of his property to a son and the gift would remain the son's in perpetuity. (2) The Prince's land could be loaned but not gifted in perpetuity to a servant. It returned to the Prince in "the year of liberty," i.e., the fiftieth year. (3) The Prince must endow his sons (and others) out of his own possessions, not those of his subjects (46:16-18).

E. The Sacrificial Kitchens (46:19-24).

Two sets of sacrificial kitchens were mentioned by Ezekiel—those for the priests and those for the people. Ezekiel was led to both of these areas by his angelic guide. Portions of the sacrifices which the priests were to eat were prepared in kitchens conveniently situated at the rear of the priests' chambers. The kitchens for the people were located in the four corners of the outer court. Here the Levites would cook the portions of sacrificial offerings which were allocated to the people.

THE FUTURE LAND
Ezekiel 47-48

Ezekiel's vision reached a climax as the prophet pictured the blessings which would belong to those who served Yahweh in the new land. Three words summarize those blessings: health, happiness and holiness.

A. The Healing Stream (47:1-12).

From the Temple kitchens Ezekiel was brought back to the door of the house. There he discovered a stream of water trickling forth from "under the threshold of the house." The stream was flowing through the inner and outer courts and beneath the eastern wall. The angelic guide measured a thousand cubits eastward from outer wall. He led Ezekiel through the waters, which at that point were ankle deep. At thousand cubit intervals the guide and the prophet found the waters to be knee deep, waist deep, and finally a river which could not be forded (47:1-5).

The guide then brought Ezekiel to the banks of the river. A great number of trees had grown up along the river. The guide explained that the river eventually made its way down through the mountains of Judah to the Dead Sea. The river of life actually purified the lifeless waters of that sea. The waters would teem with fish of all kinds. Fishermen would spread their nets along the shores. On both banks of the river trees would grow in profusion. They would bear fruit every month. Their leaves would have healing properties. Wherever the Temple river flowed there was abundant life. Only the swamps and marshes around the sea would remain too salty for living organisms (47:6-14).

B. Apportionment of the Land (47:13-48:29).

The Lord now directed Ezekiel to do what was hinted at in 45:1, viz., divide the land for an inheritance. As in the earlier land division, Joseph through his two sons would have two portions. The territory to be divided would be somewhat smaller than that apportioned by Moses and Joshua because the territory east of Jordan is not included (47:13-20).

Individual portions were to be divided by lot for an inheritance. Strangers who permanently dwelt among the tribes of Israel were to receive permanent portions according to the tribe where they lived. Thus Gentiles as well as Jews would be welcome in the new land (47:21-23).

The portions assigned to each tribe apparently were equal. These portions of approximately twenty miles in width stretched from the Mediterranean Sea to the Jordan River. The tribes apportioned territory north of the sacred district were Dan, Asher, Naphtali, Manasseh, Ephraim, Reuben and Judah (48:1-7). The sacred district which was described in 45:1-8 is again described (48:8-22). South of

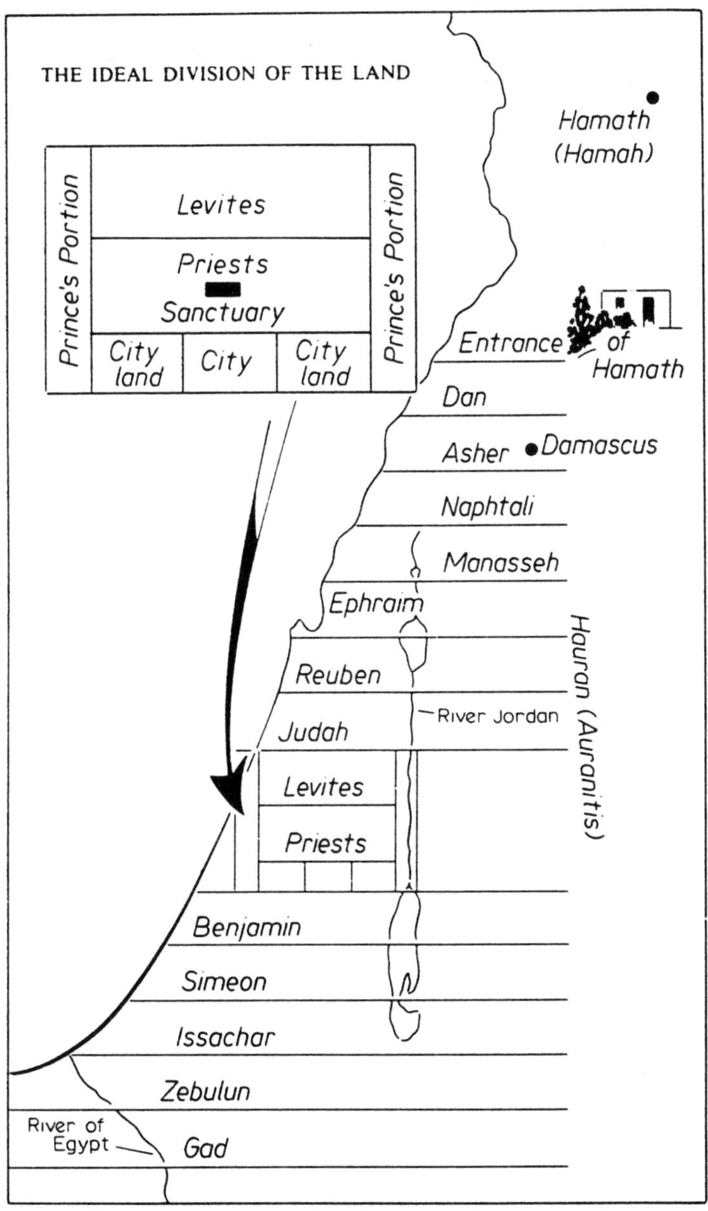
THE IDEAL DIVISION OF THE LAND
Hamath
(Hamah)
Prince's Portion
Levites
Priests
Sanctuary
City land
City
City land
Prince's Portion
Entrance of Hamath
Dan
Asher
Damascus
Naphtali
Manasseh
Ephraim
Reuben
Judah
River Jordan
Hauran (Auranitis)
Levites
Priests
Benjamin
Simeon
Issachar
Zebulun
River of Egypt
Gad

that district five tribes had their inheritance: Benjamin, Simeon, Issachar, Zebulun, and Gad (48:23-29). The significance of this arrangement is that in the New Israel the worship of God would be central.

C. The New City (48:30-35).

The final paragraph of Ezekiel describes the twelve gates of the new city. The gates were named for the tribes. The gates leading northward were those of Reuben, Judah and Levi, all children of Leah.[23] The gates of Joseph, Benjamin and Dan led eastward. The first two of these were sons of Rachel; the third a son of Rachel's handmaid (cf. Gen 30:6,24; 35:18). The southern gates received the names of Simeon, Issachar and Zebulun, again all sons of Leah. The western gates were those of Gad, Asher and Naphtali, all sons of handmaids. An interesting point is that whereas Joseph had two tribal inheritances (Ephraim and Manasseh), Joseph had only one gate. The tribe of Levi had no tribal inheritance, but did have a gate named for it (48:30-34).

The name of the new city no longer would be Jerusalem, but "Yahweh-shammah," i.e., Yahweh is there. The name points to the thought that God would dwell in the midst of the new Israel (48:35).

Endnotes

1. On the future city of God being on a high mountain see Isa 2, Mic 4:1 and Zech 14:10.

2. The guide spoke to Ezekiel in 40:4, 45-46; 41:4, 22; 42:13-14; 46:20, 24. The guide made a lengthy speech in 47:8-48:35. In 43:18-27 it is not clear whether Yahweh or the guide is the speaker.

3. There were twelve tables in all, of which eight were used for slaughtering purposes, and the remaining four for depositing the instruments used in the killing of the animals. Of the eight, four stood within the porch of the gate, two on each side, and four without.

4. Two bodies of priests are distinguished: (1) those who had charge of the Temple (v. 45); and (2) those who kept the charge of the altar (v. 46). The former were those who superintended the Levites in their chores around the Temple. The latter were those who made sacrifice and burned incense on the altar.

5. Ezekiel's visionary Temple building proper had the same dimensions as Solomon's Temple (cf. 1 Kgs 6:2-5).

6. The *gizrah* or separate place was a space behind the west end of the Temple which was marked off from the rest of the ground on which the Temple complex stood. This area was most likely devoted to less sacred purposes. A similar area behind Solomon's Temple had buildings upon it and a separate exit (2 Kgs 23:11; 1 Chr 26:18).

7. The same altar in Solomon's Temple was overlaid with gold. Perhaps Ezekiel anticipated that the Temple would be rebuilt in a time of impoverishment.

8. The problem concerns the interpretation of 42:10. Does it merely repeat what had previously been stated about the north chambers or does it allude to a third building of priests' chambers on the eastern side of the inner court?

9. On Yahweh dwelling between the cherubim see Exod 35:22; I Sam 4:4; 2 Kgs 19:15; Ps 80:1; Isa 37:16.

10. On the ark of the covenant as the footstool of Yahweh see 1 Chr 28:2; Pss 99:5; 132:7. On the Temple as God's footstool see Isa 9:13; Lam 2:1.

11. Regarding the Tabernacle God had said: "And let them construct a sanctuary for me, that I may dwell among them" (Exod 25:8; cf. 29:45). Regarding the Temple he declared: "And I will dwell among the sons of Israel, and will not forsake my people Israel" (1 Kgs 6:13).

12. The NASB and NIV regard the citation of the measurements of the altar as a continuation of the speech of Yahweh which began in 43:7.

13. Thus 43:19-25 is in the second person singular. The pronoun, however, shifts to third masculine plural in 43:26-27.

14. Cf. 34:24; 17:22-24. Most commentators reject the messianic identification of the prince in Ezekiel 40-48. For a defense of this view, see James E. Smith, *What the Bible Says About the Promised Messiah* (Joplin: College Press, 1984) 372-377.

15. Under the law of Moses those who were uncircumcised could not participate in Passover (Exod 12:48-49). Aliens who gave some measure of obedience to the Law (Exod 12:19; 20:10; Lev 17:10, 12; 18:26; 20:2; 24:16, 22) might be permitted to enter the court to present offerings to the Lord (Lev 17:8; Num 15:14, 29). The aliens mentioned here were uncircumcised in heart as well as body, i.e., they were destitute of the most basic elements of Hebrew piety.

16. In the Mosaic code priests could marry a widow. The more stringent regulation here underscores the greater sanctity of the future Temple.

17. The comment of Plumptre is appropriate: "That no such methodical distribution of Canaan ever took place, or for that matter could have taken place amongst the returned exiles, should be proof sufficient that the prophet here moves in the region of the ideal and symbolical rather than of the real and literal." "Ezekiel" in *The Pulpit Commentary* (New York: Funk & Wagnals, 1909) 2:410.

18. Neither the Hebrew nor the Greek text gives the unit of measure used for the Lord's portion. While some commentators prefer to understand *reeds,* most prefer *cubits* because the entire context is built upon that unit of measure. If *reeds* is intended, the holy district would be forty miles square.

19. In 45:8 the term *princes* is used. Some think the messianic understanding of the *prince* in these chapters flounders on this plural. Ezekiel, however, was thinking of Israel's past rulers, and contrasting with them the rulers Israel might have in the future, without affirming whether these should be many or one.

20. The *ephah* was a dry measure, the *bath* a liquid measure. Each was to contain the tenth part of a *homer,* about seventy-two gallons or thirty-two pecks. The *shekel* was the standard money weight. It equaled twenty *gerahs,* the smallest silver coin. The *maneh,* formerly equal to a hundred shekels, would come in three denominations of fifteen, twenty and twenty-five shekels.

21. "Ezekiel" in *The Pulpit Commentary* 2:414.

22. In the Mosaic Law an evening as well as a morning sacrifice was required. Why the evening sacrifice was omitted by Ezekiel is not clear.

23. Keil observes: Reuben was the firstborn in age, Judah the firstborn by virtue of the patriarcial blessing, and Levi the one chosen by Yahweh for priestly service in lieu of the firstborn. The same three sons occupy the first three places and in the same order in the blessing of Moses (Deut 33:6-8).

THE BOOK OF
DANIEL

CHAPTER THIRTY-FIVE

Getting Acquainted With Daniel

The Book of Daniel has attracted more interest than any book of the Old Testament. Sunday School children are very familiar with the stories about Daniel and his companions in Babylon. Their fidelity to God in these seductive circumstances has encouraged believers through the ages. On the other hand, the prophetic portions of Daniel generally have been ignored in the educational program of the church. This apocalyptic material with its numerical symbolism and weird animal figures has been relegated to the happy hunting ground of full-time "students of prophecy."

In his book *Thy Kingdom Come*, Rushdoony has a chapter entitled "The Offense of Daniel." Here Rushdoony explains why Daniel is "one of the most explosive books in all human history." This book assumes at every point a philosophy of history which is the antithesis of every opinion held by modern man. Rushdoony sets forth five particulars in which modern man would take exception to Daniel.

First, Daniel underscores the Biblical concept of God. Daniel's

God is totally self-sufficient, omniscient, and omnipotent. He is willing and able infallibly to reveal future events. He is far above anything man is or could ever hope to be. Second, Daniel sets forth unvarnished predictive prophecy—blunt, unmistakable, confident and specific. The God of Daniel uses history and is not used by it. Third, Daniel unapologetically narrates miraculous events. Fourth, Daniel asserts the total government of God. Modern man prefers the anarchy of chance and a god who can be manipulated. Fifth, Daniel reveals the fundamental discrimination which exists within the human race between the saved and the lost.[1]

THE PROPHET DANIEL

Four great races of people considered Daniel an outstanding hero while he was still alive—the Jews, the Chaldeans, the Medes and the Persians. Not much is known of Daniel's life. Nevertheless, this prophet is revealed as "a man of stalwart character and priceless convictions." Because he was willing at all times to stand up for what he believed he is a true hero of the Faith.[2]

The name Daniel means something like "God is my judge." The famous prophet is not the only character in the Bible to wear this name. David had a son named Daniel (1 Chr 3:1). Among those who returned from Exile with Ezra in 457 BC was a Daniel (Ezra 8:2; Neh 10:6). This man may have been named after the great prophet. Outside the Bible the name is also attested in ancient sources. In the Canaanite Ras Shamra literature which dates to about 1400 BC one named Daniel is quite prominent. Still another Daniel is found in the pseudepigraphical Book of Jubilees which dates to about 150 BC.

Scripture reveals the following facts about Daniel. He was born into the royal family (1:3). As a youth he was carried away to Babylon. He was selected to receive special training in the royal academy of Nebuchadnezzar. Daniel served as a high official under three kings—Nebuchadnezzar, Belshazzar and Darius. He gained a reputation for his ability to interpret prophetic dreams. He received a series of divine revelations which outlined God's dealings with his people from the sixth century to the end of the Old Testament era. Accused of disloyalty by his fellow officials, he was condemned to die in a den of lions. His miraculous deliverance from that fate resulted in the conversion of Darius the Mede. The chronological notes in the book suggest that Daniel's prophetic career lasted roughly seventy years.

Chart No. 14

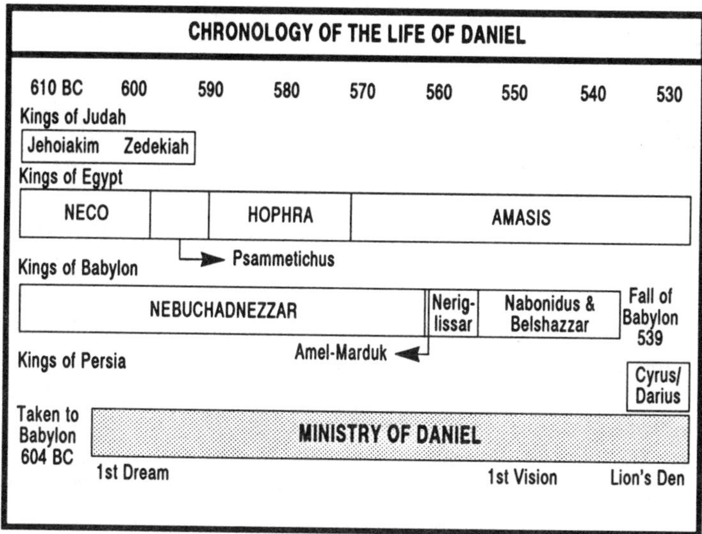

Three times Ezekiel alluded to Daniel (Ezek 14:14,20; 28:3). The careers of these two prophets parallel each other. Ezekiel was taken to Babylon about eight years after Daniel. He began to preach five years later, eleven years after Daniel's elevation in the royal court. He certainly must have known of Daniel, and probably knew him personally. These references show that Daniel was regarded as a righteous and wise man by his fellow exiles in Babylon.[3]

The curtain of authentic history closes on the life of Daniel in the third year of Cyrus (536 BC). Several traditions, however, circulated relating to this prophet. One such tradition was that Daniel delegated his office and honors in Babylon to Zerubbabel, and then retired with royal blessing to Shushan. There he supposedly spent the rest of his life in great piety. A contradictory tradition—one which has found some support among modern scholars—is that Daniel returned to

Jerusalem at the command of Cyrus. Some think the Daniel mentioned in Ezra 8:2 and Nehemiah 10:6 is the famous prophet. Daniel's tomb is shown in two places: in the royal vault in Babylon, a little west of the acropolis; and in one of the synagogues of Susa.

DANIEL IN THE CRITICS' DEN

If Daniel spent one night in a den of lions, his book has spent several centuries in a den of critics. Perhaps in no other book of the sacred sixty-six is the demarcation between conservative and liberal views of divine revelation more clearly drawn. The book purports to have been written in the sixth century before Christ. It claims to be the fruit of the ministry of a Jewish captive named Daniel who occupied high positions in the courts of the kings who ruled Mesopotamia.

Critics, however, have a very different view of the book. They regard the book as a pseudepigraph coming from an unknown author of the second century BC. The book was supposedly written to give encouragement to faithful Jews in their conflict with Antiochus Epiphanes (cf. 1 Macc 2:59f.). A few citations of scholars of this school will serve to document the critical position.

In 1899 J. D. Prince wrote: "It is now the general opinion of most scholars who study the Old Testament from a critical point of view that this work cannot possibly have originated according to the traditional theory at any time during the later Babylonian monarchy when the events recorded are supposed to have taken place."[4] In 1929 R. H. Charles stated the same position: "As a result of modern research it is now generally agreed amongst scholars that the Book of Daniel was written about or shortly before 165 BC."[5] More recent writers have questioned whether the Daniel of the book was even an historical figure.[6]

This weighty scholarship notwithstanding, the observation by E. J. Young is still valid: "If the book of Daniel comes from the age of the Maccabees, I do not see how it is possible to escape the conclusion that the book is also a forgery, for it claims to be a revelation from God to the Daniel who lived in Babylon during the exile."[7] E. B. Pusey makes a similar observation: "The book of Daniel is especially fitted to be a battlefield between faith and unbelief. It admits of no half-measure. It is either Divine or an imposture."[8]

On what basis do the critics deny the authenticity of the Book of Daniel? Older critics spoke about the historical blunders of the book. Those "blunders," however, have evaporated in the light of further research in Mesopotamian history. The situation today is such that John C. Whitcomb can write: "The author gives evidence of having a more accurate knowledge of Neo-Babylonian and early Achaemenid Persian history than any known historian since the 6th century BC."[9]

Why, then, do the critics continue to deny a sixth century date for Daniel? Because the book contains prophecies of post-Babylonian events which supposedly become increasingly accurate as they approach the date 165 BC, and vague thereafter. Stated in its simplest terms, the real issue is whether the God of the Bible can predict the near and distant future with pin-point accuracy. This book claims that God not only can reveal the future, he has done so in a most convincing manner through his servant Daniel.

CHARACTERISTICS OF THE BOOK

The Book of Daniel contains 357 verses, organized into twelve chapters. It can be read in fifty minutes or less by an average reader. Four adjectives describe the Book of Daniel.

A. A Bilingual Book.

The Book of Daniel is written in two languages, Hebrew and Aramaic. The book begins and concludes in Hebrew (1:1-2:4a; 8:1-12:13). The middle portion is in Aramaic, the international language of the sixth century. Apparently the author himself wrote the book in this Hebrew-Aramaic pattern.[10] His reasons for doing so are not entirely clear. It appears, however, that Aramaic was used in those portions of the book which deal with the future of Gentile empires while Hebrew was used where the text has direct bearing on Israelites.

B. A Unified Book.

Some liberals argue for a multiple authorship of the Book of Daniel with various chapters being assigned to different centuries. Some assign the different language sections to different authors, while others assign the material to various authors on the basis of contents. Some liberal scholars, however, join conservatives in defending the unity of the book.[11]

Chart No. 15

THE UNITY OF THE BOOK OF DANIEL

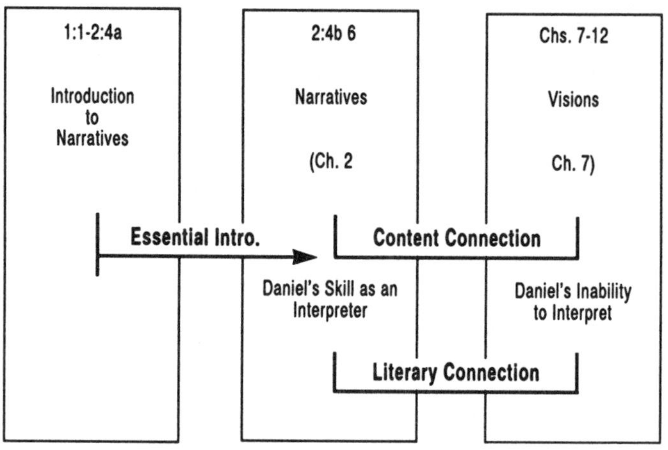

A credible defense of the unity of Daniel has been penned by the Jewish scholar Slotki.[12] Slotki points out that 1:1-2:4a is essential as an introduction to the narrative section of the book (chaps. 2-6). Furthermore, the narrative section is necessary for the full appreciation of the obscurity of the visions (chaps. 7-12). A twofold connection between the two major divisions of the book is apparent. First, the two divisions are connected by content. Chapter 2 in the narrative portion parallels chapter 7 in the visionary portion. Using different symbolism, both chapters speak of the four great world empires. Second, a literary connection between the two divisions is evident. The narrative portion serves to impress the reader with the skill of Daniel as an interpreter of dreams. On the other hand, the visionary portion underscores Daniel's inability to interpret his visions unaided.[13]

C. An Apocalyptic Book.

The revelations concerning the future which are found in Daniel are given in dreams and visions in which symbolism plays an important part. Such literature is called *apocalyptic* by scholars. A casual reading of Daniel reveals that bizarre animal and numerological symbols predominate. An element of obscurity is present in spite of the efforts of an interpreting angel to make it clear. The Book of Daniel was the Biblical prototype for the rather extensive collection of books of this genre which appeared during the intertestamental period.[14] The New Testament Book of Revelation is also modeled after Daniel. In reality, however, Daniel and Revelation are in a class by themselves. They are the only genuinely inspired apocalyptic books ever written.

D. A Miraculous Book.

The Book of Daniel records a cluster of miracles which God wrought during the period of the exile. This was the third of four Biblical periods of approximately forty years each in which God demonstrated his omnipotent power in the affairs of men. In the time of the Exodus and subsequent wilderness wandering God demonstrated his superiority to the gods of Egypt through almost daily miracles. Some five hundred years later in the age of Elijah another outburst of the miraculous is documented. At that time Israel, the northern kingdom, was about to follow queen Jezebel into the worship of the Tyrian Baal.

In Daniel's day the issue was again the allure of idolatry. The destruction of the Temple and deportation of the Jews to Babylon had shaken their faith in God. So another mighty outpouring of the miraculous was in order. Four young Jews were rewarded with visibly superior health after only ten days on a diet of vegetables. Shadrach, Meshach and Abednego were preserved in the midst of a fiery execution chamber, and were joined in that place by a heavenly being. A hand wrote a message of doom on the wall of Belshazzar's palace in the midst of a drunken banquet. The mouths of lions were sealed so that Daniel experienced no harm in their den. The greatest miracles in the book, however, are Daniel's revelations concerning the future of the world kingdoms and the people of God.

THE CONTENTS OF THE BOOK

What is the purpose of the Book of Daniel? Certainly the purpose was not autobiographical. One chapter omits any reference to Daniel. Few events from the prophet's long life are narrated. No genealogy appears. These facts would argue that the author was not attempting to give an account of Daniel's life. It is equally obvious that the author did not intend to provide for Bible students a history of the exilic period. Certainly a Bible believer cannot entertain the liberal notion that this book was written to mask a well-meaning mystic of the second century who wished to stress the rewards of fidelity to God in the midst of idolatrous surroundings. So what is the purpose of Daniel?

Four adjectives describe the dimensions of the author's purpose. First, the author had a *polemic* purpose. He intended to place in sharp contrast the omnipotence of God and the impotence of the deities of Babylon. Second, the book has a *didactic* purpose. It teaches the valuable truth that God frustrates the designs of the mightiest monarchs but defends the servants who remain faithful to him. On a third level, the author intended his book to be *consolatory*. Believers through the centuries have taken comfort in Daniel's revelation that the course of history is determined by a divine plan. In God's own time the trials of the saints end. One day oppressors will be destroyed, and the saints shall inherit the kingdom. Finally, the book is obviously *predictive*. Here the Holy Spirit intends through Daniel to outline the course of world history as it relates to the people of God.

The Book of Daniel is a literary bifid, a book of two major divisions. The first division (chaps. 1-6) contains six narratives dealing with the experiences of Daniel and his companions under Nebuchadnezzar, Belshazzar and Darius the Mede. In each chapter the Gentile king confesses with ever increasing forcefulness, his conviction that the God of the Hebrews is truly God. The second half of the book (chaps. 7-12) contains four reports from Daniel concerning a dream and three visions which he received under Belshazzar, Darius and Cyrus. These chapters offer a broad perspective on human history from the time of Nebuchadnezzar to the end of the world. The focus, however, is on events which would occur during the last centuries of the Old Covenant age.

Chart No. 16

<table>
<tr><th colspan="4">THE STRUCTURE OF THE BOOK OF DANIEL</th></tr>
<tr><td colspan="2">NARRATIVES ILLUSTRATING THE SOVEREIGN RULE OF GOD

Chapters 1-6

Daniel Interprets Dreams.
Historical Incidents.
Includes Daniel's Friends.
God Speaks Through History.
Third Person.</td><td colspan="2">PROPHECIES ILLUSTRATING THE SOVEREIGN RULE OF GOD

Chapters 7-12

An Angel Interprets Visions.
Visions and Prayers.
Daniel's Friends Absent.
God Speaks Through Prophecy.
First Person.</td></tr>
<tr><td>Heb.
Intro.
Ch 1</td><td>ARAMAIC
(Concerns Gentile Nations)
2</td><td></td><td>HEBREW
(Concerns God's People)
8 12</td></tr>
</table>

THE CHRONOLOGY OF THE BOOK

Ten of the twelve chapters in Daniel are dated according to the regnal years of the reigning Gentile ruler. The remaining two chapters (chaps. 3,4) are assigned dates in the Septuagint version but not in the Hebrew text. As indicated above, the arrangement of the book has a certain logic to it. The author, however, has not elected to arrange his material according to the time principle. Chronologically the book can be divided according to the following scheme.

A. The Reign of Nebuchadnezzar (605-562 BC).

1. Chapter 1: Daniel raised to power (604 BC).
2. Chapter 2: The image dream (602 BC).
3. Chapter 3: The fiery furnace episode (600 BC?).
4. Chapter 4: The tree dream (570 BC?).

B. The Reign of Nabonidus/Belshazzar (556-539 BC).

1. Chapter 7: Vision of four beasts (c. 556 BC).
2. Chapter 8: Vision of the ram and goat (c. 554 BC).
3. Chapter 5: Handwriting on the wall (539 BC).

C. The Reign of Cyrus/Darius (539-530 BC).

1. Chapter 9: Vision of seventy heptads (538 BC).
2. Chapter 6: The lions' den (537 BC).
3. Chapters 10-12: The final vision (536 BC).

THE HISTORY OF THE BOOK

Subsequent to its composition, the Book of Daniel had a turbulent history. An overview of that history is essential to an understanding of issues which are raised by this controversial book.

A. Used by the High Priest.

According to the testimony of Josephus,[15] an attack against Jerusalem by Alexander the Great in 332 BC was diverted by a citation from the Book of Daniel. Alexander was enraged that the Jews had refused to send him aid when he was besieging Tyre. He was determined to destroy their capital. A priestly procession met the Macedonian as he was approaching Jerusalem. The high priest showed Alexander "wherein Daniel declared that one of the Greeks should destroy the empire of the Persians." Alexander saw himself reflected in the prophecy. Instead of attacking Jerusalem, he went to the Temple and provided sacrifices to be offered in his behalf.

B. Enlarged by Anonymous Writers.

During the intertestamental period various legends arose about the characters in the Book of Daniel. Some of these legends were circulating in written form at the time the Septuagint was translated about 250 BC. The translators of that Greek version incorporated those legendary accounts into the historical Book of Daniel. The Roman Catholic Church accepts these additions to Daniel as genuine. These additions, however, were never so regarded by the Jewish community to which the oracles of God had been committed (Rom 3:2).

The first of the additions is called "The Song of the Three Holy Children." These sixty-seven verses are sandwiched between verse 23 and verse 24 of Daniel 3. This addition consists of (1) a lengthy prayer attributed to Azariah; (2) a narrative describing the heating of the furnace and the death of the Chaldean soldiers; and (3) a song of praise supposedly sung by the three Hebrews within the fiery furnace.

The second addition is known as "The History of Susanna". In the Septuagint version this comes just before the canonical Book of Daniel. In the Latin Vulgate (which is based on the Septuagint) this addition appears as chapter 13 of the book. In this well-written narrative, Daniel does some nifty detective work to expose two lying nobles who falsely had accused Susanna of committing adultery.

The third addition, "Bel and the Dragon," follows 12:13 in the Septuagint. It is chapter 14 in the Latin Vulgate. In this two-fold narrative Daniel demonstrated to the Persian king first that his god Bel was impotent. The food which disappeared from the temple of Bel was not being eaten by the god. Daniel showed the king the secret passage by which the priests entered the locked temple each night to confiscate the food which had been offered to the god. Then Daniel exposed the lack of power of the dragon which the Persian king worshiped. He fed the beast an explosive cake which killed it. Daniel was then thrown into a den of starved lions, but he was miraculously untouched. While there Daniel was fed by the prophet Habakkuk.

C. Translated into Greek.

The Septuagint translation of Daniel is defective. Translation errors abound. Their presence indicates that already by 250 BC the

Hebrew words used in this book were unfamiliar to the translators. This fact supports the sixth century date for the origin of the Book of Daniel.

D. Quoted by Ancient Sources.

In at least three pre-Christian sources allusions to Daniel have been detected. The Sibylline Oracles (3:397-400) in c. 140 BC seem to allude to Daniel 7:7-8. The first book of Maccabees (2:59f.) alludes to the narratives of Daniel 3 and 6 at ca. 80 BC. The Book of Baruch (1:15-2:19) contains many verbal similarities of expression with Daniel 9:4-19.[16]

Critics have made a great deal of the non-mention of Daniel by the intertestamental sage Ben Sira. In his list of Old Testament heroes Ben Sira mentions Isaiah, Jeremiah, Ezekiel and the Twelve Minor Prophets as a group. Why does he omit Daniel? Critics argue that this silence proves that the Book of Daniel had not yet been written in 180 BC when Ben Sira is usually dated. Ben Sira, however, does not mention Job, the Judges, Asa, Jehoshaphat, Mordecai or even the great scribe Ezra. If Ben Sira regarded Daniel as more of a statesman than a prophet that would explain why he did not mention him along with the other writing prophets. Others have suggested that Ben Sira mentioned the Old Testament worthies in their relation to the Temple. Since Daniel had nothing to do with the Temple directly, he was not mentioned. In any case, an argument from silence is not weighty enough to overthrow the claims of the book and the testimony to its existence cited above.

The most important ancient citation of Daniel is that of Jesus. Several allusions to Daniel are found in the Gospel of Matthew[17] as well as one direct quotation (24:15). Of importance is the fact that Jesus referred to Daniel as a "prophet." This seems to negate the idea popularized by W. H. Green that Daniel possessed the gift of prophecy but was not in fact a prophet.[18] Jesus' use of the title "Son of man" and the term "kingdom" seems to reflect the Book of Daniel.

E. Placed among the Prophets.

Daniel was placed alongside of Isaiah, Jeremiah, Ezekiel and the

Twelve in the pre-Christian Septuagint translation. Testimony from the Jewish historian Josephus indicates that Daniel held the same position in the sacred collection in his day, the close of the first Christian century.[19] The Syriac version—the oldest translation of the entire Bible—also placed Daniel among the prophets.

F. Relocated in the Writings.

Daniel is found in the third division—the *kethubhim* (Writings)—of the modern Hebrew Bible. At some undetermined point after AD 100 Jewish scholarship removed the book from the Prophets where it was reckoned in the days of Josephus. The second division of the Hebrew canon today consists of eight books: Joshua, Judges, Samuel, Kings, Isaiah, Jeremiah, Ezekiel and the Twelve Minor Prophets counted as one book. The earliest list of Old Testament books agreeing with the divisions of the modern Hebrew Bible is found in the Talmud which dates to about AD 400. Why the relocation of Daniel took place is not entirely clear. Perhaps the prominent use of Daniel in the Jewish Christian debates of that period had something to do with this decision. Since the Jewish concept of the Scriptures allows for degrees of inspiration, the authority of Daniel could be "downgraded" if the book were shifted to the third division.

G. Attacked by Enemies.

One of the most brilliant opponents of Christianity in its early years was Porphyry. He was born about AD 232 in Tyre. He studied in Athens, and later in Rome. At the age of forty he wrote his major work *Against the Christians* in fifteen books. The emperor Constantine tried to suppress this work. By the end of the fifth century the writings of Porphyry were no longer extant. Jerome in his commentary on Daniel preserved the criticism of Porphyry's twelfth book which dealt with the Book of Daniel. The basic position of this anti-Christian writer was essentially the same as modern liberals. Porphyry believed the book was a forgery written by someone in Judea in the days of Antiochus Epiphanes about 165 BC. He argued that the book contained no prophecy, but was in fact a narration of things already past at the time the book was written.

H. Abused by Friends.

Throughout church history the Book of Daniel has been abused by its friends.[20] Almost all of the many computations which men have made about the date of the Second Coming have been based on numbers found in Daniel. In certain cults like the Adventists and the Jehovah's Witnesses the prophecies of Daniel form the bedrock of their entire movement.

In Fundamentalist circles Daniel mania is prevalent. Those riding the prophetic hobby horse crank out literature on Daniel at a phenomenal rate. Televangelists hold audiences spellbound with messages on "Daniel's Seventieth Week" or "The Key to the Book of Daniel." Most of these interpreters come to the book with a prophetic "axe to grind." That is to say, they attempt to superimpose upon the book modern schemes of prophetic interpretation. Fanciful exegesis is supported by irrelevant cross-references based upon mere coincidence of terminology. Often Daniel is pried loose from its historical setting. Prophecies long since fulfilled to the letter are projected into the future. The result is that the vast majority of the voluminous literature on Daniel is largely worthless.[21]

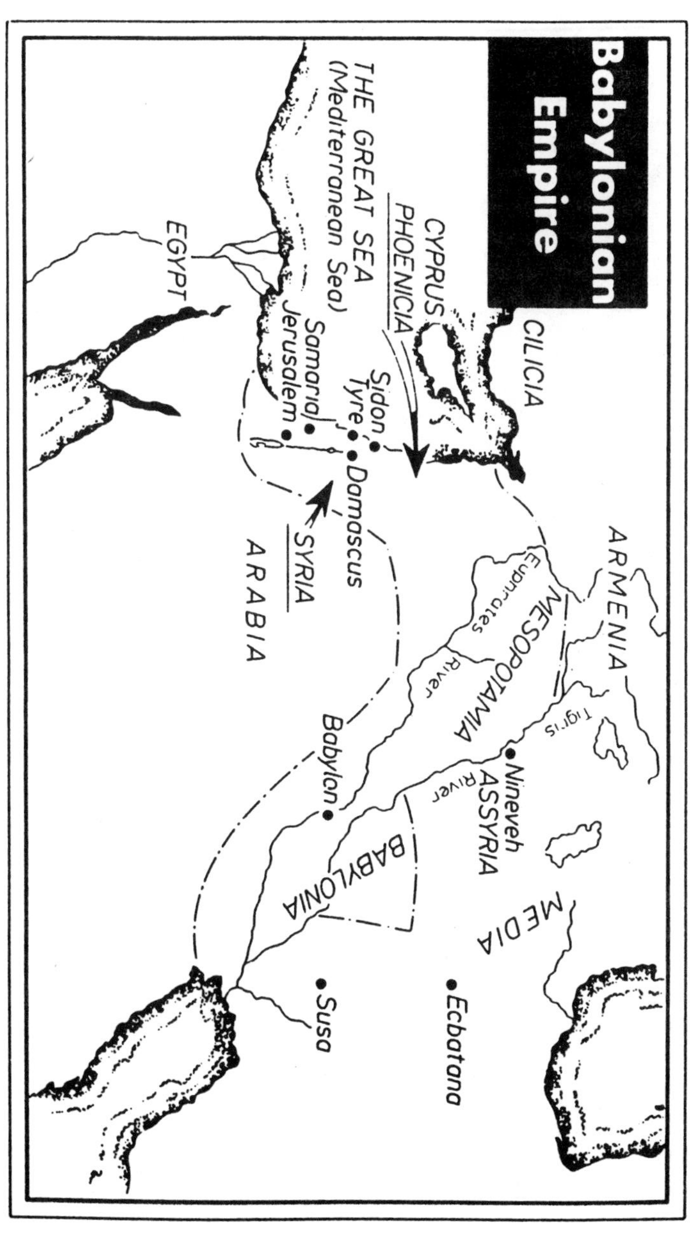
Babylonian Empire
CILICIA
CYPRUS
PHOENICIA
THE GREAT SEA
(Mediterranean Sea)
EGYPT
Sidon
Tyre
Samaria
Jerusalem
Damascus
SYRIA
ARABIA
ARMENIA
MESOPOTAMIA
Euphrates
River
Tigris
River
Nineveh
ASSYRIA
Babylon
BABYLONIA
MEDIA
Ecbatana
Susa

Endnotes

1. Rousas J. Rushdoony, *Thy Kingdom Come* (Fairfax, VA: Thoburn, 1970) 1-10.

2. E.J. Young, *The Prophecy of Daniel* (Grand Rapids: Eerdmans, 1949) 19.

3. That Ezekiel may have been referring to someone other than the prophet Daniel has been suggested for two reasons. (1) The spelling of the name in Ezekiel is slightly different—*Danel* rather than *Daniel*. (2) Ezekiel sandwiches Daniel's name between that of Noah and Job. Ezekiel, then, must be alluding to a Daniel of antiquity, perhaps the one mentioned in the Ras Shamra texts. The positioning of the name, however, serves a rhetorical rather than an historical purpose. Noah through his righteousness was able to save his family. Daniel was able to save his friends. But Job was able to save neither. On Ezekiel's reference to Daniel, see H.C. Leupold, *Exposition of Daniel* (Minneapolis, MN: Augsburg, 1949) 7.

4. J.D. Prince, *A Critical Commentary on the Book of Daniel* (New York: Lemcke & Buechner, 1899) 24.

5. R.H. Charles, *A Critical and Exegetical Commentary on the Book of Daniel* (Oxford: Clarendon, 1929) lxx.

6. Cf. Georg Fohrer, *Introduction to the Old Testament* (New York: Abingdon, 1968) 472.

7. E.J. Young, *op.cit.* 5.

8. E.B. Pusey, *Daniel the Prophet* (New York: Funk & Wagnalls, 1885) 75.

9. John C. Whitcomb, "Daniel, Book of" in *New Bible Dictionary* (2nd ed; Wheaton, IL: InterVarsity, 1982) 263.

10. Conservative scholars generally support the originality of the Hebrew-Aramaic pattern, while more liberal scholars are divided on the issue. Rowley and Eissfeldt believe the pattern is original; Bevan, Ginsberg, Charles and Montgomery hold that it is editorial.

11. Liberal scholars who defend the unity of the Book of Daniel include Rowley, Bentzen, Charles and Eissfeldt.

12. Judah J. Slotki, *Daniel* in Soncino Books of the Bible (London: Soncino, 1951) xiii.

13. In the following passages Daniel's inability to interpret his dreams unaided by God is in evidence: 8:27; 9:22; 10:2, 11, 14; 12:4, 9.

14. The intertestamental apocalyptic literature is unlike the Book of Daniel in two important respects. Most of the later books are pseudonymous, i.e., the prophecies are attributed to some prominent character; and they are pseudo-predictive. Generally some Old Testament saint is said to have foretold in detail what in reality was already history as far as the writer was concerned.

15. Josephus, *Antiquities* 11.8.4,5.

16. For various allusions to Daniel see D.S. Margoliouth, *Lines of Defense of the Biblical Revelation* (London: Hodder & Stoughton, 1900) 177-182.

17. The allusions to Daniel in Matthew's Gospel are as follows: 10:23; 16:27ff.; 19:28; 24:30; 25:31; 26:64. On the New Testament use of the Book of Daniel see C.H.H. Wright, *Daniel and his Prophecies* (originally published 1906; Minneapolis, MN: Klock & Klock, 1983 reprint) 97-100; and John Kennedy, *The Book of Daniel from the Christian Standpoint* (London: Eyre & Spottiswoode, 1898) 5-28.

18. W.H. Green, *General Introduction to the Old Testament: the Canon* (New York: Scribners, 1926) 84f.

19. Josephus (*Against Apion* 1.8) reports that the Scriptures were organized into three divisions. The first five were the books of law, the equivalent of the Pentateuch. The last four are said to contain "hymns to God and precepts for the conduct of human life" (i.e., Psalms, Proverbs, Ecclesiastes, Song of Solomon). Since Daniel was certainly a part of Josephus' Bible, and since the book could not possibly have been a part of the first or third division of the Scriptures, Daniel must have been placed among the thirteen books which Josephus attributes to prophets. For a more extended discussion of this point, see Norman L. Geisler and William Nix, *A General Introduction to the Bible* (Chicago: Moody, 1968) 151-160.

20. LeRoy E. Froom indictes the positions adopted throughout church history regarding certain key prophetic issues in Daniel in his monumental four-volume work *The Prophetic Faith of Our Fathers* (Washington: Review and Herald, 1950). The work is written from the view point of the Adventists.

21. On the value of this avalanche of exegetical material on Daniel, C.H.H. Wright comments: "The commentaries on Daniel are innumerable. On no other book, save the Book of Revelation in the New Testament, has so much worthless matter been written in the shape of exegesis." *An Introduction to the Old Testament* (London: Hodder and Stoughton, 1904) 197. H.H. Rowley in his book *Darius the Mede and the Four World Empires* (Cardiff: University of Wales, 1935) lists four hundred works he consulted in the investigation of only one problem in this book.

DANIEL: A BIBLIOGAPHY

Baldwin, Joyce. *Daniel* in Tyndale Old Testament Commentaries. Downers Grove, IL: InterVarsity, 1978.

Boutflower, Charles. *In and Around the Book of Daniel.* Grand Rapids: Kregel, 1977. Reprint of the 1923 ed.

Bultema, Harry. *Commentary on Daniel.* Grand Rapids: Kregel, 1988.

Butler, Paul. *Daniel* in Bible Study Textbook Series. Joplin, MO: College Press, 1970.

Gurney, Robert. *God in Control.* West Sussex, England: Walter, 1980.

Johnson, Philip C. *The Book of Daniel* in Shield Bible Study Series. Grand Rapids: Baker, 1964.

Leupold, H. C. *Exposition of Daniel.* Minneapolis: Augsburg, 1949.

McGuiggan, Jim. *The Book of Daniel.* West Monroe, LA: Let the Bible Speak, 1972.

Mauro, Philip. *The Seventy Weeks and the Great Tribulation.* Swengel, PA: Reiner, n.d.

Pusey, E. B. *Daniel the Prophet.* New York: Funk & Wagnalls, 1885.

Rushdoony, Rousas J. *Thy Kingdom Come.* Fairfax, VA: Thoburn, 1978.

Wallace, Ronald. *The Lord is King; The Message of Daniel.* Downers Grove, IL: InterVarsity, 1979.

Whitcomb, Jr., John C. *Darius the Mede* in Biblical and Theological Studies Series. Philadelphia: Presbyterian and Reformed, 1963.

Wilson, R. Dick. *Studies in the Book of Daniel.* 2 vols. in 1. Grand Rapids: Baker, 1972.

Wright, Charles H. H. *Studies in Daniel's Prophecy.* Minneapolis: Klock & Klock, 1983. Reprint of 1906 ed.

Young, E. J. *The Prophecy of Daniel.* Grand Rapids: Eerdmans, 1949.

CHAPTER THIRTY-SIX

The God of Gods
Daniel 1-2

Background of the Unit.

Daniel was taken as a captive to Babylon in 604 BC. Shortly thereafter Daniel and three Hebrew companions were selected to be trained for royal service. This training program lasted the better part of three years. Even before this period had ended, Daniel began to exercise his God-given ability to interpret dreams. As a result he was named ruler over the entire province of Babylon and chief of the prefects over all the wise men of the realm. In this position Daniel remained until the fall of the Babylonian empire in 539 BC.

Critics refer to the accounts in Daniel 1-6 as "martyr legends" and "oriental court tales."[1] These narratives give all the appearance, however, of being eye-witness accounts of actual events which transpired during the Babylonian captivity. Throughout these chapters Daniel is referred to in third person. Yet it is theology, not biography, which is prominent here. The author's purpose is obviously to demonstrate the superiority of the God of Heaven. In each of the six chapters pagan kings or their agents are forced to acknowledge the superiority of Daniel's God. Such acknowledgements are explicit in chapters 2-4 and 6, implicit in chapters 1 and 5.

Outline of the Unit.

A. The God of Intervention (chap. 1).
B. The God of Revelation (chap. 2).

THE GOD OF INTERVENTION
Daniel 1

The God of Daniel is introduced by two names in chapter 1. He is *'adonay*, i.e., "master, lord, or sovereign" (v. 2); he is *ha'elohim*, i.e. the God or simply *God* (vv. 9,17). In these three verses the same Hebrew verb *(nathan)* is used. This verb is translated in the NASB "gave" in verses 2 and 17, and "granted" in verse 9. The verb seems to point to the active involvement of God in the life of his people.

A. Intervention in Judgment (1:1-2).

The events of chapter 1 are dated to the third year of King Jehoiakim of Judah.[2] On the current calendar that would equate to parts of the years 605-604 BC. In 605 BC Nebuchadnezzar defeated the Egyptian-Assyrian coalition at Carchemish on the Euphrates river. He pursued Pharaoh Neco down the coast of Palestine to the borders of Egypt. At that time, apparently, Nebuchadnezzar came against Jehoiakim, an ally of the Pharaoh (2 Chr 36:6). The sovereign Lord "gave" Jehoiakim into the hand of Nebuchadnezzar; i.e., the king of Judah was forced to capitulate and recognize Nebuchadnezzar as his overlord. Jehoiakim was left on the throne (2 Kgs 24:1). He was forced, however, to give to the Babylonian some of the Temple vessels and hostages of the royal family as symbols of his submission. The Temple vessels were taken by Nebuchadnezzar "to the land of Shinar,[3] i.e., Babylonia. There they were deposited in "the house of his god," i.e., the god Marduk. The vessels were regarded as trophies of Marduk's victory over Judah's God.

B. Intervention in Confrontation (1:3-16).

The deportation of the hostages to Babylon led to a confrontation between the God of the Hebrews and the gods of Babylon. Through the lives of four faithful young men the Lord immediately began to demonstrate the wisdom of his law and the power of his presence.

1. The training (1:3-7). Having returned to Babylon, Nebuchadnezzar ordered "the chief of his officials,"[4] Ashpenaz, to select some of the hostages to be trained for royal service. Those selected had to meet five qualifications. They had to be (1) young men (2) of royal or noble birth. (3) Physically and (4) intellectually they had be superior. (5) They had to possess the poise required of those who would stand in the presence of the Great King (1:3-4a).

Those selected were to undergo a thorough program of education and indoctrination—a virtual Babylonian brainwashing! They studied the literature and language of the Chaldean people.[5] The subject matter no doubt included language, astronomy, mathematics, natural history, mythological literature, agriculture, and architecture. These young men were not being trained as soothsayers, but as upper-level administrators and advisors.[6] Nonetheless, the purpose of this curriculum was to change the way these young men thought—their world view, their value system (1:4b).

During the three years of training these selectees were to eat the king's choice food and wine. Perhaps this was meant as a privilege, and no doubt was regarded as such by most in the program. Here, however, is yet another aspect of brainwashing. The goal was to change the way these young men lived (1:5).

Those in the program were given new names, names which honored the gods of Babylon. For most in the program this would be no problem. For four Hebrew youths this would represent another aspect of brainwashing. The goal here was to change the allegiance of these young men. The following chart summarizes the result of the name changes.

Chart No. 17

BRAINWASHING THROUGH NAME CHANGE			
HEBREW NAME	MEANING	BABYLONIAN NAME	MEANING
HANANIAH	"The Lord is Gracious"	SHADRACH	"Command of Aku"
MISHAEL	"Who is What God is?"	MESHACH	"Who is what Aku is?"
AZARIAH	"The Lord has helped"	ABED-NEGO	"Servant of Nebo"
DANIEL	"God is my Judge"	BELTESHAZZAR	"May Balak protect"

2. The test (1:8-16). The Chaldeans changed Daniel's name, but they could not change his nature. This young man made up his mind that he would not defile himself with the king's food and wine. His decision was based on spiritual, not physical considerations. This food was unclean by the standards of the Law of Moses, and doubly unclean because it had first been dedicated to idols. Daniel asked the commander of officials for a special dispensation with regard to the food. The official was reluctant to grant this request. He knew it would mean his head should Daniel and his friends not fare well on their diet (1:8-10).

Daniel would not take "no" for an answer. He went to his more immediate overseer and asked for a ten day test. He and his companions would eat vegetables and grains and drink only water. Then after ten days he challenged the official to compare their appearance to that of the trainees who continued on the prescribed royal diet (1:11-13). Two questions arise here: What right did Daniel have to propose such a test? Why did he propose a vegetarian diet? The test was not a wager of faith nor even an example of the confidence of living faith.

Daniel must have received a revelation from the Spirit and he was acting in accord with that revelation.[7] The vegetarian diet was proposed because it would be impossible to obtain and prepare meat that would conform to the Mosaic code. Furthermore, vegetables and grains were not generally consecrated to pagan gods before regular use as was meat.

The overseer accepted the challenge proposed by Daniel. At the end of the ten days he found the appearance of the four Hebrew youths healthier than that of the others in the program. He found them "fatter of flesh," a idiom which refers, not to their weight as implied in the NASB, but to the texture of their skin. They had firm flesh, i.e., they were "better nourished" (NIV). So impressed was the overseer that he removed the four Hebrews from the royal diet permanently (1:14-16). Thus God was beginning to exercise his power among the Babylonians. The change in the appearance of the young men was the result of God's grace, not the properties of the foods consumed.

C. Intervention in Vindication (1:17-21).

In addition to the physical blessing, God bestowed on Daniel and his friends other gifts. He gave them "knowledge and intelligence in every branch of literature." This would involve a divine insight which would give them the ability to accept what was true and to reject what was false in their instruction. Along with that, God gave them "wisdom" to conduct their lives in such a way as to get along both with their superiors and their peers. To Daniel was given yet another gift, that of understanding all kinds of visions and dreams. Part of this gift, no doubt, was the ability to distinguish between natural and supernatural dreams (1:17).

At the end of the specified period of training, the students were brought before Nebuchadnezzar for their final exam. The king "talked with them." The Hebrew implies an intensive interrogation. Among all the candidates none was found who was the equal of Daniel and his friends. They thus entered the king's service. The king found these four consistently to be "ten times better" than all the magicians and astrologers (NASB conjurers) in the realm when it came to offering counsel. Daniel maintained his position in the court until Babylon was conquered by Cyrus in 539 BC (1:18-21).

The overriding lesson of chapter 1 is that the God of the Bible is active in the affairs of his people. He gave Jehoiakim into the hand of Nebuchadnezzar in an act of judgment. On the other hand he preserved his faithful ones by giving them favor in the eyes of their captors, and by giving them gifts of superior worth.

THE GOD OF REVELATION
Daniel 2

Daniel 2 contains a dream revelation and its interpretation. The chapter is dated to the second year of Nebuchadnezzar, i.e., 603 BC.[8] This chapter demonstrates that Yahweh, not the god Nebo, is the "revealer of mysteries" (v. 29).

A. The Problem in the Court (2:1-16).

In a dream state one night Nebuchadnezzar experienced a revelation from God which unnerved him. His spirit was troubled and his sleep left him as he puzzled over the meaning of the ominous nightmare. In the middle of the night he summoned his court advisors—magicians, conjurers, sorcerers, Chaldeans, and soothsayers. Exactly what the differences were between these officials is not known. The king demanded of them that they explain to him the meaning of his dream. The Chaldeans, acting as spokesmen for the rest, answered Nebuchadnezzar in the Aramaic language.[9] Following standard procedure they asked the king to relate to them the dream so that they might give the interpretation of it (2:1-4).

This night Nebuchadnezzar was in no mood to do business as usual. He demanded as proof of the supernatural ability of his advisors that they tell him the dream, then interpret it.[10] Should they not be able to do both, the king would order the charlatans torn limb from limb and their houses demolished for good measure. On the other hand, should they declare both the dream and its interpretation these advisors would be well rewarded with gifts and honors (2:5f.).

Presuming there was some mistake, the Chaldeans requested a second time that the king relate the contents of his dream. They would then be able to consult the standard reference books to find an interpretation for the dream symbols. The king at this point became annoyed. He accused his advisors of stalling in hopes that the original decree would be lifted. Only by declaring the dream to him could Nebuchadnezzar be assured that the interpretation which they offered was reliable (2:7-9).

The Chaldeans responded with a four-fold defense. (1) They argued that no man could comply with the demands of the king. (2) Such a request was totally unprecedented in the annals of Babylonian history. (3) They appealed for sympathy by complaining that the king's demands were too difficult. (4) Finally, they dumped the whole matter on the gods. Only those whose dwelling place is not with mortal flesh could reveal to the king the dream which he had experienced (2:10f.).

Nebuchadnezzar yielded to none of these arguments. He became enraged and consequently issued the edict which ordered the execution of all the wise men of Babylon. This command included Daniel because he had been trained under the wise men and in the broad sense at least was considered one of them. The soldiers searched for Daniel and his friends in order to carry out the order. They were probably not with the group which initially was summoned to the king because they were as yet considered novices (2:12f.).

Daniel faced his potential executioners with calmness. He knew that as long as God had a purpose for his life no man could take it from him. First, he inquired of Arioch, the captain of the king's personal police force, as to the reason for the edict. Daniel then went immediately to the king and requested time that he might declare to Nebuchadnezzar the interpretation of the dream. The confidence of this novice advisor impressed the king. Not for a moment did Daniel doubt the ability of his God to provide all that the king required. Nebuchadnezzar granted a temporary reprieve (2:14-16).

B. The Prayer for Enlightenment (2:17-24).

Daniel went immediately from the throne room to his house where he enlisted the help of his friends in a prayer vigil. The prayer itself is not recorded but the thrust of it is. Their purpose was to request compassion from "the God of heaven"[11] concerning the mystery of the king's dream and concerning the safety of the four faithful

Hebrews. That very night in a "vision of the night"[12] the mystery was revealed to Daniel (2:17-19).

Instead of rushing impulsively to the king, Daniel paused to bless the God of heaven, i.e., worship. He began his praise psalm with an exhortation: "Let the name of God be praised forever." The *name* of God in Scripture is equivalent to all that God has revealed about himself. The praise here is sevenfold. (1) Wisdom and power belong to the Lord. He, and not the wise men of Babylon, has the wisdom to order the world and the might to carry out his purposes. (2) The Lord controls, either in an active or permissive manner, the times and the epochs of history. This is a direct challenge to the fatalism of Babylonian astral religion. (3) The Lord removes and establishes kings. He is ultimately the King of kings. (4) He gives wisdom and knowledge to men who are prepared to receive it (2:20f.).

(5) The God of Heaven reveals the profound and hidden things. Only through revelation can men have any insight into the future. (6) The Lord knows what is in the darkness. He knows the inner darkness of men's hearts, the darkness of the unseen realm of Satan, and the darkness of distant past and future. (7) The light dwells in God. This is another direct rejection of Babylonian theology which deified the heavenly luminaries (2:22).

Daniel regarded the Lord as worthy of praise, not only because of his character, but for what he had done. God had now given to Daniel wisdom and power as well as the revelation which had been requested. All four of the Hebrew young men now understood the dream of the king. Immediately Daniel rushed to Arioch and urged him to stay the execution order. Though he had just received a special revelation from the Lord, Daniel was not so puffed up that he failed to think of the well-being of others. Daniel urged the official to take him to the king. He was now confident that he could interpret the dream of the king (2:23f.).

C. A Presentation of the Dream (2:25-35).

Arioch hurriedly brought Daniel into the king's presence. He took all the credit for having found someone who could make the interpretation known to the king. Turning to the Hebrew, Nebuchadnezzar asked if he were able to make known both the dream itself and its interpretation. In response, Daniel was bold to point out that his superiors—the magicians and such—were unable to give the information which the king demanded. Daniel did not want these men later to claim that he had gotten his revelation from them! While men had not been able to reveal this mystery, the God of heaven had given to Daniel the ability to make it known to the king (2:25-28).

God had revealed to Nebuchadnezzar in his "dream and visions" what would take place "in the latter days." This expression is found fourteen times in the Old Testament. It appears to refer to an extended period of time which culminates in the messianic age. Specifically in this passage the phrase must include all of the period covered by the king's dream, viz., the period from 600 BC to the inauguration and ultimate triumph of Christ's kingdom. The New Testament frequently refers to the Christian age as the last days.[13]

Daniel began his presentation by revealing the circumstances of the dream. Nebuchadnezzar was on his bed musing about what would take place in the future. The God who reveals mysteries had revealed to the king that which he had longed to know. Daniel, however, deflected any personal honor which might have been bestowed upon him. He was not a man of more wisdom than others. All credit for the revelation belonged to God. It was his gracious purpose to make known to the king the meaning of the thoughts which had filled his mind (2:29f.).

The king's dream centered on a great statue of extraordinary splendor. The image was essentially human in form. Its appearance was awesome, i.e., it exhibited strength and power. The image, as it turned out, represented worldly government which is impressive in its grandeur and might. The head of the statue was made of fine gold. Its breast and arms were of silver, its belly and thighs of bronze, its legs of iron. The feet of the statue were partly of iron and partly of clay. The materials viewed from head to toe thus declined in value. This apparently symbolizes in some sense a deterioration of the power, might and majesty of the kingdoms of this world (2:31-33).

The king then observed a strange sight. A little stone was being cut out of a mountain without hands. The stone seemed to catapult through the air like a missile. It struck the statue with incredible force in its feet of iron mixed with clay. The entire image fell, and all the valuable metals of the upper body were pulverized. The wind carried away the dust so that there was not a trace of the gold, silver, bronze or iron. The stone, however, became a great mountain and filled the whole earth. The dream began with a great image filling the stage; it closed with the great stone filling the whole earth (2:34f.).

D. The Prediction Regarding Kingdoms (2:36-45).

Daniel proceeds with confidence from the presentation of the dream to the predictive interpretation of it (2:36).

1. The head of gold (2:37-38). Nebuchadnezzar was the king of kings to whom the God of heaven had given sovereignty over the world (cf. Jer 27:6-8). The head of gold symbolized him. Since Nebuchadnezzar was the embodiment of all that Babylon was, the head represented the Babylonian kingdom as well as its king. This symbolism was most appropriate for two reasons. First, Babylon was called the golden city (Isa 14:4) because gold was used profusely to decorate its shrines and public buildings. Second, the idea of world empire originated with the Babylonians. The policies which were formulated in Babylon continued to control succeeding empires even as the head controls the body (2:37f.).

2. The breast of silver (2:39a). The breast and arms of silver represented a kingdom inferior to Babylon which would subsequently arise. Most likely this is the Medo-Persian empire which assumed sovereignty over the Near East in 539 BC when Cyrus conquered Babylon. The symbolism here was significant for three reasons. First, the two arms appropriately indicate the two major ethnic components of this empire, viz., the Medes and the Persians. Second, the breast encloses the heart. Cyrus, the founder of this empire, is reputed to have displayed heartfelt charity on friend and foe alike. Third, silver was virtually equivalent to money. Thus the silver here may be intended to portray the more commercial spirit of this empire.

The question as to how the Medo-Persian empire was inferior to that of Nebuchadnezzar is difficult. Certainly the inferiority did not lie in geography, for the territory administered by Cyrus far exceeded anything Nebuchadnezzar ever ruled. The assertion of the moral inferiority of the Medo-Persian empire is debatable. Perhaps the inferiority of the second world empire was in the following areas. First, the

Babylonian empire in the broadest sense was basically uninterrupted for two millennia. On the other hand, the Medo-Persian empire survived for but two centuries. Second, the second empire lacked the inner unity of the first.[14] Third, in terms of influence and achievement the old Babylonian empire outranked the Medo-Persian by far.[15]

3. The belly of bronze (2:39b). The third kingdom appears to be the Greco-Macedonian kingdom founded by Alexander the Great. Again the symbolism was appropriate. First, bronze was the primary metal in instruments of war, and Alexander's army was noted for its military prowess. Second, what began as a unit (the abdomen) divided itself into two separate parts which were never reunited. This may point to Syria and Egypt, the two great Hellenistic kingdoms which grew out of the empire of Alexander.

4. The legs of iron (2:40). Assuming that the second and third empires have been correctly identified, the fourth kingdom most likely is Rome. The iron might of Rome crushed and broke "all these in pieces." Each successive kingdom had assumed the elements of the previous kingdom which it supplanted. So when Rome crushed the Hellenistic kingdoms (Syria and Egypt), it in effect crushed all the previous kingdoms.

5. The feet of iron and clay (2:41). The Roman empire would experience a second phase in which it would be a mixture of firmness (iron) and weakness (clay). This may represent the decline of Rome as it absorbed Germanic tribes and became a decadent dictatorship. No rival empire conquered Rome. The fourth empire did not fall so much as it crumbled from within.

6. The toes (2:42-43). Presumably the statue had ten toes. A wide divergence of opinion exists as to the meaning of this symbolism. The Adventists think in terms of ten kingdoms which at one point constituted the Roman Empire. Some modern students of prophecy suggest that a ten nation confederacy, a revived Roman Empire, will appear on the territory once ruled by Rome. Recent political and economic developments in Europe are regarded as the fulfillment of this prophecy. Ten, however, is the number of completeness. It probably was not intended to be taken literally here. Therefore, attempts to identify ten specific kingdoms are unreliable. The toes may designate all the kingdoms which would follow Rome on the stage of history. The iron and clay mixture could be a way of portraying attempts to forge alliances of diverse ethnic and linguistic groups.[16]

7. *The stone (2:44-45)*. The stone cut out of the mountain without hands represented the messianic kingdom. God would set up that kingdom "in the days of those kings." Daniel seems to use the terms *kings* and *kingdoms* interchangeably (cf. 7:17,23). Therefore, the reference here is probably to the *kingdoms* just enumerated. During the span of time represented by the image, the God of Heaven would establish a kingdom of a different sort. That kingdom would be (1) indestructible, (2) non-transferable, (3) irresistibly powerful, and (4) eternal. Although it would coexist with the kingdoms of this world for a time, eventually it would triumph over all human government. Since this kingdom endures forever it cannot be the millennial kingdom which some anticipate. Daniel described the smashing of the image as a sudden, powerful and decisive blow. This probably represents the sweeping away of the world powers at the second coming of Christ.[17]

E. The Promotion of Daniel (2:46-49).

To say the least, Nebuchadnezzar was impressed by the abilities of Daniel. He fell on his face and did homage to him. He ordered his servants to present to Daniel an offering and fragrant incense. In these worship acts he probably was recognizing Daniel as the representative of the unseen God of heaven. The prophet certainly would not have accepted worship had he thought that it was being directed to him rather than his God (2:46).

Nebuchadnezzar's comments confirm this interpretation. He confessed nothing regarding Daniel, but made far-reaching admissions about Daniel's God. The interpretation of the dream had convinced the king of three things. Daniel's God was (1) a God of gods; (2) a Lord of kings; and (3) a revealer of mysteries. Speaking here as a polytheist, the king acknowledged the supremacy, sovereignty and sapience of Daniel's God. He had not yet, however, come to see Yahweh as the only true God (2:47).

Nebuchadnezzar promoted Daniel to be ruler over the whole province of Babylon and chief prefect, i.e., overseer, over all the wise men of the realm. His duties in these capacities are not indicated. The

REPRESENTS IN ITS TOTALITY ALL HUMAN GOVERNMENT

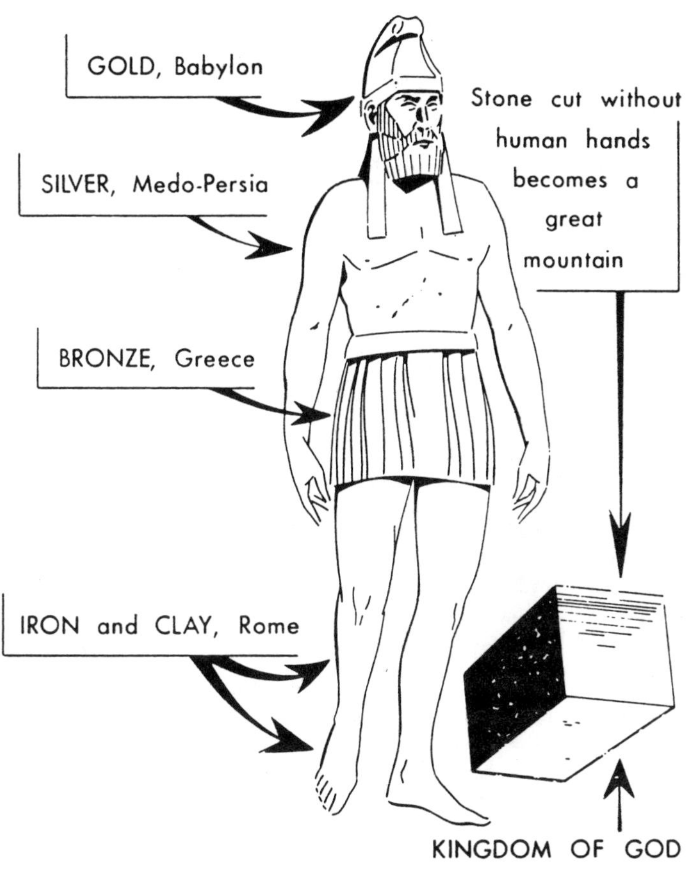

king also gave the prophet "many great gifts" as tokens of his appreciation. For his part, Daniel did not forget his three friends. He requested that they be given greater responsibility within the kingdom. Nebuchadnezzar then appointed Shadrach, Meshach and Abed-nego to administrative positions in the province of Babylon. Because of his position, Daniel himself remained in the court of the king (2:48f.).

Chapter 2 underscores four great truths which Christians can ill afford to ignore as articles of their faith. First, God and not man is sovereign in world affairs. Second, God has a plan for the world. Third, God is ordering history according to his plan. Finally, the kingdoms of this world are human and temporary. Only God's kingdom is of eternal duration.

Endnotes

1. Georg Fohrer, *Introduction to the Old Testament* (New York: Abingdon, 1968) 474f.

2. According to Jer 46:2 Nebuchadnessar smote Carchemish in Jehoiakim's fourth year. In Daniel the years are reckoned acording to the Babylonian method whereas in Jeremiah they are reckoned according to the Palestinian method. In the Babylonian method the partial year which a king reigned prior to the beginning of a new year was not counted. Thus Jehoiakim's fourth year according to Jeremiah would be the same as the third year according to Daniel.

3. Since the Tower of Babel episode (Gen 11) the term *Shinar* carried the connotation "center of wickedness." Daniel's thought is that the wicked spirit of ancient Shinar was revived in the oppression of God's people by Babylon.

4. The term literally means *eunuchs*. The Hebrew term is sometimes applied to those filling important posts, without regard to corporeal mutilation. Merrill F. Unger, *Unger's Bible Dictionary* (Chicago: Moody, 1961) 328.

5. The Chaldeans appeared as early as Abraham (Gen 11:28) dwelling near the mouth of the Euphrates River. After a millennium and a half of obscurity they emerged as the dominant power in Mesopotamia. At times in Daniel the term is used in its broad ethnic sense; at other times it is used in a restricted sense to refer to a class of magicians.

6. On the curriculum of Chaldean schools see T.G. Pinches, s.v. "Chaldea" in *The International Standard Bible Encyclopaedia* (Grand Rapids: Eerdmans, 1939) 1:591.

7. So E.J. Young, *The Prophecy of Daniel* (Grand Rapids: Eerdmans, 1949) 46.

8. Most likely the first and third years of Daniel's training (Dan 1:5) were not full years. The training period would include Nebuchadnezzar's accession year, his first full year of reign, and a portion of his second full year.

9. Because this portion of Daniel deals primarily with Gentile nations, a Gentile language is used from Dan 2:4 through chapter 7, at which point the Hebrew language is resumed.

10. The KJV unfortunately mistranslates: "The word is gone forth from me." The LXX misses the mark even more with: "I have forgotten." The NASB is corrrect: "The command from me is firm."

11. During the exile the title "God of heaven" came into prominence among the Jews. See Ezra 1:2; 6:10; 7:12, 21; Neh 1:5; 2:4; Ps 136:26.

13. E.g., Acts 2:16f.; Heb 1:1f.; I Tim 4:1; 1 John 2:18.

14. E.J. Young, *op.cit.* 74.

15. H.C. Leupold, *Expostion of Daniel* (Minneapolis, MN: Augsburg, 1949) 116-118.

16. Phillip Johnson has suggested that the phrase "they will combine with one another in the seed of men" refers to democracy which brings ordinary men into positions of leadership once reserved for a certain class. See *The Book of Daniel* in The Shield Bible Study Series (Grand Rapids: Baker, 1964) 25.

17. Gareth Reese, *Let's Study Prophecy* (Moberly, MO: Central Christian College of the Bible, n.d.) Reese cites in support of his position 1 Cor 15:20ff.; Matt 21:44; and Rev 11:15.

CHAPTER THIRTY-SEVEN

The Only True God
Daniel 3-4

Background of the Unit.

The Greek version of the Old Testament dates both chapters 3 and 4 to the eighteenth year of Nebuchadnezzar, i.e., 587 BC. That note in the Septuagint is not original. The translators apparently tried to tie these chapters to the destruction of Jerusalem which occurred in the same year. Most likely the events in chapter 3 transpired shortly after those of chapter 2. On the other hand, chapter 4 most likely comes from the closing years of Nebuchadnezzar's reign when his extensive building program in Babylon had been completed. Thus dates of about 600 BC for chapter 3, and about 570 BC for chapter 4, are appropriate.

The two chapters are quite different from the literary standpoint. Chapter 3 is written in a style similar to that which is found in the monumental inscriptions from Mesopotamia. It displays a certain formal dignity, with long lists of high officials and names of musical instruments repeated three times. On the other hand, chapter 4 is autobiographical. King Nebuchadnezzar describes what must have been the most embarrassing incident of his life.

Outline of the Unit.

Those who outline chapters 1-6 in terms of Daniel's activities have a difficult time demonstrating the connection between chapter 3 and the other five chapters in the first half of the book. The real focus of these chapters is not on Daniel, but on the continuing self-revelation of God. In chapters 3-4 Yahweh revealed himself as the God of salvation. The following outline, then, seems most appropriate:

A. Salvation for the Faithful (chap. 3).
B. Salvation for the Penitent (chap. 4).

SALVATION FOR THE FAITHFUL
Daniel 3

Farrar refers to chapter 3 as "historic fiction." Montgomery says the writer drew upon the materials from popular legend. In truth, however, nothing in this narrative savors of unreality, fiction or untruth.[1]

A. The Test (3:1-7).

Nebuchadnezzar made an image the exact nature of which is not stated in the text.[2] That the king intended this image to symbolize his universal and abiding sovereignty is certainly implied. Perhaps the head of gold on the visionary image of chapter 2 triggered Nebuchadnezzar's lust for power. If he were the golden head, why not the whole image? The king apparently intended to consolidate his power by creating an official religion in which the state, symbolized by the image, was the object of worship.

The statue was of enormous size, some sixty cubits or ninety feet high. Yet the width of the image was but six cubits or nine feet. This would make for a grotesque figure if indeed the statue was in human form. The suggestion has been made that perhaps as much as twenty-four cubits of the height should be assigned to a pedestal. That would make for better proportion. The image was of gold. Most likely gold overlay rather than solid gold is intended.

Nebuchadnezzar erected his image on the plain of Dura in the province of Babylon (3:1). Mesopotamian tablets mention three places which bear the name *Duru*. Several cities in the region have names compounded with *dur*. The name means "walled place." About six miles south of Babylon is a place by this name where archaeologists have found a large brick construction forty-five feet square and twenty feet high. The suggestion has been made that this structure may be the ruins of the pedestal upon which the statue of Daniel 3 was erected.

Nebuchadnezzar ordered the top officials of the empire to assemble for the dedication of the statue. In typical oriental emphasis by enumeration, eight different kinds of judicial, military and administrative offices are mentioned. A herald loudly proclaimed the purpose of the gathering as he moved through the great crowd. The king had decreed that when a musical signal was given by the national orchestra,[3] all present were to fall down and worship the image. Those who refused to comply with the edict would be cast into a furnace of blazing fire (3:2-6). Not even the Creator coerces outward acts of submission to heavenly authority. Yet earthly tyrants require absolute allegiance, virtual worship, from their subjects.

The reactions to the king's edict were mixed. Probably most who were present owed their position, prestige and wealth to the Great King. They were anxious to curry favor with Nebuchadnezzar no matter what eccentric demands he might make. Some of those who represented conquered peoples may have hated the king and despised all that the image represented. Yet these too bowed to the image. When the musical fanfare sounded thousands fell in unison before the image (3:7). Three young men, however, refused to bow.

B. The Accusation (3:8-12).

Certain Chaldeans came forward immediately to bring charges against the Jewish young men. No doubt they were motivated by a jealous spirit which arose after the promotion of the Hebrews to positions of prominence in the province of Babylon. That these men were wise in the ways of manipulating monarchs is clear in the text. They addressed Nebuchadnezzar with traditional respect. They repeated his commandment to him. They reminded the king of the punishment which he had stipulated for violators (3:8-11).

Instead of naming the offenders immediately, the Chaldeans spoke of them in a demeaning way: "certain Jews." The implication here is that the offenders were part of an inferior race. Lurking behind these words is the ugly specter of anti-semitism. They then further identified these "certain Jews" as men that Nebuchadnezzar had appointed over the administration of the province of Babylon. The innuendo is that these Jews were unworthy of the high honor bestowed upon them. Their ingratitude was manifested in their disobedience to the royal command. Finally, the Chaldeans specifically named the accused: Shadrach, Meshach and Abed-nego.

A three-fold charge was leveled against the three. First, they charged the Hebrews with showing disrespect for the king himself. Second, the Hebrews refused to worship the gods which Nebuchadnezzar revered. Third, the young men would not worship the golden image which the king had erected in the plain of Dura (3:12).

C. The Arraignment (3:13-18).

The king was furious (lit., burned up) when he heard the accusation. He immediately summoned Shadrach, Meshach and Abed-nego. Nebuchadnezzar had four things to say to the Hebrews. First, he sought to verify the facts. "Is it true[4] that you do not serve my gods or worship the golden image that I have set up?" In this moment of truth the three were being given the opportunity to explain away their noncompliance and to denounce their accusers. Second, he offered them another opportunity to comply with the edict. He could see in their faces, however, that they had no intention of obeying. Third, the king repeated the warning, which now had greater weight since it came directly from his lips. If they failed to comply with the edict they would be immediately thrown into the fiery furnace. Finally, he mocked their faith in God: "What God is there who can deliver you out of my hands?" He knew that the God of the Hebrews could reveal secrets, but he refused to believe that this God could deliver from physical death (3:13-15).

The response of the Hebrew young men was respectful, but at the same time, heroic and theologically sound. They made no attempt to rationalize to themselves compliance to the king's edict. Six aspects of their response are worthy of note.

First, the young men refused to apologize for their action. "We do not need to give you an answer concerning this." They were not being reckless. They realized that the king could snuff out their lives by one command; yet they were not afraid. These men had such a reverent awe for God that there was no room in their mind for fear of man. Second, the Hebrews confessed their allegiance to God. They referred to him as "our God whom we serve." If ever there was a time to compromise their commitment to the Lord, this was it. Yet they stood fast, unashamed of their years of faithful service to their Creator. Third, they testified to God's power. "Our God is able to deliver us from the furnace of blazing fire." The Hebrew conveys the strongest possible assurance. The thought might be paraphrased: "He is infinitely able to rescue us."

Fourth, the three also acknowledged the sovereignty of God. They said, "if it be so," i.e., if he wills it; if it is part of his purpose for our lives. Fifth, they expressed confidence in the grace of God. "He will deliver us out of your hand." If our deliverance is within his will he will bring it about. Finally, the Hebrews declared unwavering fidelity to God. "But even if he does not, let it be known to you that we are not going to serve your gods or worship the golden image that you have set up." The faith of these three youths was unconditional. Theirs was not a *quid pro quo* relationship with God.

D. The Sentence (3:19-23).

Though the reply had been framed in a courteous manner, Nebuchadnezzar was "filled with wrath." His fury was manifested in his face. He ordered that the furnace be heated "seven times more than it was usually heated." The phrase "seven times" is a judicial expression indicating "to the legal maximum."[5] Certain valiant warriors were commanded to tie up the offenders and cast them into the furnace. The king knew that these soldiers would be sacrificed in the process of carrying out their orders (3:19f.).

The three Hebrew youths were tied up immediately, without even removing their outer garments. They were cast into the midst of the furnace. They "fell into the midst of the furnace of blazing fire."

Apparently the furnace was built up against an embankment. The victims were thrown in from the top. In any case, because of the intense heat of the furnace the soldiers who carried out the execution order were slain in the process (3:21-23).

E. The Deliverance (3:24-27).

The king, sitting at ground level, apparently could peer through an opening in the furnace. What he saw astonished him. He verified with his advisors the number of young men who had been bound and cast into the furnace. He declared that he saw *four* men walking about within the furnace. The ropes had burned off the prisoners, yet the flames had not harmed them. The king likened the fourth man to "a son of the gods," i.e., a supernatural being (3:24f.). Jews identify the fourth man in the fire as an angel; Christians usually regard him as a Christophony, i.e., a manifestation of Christ. What a blessed thought this text suggests: The furnace of adversity provides an opportunity for the Lord to be close to his servants.

After some time the fire died down and the king was able to approach the door of the furnace. He respectfully addressed the Hebrews as "servants of the Most High God." He invited the youths to come out of the furnace. The various officials gathered around the three and verified what Nebuchadnezzar already knew. The fire had done no damage to the youths, not even so much as to singe a hair of their heads. Their clothing was not damaged, nor did they even smell as though they had been through a fire! (3:26f.).

F. The Acknowledgement (3:28-30).

Nebuchadnezzar was astonished at the power of a God who could accomplish such a spectacular feat. By his own admission, no god with whom he was familiar could do such a thing. Therefore the king burst forth with praise for the God of Shadrach, Meshach and Abed-nego. The king was impressed with the trust of the three who had been willing to put their lives on the line rather than worship what they did not recognize as God. Such trust had been rewarded. This God had sent forth his *angel* to deliver his servants (3:28). Nebuchadnezzar's praise should not be regarded as the utterance of a truly converted soul. The king was impressed with the *manifestation* of the power, rather than the *source* of it.

The king issued a proclamation regarding the God of the three Hebrew youths. From that day forward no one would be permitted to speak evil of the God of the Hebrews. The rationale for singling out this God was simply that "there is no other God who is able to deliver in this way." The edict was backed by a threat that violators would be "torn limb from limb and their houses reduced to a rubbish heap." Such grotesque intimidation apparently was the only way Nebuchadnezzar knew of gaining compliance with his wishes (cf. 2:5). To apologize to the youths for the way he had treated them, the king "caused Shadrach, Meshach, and Abed-nego to prosper in the province of Babylon." This probably means that he gave them some kind of administrative promotion (3:29f.).

SALVATION FOR THE PENITENT
Daniel 4

Chapter 4 is structured in a peculiar way. The introduction to the narrative is actually a conclusion. The chapter might be diagramed like this: *results—circumstances—results.* It begins with a proclamation in which Nebuchadnezzar declared his personal faith in the Most High God. At the end of chapter 2 the king had been impressed with the superior wisdom of Daniel's God. At the end of chapter 3 he acknowledged the superior power of this God. In chapter 4 Nebuchadnezzar came to a new level of spiritual awareness, perhaps even to salvation. This awareness grew out of a painful and humiliating experience which the king described in some detail.

A. Faith Proclaimed (4:1-3).

Some thirty years—perhaps longer—had passed since the events of chapter 3.[6] Nebuchadnezzar had experienced a wonderful conversion and he wanted the whole world to hear his testimony.[7] The standard greeting of the day, "may your peace abound," was no doubt energized by the personal peace which the king now possessed (4:1).

Because the words of the proclamation sound so Biblical, some have questioned whether in fact they were derived from Nebuchadnezzar. Two observations may help account for the language. First, in places the Babylonian psalms of praise sound remarkably like the Biblical psalms. Second, Daniel may have helped the king phrase his new-found faith in traditional Hebrew praise language.

In his testimonial tract the king wishes to declare the "signs and wonders" which the Most High God had done for him. He described these signs and wonders as "great" and "mighty." The reference here is to the interpretation and fulfillment of the dream which he was about to relate. He boasted here, not of what he had done, but of what God had done. The king praised God's kingdom as "an everlasting kingdom." Nebuchadnezzar recognized God's dominion as enduring "from generation to generation" (4:2f.). With these words Nebuchadnezzar repudiated the image of gold which he had built, and the kingdom which he was determined to perpetuate. He recognized that earthly kingdoms, his own included, only survive as long as God wills it.

B. His Anxiety Confessed (4:4-9).

Nebuchadnezzar began his account with a description of the prosperity which he had achieved during his long reign in Babylon. He was "at ease" and "flourishing" (lit., growing green), i.e., enjoying the fruits of his many conquests and enormous wealth. Then came the dream which was to change his life completely. He sensed that this was another dream revelation from God. The dream seemed to be an evil omen which was a portent of impending catastrophe. The king, however, grasped the significance of the revelation. Therefore he became restless and troubled in his mind (4:4f.).

Nebuchadnezzar sent for his wise men and requested that they make known to him the interpretation of the dream. As to why he did not call Daniel immediately the text is silent. A number of possible explanations can be offered. (1) That this *may* be a new Nebuchadnezzar is possible, but not likely. (2) Daniel may have held back, waiting for "center stage." (3) Daniel may have had responsibilities that kept him away from the city of Babylon. (4) The king may have been resisting the implications of Daniel's superior wisdom. (5) The king may have forgotten the earlier dream and Daniel's interpretation. (6) The king may have had a general idea as to the import of the dream. He may have sensed that he would suffer humiliation, most likely at the hands of Daniel's God. Therefore, he wanted nothing to do with him for the moment.

Finally Daniel came in before the king. In this meeting five points are worthy of note. First, Nebuchadnezzar used Daniel's Babylonian name: "Belteshazzar." What irony! Daniel had been given a name honoring a Chaldean god. Now the Chaldean king was explaining how he came to embrace the God of Daniel. Second, Nebuchadnezzar described Daniel as one "in whom is a spirit of the holy gods." The expression could also be translated "the Spirit of the Holy God." The translation here depends on the translator's overall impression as to whether the king experienced genuine conversion as a result of his experiences in this chapter.[8]

Third, Nebuchadnezzar addressed Daniel as "chief of magicians," i.e., he was the highest ranking member of the Chaldean court. To this position the king had appointed him many years earlier (cf. 2:48). Fourth, Nebuchadnezzar recognized Daniel's supernatural wisdom. No mystery baffled this man who was filled with a divine spirit. Fifth, Nebuchadnezzar requested that Daniel tell him the meaning of the visions which he had seen in his dream (4:8f.).

C. His Dream Described (4:10-18).

In his dream the king's attention was fixed on a tree. Trees were used as symbols for royalty in the ancient Near East.[9] The king briefly described seven attributes of this tree. The tree was (1) central in position, (2) enormous in height, (3) continuing in growth, (4) visible to all, (5) beautiful to behold, (6) abundant in fruit, and (7) providing lodging for bird and beast (4:10f.). Nebuchadnezzar may have recognized in the huge tree in the center of the earth a figure of himself.

Nebuchadnezzar then saw a "watcher"[10] or angel descending from heaven. The watcher gave the order for the tree to be hewn down. The meaning here is clear. The cutting down of a tree is a Biblical symbol of judgment (Matt 3:10; Luke 13:7). Only the stump and roots were to be left untouched. A band of iron and bronze was to be put about the stump. This act prevented the stump from splitting, thus making it possible for the tree to grow again (4:12-15a).

The watcher interpreted the dream in part by showing that the tree represented a person. The mind of that person would be changed, i.e., he would become insane. He would begin to act like an animal. This particular form of mental illness is known as zoanthropy. Living outdoors, Nebuchadnezzar would be "drenched with the dew of heaven.""Seven times," i.e., years, would pass over this person in this dehumanized state (4:15b-16).

Why would such a fate befall any man? The watcher answered that question. "This sentence is by the decree of the angelic watchers, and the decision is a command of the holy ones." The angels in heaven pleaded against this person who in his great pride ignored and obscured the glory of God. Since the angels were in full accord with God's plan, the decree or decision may rightly be described as being theirs. Behind this judicial decree was a higher purpose. This afflicted person would be brought low so that "the living may know that the Most High is ruler over the realm of mankind." The Lord bestows the rule of the human realm on whom he wishes, even sometimes the lowliest of men (4:17).

After Nebuchadnezzar had finished reciting his dream, he requested that Belteshazzar, i.e., Daniel, relate the interpretation. He admitted that the wise men of the realm were unable to explain the dream. Yet the king was confident that Daniel would meet the challenge because he had a supernatural spirit in him. The tree itself presented no problem to the king. When the tree, however, was spoken of as if it were a man, he failed to see the significance. He suspected that it applied to himself. That was why the king was uneasy when he first saw the dream (4:18; cf. v. 5).

D. His Fate Predicted (4:19-27).

Daniel was shocked into silence for awhile as he contemplated the implications of the dream. He did not wish to bear the bad tidings to the king. Nebuchadnezzar sensed his agitation, and urged him not to be alarmed. Daniel sincerely expressed his desire that this dream would apply to adversaries of the king rather than to the king himself. This statement suggests that a warm personal relationship existed between Daniel and Nebuchadnezzar (4:19).

Daniel then plainly explained the meaning of the details of the dream. The tree represented Nebuchadnezzar. Like that tree, this king had grown strong. His majesty had become great and "reached to the sky." The birds and beasts which found shelter in that tree symbolized the world-wide dominion of Nebuchadnezzar. The watcher who descended from heaven with an order concerning the tree symbolized the fact that the Most High had issued a decree which pertained to the king. The stump exposed to the elements represented the humiliation of Nebuchadnezzar. The king would be driven away from mankind. His dwelling would be with the beasts of the field. He would be given grass to eat like cattle. He would be drenched with the dew of heaven. For seven periods of time, i.e., years, this would be the status of Nebuchadnezzar. He would remain in this condition until he recognized that "the most high is ruler over the realm of mankind." That the stump had roots and a metal band signaled that the kingdom would be restored to Nebuchadnezzar once he learned that "it is heaven," i.e., the God of heaven, "that rules" (4:20-26).

In view of the ominous thrust of the dream, Daniel had some advice which he prayed Nebuchadnezzar would find pleasing. The king needed to "break away" from his sins. He could demonstrate his repentance by doing what was right. Such action might prolong his period of tranquility and result in cancellation of the threat (4:27).

E. His Discipline Implemented (4:28-33).

Twelve months elapsed before the divine sentence was executed against Nebuchadnezzar. The king was walking on the flat roof of his palace surveying his capital. His heart was filled with pride as he contemplated all he had accomplished.[11] He congratulated himself on his power, glory and majesty. While this word was still in the king's mouth, he heard a voice from heaven repeating the sentence which Daniel had made a year before. Immediately the threat of the heavenly voice was fulfilled. Nebuchadnezzar was smitten with zoanthropy. He lived outside with the animals. He ate grass like cattle. His hair grew long, his nails became like claws (4:28-33).

F. His Sanity Restored (4:34-37).

Returning to first person, Nebuchadnezzar described what transpired at the end of the seven years of discipline. He said, "I raised my eyes toward heaven." This upward look was an acknowledgment of the sovereignty of God, a token of a newfound sense of dependence and humility. At that same moment reason returned to the king. He immediately praised the Most High because (1) he is eternal; (2) his kingdom is everlasting; and (3) his will is supreme both in heaven and on earth. No one can "ward off his hand" (lit., strike his hand, i.e., hinder him or chasten him). No one had the authority to question actions of the Most High (4:34f.).

As a result of his recognition of the rightful place of God, Nebuchadnezzar experienced a fourfold restoration. First, he was restored *mentally*. He was cured of the psychosis of zoanthropy.

Second, he was restored *physically*. His "majesty and splendor" returned. This would include his physical features and all the external trappings of kingship. Third, he was restored *politically*. Those who had acted as regents during his incapacitation handed the reins of government back to Nebuchadnezzar. Once again he ruled a glorious kingdom. Fourth, he was restored *socially*. His counselors began to seek him out. Thus was Nebuchadnezzar's "sovereignty" re-established. God, however, did even more for this king, for "surpassing greatness was added" to him (4:36).

Was Nebuchadnezzar truly converted through his experience in chapter 4? Some writers feel that the evidence is insufficient to make such a claim. Yet his own testimony strongly suggests that the Chaldean now worshiped only the Most High. He offered three reasons for praising, honoring and exalting the King of heaven. First, God's works are true, i.e., he really does the things which he claims to do. Second, God's ways are just, i.e., he does not act capriciously or vindictively or excessively. He does what is right in all circumstances. Third, God's power is unlimited, for "he is able to humble those who walk in pride." No one in history was better qualified to make this observation! (4:37).

Endnotes

1. H.C. Leupold, *Exposition of Daniel* (Minneapolis: Augsburg, 1949) 132-134.

2. Scholars have suggested that the image in chapter 3 was (1) that of one of the gods of Babylon; (2) that of Nebuchadnezzar himself; (3) a reproduction of the image in chapter 2; and (4) a monument rather than a statue.

3. The brass section was represented by the *horn* (KJV cornet); the woodwinds or reed section by the *flute*. The string section was represented by the *lyre* (KJV harp; NIV zither), *trigon* (KJV sackbut; NIV lyre), and *psaltery* (NIV harp). The word translated *bagpipe* is of uncertain origin. It is rendered *dulcimer* in KJV and *pipes* in NIV.

4. Some think that Nebuchadnezzar is registering amazement rather than seeking to verify the accuracy of the accusation. Others think the phrase should be rendered, "Is it on purpose" that you have acted as you have? i.e., Is your action deliberate or inadvertent?

5. On the expression "seven times" see Lev 26:18-24; Prov 6:31; Matt 18:21ff.

6. Possibly the "Nebuchadnezzar" of chapter 4 is a successor of the Great King using a throne name. A Dead Sea scroll attributed to King Nabonidus, last king of Babylon, describes a sickness which he experienced for seven years. The king was healed through the intervention of a Jewish diviner. See discussion by E.M. Yamauchi, "Nabonidus" in *The International Standard Bible Encyclopedia* Vol. 3. ed. Geoffrey W. Bromiley (Grand Rapids: Eerdmans, 1986) 3:469f. Yamauchi is not inclined to make the Nebuchadnezzar = Nabonidus connection. If, however, the "Nebuchadnezzar" of Dan 4 is Nabonidus, then the failure to call immediately for Daniel's assistance in interpreting the dream is explained.

7. "The Assyrian and Babylonian kings regarded themselves as kings of all the earth and in their inscriptions they were accustomed thus to speak of themselves." E.J. Young, *The Prophecy of Daniel* (Grand Rapids: Eerdmans, 1949) 97.

8. Perhaps prior to the interpretation of the dream in verse 9 the plural should be used. Since verse 8 reflects the attitude of the king after the interpretation of the dream, the singular perhaps is best.

9. See Ezek 32:3ff; 17:1ff., 22-24; Isa 2:13; 10:18f.; Jer 22:7, 23. See also Herodotus 1.108; 6.37; 7.19.

10. The term "watcher" is used only in this chapter in the Bible. Later Jewish writing, however, used it frequently. Angelic beings were known to the king through his Babylonian religion.

11. Archaeologists testify that virtually every brick found in the ruins of ancient Babylon bear the imprint of Nebuchadnezzar. This king's literary texts boast repeatedly of his building accomplishments.

CHAPTER THIRTY-EIGHT

The God of Vindication
Daniel 5-6

Background of the Unit.

Nebuchadnezzar died in 562 BC. He was followed briefly on the throne by his son Amel Marduk (562-560 BC) who is known in the Bible as Evil-Merodach (2 Kgs 25:27). This king was assassinated by Nebuchadnezzar's son-in-law Neriglissar (Biblical Nergal-sar-ezer, Jer 39:3). Neriglissar died in 560 BC. His son, Labashi-Marduk, succeeded in holding the throne for nine months. Nabonidus then became king. This archaeologist and religious zealot infuriated the leadership in Babylon. He was forced to spend most of his reign in the Arabian desert. While absent from the capital his son Belshazzar acted as co-regent.

Daniel 5 focuses on the final hours of the Neo-Babylonian empire. Nabonidus had gone north to attempt to stop Cyrus the Persian from advancing against Babylon. He was unsuccessful. Belshazzar was holed up behind the massive walls of the capital. To show his disdain for all that was transpiring outside those walls, Belshazzar ordered a massive feast to be prepared. Before that night was over, Belshazzar was dead, and world hegemony had passed to the Medo-Persian empire. About sixty-five years had elapsed since Daniel was carried away captive in chapter 1. The prophet would be in his eighties.

Before he pressed on to further conquests in the east, Cyrus appointed a subordinate over the territories formerly controlled by Babylon. This ruler was known to the Jewish captives as Darius the Mede. Early in Darius' administration Daniel got caught up in some court intrigue and was sentenced to die in a den of lions. That is the thrust of Daniel 6.

Outline of the Unit.

As in the previous narratives in the book, chapters 5 and 6 focus on the actions of God. In chapter one he was the God of intervention, in chapter 2, the God of revelation. In chapters 3-4 he is the God of salvation. Now in chapters 5 and 6 he is the God of vindication. This observation suggests the following outline:

A. Vindication of God's Honor (chap. 5).
B. Vindication of God's Servant (chap. 6).

VINDICATION OF GOD'S HONOR

Daniel 5

The position of Belshazzar in the Babylonian kingdom has been illuminated by several important cuneiform inscriptions. One text declares that Nabonidus "entrusted the kingship to his son Belshazzar."[1] Other texts relate how Belshazzar performed royal functions. His name was used in oaths and prayers. In short, Belshazzar acted as king in the absence of his father Nabonidus. As far as the Jews were concerned, he was the king of Babylon. When Belshazzar ordered a feast for a thousand of his nobles, this king set the stage for one of the most memorable nights in Biblical history.

A. A Night of Revelry (5:1-4).

A banquet for a thousand nobles seems incredible. Yet history attests much larger banquets than this.[2] Before his guests Belshazzar drank wine (5:1). The Oriental custom was for the king to sit at a separate table on an elevated place so that the guests were before him. As the text unfolds, it becomes clear that this was a religious feast. The disastrous defeat of Babylon's armies at Opis and the consequent unimpeded advance of Cyrus against the capital convinced the king that the gods of the realm were offended. Belshazzar was calling for a pagan revival. He wanted his people to placate the offended gods of the realm, especially the god Marduk.

Belshazzar "tasted the wine." The text actually suggests a bit more than that. Driver paraphrases: "When Belshazzar began to feel the influence of the wine."[3] This suggests a degree of inebriation. The drunken king gave orders for the Temple vessels which Nebuchadnezzar had taken from Jerusalem to be brought to the banquet hall. Belshazzar and his nobles and their consorts wished to drink wine from those vessels. The king's intention here was to please his own gods by insulting the God of Israel (5:2).

A problem arises in the reference to Nebuchadnezzar as the "father" of Belshazzar. Cuneiform documents make it clear that he was actually the son of Nabonidus. How is this reference to be explained? R. D. Wilson has enumerated at least eight different senses in which the word *father* is used in ancient sources.[4] The best explanation is that Nebuchadnezzar was the *father* of Belshazzar in the sense that he was his predecessor on the throne.

The vessels were brought to the feast. Belshazzar and his guests drank from them as they praised the gods of the realm. No doubt this praise was directed primarily to the four chief gods of Babylon: (1) Marduk, the patron god of the city; (2) Nebo, god of wisdom, literature and education; (3) Nergal, god of war; and (4) Ishtar, goddess of fertility. The text does not explain why Belshazzar chose to use the sacred vessels from Jerusalem in this drunken praise service. That he wished to denigrate the God of the Hebrews seems clear. Perhaps he had heard of Isaiah's prophecies which predicted the conquests of Cyrus and the fall of Babylon to him (Isa 44:25-45:5). In any case, Belshazzar, whether deliberately or inadvertently, committed the worst sacrilege (5:3f.).

B. A Night of Reflection (5:5-12).

During the banquet the king and his guests witnessed a baffling event. The wisest men in the land could not explain what had transpired. The mystery triggered terror on the part of all present in the chamber. Only the suggestion of the queen mother gave any hope of solving the riddle.

1. The writing on the wall (5:5-6). The drunken feast was interrupted when someone noticed "the fingers of a man's hand" emerging out of thin air. The fingers began slowly to write on the wall plaster opposite a huge lamp stand. This was most appropriate because kings in antiquity depicted their own imagined heroic deeds on their palace walls. When the king observed the back of the hand that did the writing, he was terrified. His face turned pale. His knees began knocking. He "went to pieces."

2. The silence of the advisors (5:7-9). Belshazzar's first thought was to summon the wise men and counselors to the banquet chamber. He made an outlandish three-fold pledge to anyone who could decipher the strange writing. That man would be (1) clothed in the purple robes of royalty, i.e., elevated to nobility; (2) given a necklace of gold, the badge of highest rank, to wear about his neck; and (3) made third ruler in the kingdom. This could mean that the interpreter would be third ruler in succession immediately beneath Belshazzar the co-regent. Others take the expression to mean that he would be one of three equal rulers, the other two being Nabonidus and Belshazzar (5:7).

The king's wisemen were unable to make any sense out of the writing on the wall.[5] The king became even more terrified. The nobles were perplexed (lit.,*mentally shattered*). No one could bring any calming word to the king.

3. The suggestion of the queen (5:10-12). The alarm spread throughout the palace. Hearing of what had taken place, the queen entered the hall. She was probably Belshazzar's mother, not his wife. A woman of her station and age would not have been in attendance at the wild feast that night. She was the only one in the room who remained composed as she urged her son not to be alarmed (5:8-10).

The queen reminded Belshazzar of a man in the kingdom who possessed supernatural inspiration. Some years before Nebuchadnezzar had found in this man "illumination, insight and wisdom" such as that which was attributed to the gods. For that reason, the man had been appointed chief of all the wise men.[6] This man could interpret dreams, explain enigmas and solve difficult problems. At last the queen named the man of whom she spoke: "This Daniel whom the king named Belteshazzar." The queen urged that Daniel be summoned. She was confident that he would be able to declare the interpretation (5:11f.). Why did Belshazzar have to be reminded of the skills of Daniel? The prophet had either lost his office, become obscure, or had been engaged in business which kept him out of the attention of Belshazzar. Perhaps the king assumed he was dead.

C. A Night of Rebuke (5:13-24).

Finally Daniel was brought in before the king. Belshazzar seems to have been acquainted with Daniel's background. He knew that he was one of the exiles whom Nebuchadnezzar had brought from Judah. He repeated to Daniel the compliments which his mother had just paid the prophet. He informed him about the failure of the wise men to read the inscription or make known its interpretation. He repeated the promise he had earlier made concerning the rewards which would be given to the one who could explain the mysterious writing. His cautious "if you are able" suggests that Belshazzar was not as confident as the queen about the abilities of the old prophet (5:13-16).

Daniel indicated clearly that he was not interested in the rewards which the king offered. The gift of prophecy was not for sale. Nevertheless, he did accept the king's challenge. He promised to read the inscription and give its interpretation. First, however, he seized the opportunity to preach to Belshazzar. This king had never been in a more receptive mood to hear God's word! (5:17).

Daniel began by reminding the king of what God had done for and to Nebuchadnezzar. God had given his "father" world-wide sovereignty and absolute power over the affairs of men. When, however, Nebuchadnezzar behaved arrogantly, he was deposed from his throne and his glory was taken away. God literally put Nebuchadnezzar out to pasture for seven years. He was only restored to his position when he recognized that the Most High was the only absolute sovereign in the realm of mankind (5:18-21).

Having set forth this historical background, Daniel proceeded boldly to rebuke the king before his thousand nobles and their ladies. He made four charges. First, the king had sinned against the light of knowledge. He had failed to profit from the humbling experience of his predecessor. Second, he had defied the Lord of heaven by his sacrilegious abuse of the Jerusalem Temple vessels. Third, Belshazzar was guilty of worshiping idols "which do not see, hear or understand." Finally, the king failed to glorify the God who held in his hand Belshazzar's "life-breath and ways." This very God whom Belshazzar had offended so grievously had sent forth this hand to write the inscription on the wall (5:22-24).

C. A Night of Revelation (5:25-29).

The ominous words on the wall were "*mene, mene, tekel* and *peres.*" In rough translation these words mean: *numbered, numbered, weighed* and *divided.* Daniel gave a two-fold interpretation to each word. *Mene* is repeated for emphasis. It means (1) God has numbered your kingdom, i.e., numbered the days of your kingdom and (2) put an end to it. The duration of the Babylonian kingdom was so counted out that it now had come to an end. *Tekel* was applied to Belshazzar personally. He had been (1) weighed in the scales and (2) found deficient. He failed to measure up to the divine standards. *Peres* (plural *upharsin*) indicated that the Babylonian kingdom had been (1) divided or destroyed and (2) given over to the Medes and Persians (5:25-28).

Belshazzar must have been shaken by Daniel's explanation. Nonetheless, he fulfilled the commitment which he had made. Daniel was dressed in purple. A gold necklace was placed around his neck. A proclamation was issued naming Daniel as the third ruler in the kingdom. Some interpret Belshazzar's actions as mockery of Daniel and defiance of his announcements. The text, however, gives no hint of insincerity on the part of the king (5:29).

D. A Night of Reckoning (5:30-31).

That very night Belshazzar the Chaldean king was slain. Apparently the invaders marched into the banquet hall and slaughtered the king and his company of merrymakers. Another possibility is that Belshazzar died in a conspiracy. The Biblical account does not indicate that a bloody siege of the city took place. The cuneiform sources are silent as to what was going on when Babylon fell. For the most part, the city welcomed the armies of Cyrus as deliverers from the oppression of the current regime. The Greek historians Herodotus and Xenophon, however, confirm that Babylon was engaged in a riotous feast at the time of the overthrow. Critics have pointed out that no positive evidence exists that Belshazzar was present at the fall of Babylon. No evidence, however, has been presented that he was elsewhere that night.

So Darius the Mede "received the kingdom." The identification of this king is as yet unknown, since secular historical sources are silent concerning him. Critics regard Darius as a fictitious character invented by an author who knew nothing about the history of the period. Conservatives have offered several conjectures regarding the identity of Darius. Whitcomb has proposed that Darius was the Gubaru who was appointed governor over Babylon by Cyrus.[7] Wiseman has suggested that Cyrus the Persian was also known as Darius the Mede.[8]

Critics use 5:31 to prove that Daniel erroneously believed in a separate Median kingdom which ruled over Babylon before the Persians took over. The verse does not say, however, that the *kingdom* was Median, only that the *king* was a Mede. The phrase "he received the kingdom" fits with the historical circumstances that Cyrus was the supreme king of the Medo-Persian empire and Darius was his subordinate.[9] Daniel mentioned Darius' age (sixty-two) to suggest that his tenure was not of long duration.

VINDICATION OF GOD'S SERVANT
Daniel 6

On several occasions under Babylonian rule God had demonstrated through Daniel the superiority of his servants over those who served pagan gods. The greatest king of Babylon had proclaimed the greatness of the God of Daniel more than once. Now, however, a new administration was in power. The purpose of chapter 6 is to illustrate how God continued to work for his servant and through him to influence mighty rulers to acknowledge the greatness of the Most High God.

A. The Position of Daniel (6:1-3).

Darius quickly organized the kingdom which had been delegated to him by Cyrus. He appointed a two-tiered bureaucracy of 120 satraps who were accountable to three commissioners. A *satrap* was a "kingdom protector."[10] The satraps were appointed in order that "the king might not suffer loss." Darius was making sure that his superior, Cyrus, was not cheated out of any tribute which was due him (6:1f.).

Daniel was one of the three commissioners. As he had done during the Chaldean kingdom, the prophet began to distinguish himself among the king's administrators. Daniel would be about eighty-two at this time. The text explains his excellence as due to the "extraordinary spirit" which he possessed. The prophet was filled with the Holy Spirit (5:12) as well as a human spirit saturated with the principles of divine Scripture.[11] King Darius planned to appoint Daniel "over the entire kingdom," i.e., elevate him to be prime minister of the realm (6:3).

B. The Plot Against Daniel (6:4-9).

The commissioners and satraps were jealous that a Jew was being considered as top administrator over the kingdom which they had helped conquer. They began seeking some ground upon which they might fault Daniel with regard to government affairs. Daniel was such an outstanding public official that his antagonists could find no ground of accusation or evidence of corruption in his professional life. Because Daniel was faithful to his God, he was also faithful to his king. No negligence or corruption could be found in him. His enemies realized that Daniel's faith was the only point in which he might be vulnerable to their attack (6:4f.).

The officers devised a plan in which they would persuade the king to proclaim himself the sole representative of the deity for a period of thirty days. Since some Persian kings regarded themselves as deities,[12] such a suggestion was not at all inconceivable. All petitions were to be addressed to him. Any person offering a religious petition to man or god during the thirty days would be executed in the lion's den.[13] Such an edict would place Daniel in an awkward position. If he obeyed it, he would not be able to pray openly to his God. Yet if he disobeyed it he would appear to be disloyal to the king whom he devotedly served (6:6f.).

The suggestion appealed to the ego of the new king. He apparently did not hesitate to sign the document which his subordinates had prepared. Once he did, however, that edict became irrevocable (6:8).[14]

Daniel knew that the document had been signed. He understood the implications of that law. He knew that the king had been manipulated into issuing an edict aimed solely at him. Yet Daniel did not alter his prayer habit. As was his custom, he entered the upper story of his house where the windows opened westward toward Jerusalem. Three times each day he prayed there in full view of the enemies who had those windows under surveillance. Any attempt on his part to evade the issue by continuing his prayers in secret or at such times when he could not be detected would have been a confession of fear and unbelief (6:9f.).

Then the "men" (lit., heroes!) met at a spot where they could observe the windows of Daniel's house. Just as they had anticipated, the old prophet appeared right on schedule to make petitions and supplications (lit., seek grace for himself) before his God. They went immediately before the king. Before accusing Daniel, these clever courtiers led the king to reaffirm the intent and irrevocability of the edict which he had signed (6:11f.).

The enemies then made their accusation. They contemptuously referred to Daniel, not by his proper title as the presiding commissioner, but as "that Daniel, one of the exiles of Judah." Perhaps they were suggesting that such misconduct as they were about to describe was to be expected from one who was a foreigner. Their charge was twofold. They charged that Daniel paid no attention (1) to the king or (2) to the royal injunction. They supported this charge with eyewitness testimony that Daniel continued to offer petition three times each day to his God. Apparently they had waited an entire day so as to marshal irrefutable proof that Daniel deliberately was flaunting his disdain for the royal command (6:13).

Darius was distressed at the report. He realized that he had been used as part of a vendetta against his best subordinate. He had been misled into forcing his subjects to relinquish their religious convictions. Throughout that entire day he considered various means by which he might rescue Daniel from the unjust entrapment. Apparently the king had until sunset to execute the sentence before he was in violation of his own edict. At the end of the day, however, the commissioners and satraps reappeared to force the king's hand. They reminded him that under the law of the Medes and Persians, no injunction or statute which a king established could be rescinded or altered. Darius was forced to take action against Daniel or lose his crown and possibly his life (6:14f.).

C. The Punishment of Daniel (6:16-18).

Darius reluctantly gave the orders for Daniel to be brought forth and cast into the lions' den. The prophet was thrown into the den. Nothing is known of the construction of lions' dens. It may have been a subterranean cavern with an opening in the top and possibly also one at the side through which the animals were admitted. In any case, the king called to Daniel, "may your God, whom you serve continually, rescue you" (NIV).[15] Had Darius heard about Shadrach, Meshach, and Abed-nego? Be that as it may, the king was evidencing an initial step in his God-consciousness, viz., recognition of a power greater than his own (6:16).

A stone was brought and laid over the opening of the den. Hot wax was applied in such a way that tampering would be impossible. The king impressed his signet ring in the wax. He then required his nobles—possibly Daniel's accusers—to impress their rings on the wax as well. This act may have been a legal formality in the Medo-Persian empire, an indication of the official character of the proceedings. On the other hand, Darius may have wanted physical proof that his lords had contributed to the treacherous execution which had now been set in motion. Another view is that Darius was trying to spare Daniel from further dangerous intervention by the jealous satraps (6:17).

Darius spent a miserable night in his palace. He fasted and canceled the evening's "entertainment." Although the precise meaning of this word is not known, the best suggestion is that it refers to entertainment provided by concubines or dancing girls. Darius wanted none of that. His mind was so tormented by the day's events that he could not sleep the entire night (6:18).

D. The Protection of Daniel (6:19-24).

As early as possible in the morning, Darius rushed to the lions' den. As he approached the place he cried out (lit., screamed), "Daniel, servant of the Living God, has your God, whom you constantly serve, been able to deliver you from the lions?" Here is an advance in the God-consciousness of this monarch. He recognized Daniel's God as the *Living God* in contrast to the idols which were so prevalent in that land (6:19f.).

How relieved the king must have been when Daniel responded from the den. The prophet had survived his night with the wild beasts. God had sent his angel to shut the mouths of the lions. The Supreme Judge had found Daniel innocent in respect both to his God and his king. Whereas the prophet was guilty of the charge of praying to another, he was innocent of the implied charge of treason. Darius was very pleased that Daniel was unharmed. He immediately ordered the prophet to be brought forth. Upon examination, no injury whatever was found on the person of Daniel. The text attributes this deliverance to the fact that Daniel "trusted in his God" (6:21-23).

Darius then vented his anger on the nobles who had accused Daniel. He realized now that they, not Daniel, had shown disdain for his sovereignty. These nobles could not deny their involvement in the plot since their seals appeared on the rock. The conspiracy boomeranged on them. True to Persian custom, both the nobles and their families were thrown to the lions.[16] Before these victims had reached the bottom of the den, the lions overpowered and crushed them.[17] The ravenous appetites of the lions underscored the miracle of Daniel's deliverance (6:24).

F. The Proclamation of the King (6:25-27).

Because of the lions' den experience, Darius had reached the same conclusion about God as had Nebuchadnezzar before him. Unfortunately he made the same mistake as the Chaldean ruler as well. He thought that he would be able to legislate allegiance to the Lord. A decree was sent throughout his realm, a geographical area nearly coextensive with the former Chaldean Empire. The edict ordered all men "to fear and tremble before the God of Daniel" (6:25f.). Thus Darius was trying to undo the effects of his previous edict by issuing another which was equally wrong headed. Men must be free to choose whether or not they will bow before the Living God.

In his edict Darius did not rise above the level of a polytheist. He did not confess Daniel's God to be the only true God. He did, however, elevate him to a level above other gods. Darius cited four reasons for requiring his subjects to recognize the God of Daniel. First, Daniel's God was the Living God, active in the affairs of men. Second, he was the eternal God whose reign would never be destroyed. Third, Daniel's God "delivers and rescues" for he had delivered his servant from the power of the lions. Finally, Daniel's God "performs signs and wonders in heaven and on earth." Perhaps the king had learned from Daniel other great deeds which had been performed by the Lord in the history of his people (6:27).

Chapter 6 concludes with a footnote which indicates how Daniel fared in the Medo-Persian empire after the lions' den incident. He enjoyed success "in the reign of Darius and in the reign of Cyrus the Persian." These words are capable of more than one interpretation. Critics assume that Daniel believed in a separate Median kingdom which ruled Babylon prior to the conquest by Cyrus. That view would mean that the Book of Daniel is historically inaccurate. The words could also be interpreted to mean that the reigns of Darius and Cyrus were contemporaneous. Cyrus was the ruler over the still expanding Persian empire. Darius was appointed by Cyrus to be king over what had formerly been the Chaldean empire. The men were of two different races, but were part of the same empire. Still another view is that the verse should be rendered: "In the reign of Darius, *even* in the reign of Cyrus the Persian." This view would make Darius and Cyrus two names for the same person. In any case, the book dates the last prophecy of Daniel to the third year of Cyrus. That means that Daniel lived until at least 535 BC.

Endnotes

1. The Persian Verse Account of Nabonidus was first published by Sidney Smith, *Babylonian Historical Texts Relating to the Fall of Babylon* (London: Methuen, 1924) 87-91. A lucid paraphrase of this text is found in A.T. Olmstead, *History of the Persian Empire* (Chicago: University of Chicago, 1948) 53-55.

2. James A. Montgomery mentions a marriage festival of Alexander the Great at which ten thousand guests were present. See *A Critical and Exegetical Commentary on the Book of Daniel* in The International Critical Commentary (Edinburgh: T. & T. Clark, 1926) 250.

3. S.R. Driver, "Daniel" in *The Cambridge Bible for Schools and Colleges* (Cambridge: University Press, 1922) 62.

4. R.D. Wilson, *Studies in the Book of Daniel* (Grand Rapids: Baker) 1:117-122.

5. Some reasons which have been suggested for the inability of the wise men to interpret the writing: (1) they knew the words, but not the extended meaning; (2) the words appeared in the Hebrew language which they could not read; (3) the words were written in a Babylonian cuneiform "shorthand" and needed a context for interpretation; (4) the message was written in ideograms; and (5) the characters were written vertically.

6. The text never asserts that Daniel was himself a wise man, but that he was the administrative officer who supervised their activities.

7. John C. Whitcomb, Jr., *Darius the Mede* (Philadelphia: Presbyterian and Reformed, 1963).

8. D.J. Wiseman, "Darius" in *The New Bible Dictionary* (Grand Rapids: Eerdmans, 1965) 293-94.

9. Others interpret the phrase to mean that Darius received the kingdom from God. E.J. Young thinks the phrase merely means that Darius succeeded upon the throne. *The Prophecy of Daniel* (Grand Rapids: Eerdmans, 1949) 131.

10. The later Persian king Darius the Great divided his empire into twenty satrapies. Critics of the book believe that in Darius the Mede, Daniel has created a fictitious character based loosely on the famous Darius. The 120 satraps would then be an exaggeration on his part. The text, however, does not say there were 120 satrapies, but 120 satraps. No doubt they were of various rank.

11. That Daniel studied the Scriptures is indicated in 9:1,2.

12. E.J. Young (*op. cit.* 134) documents the claims to deity of Persian kings.

13. The mention of the den of lions testifies to the historicity of the book. The Babylonians used fire to execute. The Persians, however, included the god of fire in their pantheon. They would not likely use fire as a means of capital punishment.

14. Cf. Esth 1:19; 8:8. Diodorus Siculus 17:30 confirms the irrevocable nature of Persian royal edicts.

15. NASB renders the words of the king as an assertion: "for God whom you constantly serve will himself deliver you." Either translation is possible.

16. Sentencing of entire families of the guilty was expressly forbidden in the Mosaic law (Deut 24:16).

17. Josephus records the tradition that the enemies of Daniel scoffed at the deliverance, charging that the king had fed the lions before throwing Daniel into the den.

CHAPTER THIRTY-NINE

The Triumph of God's Kingdom
Daniel 7

Background of the Unit.

Chapters 7-12 stand in sharp contrast to chapters 1-6. The first half of the book focuses on historical incidents. Daniel and his friends are the main actors. The monarchs of Babylon are shown to be subject to the God of the Hebrews. The practitioners of occult sciences are humbled by the superior wisdom of divine revelation. Those chapters are written in the third person. God spoke through history. In chapters 7-12, however, the focus is on visions and prayers. Daniel's friends disappear. Monarchs are mentioned only for the purpose of dating material. No mention is made of Babylon's wise men. These chapters are written in the first person. God is speaking through prophecy.

Daniel's first vision is dated to "the first year of Belshazzar king of Babylon." Though Belshazzar was not mentioned by the ancient historians, the first of many inscriptions bearing his name was translated from a cuneiform tablet in 1854 by Sir Henry Rawlinson. Belshazzar began to share the rule with his father Nabonidus perhaps as early as 556 BC. According to Daniel 5, Belshazzar was slain on the night Babylon fell to the armies of Cyrus in 539 BC.

As he lay upon his bed Daniel had "a dream and visions in his mind." This was not the dark premonition of some nightmare, but the clear perception of a divine revelation. While the whole matter was fresh on his mind, Daniel immediately wrote down the dream. Chapter 7 contains a summary of this vision.

Outline of the Unit.

A. Introduction: The Setting of the Vision (v. 1).
B. Presentation of the Vision (vv. 2-14).
C. Explanation of the Vision (vv. 15-27).
D. Epilogue: The Effect of the Vision (v. 28).

PRESENTATION OF THE VISION
Daniel 7:2-14

Interpreters generally agree that Daniel 7 depicts in somewhat greater detail what was presented in a dream in chapter 2. The Babylonian king had seen four world empires in their outward glory represented by various types of metal in a huge image. Daniel saw those same kingdoms in their inward character as vicious beasts. The king had seen the kingdom of God as a stone which eventually grew to fill the whole earth. Daniel saw that same kingdom in the trials which would precede the glorious triumph.

A. The Future: The Geocentric View (7:2-8).

Daniel was first given a glimpse of the future from a geocentric, i.e., earth-bound, focus. In vivid and terrifying symbolism he foresaw that which would unfold on the stage of history.

1. The turbulent sea (7:2-3). In his vision Daniel first noticed that "the four winds of the heaven were stirring up the great sea." The "sea" (the Mediterranean?) here represents humanity.[1] The churning waters depict the restlessness in which the nations continually find themselves.

Daniel saw four different beasts coming up from the sea. They represented the great world empires of history. The world empires are human in origin and vicious in character. The beasts are four in number because four is the number of the world in biblical symbolism. The four beasts represent the sum total of the power that the world produces in the course of its development.[2] That the beasts were different from one another indicates that each of the world empires had distinct traits of its own (7:2f.).

2. The winged lion (7:4). The first beast was "like a lion." It had wings "like an eagle." Sculpted winged lions guarded the palaces of Babylon. Since the lion and eagle are dominant in their spheres, the beast represented the true regal character of the first world empire. As Daniel kept watching, he saw the wings plucked from the lion. The beast was lifted up and made to stand on two feet like a man. A human mind was given to it. The winged lion assumed human form.

That the winged lion is equivalent to the head of gold in chapter 2 is the consensus of those who have made careful study of Daniel. The change in the character of the beast probably points to the fact that the Neo-Babylonian Empire, in its later stages, was less aggressive and more humane. This change may have been triggered by the humbling experience of Nebuchadnezzar mentioned in chapter 4. In that seven-year stint in the wild, the king's lust for conquest was removed. After his sanity was restored Nebuchadnezzar never again led his armies into battle.

3. The lopsided bear (7:5). The second beast resembled a bear raised up on one side. This beast is equivalent to the chest and arms of silver in chapter 2. The posture of the bear may have no significance other than the contribution it makes to the imagery. On the other hand, some envision the bear in a crouching position which symbolizes the Medo-Persian empire poised to attack neighboring nations. Others see the bear as leaning to one side, symbolizing Persian domination of Media in the uneven alliance between the two nations.

The bear held three ribs between its teeth. Some see in this symbolism the voraciousness of the beast. Even as Daniel saw his vision the Medo-Persian empire was in the process of devouring the nations of the Near East. Others see the three ribs as specifically pointing to the three greatest conquests of Cyrus the Great, viz., Lydia, Babylon and Egypt. In addition to the ribs which were already in the bear's mouth, the creature was told to "arise and devour much meat." This must refer to conquests in addition to those symbolized by the ribs.

4. *The four-headed leopard (7:6).* The third beast was like a leopard. It had four wings which symbolize the extreme swiftness with which it moved. Like the belly and thighs of the image in chapter 2, this beast symbolizes the Greco-Macedonian empire which Alexander the Great founded. The beast had four heads which may have faced the four directions of the compass. Some take these heads to symbolize the four major territories of Alexander's kingdom.[3] Others see them as representative of the four Hellenistic monarchies ruled by the former generals of Alexander, the so-called *didachoi.*[4] Divine providence had singled out this kingdom to have world dominion for a time. However powerful kingdoms seem in the eyes of men, it is God who determines the times and extent of their dominion.

5. *The fourth beast (7:7a).* The fourth beast is not likened to any wild creature known to man. Daniel described it as "dreadful and terrifying and extremely strong."[5] Its teeth of iron remind one of the legs of iron in chapter 2. Those iron teeth "devoured and crushed" its victims. Others were "trampled down" with its feet. Everything in the description of the fourth beast points to Rome including the fact that "it was different from all the beasts that were before it." The imperial power of Rome was more syncretistic than the predecessors. That which held Rome together was commitment to an ideal rather than commitment to an individual. The unity was legal rather than regal.

6. *The ten horns (7:7b).* Daniel noted that the fourth beast had ten horns. In prophecy, ten is usually a round number, the number of completeness.[6] As to the meaning of the ten horns, four major schools of interpretation have arisen. Some see *historic Rome* in the horns. They suggest that the horns represent ten emperors of Rome or perhaps ten contemporaneous kings ruling in various parts of the old Roman empire. Others see *post Rome* kingdoms represented by the horns. These interpreters attempt to identify ten kingdoms which occupied the territory of Rome after the fall of the empire in AD 476. Another school of interpreters advocate what might be called the *continuing Rome* view. The ten horns represent successive kingdoms

which partake of the nature of Rome. These kingdoms span the years between the fall of Rome and the rise of the little horn. Thus the state of world government at any time subsequent to the fall of ancient Rome would be depicted by the horns. If this interpretation is correct, modern believers are living in the period of the ten horns. A final approach to the ten horns sees in them *revived Rome*, a future empire consisting of ten constituent nations on the territory of the old Roman empire. These interpreters generally point to the European Common Market as the initial stage in the formation of this revived Roman empire.

7. The little horn (7:8). While Daniel was contemplating the ten horns he observed a little horn growing up among them. It uprooted three of the original horns. This suggests that the little horn would have greater power than any one of the ten horns, but not so much as all ten taken together. The little horn is further described as possessing "eyes like the eyes of a man" and "a mouth uttering great boasts." These phrases may suggest that the little horn is a person rather than a government or kingdom.

On the identity of the little horn wide diversity of opinion exists. To a large measure the interpretation of the little horn depends on one's understanding of the ten horns. According to the *emperorial view* the little horn represents a Roman emperor (or emperors) who waged vicious war against the people of God. Those who hold to the *ecclesiastical view* see in the little horn the Roman Catholic papacy. This is the traditional Protestant view. According to the *eschatological view* the little horn is that individual who leads the final assault against the people of God just before the second coming of Christ.

B. The Future: The Theocentric View (7:9-14).

Looking at the future with a theocentric, i.e., God-centered, view Daniel learned two things. First, he learned that history is under the ultimate control of God. The beasts may roam the earth, but they were subject to the oversight of heaven. Second, the prophet saw that history was moving toward a climax in which righteousness would triumph over evil.

1. A court scene (7:9-10). Daniel saw thrones being set up. He did not say he saw anyone sitting on the thrones. They may be just part of the setting.[7] As the scene unfolds it becomes clear that Daniel was viewing the heavenly courtroom.

When all was ready, the Ancient of Days, God himself, took his seat. His clothing was like snow symbolizing his purity. His wool-like hair indicated his age. He sat upon a blazing throne, symbolizing his irresistible might. The wheels of the throne pointed to the fact that God is not bound to one place. He is omnipresent. Only the Ancient of Days is qualified to render judgment regarding the nations (7:9).

A river of fire was flowing forth from the throne. This fiery river symbolized the judgment of God. Innumerable angels were standing before the throne ready to carry out the bidding of the Ancient of Days. As the court sat the books of judgment were opened. These books contained the records of crimes against God and man of which the beastly empires were guilty (7:10).[8]

2. A judgment scene (7:11-12). The boastful and ungodly words of the little horn kept Daniel's attention fixed on the scene unfolding in his vision. Eventually he saw the fourth beast slain, i.e., the fourth empire was destroyed by God. "Its body," the political organization of the state, was totally destroyed. The fourth beast was given over to "the burning fire," i.e., eternal punishment. The fate of the fourth beast is mentioned first for emphasis. Strict chronology is not observed here (7:11).

Parenthetically Daniel indicated that the Ancient of Days had already dealt with the first three beasts. They were not judged so dramatically or drastically as the fourth beast. The first three empires lost their dominion over the earth, but "an extension of life was granted to them." Each had been required to relinquish its position of supremacy, but each also had been permitted to continue under a new regime "for a time and a season," i.e., for an unspecified but predetermined time (7:12).

3. A coronation scene (7:13-14). As Daniel kept looking he observed "one like a son of man coming with the clouds of heaven." Clearly this one is a *person,* not a *personification* of the redeemed of Israel. Verse 14 declares that "all peoples . . . should serve him." That this one is the Messiah was recognized by the ancient rabbis.[9] Jesus' use of the title "son of man" appears to be based on this chapter.

To what *coming* of Jesus does this passage refer? Jesus repeatedly used the designation *son of man* to refer to his coming in glory.[10] In this passage, however, Messiah does not appear to be coming from heaven to earth, but rather from earth into the presence of the Ancient of Days. "He came up to the Ancient of Days and was presented before him." The predictive picture here may be that of the ascension which was also connected with clouds (Acts. 1:9).

There in heaven's throne room the one like unto a Son of Man was given "dominion, glory and a kingdom."[11] Two points are emphasized about Messiah's kingdom. First, it is universal, consisting of "all the peoples, nations and men of every language." Second, it is everlasting. The triple emphasis on the eternality of Messiah's kingdom seems to rule out any notion that the Millennial kingdom is in view. Messiah's kingdom shall never pass away because no flaw would be found in it. It is permanent because it is perfect.

That Christ entered into heavenly glory and received a kingdom at his ascension is the clear teaching of the New Testament.[12] The manifestation of that kingdom on earth is the church of Christ. This comports well with the dream of Nebuchadnezzar in chapter 2 in which the kingdom of heaven would be established "in the days of those kings," i.e., during the course of history, not at its close. Chapter 7 obviously is constructed topically, not chronologically. That is, the one like unto a son of man does not receive his kingdom chronologically after the destruction of the little horn. Such an interpretation would pit chapter 7 against the kingdom teaching of chapter 2.[13] That the heavenly kingdom existed prior to the destruction of the fourth kingdom clearly is taught in the earlier chapter.

EXPLANATION OF THE VISION
Daniel 7:15-27

Prophets often did not understand the significance of what they saw in vision or heard in verbal revelation. So it was with Daniel. Though he may have made some connection between this vision and the dream revelation of Nebuchadnezzar in chapter 2, the new elements here were so startling that he made two inquiries as to their meaning.

A. A General Inquiry (7:15-18).

Daniel was perplexed and alarmed by what he had witnessed in his vision. He then walked on the stage of this vision and became an active participant. He approached "one of those who was standing by," i.e., an angel, and requested an authoritative explanation of what he had seen (7:15f.).

The angel offered Daniel a brief summary of the import of the vision. The four beasts represented "four kings who will arise from the earth." Later the angel identified the four beasts as "four kingdoms" (v. 17). Hence, in prophecy the terms "kings" and "kingdoms" are used interchangeably. The four beasts would arise "from the earth." Thus the tumultuous sea of verse 3 represented the earth. These worldly kingdoms, however, were temporal. "The saints of the Highest One,"[14] i.e., God's people, would receive a kingdom which is permanent. Thus the angel introduced those who would be citizens of the kingdom which would be given to the one like unto a Son of Man. He called them *saints,* those separated from the world. They are the true people of God whether Jew or Gentile. Ultimately God's people would win the victory over all opposing forces of the world (7:17f.).

B. A Specific Inquiry (7:19-20).

The angel's brief summary of the import of the vision did not satisfy Daniel. He desired to know the exact meaning of the fourth beast and the horns associated with it.

Some find it strange that Daniel who lived during the days of the first kingdom would inquire further about the fourth kingdom. His interest in the fourth beast was piqued by five factors. First, greater emphasis had been placed on that kingdom in the revelation itself. Second, the fourth beast was totally different from the others. Third, this beast was shockingly terrifying. Fourth, it had unbelievable destructive power which is attributed to its "teeth of iron" and "claws of bronze." This beast "crushed and devoured its victims and trampled underfoot whatever was left." Fifth, the revelation clearly implied that the fourth kingdom at some point would be utterly hostile to God and his people (7:19).

Daniel also wanted to know more about the ten horns, and especially the "other horn." His attention was drawn to the eleventh horn for several reasons. First, this horn "was larger in appearance," lit., sturdier, "than its fellows." During the course of the vision the "little horn" of verse 8 had become stronger than the others. Second, the eleventh horn had uprooted three of the previously existing horns. Daniel puzzled as to what this might mean. Third, this horn "had eyes and a mouth that spoke boastfully" (7:20).

C. A Visional Explanation (7:21-22).

As if to answer the prophet's inquiry concerning the little horn, another scene unfolded before Daniel. He saw the little horn "waging war against the saints." For a while the little horn prevailed in his campaign against God's people. The reign of terror, however, would come to an end when the Ancient of Days "came and judgment was passed in favor of the saints of the Highest One." The reference is obviously to the same judgment mentioned earlier in verse 11, i.e., the final judgment. God has predetermined that heathen domination of the world will cease. The final judgment will usher in the new heavens and new earth wherein dwells righteousness (2 Pet 3:13; Rev 21:1). Dominion in that day will belong to the saints of God.

D. A Verbal Explanation (7:23-27).

The angel added his verbal explanation to the supplemental vision. He responded to the three points of inquiry respecting the fourth beast, the ten horns and the little horn.

1. The fourth beast represented a fourth kingdom which would "devour," "tread down" and "crush" the whole earth (7:23). As in chapter 2, this fourth empire is Rome.

2. The ten horns represented ten kings (or kingdoms) which arise out of the old Roman empire (7:24a). Embraced in this symbol are all the worldly powers which have dominated the political scene since the fall of Rome AD 476. See discussion on verse 7 above.

3. The little horn represented a king (or kingdom) which would arise after the ten horns appeared. What had been implied earlier was now made explicit, viz., that the little horn would be "different from the previous ones." While the ten horns seem to represent kingdoms in the abstract, the little horn appears to be an individual. This individual would achieve enormous power by subduing three of the kings (or

kingdoms) which would be dominating the political scene when he arises (7:24b; cf. v. 8).

The kingdom of the little horn would be anti-God to the core. His opposition to the kingdom of God would be vocal, physical and legal. He would speak out boastfully "against the Most High." He would "wear down the saints of the Highest One," i.e., launch a vicious program of persecution. As part of the persecution, he would "intend to make alterations in times and in law." This not only indicates the power of the little horn, but also his pretensions to divine authority. His law replaces God's law; his calendar is substituted for God's. Speculating as to the exact nature of these enactments is useless.[15]

The saints would be given into the hand of the little horn "for a time, times and half a time." A *time* is a year. If the expression is meant to be interpreted literally it would mean a period of three and a half years. In Biblical prophecy, however, the expression seems to point to a short but indefinite period of intense persecution (cf. Rev. 12:14). As with the "seven times" of Daniel 4, some writers insist that this expression should be interpreted according to the year-day theory. According to this theory, a day in symbolic prophecy is equal to a calendar year. These writers insist that a prophetic year has 360 days. The "time, times and a half time" (3 1/2 years) would then contain 1260 days, which, according to the theory, should then be converted into years. These writers then search history for a suitable period of 1260 years to nominate as the fulfillment of the prophecy.[16] This approach to the passage is manifestly incorrect on two counts. First, the "time, times and a half time" is not part of the symbolism in the prophecy, but part of the explanation. Second, the expression points to a period of years. Converting these years into days in order to convert those days back into years makes no sense.

The period of the "time, times and a half time" would continue to the final judgment. Then "the court will sit for judgment." The little horn would then lose his dominion. The horn would be annihilated and destroyed forever. With his demise the kingdom, "the sovereignty, the dominion and the greatness of all the kingdoms under the whole heaven will be given to the people of the saints of the Highest One." Their kingdom is his kingdom, the kingdom given to the one like unto a Son of Man at his ascension. His kingdom is an "everlasting kingdom." All rulers would worship and obey him.[17] This is that day described by the Apostle Paul as the day Christ comes "to be glorified in his saints" (2 Thess 1:10).

EPILOGUE
Daniel 7:28

At this point the revelation ended. Nothing more was divulged to Daniel at this time. In the three subsequent visions, however, segments of the prophetic period covered by chapter 7 are amplified. Meanwhile, Daniel had a great deal to ponder. He described for his readers his reaction to this stupendous vision. "My thoughts were greatly alarming me." His inner turmoil produced outward physical consequences as his face grew pale. He kept all this information to himself, awaiting the day when he would make his visions public through the publication of his book.

Chapter 7 traverses the same prophetic terrain as chapter 2. The four metals there have become the vicious beasts of this chapter. But chapter 7 goes beyond chapter 2 in some important respects. The earlier chapter knows nothing of the glorious person to whom the Ancient of Days would give the kingdom. Nor does chapter 2 speak definitively about the course of earthly government following the collapse of historic Roman empire. No hint of the powerful anti-God personality appears in chapter 2. The earlier chapter pictures the smashing of the worldly powers by the kingdom of God; but it gives no hint of the terrible persecution which God's people must endure before that day of triumph.

Chart No. 18

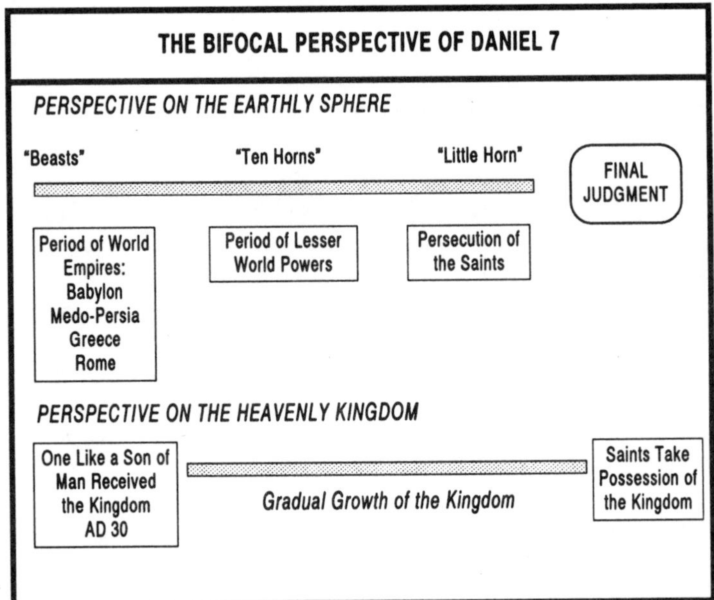

Endnotes

1. On the sea as symbolic of mankind, see Isa 17:12f. Rev 17:1, 15,16.

2. H.C. Leupold, *Exposition of Daniel* (Minneapolis: Augsburg, 1949) 285f.

3. The four major areas conquered by Alexander were Greece, Western Asia, Persia and Egypt.

4. The *didachoi* were (1) Lysimachus in Thrace and Asia Minor; (2) Antigonus and Cassander in Macedonia; (3) Ptolemy in Egypt; and (4) Seleucus in Syria and Palestine.

5. The composite beast of Revelation 13 may be the same as the fourth beast of Daniel 7. John described the beast as a mixture of leopard, bear and lion.

6. E.J. Young, *The Prophey of Daniel* (Grand Rapids: Eerdmans, 1949) 148-150.

7. Commentators have suggested that the thrones were intended for (1) the angelic keepers of the heavenly books; (2) the twenty-four elders; (3) the redeemed; (4) God and Messiah. Others think the plural is used in the abstract sense and simply represents the judicial bench or the one throne of God.

8. The Old Testament speaks of a book of life in which the names of God's own are written. See Exod 32:32; Pss 69:28; 139:16; Mal 3:16. The New Testament speaks of this book plus other books which apparently contain a record of ungodly acts. See Rev 20:11-15. The concept of a book in which human deeds and destinies are recorded is also found among the ancient Egyptians and Babylonians.

9. The rabbis had a problem reconciling Dan 7:13 with Zech 9:9. One explanation was that if Israel was worthy, Messiah would come riding the clouds; if not, he would come in the guise of a poor man riding an ass. *Sanh.* 98a.

10. On the Son of Man coming in glory see Matt 16:27,28; 19:28; 24:30; 25:31. See also Rev 1:7; 14:14.

11. The doxology of the Model Prayer is based on this passage. See also Matt 28:18-20; Acts 2:32-36; 1 Cor 15:23-26; Col 1:13.

12. In the parable of the ten minas, a man of noble birth went to a distant country to have himself appointed king and then return (Luke 19:12). Christ now sits at the right hand of the Father (Rom 8:34; Eph 1:20; Col 3:1; Heb 1:3; 8:1).

13. Commentaries generally acknowledge that verse 12 relates information which is chronologically prior to verse 11. The logic of the chapter is simply this: Daniel described the affairs of the world powers to their final destruction at the end of time. He then lifted his eyes heavenward to describe what would take place there during at least a part of that period in which the beasts held sway on earth.

14. The "Highest One" is plural in the original. Most likely this is the plural of majesty as in Prov 9:10.

15. Sabbatarian sects see here a prediction that the papacy would change the day of worship from the Sabbath to Sunday.

16. Uriah Smith, for example, started counting the 1260 years from AD 538 when the Bishop of Rome declared himself to be the head of all churches. The period ended in AD 1798 when the victories of Napoleon in Italy placed the pope at the mercy of French revolutionary government thus ending the political rule of the papacy. *Daniel and Revelation* (Portland: Pacific Press, 1912) 146-162.

17. Some take the pronominal suffix ("his") to refer to "people." This is grammatically possible. But the Hebrew word *pelach* ("serve") everywhere else is used in reference to service which is rendered to the deity. Hence the possessive pronoun must refer to the one like unto a Son of Man.

CHAPTER FORTY

The Initial Challenge
Daniel 8

Background of the Unit.

In chapter 8 the author reverts to the Hebrew language. This change was appropriate because from this point on God revealed to Daniel what would happen to his people in the more immediate future.

Chapter 8 focuses on a small section of the time-span covered in chapters 2 and 7, viz., the second and third world empires. Leupold observes that "the more immediate future is subjected to a more microscopic examination."[1] This second vision is dated to the third year of the reign of Belshazzar, two years after the vision of chapter 7. This is thought to be the last year of Belshazzar, the year of the fall of Babylon or 539 BC. The Hebrew implies that Daniel was surprised that he was granted the privilege of seeing a second vision. Three times in verse 2 the prophet records the intensity with which he observed every detail of this vision.

With regard to the geographical setting of the vision, three facts are stated. First, Daniel says he was in Susa (Shushan in KJV). Second, he notes that Susa was "in the province of Elam." Elam at this time was not part of the Chaldean Empire. This raises the question as to whether Daniel was present in Susa in person or in vision. Third, Daniel says he was beside the Ulai canal. This canal, mentioned in Assyrian literature, connected two rivers of the region. It passed Susa on the northeast. The vision was set in Susa because this city would later become one of the chief centers of the Persian Empire.

Outline of the Unit.

The structure of chapter 8 is identical to that of chapter 7. The vision is first presented and then explained.

A. Introduction: The Setting of the Vision (vv. 1-2).
B. The Presentation of the Vision (vv. 3-14).
C. The Explanation of the Vision (vv. 15-26).
D. Epilogue: The Reaction to the Vision (v. 27).

THE PRESENTATION OF THE VISION
Daniel 8:3-14

Daniel's second vision, like the first, employed animal symbolism. In this vision Daniel saw a ram and a he-goat clash. Another "little horn" appeared. In the climax, however, the animal symbolism was dropped. Daniel described the persecution of God's people and the desecration of their holy Temple.

A. The Ram (8:3-4).

Daniel first observed a ram standing in front of the Ulai canal. The ram was an emblem of princely power in the ancient Near East (Ezek 34:17; 39:18). This animal was especially significant in Persian statuary and symbolism. The guardian spirit of the Persian Empire appeared under the form of a ram. Persian kings standing at the head of their armies bore the head of a ram. The text later confirms (cf. v. 20) what these facts suggest, viz., that the ram in this vision symbolizes the kings of Media and Persia. Daniel noted that one of the two horns of the ram was longer than the other, and that the longer horn came up last. This points to the supremacy of Persia over Media in the second empire. Thus the ram is the counterpart of the chest of silver in chapter 2 and the lopsided bear in chapter 7.

From his base near Susa the ram roamed extensively to the west (Syria, Asia Minor, Babylonia), to the north (Armenia), and to the south (Egypt).[2] He roamed freely ("no other beast could stand before him"), powerfully ("nor was there anyone to rescue from his power"), and arrogantly ("he did as he pleased and magnified himself").

B. The He-goat (8:5-8).

Daniel next noticed a he-goat "coming from the west." He virtually flew over the ground until in short order he had covered the surface of the whole earth. The goat had a conspicuous horn between his eyes which, according to verse 21, represented the first king of the empire represented by the goat. The description of the goat thus far and in the verses which follow confirm that he represented the Greek Empire. He is the counterpart of the belly of bronze in chapter 2 and the four-headed leopard in chapter 7.

The he-goat entered the territory defended by the ram. He rushed upon the ram in his mighty wrath. The animosity of the he-goat toward the ram is underscored by the words, "he was enraged at him." The he-goat struck the ram, shattering his two horns. He hurled the ram to the ground and trampled him. "There was none to rescue the ram from his power" (8:7). Without question Alexander's triumphs over the Persian king Darius are depicted here. The Persians experienced crushing defeats at Granicus, Issus and finally at Shushan and the river Eulaeus. Within a few months Alexander had crushed the greatest empire known to man.

Following the victory over the ram, the he-goat "magnified himself exceedingly." At the height of his power, however, the large horn was broken. This is an obvious reference to the unexpected death of Alexander the Great at Babylon in 323 BC. In place of the single large horn, four conspicuous horns appeared. These horns, which pointed toward the four directions of the compass, have the same significance as the four heads of the leopard in chapter 7. They point to the four Hellenistic kingdoms which emerged from the empire of Alexander.[3]

C. The Little Horn (8:9-14).

Out of one of the four horns of the he-goat a little horn came forth (8:9a). This little horn represents a Hellenistic ruler. It is not to be confused with the little horn of chapter 7 which represented a ruler emerging from the fourth or Roman empire. Commentators are all but unanimous in identifying this little horn as Antiochus Epiphanes (174-164 BC), the eighth king of the Seleucus dynasty. Concerning this little horn the prophecy speaks of seven factors.

First, the campaigns of the horn were wide-ranging. He "grew exceedingly great toward the south" (i.e., Egypt), "toward the east" (i.e., Elymais and Armenia), and toward Canaan, "the Beautiful Land" (8:9).[4] Second, the horn threatened the people of God. "It grew up to the host of heaven" (8:10a). In Daniel and Revelation the host of heaven is a symbol for the people of God (see 8:24; 12:3; Rev 12:4). The figure is based on the promise made to Abraham that his descendants would be as numerous as the stars of the sky (Gen 15:5; 22:17). Jesus used a similar figure when he said: "then the righteous will shine like the sun in the kingdom of their father" (Matt 13:43).[5]

Third, the horn would be brutal in his persecution. It would cause "some of the host and some of the stars to fall to the earth, and it trampled them down" (8:10b). The mechanics of the vision at this point are hard to comprehend. How could a *horn* pluck stars from the heavens? That he would *trample* on them suggests that the horn was still viewed as attached to the he-goat. The meaning here is more important than the mechanics. Some of God's people would be brought down to earth and destroyed by Antiochus.

Fourth, the horn would manifest intolerable arrogance. "It even magnified itself to be the equal with the commander of the host" (8:11a). If the host is the Lord's people, then the commander of the host must be God himself. Antiochus called himself *Epiphanes*, a word often used by the Greeks of a glorious manifestation of the gods. This man obviously had delusions of deity!

Fifth, the horn would commit sacrilege. "It removed the regular sacrifice from him" (8:11b). Literally, he took away the *continual*. This term is used five times in Daniel. It refers either to the regular sacrifices offered morning and evening at the Jerusalem Temple, or to the entire regular Temple ritual. The Temple was so completely desecrated by this king that the sacred writer describes it as "thrown down" (NASB) or "brought low" (NIV). The place was no longer fit for the sacred functions for which it was intended.

Sixth, the horn would be used by God to punish his people. Though the horn did not realize it, he was simply a tool used by God in furthering the divine purpose as regards Israel. God would use the horn to punish his people for their *transgression* (8:12a). Most of the leaders of the Jews and perhaps even a majority of the population in the early second century BC were too willing to compromise with the pagan principles which undergirded Hellenization, i.e., the spread of Greek culture. The desecration of the Temple and the temporary removal of the regular sacrifice there was a jarring chastisement to intertestamental Israel.

Seventh, the horn temporarily would be successful. "It will fling truth to the ground and perform its will and prosper" (8:12b). For a time the horn would succeed in his ruthless and reckless assault upon all that was sacred in Judea.[6]

D. The Desecration of the Sanctuary (8:13-14).

At this point the prophet overheard a conversation between two holy ones, i.e., angels. He "heard a holy one speaking," presumably concerning the little horn (8:10-12). A second holy one asked the first, "How long will it take for the vision to be fulfilled?" The question is immediately sharpened. His request did not pertain to the *entire* vision, but to that portion of it which pertained to the desecration of the sanctuary and the trampling of the saints (8:13).

The first angel responded that it would require 2,300 "evenings and mornings" before the sanctuary could be restored to its proper use. This figure has been understood in various ways. Some have insisted that none of the numbers in Daniel's visions are in the nature of exact arithmetical calculations.[7] The 2300 days represent a period a little short of seven years. Thus the judgment which fell on Jerusalem at the hands of the little horn was not quite a full duration of divine judgment. The full judgment would be administered by the Romans in AD 66-70.

Of those who take the 2300 days literally (i.e., arithmetically) two interpretations have surfaced. (1) Because of the reference to the evenings *and* mornings, some have assumed that the figure represents the count of the regular twice-a-day sacrifices which would be missed during the period of desecration. The actual length of the desecration would then be 1150 days or roughly three years, two months and ten days. (2) Those who take the expression *evenings and mornings* as a way of speaking of ordinary days are probably correct. Thus the period of the desecration of the sanctuary *and* the trampling of the host would be roughly six years and four months. The entire period of the persecution by Antiochus is represented by the 2300 days.[8]

After the period of the 2300 days the "sanctuary" (NIV) or "holy place" (NASB) would be properly restored (8:14b). The Hebrew term used here *(qodesh)* is broader than the term translated "sanctuary" *(miqdash)* in verse 11. In Psalm 114:2 this term is used of the entire country of Judah. Thus the reference may be to the purging of the entire *land*, a purging which began with the rededication of the Temple by Judas Maccabaeus in December of 165 BC. Antiochus died a few months later in 163 BC. This seems to be the conclusion of the 2300 days.

Chart No. 19

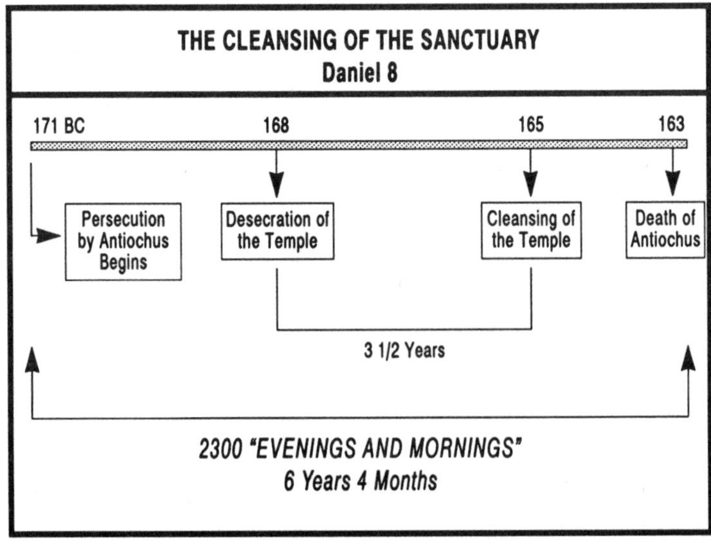

THE EXPLANATION OF THE VISION
Daniel 8:15-26

The vision which he had seen perplexed Daniel. He prayed for (or a least wished for) an explanation of it. God dispatched a high-ranking angel to explain the significance of what he had just seen.

A. Gabriel the Interpreter (8:15-18).

Suddenly one who looked like a man appeared before Daniel. He then heard the voice of a second "man" speaking to the one standing before him. The voice came from "between the banks of the Ulai," i.e., the voice seemed to be hovering in mid air over the canal. The voice appears to be the voice of God. He addressed the man who was standing before Daniel as "Gabriel."[9] The angel was directed to give Daniel an explanation of the vision (8:15f.).

At the approach of Gabriel, Daniel was terrified. He fell on his face to the ground. The mighty heavenly warrior was quite aware of the frailties of human flesh. He addressed Daniel with the title "son of man," which is used here, as in the Book of Ezekiel, to indicate the weakness of man. The angel first gave chronological orientation to the vision by announcing that "the vision pertains to the time of the end." Before Gabriel could proceed any further in his explanation he had to deal with a more immediate problem. Daniel had fainted and was prostrate on the ground! Gabriel, however, touched the prophet and empowered him to stand upright (8:17f.).

B. The Time Frame of the Vision (8:19).

What Daniel had seen in his vision had to do with what would occur "in the final period of the indignation." The *indignation (hazza`am)* is a technical term which designates the wrath of God.[10] The *indignation* began with the Babylonian domination of Judah. The present passage suggests that the *indignation* culminated in the persecutions of the little horn. If any light is found in this dark prediction it is only that the persecutions of Antiochus would mark "the final period" *('acharit)* of the *indignation*. People could then be confident that the Old Testament age was drawing to a close, and the Messianic age was at hand.

Gabriel assured Daniel that "at the appointed time the end shall come." The vision does not contemplate the end of all the ages such as a Christian might anticipate, but the end of the Old Testament era. The wording of the NASB suggests that the end of that era was predetermined. The NIV rendering ("the vision concerns the appointed time of the end") suggests that the period known as *the end* would endure for a predetermined period of time. Either interpretation of Gabriel's words is possible (8:19).

C. Explanation of the Ram and Goat (8:20-22).

Gabriel next explained the symbolism of the ram and the he-goat. The "ram" with its uneven horns represented "the kings of Media and Persia." The "shaggy goat" represented "the kingdom of Greece." The large horn which had been so conspicuous on the goat represented "the first king" of the kingdom of Greece, i.e., Alexander the Great. The "four horns" which arose after the large horn was broken represented "four kingdoms" which would arise from the kingdom which had been ruled by Alexander. As far as the Jews were concerned, the two most important of these kingdoms were those of Ptolemy who ruled Egypt, and Seleucus, who ruled Syria and Mesopotamia. The Ptolemies controlled Palestine from 321 to 198 BC when the Seleucid ruler Antiochus the Great conquered the land.

D. Explanation of the Little Horn (8:23-25).

The little horn which came out of one of the four horns of the goat represents a king who would arise. Two statements are made regarding the time when this king would arise. He would appear "in the latter period of their rule," i.e., the rule of the four kingdoms which arose out of Alexander's kingdom. Alexander died in 322 BC. The Greek kingdoms which succeeded Alexander maintained their independence until 63 BC. The Seleucid kingdom which produced Antiochus was over a century-and-a-half old at the time the evil king arose. During his reign the Romans began to assert themselves through the Mediterranean world, and the Greek kingdoms entered a period of decline.

Gabriel further identified the time of the rise of the evil king as being "when the transgressors have run their course," i.e., they had become as wicked as they could become (cf. v. 12). Under both the Ptolemies and the Seleucids, the Jews were exposed to Hellenism, an intensive promotion of Greek ways and thoughts. Many abandoned the faith of their fathers. Apostate Jews constructed a heathen gymnasium in Jerusalem and participated in the Greek games in the nude. Some Jewish men underwent a surgical procedure which camouflaged their circumcision. The high priesthood was bought and sold. Some of the high priests were the most ardent promoters of Hellenism. During this period Antiochus came on the scene.

Three phrases are used to describe the king, i.e., Antiochus. (1) He would be "insolent," lit., strong of face. The NIV renders, "a stern-faced king." The expression pictures Antiochus as hard, determined, unyielding and adamant. He would be (2) "skilled in intrigue." He would practice cunning and deceit. He would be a master of dissimulation. (3) This king's "power will be mighty." That power, however, would not be "by his own power." Like so many tyrants before him, Antiochus was but a tool in the hand of the Almighty. God would give him the might to punish his people because of their rebellion (8:23).

Four powerful words describe the work of Antiochus: *destroy, prosper, magnify* and *oppose*. He would "destroy to an extraordinary degree." Amplifying that point, Gabriel said (1) he would destroy "mighty men," i.e., powerful enemies in the south and east (cf. v. 9). He would also destroy (2) "the holy people." By these words Gabriel explained what was meant by the "host of heaven" and the "stars" of verse 10. Antiochus would also destroy (3) "many while they are at ease." He would lull the Jews into a false sense of security, and then attack.

The king would "prosper." He would do as he pleased, at least as respects the Jews. "Through his shrewdness he will cause deceit to succeed by his influence." Antiochus used false treaties, and lies to gain his ends. The king would "magnify" himself in his heart. He would even "oppose the Prince of princes," i.e., God himself (8:23b-25); cf. v. 11).

The career of the stern-faced king would end abruptly. "He will be broken without human agency" (8:25). His death would be an act of divine judgment. The mention of the demise of the king confirms the interpretation given to verse 14 that the 2300 day period ended with the death of Antiochus.

D. Concluding Words (8:26).

Gabriel concluded his explanation of the vision with three important statements. First, he gave a word of *confirmation.* "The vision of the evenings and mornings which has been told is true." Gabriel thus underscored the accuracy of the figure which Daniel had heard the angels discussing in verse 14. The period of persecution by Antiochus Epiphanes would last for six plus years.

Second, Gabriel gave a word of *instruction.* He directed Daniel to "keep the vision secret," lit., shut it up, keep it. He should preserve this vision for posterity.

Finally, the angel gave a word of *specification.* The revelation of the 2300 days of persecution "pertains to many days in the future." Daniel would not live to see the fulfillment of this prediction.

EPILOGUE: THE REACTION TO THE VISION
Daniel 8:27

Daniel described three different reactions which he experienced following the vision. First, he mentions his *physical* reaction. "Then I, Daniel, was exhausted and sick for days." For a man to receive a revelation from God is a traumatic experience. Next came the *practical* reaction. "Then I got up again and carried on the king's business." A man cannot linger for long in the mount of revelation rubbing elbows with the archangels. He must at last return to the valley of service. Third, Daniel described his *psychological* reaction. "But I was astounded at the vision and there was none to explain it." This revelation is hard enough to understand when viewed through the perspective of history. That Daniel would be perplexed by these announcements made centuries before their fulfillment is certainly understandable.

Chart No. 20

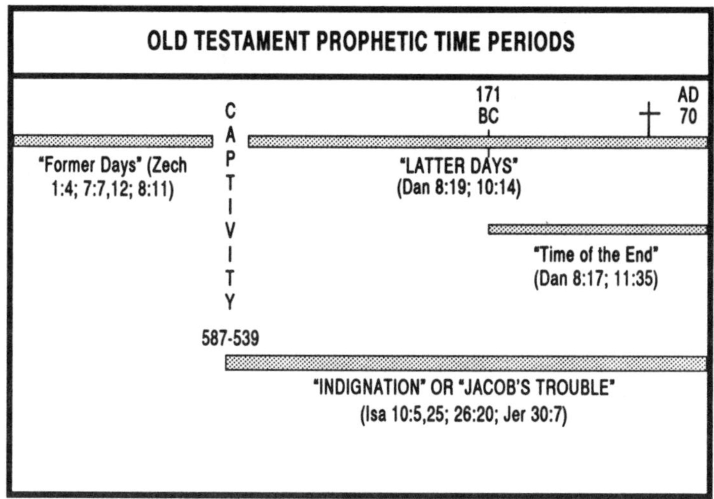

Endnotes

1. H.C. Leupold, *Exposition of Daniel* (Minneapolis: Augsburg, 1949) 332.

2. The Persian Empire did not advance to the east in the early days of its existence.

3. Initially Alexander's kingdom was carved up into five divisions: (1) Cassander ruled Macedonia; (2) Lysimachus ruled Thrace and Asia Minor: (3) Seleucus ruled Syria and Babylonia; (4) Ptolemy ruled Egypt; and (5) Antigonus ruled Asia Minor. In 301 BC Lysimachus and Seleucus defeated Antigonus in the battle of Ipsus.

4. On Antiochus' invasion of Egypt, see Dan 11:5; 1 Macc 1:16f. His campaigns in the east are documented in 1 Macc 3:31, 37; 6:1-4. His invasion of Canaan is also prophesied in Dan 11:16, 41.

5. 2 Macc 9:10, probably quoting Daniel, speaks of Antiochus as "the man that thought himself to touch the stars of heaven."

6. The primary source for the persecution of Antiochus is 1 Macc 1:41-64. See also Josephus *Antiquities* 12.5.2-4.

7. E.g., H.C. Leupold, *op. cit.* 355.

8. E.J. Young, *The Prophecy of Daniel* (Grand Rapids: Eerdmans, 1949) 173-75.

9. Daniel is the only book in the Old Testament in which angels are given their personal names. Gabriel appears again 9:21 and in Luke 1:19, 26. His name means "man of God."

10. The indignation (wrath) is a period during which God gave up his people to punishment because they had sinned against him. See Isa. 10:5, 25; 26:20.

CHAPTER FORTY-ONE

The Ultimate Champion
Daniel 9

Background of the Unit.

Chapter 9 of Daniel is dated to the first year of Darius the son of Ahasuerus (Xerxes NIV). This is the same king called Darius the Mede in 5:30. After the fall of Babylon to the armies of Cyrus in 539 BC this Darius was appointed king. On behalf of Cyrus he administered a large territory comprised, it would seem, of the entirety of the realm formerly ruled by the Chaldeans. On the problem of the identity of Darius the Mede, see the background material to Daniel 6.

The events of Daniel 9 were triggered by the reading of Scripture. Daniel had access to a collection of prophetic literature which included the scroll of Jeremiah. He noted in Jeremiah 25:11 that the desolations of Jerusalem were to end after the termination of the seventy years of Babylonian world rule.[1] Since as yet the liberation of the Jews had not taken place, Daniel was moved to pray for the fulfillment of the good word spoken by Jeremiah. To underscore his distress and demonstrate his repentance, Daniel fasted, donned sackcloth, and poured ashes over his head (9:2).

Since Darius received the kingdom shortly after the fall of Babylon (5:30), the first year of Darius would probably equate to the first year of Cyrus. In the first year of his reign Cyrus issued a decree which allowed the Jews to return to their homeland from Babylon. A contingent led by Zerubbabel the governor and Joshua the high priest took advantage of the king's gracious decree. A list of the families who returned is given in Ezra 2. The figures listed for each family indicate that 29,744 men made the trip back to Judah. This figure apparently does not include women and children.

That Daniel chose to remain in Babylon is no indication of lack of spiritual commitment on his part. His advanced age—he was in his eighties—and his prominent position in the administration of Darius (Dan 6:2) would have prevented him from making the trip.

Outline of the Unit.

A. The Prayer of Daniel (9:1-19).
B. The Appearance of Gabriel (9:20-23).
C. The Decree of God (9:24-27).

THE PRAYER OF DANIEL
Daniel 9:1-19

Daniel's prayer in this chapter ranks as one of the finest in Biblical literature. Unfortunately, because of the tremendous impact of the prediction found at the conclusion of chapter 9, the prayer in the opening section has received scant attention. The prayer has two main divisions: (1) an acknowledgment of sin; and (2) a plea for mercy.

A. Acknowledgment of Iniquity (9:4-14).

The prayer began with praise. Daniel addressed God as "great and awesome." He is a God who keeps his covenant. He extends "loving-kindness" to all who love him and keep his commandments (9:4).

Praise was followed by honest confession. "We have sinned,

committed iniquity, acted wickedly and rebelled." Daniel here modeled effective intercession by including himself among the guilty. Israel had turned aside from the Lord's commandments and ordinances. The Lord sent his servants the prophets to call the nation back to paths of fidelity. The prophets spoke in God's name to "our kings, our princes, our fathers and all the people of the land." No one listened (9:5f.).

Daniel next described the "open," i.e., obvious, "shame" of Israel. Lest anyone conclude that Daniel was complaining about the fairness of the present circumstances, he declared that "righteousness" belongs to the Lord. Even as the prophet prayed, however, the men of Judah, inhabitants of Jerusalem, and all Israel were in captivity. Some were nearby in Babylon; others were in surrounding countries. To these distant lands God himself had driven them because of their unfaithfulness. Kings, princes and fathers had all experienced open shame because "we have sinned against thee" (9:7f.).

The punishment of Israel was just. In spite of the Lord's compassion and forgiveness, Israel rebelled against him. They had not obeyed his voice nor followed his teaching as set forth by the prophets. Because all of Israel had transgressed the Law of Moses, the curse of that law had been poured out on the nation (9:9-11).

The exile to Babylon had confirmed the words which God had spoken against his people and their rulers. Jerusalem had experienced a tragedy beyond comparison. In spite of warnings along the way, God's people had not sought the favor of the Lord. They had not turned from their iniquity to give attention to the divine truth. The Lord "kept the calamity in store" and finally brought the full measure of it on his people in 587 BC. The great Yahweh, who had bonded himself to Israel when he brought them forth from the land of Egypt, was absolutely righteous in the judgment which he had inflicted. In essence, Daniel was saying, You were in the right, Lord; we were in the wrong! (9:12-15).

B. Appeal for Intervention (9:16-19).

Daniel's prayer contained a four-fold appeal to the Lord. First, he asked that the Lord might turn away his anger and wrath from Jerusalem. Daniel supported this appeal with four considerations. (1)

For God to intervene on behalf of Jerusalem would be harmonious with all his prior righteous acts. (2) The city of Jerusalem belonged to God as much as to Israel. (3) That mount upon which Jerusalem was built was holy. (4) Jerusalem and its former inhabitants had become "a reproach" to all those around about (9:16).

The second appeal focused on the "desolate sanctuary." Daniel asked that God's face might shine on those ruins, i.e., that God might cause a new day of blessing to dawn for his Temple. Daniel presented three grounds for this second appeal. (1) The Lord is *our* God, i.e., the Lord had a special relationship to Israel. (2) He who presented this earnest supplication was God's faithful servant. (3) The restoration of the Temple would be in God's own self-interest. He should therefore act for his own sake (9:17).

The third appeal called upon the Lord to open both his ear and his eye. Daniel wanted the Lord to take note of *your* desolations, to see the condition of that city "which is called by Thy name," i.e., which belonged to the Lord. Even though the petitioners could claim no personal merit before God, the sight of Jerusalem's desolations would stir the "great compassion" of the Lord (9:18).

In the fourth petition Daniel called upon the Lord to forgive his wayward people and to take action regarding their land and Temple. Again he urged God to consider that both Israel and Jerusalem belonged to him. For his own sake, i.e., for the sake of his reputation, God should reverse the fortunes of Jerusalem without delay (9:19).

THE APPEARANCE OF GABRIEL
Daniel 9:20-23

Daniel's season of prayer was interrupted by the second appearance of the angel Gabriel.[2] Two things are said with regard to the time of the angel's visit. First, Gabriel came when Daniel was extremely weary from his long prayer vigil.[3] Second, the angel appeared "about the time of the evening offering," i.e., about 3-4 PM. Faithful Jews could not sacrifice on foreign soil, but they did not forget the appointed hour (9:20f.)

Daniel described what the angel did by saying, "he gave me instruction and talked with me." Gabriel himself described his mission in these words: "I have now come forth to give you insight and understanding." These words must have reference to the matters about which Daniel was praying, viz., the forgiveness of God's people and the restoration of Jerusalem and the sanctuary (9:22).

How long Daniel had prayed before the appearance of Gabriel is not stated in the text. At the very beginning of his supplications, however, a divine command (lit., word)—the verbal revelation of 9:24-27—went forth from God. Gabriel was dispatched with this revelation because Daniel was "highly esteemed," lit., most desired. The angel exhorted Daniel to pay special attention to the message and understand "the vision" (9:23). The reference is not to the vision of the preceding chapter, but rather to the prediction which Gabriel was about to make.

THE DECREE OF GOD
Daniel 9:24-27

Gabriel's announcement in the last four verses of chapter 9 are the continental divide of Biblical prophecy. Montgomery called the passage "the dismal swamp of Old Testament criticism."[4] Leupold called it "an exegetical crux."[5] Young regarded it as "one of the most difficult in all the Old Testament."[6] The German scholar C. F. Keil devoted sixty-five pages to the consideration of these four verses. The leading features of this passage can be summarized under seven headings.

A. The Seventy Heptads (9:24).

Gabriel announced that "seventy weeks," lit., seventy units of seven, seventy heptads, had been decreed. That the passage envisions "weeks" of years and not days is all but the consensus among scholars of all prophetic schools.[7] [8] Just as westerners think in terms of units of ten years, the Israelites divided time into seven-year units which terminated in a sabbatical rest for the land. If a heptad here equals seven years, seventy heptads would equal 490 years.

The angel said that the seventy heptad period (490 years) concerned God's dealings with "your people and your holy city." The holy city is obviously Jerusalem. Daniel's people are the same people for which he earnestly was praying only moments before the arrival of Gabriel, viz., the Jews. Six objectives were to be accomplished during the seventy heptads. Each is stated in the form of an infinitive. These objectives are further developed as the prophecy unfolds.[9]

First, the expression "to finish the transgression" suggests that Israel would continue to rebel against God. Daniel's prayer alluded several times to Israel's transgression and the consequent curse which the nation had experienced. He now learned that the full measure of Israel's transgression was yet future.[10]

The second infinitive phrase, "to make an end of sin," literally means "to seal up sin." Israel's sins and transgressions would be sealed up, i.e., completed or terminated, during the seventy heptads. The crucifixion was the breaking point of God's patience with the Jews.[11]

The third phrase, "to make atonement for iniquity," surely must point to the work of Christ on the cross. The atonement or covering of sin is a major theme of the Christian Gospel (cf. Heb 10:12ff.; 2 Tim 1:10).

Once sin had been covered, then God could "bring in everlasting righteousness." The reference is to the right relationship to God which comes to a sinner through Christ (Rom 3:21-26).[12] This righteousness is called *everlasting* because (1) it originated in the eternal counsel of God; and (2) it has eternal duration.

Fifth, God would also "seal up vision and prophecy" during the seventy heptads. The Old Testament messianic prophecy was accredited by the life, death, resurrection and ascension of Jesus.[13] [14]

Finally, God would "anoint the most holy" (NIV) during the seventy heptads. The NASB inserts *place* after the words *most holy.* If a *place* is intended, then the Temple may be in view, or perhaps heaven itself. The centrality of Christ in the verses which follow, however, suggests that the *most holy* is a *person*, viz., Christ. He was anointed by the Holy Spirit at his baptism.[15] [16]

B. Issuing of a Command (9:25).

Daniel was told that the countdown for the seventy heptads would begin with "the issuing of a decree" (lit., word) "to restore and rebuild Jerusalem." The reference is probably not to the decree of some Persian king,[17] but to the command of God himself.[18] The first two attempts to rebuild Jerusalem's walls occurred during the reign of Artaxerxes (464-423 BC). The second of these attempts was the effort of Nehemiah who, with royal permission, successfully rebuilt the walls in 445 BC. A letter to the king from the adversaries of the Jews documents that an attempt was made to rebuild the walls prior to Artaxerxes' approval (Ezra 4:7-16).

The unauthorized wall construction is attributed to a group of Jews who recently had returned from Persia (Ezra 4:12,16). The only group known to have returned to Jerusalem from the Persian capital prior to Nehemiah was that group led by Ezra the scribe in the seventh year of Artaxerxes (Ezra 7:8). This group arrived in Jerusalem on August 4, 458 BC. The record indicates that Ezra was occupied with correcting the marriage abuses of the inhabitants of the land until New Year's day (Ezra 10:17). On the modern calendar this would fall within the spring of 457 BC. During the next few months Ezra exceeded the stipulations of his royal commission by leading his countrymen in the restoration of Jerusalem.

Thus the word to restore Jerusalem would have been issued by God through Ezra in the year 457 BC.[19] That this attempt to rebuild the walls failed (Ezra 4:17-23) in no way negates the fact that this was the first "word" to restore Jerusalem. The year 457 BC, then, is the *terminus a quo* for the seventy heptad prophecy.

Chart No. 21

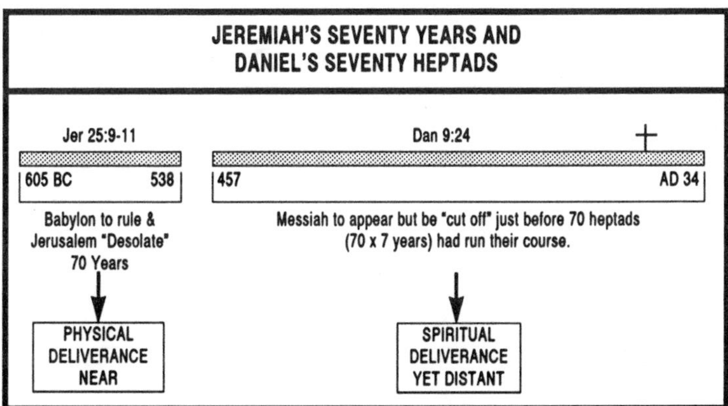

C. Appearance of the Anointed One (9:25).

The climax of the seventy heptads is the appearance of "the Anointed One, the ruler" (NIV). In the Old Testament both kings and priests were anointed. Hence the language points to one who is not only a priest (anointed one), but also a king. The reference can only be to Christ. Daniel was here addressing the last of the six infinitives of purpose from the preceding verse using precisely the same verbal root with which verse 24 closed.

This amazing prophecy stipulates the exact amount of time which must elapse between the word to restore Jerusalem and the appearance of Messiah as "seven weeks and sixty-two weeks." Sixty-nine heptads equals 483 years. Counting 483 years from 457 BC when the word to restore Jerusalem was issued places the appearance of the Messiah in the year AD 26. In that year Jesus of Nazareth was baptized by John in the River Jordan. Shortly thereafter he commenced his messianic ministry.[20]

D. Restoration of the City (9:25).

The sixty-nine heptads between the issuing of the word to restore Jerusalem and the appearance of Messiah are divided into two periods of seven and sixty-two heptads. Apparently in reference to the first of these two periods, the text declares that "it will be built." The period of the physical restoration of Jerusalem would be gradual, extending over a period of seven heptads or forty-nine years. Thirteen years after the failed attempt of Ezra, Nehemiah the governor succeeded in rebuilding the walls of Jerusalem. The curtain closes on Old Testament history with the second governorship of Nehemiah in 432 BC. References to the Jews in Palestine immediately subsequent to the period of Nehemiah are non-existent.

Other projects undoubtedly were undertaken during the seven heptads of reconstruction. The expression "with plaza and moat" is figurative for complete restoration. This language would be appropriate for one living in Babylon in the sixth century BC. The difficulties of achieving complete restoration of Jerusalem is indicated by the phrase "even in times of distress." The opposition faced by both Ezra and Nehemiah in their reconstruction efforts is in view here.

Chart No. 22

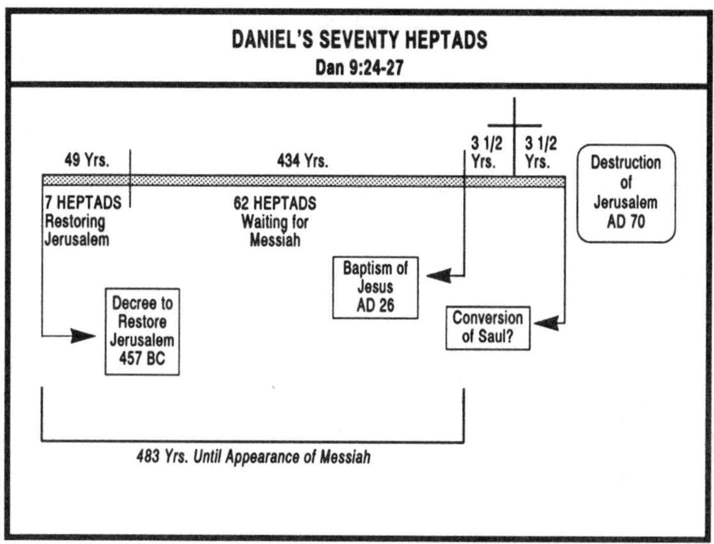

E. Cutting off of Messiah (9:26).

The first seven heptads was a time of reconstruction for Jerusalem. The sixty-two heptads was the time of waiting for Messiah. After the sixty-two heptad period the "Anointed One will be cut off." The text does not indicate in verse 26 how long after his appearance this cutting off takes place. The language points to a premature death. At the time of his death the Anointed One would "have nothing." This is a forceful way of indicating Messiah's utter rejection. The fulfillment is evident in the life of Jesus. He was arrested, tried and executed on a cross at the age of thirty-three after a brief ministry of three and a half years. Christ was stripped of even his clothes. The Roman soldiers gambled over his robe on the brow of Calvary. Of his closest followers only five are identified as having been present to render moral support in the hours of his agony.

F. Judgment on Jerusalem (9:26).

In consequence of the cutting off of Messiah, the people of a prince would come against Jerusalem. The time of this attack is not specified except that it would occur after the sixty-two heptads. This prince is obviously not the same as the Anointed One, the ruler or prince of the preceding verse. That prince would be "cut off" before the arrival of the people of this prince. Conservative commentators generally identify "the people of the prince who is to come" as the Roman armies which destroyed Jerusalem in AD 70. The prince must therefore be Titus, the one who commanded these armies.[21]

Concerning this judgment against Jerusalem four facts are predicted. First, the enemy would "destroy the city and the sanctuary." Such was the case in AD 70. Second, the "end" of the city would come "like a flood." Jerusalem would not just fade gradually from the scene of history. The climactic end of the struggle would come when the armies of the prince overwhelmed Jerusalem. Third, war would "continue unto the end." The final collapse of the city would be preceded by a long struggle. The Romans besieged Jerusalem from AD 66 to the final collapse of the city in AD 70. Rather than joining forces against a common enemy, factions within the city were fighting one another during that same period of time. Finally, that Jerusalem would become "desolations" was *determined* during the seventy heptads. The actual execution of the sentence occurred some forty years later in AD 70.

G. Amplification of the Prediction (9:27).

The last verse of chapter 9 contains information which augments the prophecy which has unfolded to this point. Four additional pieces of information are contained here. First, "he will confirm a covenant with many for one seven" (NIV). The pronoun refers back to the leading figure of the previous verse, viz., Messiah.[22] By his miracles and his fulfillment of prophecy Jesus confirmed God's covenant to send the Messiah into the world. The *many* are the thousands of Jewish people who responded to the words and works of Jesus and his Apostles. From the beginning of Christ's ministry to the conversion of Paul was about seven years (one heptad). During that period God's covenant to send a Messiah was confirmed with Israel. After Paul, Gentiles more than Jews were brought into the church.

Second, "in the middle of the week he will put a stop to sacrifice and grain offering." The middle of a heptad would be after a period of three and a half years. The reference again is to what the Messiah would do. After a ministry of three-and-one-half years, Jesus offered himself on the cross as the perfect sacrifice for sin. He thus brought to an end the Old Testament sacrificial system. It is true that sacrifices continued to be offered in Jerusalem's Temple until AD 70. Nonetheless, the grand argument of the Book of Hebrews is that the sacrificial system ceased as a divine appointment when Jesus died on the cross.[23]

Third, "on the wing of abominations will come one who makes desolate." This difficult clause has been interpreted in two ways. Some understand "the wing of abomination" to refer to the idolatrous eagles carried against Jerusalem by the Roman legions. Others think the reference is to the "wing" or pinnacle of the Temple which would become so desolated that it could no longer be regarded as part of God's house.[24] The "one who makes desolate" is the Roman general Titus who was mentioned as the "prince who is to come" in the previous verse. This is the "abomination of desolation" of which Jesus warned (Matt 24:15; Luke 21:20).

Fourth, "even until a complete destruction, one that is decreed, is poured out on the one who makes desolate." God had also decreed the complete destruction of the one who makes Jerusalem desolate.

Endnotes

1. Scriptures related to the issue of the seventy years are these: Jer 29:10; 27:6f; 25:11f.; and Dan 9:2. The emancipation edict of Cyrus fulfilled the word of the Lord spoken through Jeremiah the prophet concerning the desolations of Jerusalem (Ezra 1:1). Another seventy year period is mentioned in Zech 1:12; 7:5. For a discussion of these two periods see James E. Smith, *Jeremiah and Lamentations* in Bible Study Textbook Series, (Joplin: College Press, 1972) 443-456.

2. Gabriel appeared initially in 8:16 to explain to Daniel the vision of the 2300 evenings and mornings.

3. The expression is literally "to be weary in weariness" and could refer either to the angel or to Daniel.

4. James A Montgomery, *A Critical and Exegetical Commentary on the Book of Daniel* in The International Critical Commentary (Edinburgh: Clark, 1979; reprint of 1926 ed.) 400.

5. H.C. Leupold, *Exposition of Daniel* (Minneapolis: Augsburg, 1949) 403.

6. E.J. Young, *The Prophecy of Daniel* (Grand Rapids: Eerdmans, 1949) 191.

7. A period of 490 days would not serve to meet the requirements of the prophecy. By the third year of Cyrus (10:1) 490 *days* would have passed and the prophecy would have failed. Yet Daniel gives no indication in chapters 10-12 that such was the case. Also a connection seems to exist between the *seventy years* of Jeremiah's prophecy mentioned earlier in this chapter, and the *seventy times seven* years which are the focus here.

8. Leupold follows Keil in dissenting from the view that a heptad here equals seven years. Both scholars prefer to view the seventy heptads as an intentionally indefinite designation of time. That the numbers *seven, three* and *ten* often have symbolic significance is certainly true. Yet the seventy heptads are divided into units of seven, sixty-two and one. The latter two numbers are devoid of symbolic significance. This seems to indicate that the entire figure is intended to be taken arithmetically and chronologically.

9. J. Barton Payne, *Encyclopedia of Biblical Prophecy* (New York; Harper & Row, 1973) 386f.

10. The first infinitive phrase has also been taken to mean (1) the forgiveness of sin (Young); (2) the cessation of sin (Keil); and (3) the restraining of sin through the presence of Jesus and the power of the Gospel (Payne).

11. See Matt 23:29-39; 1 Thess 2:14-16. Keil interpreted the second infinitive phrase to refer to the total removal of all sin from the world. Young thought that this sealing up of sin was equivalent to forgiveness of sin.

12. Righteousness is frequently mentioned as a characteristic of Christ's kingdom. See Matt 6:33; Rom 14:17; 1 Cor 1:30.

13. Cf. John 3:33—The man who accepts the testimony of Jesus "has certified" (lit., sealed) "that God is truthful." In Luke 18:31 Jesus may have been elaborating on this phrase from Daniel 9. Young has pointed out that the word *vision* here is the technical name for revelation given to Old Testament prophets.

14. Two other interpretations of the phrase have been offered: (1) to close up prophecy as a punishment as in Matt 13:14f and John 12:39-41; (2) to remove prophecy from the scene because its functions are finished.

15. On the anointing of Christ see Luke 3:22; 4:18; Acts 10:38.

16. Those who understand the reference to be to the anointing of a holy place suggest (1) the Millennial temple (Gaebelein); (2) the Holy City, the New Jerusalem (Keil); and (3) heaven (Allis).

17. Those who hold that some Persian edict is intended have taken three positions: (1) Keil, Mauro, Young and Leupold opt for the decree of Cyrus in 538 BC. Isaiah 45:13 and 44:28 predict that Cyrus would order Jerusalem rebuilt. But Cyrus' decree said nothing about Jerusalem's walls which were essential to the reconstruction of the city. (2) Archer points to the edict of

Artaxerxes in 458 BC, but that edict did not order the restoration of Jerusalem's walls either. (3) Anderson points to the second decree of Artaxerxes in 445 BC which did in fact authorize the rebuilding of the walls (Neh 2:7, 8). That, however, was not the initial effort to reconstruct the walls.

18. The word *decree* in v. 25 is the same Hebrew word as the word *command* in v. 23 where God is the subject.

19. Jack Finegan, *Handbook of Biblical Chronology* (Princeton: University Press, 1964) 213.

20. Finegan, *op. cit.* 267.

21. Keil and Leupold identify the prince as the Antichrist whose coming was foretold in the Little Horn of Chapter 7. Some commentators incredibly identify the *prince* as Antichrist, but *the people of the prince* as the Roman armies of AD 70.

22. The other alternative is that the one who makes firm a covenant for one heptad is "the prince" whose armies destroy Jerusalem. Against this interpretation are the following points: (1) The "prince" in verse 26 occupies a subordinate position grammatically. (2) The prince and the people in verse 26 must be contemporaneous. (3) Scripture knows nothing of a future prince who makes a covenant with the Jews for seven years.

23. On the cessation of the sacrificial system, see Heb 7:11; 8:13; 9:25f.; 10:8f., 12.

24. According to Josephus, immediately prior to Jerusalem's fall to Titus the zealots "polluted the temple of God" and "made the house of God full of many abominations" (*Wars* 4.2.1; 4.3.10), Cf. Matt 24:15.

CHAPTER FORTY-TWO

The Last Days of National Israel Daniel 10-11

Background of the Unit.

Two notes are given as to the chronology of Daniel's final revelation. The year was the third of "Cyrus king of Persia,"[1] i.e., 536 BC (10:1). In his first year this Persian king had issued a decree which permitted the Jews to return to their homeland (Ezra 1:1). Not many took advantage of the opportunity; those who did experienced difficult times. To be more precise, the revelation came on the twenty-fourth day of the first month, the month of Nisan (10:4). The Passover season, when Israel commemorated deliverance from Egyptian bondage, had just been completed.

Because of the sad condition of his people, Daniel[2] was unable to enjoy the Passover season. He had been mourning for three entire weeks.[3] He took no food nor drink during that period. He used no ointment upon his body such as one might do during a festive occasion (10:2f.).

The vision occurred while Daniel was away from Babylon by the bank of the great river Tigris. Was he there on administrative duty? Was he there to urge the Jews to return to their homeland? Speculation is useless.

Three words describe the vision which Daniel received. First, the message was *true*. The vision was also *turbulent*, "one of great conflict" or suffering. Finally, the vision was *transparent*. Daniel "understood the message and had an understanding of the vision" (10:1).

Outline of the Unit.

A. The Heavenly Messenger (10:5-11:1).
B. The Immediate Future (11:2-20).
C. The Contemptible Person (11:21-35).
D. The Arrogant King (11:36-45).

THE HEAVENLY MESSENGER
Daniel 10:5-11:1

God responded to the fasting and prayer of Daniel by dispatching an angel to speak to him.

A. The Appearance of the Angel (10:5-9).

In the midst of his meditation, Daniel became conscious of the presence of one who had the appearance of a man. The man was dressed in linen, emblematic of purity. His waist was girded with a belt of pure gold of Uphaz,[4] i.e., with a heavy cloth embroidered with gold. This girdle was the insignia of one of high rank (10:5).

The man had a body "like beryl" (NIV chrysolite). This particular stone has not yet been identified, but undoubtedly a gem of rare beauty and color is meant. His face had the appearance of lightning, i.e., it had a startling brilliance, and perhaps was flashing. His eyes were "like flaming torches." They burned with a bright light. His arms and feet were "like the gleam of polished bronze." His voice sounded "like the sound of a tumult," i.e., like a roaring crowd (10:6).

Who was this "man" who appeared to Daniel beside the River Tigris? Because of the similarities to the description in Revelation 1:13-15, some have argued that the man was Christ. That this "man" had recently required the assistance of the angel Michael seems to suggest that he was not Christ. The "man" was obviously an angel of the highest rank, one who was the equal of Michael the archangel.

Only Daniel saw the vision of the heavenly messenger. Those who accompanied the prophet experienced a feeling of great foreboding, even though they did not see the "man." They fled the scene to hide themselves. Daniel himself became weak and pale. The impact of the vision added to the weakness caused by three weeks of fasting. When he heard the voice of the angel, Daniel fell to the ground in a trance (10:7-9).

B. The Assurance of the Angel (10:10-14).

Daniel next felt the touch of a hand. The angel set him trembling on his hands and knees. Then the angel addressed the prophet in order to assure him of several things. First, the angel assured Daniel that he had standing with God for he was a "man highly esteemed." Second, he assured Daniel that he had important information which the prophet must seek to understand. Third, he assured Daniel that he had nothing to fear. Therefore he should stand up like a man to receive the revelation from God. Fourth, he assured Daniel that his words of prayer had been heard from the first utterance. The prophet had been trying to understand the weighty revelations of chapters 8 and 9. By humbling himself he thought that God might grant additional insight. This angel had been dispatched in response to Daniel's petitions.

Fifth, he assured Daniel that he had a legitimate reason for not appearing sooner. His last post had been "with the kings of Persia." For twenty-one days he had been engaged in a struggle with "the prince of the kingdom of Persia." Obviously this must refer to some powerful demonic personality. Michael, "one of the chief princes" in the heavenly hierarchy came to help this angel in the struggle. The text depicts a spiritual warfare to influence the Persian court, especially King Cyrus, to be favorable to the Jews. Finally, he assured Daniel that he had come to give him understanding of what would happen to the Jews "in the latter days." In Old Testament prophecy this phrase always reaches out to the Messianic age. The New Testament identifies the Christian age as being the last days.[5] Some portion of the vision would pertain to the present age which began with the outpouring of the Spirit on the day of Pentecost.

C. The Assistance of the Angel (10:15-19).

When Daniel heard the words of the angel he turned his face to the ground and became speechless. "One who resembled a human being," i.e., the angel, at that point touched the lips of Daniel. The purpose of this touch was to impart to his mouth the ability to present his petition before the angel in the form of a complaint. The prophet opened his mouth to complain of the anguish and weakness which had come upon him as a result of the vision which he had just experienced. Daniel felt totally unworthy to converse with such an exalted being as this angel (10:15-17).

Again the angel touched Daniel and strengthened him. Again he addressed the prophet with words which reassured him of his standing with God. He encouraged Daniel with the traditional friendly greeting "peace be with you." He exhorted the prophet to take courage. To all this Daniel responded positively. Once strengthened he was ready now to listen to what the angel had to say (10:18f.).

D. The Assertion of the Angel (10:20-11:1).

Why had this warrior angel come to Daniel? The angel asserted the importance of the following revelation in two ways. First, he indicated the priority which had been assigned to the communication of this message. God had dispatched a most prominent messenger to bring the word to Daniel. Once he had completed this mission, the angel must return to his post to renew the battle against "the prince of Persia." That demonic spirit would continue to try to influence the Persian kings to be hostile toward the people of God. When that battle ended, "the prince of Greece" would come, i.e., a demonic spirit which would endeavor to enlist another power in the war of destruction against God's people. Only Michael "your angel," i.e., an angel assigned to the watch care of God's people, was of sufficient rank and power to engage in the high-level warfare alongside this warrior angel. Apparently the two worked as comrades in arms. Two years earlier, in the first year of Darius the Mede, this warrior angel had come to the assistance of Michael in a similar spiritual battle. Second, the angel underscored the importance of the subsequent revelation by his summary of its contents. "I will tell you what is inscribed in the writing of truth." Here heavenly truth is expressed in earthly terms. In the ancient world that which was written was taken far more seriously than that which was spoken. The "writing of truth" points to God's foreknowledge of future events. That which God foreknows will certainly take place. He is not, therefore, embarrassed to put down in writing his revelations.

THE IMMEDIATE FUTURE
Daniel 11:2-20

The final revelation was designed to amplify the vision of the seventy heptads in chapter 9. Because of its pin-point predictive prophecy this chapter is utterly amazing! The prophetic range here is roughly six hundred years, from Daniel's day to the fall of Jerusalem to the Romans in AD 70. In the first nineteen verses in rapid succession the prophecy speaks of the last of the Persians, the rise of the Greeks and the rivalry of the Ptolemaic and Seleucid kingdoms.

A. The Last of the Persians (11:2).

The angel first announced that three more kings would arise in Persia. Since the prophecy was given in the days of Cyrus, the reference must be to Cambyses (530-522 BC), Smerdis (522), and Darius the Great (521-486 BC). "Then a fourth king" would amass enormous wealth and with it launch an invasion against "the realm of Greece." The reference is to Xerxes (486-465 BC) who is also known in the Bible as Ahasuerus. In 480 BC Xerxes attempted to avenge the Persian defeat at the battle of Marathon (490 BC) when his predecessor invaded Greek territory. Xerxes was delayed by the Trojans at Thermopylae and finally defeated at the battles of Salamis and Plataea. The invasion of the Hellenistic homelands was the pretext of Alexander's invasion of the Persian empire in the fourth century.

B. The Arrival of the Greeks (11:3-4).

The angel-prophet announced the rise of a "mighty king," one who would rule "with great authority and do as he pleases." Obviously the reference is to Alexander the Great. Almost as soon as he assumed power, the great king's kingdom would be "broken up." After demolishing the Persian empire and extending his hegemony from Egypt to the Indus river, Alexander died in Babylon in 323 BC. His kingdom was then "parceled out toward the four points of the compass." The "sovereignty" would be "uprooted and given to others" outside the royal bloodline. These successors would not rule with the authority once wielded by Alexander. The prediction found fulfillment in the four Hellenistic empires which grew out of the imperial dream of Alexander. Cassander ruled in Macedonia. Thrace and Asia Minor were ruled by Lysimachus. Seleucus ruled Syria and Babylonia. Ptolemy ruled Egypt.[6]

C. The Rival Kingdoms (11:5-20).

The Ptolemaic and Seleucid kingdoms received special attention in the prophecy because of their proximity to the people of God. Palestine was a prize coveted by the successive rulers in both of these kingdoms. The Ptolemies wanted to control Palestine as a buffer against invasion by the rival Seleucid kings. The Seleucids wanted control of Palestine as a staging area for invasions into Egypt. The people of God were brutalized by both regimes. The prophecy focuses on four pairs of rival rulers.

1. The first pair (11:5). The first "king of the south," i.e. Egypt,[7] was Ptolemy Soter, one of Alexander's generals. He ruled from 322-305 BC. Seleucus (later called Nicator) was forced to flee from his claimed territory in Syria. He temporarily cast his lot with Ptolemy. From the Egyptian point of view, Seleucus was one of Ptolemy's princes. Ptolemy helped Seleucus gain control over Syria in 312 BC. He ruled his kingdom until 281 BC. The Seleucid dynasty eventually came to surpass that of the Ptolemies in Egypt (11:5).

2. The second pair (11:6). The successors of Ptolemy and Seleucus became bitter rivals. Thirty-five years after the death of Seleucus, Ptolemy Philadelphus (285-246 BC) and Antiochus II Theos (261-246 BC) attempted to work out an agreement which would keep the peace. The accord was sealed by the marriage of Philadelphus' daughter Bernice to Antiochus II. Two years later, however, Antiochus abandoned his Egyptian wife. Shortly thereafter Antiochus was assassinated by his new wife. Bernice and her child by Antiochus were also murdered.

3. The third pair (11:7-9). To avenge his sister's death, Ptolemy III Euergetes (246-222 BC) carried out a military expedition against Seleucus II Callinicus (246-226 BC). He executed Bernice's murderers. At the same time Euergetes captured paraphernalia connected with the gods of Syria. About 240 BC Callinicus attempted to retaliate by invading Egypt, but with no success.

4. The fourth pair (11:10-19). Under the sons of Callinicus, Seleucus III Ceraunus (226-223 BC) and Antiochus III (223-187 BC), the Seleucid dynasty began to grow in power. The latter king enjoyed great military success. He took Phoenicia and Palestine and fortified himself at Gaza. Antiochus raised a huge army[8] in preparation for an Egyptian invasion. Ptolemy IV Philopator (222-205 BC) attacked and defeated Antiochus in the battle of Raphia. Antiochus suffered enormous loses. Philopator did not, however, press his advantage. He was more interested in self-indulgence than in conquest (11:10-12).

Thirteen years after the battle of Raphia, Antiochus III was ready for another attempt to settle the score with the Ptolemies. Philopator was dead, and his four-year old son Ptolemy V Epiphanes (204-180 BC) was on the throne. Jews who were in league with Antiochus worked from within to overthrow Ptolemaic rule of Palestine. Soon they would realize that switching from Ptolemaic to Seleucid rule was like being cast from the proverbial frying pan into the fire. The showdown finally occurred at Sidon. There Scopas, chief lieutenant of Ptolemy, was defeated by Antiochus. After the battle Antiochus stayed for a time "in the beautiful land," i.e., Palestine, "with destruction in his hand." The Jews now realized that one tyrant is no different from another (11:13-16).

Antiochus next attempted to gain control of Egypt through political means. He married his daughter Cleopatra to the seven-year old Ptolemy.[9] The plan failed, however, because Cleopatra constantly took the side of her young husband against her father. Meanwhile Antiochus campaigned against the islands and coasts of the Mediterranean Sea. At the instigation of the now armyless Hannibal, Antiochus invaded Greece. There he was defeated by the Romans. Antiochus retreated to Asia Minor where the Romans crushed him at

Magnesia. He was forced to pay huge indemnity as well as surrender his navy and elephants. The Romans also took hostage his son, later known as Antiochus Epiphanes, and kept him in Rome for twelve years (11:17f.).

In his last days Antiochus the Great could no longer think of expansion. The best he could do was to maintain his own territory. He was killed in 187 BC by fierce tribesmen in Elamais where he had gone to seize treasure to help pay his debt to the Romans. Seleucus IV Philopator (187-175 BC) succeeded his father. He dispatched Heliodorus the prime minister to appropriate a part of the Temple treasury in Jerusalem. Seleucus died mysteriously. Poisoning is suspected, possibly at the hand of Heliodorus (11:19f.).

THE DESPICABLE PERSON
Daniel 11:21-35

The first twenty verses of Daniel 11 are background to the predictions concerning the "despicable person," i.e., Antiochus Epiphanes (175-163 BC). The angel spoke of his rise to power, his two invasions of Egypt, and his persecution of the people of God.

A. The Rise of Antiochus (11:21-24).

Antiochus Epiphanes was not born to the throne. He took advantage of political and military confusion to carve out for himself a power base. In those troublous times the "prince of the covenant," i.e., the high priest, would be murdered. The prediction points to the death of Onias III, the last godly high priest of the Mosaic system (11:22).

By means of a covenant Antiochus lulled his rivals into a false sense of security. After some time with only a small number of partisans he was able to gain control of the Syrian government. He then took advantage of the tranquility of the area to seize personal and national wealth to finance his extravagant life style (11:23f.).

B. Egyptian Campaigns (11:25-30a).

Antiochus Epiphanes moved on Egypt in 170 BC. The regents of Ptolemy VI Philometor (180-146 BC) could not withstand him. Ptolemy's advisors treacherously had the boy king flee Alexandria by sea. He was intercepted by Antiochus. The citizens of Alexandria Egypt proclaimed his younger brother king under the title Euergetes II. Antiochus pretended to back Philometor against his brother. With Egypt divided between two rival bothers, Antiochus seemed to be in a position to annex Egypt. Yet his plans would not succeed "for the end is still to come at the appointed time." God had another destiny in store for Antiochus, one which he would fulfill in frustration over his failures in Egypt (11:25-27).

En route to his homeland, Antiochus Epiphanes marched with a strong force against Jerusalem. There he entered the Temple and carried off the sacred furniture. He stripped off all the gold plating from the front of the Temple. He seized the silver, gold and precious vessels, and whatever secret treasures he found (11:28).

At God's appointed time, Antiochus attempted a second invasion of Egypt in 168 BC. This last time "it would not turn out the way it did before." On Egyptian soil he was confronted by "ships of Kittim," i.e., invaders from the west. A small contingent of Roman soldiers ordered Antiochus to desist from his ambitions to annex Egypt or face war with Rome. Recalling the devastating defeat which his father had experienced at the hand of the Romans, Antiochus Epiphanes returned in frustration to his own land (11:29-30a).

C. Persecution of the Jews (11:30b-35)

Antiochus Epiphanes took out his frustration on "the holy covenant," i.e., the people of the covenant or Jews. He would attack "the sanctuary fortress." With the temple under pagan control, the regular sacrifices would no longer be offered. The king would set up in the Temple "the abomination of desolation," i.e., an idol (11:30b-31). All these sacrileges are documented in the first chapter of 1 Maccabees.

Antiochus found a number of turncoats who would make common cause with him, "those who forsake the holy covenant" as the prophecy calls them. The king's "smooth words" persuaded many to "turn to godlessness." Those, however, who "know their God" would form a resistance movement. In those desperate times leaders would arise, "those who have insight," to teach and thus preserve the true faith (11:32f.). The reference appears to be to the Hasidim, a pious sect which arose to preserve the Law. The Greeks took advantage of the fanatical refusal of these devout men to fight on the sabbath. Hundreds were slain.

When the Hasidim faced virtual extinction, God granted them "a little help." The reference appears to be to the charismatic leader, and brilliant military tactician, Judas Maccabee, lit., the hammer. Judas was able to relieve some of the pressure on the Jews by a series of battlefield triumphs over huge opposing forces. He, however, was never able to completely rescue his people from the Syrian Greeks. Nor was he able to stem the tide of paganism in Judea. Some Jews hypocritically pretended to support the popular Judas, but their hearts inclined toward Hellenization (11:34).

Judea would suffer through a time of testing and purging "until the end time," i.e., the end of the Old Testament era. At the "appointed time" the testing would end and the new age, the age of Messiah, would commence (11:35). These words are reminiscent of what Paul wrote: "But when the fullness of the time came, God sent forth His Son, born of a woman, born under the Law, in order that He might redeem those who were under the Law, that we might receive the adoption as sons" (Gal 4:4f.).

THE ARROGANT KING
Daniel 11:36-45

The identity of the king who does as he pleases in 11:36 is disputed. The two most popular views are (1) that this is a further description of the career of Antiochus Epiphanes; and (2) that he is the eschatological Antichrist who has yet to appear on the earth. The details here do not snugly fit what is known of the career of Antiochus. The view that this king is Antichrist is sheer imagination. A better interpretation is that this king represents that great king who ruled just prior to the birth of Christ, Herod the Great (40-4 BC).

A. The Pride of the King (11:36-39).

In some respects this king would repeat the indignation visited upon Israel by Antiochus Epiphanes. His arrogance would be manifested in five ways. (1) He would do as he pleased. (2) He would exalt himself over every god. (3) He would speak "monstrous things against the God of gods." (4) He would reject the traditional religion of his fathers. (5) He would have no regard for "the desire of women." This last phrase has been interpreted in various ways. Some think that the phrase means he would have no desire for women, i.e., he would be homosexual or perhaps celibate. Others think the reference is to his disregard of those desired by women, i.e., children in general, or the Messiah in particular (11:36f.). If the king here is Herod, the slaughter of the Bethlehem infants might be in view.[10]

The king (Herod) would prosper "until the indignation is finished." The period of wrath against national Israel which began with Antiochus Epiphanes would continue under the new dynasty. This king's only god would be war, and he would build fortresses for his temples.[11] With the support of his allies, the Romans, Herod undertook the most daring military adventures. He used bribery to raise up a host of fanatics loyal to his cause (11:38f.).

B. The Demise of the King (11:40-45).

At the "end time," i.e, the last period before the appearance of Messiah, this king would become allies with "the king of the south." The famous Cleopatra was the representative of the old Ptolemaic dynasty in Egypt. She, Mark Antony and Herod joined together to capture the Roman province of Syria.[12] This was the beginning of the Actian War. The "king of the north," the Romans who now controlled Syria, would retaliate by a full-blown attack against Herod and surrounding lands (11:40).

En route to Egypt, the king of the north (the Roman Augustus) would enter the Beautiful Land, i.e., Judah. History records that Herod saved his crown at this time by switching allegiance and aiding Augustus. According to Josephus, Pliny and others, the Roman sent an unsuccessful expedition against Edom and Moab at this time. Other lands, however, did not escape. Augustus took possession of the wealth of North Africa. Libya and Ethiopia submitted to his authority (11:41-43).

After the brief parenthesis describing the movements of the "king of the north," the attention is again focused on Herod. That arrogant king would be troubled by "reports from the east" which troubled Herod was probably the news brought by the Magi (Matt 2:1-3). To protect his throne Herod ordered the slaughter of the Bethlehem innocents. The "reports from the north" came in a letter from his son in Rome. The letter reported that Herod's other two sons and heirs apparent had written a slanderous letter to Rome about their father (11:44). Herod had those sons killed.[13]

The king would "pitch his royal tents between the seas at the beautiful holy mountain" (NIV). The *seas* here are probably the Mediterranean and the Dead seas. The beautiful holy mountain would be Mt. Zion or Jerusalem. Herod had two palaces in Jerusalem, one in the temple area, and one in the upper city. Though he would be successful for a time in dominating the Holy Land, he would "come to his end, and no one will help him." Josephus describes the terrible end of Herod. He literally rotted away and suffered convulsions. Herod ordered that Jewish leaders should be executed upon news of his death in order that there be mourning at the time of his funeral.

Chart No. 23

DANIEL'S LAST VISION 536 BC *What will Happen to the Jews during the Seventy Heptads*						
10:1 - 11:1	11:2 - 12:3					
	11:2	11:3	11:4-19	11:20-35	11:36-45	12:1-3
Introduction Delay Visit of the Angel	Four More Persian Kings	Alexander the Great	King of the North (Seleucids) Vs. King of the South (Ptolemies)	Career of Antiochus Epiphanes	Herod the Great	Time of Trouble and Gospel Awakening
	536 - 336 BC 200 Yrs	336 - 323 BC 13 Yrs	323 - 175 BC 148 Yrs	175 - 164 BC 11 Yrs	37 - 4 BC 33 Yrs	4 BC - AD 70 74 Yrs

Endnotes

1. The title "king of Persia" does not conform to the known usage in monuments and documents from the sixth century BC. One should note, however, that (1) monuments and documentary evidence are fragmentary; (2) Cyrus was king of Persia; and (3) Daniel was not writing for Persians in their idiom, but for Jews in theirs.

2. Daniel's Babylonian name, as well as his Hebrew name, was used to emphasize that, in spite of the many years which had passed, the same Daniel who had come to the court in 604 BC was the subject of this chapter.

3. The text reads literally, "three heptads as to days," i.e., three ordinary weeks of days. The text is careful to distinguish these heptads from the heptads of years in the preceding chapter.

4. Uphaz is elsewhere mentioned only in Jeremiah 10:9. The location is uncertain. Perhaps Uphaz is the same as Ophir, a location mentioned ten times in the Old Testament. It was reached by sea from the port at Ezion-geber on the Gulf of Aqabah. From the time of the Septuagint (second century BC) Ophir was identified as India. Fine gold was the principal product of Ophir (Job 22:24).

5. Acts 2:17; Heb 1:2; 1 John 2:18; 1 Pet 1:20.

6. On the partitioning of Alexander's empire see the prophecies in 7:6 and 8:8.

7. The Greek version always renders *Egypt* instead of *the south.*

8. Antiochus' army consisted of 70,000 infantry, 5,000 cavalry, and 73 elephants.

9. Due to the age of the king, the marriage of Cleopatra to Ptolemy V Epiphanes was delayed five years.

10. The king's disregard for the desire of women is sandwiched between two clauses depicting his arrogant disregard for deity. The "desire of women" might be the Messiah whom Herod tried to destroy at Bethlehem.

11. Antonia in Jerusalem, the Herodion near Bethlehem, and Masada are examples of fortresses built by Herod.

12. Plutarch's "Life of Mark Antony" lists Herod as contributing supplies to the effort to capture Syria. The NIV and NASB would make it appear in verse 40 that the king of the south went to war *against* "the king" who ruled Palestine. The Hebrew could just as easily be understood to say that the two were allies against someone else. See Philip Mauro, *The Seventy Weeks of Daniel and the Great Tribulation* (Swengel, PA: Reiner, n.d.)

13. Josephus, *Antiquities* 17.4.7; *Wars* 1.30-33.

14. Josephus, *Antiquities* 17.6.5.

CHAPTER FORTY-THREE

The Time of Great Distress Daniel 12

Background of the Unit.

In Daniel 12 the prophecy from chapter 11 continues. Thus far the angel prophetically had outlined the events from Daniel's day through the demise of Herod the Great. He had alluded to events connected with the birth of Christ, viz., the disturbing news from the east, and Herod's disregard for the desire of women. In chapter 12 the angel spoke of the dawn of the Messianic Age and the closing events of God's dealings with national Israel.[1]

Outline of the Unit.

A. An Angelic Proclamation (12:1-4).
B. An Angelic Conversation (12:5-6).
C. An Angelic Explanation (12:7-13).

AN ANGELIC PROCLAMATION
Daniel 12:1-4

The angel who had been outlining Israel's future for Daniel in chapter 11 now made a dramatic proclamation concerning the final events of that nation's existence. He announced that a great distress and a great awakening would take place in Israel in days to come.

A. A Great Distress (12:1).

The angel made four points regarding the great "distress" which would befall the Jewish nation. First, he pointed out that the distress would be unprecedented. Israel had been through many trying experiences in its history. The angel, however, spoke of "a time of distress such as never occurred since there was a nation until that time." This ordeal seems to be the same as that prophesied in the closing verses of chapter 9. The Roman war of AD 66-70 is in view.

That national Israel came to its end with a time of tribulation, distress and sufferings of unsurpassed severity is a well-known fact. Flavius Josephus, an eyewitness of these events, renders this opinion: "Accordingly, it appears to me that the misfortunes of all men, from the beginning of the world, if they be compared to these of the Jews are not so considerable as they were."[2] After reading this historian's vivid chronicle of the fall of Jerusalem one is forced to agree with him "that neither did any other city ever suffer such miseries, nor did any age ever breed a generation more fruitful in wickedness than this was, from the beginning of the world."[3] Jesus foretold that the calamities which would befall the Jewish people in the siege of Jerusalem would be the greatest that had ever been since the beginning of the world.[4]

Second, the angel pointed out that the unprecedented distress would occur "at that time," i.e., during the period of the Herodian dynasty. Chapter 12 is obviously a continuation of chapter 11. If "the king" in 11:36-45 is Herod the Great as seems most probable, the events of chapter 12 must follow shortly after his reign. Herod the Great died in 4 BC. His sons and grandsons ruled greater or lesser portions of Palestine as puppets of Rome throughout the first Christian century. King Agrippa, the last representative of the Herodian dynasty, died childless in AD 100.[5]

Third, the angel revealed that the unprecedented distress would provoke intervention by an angel of great authority. Michael is described as "a great prince." i.e., he is one of the most powerful of the heavenly host. Michael would "arise," i.e., intervene, on behalf of God's people, for it was his duty to protect them.

Fourth, the angel promised that some of Daniel's people, i.e., the Jews, would be delivered from this unprecedented time of distress. Those of Daniel's people who were found "written in the book" would be rescued in those desperate days. Jesus told his disciples that their names were written in heaven (Luke 10:20). History attests that Jewish believers in Christ heeded the warnings of their Master and fled Jerusalem before the terrible ordeal of AD 70.

B. A Great Awakening (12:2-4).

The angelic interpreter painted three pictures of a great awakening which would also be a part of the events "at that time," i.e., during the days of the Herodian dynasty.

First, the angel spoke of a great resurrection. "Many of those who sleep in the dust of the ground will awake." Death is frequently compared to sleep in the Scriptures.[6] The "dust of the ground" is figurative for the grave. Commentators are all but united in seeing this as a reference to the final resurrection of the body. The Old Testament certainly knew of a bodily resurrection.[7] Many passages, however, use the language of resurrection to refer to great moral and spiritual awakenings.[8] In the days of the Herodian dynasty the whole nation of Israel was "awakened" out of the sleep of centuries through the preaching of John the Baptist, Jesus, the New Testament apostles and evangelists.[9] *Many* who slumbered in spiritual indifference would hear the Gospel call. Some would arise to receive by faith the gift of everlasting life. Others would be stirred by that message to hostility and persecution. They would receive "disgrace and everlasting contempt" (12:2).

Second, the angel spoke of teaching stars. The great awakening would be stirred by "those who are wise," literally, those who cause others to be wise. The reference is to teachers of the Gospel who are in the business of leading "the many to righteousness." These soul winners would have lasting honor. They would shine with eternal glory like the stars which fill the night sky (12:3; cf. Matt 13:43).

Third, the angel spoke of the sealed book. Daniel was directed to seal up the book he was writing. This signals that the fulfillment of these predictions would occur long after the death of the prophet.[10] Only at "the end of time" would these predictions be understandable. What end of time? Throughout this final vision the phrase has referred to the end of God's dealings with national Israel. Why would the book of Daniel be easier to interpret at the end of time? Because "many will go back and forth,[11] and knowledge will increase" (12:4). Those who go back and forth are probably the same as those who cause others to be wise in the previous verse. The *knowledge* which increases is that spiritual insight cast upon Old Testament revelation through the preaching of the Gospel of Christ.[12]

AN ANGELIC CONVERSATION
Daniel 12:5-7

Two angels now appeared on the scene. They functioned as witnesses to an oath about to be taken. The two angels stood on either side of the Tigris river while the superior angel who had been conducting Daniel through this final vision was stationed "above the waters of the river." The exact significance of this position is not indicated.[13] One of the angels directed a question to the superior angel: "How long will it be until the end of these wonders?" The question is *not* How long *until* the end, but How long *is* the end. How long would the terrible period of tribulation alluded to in 12:1 last? (12:5f.).[14]

The answer came in the form of a solemn oath. The superior angel raised both his hands toward heaven to signify the most solemn assurance. He swore "by him who lives forever." In his oath the celestial messenger made known first what would be the duration of the period of great distress; and second, what would be the result of the events which transpired during the great distress.

The period of great distress would last "for a time, times, and half a time." Since *time* in Daniel indicates a year (see 4:25), the cryptic expression used here would be equivalent to three years and part of a fourth. Always in the Bible this expression indicates a period of intense suffering.[15]

The *terminus ad quem* of the prophecy is clearly set forth. "The power of the holy people" would be shattered (12:7). The entire prophecy spoken by the heavenly messenger must have been fulfilled prior to the destruction of Jerusalem in AD 70 when the Romans smashed through the walls of Jerusalem. In that year the power of national Israel was shattered.[16]

AN ANGELIC EXPLANATION
Daniel 12:8-13

No event was mentioned from which the time, times and part of a time were to be counted. Thus Daniel did not comprehend what he had been hearing. He respectfully asked his guide, "What will be the outcome of these events? He wanted to know who would win in the struggle, and how the participants would fare. The angel replied: "Go your way, Daniel, for these words are concealed and sealed up until the end of time." The vision did not concern Daniel directly. Trying to gain any further insight concerning these matters was futile. As time goes on these events would unravel themselves. History would shed light on prophecy. "At the end of time," i.e., at the end of God's dealings with national Israel, men would understand these matters (12:8f.).

The predictions here recorded would not be understood by all men even in the day of fulfillment. Many Jews would be "purged, purified and refined" both by the ordeal of those days, and by the preaching of the Gospel. Some would "have insight," i.e. they would recognize their Messiah. With the help of Jesus, their teacher, these would understand the words of the angel. The obstinately wicked, however, would continue to act wickedly even as prophetic judgment crashed down upon them (12:10). In Matthew 24 Jesus discoursed at length about the impending destruction of Jerusalem by the Romans. He gave his disciples warning signs and urged them to flee the city when they observed these signs. Christians heeded these warnings and were unaffected by the destruction of Jerusalem in AD 70.

The time of great distress would be marked by two pivotal events. Both are reminiscent of events in the days of Antiochus Epiphanes (cf. 8:13; 11:31).[17] During the tribulation the "daily sacrifice" would be abolished.[18] Only the most desperate straits would cause loyal Jews to cease offering the morning and evening Temple sacrifices required by the Law of God. The Jews had every intention of renewing those sacrifices once the war was over. As it turned out, however, the last sacrifices ever offered by a Jewish priest were placed on the altar on July 13, AD 70.[19]

What circumstances would bring about the total cessation of the Old Testament sacrificial system? One would come who would set up "the abomination that causes desolation."[20] Jesus alerted his disciples to watch for the abomination of desolation standing in the holy place (Matt 24:15). In the parallel passage in the Gospel of Luke Jesus explained Daniel's prophecy as referring the the armies which would surround Jerusalem (Luke 21:20). This clue from the teaching of Jesus makes it clear that Daniel mentioned the two pivotal events of the great distress in *reverse* chronological order.

The angel specified the length of time between the two pivotal events as 1,290 days. Forty-three months after the abomination that causes desolation was set up (i.e., the Roman armies surrounded Jerusalem), the daily sacrifice would cease. According to Josephus, the Roman armies approached Jerusalem on the twenty-seventh day of the month Hyperberetaios (October) AD 66.[21] Under pressure of the siege, the daily sacrifice was suspended July 14, AD 70. In July AD 70 Titus the Roman general forced his way into Jerusalem and utterly destroyed the place. The 1290 days would thus represent the period of most intense suffering for the inhabitants of Jerusalem.

The angel pronounces as "blessed" that person who "keeps waiting and attains to the 1335 days" (12:12). This would be forty-five days longer than the 1290 days.[22] The city was set to the torch on August 6, AD 70. The ordeal was over.

Daniel would not live to see the events which the angel had prophesied. He would rest in death. "At the end of the days," however, he would rise from the dead to receive his inheritance in the eternal kingdom (12:13). With this note the Book of Daniel comes to a close.

Chart No. 24

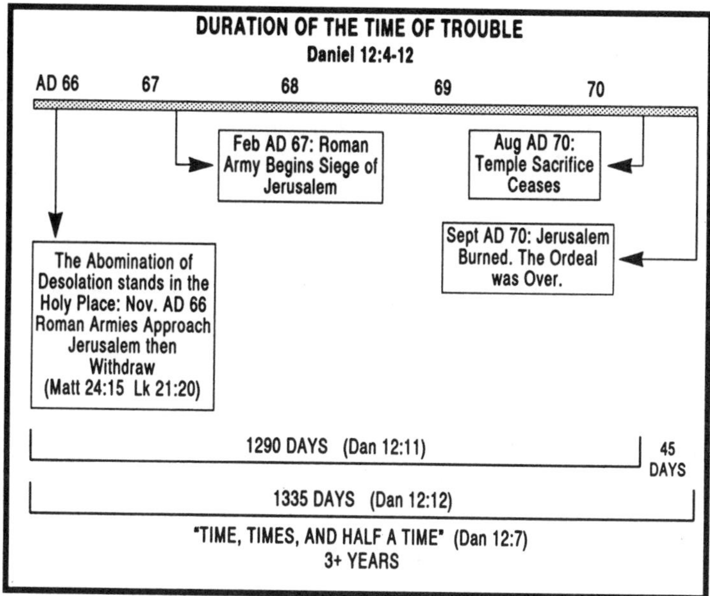

Endnotes

1. Futurists see in Daniel 12 predictions of "the Great Tribulation" which is supposed to take place in conjunction with the "Rapture of the church." Some hold that the Church is raptured during the Great Tribulation, and some say after. On the basis of Jeremiah 30:7 this "Great Tribulation" is sometimes called, "Jacob's Trouble."

2. Josephus, *Wars* Preface 6.

3. Josephus, *Wars* 5.10.5.

4. See Matt 24:21; Mark 13:19; Luke 21:23, 24.

5. This king is famous in early church history because of his encounter with Paul. See Acts 25:13-26:32.

6. Death is compared to sleep in the following passages: Ps 13:3; Job 3:13; Jer 51:39, 57; John 11:11; Acts 7:60; 1 Thess 5:10.

7. Bodily resurrection in the Old Testament: Ps 16:9-11; Job 19:25-27; Isa 26:19.

8. In the following passages the language of death is used to describe a state of spiritual indifference and sin. Arising from death in these cases is equivalent to revival or renewal or conversion. See Isa 9:2; 29:10; 60:1; Ezek 37:1-14; Matt 4:15-16; John 5:25; Eph 5:14.

9. The interpretation of Daniel 12 adopted here is that of Philip Mauro, *The Seventy Weeks and the Great Tribulation* (Swengel, PA: Reiner, rev. ed., n.d.) 165-181.

10. H.C. Leupold thinks that only the present vision is to be sealed. E.J. Young, however, is probably correct in applying the sealing to the entire book of Daniel.

11. Those who go back and forth are those who are trying to carry out the commission of the Lord (Matt 28:19). Mark reports that the disciples "went forth and preached everywhere, the Lord working with them" (16:20). A messenger is frequently depicted as one who runs, because of the urgency of the tiding he bears. See Hab 2:2f.; Rom 10:14f.

12. The times prior to Christ are characterized as "the times of this ignorance" (Acts 17:30). Knowledge of the true God removed the darkness of this ignorance. See John 17:4; 1 Cor 15:34; Col 1:10.

13. Leupold suggests that the superior angel was above the river to indicate that God still ruled over the turbulent forces of opposition just as he once stood over Egypt and the Nile. *Exposition of Daniel* (Minneapolis: Augsburg, 1949) 536f.

14. Jesus was referring to this same time of distress when he said: "These be the days of vengeance that all things that are written may be fulfilled" (Luke 21:22). Again he said: "And except those days be shortened there should no flesh be saved, but for the sake of the elect those days shall be shortened" (Matt 24:22).

15. See Rev 11:2; 12:6, 13-14; 13:5. Time, times and half a time is equivalent to 42 months or 1260 days.

16. Moses may have predicted the result of the Roman destruction of Jerusalem in Deut 28:49-68, especially the words, "And the Lord shall scatter you among all people, from the one end of the earth even to the other," (v. 64).

17. That the prophecy in Daniel 12 cannot refer to what transpired in the days of Antiochus is proved by the fact that Jesus still regarded the setting up of the abomination of desolation as a future event, not a past fact. See Matt 24:15.

18. This abolishment of the daily sacrifice is not to be confused with the causing of the sacrifice and oblation to cease, as foretold in Dan 9:27, which is a very different thing.

19. See Josephus *Wars* 6.2.1.

20. In his earlier prediction of the fall of Jerusalem to the Romans, the angel spoke of the coming of one who makes desolate. See 9:27.

21. *Wars* 2.19.4. Josephus employs the Macedonian calendar but frequently indicates correlations with the Jewish calendar. Hyperberetaios is equivalent to Jewish Tishri which overlaps September-October of the modern calendar.

22. The measures of time here given, the 1290 days and the 1335 days, both fall within the period of three years and a part of a fourth which is given in verse 7.